ALSO BY HARVEY SACHS

Toscanini
Virtuoso
Music in Fascist Italy
Reflections on Toscanini
Rubinstein: A Life

AS COAUTHOR:

My First Forty Years with Plácido Domingo
Memoirs with Sir Georg Solti

The Letters of Arturo Toscanini

The Letters of

ARTURO TOSCANINI

Compiled, edited, and translated by

HARVEY SACHS

Alfred A. Knopf *New York* 2002

Library of Congress Cataloging-in-Publication Data
Toscanini, Arturo, 1867–1957.
{Correspondence. Selections. English}
The letters of Arturo Toscanini / compiled, edited, and translated by Harvey Sachs.
p.   cm.
Includes bibliographical references and index.
ISBN 0-375-40405-8 (alk. paper)
1. Toscanini, Arturo, 1867–1957—Correspondence.   2. Conductors (Music)—Correspondence.   3. Toscanini,
Arturo, 1867–1957—Relations with women.   4. Toscanini, Arturo, 1867–1957—Views on fascism.
5. Fascism—Europe—History—20th century.   I. Sachs, Harvey, 1946—   II. Title.

ML 422.T67 A4 2002
784.2'092—dc21
{B}   2001038627

Manufactured in the United States of America
First Edition

PHOTOGRAPH CREDITS

*Robert Haas: pp. 140, 202; Courtesy RCA Victor Group/RCA Red Seal: p. 290;
Courtesy of the family of Arturo Toscanini: p. 360; Robert Hupka: p. 406.*

To Maria Cristina,

my love and now also my wife,

who has stood by me

through my most difficult years

Contents

Acknowledgments

My thanks go above all to my wife, Maria Cristina Reinhart-Sachs, who has given me inestimable assistance throughout the duration of this project, everything from suggestions about content and translation to help with photocopying and transport. She, our little daughter, Lyuba, and my son, Julian, have had to put up with the disagreeable aspects of the various moves and absences that the project has necessitated, and I beg their pardon for these disruptions in their lives.

This book could not have been completed without the extraordinary participation of three sets of individuals and organizations. The first set consists of the Fondazione Sergio Dragoni of Milan, in the person of its president, Antonio Magnocavallo, and the Fondazione Omina-Freundeshilfe of Vaduz, in the persons of three of its directors—Hans Deichmann, Maria Deichmann Lauper, and Mathias Deichmann. Had these individuals and the organizations they represent not intervened to save Toscanini's letters to Ada Mainardi from purchase by private collectors and possible eventual dispersal to the four corners of the earth, one of the main components of this book might well have remained an unknown quantity. As I write these words, the process of transferring possession of these documents to the Fondazione Arturo Toscanini in Parma has begun, but the foundation directors who generously undertook the stopgap measure of acquisition back in 1995 deserve the gratitude of every reader of this book.

In the years since my biography of Toscanini was first published,* Emanuela di Castelbarco and Walfredo Toscanini have become real friends of mine, and they make up the second set of people to whom I am especially indebted. Above and beyond communicating to them my sincerest gratitude for their cooperation in this project— cooperation that included not only the provision of a great deal of original source material but also help in identifying some of the people and situations mentioned in the letters and permission to use the documents that I am publishing in this book—I want to tell them in print what I hope they already know: that I cherish them for who and what they are as individuals, and not because they are Arturo Toscanini's grandchildren. (Both of them are now grandparents in their own right, which means that the Maestro's descendants have reached the fourth generation.)

As I mention in the introduction, a fellowship at the New York Public Library's newly instituted Center for Scholars and Writers enabled me to do the bulk of the primary and secondary research for this book in Manhattan from September 1999 through

---

* *Toscanini* (New York: Lippincott, 1978)

May 2000. I am infinitely grateful to the center's director, Peter Gay; to his assistant, Pamela Leo; to the center's assistant, Rachael Kafrissen; to Dorothy and Lewis B. Cullman, who more than anyone else made the center's existence possible; to Paul LeClerc, the library's president, for the opportunity to exchange views on a variety of subjects; to Susan T. Sommer, who was then acting director of the New York Public Library for the Performing Arts; to Linda Fairtile, who had organized the library's Toscanini Legacy and answered my endless questions with expertise and unfailing patience; to all the other library staff members who assisted me throughout the term of the fellowship; and to the fourteen other Fellows—Sven Beckert, Paul Berman, Graham Burnett, Kathleen Cleaver, Pamela Clemit, Andrew Delbanco, Gregory Dreicer, Christian Fleck, Anthony Holden, Ada Louise Huxtable, Marion Kaplan, Allen Kurzweil, Howard Markel, and Francine Prose—for all the useful knowledge they generously shared with me from their various areas of study, and for their delightful companionship.

Further thanks to the following individuals (in alphabetical order) for their direct or indirect assistance: Maria Antonelli, Rome; Maria Grazia Boccuni, Bologna; Eva Bucek, Vienna; Iris Cantelli, Morlupo (Rome); Andrea Carandini, Rome; Maria Montarsolo Cecchini (deceased); Aline Cholmondeley, London; Richard Cooley, Baltimore; Ken Crilly, New Haven; Everett Fox, Newton, Massachusetts; Howard Gotlieb, Boston; Anne Chotzinoff Grossman, Babylon, New York; Michael Holroyd, London; Robert Hupka (deceased); Fritz Janschka, Greensboro, North Carolina; Adrian Lyttelton, Florence; Francesca Marciano, Rome; Fanny Mavromichalis, Paris; Sean Noel, Boston; Stefano Rossini, Pisa; Erik Ryding, New York; Jay Shulman, New York; Elena Cesari Silva (deceased); Peter Stansky, Stanford, California; Allan Steckler, New York; Elisabetta Stefanini, Rome; Neill Thornborrow, Düsseldorf; Iwa Aulin Voghera, Stockholm; William Weaver, Annandale-on-Hudson, New York; Larry Weinstein, Toronto; Piero Weiss, Baltimore; and Philip Wults, Victoria, British Columbia. And thanks to the following institutions (in alphabetical order): Accademia di Santa Cecilia, Rome; Anthony Capraro Collection, Immigration History Research Center, University of Minnesota; Archivio Centrale dello Stato, Rome; Archivio Municipale, Turin; Archivio del Teatro Regio, Turin; Biblioteca Palatina, Parma; Boston University, Papers of Samuel Chotzinoff; Casa Natale di Arturo Toscanini, Collezione Aureliano Pertile, Parma; Conservatorio Giuseppe Verdi (Biblioteca), Milan; Edizioni della Scala, Milan; Fondazione Arturo Toscanini, Parma; Franklin D. Roosevelt Library, Hyde Park, New York; La Pilotta (publisher), Parma; Library of Congress, Damrosch-Blaine Collection and Koussevitzky Collection, Washington, D.C.; Metropolitan Opera Archives, New York; Morton Gould Archives, New York; Museo Teatrale alla Scala, Milan; New York Philharmonic Archive, New York; Olin Downes Papers, Hargrett Rare Book and Manuscript Library, University of Georgia, Athens, Georgia; The Pierpont Morgan Library, Mary Flagler Cary Music Collection, New York; Richard Wagner Gedenkstätte der Stadt Bayreuth. Thanks also to any individuals or institutions I may have forgotten to mention—and I imagine that there will be a few.

Jonathan Segal, my editor at Knopf, and his assistant, Ida Giragossian, have stood firmly behind this project from start to finish and have given me every sort of assistance, and Rita Madrigal, the production editor, and Lynn Anderson, the copyeditor, have done a first-rate job with a highly complicated text. My thanks go to them as also to Ned Leavitt, my agent for this book, and his assistants.

H.S.

Explanations and Abbreviations

The original source of every document by Toscanini quoted in the following pages is a handwritten letter in Italian, unless otherwise indicated. Drafts, telegrams, postcards, typewritten items, transcripts, photocopies, documents taken from books or other published sources, and so on are clearly identified for what they are, and so are documents that were written in languages other than Italian.

The line that precedes each document (whole or excerpted) gives the following information:

1. Type of document (draft, telegram, postcard), if the document is not a letter
2. Place and date of postmark (if a postmarked envelope exists)
3. Location (in parentheses if not stated in document; with question mark if uncertain) and date (or estimated date) of document's provenance, if the information is not displayed elsewhere
4. Content of printed letterhead, if there is one
5. Name and location (as in No. 3 above) of addressee
6. Language in which the document is written, if other than Italian
7. Source from which document was obtained, preceded by "pc" if the source was a photocopy

Here are a few examples:

E.P. BRESCIA, 17 AUGUST 1896; TO CDM, HSSLG; EC
Envelope postmarked Brescia, 17 August 1896; to Carla De Martini, Hotel Salò, Salò, Lake Garda; collection of Emanuela Castelbarco.

P.S., STAZIONE CLIMATICO [SIC] ALPINA/HÔTEL CADORE/TAI DI CADORE/ A. REGAZZI; TO ROSINA STORCHIO, (MI); NYPLTL
Printed stationery, Stazione [etc.]; to Rosina Storchio (presumably in Milan); New York Public Library, Toscanini Legacy. The place and date of the letter's provenance are not given here because they appear in the letter.

TG, MI, 24 DECEMBER 1915; TO BERNARDINO MOLINARI, [ADDRESS] AS IN PREVIOUS TELEGRAM; ASC
Telegram sent from Milan on 24 December 1915; to Bernardino Molinari, Via Cicerone 28, Rome; from the archives of the Accademia di Santa Cecilia, Rome.

Rather than interrupting the flow of each document with footnotes attached to names and other items in the various letters, I have added a note at the end of each letter that required one and have explained whatever seemed to require an explanation.

In translating the letters, I have corrected misspelled names; only in the letters that were originally in English have I left AT's misspellings and added [sic] wherever necessary.

Toscanini usually wrote letters quickly and did not reread them, which accounts for occasional syntactical and other slips, but in general his Italian was literary, clear, pungent, and often beautiful. His punctuation, like that of many other Italians of his generation, was erratic. He often used three or more dots or a dot-dash-dot combination instead of a comma or period, and if the right edge of the page corresponded to the end of a phrase or sentence, he would often omit any sort of punctuation, as if the edge served somehow as a partial or full stop. For the most part, I have eliminated the series of dots and replaced them with commas, periods, and even dashes, in order to make the text as clear as possible. I have not, however, eliminated either Toscanini's abundant exclamation points or his frequent underlinings (double, triple, and even more emphatic underlinings are shown in boldface type), which are also typical of the Italian epistolary style of the period; see, for instance, the letters of Eleonora Duse. I have applied the same criteria to my translations of the relatively few letters that he wrote in French. In the letters that Toscanini wrote in English, however, I have reproduced everything as he wrote it and have added corrections in brackets. (Toscanini's written English ranged from respectable to unintentionally funny to appalling, depending on how much time he dedicated to a given letter.) In all the letters, I have preserved his quirky underlinings (or, more often, lack of them) of titles of compositions, books, and so on, and his equally quirky paragraphing.

The following is an alphabetized list of the abbreviations that I have used.

AT Arturo Toscanini
25VBMMi 25 Via Bianca Maria, Milan
26W68NY 26 West 68th Street, New York
28CSL 28 Chester Street, London
29W85NY 29 West 85th Street, New York
46VMPMi 46 Via Mario Pagano, Milan
ACS Accademia di Santa Cecilia, Rome (archives)
AIV Albergo [Hotel] Italia, Voghera
AM Ada Mainardi
AMT Archivio Municipale, Turin
AOLCV Albergo Oceano, Lido di Camaiore, Viareggio
ASP Albergo Salvadori, Piazze, Province of Siena
Barblan Guglielmo Barblan, and Eugenio Gara, *Toscanini e la Scala* (Milan: Edizioni della Scala, 1972)
Bo Bologna
CDM Carla De Martini, before she became Carla Toscanini
coll. From the collection of
CT Carla (De Martini) Toscanini
D20Mi Via Durini 20, Milan

Della Corte Andrea Della Corte, *Toscanini visto da un critico* (Turin: ILTE, 1958)

e. Envelope

EC Emanuela di Castelbarco, AT's granddaughter (daughter of WyT)

EK Elsa Kurzbauer

e.p. Envelope postmarked

FDRL Franklin Delano Roosevelt Library, Hyde Park, New York

Fiorda Nuccio Fiorda, *Arte, beghe e bizze di Toscanini* (Rome: Fratelli Palombi, 1969)

FSD-FOF Fondazione Sergio Dragoni, Milan, and Fondazione Omina-Freundeshilfe, Vaduz

GHS Grand Hôtel, Strobel, St. Wolfgangsee, Austria

GS Gelsa (Gelsina) Salvadori

HAAF Hotel Anglo-Americano, Florence

HAZB Hotel am Zoo, Berlin

HBG Hôtel Bellevue, Gstaad

HBGr Hotel Baer, Grindelwald

HBM Hotel Bristol, Merano

HDKM Hôtel Deutscher Kaiser, Munich

HH B. H. Haggin, *Arturo Toscanini: Contemporary Recollections of the Maestro,* ed. Thomas Hathaway (New York: Da Capo, 1989)

HIR Hotel Imperiale, Rome

HLBVB Hotel Lago di Braies, Villabassa Bolzano

HMP Hôtel Majestic, Paris

HQR Hotel Quirinale, Rome

HRG Hôtel Riessersee, Garmisch (Germany)

HSSLG Hotel Salò, Salò, Lake Garda

HVM Hôtel de la Ville, Milan

HWMC Hôtel Windsor, Monte Carlo

ISG Isolino San Giovanni, Lake Maggiore

LOC Library of Congress, Washington, D.C.

Mi Milan

MTS Museo Teatrale alla Scala, Milan

n.d. No date given

NY New York

NYPA New York Philharmonic Archives

NYPL New York Public Library

NYPLSC New York Public Library, Special Collections

NYPLTL New York Public Library, Toscanini Legacy

ODUGA Olin Downes Papers, Hargrett Rare Book and Manuscript Library, University of Georgia

orig. Eng. Original document in English

orig. Fr. Original document in French

orig. Ger. Original document in German

pc Photocopy

PFB Pension Fürstenhaus, 69 Kurfürstendamm, Berlin

PH22MB Pension Herbke, 22 Meinekestrasse, Berlin

PN Pallanza-Novara (Pallanza, the town opposite the Isolino San Giovanni in Lake Maggiore, is in the Province of Novara and had the post office that Toscanini usually used when he was staying on the Isolino)

PS Piazze, Province of Siena

p.s. Printed stationery (letterhead)

PVBCA c/o Pizzetti, Villa Borgatto, Cortina d'Ampezzo

RWGSB Richard Wagner Gedenkstätte der Stadt Bayreuth

S8Mi Via Speronari 8, Milan

Sacchi 1951 Filippo Sacchi, *Toscanini* (Milan: Mondadori, 1951; there were later
   editions of the book)

SC Samuel Chotzinoff

SCBU Papers of Samuel Chotzinoff, Boston University

SNNS Schloss Neudeck, Nonnthalhauptstrasse 51, Salzburg

SR Stefano Rossini (great-nephew of Gelsa Salvadori)

tg Telegram

Tu Turin

VB8R Via Bruxelles 8, Rome

Ve Venice

Vetro Gaspare Nello Vetro, *Arturo Toscanini alla Regia Scuola del Carmine in Parma*
   (Parma: Tipolito la Ducale, 1974)

VSCA Villa Sella, Cortina d'Ampezzo

WaT Wanda Toscanini (later Wanda Horowitz), AT's daughter

WoT Walfredo Toscanini, AT's grandson (WrT's son)

WrT Walter Toscanini, AT's son

WyT Wally Toscanini (later Wally di Castelbarco), AT's daughter

To avoid confusion, European dating (day-month-year) has been used throughout
except in cases in which Toscanini himself used American dating (month-day-year).

Introduction

Arturo Toscanini was born in the city of Parma, in Italy's fertile Po plain, on 25 March 1867. He was the oldest of four children and the only son of Paola (*née* Montani) and Claudio Toscanini. Both parents came from middle-class families, but Claudio had the temperament of an adventurer and had gone off in his youth to fight in Garibaldi's forces during Italy's wars of independence and reunification. Thereafter, he never managed to settle down seriously to domestic life, and his drinking, philandering, and general irresponsibility made life difficult for his wife and children. Arturo entered Parma's Royal School of Music at the age of nine and graduated from it at eighteen, with maximum honors in cello and composition and with a reputation, among local musicians, not only for his virtually photographic memory and other remarkable talents but also for his wide-ranging musical interests and passionately held ideals. The following year, he was engaged as principal cellist and assistant chorus master of an Italian opera company that was to tour South America, and one evening, in Rio de Janeiro, the nineteen-year-old musician was called upon at the last moment to replace the ensemble's regular conductor in *Aida,* which he led by heart. Thus began one of the most extraordinary careers in the history of musical performance.

On his return to Italy, Toscanini immediately began to acquire experience by conducting one short season after another in many of the country's opera houses. During one of those seasons, at Milan's Teatro Dal Verme in 1892, he conducted the world premiere of Leoncavallo's *Pagliacci.* Three years later he became what would today be called artistic director of Turin's prestigious Teatro Regio, where he conducted—among many other works—the world premiere of Puccini's *La bohème,* the first Italian production of Wagner's *Götter-dämmerung,* the local premiere of *Tristan und Isolde,* and a host of new or recent symphonic pieces.

In 1898, at the age of thirty-one, he assumed the directorship of Milan's Teatro alla Scala, the most important opera ensemble in Italy. He spent seven of the following ten seasons there (1898–1903, 1906–08), conducting the first Italian productions of Wagner's *Siegfried,* Tchaikovsky's *Eugene Onegin,* Strauss's *Salome* (contemporaneous with a Turin production conducted by the composer), Debussy's *Pelléas et Mélisande,* and symphonic works by some of the most promising talents of his generation, including Debussy, Strauss, and Sibelius. He also introduced *Tristan,* Puccini's *Tosca,* Charpentier's *Louise,* and works by Mascagni, Giordano, Cilea, Franchetti, and other leading Italian composers of the day to the Milanese public; initiated a series of revolutionary revivals of the Verdi repertoire; and undertook many important reforms in the theater's artistic and administrative sectors.

Toscanini quickly established himself as the first Italian conductor of world-class talent who was as interested in foreign repertoire as in domestic works, in symphonic music as in opera, in the classics as in the moderns. He performed Wagner's music with passion and intellectual rigor—in Toscanini's student days Wagner had embodied Europe's musical avant-garde—but he performed with equal passion and rigor the works of many composers whom Wagner had detested, notably Verdi and Brahms. In the lyric theater, which had often been held hostage by star singers and their caprices, Toscanini gradually imposed a system in which solo voices, chorus, orchestra, stage movement, sets, costumes, and lighting were all given maximum attention in order to create what Wagner had called the *Gesamtkunstwerk*—the complete work of art. At the same time he began to demand more highly skilled playing from orchestra musicians than his predecessors had considered necessary. To his way of thinking, the sense and spirit of a piece of music could not be expressed if the notes were not played in tune, with their proper rhythmic values, at a tempo close to the one indicated by the composer, and in correct textural balance against all the other notes being played at the same time. All of this was merely a point of departure for achieving something much deeper and more valuable, but it was nevertheless a sine qua non. To achieve these goals Toscanini fought great battles, and his terrifying temper became a legend in the musical world. The result, however, is that most professional musicians from his day to ours—even those who disagree with his recorded interpretations—are direct beneficiaries of his lifelong struggle.

Toscanini conducted four substantial seasons in Buenos Aires during the first decade of the twentieth century, seasons that included the Argentine premieres of *Tristan,* Berlioz's *The Damnation of Faust,* Cilea's *Adriana Lecouvreur,* Puccini's *Madama Butterfly,* and many other works. From 1908 to 1915 he was in effect principal conductor (together with Mahler, during the first two seasons) of New York's Metropolitan Opera Company, with which he led the world premiere of Puccini's *La fanciulla del West,* the American premiere of Mussorgsky's *Boris Godunov,* and important revivals of works that ranged from Gluck's *Orfeo ed Euridice* and *Armide* and Weber's *Euryanthe* through the best-known mid- and late-nineteenth-century repertoire, to the most recent works of Giordano, Montemezzi, Wolf-Ferrari, and Dukas.

During World War I, Toscanini stayed in Italy, conducting only military bands at the front and special benefit events in the cities. In 1920–21 he took the Scala orchestra on a marathon tour of Italy, the United States, and Canada, and masterminded the rebirth of his country's most glorious opera company, which had been virtually defunct since 1917. In December 1921 he inaugurated the overhauled Scala ensemble's first season, and he presided over the house's fortunes with tremendous success almost to the end of the decade. This period was in many ways the culmination of his life as an opera conductor.

Toscanini made his first guest appearances with the New York Philharmonic in 1926, and by 1930, when he took the ensemble on a history-making European tour, he had become its principal conductor. Also in 1930, Toscanini became the first non-German-school conductor to perform at the Bayreuth Festival, to which he returned in 1931; he canceled a further scheduled return in 1933 because Hitler had come to power in Germany. From then until the outbreak of the Second World War, Toscanini conducted a circle around Nazi Germany and Fascist Italy (he had been attacked and hit in the face by Fascist thugs in his own country in 1931 for refusing to play the ruling party's official anthem at the start of a concert): He worked occasionally as guest conductor with Paris's Orchestre Walter-Straram beginning in 1932, with the Vienna Philharmonic and the Stockholm Concert Society Orchestra from 1933 to 1937, with the BBC Symphony Orchestra in London from 1935 to 1939, and with the Residentie-Orkest in The Hague in 1937 and 1938. At the Salzburg Festivals of 1935 to 1937 he gave what proved to be his last performances of complete, staged operas, and in 1938, when he withdrew from Salzburg for political reasons, he helped to create the new Lucerne Festival by agreeing to conduct concerts in the Swiss city. But his most celebrated political gesture was his trip to Palestine, at his own expense, at the end of 1936, to conduct a new orchestra (later known as the Israel Philharmonic), that was made up largely of Jewish refugees from Central Europe.

In 1937, a year after his retirement from the New York Philharmonic, the seventy-year-old Toscanini accepted an offer from the National Broadcasting Company in New York to conduct a new orchestra made up of musicians of the highest caliber, for weekly radio broadcast concerts and frequent recordings. He remained in the United States throughout the Second World War and returned to Europe only in 1946, to reconsecrate La Scala, which had been heavily damaged by Allied bombs in 1943. Thereafter he returned to Europe every year, but his principal center of activity remained the NBC Symphony. Toscanini retired for good in 1954, at the age of eighty-seven, and died at his home in Riverdale (Bronx, New York) on 16 January 1957, a few weeks before his ninetieth birthday.

My biography of Arturo Toscanini contained its fair share of minor mistakes (most of them corrected in subsequent editions) and one glaring error: "Toscanini's letters . . . are relatively few and often uninformative," I wrote in the book's foreword. Little did I know! The truth was that most of his extant letters had not yet come to light, although he had already been dead for two decades when the book was written. Not until two or three years after the biography was published did I have an inkling that his correspondence might have been extensive. I was living in London at the time, and a BBC producer who took me to lunch one day to discuss an unrelated project mentioned, *en passant,* that a friend of his owned some Toscanini letters. I contacted the friend—a professor of anthropology at the University of London—and soon found myself in possession of photocopies of about forty letters that Toscanini had written to one Elsa Kurzbauer, the professor's aunt, between 1939 and 1947. These largely pornographic documents were of little musical-historical value, except as reminders of the fact that overheated sexuality is often a concomitant and sometimes an important component of intense spirituality. But they made me wonder whether Toscanini, who had clearly enjoyed writing about certain pleasures of the flesh, had been inclined to set down his thoughts on other subjects as well.

At the New York Public Library in the mid-1980s, I came across a recently catalogued folder of documents that concerned Toscanini's announcement, in February 1938, that he would not return to the Salzburg Festival because of his anger and dismay over Austrian Chancellor Kurt von Schuschnigg's first political compromises with Hitler. Most of the items were addressed to Toscanini, but the few that were written by him revealed a good deal about his character. Then, in 1995, nearly a thousand letters and telegrams written by Toscanini to a single correspondent—Ada Colleoni Mainardi—mainly during the period 1933–39, were auctioned off as a lot by the Stargardt auction house in Berlin, and after many strange vicissitudes the lot was jointly acquired, at my instigation, by two foundations and taken by me to Milan. These letters and telegrams amount to a total of more than 240,000 words—much longer than this entire book—and constitute by far the largest single collection of Toscanini's writings known to exist. In no other correspondence does the conductor so frequently and frankly reveal his thoughts and feelings on so great a variety of subjects—himself, his family, other people, the music he studied and performed, his work, travels, early years, reading, political beliefs, and attitudes toward love and sex—and the fact that these letters date from the period during which both his musical career and his anti-Fascist activities were at their apogee further increases their importance. Within a few months of their acquisition, I had begun to organize and transcribe them for the two foundations, and as I did so the idea of publishing a collection of Toscanini's letters began to take shape in my mind.

In April 1998 my partner (now wife), Maria Cristina Reinhart-Sachs, and I borrowed a photocopying machine, made the three-hour drive from our home in east central Tuscany to the home of Countess Emanuela di Castelbarco, Toscanini's granddaughter, in southwestern Tuscany, and spent many days copying some two thousand pages of documents that Countess Castlebarco had inherited from her mother, Wally Toscanini Castelbarco. This material, which included a great deal of family correspondence, made the idea of a volume of Toscanini's letters even more plausible.

Finally, during the 1999–2000 academic year, a fellowship at the New York Public Library's newly instituted Center for Scholars and Writers enabled me to study the documents in the library's Toscanini Legacy and to transcribe those that I needed for what had by then become a concrete undertaking with my publisher, Alfred A. Knopf. Most of the legacy, which had been acquired by the library from the Toscanini family in 1986 after having lain dormant and untouched for nearly twenty years, had been assembled by Walter Toscanini, the conductor's son. In addition to thousands of hours of recordings and a vast collection of printed music and other printed matter, the legacy contains an enormous quantity of documents, most of which were catalogued in the mid-1990s by Linda Fairtile of the library's staff. This material kept me busy for much of my eight-month fellowship period.

There were many other sources as well for the letters contained in this volume. Walfredo Toscanini, Walter's son, contributed items from his private collection, which now includes the letters that had belonged to the professor in London. Copies of letters to Samuel and Pauline Chotzinoff were obtained from Boston University; copies of letters to Olin Downes were obtained from the University of Georgia; at the Morgan Library in New York I was allowed to copy a letter and a telegram from Toscanini to Debussy; and there were letters in the Franklin Delano Roosevelt Library, in the Library of Congress, in various collections (besides the Toscanini Legacy) at the New York Public Library, and in many other public and private archives. Several individuals came forward with items of interest from their own or their parents' or grandparents' papers.

I do not doubt that dozens and perhaps hundreds of Toscanini's letters are still in the hands of various sources unknown to me (one source well known to me refused even to reply to my request to be allowed to see the documents in her possession), and I am sure that a week, a month, or ten years after this book is published someone will contact me and ask, "How is it possible that you didn't print any of the seventy-three Toscanini letters that are in the Discordia Conservatory library? The addressees include Bruckner, Lenin, Babe Ruth, and Mata Hari!" I shall duly hang my head in shame.

What these letters reveal above all else is a man whose psychological perceptions in general and self-knowledge in particular were much more acute than most people who have studied his life and work have thought likely. Various elements in Toscanini's character—enormous pride, inability to suffer the company of fools and hangers-on, disgust with everything that smacked of servility and opportunism, intolerance of superficial or slipshod music making, and just plain generalized anger—would sometimes overwhelm his capacity to make rational judgments, but when the Apollonian and Dionysian sides of his nature were working in tandem rather than pulling him in opposite directions, his observations were sharp and wise.

A whole psychology textbook could be written about Toscanini and anger. Although no significant letters from his student days have been found, statements made in a few letters written much later indicate that he always looked back on that period as the happiest in his life, when he was discovering music and literature and beginning to come to terms with his talent but before he realized what an infernal burden the talent would impose on him once he had chained it forever to his impossibly high artistic and professional ethic. And one talent that he possessed in an unusually small measure was the talent for being happy. Whether his bad digestion (which he mentions in several letters), his grumpy and unaffectionate mother (whom he blames for his "unhappy nature" in several others), or (most likely) some combination of these and many other elements had created his lack of ability to feel fulfilled, the fact is that Toscanini's specialty was dissatisfaction. He was dissatisfied with his artistic accomplishments, with himself as a human being, with his destiny (he was a fatalist through and through), with other people, and indeed with the way in which the whole world had been put together. He was dissatisfied when he was working, but he was even more dissatisfied when he was not working. He loved or at worst felt compassion for his wife, and he certainly loved his children, but he was thoroughly dissatisfied with his marriage. He was tremendously attracted and attractive to women and had virtually numberless affairs and quick sexual encounters until he had long surpassed the average lifespan, but he swung back and forth between feeling unworthy of being loved and feeling that his love was undervalued.

He believed himself superior to all but a few other interpretive musicians but on the whole completely inadequate to the task that had been put in his hands. Readers of this book will notice that time and again Toscanini expresses satisfaction over a performance that has just taken place but subsequently remembers the performance only for its defects—the opposite reaction to that of most musicians, who, in the immediate aftermath of a performance, remember all too clearly the mistakes they have just made but eventually allow the memory of the event as a whole to take on a generically golden, if somewhat faded and inchoate, glow. One has to smile, after having read Toscanini's expressions of pleasure over his *Fidelio* and *Falstaff* performances at Salzburg in 1935, to read his statements in 1936 and then again in 1937 to the effect that the cast and orchestra for both operas were "better this year than last": one knows exactly what mental process has been at work.

My impression is that Toscanini was happiest when he was studying (either in silence or at the piano) pieces of music that he loved, discovering new pieces of music to love, reading books that fascinated him, looking at paintings that gave him pleasure, and occasionally spending half an hour or an hour—a mealtime, perhaps, but not much longer—with one or another of his children or grandchildren. Maybe, but only maybe, he was happy in bed with a woman who offered him sensual gratification and who he (temporarily) believed understood him. He was curious about the world around him, enjoyed visiting places that he had never seen before, and took an active interest in world events, but his love for the peaks of human achievement was forever at war with his contempt for the vast majority of human beings—often himself first and foremost. And his dissatisfaction and contempt were expressed by outbursts of excessive anger and rage. Today Toscanini might be on Prozac or the like, and much the happier for it. But all of those startling, stimulating, questing, controversial performances that he gave the world would not have existed.

Would Toscanini have wanted these letters to be published? As a matter of fact, a few private letters that dealt with artistic matters were published in his lifetime, and he did not object—not publicly, at any rate. He may even have given permission to Filippo Sacchi, for instance, to publish, in 1951, a facsimile of part of his letter of 1 January 1905, to Enrico Polo. (A translation of as much of that letter as I have been able to find is included in this volume.) In short, I think that not much soul-searching need be done about publishing his comments on music and musicians or those that deal with his patriotic efforts during the First World War and his anti-Fascist ideals and activities during the 1930s and 1940s, which he was always ready to discuss.

There is no doubt, however, that he would have objected, and strenuously, to the publication of letters that deal with private matters—his states of mind and health, family problems, his relations with his friends, and especially his love affairs and sexual behavior. "[W]hy stick one's nose into others' boudoirs?" he rhetorically asked Ada Mainardi (letter of 7 November 1936) regarding the question of whether or not the musicologist Carlo Gatti had the right to publish information about Verdi's private life. "I gave Gatti my frank opinion. Judge the man and the artist—his life, as honest and upright as his art—but for pity's sake, stop short at the bedroom threshold."

On the other hand, in the same letter Toscanini gleefully recounted gossip that he had heard as a young man—when Verdi was still very much alive (Toscanini eventually encountered him personally on at least five occasions)—about the composer's "exaggerated" love of women and enthusiasm for oral sex, and he commented, "[I]f he liked women, what harm was there in that? He wrote Falstaff when he was eighty years old, Otello when he was seventy-four; do you think that a man of such fiber would be satisfied doing nothing but reciting the Ave Maria?" In other words, Toscanini thought that *he* was entitled to know the intimate details of Verdi's life and to pass them on to his friends, and that this knowledge could do no harm to Verdi's reputation in his or their eyes, but that such information ought to be denied to people he did not know because they could not be trusted to put it into the proper perspective.

Today, his point of view on this matter seems hypocritical, but to fault him for it would be to make an anachronistic judgment. It is all very well for a modern scholar to say that whenever a celebrity writes something down he or she runs the risk of having it read sooner or later by people for whom it was not intended. Likewise, it is all very well to theorize about letter writers' awareness of a Third Eye—an unknown, invisible, over-the-shoulder, omniscient reader who sees all letters and bestows the absolution of sympathetic understanding upon all who bare their souls in correspondence. No person born in 1867, however, would have believed that letters on family matters, let alone erotic-pornographic ravings to lovers, would someday find their way into mass-market publications for a Fourth Eye and a Fifth Eye and (depending on sales) a Ten Thousandth Eye to glint over. In our day the sex lives of celebrities have become so prominent a public fixation that whatever talents and activities initially brought the celebrities their fame are often overshadowed by the piquant details, real or invented, of their private carryings-on. In Toscanini's day such carryings-on were rarely reported to the masses. His greatest worry was that certain letters might be discovered by his wife or his girlfriends' husbands, not that they would find their way into the clutches of a curious biographer and end up before the eyes of the public—an entity he always regarded with suspicion and often with disdain.

For more than a generation, however, even the most sober and serious readers of biographical works have wanted to know more about biographees' whole personae than used to be considered necessary or, for that matter, permissible. To present Toscanini to this century only as he would have wished to be presented would do a service to no one, least of all Toscanini. In my opinion, his no-holds-barred sexuality was nothing more (or less) than an example of the same tremendous vitality that made every rehearsal and performance a life-and-death issue for him, and the fact that sex continued to play a large part in his life even at an age at which most pre-Viagra-era men had long since consigned their sexuality to their mental trophy cases means merely that he understood the nature of the current that runs from the vital juices to the emotions and the thought processes—and that he was lucky.

At least as difficult as the matter of dealing with Toscanini's writing on sex is the matter of dealing with his violently categorical pronouncements on a variety of subjects. In the end, all one can do is to caution the reader to try to understand such declarations in context. Whenever Toscanini mentions "the Germans," for instance, as a nation or an ethnic unit, his comments are scathing and at times downright racist, but when he writes about individual Germans—the great composers, his friend Adolf Busch, Goethe, a few of Wagner's descendants, and others—his words glow with admiration. Conversely, his occasionally intolerant remarks about individual Jewish friends when they have upset him in some way (e.g., "those Jews" David Sarnoff and Samuel Chotzinoff) are offset by his heartfelt defense of the Jews as a people, not only in his public stance during the Nazi years but even in his most intimate letters to Ada Mainardi, whose anti-Semitism he found repugnant. The fact is that in these letters he often lets off steam over people he loves (including his children) when they have irked him for some reason or other; if a good old ethnic slur is the first insult that pops into his mind, he uses it.

Entirely defensible, on the other hand, are his negative and sometimes devastatingly critical remarks about other performing musicians. All outstanding musicians have strong points of view about the music they perform; their points of view may change dramatically over the years, but they are held doggedly at any given moment. Attentive readers will notice that although Toscanini attacks a few of his colleagues over specific interpretations, his criticisms usually have to do with general approach or even nonmusical matters. Thus he demolishes Bernardino Molinari for being generally uncultivated and for treating accomplished orchestra players like schoolchildren, making them overrehearse music that they were already playing excellently; he calls Stokowski and Mengelberg "clowns" because of their thirst for publicity and refers to the former as a "gangster" because Toscanini believed that he was intentionally distorting certain pieces of music; he is driven to frenzies of frustration, especially in his younger years, by singers who are ill prepared; and he castigates Wilhelm Furtwängler and Sir Thomas Beecham over political issues. For the most part, however, he leaves people alone on matters of interpretation.

Some three to four dozen Toscanini letters have previously appeared in print, in whole or in part, most of them only in Italian. The most important ones among these have been inserted into this collection, too.

Because Toscanini's letters to Ada Mainardi and Elsa Kurzbauer (the professor's aunt) happen to have survived and come to light, whereas his letters to many other people outside his family (e.g., Giulio Ricordi) have not, the aforementioned erotic-pornographic ravings occupy a disproportionate segment of his extant correspondence. Several thousand declarations of love and descriptions of sexual activities may not be excessive if they are written and read over a substantial number of years, or if they were produced by someone who had a special talent for writing such things, but they are cloying and indeed boring in a single collection of writings by someone whose sole gift in this area was his enthusiasm. Inasmuch as I realized early in my work on this book that its preset word limit would have to be exceeded by a good deal, I decided to restrict the ravings to a few choice examples and to concentrate instead on letters that have more to offer readers whose principal interest in Toscanini presumably has to do with his music making and his whole persona. I am only too well aware, however, of how this volume's contents are likely to be treated in the press. About 15 percent of the text of my biography of Arthur Rubinstein* was dedicated to his relations with his wife, his children, and the various women in his life, but that subject occupied about 80 percent of the space that many reviewers dedicated to the book.

Throughout the following letters, frequent and sometimes substantial cuts have been made to avoid repetition, lengthy references to family friends whose names are unknown to the public, and other material of minimal cultural, historical, or biographical value; these cuts are all clearly indicated by the use of brackets and ellipses: [. . .]. Dozens upon dozens of letters that I judged to be uninteresting or that merely repeated statements made more fully elsewhere do not appear here at all. But I wish to state in the strongest way that I have acted only as an editor, not as a censor. I have not tried to alter, hide, or eliminate controversial opinions or aspects of Toscanini's character that I do not like or that I thought others would find objectionable.

So I can make this unfashionably judgmental declaration: In these letters, Toscanini appears with all of his flaws and in all of his greatness.

---

* *Rubinstein: A Life* (New York: Grove Atlantic, 1995)

Part One

JANUARY 1885–
SEPTEMBER 1897

MAJOR EVENTS IN TOSCANINI'S LIFE
BEFORE AND DURING THIS PERIOD

1867   25 March: Born in Parma, Italy, the first of four children and only son
        of Claudio Toscanini (1833–1906) and Paola Montani Toscanini
        (1840–1924).
1876   Enters Parma's Royal School of Music.
1885   Graduates with highest honors in cello and composition and maximum
        points in piano, taking first prize in graduating class.
1886   30 June: Makes unanticipated debut as conductor in Rio de Janeiro while
        touring as principal cello and assistant chorus master of itinerant Italian
        opera company. 4 November: Makes Italian conducting debut in Turin.
1892   Conducts world premiere of Leoncavallo's *Pagliacci* in Milan.
1895   Becomes principal conductor of Teatro Regio, Turin, and conducts there
        the first Italian production of Wagner's *Götterdämmerung*.
1896   Conducts world premiere of Puccini's *La bohème* at the Regio, where he
        also conducts his first complete symphony concerts.
1897   Marries Carla De Martini (1897–1951) of Milan.

Parma, 12 January 1885

Hon. Mr. Director.

The serious incident of which I am guilty toward you obliges me to write a few lines, which may serve to familiarize you with my great repentance for having committed so serious a mistake.

I did it not at all because I wished to disobey your orders, but rather because I had not reflected much about what I was doing, and because I allowed myself to succumb to a moment of anger.

I am very sorry for having caused such great displeasure to you and to my Teachers, but I hope that the goodness that you have always shown me will not fail at so critical and sad a moment for me, and that you will be so kind as to pardon my involuntary error, as I promise you that my gratitude toward you will never fail and that you will never have cause for complaint about me.

Anxiously hopeful, and with all my esteem, I sign myself your very Aff. pupil

A. Toscanini

Giusto Dacci (Parma, 1840–1915), composer and pedagogue, directed his home-town's excellent conservatory throughout AT's student years. According to Dacci's diary, on Sunday, 11 January 1885, fifteen students, including the seventeen-year-old AT, who was in his last year at the conservatory, refused to get up early to attend mass. When Dacci told them that they would have to attend a later mass during the time reserved for weekly family visits, and ordered them to go immediately to their respective study rooms, they refused. Dacci, who was accustomed to being obeyed, told an assistant to take the names of the disobedient boys and remarked in his diary that "Toscanini, in the presence of his companions, declared that he wanted his name to be first on the list. [. . .] I had his father sent for at once and told him that if his son did not write a letter asking to be pardoned, he would certainly be expelled from the school. [. . .] The young Toscanini, who was also in the office, walked out of the room—another scornful act. The same day I informed the Royal Commissioner of the occurrence. [. . .]" Only after Dacci had persuaded some of the professors to write the letter and persuade AT, the school's star pupil, to copy and sign it was the problem resolved.

POSTCARD, VIA SAN SIMONE 7, MI, N.D. BUT FROM SUMMER 1887;
TO ENRICO POLO, PARMA; BARBLAN, P. 28

Since I'll be returning to Casalmonferrato this October to conduct, I would need a concertmaster, in addition to several first violins; and of course I thought of you immediately, because after Gioconda we'll do Lombardi, and you understand what there is in this opera. I think the pay will be as much as 7 lire a day. [. . .]

The violinist Enrico Polo (1868–1953) had been a schoolmate of AT's at the Parma Conservatory. He later studied under Joseph Joachim in Berlin, then returned to Italy, became AT's concertmaster at Turin's Teatro Regio (1895), married AT's wife's older sister, and was an influential professor of violin at the Milan Conservatory for more than thirty years. · The nineteen-year-old AT's remarkable conducting debut in Rio de Janeiro in June 1886 and his Italian debut in Turin the following November did not solve his employment problems. He successfully auditioned for the position of second cello in La Scala's orchestra for the 1886–87 season (which included the world premiere of *Otello* under the composer's supervision) and conducted very little throughout 1887. He did, however, conduct Meyerbeer's *L'Africaine* in the Piedmontese town of Casale Monferrato in June of that year and returned in the fall to conduct Ponchielli's *La Gioconda* and Verdi's *I lombardi.* "What there is" in *I lombardi* is a lengthy, elaborate violin solo in the Trio in Act III; a first-rate violinist is required, and AT thought immediately of his friend Polo.

TO ?; NYPLTL

Casale [Monferrato] 28 November 1887.

Dear Sir.

As the performances of La Gioconda are coming to an end, and as next Saturday will be the evening of the prima donna, Sig.a Peydro, the town would wish to have the artist appear in a new piece of some sort; I therefore ask you to be so good as to demonstrate your great courtesy by allowing one of my songs to be performed, if not between the acts then at least before or after the opera. You will be doing me an enormous favor.

I therefore declare to you my most deeply felt thanks, and believe me your
Most humble servant
A. Toscanini

This letter was intended for the impresario or director of Casale Monferrato's opera house. In those days, leading singers were often given *serate d'onore* (evenings of honor) during which they were presented with gifts and laurel wreaths between two acts of an opera or at the end of the performance. Lola Peydro, the leading soprano in *La Gioconda,* did indeed sing AT's song "Son Gelosa" (composed during his student years) at her *serata,* with the young maestro accompanying her at the piano.

TO LUIGI PIONTELLI, (MI?); MTS

Genoa 7-3-92.

My dear Piontelli.

I need to ask a great favor of you, thus I ask you not to deny it of me and to be understanding if I'm bothering you for the second time.

As a result of various (not trifling) family obligations, I find myself in very great need. I require three hundred lire and I don't know which wall to bash my head against; I beg you to be so kind as to get me out of this mess, and I hope that the occasion to pay you back can't be far off: for now, all I can do is be grateful. The bearer of this letter is a trustworthy friend of mine (Attorney Oreste Ventura). You could give him the three hundred lire or, if you prefer, send them to me in Genoa, Via Fieschi 19, apartment 8. Again, I ask you to do this for me if you can, and I thank you in advance. I shake your hand and ask you to think of me as

Your Affec.

Arturo Toscanini

AT, in his early letters to Luigi Piontelli—one of the most important Italian opera impresarios of his day, who, later in the decade, acted as a sort of agent-manager for AT—addresses the older man with the extraformal *voi* form of the second person; in correspondence from the mid-1890s on, the informal *tu* is used. · The financial difficulties in which AT found himself off and on for several years were the result of his eccentric (and alcoholic) father's shaky business dealings. AT's relations with his parents and sisters were fundamentally affectionate but often strained.

TO LUIGI PIONTELLI, (MI?); MTS

Genoa 17-3-92.

My dear Piontelli.—Yesterday, after two supplicating letters and a telegram, I received from you a message saying that a telegraphic money order would be sent to me that morning. The morning went by, the evening went by, and another morning, and . . . nothing, nothing, nothing. My dear Piontelli, I absolutely can't believe that you're laughing at my present, highly critical position: I believe that you've forgotten; so for the last time, I beg and plead with you to send me three hundred lire; I'm in an impossible position, I can't leave Genoa until I have this sum; and believe me, I'm in this situation because of my goodness, too much goodness, toward a family that is very ungrateful to me. Superti can tell you something about this.

So be good, be kind, dear Piontelli, do me this favor; my gratitude will be boundless if you get me out of this situation, and if you wish I'll sign a promissory note that I will pay back as soon as I have a contract. You, who told me that I would be engaged in the fall, at Carnival and at Lent in your theaters, should trust that I will be able to pay off all of my debts, if not today then tomorrow. So do me this immense favor, think about my situation, which costs me more with every passing day and continually eats away at my heart. And I don't know where to turn. I hope that tomorrow (Friday) a money order from you will reach me, or at least a telegram disabusing me of my hopes—even that—but answer—it's not a matter that's not worth answering.

Once again, I heatedly implore you, I thank you in advance, and I send you my greetings. A handshake from

Your Aff.

A. Toscanini [. . .]

AT had known the violinist and conductor Carlo Superti at least since 1886: Superti had been assistant conductor and coimpresario of the Italian opera company with which AT had made his unanticipated conducting debut in Rio de Janeiro that year. Later, Superti worked as AT's assistant at various theaters.

OPEN LETTER ORIGINALLY PUBLISHED IN *TRIBUNA,* ROME, OCTOBER OR NOVEMBER 1892; REPUBLISHED IN A. DE ANGELIS, "LE DIREZIONI DI TOSCANINI A ROMA," IN *SANTA CECILIA,* ROME, 1957, NO. 2

The Fanfulla [newspaper] would like to have it believed that it was I who spontaneously offered Mascagni the honor of conducting I Rantzau. This is not true. Far from having given up this honor, I would rather have kept it for myself, and I would have felt fully equal to the task, and with no effort, notwithstanding the limited time available; but Mascagni wanted to keep for himself the honor of the first three performances. As far as I'm concerned, he can keep the remaining ones as well.

AT made his Rome debut at the Teatro Costanzi (now Teatro dell'Opera) in October–November 1892, conducting *Carmen, La forza del destino,* and the world premiere of *Gualtiero Swarten* by the now-forgotten Andrea Gnaga. He was also to have conducted the local premiere of *I Rantzau,* the latest opera of Pietro Mascagni (1863–1945), but Mascagni then decided that he would like to conduct the first performances himself. This letter is the result of what was to be the first in a series of clashes between AT and Mascagni, whose characters were poles apart. It is the only example of a published self-defense on AT's part in such a case.

P.S., HOTEL MILAN, PALERMO; TO GIACOMO PUCCINI, STABILIMENTO RICORDI, VIA OMENONI, MI; PC; NYPLTL

6-4-1893

My dear Maestro Puccini,
Some days ago I had the pleasure of being contacted by the Cambiaggio Agency to conduct Manon in Trent during the coming season.

I've heard nothing more about it . . . has it perhaps come to naught? I hope not.—In the event that the business were to come off, I would ask you to be so good as to bear in mind the following excellent orchestra musicians— Uldarico Giraud and Adolfo Melò; the former is a principal cellist with few rivals, the other an outstanding principal double bass, and both are currently working under my direction. In the event that I were not engaged, if some other plans for Manon are made without my participation, do propose [the two musicians] all the same to the management, and you will be very satisfied.

My dear maestro, I shall add my modest applause to the many praises unanimously heaped on your Manon by Turin's audiences and newspapers. Please accept it, because if nothing else it certainly has the virtue of sincerity.—I send you my best regards and I shake your hand affectionately.—Your

A. Toscanini

Quite a few letters from Puccini (1858–1924) to AT exist—most or perhaps all of the significant ones have been published—but there are very few known communications from AT to Puccini. In this letter, the conductor addresses the composer with the formal *Lei* form of the second person singular; by the letter of 1 March, below, written less than a year later, AT was using the informal *tu*. AT was finishing up a tumultuous five-month season at Palermo's Politeama Garibaldi when he wrote this letter. Puccini's *Manon Lescaut* had had its world premiere in Turin two months earlier and was beginning to make the rounds of other major theaters. AT could not have heard it performed, but he had read the score. In the event, he did not perform *Manon* or anything else in Trent the following season, and he first conducted *Manon* in March 1894 in Pisa.

P.S., GRAND HOTEL NETTUNO, PISA; TO CESARE BLANC (MI); NYPLTL

My dear Blanc—Let me refresh your memory. If by chance they decide to give Lohengrin at the Dal Verme, don't forget that I am eager to conduct this opera in Milan and that I am counting on your friendship in order to succeed with this plan.—From Milan I've learned that <u>Cimini</u> is favored by the management. Is this true? I put myself in your hands; by all means remind Signor Giulio to think of me, so that I can at least make up for the damage done me last year and rid myself of the curse thrust upon me by the infamous Viscount D'Afa [?]. . . . . I'm hoping to open here tomorrow. Following enormous problems with the orchestra and chorus everything has been mended, and I think the production will be a success.

Good-bye, my dear Blanc. If you have a couple of free minutes, let me know about the Dal Verme productions. Remember me. I shake your hand affectionately. Your

A. Toscanini

Pisa, 17-2-94

Blanc was an administrator in the Ricordi publishing company, which controlled much of Italy's musical life in those days (see below). *Lohengrin* was indeed performed at the Teatro Dal Verme (which, after La Scala, was considered the best of Milan's various opera houses) in September 1894, but with Vittorio Maria Vanzo (1862–1945) conducting. (Cimini, mentioned by AT, could conceivably have been Pietro Cimini, who later made a name for himself as a conductor, but he was only eighteen in 1894.) Vanzo, an early Italian Wagnerite, had conducted *Lohengrin* in Parma in 1883 (the sixteen-year-old AT was playing in the cello section) and the first Italian production of *Die Walküre* in Turin in 1891. · "Signor Giulio" was Giulio Ricordi (1840–1912), head of the G. Ricordi & Co. publishing firm, a powerful worldwide force in the opera industry; he and AT were not fond of each other, but AT needed the right to conduct operas of which Ricordi owned the copyright, and Ricordi soon came to need the services of the brilliant young conductor as a propagator of new operas by Puccini and other rising stars. What the "damage" AT refers to might have been is not known, but his artistic intransigence prevented him from getting as much work as he might otherwise have had during the first decade of his career. As he wrote to a friend many years later, "At that time, *no one* wanted me as a conductor, and I spent many a month inactive, *by others' lights.* They didn't deny that I had a certain amount of talent, but they were frightened by my *nasty character* and my exacting demands." This statement certainly applied to his relations with Giulio Ricordi. · Viscount d'Afa has not been identified. · The production with which AT was having "enormous problems" in Pisa was *Otello:* the orchestra was not up to the task.

TO GIACOMO PUCCINI, (MI?); COLL. ROBERT HUPKA, NY

Pisa 1-3-94.

My dear Puccini.

Tomorrow is the first orchestra rehearsal with everyone, singers and chorus. If you want to honor us with your presence, do so, and as soon as possible. We ought to open next Wednesday. I don't need to tell you that the impresa is at your disposal with respect to expenses, etc. etc. The tenor Rosati is a cretin, but he makes up for this misfortune of his with a beautiful, warm, and expressive voice. The baritone Bucalo, a gift from D' Ormeville, doesn't convince me at all, but he already sang it [the role of Lescaut] in Ferrara and it went well. The rest is going along.—Come very soon and let me know either by letter or by telegram.

Tell Blanc to send me two copies of the latest edition of Manon.

Ciao. Greetings from Corsi and a handshake from your

Aff. A. Toscanini

An *impresa* was a group licensed to run a given opera season at a given theater; the head of the *impresa* was the impresario, who engaged singers, conductor, and extra orchestra musicians and chorus members (if necessary) and provided sets, costumes, and whatever else was needed for the productions. The *impresa* is not to be confused with the theater administration, which was a permanent organization, usually under the control of the municipality. The administration engaged an *impresa* on a season-by-season basis: Theater A in City B might engage Signor X's impresa one year and Signor Y's the next. Most, but by no means all, *imprese* were based in Milan. · The "cretin" may have been Enrico Rosati (1874–?), whose main claim to fame is that he was Beniamino Gigli's teacher. · Carlo D'Ormeville (1840–1924) was a playwright, librettist (Catalani's *Loreley* is his best-known text), impresario, and theater agent; he seems to have been something of an intrigant, and AT had little use for him. · "La Corsi": Emilia Corsi (1870–1927), soprano, was a well-known Manon Lescaut.

Sunday evening 29-3-96

I've returned from having walked Signora Lucia home. This unpleasant woman had to disturb my joy in having spent an evening near my dearest Carla, turning the conversation onto a subject that caused me displeasure. Unpleasant a thousand times over, that woman. I'm sad and discouraged, and I need to tell you, because I'm so close to you in spirit and you don't know it. I don't have the consolation of talking to anyone about you, about what I feel, about what I'm going through. The only friend with whom I could do this is far away. To whom can I turn if not to the most kind Miss Carla? "Can it be true that she loves me?" This is the incessant thought, this is the doubt that pursues me ceaselessly, implacably. I make every effort to distract myself, but in vain: my mind's dreams won't be able to destroy my heart's dream. If it's true that you've given me a little of your affection as I've given you my whole soul, write a few words to me. They will be very dear to me. As always, your

Aff. A. . . . .

This letter was probably hand-delivered by a servant. AT had met Carla De Martini (1877–1951), his future wife, during the summer of 1895, while he was preparing singers for the first Italian production of Wagner's *Götterdämmerung,* which he was to conduct in Turin the following December. Carla's older sister, Ida, had been chosen for the roles of a Norn and Woglinde in that production, and Francesca De Martini, Ida and Carla's widowed mother, chaperoned Ida wherever she went, with Carla in tow. This is the first substantial letter that AT is known to have sent to CDM. · The Signora Lucia in question seems to have been an agent for singers, thus the "subject" that displeased AT may have had to do with that area of activity. · The "only friend" with whom AT could discuss his private life and thoughts was probably Enrico Polo. · In this letter, AT still addresses CDM with the formal *Lei,* but during the following two months, which he spent mainly in Milan (where CDM was born and had always lived, and which was by then AT's home when he was not conducting elsewhere), they evidently decided to use the informal *tu,* because in his next letter AT addresses CDM with it. At the request of a member of AT's family, who may eventually want to use the AT-CDM courtship correspondence for other projects, I have restricted my use of private content in this material to a few examples and have concentrated on AT's references to musical matters. Nevertheless, no censorship has been applied here: the letters are as chaste as any average nineteen-year-old, middle-class girl would have been allowed to receive in those days.

4-6-96 6 in the morning

My first thought on awaking is for you, and I send it to you with my good morning and a big kiss in which you will find all of my soul. On Tuesday I received your dear note, which filled my heart with joy, both for the sweet, affectionate assurances of love that it contains and for the good news that it brings me. Thanks, a thousand times thanks. I'm picturing you with a long,

long face and a reproachful expression because I didn't keep my promise of writing to you immediately. Am I or am I not mistaken? Well, if this is so, I beg your pardon, even if my crime was involuntary. The work I've done in the last few days has been enormous, and it has robbed me of many precious hours that I would rather have devoted to the little woman of my heart, to my Carla. And it's not yet finished. You see? I'm writing to you at this hour so that you will at least have this letter of mine this evening, with the six o'clock delivery, otherwise I wouldn't be able to do it today! So be patient again for this part of the week. You will be so good, won't you?

So your mother is happy that we love each other? I'm glad. I was already very fond of her, but now I adore her! Yes, very, very much. I'll write to her on Saturday, and on Monday I'll be in Milan without fail. So she told you that she's afraid that I won't be able to put up with your character? That she finds it impetuous, capricious? For that matter, this doesn't necessarily mean that you're not good and capable of creating the happiness of the person who loves you, isn't that so? And then, I love and adore you just this way, as you are! You were absolutely right not to talk to your mother about Polo. I don't think the moment is yet ripe. I won't dwell on this, because I fear not being in time to get this letter off, which I wouldn't like at all. I'll tell you only that I would like to shrink into a little, tiny object, so as to rest on your heart, always! But I'll take my revenge from afar by thinking of you, my beautiful treasure, every minute, and by giving you at every instant that vast, infinite love which I feel for you and will always have for you to my dying moment. Farewell my joy, my all—I can't wait to see you so that I can tell you aloud the things that I'm happy to write to you now, in other words that I am and will be yours, all yours, today as yesterday and as forever.

Aff <u>Arturo</u>

Best regards to dearest Ida.

AT had gone to Trent (Trento)—which until 1918 was part of the Austro-Hungarian Empire—to conduct the local premiere of *La bohème* and a revival of Verdi's *Un ballo in maschera.* · The reference to Polo concerns the violinist's budding courtship of Ida De Martini, CDM's sister; this was still being kept secret from the girls' mother.

TRENT 7 JUNE 1896; TO CDM, (MI?); EC

<u>Sunday six o'clock p.m.</u>

[. . .] Yesterday evening La Bohème was accorded a truly enthusiastic success— much greater than in Turin. The truth is that the opera gained a lot from a small venue like this theater in Trent. And Ferrani, Pasini, Gorga, and Polonini also profited from it. Wigley, the baritone, is a very handsome, elegant Marcello—the voice is <u>what it is,</u> but he is good on stage and enunciates well. The other baritone, in the role of Schaunard, is a real dog, and always will be, for all eternity. I also listened to that tenor Peirani, whose grandiosely bestial ignorance frightened me. He is the real, genuine Liebig of tenors, in other words a cretin of the highest order. But enough! May God help us, and him, because expectations are high here for Ballo in maschera, an opera that hasn't been performed in twenty-seven years, and I think those expectations will be disappointed. [. . .]

The sopranos Cesira Ferrani (1863–1943) and Camilla Pasini (1875–1935) and the tenor Evan Gorga (1865–1957) had been Mimì, Musetta, and Rodolfo, respectively, at *La bohème*'s world premiere in Turin four months earlier, under AT's direction, and were repeating their roles in Trent. Alessandro Polonini (1842–1920), baritone, had been Benoît at the *Bohème* premiere. · Giovanni Peirani (1868–1901) enjoyed a brief success before his early death. · Liebig was a company that produced bouillon cubes and packaged them with collectible illustrated figures from popular operas.

There are several telling bits of information in this letter, which demonstrates that even idealistic musicians like AT were tremendously interested in the degree of popularity that a production achieved: the number of performances given depended on how many times the house could be reasonably well filled, and the *impresa*'s economic survival depended on filling the house as many times as possible. As with Broadway musicals today, the box-office take was all-important; a season's day-by-day details could not be planned far in advance. Another fact that leaps out from this page is the emphasis on singers' stage presence and clear diction. And what is interesting about this is not that AT—one of the earliest and most convinced followers of Wagner's ideas about the *Gesamtkunstwerk,* the "complete work of art"—was willing to put up with an unremarkable voice if the singer's general communicative ability was good, but that most of the public evidently felt the same way; otherwise, the singer in question would not have been so warmly received. In Italy in 1896, three centuries after the birth of opera, the form was still considered *dramma per musica,* and for AT it remained so. Equally striking is the revelation that in a good-sized town like Trent, with an active opera house, Verdi's *Un ballo in maschera,* which is today considered a repertoire staple, had not been performed in twenty-seven years. Eighteen-ninety-six minus twenty-seven leaves 1869—ten years after *Ballo* was written. By the age of ten, an opera ceased to be fashionable and therefore tended to fade away. In 1896, at the age of thirty-seven, *Ballo* was about to reappear as a classic, and AT was by no means certain that it would still be deemed interesting.

(TRENT?, MID-JUNE 1896?); TO CDM, MI; EC

<u>five o'clock p.m.</u>

[. . .] I wanted to write to you last night, but I didn't have the strength. I was too tired when I came back from the theater. I've rehearsed a great, great deal today, and at seven-thirty I have to rehearse some more. After several rehearsals at the piano and with orchestra, I had to release Decima, who didn't know her part and has become even more of an ass, as well as Baccini, and Guerras, the baritone, replacing them with Ceresoli, Bianchini-Cappelli, who sang in Guarany and Maruzza recently at the Dal Verme, and Bellati. This last has arrived, and he, too, doesn't know his part. You can imagine the work that's cut out for me, with so great a fool! The worst of it is that we've had to postpone the opening to Tuesday, so good-bye to my quick trip to Milan; maybe we'll see each other on Wednesday, if they don't do three performances in a row. God, how sad I am! And it's simply intolerable that I can't write to you as I'd like or tell you everything that goes through my mind, everything I feel!

I'm not feeling well either, but it's nothing serious—only my usual lack of appetite and my unpleasant irritability. [. . .]

My guess is that the production in question in this undated letter (the envelope is missing) was the Trent *Ballo in maschera*. · Emma Decima had sung the roles of a Norn and Flosshilde with AT in Turin at the Italian premiere of *Götterdämmerung;* Elena Bianchini-Cappelli would sing the role of Brünnhilde with AT at La Scala in 1899, in the Italian premiere of *Siegfried*.

TRENT, 25 JUNE 1896; TO CDM, (MI?); EC

<u>six in the morning 25th</u>

[. . .] Last week Piontelli and the inseparable Signora Giulia were here; he attended the opening of Ballo in maschera and a performance of Bohème, then he left for Milan, where La Scala's Theater Commission was waiting for him to arrange the ceding of the Sonzogno management. If this transfer takes place, the productions that Piontelli would give would be: Götterdämmerung, Andrea Chénier, Bohème, etc., etc., and it seems to me that I'll have to release myself somehow from my Turin contract. Would you be pleased?

When I come to Milan, I'll amuse you by showing you the letters with which that unpleasant imbecile of a Russian woman to whom I gave a few lessons tormented me here in Trent. They're very amusing. When you realize that she never got even the slightest sign of interest out of me, you can only laugh and call her crazy, a thousand times crazy. And just think that she had threatened to visit me if I didn't reply! It's clear that she gave the matter some thought and persuaded herself that she was dealing with someone even madder than herself. [. . .]

Signora Giulia was Piontelli's wife. · The name of the Russian singer, or would-be singer, who tried to seduce AT is not known, but her letter to him is indeed included among his letters to CDM. This was by no means the only occasion on which he demonstrated (or tried to demonstrate) his faithfulness as a lover by sending to one woman a letter he had received from another.

[. . .] You may well believe that I am truly a wretch! No one's life is as embittered by this cursed theater as mine is! The worst of it is that I in turn embitter others' lives, unconsciously, through no fault of my own.

And I can tell you that I am very unhappy here in Trent, where the air does nothing for me, where everything around me is unpleasant, and where even the customs are intolerable. [. . .] As a result you can easily imagine this highly agitated creature's state of mind these last few days, the more so inasmuch as I am the victim of nasty pains that take hold of my back and right arm, making it painful even to breathe! I've often been on the verge of writing to Carla or to your mother but have then given up because I've felt incapable of formulating a single thought. [. . .]

In this letter AT is still using the formal *Lei* form of "you" with his future sister-in-law. · This is one of the earliest known references to AT's conducting-related physical problems, which became acute more than thirty years later; see also the letter of 16 April 1897.

29-6-96

My dear Depanis,

You have been too nice in not sending me a bunch of insults. They would have been like so much manna to me. You have to understand that I'm one of those brats for whom a few smacks on the head have a greater effect than any serious sort of admonition. Good God! If you knew how much I suffer as a result of this exaggerated laziness and how ashamed I am of myself, you wouldn't upset yourself but would instead double the dose of mercy you've shown toward me so far. Enough: be as good as ever once again, shake my hand affectionately, and forget this most recent childish prank, since you mustn't give it any deeper significance.—And now we come to our orchestra. The first violin section will be fine when it's completed by Genesini (who, if he accepts at a lower salary, will surely not want to play the ballets), Villa, and Superti. If the last doesn't accept, we could engage Prof. Minelli, a most excellent first violin. The second violin section, too, seems to me complete and good. Remember to reprimand severely Bertazzi, who got drunk every Saturday, and Sesia, who was late to rehearsals and deserted several performances with the aim of carrying on behind his wife's back.

I fear that Sabbia won't accept—and I would be very sorry, because besides being an excellent player he is a dear and distinguished young man. In any case, let me know and we'll replace him as best we can. For the violas, once you've signed up De Marzi we'll be all right.

As to the cellos, I've asked Serato in Bologna to recommend some of his distinguished pupils who could replace Melluzzi and Forzano, and in a few days I'll send you the names of these new members. In sending the contract to Guarnieri, warn him that I absolutely won't accept him in the orchestra except with a different instrument, because the one he had last year was impossible. Instead of <u>Morini</u> I'd like to propose <u>Agesilao Villani,</u> who is far superior to the other and who will accept the same terms. His address is simply [the town of] Correggio. The others are fine.

I hope that the question of Beniamino [flute] will be resolved to our advantage, that is, by excluding him altogether and replacing him with a competent young man who is now at <u>Saint Moritz:</u> Abelardo Albisi. Instead of making Nizza [piccolo] change instruments, I would have him change brains—but as the operation would be painful and might not work, I advise you to change the whole person by replacing him with Prof. <u>Gennaro Giuliani,</u> who is also currently under contract at Saint Moritz.

And now for pity's sake, let's not ruin the excellent quartet of horns that we would have by engaging Caletti, Naglia, and Pasetti, in addition to Fontana as first. Moressi may be all that you say—a good man, good player, good-looking, and virtuous—but his sound is impossible. He doesn't fit in, doesn't blend with the other three, and what's more, he plays out of tune. If a fifth horn should be engaged, however, <u>Moressi</u> would be my preference, because he's better than Forzano and Savino. But remember for pity's sake not to touch the quartet of horns that I had last year.

Filippa, the third trombone, I can manage to swallow again if, before renewing his contract, you give him a good punch in the head and tell him that I wasn't at all happy with him either as a player or as a person—but I absolutely don't want that fourth trombone. He may be wonderful for the band and for Maestro Vaninetti [the bandmaster], but he's worthless in the orchestra—in fact he ruins things—because he has no sound, he can't hold a note for four quarter beats without running out of breath, and furthermore he blithely and cold-bloodedly plays out of tune.

As to the first clarinet and bass clarinet, I want to hear them—because I remember the first's audition, which <u>wasn't very satisfactory</u>—therefore his nomination didn't convince me, and furthermore, I wouldn't want to make the same mistake as last year by trusting Maestro Vaninetti's assurances.

With that, I've finished the chat about the orchestra. I'll tell you now that I probably won't go to America—so it will be easy to arrange the concert business.

Write to me soon. I'm leaving for Milan tomorrow, and you can address letters to me at the usual address—Via della Maddalena, 5.

I promise to reply by return of post and not to disquiet you anymore. A strong, hearty handshake from your

Aff. A. Toscanini

Giuseppe Depanis (1853–1942), chief administrator of Turin's Teatro Regio, was the son of Giovanni Depanis (1823–89), who had arranged AT's Italian debut at the Teatro Carignano in Turin in 1886. Giuseppe, a lawyer by training, was an art, music, and literary critic by preference and a man of the theater by instinct. In 1895 his far-sightedness had been the main force behind the creation of the system that allowed the Regio's thoroughly overhauled orchestra—under AT's direction—to become Turin's Municipal Orchestra, and for the principal members of the orchestra to augment their earnings and simultaneously contribute to the city's musical life by teaching at the local music academy. · For explanations of AT's apologies to Depanis, see the following letter. · All professional Italian orchestra musicians are called *professori,* thus the denomination "Prof." for various orchestra members. · "Genesini [. . .] will not want to play the ballets": In those days, in major Italian opera houses, an opera performance, no matter how long it lasted, was generally followed by a ballet, which could last half an hour or even longer. The conductor changed, but most of the orchestra personnel remained. AT opposed this practice, which left players exhausted, but it was not eradicated until some years later. · Francesco Serato (1843–1919) was a well-known cellist and teacher, and father of the concert violinist Arrigo Serato. · This letter demonstrates the detailed seriousness with which AT chose players for his orchestras, and his memory for the playing of various musicians. In later years, when he was working with first-rate ensembles, he would go to almost any lengths to avoid firing or demoting players, but in his youth, when he was trying to put (and keep) together orchestras with whatever material was available, and when players did not in any case expect to be engaged for more than a year at a time, he replaced players as he thought best and, it seems, with an easy conscience. · There had been a plan for AT to conduct in New York in the autumn of 1896, but it fell through; the details are not known.

<hr>

TRENT, 29 JUNE 1896; TO CDM, S8MI; EC

29th—10 o'clock in the morning

Yesterday I wrote a long, interminable letter to my friend Depanis, [. . .] to make up for a grave lack of respect that I had committed toward that good, kind friend—I could do no less. Since June first he had been awaiting an answer to a very important letter, which he followed up with another and with four telegrams, the last of which had a prepaid reply form, plus one from the mayor. In short, I can tell you that I'm ashamed to put this in writing. It's a real enormity, and I didn't believe myself capable of it, although I'd given proof that I would achieve sublime things in the way of epistolary correspondence.

Poor Depanis was at first mortified, then irritated by this ill-mannered behavior of mine; he sent the mayor his resignation as head of the municipal orchestra. I trust that my fat letter, in which all the sweetest and most persuasive words of friendship have been joined together, will make him change his mind about this resolution and will restore to me his friendship and his most precious affection. [. . .] Tomorrow I'll have finished my ascent of Calvary and I'll set down my cross, to pick it up again—when?? When you leave for the country! Away, away, nasty thoughts. Now I'll get up and rush off to the theater. [. . .]

5-July 1896.

[. . .] I signed the Turin contract on <u>Friday,</u> and I lost the Scala contract—but since every cloud has a silver lining, let's hope and hope again. I wrote twice to <u>Depanis</u> and made an act of contrition. Nothing new so far. He's silent, shows no sign of life. Will I have to send him to the gallows?

[. . .] Is it necessary for me to tell you that P.P. is fond of you and that Bocchio sends her greetings? And I add: and that I'm happy? Giraud, present, says hello. He's finished eating the risotto and is about to devour a contemptible chicken. And he continues to say that he has a stomachache!

AT had been approached to assume the conductorship of La Scala, which was in the midst of an administrative and financial crisis, but he wisely decided to stay in Turin (once he had successfully pressed for a very large salary increase) until circumstances in Milan seemed more propitious. · P.P. and Bocchio or Bocchietto were the nicknames of Ida and Carla De Martini, respectively. · Fiorello Giraud (1868–1928), a fellow Parmesan and friend of AT's and Polo's, was a well-known tenor who had sung Canio in the world premiere of *Pagliacci* (1892) under AT's direction. He eventually sang many other roles with AT, including Siegfried in *Götterdämmerung* (La Scala, 1907) and Pelléas in the Italian premiere of Debussy's *Pelléas et Mélisande* (La Scala, 1908).

(MI), 8 JULY 1896; TO COUNT TORAZZO, (TU); AMT

[. . .] I've saved the best for last! Regarding Campanella, I repeat yet again what I said in my last letter: He is impossible. If he made no horrible mistakes in <u>Götterdämmerung</u> or in the other operas, it was because he <u>preferred keeping silent</u> or <u>reading the newspapers</u> to playing, and in the end I let the matter ride so as not to upset myself more than usual. I took pity on him. I don't intend to hear the same refrain again this year, but since <u>the need to replace him</u> doesn't <u>seem clear</u> to the City of Turin (I'm repeating his [the mayor's] words verbatim), I wouldn't dream of upsetting exquisite sensibilities by exerting pressure to replace this precious player—as long as he plays only in the band. But allow me to tell you that although the aforementioned phrase struck me as neither nice nor flattering toward me, it did seem lovely and new in its genre—so much so that it amused me. [. . .]

Count Ignazio di Torazzo was in charge of engaging orchestra players in Turin. · Campanella was the fourth trombone in AT's orchestra. · Small bands are used for playing offstage pieces (usually short) in operas that call for them; weak or inexperienced players were sometimes used for them.

[. . .] And now, my dear Torazzo, I'll tell you completely confidentially but with my heart on my sleeve that I am happy, extremely happy, about having brought off these changes—necessary ones—and I send my heartfelt thanks to Depanis, to you, and to all who have taken my complaints to heart. They were justified by what they were aiming for, that is, to bring Turin's orchestra to a level of perfection that has perhaps never before been achieved in Italy. [. . .]

E.P. NOVI–MILAN (RAILROAD LINE FROM NOVI LIGURE TO MILAN), 7 AUGUST 1896; TO CDM, POSTE RESTANTE, SALÒ, LAKE GARDA; EC

Voghera 6-August 96—6 o'clock p.m.

[. . .] I've been in Voghera for three days, and I'm already bewildered by the fearful number of outings. To walk—that's the only amusement allowed me: I can't even think, what with this uncle of mine, as dear as he is eager to be near me and to introduce me to this or that person. Only this morning I had some delightful moments during a peaceful walk in the garden that's part of the villa of some people whom I'd gone to visit but who weren't home at that moment. Completely alone, while waiting for them I savored the joy of losing myself in the greenery and amid the shadows; I walked around a nice green lake, as melancholy as my thoughts, until at last I sat down at the edge of a lit-tle grotto for capricious fairies, and I thought about many <u>high, sweet</u> things; then I wanted my thoughts to soar even higher, toward a beautiful <u>sunbeam, toward my Carla!</u>

[. . .] And how is Ida? Having fun? Continuing to put on weight? Everyone here is asking me about her, and I diligently sing the praises of her artistic qualities as well as her physical and moral ones. I don't have to tell you that the theater administration as well as other people who take an interest in the-ater matters have declared their satisfaction at knowing that she has already been signed up. Remember, as soon as you've found lodgings, rent a piano. Ida very much needs to keep always in mind everything that she studied with me last month. She must look hard at the words and try to become familiar with Abbé Prévost's novel. She must declaim her part. This will be an excel-lent exercise for learning to phrase well and, what's more important, to <u>recite warmly.</u> [. . .]

The De Martini sisters and their mother were spending a brief summer holiday at Salò, on Lake Garda. · So far as can be determined, the uncle whom AT was visiting in Voghera was a Montani, one of AT's mother's brothers, with whom AT had had an affectionate relationship during his childhood in Parma. Voghera is a small town in southern Lombardy some forty miles southwest of Milan and sixty miles northwest of Parma; its Teatro Sociale provided local citizens with short opera seasons, and AT had conducted *Aida* and *La favorita* there in 1889. Ida had been engaged to sing *Manon Lescaut* at the Sociale in the fall of 1896, thus the reference to the Abbé Prévost novel on which Puccini's opera was based. This is another example of AT's overriding concern with the literary-dramatic quality of opera performances.

E.P. BRESCIA, 14 AUGUST 1896; TO CDM, HSSLG; N.D.; EC

<u>eleven o'clock p.m.</u>

[. . .] Yesterday evening I ran a short, partial rehearsal with the baritone who is supposed to do the part of Schaunard, a Spaniard whose name I don't recall. He has a nice voice, but he's a bit cold; he may be intelligent—he certainly is ugly. I rehearsed with everyone at one this afternoon and at nine this evening. [. . .]

AT had gone to Brescia, a major Lombard town, to conduct the local premiere of *La bohème,* which opened at the Teatro Grande on 22 August.

E.P. BRESCIA, 15 AUGUST 1896; TO CDM, HSSLG; EC

eleven o'clock in the evening

[. . .] How has Ida replied to La Scala? Superti told me that Vanzo didn't intend to give her the parts of [both] Gutrune and the first Rhine Maiden, as he finds the idea not very artistic and even less decorous for the house. So what have you ladies arranged?

I'm dying of boredom here. I feel a general malaise that oppresses my heart. This stiff neck doesn't want to go away; it torments me and adds to my ill humor. I'm doing orchestra rehearsals only with the players from Brescia, and it would strike terror to the hearts of anyone who heard them. The most unmusical of ears would be offended and revolted. I'm not doing any more rehearsals with the singers—they've all done the opera before. I'm working on that poor devil who is doing Schaunard; I'm trying to put some life in him by shouting his part into his ears with my beautiful voice. Vain efforts! He becomes more and more of a goose. He's not lacking in intelligence, but he lacks the sort of comic talent that a part like this requires, and I'm oddly heartsick at the thought that we may have to replace him with Pini-Corsi or with Cerratelli[?].

[. . .] The poets tell you that life is made up of illusions and that reality is . . . . a dream—isn't that so? Now then, wouldn't you like to nourish yourself on illusions until life's very last moment? I would! Do you care so much about reality? I don't believe in it—it's inhuman. What's terrible and awful in life are the disappointments—those are what kill the soul and lacerate the body! And you <u>won't have any</u>—you <u>mustn't have any.</u> Your life must be <u>calm, azure</u>—that's how I desire and wish it to be for you. [. . .]

AT was "heartsick" at the thought of having to fire the inadequate singer, not at having to work with Antonio Pini-Corsi (1858–1918), who had sung Schaunard with AT at *La bohème*'s world premiere and who would work with him on countless other occasions at La Scala, the Metropolitan Opera, and elsewhere. · As to CDM's "calm, azure" future life as AT's wife: rarely do things turn out thus even among couples who live "normal" lives, let alone among couples whose lives are determined by the world of the theater.

E.P. BRESCIA, 17 AUGUST 1896; TO CDM, HSSLG; EC

[. . .] So you really want to know why I went to the Hotel Italia instead of the Cappello? What a child you are! But that's how I like you.—My reason for staying at the Italia is that at the station, the coachman who drives the [hotel's] omnibus came to take my suitcase as soon as he saw me, and I didn't have the heart to embarrass him—so this time, too, I've come to this hotel. <u>For no other reason.</u> Or rather, I've been lying: <u>it was to run after a beautiful young woman who got off the train with me.</u> Are you happy?—The tenor Apostolou is also staying at the Italia, and he's taken the room that I had the last time. Ferrani is at the Cappello and Pasini in a private home.

Will I go to Genoa? I don't know, either. The other day, everything seemed to have been arranged with Superti. This evening I received a letter in which questions about the fee were raised. I wired back withdrawing from all obligations. We'll see how it all ends this time. [. . .]

Is it true that Vanzo wants to listen to Ida for Götterdämmerung? I wouldn't advise her to agree to this request. She did the opera 18 times in Turin, and well. The press was unanimous in judging her favorably—what more does our friend Vanzo want? He ought to sign her up without hesitation. This is my opinion—Ida will do what she thinks best.

[. . .] Franchi's arrival was the cause of a staging rehearsal for chorus and extras. Steffanoni, the chorus master, is away, now that the fair is on, busy with activities all over the place, and I couldn't avoid staying around to play the piano. Tomorrow morning I'll run another staging rehearsal for chorus and singers; tomorrow evening will be the first rehearsal for the whole orchestra. [. . .]

The Greek tenor Yannis Apostolou (1860?–1905) sang Rodolfo with AT in the Brescia *La bohème*. · AT did not conduct in Genoa in 1896. · Franchi was a stage manager who also worked with AT in Turin. · Indicative of AT's now-legendary artistic seriousness is the fact that in the midst of his tenure as artistic director, in effect, of Turin's Regio—one of the three or four most important opera houses in Italy—and after having achieved international renown for such accomplishments as the first Italian production of *Götterdämmerung,* he would sit down and play the piano for a staging rehearsal for chorus and extras in a provincial theater if no one else was around to do the job. His main goal was to bring a production to the highest level possible with whatever forces were available.

[. . .] I didn't write to you yesterday evening because I was rabid with anger and I didn't feel well. In that damned 2nd act of Bohème the chorus and orchestra made me curse the day I was born. I walked out of the rehearsal and ran off to bed. All will be over on Saturday, God willing, and I won't have to trouble myself anymore. [. . .]

<u>eleven forty-five in the evening</u>

Beautiful house, great applause, curtain calls, encores of [Musetta's] waltz and of the quartet in the third act's finale: that's the report on the evening. No. 11 in the third row of boxes was occupied by a gentleman and a lady. My dear Bocchietto wasn't there as on the other evenings, and I conducted listlessly, yawning every five minutes. Without you, the evening held no attraction for me.

The trip today was endless, boringly endless. I arrived twenty-five minutes late. We stopped more than half an hour at Tormini[?]. I was in the black mood that I'm always in when I leave you and when I have to spend two or three truly agonizing hours in these blessed trains that raise hell's own dust. I don't want to take that route back anymore.

[. . .] I heard about the incident that took place at the opening of Bohème in Vicenza. Corsi suddenly lost her voice and did the performance as best she could. The next evening she was replaced by Zampini, who was so-so. I heard this from the tenor Moretti, who attended the second performance. It now seems that Angeloni, the impresario, wants to release Corsi, but the theater's administrators won't hear of it.

Maestro Pomè was in the theater this evening; he had come just to hear La Bohème, which he will have to conduct in Genoa instead of me. He'll stay on tomorrow evening as well.

AT had not yet begun his campaign in opposition to the antidramatic practice of encoring arias in the middle of opera performances; indeed, he was still using the number of encores at a performance as a gauge of a work's success. · CDM, no doubt with her mother and sister, had attended the first two *La bohème* performances in Brescia, which is only about twenty miles from Salò, where they were spending their summer holiday. And AT had evidently returned to Salò with them when he had a day and a half between performances. · Regarding Emilia Corsi, see the letter of 1 March 1894. The story of her indisposition is interesting only because it demonstrates how closely AT observed even the most provincial of singers, impresarios, administrators, and others who inhabited his world. · The soprano Gisella Zampini did not leave much of a mark. · Alessandro Pomè (1851–1934) was a noted conductor in his day; historically, his claim to fame is that he conducted the world premiere of *Manon Lescaut*. AT had worked briefly as his assistant at the Teatro Carignano in Turin in the fall of 1886, but by 1896 AT's reputation had greatly overshadowed that of Pomè.

[. . .] I am very worried about a telegram from my father that I received at the theater yesterday evening, not preceded by any other advance news regarding the health of my sister Zina, who is in Parma right now. It reads: "Just received telegram Zina Parma she is better no danger to our peace of mind." As you see, it talks about danger—averted, so it seems—but no letter or card had warned me that my sister was ill. On the contrary, I thought she had completely recovered. Early this morning I wired home; I'm awaiting an answer, but in the meantime my mind isn't at peace in the least.

[. . .] Yesterday evening there was another magnificent house—the take was nearly three thousand lire. De Comis goes into ecstasies over La Bohème's music—he says that for the time being it is the most beautiful music in the world—very melodic and—even more—harmonic.

AT was the oldest of four children and the only son; he and his family were living mainly in Milan by the mid-1890s, but his parents seem to have maintained some sort of residence in Parma. Narcisa, the oldest of his sisters, had died in about 1878 at about ten years of age. Ada lived from about 1875 to 1955 and Zina from 1877 to 1900. He had been very fond of Narcisa—her death when he was still a child had been a terrible blow to him—and he loved Zina, too. With Ada he seems to have had little to do, although she lived nearly as long as he did. · "De Comis goes . . .": AT's irony about La bohème is telling. He understood what a well-made opera it was, and he seems to have enjoyed conducting it, but to the end of his life he often expressed qualms about Puccini's originality and musical taste.

5 p.m.

I've received very bad news from Milan and Parma about my sister Zina's health. She has caught a bad fever-related infection and intestinal inflammation. The doctor fears that she could get intestinal peritonitis, which would mean intestinal tuberculosis. My mother left for Parma yesterday with my sister Ada; she wrote to me today, and however reassuring her letter may be, I'm very much afraid, knowing how weak Zina is physically.

I can't begin to tell you how agitated I am right now. This is a blow that I wasn't expecting, the more so because I thought that my sister had recovered within two weeks of having gone to Parma. She would like me to go visit her. [. . .]

According to Dr. Howard Markel, director of the University of Michigan's Historical Center for the Health Sciences, there is "a form of intestinal tuberculosis" that was often contracted "from drinking unpasteurized milk"; the lesions (tubercles) "can perforate the intestines and cause a peritonitis—an infection of the abdominal space caused by a hole in the actual gut."

I haven't been able to write to you since I arrived. I've just this moment left Zina to wire you. Yesterday she was very ill[,] this morning better, I'll manage to write you today. [. . .]

Yesterday Zina worsened, so I postponed departure hoping to leave her improved. Today she's better [,] tomorrow morning I'll go to Milan [. . .]

11-10-96 3 p.m.

[. . .] Please keep me informed of everything that concerns the Manon rehearsals. I would like to be near Ida, and at the same time I know that it would be a bad thing because I would frighten her uselessly. Do yourself what I could do: <u>liven her up, repeat a thousand times what you've heard a thousand times from me,</u> and <u>encourage her</u> to <u>look at</u> the <u>vocal score after the rehearsal too, maybe</u> in <u>bed; she can never know the opera well enough,</u> and <u>when she goes before</u> the <u>orchestra she will still find herself in difficulty, even if she knows [the opera] perfectly;</u> and <u>above all</u> she mustn't <u>drag</u> the <u>tempi.</u> [. . .]

"She can never know the opera well enough": This could be called AT's credo with respect to his own work and the work of everyone who worked with him throughout his career. "She mustn't drag the tempi": Similar *cris de coeur* to singers echo and reecho through the letters of Verdi and many other opera composers.

[. . .] This morning Piontelli sent me a guaranteed-delivery letter, heatedly exhorting me to deal with putting together the ensemble, as he has to present the complete list of repertoire and singers to the municipality at the end of the month, and I can't continue to wash my hands of the matter, like Pilate, as I've done till now, but must rather deal with it seriously, because in the end it's also in my interest.—I hope for that matter that the [*Manon Lescaut*] rehearsals are moving along well and that Ida isn't arousing Perosio's anger like the tenor and some of the other artists. If you continue to keep me informed you'll reassure me more and more, in addition to doing something that I appreciate.

It seems to me a bit early to go before the orchestra! Advise Ida to sing out immediately the main items, such as, for example: <u>In quelle trine morbide,</u> <u>L'ora, o Tirsi,</u> the love duet from the second act, and the fourth act. Remind her above all that if one makes an honest mistake, one is only half a jackass; the other half is the listener who swallows it. In short, repeat the usual refrains, which will always be useful.

Your concierge came to call me in a great hurry yesterday evening. Half afraid, I ran to your house and found a letter from Zina's doctor. Fortunately, it wasn't alarming. Zina has improved remarkably over the last few days, and although one can't yet say that the disease has run its course, the doctor's prognosis is highly favorable. Let's hope for the best! [. . .]

Piontelli's letter no doubt referred to AT's Turin season, which was to begin only two months later. The fact that at that late date a major opera company had not yet settled on its artists and repertoire indicates how different the opera world was then from what it has become now, when seasons are often planned four or five years in advance, despite the fact that no one knows what condition a singer's voice will be in so far in the future. · Perosio was a conductor of modest repute toward whom AT seems to have been fairly well disposed. · However much Zina's health seemed to have improved, she died four years later at the age of twenty-three.

E.P. MI, 13 OCTOBER 1896; TO CDM, AIV; EC

This morning I received a letter from Bolelli, my impresario in Bologna, announcing his idea of exchanging <u>Le Villi and the ballet</u> for <u>Chénier.</u> If this were to happen, you can imagine what a job I'll have dealing with Sonzogno to put the cast together! I already began this morning to write very long letters to both Piontelli and Bolelli. I've never written so much in my life! [. . .] Has Ida sent her visiting card to various journalists? I'll find out from my uncle whether or not this is the custom. [. . .]

AT was scheduled to conduct *La bohème* and *Le villi*—both by Puccini and both published by Ricordi—in Bologna, with rehearsals scheduled to begin only two weeks after the date of this letter; Umberto Giordano's new *Andrea Chénier,* on the other hand, was published by Edoardo Sonzogno, whom AT found even more difficult than Sonzogno's rival Giulio Ricordi in the matter of arranging casts. Besides, as the next letter indicates, a diplomatic effort was required if operas that belonged to competing publishers were to appear back to back. · It is amusing to observe AT solicitously trying to discover whether or not his future sister-in-law ought to butter up the press in a small town such as Voghera, whereas he had always been (and continued to be) far too proud to do any such thing on his own behalf, even in Italy's musical capitals.

E.P. MI, 14 OCTOBER 1896; TO CDM, AIV; EC

My dearest, I was hoping to receive news regarding the latest rehearsals and especially the first one with orchestra, but here I am empty-handed. [. . .] I certainly hope that everything is going normally, and this is what I ardently desire. Have they done a staging rehearsal? And how did Ida bring it off? I'm curious to know also whether she <u>faltered</u> in rehearsing with the orchestra or whether she found less difficulty and greater support in watching the maestro's beat. Write to me—keep me informed.

And you, my dear Bocchietto, what are you doing? I can imagine you running up to the stage and back, following the rehearsals' progress with anxiety, with trepidation! I, too, am a bit nervous, knowing Ida's excessively impressionable and cold character, and I won't hide the fact that my nervousness won't stop until after the first or second performance, although I know that she can do quite well.

[. . .] Between answering the extremely long letters of Piontelli, who has woken up at last, and Bolelli, and busying myself with the choice of singers, I don't have an hour's rest. I'm going to have lunch now, then I'll go look for [parliamentary] Deputy Marescalchi of Bologna, a friend of Sonzogno and Ricordi, so that he'll <u>intercede</u> with the latter for permission to perform Bohème although we're giving Chénier. [. . .]

In the end, the *Chénier* plan was abandoned and *La bohème* was followed by *Le villi,* as originally scheduled.

E.P. TURIN–PISA (RAILROAD LINE), 20 OCTOBER 1896 (ONE ASSUMES THAT THE LETTER WAS SOMEHOW REROUTED, AS AT WAS IN MILAN); P.S., GIUSEPPE BERGAMIN/THEATER AGENCY/MILAN, ... 189/ VIA CARLO ALBERTO 8 (PIAZZA DEL DUOMO)/FOR TELEGRAMS, BERGAMIN— MILAN; TO CDM, AIV; EC

My dearest, I have no choice but to write to you in a hurry while a tenor is howling here at the agency. Since this morning, when I went to the station to mail the letter I wrote to you, I haven't been back home. I've got Piontelli following me around, and I don't know how long this will go on! I wanted to write to Ida, but it isn't possible. I'll barely manage to send off these few lines. Tell her to be as courageous as possible, to go on stage straightforwardly and securely, and all will go as she and I desire. She must be straightforward on the stage, she mustn't look at the maestro—and above all, brio, brio. She must support the voice and breathe calmly. Forget about any refinements whatsoever for that audience.—Wire me.

AT's advice that Ida *not* watch the conductor seems strange at first blush, but it probably meant either that a conductor ought to be ready to follow an inexperienced singer rather than lead or collaborate with her, or that AT considered the conductor in question insecure, therefore more likely to throw Ida off than to help her.

[. . .] For three days I've been leading a dog's life. I leave home at 8:30 [a.m.] and get back at midnight. Three days of eating lunch and supper out and of running all over the Bergamin Agency listening to singers of every sex and genre, and as if that weren't enough I've had to go through the martyrdom of two sessions of three and a half hours each to audition two new operas. In short, I can't wait to get out of Milan, and I hope to do so tomorrow (Saturday), otherwise Piontelli will drive me mad.

[. . .] At 1:30 a.m. I received the telegram announcing Ida's success [in the opera's first act], and if on the one hand it gave me immense pleasure, on the other it kept me terribly worried since it wasn't followed by more news to reassure me that the success was complete. Luckily, that came the following evening [. . .]. It gave me the greatest pleasure—it truly moved me. I'm happy for Ida, for your mother, for you, and for everyone. [. . .]

My dearest, Here I am in Learned Bologna. [. . .] I've already had a rehearsal of Bohème, and I very much fear for Rebuffini and the baritone De Bernis, Schaunard. [. . .]

Bologna, where the world's first university was created in the late eleventh century, is nicknamed *la dotta* ("the learned") in Italy. · Rebuffini, a soprano, was scheduled to sing Musetta in the Bologna premiere of *La bohème*. · Emilio De Bernis (1842–1907) was a Turin-born baritone.

<u>Bologna 28-10-96</u>
[. . .] I went to the <u>Quattro Pellegrini</u> hotel, where I was awaited by the German prima donna Ella Prossi, who has been engaged by Piontelli for Turin; she has come to Bologna to study, or rather to complete her study of Tristan and Götterdämmerung in Italian with me. [. . .]

<u>midnight</u>—[. . .] I'm desperate over my rehearsals! Rebuffini is such a dog that it would be hard to find her equal. I'm heartsick at having to send her away, but neither do I want to jeopardize the production on her account, especially since the Bolognesi aren't very easygoing—on the contrary, the public here is highly intelligent. She is here with her mother and a lawyer named Sala; she has rented an apartment and it seems that she is living with this

lawyer. I've already wired Signor Giulio about the problem, and he has replied, reminding me that he's given me full power and asking me to look after replacing her. Of course, it was on his advice that Rebuffini learned this role, and he was the one who insisted that she be engaged! What rascals all these publishers are! She seems to have foreseen that her end is near, because when she saw that I was a bit put out [at the rehearsal] this evening, especially with her, she begged me to go to her place to go over the part with her. I got out of this, because however wily she may be, I could buy her, sell her, and buy her again. [. . .]

Ella Prossi: Really Ella (or Hella) Prossnitz, although the Italianized form of her name appeared even in the printed libretto of the Turin *Tristan.*

(BO); TO CDM, (AIV); EC

<u>midnight 29-10-96.</u>

[. . .] Have pity on Merolla, because she is merely one of the many mentally and spiritually unfortunate women who live in this false world of the theater. [. . .]

According to CDM, Signorina Merolla, a soprano who was performing in Voghera at the same time as Ida, had been giving Ida a hard time.

E.P. BO, 31 OCTOBER 1896; TO CDM, AIV; EC

<u>7 a.m. 31-10-96.</u>

[. . .] I'm still in bed, and with a terrible sore throat. Yesterday evening I got very, very angry with the orchestra—and so I shouted like a madman. This morning I'm feeling all the wonderful effects. [. . .] I've advised Ida not to accept the proposals she has had from Perugia and Bergamo. Those aren't operas for her. I'm surprised that Baragli is still set on Ballo in maschera and La forza del destino. <u>He might as well have proposed her for Norma, too!</u> [. . .]

Some Verdian sopranos who can sing Amelia in *Ballo* and Leonora in *Forza* may also be able to sing the title role in Puccini's *Manon Lescaut* well, but Amelia and Leonora can be sung well only by a full-fledged Verdian *lirico-spinto* soprano. AT evidently felt that Ida was not capable of dramatic roles, at least not so early in her career. And he considered the title role in Bellini's *Norma* the most difficult soprano part in the standard Italian Romantic repertoire.

1-11-96. seven o'clock a.m.

[. . .] <u>Are you perhaps a little jealous?</u> Your Rebuffini is in a very bad temper with me! She has begged and pleaded with me to let her perform, but I am steadfastly against this because I don't want to jeopardize a success that will be assured once she has been replaced by Sedelmayer.

I'm voiceless and tired. I'm working at the theater all day long, since I have to look after things that I've never had to do in the past with Piontelli, such as the sets, props, etc. I have to deal with them here because the impresario is senile and soft. [. . .]

Carla had expressed misgivings over Rebuffini's invitation to AT to visit her at her apartment, and AT enjoyed teasing Carla over this. Rebuffini was replaced by Amelia Sedelmayer.

midnight 2-11-96

[. . .] I've finished the dress rehearsal just this minute, and it went well. The first performance will take place on Wednesday and I'm hoping for a success. <u>Pandolfini</u> sings well, but she's no <u>Ferranina.</u> She doesn't have the latter's soul, the warmth of her delivery. She sings well because you can see that she's been taught by a distinguished teacher, namely her father, a famous baritone.

Nor does Sedelmayer make me forget Pasini. She has a better voice than the latter, but she lacks her grace, her flirtatiousness, and the natural verve that's necessary for bringing to life a character like Musetta.

[Umberto] Beduschi, the tenor, is perhaps more of a jackass than the other tenors I've had in Bohème, but he, too, will be liked. By forcing the Schaunard to sing his head off I've managed to make him listenable and he won't wreck things. Arimondi as Colline and Carbonetti as Benoit and Alcindoro will be liked.

The orchestra and chorus are decent. With the former I had really serious trouble. Now it's all over. But at the time I wanted to drop everything and run off to Voghera, you know. Now, as I've said, the river's rising waters have receded and the matter is finished. I'm sorry that things went differently for poor, good Maestro Perosio. [. . .]

The German woman is young—she must be 24 years old—but she isn't pretty. I haven't seen her since Thursday afternoon. [. . .]

The soprano Angelica Pandolfini (1871–1959), daughter of Francesco Pandolfini (1836–1916), was Mimì in AT's Bologna *La bohème;* AT compares her unfavorably to Cesira Ferrani, his (and the opera's) first Mimì. In 1898 Pandolfini was Eva in the production of *Die Meistersinger* with which AT began his tenure at La Scala, and in 1902 she "created" the title role in Cilea's *Adriana Lecouvreur.* · AT makes a similar comparison between Amelia Sedelmayer and Camilla Pasini, the first Musetta. Other references include the basses Vittorio Arimondi (1861–1928)—who had sung with AT in the first production of Franchetti's *Cristoforo Colombo* and had been Pistola at the world premiere of Verdi's *Falstaff*—and Federico Carbonetti (1854–1916).

E.P. BO, 6 NOVEMBER 1896; TO CDM, AIV; EC

5-11-96.

My dearest, So, La Bohème was a true, unanimous success at this delightful Teatro Comunale. Five pieces were encored: the tenor's <u>romanza</u> in Act I, <u>Musetta's Waltz</u> and the <u>Finale</u> of Act II, the final <u>quartet</u> of Act III, and <u>Addio vecchia zimarra</u> [in Act IV], not to mention the innumerable curtain calls and applause that crowned all these encores. [. . .]

E.P. BO, 6 NOVEMBER 1896; TO CDM, AIV; EC

midnight

The 2nd performance of Bohème ended ten minutes ago. [. . .] This evening's performance earned the same applause and the same encores, excepting the tenor's romanza—he didn't want to concede it. The audience was smaller than yesterday evening's, but considering that second performances of every sort of opera, however well liked, always have empty houses at every theater, the numbers were rather high. And how is the Voghera impresa's business doing? Piontelli has signed up one Dupeyron, a tenor from the Paris Opéra, for Samson and Tristan [in Turin]; I've been told that he's excellent. [. . .]

Tell Nastrucci that I may have found a good cello for him. It belongs to Prof. <u>Cremonini,</u> who is my 1st Cello here. He would give it to me to take to Turin, so that he [Nastrucci] could try it out before buying it. [. . .]

Bordeaux-born Hector Dupeyron (1861–1911) had made a name for himself in Brussels, Paris, and elsewhere. · Ugo Nastrucci, who played cello in AT's Turin orchestra, was probably a brother of the violinist Gino Nastrucci, who was later AT's concertmaster at La Scala; Ugo was probably heading the cello section in Voghera's wretched orchestra in order to survive until the 1896–97 Turin season began.

E.P. BO, 7 NOVEMBER 1896; TO CDM, AIV; EC

eight thirty p.m.

[. . .] This evening I'll go to bed very early, because I need to rest. I've played a lot of my dear Tristan and now I'm really tired. [. . .] Today I received a very kind letter from Ricordi, who thanks me for the careful preparation I gave to

Bohème and answers, at the same time, a request I made of him—that is, not to pay much for the rental of Le Villi; with the kindness typical of Signor Giulio when he's in a good mood, he agreed, thanks to his high regard for me, to give us the opera at an exceptional price—five hundred lire!

Has Sonnino spoken to Ida again about engaging her for La Bohème in Novara? Ask about this, because I think I heard that one <u>Lina Peri,</u> who is now in Asti to sing in Rigoletto, has already been engaged for it. Then tell me if there's any truth in all of this. [. . .]

<u>Bologna 6-11-96.</u>

So far as I have been able to determine, neither AT's letters to Giulio Ricordi nor Ricordi's to AT have survived. · Sonnino was an impresario who worked at provincial theaters. The statement about Lina Peri demonstrates once again that AT paid close attention to what was happening throughout the Italian opera world, even in provincial towns such as Asti and Novara.

E.P. BO, 8 NOVEMBER 1896; TO CDM, AIV; EC

<u>midnight</u>

[. . .] This evening, too, La Bohème enjoyed its usual success—there were many more people than at the second performance. At the Brunetti, on the other hand, La Traviata opened with Musiani Rizzoni [as Violetta] and was a fiasco. Is Sonnino doing good business? Has Manon attracted the interest of those ignorant people of Voghera? [. . .]

The Teatro Brunetti was Bologna's second opera house.

E.P. BO, 8 NOVEMBER 1896; TO CDM, AIV; EC

<u>five p.m. 8-11-96</u>

[. . .] It seems to me that Sonnino doesn't know how to operate successfully, and I'm surprised, because I had sized him up very differently! [. . .] I'm sending you three letters from Rebuffini, in an envelope, and they will show you how we took our leave of each other. [. . .]

The letters in question have not been found; presumably Rebuffini felt angry and humiliated at having been replaced.

eight o'clock in the morning. 14.11.96.

[. . .] I had many dreams during the night. My sleep was highly agitated. In fact, in this regard please ask your mother what meaning water has in the cabala of dreams. All night long I kept dreaming that I was swimming in the sea, and swimming splendidly—I, who don't know how to stay afloat one second. [. . .]

twelve o'clock noon 15-11-96.

[. . .] I wanted to write to you after [I left] the theater, but just as I was going up the steps of the hotel I ran into Maestro Buzzi-Peccia, who has come to Bologna specifically to play me the redone 2nd act of his opera—and as you can very well imagine, after the preliminary greetings we moved on to an endless series of chats. I went to bed at three. He's now waiting for me downstairs in the dining room so that we can go to the theater to hear the 2nd act of his opera. [. . .]

During the following Turin season AT would be conducting the symphonic poem *Re Harfagar* and the world premiere of the opera *La forza d'amore* by Arturo Buzzi-Peccia (1854–1943). The now-forgotten Milanese composer eventually ended up as a music teacher in the United States and remained in touch with AT, to whom he occasionally sent mock epic poems in doggerel, poking fun at himself, at AT, and at various common acquaintances.

My dearest, I was absolutely unable to write to you yesterday. I did eight hours of sessions at the piano, between rehearsing Le Villi and going over Tristan with the German woman—who, God willing, will go back to Milan on Thursday. A cousin of mine from Milan arrived on Sunday evening. Unfortunately! Because he brought me wonderfully comforting news about my **dear dad!** What a pleasure it is to have such a parent! He's playing the devil now, because he knows that I want to send them all to Parma at the end of March. I've already given notice to the landlord. If he continues to plague my existence, in the end I'll wash my hands of the matter and won't set foot again in my home, leaving everything in their hands. My dearest Carla, this is how one is repaid for being good-hearted, to the point of being so three times over!

Enough. So much the worse for him—I won't budge an inch from what I've planned to do. But I won't hide from you the fact that all this business upsets and afflicts me and puts me in the worst humor. On top of all this, there's the dreadful weather and the fact that I'm bored to death by this eternal, unpleasant opera season, which forces me to be far away from you and kills my soul and spirit. Never have I felt as unhappy as today. I can't begin to describe the sluggishness I feel—I hate being busy, but I must work. I'm envious of you, who can sleep as much as you please! But let's speak of cheerful things. So: did all of you go with Nastrucci to Alessandria yesterday (Monday), to hear [Boito's] Mefistofele? For that matter, you were right to rid yourselves of the boredom that you, too, must feel in Voghera! [. . .]

Here, we'll have Wednesday and Thursday free but will then do three performances in a row: Friday—the queen's birthday—Saturday, and Sunday. Puccini, specially invited by the impresa and the theater's administrators, may attend the last one. I can't tell you how much his coming annoys me! Especially since I have no desire to conduct, and since the performances of La Bohème now are worthy of the last Saturday of Carnival. [. . .]

17-11-96 five o'clock p.m.

The nature of this particular dispute between AT and his untrustworthy father is not known, nor do we know what "three times over" refers to. · Also unknown is the cause of AT's negative feelings toward Puccini at this time; there were rumors of rivalry between the two men over the soprano Cesira Ferrani, but this is not a matter to which AT would have been likely to draw Carla's attention. More likely, Puccini had promised to do AT a good turn with respect to a prestigious conducting opportunity somewhere but instead had done him a bad one. · "Worthy of the last Saturday of Carnival": Tawdry.

E.P. BO, 18 NOVEMBER 1896; TO CDM, AIV; EC

4 p.m. 18-11-96.

[. . .] I had decided to go to the [Teatro] Brunetti this evening to hear Mefistofele—me, too—but instead Arimondi advised me to go with him to the Genesini café to hear three mad people perform—two brothers and a sister, a pianist—and I'll follow his advice. I'll go after the rehearsal of Le Villi. [. . .]

E.P. BO, 19 NOVEMBER 1896; TO CDM, AIV; EC

[. . .] It's been a while since I've had so boring and unpleasant a season as this one! I'm working listlessly, contrary to my custom; I feel a need for solitude, and it kills my spirit and makes me irritable. Oh my Carla, what ever have you done to this poor Arturo! Who would have thought that the young girl I met in Treviso last year would steal my whole heart and soul! [. . .]

<u>20-11-96.</u>

[. . .] I got up at eleven and went to the theater to go over the romanza from Le Villi with Beduschi; I auditioned a baritone and I rehearsed the orchestra in the 2nd act.

This morning Puccini wrote me a postcard in which he tells me that he absolutely can't accept the invitation sent to him by the impresa and the theater committee, because tomorrow he has to leave for the Maremma as a guest of Count Gherardi. You can imagine my joy!!! It's only equaled by the impresa's displeasure at the news.

[. . .] There will be a grand evening here this evening, with the theater brilliantly illuminated—which of course means that one doesn't see [the stage] as well—for the tenth performance of Bohème. Tuesday the ballet Coppélia opens, Saturday Le Villi. [. . .]

The Maremma is an area in southwestern Tuscany.

21-11-96. <u>seven-thirty a.m.</u>

[. . .] I didn't write to you last night because I came back from the theater so tired that I couldn't stay up even five more minutes. We finished the performance at half past twelve, having begun at nine, preceded by the royal march, which was encored and repeated again before the third act. The king of Greece and his family were in the theater. It was a splendid evening—the theater was magnificent. [. . .]

The king of Greece was the redoubtable George I (1845–1913).

<u>21-11-96 four o'clock p.m.</u>

[. . .] Must I always be besieged by inexperienced young composers? One [blank space] will be following me around in a few days—he's a full-fledged pest—and I'll have to swallow whole his extremely long four-act opera. God knows how long he'll hang around, since he told me that he wants to stay awhile in Bologna to show me the orchestral score, too, and to get my advice on it. Imagine my suffering! [. . .]

21-11-96. <u>eleven forty-five</u>

[. . .] I've heard some news that I don't much like. It seems that Puccini, having heard over and over that Florence's Bohème is nothing in comparison with this one in Bologna, and not only that, but that the 2nd act can't even be compared with it, has become curious about hearing it, and it seems probable that he'll come next Thursday. Oh! What wouldn't I give to have him stay away!? How it bothers me to see Jesuits and fakes! [. . .]

See the note to the letter of 17 November 1896.

22-11-96.

[. . .] I'm not surprised in the least over Sonnino and Fauner's [Trauner's?] unkind behavior. They're impresarios, and desperate ones at that; enough said. I'm surprised only that Ida doesn't tire of wallowing in all the muck. I hope that during this season she will have learned what the theater is like and what most singers are like. Nothing of what you've written me about the impresa and the singers has surprised me at all—I knew it all in advance, and in fact I think that before all of you left Milan I warned you what would happen.

What's certain is that I can't see you [singular] happily spending much time in the theater, suffering from it! At the same time, I'm happy that Ida has been and continues to be fêted. Her pleasure is certainly not greater than mine. [. . .]

23-11-96 seven thirty a.m.

[. . .] Thanks to having shot the breeze with that chatterbox Lawyer Camber, I didn't get to bed until four a.m. tonight. I'm horribly sleepy. That pest kept nattering at me in the most indescribable way! He wouldn't hear of my saying no to signing a contract with him for a tour in Germany. What a pleasure! I hope that he'll leave at two this afternoon [. . .].

Have you heard what a <u>ridiculous</u> figure Zampini cut as Venus in Tannhäuser? And she wants to do La Bohème at La Scala! [. . .]

AT did not conduct in Germany until 1929. · Gisella Zampini sang Venus in a production of *Tannhäuser* at Milan's Teatro Dal Verme in November 1896, but had to be replaced by Giuseppina Cesareo.

five o'clock 24-11-96.

[. . .] Lucky you who are finally home in delightful Milan, which I love so much! I'm counting the days still to pass till I leave this sad Bologna, but they go by so slowly that time seems endless to me. What a tiresome season! What boredom! What martyrdom!—The ballet opens this evening, and I don't know what sort of success it can have. In my opinion, it was still very unready, with poor ensemble between the orchestra and the ballerinas' legs! We'll see what the audience thinks of it. Meanwhile, we're doing Bohème, and Saturday Le Villi will open, if there are no hitches. [. . .]

AT did not conduct the ballet, but he had attended the dress rehearsal.

E.P. BO, 26 NOVEMBER 1896; TO CDM, S8MI; EC

26-11-96. seven-thirty a.m.

My dearest, I didn't write to you yesterday evening after the rehearsal because I rushed immediately to bed; I was as angry as a dog. I was already in bed at ten. I walked out of the rehearsal less than forty-five minutes after it had begun because of the 1st trumpet, who, piqued by a repeated correction of mine, left the rehearsal like a coward, thereby cutting an extremely poor figure in front of the whole orchestra as well as the chorus and singers. A devil of a ruckus then broke out. De Bernis, the baritone, who thought that the orchestra was protesting against me, insulted a player (Cremonini, the 1st cello), and a serious incident nearly took place—all over a misunderstanding. They were both saying the same thing without understanding each other at all. Beduschi and Wilmant calmed them down and the two went back to being friends, more so than before.

I was still extremely irritated, of course, and after having wired Modena for a 1st trumpet I marched off to bed with a powerful headache. All night I did nothing but dream highly agitated dreams. These are our uncertainties. God willing, even this eternal season will come to an end! [. . .]

E.P. BO, 27 NOVEMBER 1896; TO CDM, S8MI;
LETTER PROBABLY WRITTEN ON 26 NOVEMBER 1896; EC

7 o'clock in the evening

[. . .] This morning that trumpet player came to the hotel to apologize; I refused to see him. At this afternoon's rehearsal the one I wired Modena for was already there. Le Villi won't open on Saturday {28 November} but rather on Tuesday {1 December}.

La Gioconda was a <u>monumental</u> fiasco at the Brunetti yesterday evening. The conductor was Maestro Palminteri, who, the other evening, had to stop rehearsing because he was as drunk as a lord. [. . .]

E.P. BO, 27 NOVEMBER 1896; TO CDM, S8MI; EC

<u>27-11-96. seven-thirty a.m.</u>

[. . .] At the fourteenth Bohème performance yesterday evening there was a magnificent house and great and enthusiastic applause. Coppélia, the ballet, was also applauded more than the other evening—or so Arimondi told me, because I didn't stay for it. [. . .]

E.P. BO, 28 NOVEMBER 1896; CDM, S8MI; EC

[. . .] So Signora Lucia (that sweet thing!) came over to propose that Ida sing a brand-new opera—La Forza del destino—and maybe at the theater in Roccamura. Is that all she has to offer? I'm being tortured by Mayor Dall'Olio, who, in the name of some ladies, patronesses of a charitable institution, requests that I put together a vocal concert. Isn't that nice? And one can't say no, which is what I would gladly do. [. . .]

<u>6-thirty evening—28-11-96.</u>

Signora Lucia, whose name first appears in AT's letter to CDM of 29 March 1896, was probably a minor agent or impresario. AT was of course being sarcastic about the "brand-new" *Forza del destino*, which was thirty-four years old in 1896. Roccamura is a nonexistent small town—a name used to indicate "Nowheresville," an archetypal provincial backwater.

E.P. BO, 30 NOVEMBER 1896; TO CDM, S8MI; EC

[. . .] So you went to the theater and you liked Phriné [by Saint-Saëns]? You have bad taste, because that opera is a real piece of trash. [. . .]

In this early phase of their relationship, AT rarely expressed anger toward Carla, but questions of musical taste were too serious for him to ignore.

two in the morning

My dearest, What a dreadful day this has been! I spent it at the theater, getting terribly angry. A more idiotic organization, a stupider stage director, a more undisciplined and ignorant stage crew couldn't have befallen me. After having worn myself out giving all the necessary orders so that the dress rehearsal [of *Le villi*] would proceed well, nothing was ready this evening. The stage manager didn't even know at which points the scene changes were to take place. I walked out halfway through the rehearsal, then I came back, only to leave for good toward the end, declaring explicitly to the organization and the management that I've never yet been anyone's marionette and didn't intend to start now by allowing [the production] to go onstage in such an indecent state. I hadn't been that angry in a long time. I assure you that if I were capable of pretending to be ill, as Pomè and Vanzo do, I would gladly do it to extract myself from this mess. <u>Piontelli, my Piontelli, where are you when I need you??</u> I have 28 dancers who couldn't manage to dance a waltz. Compared to them, I'm Terpsichore. Then there's Beduschi, who's such a dog in this opera that he's beyond being laughable. The only one who's all right is Wilmant (and Ricordi didn't want him). Even Pandolfini isn't quite right. The orchestra and chorus are decent, on the other hand. But the staging is something horrible, and not only that, it's also unfinished, tawdry. Tomorrow I'll run two more rehearsals, and we'll open on Wednesday. Dearest Carla, maybe it would have been better if I'd become a priest instead of a musician. At least I would have eaten <u>ostie,</u> whereas with these annoyances I run the risk of shouting them at everyone.

You're perfectly right to say that I misread the part [of CDM's letter] regarding Phrinè, Cavalleria, Pandolfini, Bertrand. I've just now reread it and, by first <u>inserting</u> the <u>periods</u> and <u>commas</u> (which are almost always missing) I've understood my error and have bowed down before the truth. Are you happy now? [. . .]

An *ostia* is the wafer (the Host) taken at Communion, but the word *ostia* (plural *ostie*) is also a mild swearword in Italian.

3-12-96.

[. . .] Yesterday evening we finally presented Le Villi. Semifiasco! Although the opera was decently performed by the singers and well performed by chorus and orchestra, it couldn't survive the comparison with La Bohème. The audience was bored to death. We'll perform it again this evening, for Wilmant's "evening," and then I think we'll go back to our first love. For several days, members of the chorus and the corps de ballet have continued to melt away. By the time we get to the last performances only half the personnel will be here. Yesterday evening a viola and a first violin ran off. At this point, I'm taking the whole thing as a joke. I'm tired of getting angry. [. . .]

With respect to the Scala business, I would advise Ida to have Vanzo hear her before she accepts. For the first Rhine Maiden an audition would be useless, but for Gutrune it would be good for that impostor to state openly whether or not Ida meets his requirements. That's my advice. Ida has enough good sense and judgment to decide. Does she remember the part a little? Does she feel up to memorizing it in a short time, to setting aside her great timidity? Vanzo may not be irritable, like a certain Toscanini, but he lacks the latter's sincerity! Ida must listen to her conscience. First of all, she must feel that she is capable of learning the part in a few days, conquering her timidity, and above all know how to figure out the maestro's personality—recognizing that at bottom he is a false individual, unreliable in everything he says and does. On the other hand, this engagement could tickle any singer's self-esteem, and especially in Ida's case, considering how recently she began her career. The most difficult thing for her will be the scene [AT forgot to specify which scene], which must be done rigorously in tempo. And that's all I have to say on the subject. [. . .]

About Ida and the Scala production of *Götterdämmerung,* see AT's letters to CDM of 15 and 17 August 1896. In the end, she did not participate.

(BO); TO ENRICO POLO, TU; BARBLAN, P. 316

3 December 1896

My dear Polo,
You seem to have become a great sluggard! Ida is very sorry that you don't write to her and don't even answer her letters. Are you so busy that you can't give her two minutes? Tell me whether the orchestra is better than last year and whether Maestro Martucci was happy with it.

I'm angry that I can't perform the 2nd part of Berlioz's Dramatic Symph. Romeo and Juliet on the first concert I conduct. The [concert] society doesn't want to cover the cost of the music, and I'll have to replace this piece with Buzzi Peccia's symphonic poem Re Harfagar. The rest of the program consists of Beethoven's 1st Symphony, Grieg's Holberg suite, Wagner's Forest Murmurs, and Bourgault-Ducoudray's Cambodian Rhapsody.

Ciao dear friend, write to Ida and then to me. Say hello to your mother.
I'll be in Turin the evening of the 9th.
Greetings
                              your aff. A. Toscanini

The composer, pianist, and conductor Giuseppe Martucci (1856–1909) gave a great impetus to concert life in opera-dominated Italy at the turn of the century, but he had also conducted (1888) the first Italian production of *Tristan und Isolde.* AT admired him as a musician and liked many of his compositions. Martucci had conducted the Turin orchestra's first concerts of the season. · In the end, AT replaced the Bourgault-Ducoudray piece (which he never conducted) with Weber's *Freischütz* Overture.

E.P. BO, 5 DECEMBER 1896; TO CDM, S8MI; EC

eight o'clock in the morning.

[. . .] Yesterday evening was the 2nd performance of Le Villi and our friend Wilmant's "evening." The attendance was poor and the gifts scarce: a little pin weighing a few milligrams and a funeral wreath from the impresa, plus another wreath, a rather pretty one, from his friend and colleague De Bernis. Applause, and an encore of his romanza. So much for the merriment of the festivities.

The impresa had asked me whether I, too, wanted my evening. I politely replied that I will have my evening when I come back again to Bologna, and very gladly. [. . .]

E.P. BO, DATE ILLEGIBLE; TO CDM, S8MI; EC

three p.m. 5-12-96.

My dearest, Tell Ida to send them all to the devil—Vanzo, D'Ormeville, and Corti, a bunch of impostors. She absolutely must not accept. She'll save herself unpleasantness and humiliation. She mustn't believe in any promises, especially if they come from Vanzo. [. . .]

Coming back to the subject of La Scala, let me say that it's useless for Ida to kill herself learning Gutrune. My Russian woman (as you call her) will certainly do that part, in the first place because she sings gratis, and then because if Vanzo said that he'll have to try to get rid of her, you have to believe the exact opposite—unless he's behaving in a manner unworthy of himself, which is highly unlikely. And I wouldn't advise [Ida] to accept the role of the Rhine Maiden. [. . .]

About Carlo D'Ormeville, see letter of 1 March 1894. · Maria Corti was a soprano. · The Russian woman, whoever she was, did not sing Gutrune in the first Scala *Götterdämmerung:* the role was taken by Corti.

I'M DEAD FROM WORKING I HAVEN'T TIME TO BREATHE BETWEEN OPERA AND CONCERT I REHEARSE FOUR TIMES A DAY FORGIVE ME FOR NOT WRITING TO YOU THANKS FOR INFINITE GOODNESS WILL FIND WAY TO WRITE TO YOU THIS EVENING AFFECTIONATE KISSES AND GREETINGS BE ALWAYS AT EASE—ARTURO

Between the previous letter and this telegram AT had finished his Bologna season, returned to Milan for a two- or three-day break, and then dashed to Turin to begin a much longer and more demanding series of concerts and operas.

14-12-96.

[. . .] My dear, from the time I left Milan until now I haven't had a moment's peace. In a little over a week I've lost a rather remarkable amount of weight. I haven't had a moment's peace, don't have one now, and won't have one for the rest of the week. I had hoped to be free Sunday morning and to be able to write to you, but instead I had to run a rehearsal of the Freischütz Overture, which was replacing a number on the program that had been eliminated at the dress rehearsal. Depanis came to bother me at ten this morning and didn't leave until twelve, when I had to run to the rehearsal for the 2nd concert without having had lunch; I finished at three and ran to the piano rehearsal of Chénier. Add to this the fact that I hadn't taken the trouble to study this unpleasant opera—so after each rehearsal I have to run home to study whichever act I have to coach at the following rehearsal. As a result, by evening I'm so tired that I don't even have the willpower to talk. [. . .] I'm staying at Piontelli's place; I have a magnificent room and I eat at home with him. We see each other only at mealtimes. The same with Polo, except that I see him at rehearsals. As you see, it's not socializing that robs me of my time for writing to you! I'm pleased that my concert was successful, artistically as well as materially, at the box office. More people attended it than Martucci's two concerts, and it's expected that people will have to be turned away from the last concert, on Sunday. I'm very pleased for the sake of my two or three enemies in the [concert] society. [. . .]

16-12-96

[. . .] In the name of justice and legitimate self-defense, I have to tell you that Polo's duties are very different from mine. When he has finished an orchestra rehearsal, he is more rested than he was when it began; the lessons, both private and at the Liceo, can be given in one's sleep, whereas I achieve nothing if I don't make use of all my nerves and energy. And then there's a bit of difference between fighting with one sole individual rather than with eighty or a hundred. And then in the end, if Polo's pupils prepare their lessons, good; if not, so much the worse for them—whereas my responsibilities are of quite a different order, don't you think? No, no, believe me, if I haven't written to you it's because I couldn't. [. . .]

E.P. TU, 18 DECEMBER 1896; TO CDM, S8MI; EC

[. . .] I'm taking advantage of the half hour that's left me before I go to rehearse the singers in Chénier to spend a little time with you. The orchestra rehearsals for the opera will begin Sunday evening [20 December] and I'm counting on doing the dress rehearsal next Thursday [24 December], in order to come to my Carlottina on Friday [Christmas Day], to receive all those little kisses that she's promised me. [. . .] The program of this last concert is very interesting. It consists of Haydn's Symphony in D Major (the one I conducted at La Scala [no. 101, "Clock"]), Mendelssohn's <u>Midsummer Night's Dream</u> Overture, [Catalani's] Danza delle Ondine (Loreley), the Adagio from Bruckner's 7th Symphony, Isolde's Love-Death by Wagner, and Chabrier's Gwendoline Overture. I had to rehearse a lot, and I'll run two more rehearsals tomorrow to clean up the whole, difficult program. I hope that this one, too, will go well! [. . .]

AT performed the Adagio from Bruckner's Seventh Symphony in memory of its composer, who had died two months earlier. He conducted the Fourth and Seventh symphonies with the New York Philharmonic during the 1930s, but those were his only other forays into the Bruckner repertoire.

(TU, 21 DECEMBER 1896); TO CDM, (S8MI); EC

<u>10 in the morning</u>

[. . .] The concerts, too, are finally finished! Everything went splendidly. The only piece on the program that was received coldly was Bruckner's Adagio. It's beautiful but very hard to grasp at first blush. For this piece, the audience split into two factions that joined together at the end in a formidable applause for all the performers. Then, in the evening, I ran a very long orchestra rehearsal of Chénier. I finished at midnight, dead tired—because the concert had already exhausted me. This morning at eleven there is a staging rehearsal for the singers, at one an orchestra rehearsal, this evening at seven another staging rehearsal for the singers, at nine a rehearsal for everyone. Illica and Barilati[?] have arrived. The Giordano-Spatz couple will arrive any day now. The full dress rehearsal takes place on Thursday [24 December]. [. . .]

Ciao, my dearest. Signora Giulia is calling me to come eat a couple of eggs. I'll go, and then I'll run to the theater. [. . .]

Luigi Illica (1857–1919) is remembered as the librettist not only of Giordano's *Andrea Chénier,* but also of Catalani's *La Wally,* Mascagni's *Iris and Isabeau,* and above all (in collaboration with Giuseppe Giacosa) Puccini's *La bohème, Tosca,* and *Madama Butterfly.* Illica and AT had been very friendly since the days when both of them were helping to look after the dying Catalani. · Umberto Giordano was married to Olga Spatz-Wurms, daughter of the owner of the Grand Hôtel et de Milan, near La Scala, where Verdi and other celebrities stayed when they visited Milan. · For Signora Giulia, see the letter of 25 June 1896.

E.P. TU, 2 JANUARY 1897; TO CDM, S8MI; EC

2-1-97. 10 in the morning

[. . .] Yesterday was an awful day for me. I felt very ill. I have a horrible cold and my head hurts a lot. I was very irritable at the rehearsal, for the first time since the season began, and I felt very badly about it. After the rehearsal I rested a bit and in fact I slept a couple of hours, contrary to my custom. This rest did me good, because yesterday evening I rehearsed more willingly and less irritably. [. . .]

I've been very sorry about never being able to write to you during the last few days, but what can I do? You'll have to agree that the fault isn't entirely mine. Both Chénier and Samson were absolutely new operas for me—you know that last summer I was taken up with nothing except my Bocchietto, and it was natural enough that I dedicate a few days to them, too! And you must realize that neither Franchi nor Piontelli knows the staging for Samson—so I've had to order a French booklet that deals with this opera's staging and then explain some of it to Franchi, who didn't even know who Samson was. [. . .]

Franchi was the Regio's stage manager. In all likelihood, the booklet in question contained what the Italians called *disposizioni sceniche,* or stage distributions. Creative opera stagings as we know them did not exist at the end of the nineteenth century; instead, composers and/or librettists often published diagrams, with accompanying descriptions, to explain where singers, chorus members, and supernumeraries were to position themselves during each of an opera's scenes, and they expected their instructions to be followed—although not rigidly—for as long as the opera survived. AT felt that inasmuch as neither Franchi nor Piontelli had taken the trouble to investigate the opera's stage distribution, the responsibility was thrust upon him.

<u>4-1-97 seven in the evening</u>

[. . .] I've not only had to attend all the staging rehearsals of Samson, as I do for all the operas, for that matter, but also to teach the chorus and extras where and how to move, point out the [singers'] various changes of position, and, last but not least, even deal with the ballet. The dress rehearsal will take place this evening, God willing. The first performance is tomorrow. I hope that everything will come off in good order. Dupeyron, the tenor, has a beautiful voice and is a fine artist. He enunciates clearly and well—better than the Italian singers. In my opinion, he has a flaw that could prove distasteful to the audience—certain vocal sounds are too nasal. But if they put up with this defect, they'll have to like him. Cucini is a bit cold, but she has a pleasant voice and sings quite well. The chorus has its good moments; likewise the ballet segments are going pretty well. The orchestra is good. All in all, it seems to me that the opera ought to be liked. The music is pretty and has beautiful moments.

<u>one a.m.</u>

I finished the dress rehearsal a half hour ago, and it didn't go well at all. The orchestra was careless to the point of forcing me to demand another rehearsal for tomorrow morning, as punishment. The tenor never sang full voice. The other singers did. The opera made a very good impression. We'll see the final results tomorrow evening.

My compliments for your detailed and judicious account of the Götterdämmerung performance [at La Scala]. Bravissima! I read that part of your letter aloud to Piontelli, who was present when I received it, and he told me that your impressions were the same as those of his daughter Carolina. I was very pleased to hear my Bocchietto discuss Götterdämmerung and its performance. [. . .]

Alice Cucini (1870?–1949) was a well-known contralto.

E.P. TU, 7 JANUARY 1897; TO CDM, S8MI;
LETTER WRITTEN 6 JANUARY 1897; EC

<u>five p.m.</u>

[. . .] I've done a rehearsal of Mefistofele, and the outcome makes me foresee that I'll have to replace Gorga—who has turned into a dog, and a breathless one at that—as well as Dufriche, whose voice isn't deep enough for the role of Mefistofele. Corsi is decent. I think that Chénier didn't go very well at La Scala, isn't that so? Here it arouses no interest. The theater is always half empty. There is great anticipation for Samson. I would never advise Ida to accept singing Musetta. Mimì is a different matter, although I would want to hear her first in the whole part, since it's a matter of performing before an intelligent and difficult audience. This time, however—in the event that this could be arranged—she mustn't accept without getting a reasonably good fee, because the responsibility would be much greater than for the Manon in Voghera. [. . .]

The production of Boito's *Mefistofele* did not open until 24 January. · Paris-born Eugène Dufriche (1848–?) sang in most of the world's opera capitals. · Regarding Corsi, see the letter of 1 March 1894. · AT was wrong about the reception that *Chénier* had received at its world premiere at La Scala on 28 March 1896: it was a triumph, and the opera quickly became popular. · Musetta is a role for a lighter soprano voice than the roles of Mimì and Manon Lescaut.

E.P. TU, 7 JANUARY 1897; TO CDM, S8MI; EC

four p.m. 7-1-97.

Samson finally opened yesterday evening. On the whole, it went well and was liked. I think it will arouse interest.

Dupeyron was an astonishing dog, enough to frighten a thousand wolves. But the audience, knowing that he sings at the Paris Opéra, felt that he was someone who had to be applauded, certainly much more than he deserved, although without enthusiasm. I assure you that he made more versi than Dante in his Divine Comedy. What's more, he continued to sing out of time all evening. Cucini, on the other hand, was much liked—in my opinion she doesn't understand a thing about the character, but since she has a nice, even voice she made an excellent impression on the audience and was applauded throughout. Polese, the baritone, was decent, but in the first act he jeopardized his aria by making a very loud error on the last note. D'Arrigo (the wretch) made it through better than I'd thought he would. The chorus was fine. The orchestra was <u>awful, nerveless and careless.</u> The musicians had undoubtedly eaten too much focaccia. The staging was nice. All in all, the production is good and will certainly improve when the tenor regains his courage after yesterday evening's enormous nervousness—because I'm sure he can't really be the dog he showed himself to be. So much for a report on the evening, or rather a review of its main features. [. . .]

". . . more versi than Dante in his Divine Comedy": A *verso* is a line (not a verse) of poetry, but in colloquial Italian it also means a stray or unpleasant noise. · Giovanni Polese (1873–1952) later sang a great deal in the United States. · G. D'Arrigo was singing the role of Abimélech (bass).

10-I-97.

[. . .] This evening we're doing Chénier instead of Samson. Cucini is ill. [. . .]

This sentence is interesting because it demonstrates the relative ease with which one opera could be replaced by another at the last minute if a key singer was indisposed. This was possible because a company of singers tended to stay put for an entire season and because sets consisted mainly of painted backdrops rather than complicated structures.

21-I-97.

[. . .] I have to dress for the performance before I eat, because at seven-thirty I'm going to the theater to listen to the boys and girls who are singing in the Prologue to Mefistofele, which will open—I don't yet know when. Dufriche has given up the part [of Mefistofele] and it will be taken by Arimondi. I'm continuing to rehearse Mefistofele morning, noon, and night, plus having a look at Tristan once in a while. We're not going to do Bohème. Ricordi absolutely doesn't want Corsi. [. . .]

23-1-97. three p.m.

My dearest, I couldn't write to you yesterday. I spent the whole day at the theater, rehearsing, and I had to dedicate my few remaining free hours to Maestro Buzzi-Peccia, who arrived Thursday evening specifically to go over his opera. I wanted to write to you yesterday evening after the rehearsal, but I admit that I didn't have the strength. I did all of Mefistofele straight through for the first time—it was and wasn't a dress rehearsal—in short, the rehearsal went on till one a.m. I was more dead than alive. [. . .] I'm waiting for Depanis, who is to take me to the site where they're building the venues for the Exposition, to see and arrange how to set up the big concert hall and connecting rooms. [. . .]

The Esposizione Generale Italiana was to be held in Turin in 1898.

My dearest, Just so as not to leave you without word from me, I'm writing you a few lines in a great hurry. Tristan doesn't leave me time to breathe. When

I'm not busy with piano rehearsals, I'm busy on my own, studying the orchestra score. I admit, however, that although working all day long—and part of the night, I may well say—tires me, I'm nevertheless working willingly and don't feel the fatigue as much as I do with other operas. I'm driving those poor singers crazy. This is their rehearsal schedule every day: from one to four-thirty, from nine to a quarter past midnight. Yesterday evening Superti and Polo came to tell me that it was past midnight! I hadn't noticed. [. . .] This evening we're doing Samson instead of the third performance of Mefistofele. Piontelli went to Milan to find someone to replace Gorga, who at this point can't sing at all. [. . .]

six p.m. 28-1-97.

E.P. TU, 29 JANUARY 1897; TO CDM, S8MI; EC

one a.m.   29-1-97.

[. . .] I'm so fond of your mama that, to tell you the truth, it would be a joy for me to have her always with us when we're married. Wouldn't she also keep you company when I'm at the theater rehearsing? Since I'm hoping to establish myself at La Scala and to travel as little as possible—excepting the American business, if it should be arranged for '98—it would make things easier for me, for you, and for her. [. . .]

Once again, it is not known what American engagement was being discussed for 1898. It did not take place.

N.D. BUT WRITTEN BETWEEN I AND 7 FEBRUARY 1897; EC

[. . .] [Regarding *Tristan:*] At noon I rehearse the strings alone until two, when the singers come and stay until five; at seven, if there's no performance, the strings return and we rehearse until nine, when the singers come back again to rehearse until eleven thirty, and often until twelve or a quarter past twelve. In the morning I have myself awakened at eight and I work on my own, on Tristan as usual, because every day it seems to become more difficult. And I'll be working like this for quite a few days, that is, it will be my fate to continue to repeat this rehearsal pattern until I put the whole business together. You can't imagine how difficult this opera is, especially for the singers, and the tenor in particular. There is no part more difficult than this one. If only all this effort were at least to be crowned with a substantial success . . . ! Let's hope so! [. . .]

one a.m.

My dearest. I'm just now getting home after four and a quarter hours of rehearsal. I'm dead tired. I began at ten-thirty this morning, teaching a little solo in the third act to the English horn player; at eleven-thirty I ate two eggs in a hurry and from noon on I rehearsed the orchestra alone; then at six I continued with the singers. In all, eleven hours of rehearsals for your poor Arturo. I can truly say that by the sweat of my brow I earn my bread! This evening, however, I feel tired even mentally. This blessed Tristan is very, very difficult. And then, to get it into the bloodstream of the imbecilic groups—orchestra, singers, etc., etc., allowing for exceptions—who make up the production requires greater patience than mine, I guarantee you. I think God is helping me to acquire it. This morning I was so very upset with the bass clarinet that in the end I chased him out of the orchestra, but apart from this outburst my nerves' thermometer is low enough. Tomorrow morning I'll rehearse all the singers and chorus. In the evening I'll rehearse the whole opera with everyone. Piontelli is intentionally keeping the theater closed, to speed up the opening. Wednesday there will be two more rehearsals, Thursday a rehearsal in the morning, Friday a rehearsal in the morning and dress rehearsal in the evening, Saturday free for the singers and maybe also for the orchestra—and Sunday, the grand premiere. Will it go well? Let's hope so. If my Carlottina were there that evening I'd be certain of victory. But since I can't hope for that, I can only sigh! My heart will be at peace, and I'll be able to say that I've done everything that my intelligence intimated to me. I hear that a great many people will come from Milan, also from Bologna and Florence. The general anticipation is high. I won't hide from you the fact that this opening makes me feel a degree of trepidation, especially after the fiascos of Götterdämmerung and Don Carlo at La Scala. [. . .]

"Piontelli is intentionally keeping the theater closed": In other words, no performances were scheduled so that rehearsals could be held in the evenings as well as during the day. "The general anticipation is high": This was not only the local premiere of *Tristan,* but also the first Italian production of the opera since its national premiere in Bologna nine years earlier. · The disastrous first Milanese *Götterdämmerung* and a badly received revival of *Don Carlo,* both under Vanzo's baton and at La Scala, contributed to the decision, made several months later, to keep Italy's leading opera house closed for the entire 1897–98 season.

[. . .] This morning I had a big rehearsal of the whole first act and part of the second [of *Tristan*], with the whole gang, and it went reasonably well. This evening I'll do the 2nd from the beginning and the third as well. I'm sorry to hear that your mama isn't feeling well; let's hope that it's purely temporary. I've had bad news from home about my father's health; all winter he's felt unwell. I thank heaven that my health is good, despite the fact that I wear myself out in a way that would arouse compassion—only I've lost a little weight. [. . .]

9-2-97. 6 p.m.

My dearest, Yesterday, during the day, I had received a letter and newspapers from the greatest <u>living evil eye caster,</u> so how could I have avoided having some disgusting accident or other happen to me? You will have learned from the newspapers I've sent you what happened at the 2nd Tristan performance— thus I have nothing to add to the report other than that I felt awful, really awful. I thought my head was going to split from one moment to the next, and yet I never for a moment stopped showing disrespect toward the audience. On the contrary, at the end of the 2nd act they were calling for me to take a bow, but I refused, declaring openly in the middle of the stage [behind the closed curtain or front drop] that I was doing it on purpose, to show disrespect toward the audience. I won't tell you what I shouted at the journalists Bersezio and Berta in the presence of the owners of La Stampa and La Gazzetta del Popolo, respectively, since all that pandemonium was their fault, a result of their asinine doings. Damn all the people who cast the evil eye! [. . .]

The first performance of *Tristan* had gone excellently, although there was a bit of grumbling from some members of the public because AT had insisted on keeping the auditorium dark during the performance: in those days, audiences were accustomed to having half-light in the auditorium so that they could walk around, chat, eat, observe one another, flirt, play cards, and follow libretti while "listening" to an opera. The next day's newspapers gave exaggerated reports of the grumbling, thus provoking a verbal battle at the second performance. AT had to stop conducting, and when the management turned the lights on he lost his temper and smashed the light on his music stand. The remainder of the performance took place in half-light, but AT was so angry that he conducted the rest of the opera sitting in his chair, his right hand resting on his knee, and barely moved his baton. Poor Polo virtually had to lead the orchestra, while the prompter tried to assist the singers. · Like most theater people, AT was superstitious, and he was especially wary of people who were said to have the evil eye.

[. . .] I've begun working on Buzzi-Peccia's opera, and as far as I can tell at this point—I've barely begun the rehearsals—I'm going to have to make quite an effort. Today I rehearsed from eleven until three-thirty. Samson and Delilah this evening. Did you see? Even the Corriere reported the incident at the 2nd Tristan performance. Sunday, at the third, there may be another demonstration in favor of the <u>forces of darkness,</u> but however great the number of these demonstrators may be in comparison with the enemies of darkness, I fear that they won't win out, because a hundred people who whistle will make more of an uproar and are more tenacious and shameless than a thousand who applaud. Enough; we shall see! [. . .]

18-2-97.

In the end, AT prevailed, but the episode had left bitter feelings on both sides and only six performances of *Tristan* were given.

(TU); P.S., IMPRESA TEATRALE PIONTELLI-RHO;
TO CESARE BLANC, (MI); NYPLTL

18-2-97.

My dear Blanc, Pardon me for not having replied immediately to your very nice letter of the 14th. I had a great deal to do and I was also feeling a little unwell. For the Bergamo season I'm going to ask for two thousand lire. Go ahead and tell that friend of yours that I have reduced my fee to the bare minimum, the more so inasmuch as the productions I'll have to conduct certainly won't fill me with pride, excepting the fact that they're being performed to mark an anniversary. Furthermore, I'd like to know when the season is to begin and end. And where are they going to hunt up the singers for these operas?

I'm rehearsing Buzzi-Peccia's opera, which I hope will be well received. Thus I would be able to declare that all of this season's productions—Boito as well as Wagner, Buzzi-Peccia as well as Saint-Saëns—have been looked after with equal love and equal passion, and appreciated by the audiences as well as the critics. Good-bye, dear friend. Accept an affectionate handshake from your <u>A. Toscanini.</u>

AT had been invited to conduct performances of *La favorita* and *Lucia di Lammermoor* in Bergamo during August–September 1897 for the hundredth anniversary of the birth of Gaetano Donizetti, a native of the town. But contractual disputes between AT and the Bergamo impresario erupted after the conductor arrived, and AT may also have had run-ins with some of the singers. He did not conduct any of the opera performances. (See letter of 25 September 1897.)

<u>25-2-97.</u>

[. . .] I've received proposals for the month of May from Barcelona—Teatro Liceo—and from Sonzogno for the Fenice in Venice, where Werther and Leoncavallo's Bohème are to be given. But if Piontelli arranges this tour I'll stay with him. We would go to Florence, Rome, Genoa, Bologna, Venice, Trieste, and Milan, and we would give two performances of Tristan and an orchestral concert [in each town]. [. . .]

AT did not accept the offers from either Barcelona or Sonzogno (Leoncavallo had wanted AT to conduct the world premiere of his own version of *La bohème*), and the *Tristan* tour with Turin's Municipal Orchestra—which was the Teatro Regio's house orchestra—never took place. If it had, AT would have conducted the local premieres of *Tristan* in all of the prospective tour cities except Bologna, where the opera's Italian premiere had taken place nine years earlier.

My dearest, I haven't felt well for two days and I have to work a great deal. I have no appetite, and I think that this is a result of my great tiredness. Never, never to have a moment's rest has become downright oppressive. After the exertions for Tristan I now have to face this nasty new opera [by Buzzi-Peccia], full of errors, that drives me crazy and puts me in a very bad mood. To continue every day to rehearse from noon until five-thirty or six and then to have a performance in the evening, and for months on end, is a little too much. But enough: this season, too, will come to an end! [. . .]

Here, they're offering me a single contract for the next carnival season together with that of the exposition, including the following carnival season. This would mean twelve and a half months' work, and they would give me 28 thousand lire—but I think they would agree to 30. By Italian standards, I think it's a splendid deal! And now that they're threatening to eliminate the Scala subsidy, as a result of the scandalous and disastrous outcome of the current season, I won't see a better deal. Naturally, I'm not giving a positive answer for now. [. . .]

<u>27-2-97. seven o'clock in the evening</u>

Clearly, AT was aiming for La Scala, but he was holding out until conditions there were more propitious. The "they" at the beginning of the last paragraph were Turin's municipal authorities; the "they" in the sentence regarding La Scala were not only Milan's municipal authorities but also the Crown (i.e., the national government), which had traditionally given money to finance the country's leading opera house.

<u>4-3-97.</u>

[. . .] the last two nights I've been up until 5 a.m., orchestrating bits of this new opera in order to help Maestro Buzzi-Peccia, who is very agitated and fearful these days over the forthcoming opening. I'll have to work tonight, too. [. . .]

<u>7</u>[*sic*, for 6]<u>-3-97</u>.

[. . .] Yesterday evening we had a sort of dress rehearsal for the new opera. This morning I'll rehearse the chorus and orchestra again, and this evening . . . ? Hmmm! God help us. I wish the maestro a great success—let's hope! Tomorrow morning I'll start rehearsing the first concert, which will take place Wednesday evening {10 March 1897} at the Regio. Maybe—I repeat, maybe—I'll be able to make a quick visit to Milan before the concerts are done. In mid-April I'll go to Venice with Piontelli to conduct La Bohème. Your mama ought to bring you there for a few days! We'll have only a few rehearsals and ten performances, and I'll have all the time in the world to keep you company. [. . .]

AT was going to conduct Puccini's *La bohème,* not Leoncavallo's, in Venice. It is safe to assume that he had three motives for doing so: he preferred Puccini's work to Leoncavallo's; he felt happier under Piontelli's aegis than under that of the Fenice's impresario; and it was more important to him to remain in the good graces of Giulio Ricordi, Puccini's publisher, than in those of Edoardo Sonzogno, the publisher of Leoncavallo's new work.

<u>12 o'clock 8</u> [*sic*, for 7] <u>-3-97</u>

[. . .] The opera opened {6 March 1897} and enjoyed a succès de — compatibilité. Too many references to other operas, by Puccini, Wagner, Mascagni, harmed Buzzi-Peccia's work, which was also damaged by the enormous errors in the orchestral parts; in the end, these tired the musicians, whose extreme lack of confidence spread to the audience. Yet we managed to get to the end of the opera, and the composer was called before the curtain several times. We'll give it again this evening. At one I'm going to do the first rehearsal for Wednesday's concert. [. . .] You will perhaps have received today the libretto of the new opera, which I sent you yesterday. You'll see that it's half a load of cr———. Sorry to write in such haste: I have to go to the theater to talk to the [chief] stagehand about the platform to be built for the orchestra, for the concerts, since they'll be given at the Regio. [. . .]

7-3-97.

[. . .] I'm going to eat and then I'll dress to go conduct the second performance of Forza d'amore. They haven't sold a single ticket. We would like to end the season in triumph with Tristan, but Dufriche's illness will certainly prevent this, and so we'll have to fall back on that unlovable and ungrateful Samson. [. . .]

A few weeks earlier, AT had described *Samson* as "pretty" with "beautiful moments," but he was now describing it as "unlovable and ungrateful." It had not worn well with him. As to the other works he gave in Turin that season: he did not like either *Andrea Chénier* or *La forza d'amore,* both of which he had had to introduce to the city. This left Boito's *Mefistofele,* for which he had a lifelong weakness, and *Tristan,* which remained a great love to the end of his days. Yet the young AT, like his contemporaries, would never have dreamed of shunning the responsibility of studying, rehearsing, and performing new music.

six in the evening

[. . .] My head has been hurting terribly since yesterday; I have no desire to work, yet I must do it; I would like to rest a little, and instead I have to keep very, very busy. Today, as soon as the rehearsal ended, I came home to study. Just think that nearly all four [concert] programs are made up of music that's completely new to me—and to the audience, of course! [. . .]

The programs contained works by Raff, Beethoven, Grieg, Weber, Smetana, Corelli, Saint-Saëns, Dvořák, Schumann, Goldmark, Berlioz, Bolzoni, Wagner, Tchaikovsky, Haydn, Cherubini, and Bach. Of these seventeen composers, five were still alive and three others had been dead for less than fifteen years.

midnight [9–10.3.97]

[. . .] Today I had a great deal to do for my concert, and the biggest annoyance of all was that cursed Belgian Ysaÿe, who is set on playing two violin concerti with orchestral accompaniment, and I absolutely don't want to accompany him in both because I'm tired of working like a horse just to satisfy others' self-esteem. [. . .]

AT won the dispute with the celebrated Eugène Ysaÿe (1858–1931), who played only one concerto (Beethoven's) and then added, on his own, the well-known unaccompanied Chaconne from Bach's Second Partita.

[. . .] Yesterday's concert went splendidly. I didn't like the violinist [Ysaÿe]. I've heard Polo play the second piece [i.e., the Bach Chaconne] better. I'm enclosing the illustrated program. [. . .]

E.P. TU, 17 MARCH 1897; TO CDM, S8MI; EC

<u>11 a.m.</u>

[. . .] I couldn't write to you yesterday after lunch because in addition to being very busy studying the Schumann symphony, I had to go to bed with a bad headache that had been bothering me since morning. I have a terrible cold. This morning I feel a little better. If I were near my Bocchietto I would be completely cured. [. . .]

AT conducted Schumann's Second Symphony in his Turin concert of 22 March 1897; it was his first performance of any Schumann symphony.

(TU); TO CDM, S8MI; EC

<u>19-3-97.</u>

[. . .] I'm off to the rehearsal now, to drive myself crazy with the Ride of the Valkyries. [. . .]

"The Ride of the Valkyries" presents few difficulties to a modern professional orchestra, but in 1897 an orchestra that had never played or even heard it would have found it enormously challenging.

E.P. TU, 21 MARCH 1897; TO CDM, S8MI; EC

<u>10 o'clock a.m.</u> [20.3.97]

[. . .] I've decided to stay in Turin next year, for the exposition and the following carnival. They're giving me thirty-one thousand lire. I thought it was a good idea to accept. After all, we'll live peacefully here, and if the business with Ida and Polo goes as I hope I think we'll live through a happy period, with all four of us keeping good company with each other.

I thought it was a good idea to accept also because with me the municipal orchestra's plans proceed, and both the city and the exposition's operating committee hand out money; without me everything would fall apart. This is why they wanted to be sure that I would accept before they confirmed the orchestra [players' contracts]. I think I've done the right thing. Do you agree?

The Scala question is highly uncertain, too, and if they also wanted to create a municipal orchestra in Milan I would undoubtedly have the annoyance of incurring enmities, just as happened here in Turin at first. And to tell you the holy truth, I don't at all want to upset myself, especially when my Bocchietto will be with me.

Write and tell me whether I've done the right or the wrong thing. [. . .]

(TU), 23 MARCH 1897; TO CDM (S8MI); EC

---

11 o'clock a.m.

My dearest, I've been in bed until now. Yesterday evening's concert killed me. It was a great success. Three pieces were encored: <u>In the Garden, The Brook,</u> and the <u>Ride of the Valkyries.</u> If the audience hadn't taken pity on us, we would almost have had to encore the Magic Fire Music, too. [. . .]

"In the Garden" is from Karl Goldmark's "Rustic Wedding" Symphony; "The Brook" is a piece for strings by Giovanni Bolzoni.

(VE, ON OR AROUND 10 APRIL 1897); TO CDM, (S8MI); EC

---

10 o'clock a.m.

[. . .] Yesterday I wandered around with Polo all day; he is enchanted with Venice, and so am I, no less than he. We went to the Lido. The weather is magnificent—there are many foreigners, especially Germans.

Amid so much harmony and beauty I'm dreaming of you, and I wish you were near, very near me. Yesterday evening I began the rehearsals. The orchestra is good but the theater [Teatro Rossini] is [acoustically] as dead as a doornail. [. . .] Three opera houses are running simultaneously: the Fenice with Werther and Leoncavallo's Bohème, the Malibran with Massenet's Manon and [Mascagni's] L'amico Fritz, and the Rossini with our company of Bohemians. [. . .]

E.P. VE, 16 APRIL 1897; TO CDM, S8MI; EC

[. . .] my shoulder is extraordinarily painful; I couldn't sleep last night. You can't imagine how hard it is for me to conduct. The dress rehearsal is this evening and the first performance tomorrow. [. . .]

My dearest, La Bohème was an astonishing success yesterday evening—
so much so that it caused the entire Venetian press to record the event as a
great triumph. Please note that the press had been bought off by Sonzogno
and would gladly have reacted negatively to our production. The theater was
packed—the Venetian nobility all turned out, and so did the foreigners—
and the applause was transformed into truly enthusiastic ovations. When I
appeared with the singers at the end of the act, a great shout went up. So much
enthusiasm has truly never been seen in Venice. How happy I would have been
had you been here! And now the terrain has been well prepared for Leoncavallo's opera. The poor wretch! [. . .]

18-04-97.

AT was fond of Leoncavallo personally and was happy to have helped him by having
launched the tremendously successful *Pagliacci.* But he considered him completely
lacking in musical subtlety and refinement, and he often used his name as a paradigm
for artistic crudity.

(CONEGLIANO VENETO, ON OR AROUND 12 MAY 1897); TO CDM, (S8MI); EC

My dearest, I'm writing from Conegliano [. . .]. The deal that seemed on the
verge of being done—to give Bohème at the [Teatro] Malibran [in Venice]—
has come to nothing thanks to the fees foolishly demanded by Apostolou and
Zeni, and Wilmant's moaning and groaning. As for me, I'm glad in the end.
[. . .] I'll stay here until Sunday because I want to arrange things with Gigio
regarding our future productions, so that I won't have to write and trouble my
soul later on. Send me precise information on Merolla; tell me whether she has
a nice voice, whether she is better than or equal to Pandolfini—in short, tell
me whether you like her. Is she better than Cruz? [. . .]

Conegliano Veneto was Luigi ("Gigio") Piontelli's town. · The plan had been to repeat
La bohème at the Malibran when the performances at the Rossini were finished. ·
Regarding Apostolou, see the letter of 17 August 1896. · The tenor Pietro Zeni sang
in AT's *Lohengrin* and *Eugene Onegin,* both at La Scala in 1900. · Augusta Cruz had sung
the roles of a Norn and Gutrune with AT in Turin in the Italian premiere of *Götterdämmerung* but had been replaced by Gisella Zampini. · AT had already begun to trust
his fiancée's ear for voices, even though Carla was musically untrained. She later
brought to his attention such remarkable singers as the tenor Aureliano Pertile and
the soprano Toti Dal Monte.

ANNOTATION IN WRT'S HAND: "22 OR 23 MAY 1897, FROM MONTEBELLUNA, ADDRESSED TO PROF. ENRICO POLO, S MASSIMO 7, TURIN"; PC; NYPLTL

My dear Enrico, Yesterday evening a highly violent and extremely saddening scene took place between myself and that **hyena** of a Mamma De Martini. It was a scene in which I had to take every imaginable injury and insult without reacting, in which my pride was offended in the most horrible and at the same time the lowest way, and in which, in the end, in order to get away from that storm of injuries that poured forth from a worse-than-vulgar mouth, I was compelled to leave the house forever—inasmuch as no one in the world could induce me to set foot there. I had just arrived; all I did was turn around and leave, and go to Piontelli's place at Montebelluna.

I'll say no more. You can imagine my pain and Carla and Ida's. The poor things wept and despaired in a way that would have aroused compassion in the very stones, but the **hyena** seemed only to become more ferocious. Poor angels, poor victims! You will easily have figured out that some of the remarks in this scene were aimed at you, too. Enough. A word to the wise . . . Send me news of your mother—if only I could take consolation in knowing that you're feeling all right about her health. Give her a kiss from me. Tomorrow I'll be in Venice—Albergo del Vapore—A kiss from your affectionate A. Toscanini

The cause and nature of Francesca De Martini's attack on her future son-in-law is not known; it seems doubly strange inasmuch as their relations had previously been excellent. I have found no further mention of her in any of AT's subsequent correspondence. AT and CDM were married at Conegliano Veneto on 21 June 1897, and they had their honeymoon at Cadore, in the Dolomites. Their son Walter was born on 21 March 1898—nine months to the day after their wedding.

CONEGLIANO VENETO, 25 SEPTEMBER 1897; TO COUNT TORAZZO, TU; AMT

My dear Torazzo.

I've been in Conegliano for a week as a guest of our friend Piontelli. I said goodbye to those worthy gentlemen who make up the Committee of Honor for Donizetti and to my dear impresario Terzi, who cheated me out of a cool thousand lire so that I would remember him forever, and I've come to these delightful hills where I can forget about that unfortunate Bergamo season. [. . .]

As to providing for the bass clarinet, it makes no difference to me whether it's in B-flat or A; so long as it has a low C and is in tune, I'll be happy. [. . .]

Now then, I heartily suggest that in the event that Superti were not to come to Turin this year—we should be so lucky!—you replace him with Giuseppe Ferrari of Modena, a <u>most excellent</u> 1st violin and a <u>most valuable orchestra member.</u> And while I'm making suggestions, let me add another: if possible, make the number of second violins equal to that of the firsts. These are no longer the days of Norma and La Sonnambula, when the criteria for building an orchestra were what they were! Do you have all the violas? [. . .] Last year the violas were very bad, and this was in part owing to the principal, who was rather worse than the year before. Enough: please, please look after this branch of the orchestra, which seems to me the <u>crappiest.</u> I hope that that student double-bass player from last year has made progress; it would be a good idea to have him with us, but with a four-stringed instrument—and while I'm <u>on the subject: it would be a good thing for you to say the same thing to all the double-bass players,</u> because last year someone—I don't recall who it was—had a three-stringed bass. And now I'll leave you in peace. [. . .]

See the letter of 8 July 1896 for a note about Torazzo. · Regarding the Bergamo episode, see also the letter of 18 February 1897. · Modern double basses have four or five strings; the three-string bass had too narrow a range for much nineteenth-century music.

Part Two

JULY 1898–
MAY 1933

1898   Son Walter born (dies 1971); Toscanini leaves Turin's Teatro Regio to become principal conductor of the Teatro alla Scala, Milan.

1899   Conducts first Italian production of Wagner's *Siegfried* at La Scala.

1900   Daughter Wally born (dies 1991); Toscanini conducts Italian premiere of Tchaikovsky's *Eugene Onegin.*

1901   Son Giorgio born (dies 1906, of diphtheria).

1901, 1903, 1904, 1906   Conducts, during Argentine winter season, at the Teatro de la Opera, Buenos Aires; gives Argentine premieres of Berlioz's *La Damnation de Faust,* Puccini's *Madama Butterfly,* Cilea's *Adriana Lecouvreur,* and other operas.

1903   Leaves La Scala; freelances for three years.

1906   Returns to La Scala; conducts Italian premiere of Strauss's *Salome* there (contemporaneous with a version conducted by the composer in Turin).

1907   Daughter Wanda born (dies 1998).

1908   Conducts Italian premiere of Debussy's *Pelléas et Mélisande* at La Scala; leaves La Scala and becomes principal conductor (together with Gustav Mahler) of the Metropolitan Opera Company in New York.

1910   Takes the Metropolitan ensemble to Paris for performances that include the French premiere of Puccini's *Manon Lescaut;* conducts world premiere of Puccini's *La fanciulla del West* at the Metropolitan in New York.

1912   May–September: Conducts at Teatro Colón, Buenos Aires.

1913   Conducts U.S. premiere of Mussorgsky's *Boris Godunov* at the Metropolitan.

1915   Leaves the Metropolitan.

1915–18   Conducts only benefit performances (concerts and operas, also military bands at the front) and only in Italy until the end of World War I.

1920–21   Conducts marathon tour of Italy, the United States, and Canada with a new orchestra formed under the auspices of La Scala; with this orchestra makes his first phonograph records, in Camden, New Jersey; completely reorganizes La Scala's artistic, social, and financial administration and becomes in effect the ensemble's general director.

1921   December 26: With a performance of Verdi's *Falstaff,* Toscanini reopens La Scala, which has had no regular season since 1917.

1926   First concerts as guest conductor with the New York Philharmonic;

conducts world premiere of Puccini's *Turandot* at La Scala.

1927   Becomes coconductor, with Willem Mengelberg, of New York Philharmonic; makes first radio broadcasts, with this orchestra.

1929   Gives historic performances with La Scala ensemble in Vienna and Berlin; leaves La Scala.

1930   Takes New York Philharmonic on its first European tour; becomes the first non-German-school conductor to appear at the Bayreuth Festival *(Tannhäuser* and *Tristan);* becomes the New York Philharmonic's principal conductor.

1931   Assaulted by Fascist hooligans in Bologna for refusing to perform their party's hymn before a concert; determines not to conduct again in Italy under the Fascist regime; returns to Bayreuth *(Tannhäuser* and *Parsifal).*

1933   Withdraws from Bayreuth Festival following Hitler's accession to power in Germany.

Dearest Bocchietto

No sooner had I arrived than I went to the Teatro Regio and continued the rehearsal that Maestro Barone had already started; afterward I went to say hello to Ida, who was a little ill, then I came home to send you only two kisses, but long and affectionate ones.

    Tomorrow evening—Monday [4 July 1898]—is the concert, unfortunately. I'm fed up with music and concerts. I long for the mountains and peace, and these last days of <u>forced labor</u> seem eternal to me! Yesterday, no fewer than four countesses came looking for me! One of them is the Duchess of Genoa's lady-in-waiting. They would like an appointment at my place, in order to talk to me. Maybe there are some other benefit concerts in view! Enough of this; set something up regarding the apartment, and come soon. Bear in mind that the ones in Piazza Umberto wouldn't be bad, if we could pay 1,200 the first year and 1,500 thereafter. Ciao. Kisses to you and to Walter.

—Arturo.

AT was in the midst of a forty-three-concert marathon (with respective rehearsals) at Turin's General Italian Exposition. · Ida De Martini and Enrico Polo had married and were living in Turin, but because AT had accepted the directorship of La Scala, effective late in the autumn of 1898, CT had left Turin—where she and AT had been living since their marriage—and was looking for a suitable apartment for her husband, their baby, and herself in Milan; she was probably staying with her mother. · Maestro Barone: evidently AT's assistant conductor.

My dear and Esteemed Prof. Romeo Orsi,

As I must deliver a complete list of the orchestra members to Engineer Gatti-Casazza, La Scala's General Director, as soon as possible, I'm turning to you for help with this difficult task. However good my memory may be, some names may very well escape me, thus if you would be so kind as to send me a complete note of the members who make up the Orchestral Society my task would be greatly facilitated and I would be most grateful to you. At the same time, I'm asking another favor of you! If by chance you were to meet Prof. Zamperoni, advise him not to leave his place at La Scala! I firmly believe that his reasons for wanting to leave that position, however eloquent and persuasive they may be, are not wholly acceptable to those who know Prof. Zamperoni reasonably well. I'm sure it's true that he suffers from nerves, but this is nothing new, and yet he has always played well. He says that he is old, but I would like to have an orchestra made up entirely of old men like himself, but who could play as he does; I would accept them with the greatest enthusiasm!

I have already written to him and advised him to reconsider seriously; not only that, but I told him that I wouldn't even dream of replacing him. We'll see what his answer will be. Meanwhile, if you have occasion to see him, persuade him to accept.

I don't know where to find a very good Bass Clarinet! Is there no Clarinet player in Milan who would agree to play the Bass Clarinet? And I hope that Sonzogno will accept [the offer] to become 1st Horn. Can you give me his address?

My dear Professor, forgive me for giving you so many headaches with this letter of mine; have pity on me and remember that I will be very happy to be of use to you whenever possible. Accept my heartfelt thanks and a hearty handshake.

Your ever

devoted A. Toscanini

Ceresole Reale is in the Canavese, a region of the Piedmontese Alps; AT and family were vacationing there. · Romeo Orsi was a member of the Scala orchestra and probably the head of the orchestral committee. AT was completing the orchestra's roster in anticipation of his first season as head of Italy's greatest lyric theater. He knew the orchestra because he had conducted highly successful concerts with it in the spring of 1896, but becoming principal conductor was another matter. · Giulio Gatti-Casazza (1868–1940), who was trained as a naval engineer but had been active in theater management for several years, assumed the administrative direction of La Scala just as AT was assuming its artistic direction; he remained there until 1908, when he and AT went to the Metropolitan Opera in New York in tandem. · Antonio Zamperoni, La Scala's principal flute, had decided to retire, but AT liked his playing and was determined to keep him in the orchestra.

<u>My dear Depanis</u>

Thank you for your sweet letter and for all the clarifications you've given me in it. I'm so little inclined to go to Milan that I'll also include in the contract the clause that your letter suggests. If it's not accepted, so much the better for me.

Joachim has written to Polo that he can't come to Italy in the autumn, having already made provisional dates for concerts in Germany and having to marry off his daughter during the same period. I was most sorry about this piece of news, and it makes me foresee that things will go badly for our approaches to other soloists as well. You'll see that Saint-Saëns, too, will be busy during that period! We should have thought about this earlier.

In the meantime, I think we'd do well to secure Serato, the violinist, and this we can do immediately by contacting his father in Bologna. I would like to have Polo play in one of the first concerts in September. This artist isn't well enough known in Turin, but I guarantee you that he is truly capable and rises above the class to which he unfortunately has to belong in order to survive. What do you think? Tell me frankly your opinion, with no hesitation whatsoever.

Please have Blanc send me the Strauss and Franck scores as soon as they arrive. [. . .]

Has Sgambati accepted? Pollini? [. . .]

The depth of AT's confidence in Depanis is indicated by the fact that he consulted with him about his Scala contract even though he knew that Depanis would have preferred to keep him in Turin. · After having graduated from the Parma Conservatory, Polo had gone to Berlin to study with Joseph Joachim (1831–1907), one of the most celebrated violinists of the nineteenth century, who had worked with Mendelssohn, Schumann, Liszt, and especially Brahms. Through Polo, AT had invited Joachim to appear as soloist in one of his Turin concerts that fall. · As AT had predicted, the invitation to composer-pianist Camille Saint-Saëns (1835–1921) was unsuccessful. · Polo played the Bruch Concerto in Turin under AT's direction on 10 September 1898, but the violinist Arrigo Serato (1877–1948) did not play with AT that season. (Earlier that year, also in Turin, AT had conducted Bruch's "Scottish Fantasy" with the celebrated Spanish violinist Pablo de Sarasate as soloist.) · Although AT was already examining Richard Strauss's music in 1898, he did not conduct any of it until 1902. He did, however, perform the intermezzo from César Franck's symphonic poem *Rédemption* three times in Turin that fall. · Giovanni Sgambati (1841–1914), a well-known pianist and influential composer in Italy, performed his own Piano Concerto in G Minor with AT in Turin on 27 October 1898, but the pianist and composer Cesare Pollini (1858–1912) did not participate in the season's programs.

<u>My dear Depanis,</u> I'm sending six programs to examine for the first concerts. I think I've managed to put them together as you wish, varied and effective.

Tomorrow, Monday, I'm going to Turin, and on Tuesday I'll start the rehearsals. [. . .]

Pardon me for not having written to you until now, but during the last two weeks I've been dedicating myself with wild passion to mountain climbing; in addition to many hiking excursions, I've made a few climbs, such as, for instance, the Colle della Galisia, the Colle della Porta, to the top of the Cuccagna, and to the Gran Paradiso—but it's clear that neither I nor my companions were worthy of setting foot on the last, because when we had reached 3800 meters—in other words, almost onto the Becca di Moncoroè [?], and at 260 meters from the summit we were caught in a fearful snowstorm that forced us to return at once to the Victor Emmanuel **Refuge,** dying of cold and—on my part, at least—absolutely famished. Really, I'll leave Ceresole most unwillingly! If I could at least have reached the top of the Paradiso! I had to say no to the Levanna because my wife absolutely wouldn't hear of it, since this is a more difficult climb. But enough: the day after tomorrow I'll replace my alpenstock with the baton of command and clamber over the less dangerous mountains of eighth notes and sixteenth notes.

And how are you doing? Having a good time? I've gained weight—I continue to have a musician's appetite. My wife and my baby are very well. [. . .]

(MI); TO GIUSEPPE MARTUCCI, (BO?); NYPLTL

My dear <u>Maestro Martucci</u>

I have already given instructions for the piano to be placed as it was in the Exposition Concert Hall. Your concerto occupies the same position as in the Turin programs, except that it will be preceded by Paër's <u>Sargino</u> [Overture] rather than the <u>Magic Flute</u> Overture, as the concert is entirely Italian.

The orchestra here is bigger than Turin's, that is, it is made up of 24 first violins, 20 seconds, 14 violas, 14 cellos, and 12 double basses. Don't you think it should be reduced to 16 firsts, 16 seconds, 10 violas, 10 cellos, and 10 basses? I would be grateful to have an opinion from you. In the meantime, I thank you very much and with all my heart for your kindness toward me and the Orchestral Society. You cannot imagine how profoundly grateful I am! I am happy to think that I shall see you and be able to shake your hand affectionately in a few days. Please give my regards to your good wife. As always, I love and admire you. Keep your precious friendship for me.

<u>Affectionately A. Toscanini</u>

21-4-99.

Martucci played his Piano Concerto no. 2 in B-flat Major, op. 66, with AT and Milan's Orchestral Society (basically, the Scala orchestra) on 27 April 1899; the other works on the program—in addition to the Paër overture—were by Luigi Mancinelli, Giuseppe Sgambati, Luigi Cherubini, Nicolò Celega, and Francesco Morlacchi.

My dear friend. I heard a good orchestral performance of Meistersinger but could only deplore the complete lack of good ensemble among orchestra, chorus, and singers; the last, I can tell you just between us, are dogs. These Bayreuth performances are a real hoax for people like me who are hoping to hear perfection. Your Arturo

Pietro Sormani was AT's faithful assistant conductor at La Scala; AT held him in high regard, and they used the informal *tu* with each other. · So far as is known, this was AT's first visit to the Bayreuth Festival. The *Meistersinger* production that he refers to had first been staged there in 1888; in 1899 it was conducted by Wagner's celebrated disciple Hans Richter (1843–1916) and sung by Leopold Demuth (alternating with Anton van Rooy as Sachs), Fritz Friedrichs (Beckmesser), Ernst Kraus (Stolzing), and Johanna Gadski (Eva)—all celebrated Wagner interpreters. AT probably heard some or all of the other works performed at the festival that summer. He would have been especially interested in *Parsifal,* which until 1913 could be performed only at Bayreuth (although AT himself would give a concert performance of Act III at La Scala in 1903) and which in 1899 was conducted by Franz Fischer and sung by Alois Burgstaller (alternating with Emil Gerhäuser and Erik Schmedes as Parsifal), Ellen Gulbranson (alternating with Milka Ternina as Kundry), Felix von Kraus (alternating with Anton Sistermanns and Ernst Wachter as Gurnemanz), Hans Schütz (Amfortas), and Wilhelm Fenten (alternating with Demeter Popovici as Klingsor). The entire *Ring* was also given at Bayreuth that year, under the baton of Siegfried Wagner (1869–1930), the composer's son (who was soon to become a great admirer of AT's work), and with van Rooy (Wotan), Burgstaller (Siegmund), Ernestine Schumann-Heink (Erda and Waltraute), Rosa Sucher (Sieglinde), Gulbranson (Brünnhilde), and E. Kraus (alternating with Schmedes as Siegfried), among others. Barblan claims that AT returned to Bayreuth in 1905, but there was no Bayreuth Festival in 1905.

My most adored Rosina

Gatti[-Casazza] has arrived just now and I've learned everything, everything from him! I haven't had word from you in two weeks. Or rather, to be clear: since the last letter that I sent you from Valle I haven't been able to pick up your letters anymore. The same day that I sent mine, it was impossible to find out whether there were letters for me, because I arrived there in a carriage, with my children, just as the post was arriving, and the office stays closed for half an hour. I couldn't wait, and I postponed the pleasure of reading your letter till the following day. But the following day, as a result of a cursed piece of bad luck, my wife found out that at Pieve I was picking up letters under the name of Antonio Trascuri. You can imagine what happened! I could no longer take a step by myself, and I couldn't get any more information about you.

Luck was with me, because I think she went to Valle, too, to ask for letters addressed to that name, and the newly adopted pseudonym served a purpose.

Enough of that. I've learned from Gatti everything you'll tell me in the letters that are lying around in Valle, and unfortunately these terrible confirmations of your state, which your mother, too, is aware of, have thrown me into consternation and pain. But what drives me even crazier is the notion that has arisen in you that my heart could beat differently toward you now than it did before! Oh, no! <u>I love you more and more, and I feel more and more unworthy of you, because I have no idea what to do to save you either before the world or before my conscience, which fills me with remorse and tortures me.</u> I even fear sleep now, because I'm spied on even then, and I talk continually. Love me and believe, believe always in my real, great, sincere love.

AT probably met the soprano Rosina Storchio (1872 or 1876–1945) when he was rehearsing for the world premiere of Leoncavallo's *Zazà* at Milan's Teatro Lirico in 1900; she was singing the title role. He admired her artistry, and she, like many other women before and after, was overwhelmed by his brilliance and intensity. They fell in love and had a tempestuous affair, of which this letter and the two following ones are the only written testimony known to me. Their son, Giovannino, was born in March 1903 (thus Storchio must have just realized that she was pregnant when these letters were written); he was palsied and died at the age of sixteen. Storchio and AT remained lovers for several years and often worked together at La Scala and in Buenos Aires until 1906, and then more rarely until 1915. Their relationship, which created a scandal in the Milanese artistic world, had a disastrous effect on her life and was responsible for the first major crisis in AT and CT's difficult marriage. Storchio had a major career (the few recordings she made are very impressive), retired in 1923, and died in obscurity after a lengthy, paralyzing illness; she never married. · Valle di Cadore, Pieve di Cadore, and Tai di Cadore are villages in the Dolomites, where AT, CT, and their three small children (after Walter in 1898 came Wally in 1900 and Giorgio in 1901) were spending their summer vacation. · AT loved to use childish and not always accurate anagrams of his name as pseudonyms; thus Antonio Trascuri here and Icinio Artù-Rostan in the letter of 11 July 1902.

N.D. BUT FROM VALLE DI CADORE, JULY 1902;
TO ROSINA STORCHIO (MI); NYPLTL

<u>My dearest,</u> I beg you, I plead with you to tell me everything your mother said to you after your confession. I am completely mortified to think about how I must look to this woman, who, it must be said, considered me a gentleman until yesterday, and who today has every right to think anything she pleases about me. <u>My Rosina, that which our uncontrollable passion drew us on to do is highly serious, and I can't forgive myself—I'm harming you in every way—</u> and I feel strongly that I must react in a way that will help to alleviate your burden. I'm beside myself, and I don't even know what to think, I'm incapable of writing you anything that would lift you out of the abyss of sorrow I've thrown you into, and that has been increased by the material and moral cer-

tainty that I'll never again be able to set foot in your home. I have betrayed your mother's good faith! Forgive this stupid letter, Rosina—I'm capable only of saying stupid things today. If the assurance of my ever-constant love is dear to you, may it reach you today more than ever in all its warmth and sweet truthfulness. You are deeper than ever in my soul, and the very thought that you might consider me a bad person wounds me cruelly. Please know this. Take all my kisses and all my soul, as always.

Your A.

Continue to write to Valle—I'll retrieve the letters as soon as I can.

P.S.; STAZIONE CLIMATICO [*SIC*] ALPINA/HÔTEL CADORE/ TAI DI CADORE/A. REGAZZI; TO ROSINA STORCHIO, (MI); NYPLTL

Valle di Cadore
Friday 11-7-902*

My dearest, Yesterday, too, I had no news from you. Are you perhaps ill? I tremble at the idea. Or else you haven't gone to the post office for a few days and my letters are still lying around there. In any case, if you want to wire me occasionally, if you don't have time to write, send telegrams to poste restante at Valle di Cadore, to Mr. Icinio Artù-Rostan, and likewise for the letters, since I don't want to pick them up at Pieve anymore. There is no telegraph office at Tai, so when dispatches arrive they come to me through the office in Pieve, and precisely through the clerk who gives me your letters—so that we could run into some unpleasant messes. Therefore, I prefer to travel a few extra kilometers but keep my peace of mind. I'll go to Pieve again today, and I hope to find your letters there. If I don't find any, my pain will certainly worsen, because I really won't know what to think about you.

My adored Rosina, if I could know that you were happy I would give up any imaginable joy, present (there are none, unfortunately) and future.

For several days I've been like a madman, pervaded by remorse that tears my heart to shreds. No, no! I can't be the cause of new, crueler sorrows in your life! I can't be condemned to this martyrdom! I feel that I'm a good person, and I love you so much!

I await, anxiously and in trepidation, some good news from you. Send it soon, along with your kisses, and tell me, repeat to me always that you love me and that I'm your constant, sole love. I throw myself into your arms, and I kiss you and kiss you.

Always yours

---

* For some reason, Toscanini often omitted the first number in years of the twentieth century.

ROME, 1 JANUARY 1905; TO ENRICO POLO, (MI?); SACCHI 1951,
REPRODUCTION (BETWEEN PP. 176 AND 177) OF PART OF LETTER;
THE REST IN BARBLAN, P. 119

My dear Enrico

So you decided to allow nothing to prevent you from sending me the Mahler
[Fifth] Symphony at any cost! So much the better for me, and—many, many
thanks to you. I can't describe how much joy and how much curiosity its unexpected arrival brought me, but you can easily imagine. I read through it
immediately, or rather devoured it—but unfortunately in the course of this
ferocious musical meal my initial joy and curiosity gradually waned, and by
the end they were transformed into sad, very sad hilarity.

No, dear Enrico, believe me, Mahler is not a genuine artist. His music has
neither personality nor genius. It is a mixture of an Italianate style à la Petrella
or Leoncavallo, coupled with Tchaikovsky's musical and instrumental bombast
and a search for Straussian eccentricities—although boasting an opposing system—without having the brilliance of the last two. At every step you fall into
something that's not so much commonplace as trivial. Let this suffice: [AT
wrote out the recurrent eight-bar theme of the opening funeral march]. This
little march tune, which Petrella and Leoncavallo would consider unworthy,
[. . .] Mahler has the shamelessness to introduce into the first movement of a
symphony. Can you imagine a more awful piece of hackwork than this other bit
that I'm transcribing here: [first thirteen bars of the trumpet solo at no. 7 in the
first movement]. And this is colored by whining violins and wailing woodwinds; Martinazzi would turn up his nose if he were accused of having fathered
it. And beyond this, add technical difficulty and overblown proportions—
thus the idea of a possible performance in Turin has faded. Where am I to
look? Tchaikovsky's fifth symphony and another in D by Dvořák will arrive
any day now. Let's hope for better luck. I'm also awaiting Elgar's Variations.
[. . .]

AT had broken with La Scala in the spring of 1903; between then and the date of this
letter, he had conducted two opera seasons (May–August in both 1903 and 1904) at
the Teatro de la Opera in Buenos Aires (the Teatro Colón did not open until 1908),
where he had already conducted in 1901. He had also conducted short seasons at
Bologna's Teatro Comunale in 1904 and 1905 and had assumed the direction of the
1905–6 season at his old haunt, the Teatro Regio in Turin. In addition, he had given
concerts in Bologna, Rome, Turin, and Milan. · Polo, who had studied in Germany
and spoke German, was responsible for bringing much new and recent music from the
German-speaking countries to AT's attention. So far as is known, this was AT's first
encounter with any of Mahler's music. Condemnation of AT for his brutal criticism of
the Fifth Symphony would be easy but antihistorical: his misunderstanding of
Mahlerian irony was shared by the vast majority of musicians of their generation
(Mahler was only seven years older than AT), including those of the German school.
Indeed, Mahler's authentic, worldwide popularity did not begin until the 1960s, by
which time AT was dead. The two musicians were colleagues at the Metropolitan
Opera during 1908 and 1909 (they even shared the podium one evening, at a gala
event), but they had little contact with each other. · Petrella and Martinazzi were com-

posers of popular Italian operas of which AT clearly did not think well. · AT never incorporated either Tchaikovsky's Fifth Symphony or Dvořák's Sixth into his repertoire, but he did like, and frequently conducted, Elgar's "Enigma" Variations.

ROME; TO PIETRO SORMANI, (MI?); PC; EC

My dear Sormani

Thank you for your good wishes—please accept the same from me, sincerely and affectionately. I've begun the new year in full, sweet closeness with my family; a few friends have sent me their affectionate greetings—I couldn't have hoped to start it off better. Carla and I are happy with our new residence, we live very privately, travel all over Rome, which constantly sharpens our interest, and make ready to receive fresh impressions from our forthcoming trip to Sicily by reading books and pamphlets about the beautiful island of fire.

The children are in excellent health, thank God, and this makes us even happier. Walter and Wally attend school, and little Giorgio keeps us company during the day.

This sweet, peaceful rest, however, hasn't kept me completely away from all musical work. I've made the acquaintance of some very interesting works. Strauss's Sinfonia Domestica—his last born—is a formidable composition from a technical point of view, with flashes of brilliance, but highly debatable as an artistic path, unless one wholly and blindly accepts the artistic dogma that has been launched by this Secessionist of great ability. Another composer, of whose very name I was barely aware, has won all my sympathy. The Frenchman Debussy with his Pelléas et Mélisande: lyric drama in five acts and twelve scenes, by Maeterlinck. He's another Secessionist. His art overthrows everything that has been done up to now. He doesn't have Strauss's technique, but he is more brilliant, more elegant, and without a doubt bolder. On first testing oneself against him, one is disoriented, but then, as one becomes a little more familiar with his language and with Maeterlinck, his inspirer, one ends up fascinated. In thinking about Maeterlinck's theater and characters, I must confirm my opinion that Debussy's music integrates that art. But our audiences, present-day audiences in all countries, aren't yet ripe, I won't say for accepting it, but rather for making some sense of it! On the other hand, I was nauseated by Mr. Mahler, director of the Vienna Opera, with his Symphony no. 5. If he conducts the way he writes, oh, what a trivial interpreter he must be! Can you imagine an individual who, in the year 1904, has the shamelessness to write down these bars [writes out the theme, bars 4 to 11 after no. 16 in the second movement] and to place his signature over them? Leoncavallo has found his redeemer. But let's cut this long chat short. Be so kind as to remember me to your wife, to the young ladies, and to your grandmother—accept our greetings and a hug from

Your Affectionate Arturo Toscanini

2-1-905 Rome.

AT and Carla seem to have reached some sort of agreement for peaceful coexistence following the Storchio episode, which had developed into a public scandal. The family spent much of the 1904–05 season more closely together than in previous years because AT had allowed himself a sort of semisabbatical, much of which was spent in Rome and Sicily. · AT's perceptive comments about his contemporaries Richard Strauss and especially Claude Debussy were ahead of their time, whereas his remarks on Mahler were, once again, very much of their time. AT became the first major Italian propagator and defender of many important works of both Strauss and Debussy.

ROME, 15 FEBRUARY 1905; TO GIUSEPPE MARTUCCI, (BO?);
NYPL, TOSCANINI MEMORIAL ARCHIVE

[. . .] Yesterday I began rehearsing the symphony and after two hours of assiduous study I was not able to get through the first movement. What a horrid orchestra! How badly they sight-read! And they play even worse! I haven't conducted their like in years. I have to think back to a rather remote period in order to remind myself of impressions similar to the ones revived in me by this Roman orchestra. These people have lost the feel for playing—I won't even say well, but at least correctly. I nearly slaughtered myself trying to put together the first concert, which the public and magna critica deemed highly successful. And here it is really the case that he who is satisfied enjoys himself. I was disgusted by it.

Today I was able to read through the first movement better and to run through the Scherzo, which turned out to be less difficult than the first movement. Tomorrow I shall dedicate to the Scherzo again and I shall read through the Adagio. I can already hear those cellos and those wretched double basses wreaking havoc on those poor notes. Enough—I've armed myself with patience. I hope it will serve to achieve everything that these not good, but good-hearted players (since that is how they have been with me) can give. And to think that you read through the whole symphony in two rehearsals in Bologna!

I told Count di San Martino that eight rehearsals will be necessary for this concert; I am sure that he will be able to satisfy my request, somehow or other. [. . .]

The symphony in question was Martucci's Second, in F Major, op. 81, completed the previous year, and the orchestra in question was that of the Accademia di Santa Cecilia, of which Count Enrico di San Martino Valperga was president.

Dear Mr. Fano

I beg your pardon for having taken so long to reply to your very kind letter, but a series of doubts, of ifs, of buts, made me and continues to make me hesitate as to whether or not to accept your proposal, which is an extremely kind one in many respects. I fear working abroad because of the dizzying rush in the preparation of both opera productions and concerts, but I especially fear London because I remember a performance of <u>Götterdämmerung</u> in which the orchestra, under the direction of Felix Mottl, was sight-reading the opera's final scene before an audience. The audience noticed nothing, and the press found the performance superb. Of course! An eminent maestro was conducting, and he was German to boot.

Now, under no circumstances would I want to find myself in such a situation, in the first place out of self-respect; in the second, because I would despair if I were to be treated in such a way by the English public and press—and this is why I would like to know what the terms for these two concerts would be—how many rehearsals would be granted me for each of them, and of what length, and what criteria I would have to apply in working out the programs.

As to my fee for each concert, you may bear in mind that the Bologna Quartet Society usually gives me 1,500 lire [roughly $300 or £60 at the time] and that, as a special favor on my part, I accept a thousand lire from the Turin Concert Society. If these negotiations haven't already fallen through, as a result of my delay in replying, I hope that you will be so kind as to refer my questions to London and to let me know the outcome as soon as you can. For the time being, I thank you with all my heart and I greet you cordially.

Your Dev. <u>A Toscanini</u>

<u>Via Sicilia 50</u>
<u>Rome 8-3-905</u>

Your interpretation of my opinion of Slezak's question was exactly right.

This exceptionally interesting letter was evidently sent to an agent who had contacts with the British musical world. In the first place, it demonstrates that AT had heard the celebrated Wagner disciple Felix Mottl (1856–1911) conduct *Götterdämmerung* in London. (The only years in which that could have happened were 1898 and 1900.) More important, AT herein reveals his thoughts on the subject of adequate preparation—that is, he explicitly states some of the conditions of artistic seriousness that were to become hallmarks of his work. Particularly significant is his statement to the effect that he would "despair" were he to be accorded an enthusiastic reception for a performance that did not merit it. The proposed engagement never materialized; indeed, AT did not conduct a British orchestra until 1935 and never conducted opera in Britain. · The Bohemian tenor Leo Slezak (1873–1946) was at the Vienna Court Opera (under Mahler's direction) in 1905; he did not sing with AT until they were both at the Metropolitan Opera, and the nature of the "question" referred to here has not been determined.

My dear <u>Marchesi</u>

[. . .] Yesterday evening Carla and I were at the Costanzi. The two operas Cabrera and Menendez were opening. The latter is a real piece of mischief by a boy of little talent; the former, a trifle that makes a few attempts at graciousness, shows to good effect a young man with a good musical background, but there is nothing new in his language—on the contrary, in general he expresses himself through the usual ingredients, however graciously he may manipulate them. They must have been liked, if one is to judge from the applause, and the uglier one in particular received an impressive demonstration that greatly irritated me. The composer, who had been sowing the aristocratic terrain of the capital for two weeks, was in attendance. So it's all clear! I very much liked Krusceniski in Menendez, but didn't at all like Zenatello in either opera; Farneti was insignificant in Cabrera.

Ciao. Give my greetings and Carla's as well to everyone in your large family, and accept a hearty handshake from us.

Your <u>Aff. Arturo</u>

<u>13-March 905</u>

Mario Marchesi (1862–1933), AT's friend and a fellow Parmesan, had taught clarinet in their hometown before becoming a prompter at La Scala during AT's first tenure there; he later held the same position at the Metropolitan Opera, again at AT's invitation. According to the Italian music historian Eugenio Gara, the prompter's function "at that time, above all after Wagner's operas had come into the mainstream repertoire, began to acquire an importance that old-fashioned conductors had not attached to it. (Formerly, singers or instrumentalists in decline had been used as prompters.)" Marchesi was one of the first of the new breed, and, again according to Gara, "even after professional duties had separated them, Toscanini remained in contact with Marchesi and often entrusted him with important tasks" (Barblan, p. 328). · *La Cabrera,* an opera by Massenet's pupil Gabriel Dupont (1878–1914), and *Manuel Menendez,* by Lorenzo Filiasi (1878–1963), had won prizes in the Sonzogno publishing house's competitions and had debuted at Milan's Teatro Lirico in 1904; AT attended the Rome premiere of both works. · The Polish dramatic soprano Salomea Kruszelnicka (known in Italy as Krusceniska, Kruscenisky, or Krusceniski; 1873–1952) had a major career in Italy, and in 1906 she sang the role of Salome at the Scala premiere of Strauss's opera, under AT's direction. According to Sacchi, in later years AT told intimate friends that she was the only woman with whom he had been in love who had shunned his advances. · The well-known tenor Giovanni Zenatello (1876–1949) sang often under AT at La Scala and elsewhere. · Maria Farneti (1877–1955) was a respected soprano in her day and worked many times with AT; she married a lawyer, Riboldi, and the couple remained friends of the Toscaninis.

[. . .] We reached the top of Mont Blanc. Dante, Beethoven, Wagner!!! We're aquiver with enthusiasm. [. . .]

AT and Gino Mella, a Milanese friend who was related to CT, had gone climbing in the French-Italian Alps that summer with the guide Giuseppe Barmaz; they and their families were spending much of the summer at Pré-St.-Didier in the Val d'Aosta.

Illustrious Master

Having been imbued with admiration of your genius and your talents for a long time, I am very happy that chance has now brought me the exquisite joy of writing to talk to you about your Salome, your next masterpiece. (Please excuse my barbaric French.) I hope that your beautiful score is finished by now, and I also hope that you will not find any difficulty in granting my ardent desire to present Salome this winter in Turin. Mr. Bossi will have spoken to you in his letter about my intentions in this regard, and in effect he reminds me about your very kind reply, your precious instructions with respect to the number and type of singers required for Salome, and your pleasing statements about me. I thank you from the bottom of my heart.

I now have another reason for wanting most ardently to fulfill my desire: I would consider myself infinitely fortunate, Illustrious Master, to be able to make your personal acquaintance on that occasion. To this I add my request to let me know the name of your publisher, so that I can know what royalties are being asked. Finally, I must let you know that I have at last found the Salome poem in French, as Oscar Wilde wrote it—it would be useful to me for the Italian translation. Accept, however, Illustrious Master, my highest compliments for your fine choice of so beautiful and musical a subject.

If you have a copy of Salome at your disposal, I would receive it from you with great pleasure, as a token of your esteem, for which I send you my thanks.

Allow me to express my feelings toward one of the men who most honor the art of music today, regardless of nationality. Please accept my profound esteem, my admiration, and my complete devotion.

Arturo Toscanini.

27 July 905
Pré St. Didier—Val d'Aosta
through the month of August

AT was requesting the privilege of conducting the Italian premiere of *Salome,* a request Strauss was happy to ask his publisher to grant, inasmuch as the outstanding reputation of AT (Strauss's junior by only three years) had already spread to the German-speaking countries. "I greatly rejoice in your interest in my works," Strauss replied (in even worse French than AT's) on 2 August 1905, but he explained that the piano score of the opera would not be off the presses until about 15 September and the orchestra score a month and a half later. *Salome*'s world premiere took place in Dresden on 9 December 1905, under the baton of Ernst von Schuch. · I have not been able to identify Mr. Bossi; he may have been an Italian representative of Strauss's Berlin-based publisher, Adolf Fürstner.

N.D. BUT FROM TURIN, 16 FEBRUARY 1906;
TO MARIO MARCHESI, (MI?); PC; EC

My dear <u>Marchesi</u>

Please show Nastrucci the list of the first and second violins engaged for Buenos Aires and urge him to tell me whether they are all good. Show him as well the names of those who live in Buenos Aires. Warn him that this year we will do Die Walküre in addition to Tristan; thus we need good players more badly than ever. One <u>Viti</u> has been recommended to me as a second violin, and I've been assured that he is very good. If there are still positions open, have him engaged.

Yesterday evening Loreley finally opened, after an uninterrupted series of illnesses, and it was a very warm success. Kruscenisky is truly exquisite in this opera. Too bad that she can do only three performances. She leaves for Lisbon on Monday [19 February].

It is uncertain whether or not our Turin orchestra will come to Milan because the Milanese theaters are all occupied. But it isn't unlikely. Today, Mayor Frole consulted with me and asked me to promise him that I would stay for the entire three-year period. I'm withholding an answer for a few days, but I didn't hide from him my wish for absolute rest, and in the end I'll insist on and succeed in doing this. I no longer want to do any opera seasons in Italy. I want to keep [South] America for myself and give myself completely to concerts [in Italy]. I'm sorry to leave Turin, the more so because if I give it up Depanis would also give up looking after the orchestra. But this time my selfishness will prevail.

Ciao, my dear friend. Write to me.

Heartiest greetings to your family, and an embrace for you from

Your Affectionate <u>A. Toscanini</u>

Gino Nastrucci was concertmaster of the Scala orchestra. · AT was organizing another opera season in Buenos Aires for the following May to August. The 1906 trip to Argentina would be a tragic one for the Toscaninis: Giorgio, their youngest son, contracted diphtheria there and died on 10 June, at the age of four. AT is said to have been with Storchio when his son died; Carla packed her bags and was ready to leave her husband forever, but he prevailed on her to stay with him. · The Turin orchestra did perform at Milan's Teatro Lirico under AT's direction on 20 March 1906, and AT did not return to Turin for the 1906–07 season—not because he had given up conducting opera in Italy, but because he had accepted an invitation to return to La Scala.

Dear Master,

I want to tell you immediately that I am not at all angry with you: I am only very astonished that when I expressed my simple and more than natural personal wish to give <u>Salome</u> in Milan on the 26th [of December], you didn't interpret this wish according to its true meaning but rather brought the matter onto commercial terrain. I repeat that it's not La Scala's administration that is requesting permission to move up the opening date in Milan, because in any case the administration could never give more than 15 performances of your opera; it is I, rather, [who request this permission] for entirely personal and artistic satisfaction. But in the end, dear Master, if you intend to continue in your determination to change the conditions of the contract [in order to grant] the favor that I had asked, then I am obliged to ask you to leave things as they are: we will give <u>Salome</u> in Milan at the time already decided upon, because I cannot allow the administration of La Scala to make a sacrifice in order to do me a favor.

In any case, I shall be at Mr. Fürstner's at 11 o'clock. Sincerely,

Your
A. Toscanini

During the fourteen and a half months that had passed since Strauss had unofficially promised the Italian *Salome* premiere to AT and Turin's Teatro Regio, AT had left the Regio and returned to La Scala. Strauss and Fürstner were interested in earning as much from the opera as they could, and as the Regio was offering more money than La Scala, Strauss agreed to conduct the Italian premiere in Turin. AT learned of this development when he returned to Milan from Buenos Aires, late in the summer of 1906. Together with CT and Polo (the latter to act as interpreter), he took a train to Berlin to try to persuade Strauss to change his mind. I gave the story of their encounter in my biography of AT; its tensest moment came when Strauss intimated that he would be willing to consider a simultaneous premiere in both theaters if La Scala were willing to pay a fee equal to the one Turin was paying. AT immediately declared that Strauss's respect for his word of honor was nothing more than a question of money and walked out. Strauss immediately sent AT a letter in which he apologized for what had happened but explained the complicated series of negotiations that had led to the misunderstanding. This letter of AT's was a response to Strauss's explanations. The fact is that Strauss saw the matter in terms of his legal right to earn a much larger sum of money, whereas AT was asking a personal favor that had nothing to do with money. AT, however, failed to recognize that Turin could not have been expected to pay more than Milan if there were going to be a simultaneous premiere in the two cities. The following letter makes one assume that the meeting at Fürstner's must have confirmed AT in his resolve to let the matter drop and to accept the fact that La Scala would give the second Italian production of *Salome.*

12 November 1906

Highly esteemed Master!

I received your letter from Frankfurt just when I wanted to give you news of La Scala's <u>Salome</u>—news that will spare further annoyances to both you and me, and for which you need not thank me for my compliance—I felt no obligation at all to be so (notice my free declaration)—but rather a situation that hadn't been sufficiently anticipated and that now turns the matter to your advantage. I began the piano rehearsals of <u>Salome</u> several days ago, and you cannot imagine what a titanic, superhuman effort the singers have to make to try to overcome the colossal difficulties, which are made even worse by a bad translation. This convinced me that I had been perfectly stupid in settling on a date for the performance of an opera without having taken its difficulties into consideration—an opera in which, for the ears of our Italian singers, there are extraordinary harmonic contrasts and great difficulties to be overcome.

I considered it my duty to inform the administration of La Scala of all this: consequently, <u>Salome</u> cannot be performed before early January, the more so inasmuch as I have to prepare the opera <u>Carmen</u> at the same time.

As you see, esteemed Master, the matter has taken a good turn, not thanks to me but thanks to your luck, as you and the Turin impresa desired. I hope that it won't be necessary to add anything else to all that has already been said and argued on this subject.

Please believe always in my admiration for your art, and accept my devoted greetings.

Your

Arturo Toscanini

"My admiration for your art" but not for you as a person, AT was clearly implying. In the end, when AT saw that his *Salome* rehearsals were going better than he had anticipated, he decided to play a trick on Strauss by presenting an open dress rehearsal at La Scala, with an invited audience and all the major critics, on 21 December 1906—twenty-four hours before the Turin premiere. Unfortunately, this trick upset not only Strauss, who may or may not have deserved what he got, but also AT's old friends in Turin, who had originally secured the rights to *Salome* to please their former music director.

(MI), ANNOTATION IN WRT'S HAND: "PROBABLY APRIL MAY 1907 OR 1908??"; TO GIUSEPPE MARTUCCI; PC; NYPLTL

<u>My dear Maestro</u>

My brother-in-law Polo will have told you about the monastic isolation that the doctor has imposed on me for two weeks. I can't begin to tell you how superirritable I've become as a result of this hard-and-fast requirement to wander around the house all day, in the dark, like a ghost, without being able to read and without being able to work at anything at all! I can't describe my displeasure over not having been able to spend a few hours in your and your good wife's company. You can surely imagine how I feel. I was hoping that the doctor would allow me to come to La Scala for a moment this evening to say hello, but he is sticking inexorably to his orders, for the health of my eyes. Therefore I'm sending you in writing my most affectionate greetings, and I beg you to present my most devoted salutations to your good wife.

Your Affectionate A Toscanini

AT was nearsighted from his youth, but not abnormally so. The often-repeated story that acute myopia had forced him to develop an extraordinary memory is nonsense: his memory, which was said to be photographic, was in any case connected with his phenomenal capacity for intense concentration, and was fully functioning at least as early as his midteens. This letter, written when AT was forty or forty-one years old, is the earliest indication known to me that he was having severe eye problems, and by then he had been conducting from memory for more than twenty years. · Martucci was conducting concerts at La Scala, and AT was explaining why he was unable to attend.

(MI?); TO CLAUDE DEBUSSY, (PARIS?); THE PIERPONT MORGAN LIBRARY, MARY FLAGLER CARY MUSIC COLLECTION, NY, MFC T713.D289 (1)

8-3-908

Dearest Maestro,

As I told you by wire, I was amazed by and sorry for the strange thing that happened to your letter. It had been thrust into a big American newspaper, which, like all the others, had gone unread, and it was really by chance that it, too, wasn't consigned to the flames.

Unfortunately, I was unable to accept the Lamoureux Concert Society's invitation because of my previous commitments at La Scala, and so I missed having the pleasure of coming to talk to you and of telling you how greatly I admire your exquisite art, and of thanking you for the profound enjoyment that you have showered upon me, like a great lord, through your incomparable art.

It is unfortunate that you cannot be in Italy before April—but by then Pelléas et Mélisande will have gone on stage without having first been heard by you, and without your having been able to give us some precious pieces of advice. And this is what has persuaded me to insist, and to beg you to come to Milan for a few days. You have already made a few little additions to the score, here and there; it may be that, when you hear it performed in as big a theater as La Scala, you may feel a need to make a few other retouchings, and these retouchings, in an opera like Pelléas et Mélisande, can only be done by the author himself. The opening is scheduled for the 26th or 27th of this month.

Please accept my sincerest greetings and believe that I have the most immense esteem for you.

Arturo Toscanini

Debussy's letter to AT, referred to in the first paragraph of this reply, has not been found. · AT never did conduct the Orchestre Lamoureux. · In any event, the Italian *Pelléas* premiere under AT's direction at La Scala—one of the first productions of the opera outside France—took place on 2 April 1908; it was the realization of a three-year-old dream of AT's (see letter of 2 January 1905). Unfortunately, Debussy was unable to attend either the rehearsals or the premiere. · The "little additions to the score" to which AT refers were written in a copy of the opera's piano-vocal score (Italian version) that Debussy sent AT, and in which AT then made considerable changes to the Italian text, so as to make the words and the musical line correspond as nearly as possible. (When he conducted the opera again at La Scala, during the 1920s, he had it sung in French because he had come to the conclusion that in this case the sound of the language was so closely married to the music as to be inseparable from it, whereas all the other operas that he conducted at La Scala were performed in Italian, regardless of their original language.)

TG, MI, 3 APRIL 1908; TO CLAUDE DEBUSSY, 80 AVENUE DU BOIS DE
BOULOGNE, PARIS; THE PIERPONT MORGAN LIBRARY,
MARY FLAGLER CARY MUSIC COLLECTION, NY, MFC T713.D289 (2)

I AM HAPPY PELLEAS HAS WON[.] IT HAS WON HEROICALLY AND DESPITE AN
IGNORANT COWARDLY HOSTILE PART OF THE AUDIENCE OF SUBSCRIBERS
PROVOKING SCANDAL [IN THE] GROTTO SCENE[,] OPERA ENDED IN A TRI-
UMPH FOR YOU [AND] FOR YOUR INCOMPARABLE ART
RESPECTFUL GREETINGS — TOSCANINI

This was AT's report immediately after the premiere; it accurately summarizes the events of the previous evening. Debussy then sent AT an autographed photograph with the inscription (in French): "To Maestro Toscanini, whom I shall never be able to thank enough." On the back, Debussy wrote the first bar of Act III, Scene 2 ("Lourd et sombre") with the comment ". . . at which point Toscanini came out victorious all the same."

(NY); P.S., THE ANSONIA/BROADWAY AT 73D STREET/NEW YORK;
TO CT, (MI?); EC

21-12-909

My dearest **Bocchietto**

[. . .] when I have nothing to do at the theater I stay home. I study, and from time to time I read in English, but . . . unfortunately, I don't speak it. And to think that I could do so rather well. As I've already written, on Sundays I have dinner with the Amatos, excepting the two occasions on which I was invited by the De Macchis and Dr. Castelli's fiancée. I went to Alda's a couple of times, but some time ago. The other day Marchesi's landlady's little girl came to lunch, and in fact she asked me to write and tell you that she would like to have a photograph of you together with the children. [. . .] Last week

Marchesi came to my place almost every day for either lunch or supper. Setti and Romei haven't yet been here. I'll invite them soon. Tomorrow is the Orfeo dress rehearsal, in the evening a performance of But[terfly; rest of letter missing]

AT had become one of the Metropolitan Opera's principal conductors in the fall of 1908, and for seven years his home in New York was the Ansonia Hotel, then considered one of the most comfortable and modern hotels in the world. CT had probably spent the entire first season with him in New York, leaving the two oldest children, Walter and Wally, in Milan in the care of Eugenia ("Nena") Rama, a trusted governess who lived with the family for forty years, and taking baby Wanda (born 5 December 1907) along. But CT spent only parts of AT's subsequent Met seasons with her husband in New York. · AT was always embarrassed about speaking foreign languages, although he eventually overcame his embarrassment with respect to English. · AT spent a good deal of his free time in New York with other members of the Italian opera community. "The Amatos" were the famous baritone Pasquale Amato (1878–1942) and his wife. · The celebrated New Zealand–born soprano Frances Alda (1879–1952), one of AT's best friends among his singers, married Gatti-Casazza in 1910 and divorced him in 1928; Gatti had gone from La Scala to the Met as general manager in 1908. · Giulio Setti was chorus master and a staff conductor at the Met from 1909 to 1935. · Francesco Romei, who had been an assistant conductor to AT in Italy, would stage the latter's 1913 production of *Il trovatore* at the Met. · The Met's new production of Gluck's *Orfeo ed Euridice* under AT's baton opened on 23 December 1909 and starred Louise Homer (1871–1947) and Johanna Gadski (1872–1932) in the title roles, with the beautiful young Alma Gluck (1884–1938) as the Happy Spirit.

(MONCENISIO); P.S., HÔTEL DE LA POSTE/MONTCÉNIS/M. 2000 S/M./ FAURE VICTOR/PROPR.; TO GIUSEPPE DEPANIS, (TU?); NYPLTL

16-8-911

My dear Depanis

I've followed my optometrist up here, and he tortures me daily with rather painful eye injections. So please excuse me if I'm very laconic and make do with only a few words. I can come to Turin around September 10th and stay until the 28th. I'm including four programs. They're not noteworthy for novelties, but not all the novelties (and I've looked over numerous ones) are interesting; I've done the best I can. Suggest some changes if you like, and I'll be happy to satisfy you. I'll be here all of August. Ciao, dear friend. I hug you affectionately. Your A Toscanini

Montcénis (Moncenisio in Italian) is a resort in the Piedmontese Alps, northwest of Turin. · AT was to conduct five concerts at Turin's International Industry and Labor Exposition in September 1911.

[. . .] I've made some progress, physically. Under the assault of the treatment, my eyes bother me a little, of course, but I try not to tire them with any sort of reading. No music, no books in English, no newspapers. I spend as much time out of doors as I can, with my big glasses perched on my nose. It's true that the place is pretty, but it's not the best place for peace. Too much noise. Automobiles, bicycles, and motorcycles pound one's ears all day long. Not to speak of the children's racket. Walter is having the time of his life. He already made a hole in his new pants yesterday, by sliding down a hill behind the hotel. [. . .] The bad news that Precerutti gave me about Walter's eyes upset me a great deal. I'll start to give him a few drops today.

Kiss Wanduccia and the little enchantress for me. Say hello to mamma and have a kiss from

Your Arturo

Make up your mind to come for a few days!

Precerutti was the opthalmologist who was looking after AT, and he discovered that thirteen-year-old Walter Toscanini also had weak eyes. · Wanduccia was of course AT and CT's daughter Wanda; the "little enchantress," eleven-year-old daughter Wally, was very pretty and enamored of her own looks. · "Mamma" was AT's own mother, who had been a widow since 1906; she lived in her own apartment in Milan not far from AT and his family.

[. . .] Concerning my programs, and with reference to your very nice last letter, I'll replace—although not without some regret for the disruption of that program's smooth rhythm—Dukas's Sorcerer's Apprentice with Sibelius's En Saga. Or, if you prefer, I could play Elgar's ["Enigma"] Variations, if they aren't yet part of your general program. I'll either have to give up on the Franck piece altogether or play the three numbers together. The first two can't stand on their own. As to Sinigaglia's Piedmont Suite, yes, it's new, nevertheless it's one of those rhapsodies knitted together out of Piedmont folk tunes. It's true that this time there's no "The Sun Is Rising" or "Ciao, Ciao, Ciao," but instead there are "The Violet" and similar popular songs. Alas, the suite is dedicated to me! Sinigaglia is Jewish, in case you didn't know it, and for several years he has been buzzing around me, making requests of me, bothering me, etc., etc. Like you, I, too, am of the opinion that this genre of popular rhapsody does not have much staying power in these parts, but what troubles me most is that the suite is in four movements—and woe unto me if the audience takes a dislike to it right from the start! Moreover, in the last analysis, I must add to all this my total lack of desire to look over new scores, especially now that Precerutti has begged and pleaded with me to let my eyes rest. They will continue to be subjected to further injections and abuses of various sorts, even during the period of my Turin concerts.

Sinigaglia has made contact several times. He wired Moncenisio that he wanted to come see me here for a few days. I answered that I had to go to Paris. In fact, he thinks I'm there, and I've received no further word from him. Has he written to you? Do you think it would be a good idea to replace the Piedmont Suite with Strauss's Heldenleben? Bye, dear friend. Stay well and accept Carla's cordial greetings and a hug from your Affectionate A Toscanini

Although AT was not a great admirer of the "Piedmontese Dances" by Leone Sinigaglia (1868–1944), he admired the composer's skill and conducted several of his other works, notably the Overture to *Le baruffe chiozzotte,* which he continued to perform in America as late as 1947. · AT tended to categorize nationalities and ethnic groups according to well-known stereotypes: the Germans were crude and violent but occasionally produced a phenomenal genius; the Austrians were untrustworthy but capable of great achievements; the English were polite but inscrutable. He regarded the Jews as brilliant but sometimes pestiferous—too insistent in trying to get whatever they wanted out of others—and this attitude is reflected in his description of Sinigaglia. In New York, where he spent about twenty years of his life, the vast majority of his non-Italian friends were Jews, and in his last decades many of his Italian friends there included Jews who had emigrated from Italy after the introduction of the 1938 racial laws. His wholehearted defense of the Jews throughout the Nazi period is a matter of record and will be observed in due course.

(MONCENISIO), N.D. BUT SUMMER 1911; P.S. AS IN LETTER OF 16 AUGUST 1911; TO GIUSEPPE DEPANIS; NYPLTL

My dear Depanis

That's fine. I'll give up Psyché, which we'll replace in one way or another, and I'll hold onto The Sorcerer's Apprentice. As to Busoni's Berceuse Elégiaque, I can give it up, too: the two Martucci pieces, which I think are new for Turin, are more than enough. Regarding the Bach Suite, I don't remember whether or not I informed you about the impossibility of finding an Arpicordo in Italy and the possibility of renting one from Bechstein, which built it explicitly for Mahler. It can be replaced, however, by a good harpsichord. In any case, we'll discuss this again in Turin Tuesday evening. I'll get there at 7 p.m. and will probably stay the night. I hug you cordially. Your Affectionate A Toscanini

In any event, AT's Turin concerts comprised works by Bach (Mahler's version of the B Minor Suite, which included parts of the D Major Suite, and which AT might have heard Mahler perform with the New York Philharmonic in November 1910), Beethoven, Brahms, Wagner, R. Strauss, Gluck, Martucci, Rossini, Handel, Dukas (in the end he did conduct "The Sorcerer's Apprentice"), Weber, Mozart, and Debussy. · AT had met the composer and pianist Ferruccio Busoni (1866–1924) in New York the previous February, and the two men seem to have been greatly impressed with each other. In any case, Busoni wrote to his wife, "Toscanini is the most intelligent musician I have met up till now (with perhaps the exception of Strauss). Tremendously lively, quick, far-sighted, and artistic." AT did not conduct the *Berceuse élégiaque* in Turin that year, but he eventually programmed both it and the *Rondò arlecchinesco* frequently in Italy and abroad. · *Arpicordo* clearly has little or nothing to do with the instrument of that name (a cross between a harpsichord and a spinet) referred to in sixteenth-century Italian texts; it was presumably a modernized version—built for bigger sound—of a harpsichord (*clavicembalo* in Italian).

(NY), N.D. BUT FROM END OF DECEMBER 1911; TO CT (MI?); EC

Dearest Bocchio

I hope you will have spent the Christmas holidays more merrily than I've done. What a contrast to last year! I had several invitations but preferred to be alone. On Christmas Eve I stayed home the whole day. I had supper alone. Marchesi was invited elsewhere. So I was already in bed at eleven, contrary to my custom.

[. . .] I'm angry with Gatti and Alda—with the former because the <u>Donne curiose</u> failed to open on December 28, the date that he had decided on and had said could not be changed; with his wife because she gossips and intervenes in matters that are none of her business—thus we didn't even wish each other happy holidays, and the same black mood still prevails.

Gatti's desire is for nothing to happen that will upset his schedule of performances, openings, rehearsals, etc., and unfortunately a lot of disturbances have occurred this year. Nevertheless, he has always managed to repair the damage, because despite everything this theater remains the easiest to run, in my opinion, inasmuch as the company is so large and the audience ideal. But as you know better than I, Gatti would like to earn 150 thousand lire [a year] without having to raise himself for a moment out of his horizontal position. The Donne curiose will open on January 3. We've worked like cart horses— one rehearsal after another, full steam ahead. Three or four staging rehearsals have lasted as long as six hours each. The singers and I, too, ate our lunches in the theater. And despite all this, dear Gatti and the beautiful Alda have had the nerve to complain. It's not [one or more pages missing]

[. . .] Am I right in assuming that you heard about the sudden death of poor Missiano? The poor man! I can't tell you how thunderstruck I was when Gatti phoned me with this sorrowful news. I thought I was going to pass out. I had such an attack of nerves that I continued to cry like a baby all evening. One hour earlier, he had finished a Tosca rehearsal with me, and the last words he sang were those of the prison guard: <u>Vi resta un'ora, un sacerdote i vostri cenni attende</u> [You have one hour left, a priest awaits your orders]. He was singing those sad words to himself. I can't begin to describe poor Caruso's reaction!

Now then, Kahn has offered me a three-year contract, and I accepted in principle, but kept my arrival time and the length of the season open. Of course I would like a salary increase, but I haven't yet spoken about that. Gatti, on the other hand, was treated rather unpleasantly, as usual. Kahn offered him the same [three-year] contract, but rescindable each year—in other words, like the first contract. He was furious, of course, and for the first time in his life he behaved proudly, disdaining and refusing the offer. Kahn then called me to explain the situation, and I of course told him that he was wrong. Thus everything ended as Gatti had wished. Are you pleased that I've accepted this reconfirmation, at least in part? You'll tell me by word of mouth, no? When do you plan to leave? Try to make it as soon as possible, I beg you. Living like this is terrible, believe me, and next year we absolutely must work things out differently. The greatest difficulty is for Walter. But if we could find a young teacher who would prepare him for his final exams and who would be thrilled to come to New York, the problem would be resolved. Wally is much easier to deal with. We could find a magnificent apartment here and furnish it as the Amatos did, spending the same amount that I'm spending for myself, and having the home paid for year-round. We'll talk about it and discuss the pros and cons when you get here. Has your sister made up her mind to come along with you? I've received two very dear letters from Wally—one in German, the other in French—but nothing from Walter. And you don't talk about him, either. Why not? Isn't he studying? Is he behaving badly? I've had word from mamma.—Consigli has been here over a week but hasn't yet signed up any singers. He wanted Farrar, whom he went to hear in Philadelphia, but there were various impediments to his success—first and foremost Gatti, who wouldn't let her go before the end of April, just as he didn't want Amato to leave—and in addition she must do a concert tour in California in October and wouldn't arrive in time, as a result of the extremely long trip. Weidt, whom I cabled in Vienna, won't accept because she doesn't feel like learning Götterdämmerung, Tristan, and Ariane et Barbe-bleue in Italian in three or four months. So we're still working on Bori and trying to cope with Krusceniski, who is demanding exorbitant fees. Did you hear Armida? How did it go? I'm so happy with the news you gave me about the house and the furniture that you've bought. [. . .]

Le donne curiose, an opera by Ermanno Wolf-Ferrari, did indeed open at the Met on 3 January 1912 (U.S. premiere), with an all-star cast headed by the American soprano Geraldine Farrar (1882–1967). Farrar was one of the most popular opera singers of her day and was almost as famous for her beauty as for her vocal artistry. She and AT had a tempestuous affair, and her ultimatum to him, in 1915, that he choose between his wife and herself was partly responsible for his departure from the Met that spring. · A salary of 150,000 lire was in those days equal to about $30,000—a considerable sum at the time. · The character baritone Edoardo Missiano sang at the Met from 1908 until his sudden death, which AT mentions in this letter. · Enrico Caruso (1873–1921), the most celebrated lyric tenor in history, had first worked with AT at La Scala during the 1900–01 season, and they worked together throughout AT's years at the Met. · Otto Kahn (1867–1934), a German-born American financier, was the Met's part owner and leading benefactor throughout AT's tenure. · Consigli was presumably the impresario who was organizing the opera season that AT was to conduct at the Teatro Colón in Buenos Aires from May through August 1912. · In the end, the Austrian soprano Lucie Weidt (c. 1880–1940) did sing *Tristan* and *Götterdämmerung* (but not *Ariane*) with AT in Buenos Aires; in those days, most operas at the Colón were performed in Italian because most of the performing ensembles were Italian. · The renowned Spanish soprano Lucrezia Bori (1887–1960) first sang with AT during the Met's visit to Paris in 1910 and became a Met regular in New York from 1912 to the end of her career; she was known more for her overall artistry than for her voice as such. There are rumors that she, too, had an affair with AT, and even that she aborted a baby of which he was the father. But Walfredo Toscanini, AT's grandson, says that he is surprised by this rumor, especially since "Bori's reputation was rather virginal, in our family." · Gluck's *Armide* was being performed at La Scala that season under Tullio Serafin (1878–1968), AT's former assistant, who now led the Milanese ensemble. · In 1909, with his Met earnings, AT had purchased a large, beautiful, seventeenth-century home at 20 Via Durini, in the center of Milan; CT was evidently still furnishing it in 1911, although the family was already living there. For the rest of his life, AT loved that home more than any of his other residences.

(NY), N.D. BUT EARLY APRIL 1912; P.S., HOTEL ANSONIA/BROADWAY, 73D TO 74TH STREETS/NEW YORK CITY; TO CT, (MI?); EC

[. . .] I will leave here <u>Saturday the 13th</u> aboard the Olympic.

I will complete my duties on Thursday [the 11th] with the last performance of <u>Meistersinger,</u> and I finally told Gatti to work things out regarding the repertoire for the first four weeks of the coming season, because I won't be at his disposal before December 10. He was appalled. He had me talk to Kahn, but this time I wouldn't budge on my decision. I want that <u>animal</u> [Gatti-Casazza] to learn once and for all to treat with greater respect those who have the right to it. I don't want to do him any harm—not at all—I want only to do a bit of working to rule, in other words, to stick to the letter of my contract, thereby reminding him every once in a while that I'm worth something, after all, and that if he shines, it's with light reflected from me. Yesterday he came over while I was in bed; I was feeling a little off. He poured out his feelings in that humble tone of voice that he knows how to put on at difficult moments, admitting that he had been the greatest of fools in allowing an ignoble performance in English of Monteverdi's Orfeo [to be scheduled], and that he knew that he had caused me great displeasure but had been obliged to do it because of a promise that he could no longer retract. He said that he would withdraw it, however, if that were my wish. I answered that I'm not accustomed to imposing my will in areas in which I have no right to do so, and that if I expressed, some time ago, my wish to avoid that botched-up mess, that piece of artistic ugliness, it was only out of respect for him, but that I didn't feel now [rest of letter missing]

The performance of *Orfeo* mentioned by AT was no doubt a greatly abridged arrangement of Monteverdi's opera because it was given as the second part of a Sunday evening concert, and in concert form; the sole performance took place on 14 April 1912, the day after AT left for Italy.

[one or more pages missing from the beginning] [. . .] I've bought two books of short stories in English for Wally and Walter. Will they be able to read them? Walter wrote to me in moderately good English. He made several spelling mistakes but, taking into account that he does the same in Italian, too, I can really take pleasure in the progress he has made. Assuming that <u>he wrote it himself.</u> [. . .] [end of letter missing]

[. . .] I spend many hours of each day in the most delightful corner of my house. It is what it is thanks to you, and it contains a goodly portion of what is best in you. It is a pleasant way in which to detach myself from life's material reality, and when I'm sitting in front of your beautiful song, "Light October Fog," I live for the thought, for the ecstasy of the thought that enlivens it. What delightful music begins to make itself heard little by little—light, elusive music, and yet so warmly harmonious! But to hear it one must have soul, not ears. You're a lucky man, Vittore, to be able to make the voice of your beautiful soul sing!

Beginning in the last years of the nineteenth century, AT collected works of art, especially by Milanese and other Lombard painters. He said more than once that he loved painting as much as music, and he would spend hours climbing up stepladders, hammer and nails in hand, hanging and rehanging paintings. He met the Milanese pointillist painter Vittore Grubicy de Dragon (1851–1920) in 1904; Grubicy painted a portrait of AT (oil on canvas, 40 × 31 centimeters, 1907–10) that now hangs in the Parma Conservatory, and the two were close friends, particularly from the World War I years until the painter's death. Grubicy was also an art collector and dealer, and he counseled AT on the acquisition of contemporary Italian paintings.

[. . .] Here everything is going along well, or at least normally. <u>L'amore dei tre re</u> has been dazzlingly successful with the public and press. Like no other opera of any other modern composer. I'm still incredulous over it.

Kahn has offered me a <u>blank</u> contract for another three or five years; but I won't make any decision about this. [. . .] If you see Walter and Wanda tell them not to study, but hug them tenderly for me. [. . .]

AT had conducted the American premiere of *L'amore dei tre re* by Italo Montemezzi (1875–1952) at the Met on 2 January 1914, with Bori, Amato, the tenor Edoardo

Ferrari-Fontana (1878–1936), and the bass Adamo Didur (1874–1946) in the leading roles. · AT's advice "not to study" was, obviously, meant facetiously.

AUTOGRAPH DRAFT, (MI?, SUMMER 1914?); POSSIBLY TO GERALDINE FARRAR; ORIG. ENG. (ALL ERRORS HAVE BEEN PRESERVED); EC

You are an adorable woman and to love you is to love something very unlike and inexpressibly superior to the greatest [word illegible] of women.

I ought to have peace of mind and soul and tranquillity. I have great need of that. But how to catch it[?]

I believe I shall take a very pleasant villa at Viareggio for the summer months[.]

I kiss you and you [your?] kiss [word illegible] for me[.]

Oh those days passed together in the most delirious [delicious?] intimity[.] How soon they fled away and how slowly helas! they will return for flying away sooner than ever and leaving us in this wretched solitude. This depression of spirits I believe will be [space left for another word] by your next arrival[.] Your [word illegible] does me good[.]

(MI?), N.D. BUT PROBABLY SUMMER 1915; TO MAX SMITH, (NY?); BARBLAN, PP. 337–8

My dear Smith,

I'm taking advantage of our friend Marchesi's trip to New York to send you and Mrs. Smith my hearty greetings and a sincere expression of my deepest friendship. My wife, Walter, and Wally also want to be remembered to you.

At the same time, let me ask you, dear friend, to accept this explicit declaration of mine regarding my spontaneous withdrawal from the Metropolitan, and even to make it public if necessary. "I have given up my position at that theater because my artistic aspirations and ideals did not find the expression that I had dreamed of reaching when I entered it in 1908. Routine is that theater's ideal and foundation. This may suffice *for the artisan not for the artist*" [italicized words in English in original].

"Renew yourself or die." Voilà tout. This is the "only" reason that distanced me from the Metropolitan. All the others that have circulated in the newspapers are false and unfounded.

I shake your hand affectionately.

Your

A. Toscanini

Max Smith (1874–1935), an Italian-speaking journalist, was one of AT's "authentic" American friends in New York, and AT occasionally requested Smith's help when he wanted to make an unofficial statement to the press. · That AT had become dissatisfied with the way the Met was run is not to be doubted, but there were two other reasons for his departure from New York, each of them probably more important than the one he gave Smith: the Farrar affair (see notes accompanying letter to CT, December 1911) and Italy's entry into World War I against Germany and Austro-Hungary in May 1915.

DRAFT OF TG, (MI? SUMMER 1915?);
TO ENRICO CARUSO, TEATRO COLÓN, BUENOS AIRES; ORIG. ENG.;
BIBLIOTECA PALATINA, SEZIONE MUSICALE, PARMA

Lusardi assures your coming Italy can I then rely upon your promise singing Pagliacci. Friendly greetings. Toscanini

AT was arranging a series of opera performances at Milan's Teatro Dal Verme from September to November 1915, for the benefit of the many Milanese musicians whom the war had left unemployed. Many star singers, including Caruso, Storchio, Claudia Muzio, Alessandro Bonci, and Tito Schipa, answered his call to participate. · Lusardi was an agent. · Why AT wrote to Caruso in English is not known.

DRAFT OF TG, (MI?), N.D. BUT PROBABLY NOVEMBER 1915;
TO OTTO KAHN, METROPOLITAN OPERA, NY; ORIG. ENG.
(ALL ERRORS HAVE BEEN PRESERVED); NYPLTL

With the greatest pleasure and satisfation I announce you my opera season ended with two hundred and ten thousand lire of benefit. You have brought me good luck. Thanks you for it and for your splendid offer and sympathetic letter. Remember me please to madame Kahn. Greetings to you Toscanini

This telegram was sent in response to a letter from Kahn (23 August 1915) in which the Metropolitan Opera's chief patron praised AT for organizing opera performances and doing other charitable war work; he had enclosed a check for 5,000 lire (about $1,000).

TG, MI, 18 DECEMBER 1915;
TO BERNARDINO MOLINARI, VIA CICERONE 28, ROME; ASC

PLEASE DO THE IMPOSSIBLE POSTPONE DATES MY CONCERTS TWO WEEKS LATER—I AM VERY BUSY DISTRIBUTION SUBSIDIES MY PRESENCE NECESSARY—VERY SORRY GIVE YOU HEADACHES BUT I AM COMPELLED BY CIRCUMSTANCES FORGIVE ME TELL ME WHETHER YOU [PLURAL] HAVE PER-FORMED MUSIC BY STRAVINSKY AND WHICH [PIECES] HEARTY GREETINGS YOU AND YOUR GOOD WIFE = TOSCANINI

Bernardino Molinari (1880–1952) was one of the leading Italian conductors of his generation. He was more successful than any other musician in fostering symphonic music in the city of Rome during the first half of the twentieth century. AT considered him an unrefined but highly competent musician. Molinari replied to this message by setting the dates of AT's concerts for January 1916 and saying that the composer Alfredo Casella (1883–1947) had conducted *Petrushka* there the previous year but that the public would welcome a repetition; Molinari had himself conducted the berceuse from *The Firebird* and was about to conduct *Fireworks*.

TG, MI, 24 DECEMBER 1915;
TO BERNARDINO MOLINARI, AS IN PREVIOUS TELEGRAM; ASC

= I SHALL PERFORM THE SAME PETRUSHKA PIECES PERFORMED BY CASELLA PLUS RACHMANINOFFS ISLE OF THE DEAD ELGARS SYMPHONIC ["ENIGMA"] VARIATIONS SIBELIUS EN SAGA IM SENDING YOU PROGRAMS GREETINGS = TOSCANINI

These performances of the *Petrushka* excerpts (Rome, 6 and 9 February 1916) were the ones that Stravinsky regarded as a turning point in his international career. AT's performance of *Isle of the Dead* on 30 January 1916 seems to have been his only performance of any music by Rachmaninoff, although he admired Rachmaninoff as a pianist.

TYPESCRIPT COPY, (MI?), N.D. BUT CLEARLY FROM 1916; EC

To the Most Illustrious Duke UBERTO VISCONTI DI MODRONE. SENATOR OF THE REALM.

La Scala's official program for the coming season, which is known to have been prepared by the impresario of the Teatro Colón of Buenos Aires, Mr. Walter Mocchi, and approved by you, Duke, has now been made public, and I am rising up to protest against you for violating a noble tradition of high moral significance, well established for years at La Scala, rooted in the conscience of the public and of the entire citizenry. The obviously secretive arrival on the scene of Mr. Walter Mocchi—the most singular exponent of theatrical speculation—to share with you the responsibility for La Scala's artistic decency, constitutes that violation; and this is happening precisely in the theater that eighteen years ago [i.e., in 1898, when Toscanini first became its principal conductor] was rescued, with noble intentions and aspirations, from the hands of speculators by your father, Duke Guido Visconti di Modrone (whom I still honor and remember with reverent affection) together with distinguished citizens worthy of him. You could not have been more badly advised, if you were advised at all in this rash act.

The joining of two theaters—Scala and Colón—which, as the orchestra's contracts demonstrate, has [already] taken place, can only be the result of selfish interests, all to the disadvantage of the Milanese institution. The two theaters diverge in their ideals, and they diverge in their means of achieving them.

You are thus initiating and establishing new criteria contrary to the spirit of the concession that was given you by the municipality and the box holders [who helped to guarantee La Scala's solvency], and therefore contrary to the raison d'être of the municipal subsidy and the box-rental fees; contrary to the meaning of the civic subscription and to the demands of public-spirited service; contrary to your immediate predecessors and to the tradition begun and scrupulously maintained by your father, who was admired and applauded by all; and they are criteria that offend all those who have given and who continue to give the best of themselves to Art, who have suffered, struggled, trembled for it, for the attainment of a high ideal, and who cherish in their hearts the living flame of a religious love for all those institutions that, like La Scala, are the pride not only of the city but of the nation. And if the legal chicanery and subtleties elude the various bodies that unite to subsidize La Scala and that have the right to raise objections to Mr. Mocchi's meddling, moral reasons, which also have power and meaning in cases like these, must absolutely take precedence. The municipality, box holders, and subscribers are wrong in not contesting the matter. Supine acquiescence is an outrage against the law.

Eighteen years ago the wisdom of entrusting the direction of La Scala to Lawyer DI GIORGI of Palermo was argued to death, because he had at times managed that city's theaters. Then Engineer Giulio Gatti Casazza, untainted by original sin, was nominated in his place. Ten years later there were again arguments over Mr. Temistocle Pozzali, a theater impresario, who gave an unfortunate interview that was published in the Corriere della Sera, I believe, and that led to the choice of Maestro Vittorio Mingardi. Mr. Walter Mocchi's arrival at La Scala is therefore a violation of this tradition, and it has sullied the steadfast purity of your management. It may also have prepared the way for a movie-house-like trash heap of performances put together in a hurry, as [was the case] last season at the Teatro Colón in Buenos Aires. He [Mocchi] has done nothing whatsoever that would give him right of access [to La Scala's administration]. This impresario had the impudence to write to me that he is creating, by agreement with you, Duke, a new technical mechanism for operating the theater and that it ought to yield above-average artistic results, in his opinion. I have already replied to him personally: "No, Mr. Walter Mocchi, you cannot create anything, but only deform everything—your career as a theatrical impresario demonstrates this. What happened yesterday will happen again tomorrow. You began with little honor at the [Teatro] Adriano in Rome—nor did you find greater glory later at the Teatro Dal Verme [in Milan]—do you remember? And so you continued, moving from one theater to another, from one scandal to another, speculating one day on a singer's fame, the next on a composer's, without ever doing anything that was artistically beautiful.

"[In 1908,] You opened the Teatro Colón in Buenos Aires, where you dominated everyone and everything—but as a result of the indecent productions and of the subsequent clamorous public protests you were shown the door and replaced after one year. With your impertinent chatter 'in the name of Art and in order to realize reforms never before conceived by anyone' (sic) you enticed and secured [the cooperation of] many ingenuous people; you set up societies that made affiliates of Italy's most important theaters, with the goal of dominating the theatrical market and putting the brakes on the singers' growing [economic] demands, and creating at the same time your famous 'technical mechanism,' with the deplorable results of which everyone is aware. The societies vanished, the theatrical market worsened, the singers' demands reached incredible levels as a result of the competition you had created, the technical mechanism either was not realized or worked poorly, and there was no glory and even less money."

This is how I answered him, Duke, and this is the list of artistic merits that, in your opinion, make him worthy of the right to enter La Scala. And in the meantime we are sadly witnessing some very strange couplings: Duke Visconti di Modrone and Walter Mocchi—La Scala and the Colón of Buenos Aires—in other words, Patronage and Speculation. Illegal couplings—not long lasting, I hope. Because if one were to lose hope that the present state of things is transitory, it would be better for La Scala to return once and for all to the impresarios, to the speculators. We would not hear, now and forever, the critics' alluring blandishments, nor would we have to witness with disgust the public's passive acquiescence—and these are the chief causes of the artistic debasement that has already taken place and of the moral one that has now begun. All would awaken from the lethargic torpor into which they have sunk [as a result of] their obsequiousness toward patronage and, as used to happen in the old days, [the audiences'] chairs would be sent flying onto the stage and the conductor would be removed or thrown down from his podium.

I have finished—I have protested and I know that I have done so in vain. I have done it, however, to carry out a compelling but sad duty.

Sincerely yours

Arturo Toscanini

This is probably the longest piece of correspondence ever written by AT, and it is certainly the document in which he most explicitly states his thoughts about the need for a lyric theater to be run by people whose honesty was unimpeachable. · As the letter makes clear, Duke Uberto Visconti di Modrone was the president of La Scala's board of governors, and Walter Mocchi (1870–1955) was an impresario whose ruthless methods were mistrusted and opposed not only by AT but also by Mascagni and many other important figures in the opera world. By most accounts, Mocchi was an opportunist, highly skilled politically as well as managerially, and he was later a Fascist spy and propagandist. · In the first three sentences of the letter's fourth paragraph ("Eighteen years ago . . ."), AT's point is that La Scala's administration had been kept absolutely clean during the previous eighteen years. In 1898, the mere fact that an otherwise qualified candidate for the general managership had previously functioned occasionally as an impresario in Palermo had been sufficient to prevent his nomination and to bring about the nomination of Gatti-Casazza. And in 1908 the candidate most likely to replace Gatti-Casazza had disqualified himself simply by giving a newspaper interview that cast doubts on his professional reputation.

WORDS ON AN OTHERWISE BLANK SHEET OF PAPER, (MI?), ANNOTATION IN WRT'S HAND: "1917"; TO VITTORE GRUBICY DE DRAGON, (MI?); NYPLTL

Hope is like the dawn. Its rosy kiss touches and gladdens even the most inhospitable terrain. Dear Vittore, you have the virtue of being able to express ineffable music to the soul through painting. Oh, the long-sought day will arrive! The hour of supreme ecstasy won't fail to arrive!

A slight impact knocks a tired man down but doesn't move a vigorous one by an inch.

FROM SOMEWHERE NEAR THE FRONT;
TO WRT, ALSO NEAR THE FRONT; NYPLTL

31-8-917

My <u>dearest Walter</u>

I didn't have time to come give you a kiss at Vipulzaro[?], because no sooner had I arrived at Quisca[?] on Friday the 24th than General Cascino called to tell me to go the next morning to Monte Santo, which had just been taken. And that's what I did. I stayed there four days. We played in the Austrians' faces, and we sang our national anthems. I observed several attacks on the San Gabriele, and I went down to Quisca[?], sorry not to have seen this other conquest. And where are you? What are you doing? I went to some trouble to obtain your address, and I'm sending you this note through Major Costantino Salvi, a nice man. I know that you're well and I'm happy about it. Write to Mama often, or at least whenever you can. As soon as they let me, I'll be over to give you a hug. <u>Send me your exact address.</u>

I kiss you affectionately. Your father

AT had been an ardent interventionist in 1915, on the eve of Italy's entry into World War I against Germany and Austria; like many other liberal-minded Italians, he believed that Austria had to be forced at last to cede its ethnic Italian territories, which included the cities of Trent and Trieste, to Italy. He refused to work for money throughout the war period and dedicated himself to musical benefit events connected with the war effort; indeed, his house had to be sold so that he and his family would have enough money to live on, although it was bought by friends who allowed them to stay on and who sold the house back to AT after the war. In the summer of 1917, at the invitation of General Antonio Cascino, he formed a military band to play for soldiers along the Isonzo front. · WrT had volunteered for military service as soon as he was of age, and at the time this letter was written he was also at the front, not far from his father. · Monte Santo is now in Slovenia and is called Sveta Gora.

FROM NEAR THE FRONT, 1 SEPTEMBER 1917; TO CT, (MI?); NYPLTL

Dearest Carla,

[. . .] Did you get the brief note I wrote you at Monte Santo? I was up there four days and four nights. I saw some marvelous things, so much so that my heart beats violently at the memory of them. A month ago, among all of you there at the Cantoniera, near my piano, rejoicing in Pelléas's exquisite sweetness, I certainly couldn't have imagined that such a new, unprecedented chapter in my life was about to begin! The same evening that I came down from Monte Santo, I received a call from His Excellency General Cappello to be at a certain place—I can't tell you right now where it was—the following morning at 10. I thought that he wanted to talk to me about the orchestra that he was thinking of putting together in his Army corps. I got there late, because the drivers didn't know the place well; the general had been waiting for me for half an hour. He took me to an enormous field, where a magnificent brigade of bersaglieri [light infantrymen] (four or five thousand men) had just finished a maneuver in his presence, and right there, with the bersaglieri presenting arms, he placed a silver medal for military valor on my chest and kissed me on both cheeks.

You can imagine my surprise and the violent emotion that followed!! I cried like a baby, and in the general's presence I was as stupid as a goose. And I feel overwhelmed by this great symbol of honor, which I don't think I deserve. What could have been more humble or simple than to take a few wind players and a little music to Monte Santo, in the midst of those dear soldiers who conquered it??—No journalists were present that morning, fortunately, so that the news will remain secret, I hope. **I beg you, don't say a word about it to anyone.** It's true that Ojetti was with me at General Cappello's for lunch, but I believe that at the moment he's not writing for any newspapers. I'm sending along General Cascino's statement of reasons [for the medal]. [. . .]

1-9-917

Cantoniera della Presolana is a pass in the Lombard Alps, north of Bergamo and Lake Iseo and not far from the Swiss border; AT and his family spent some of the summer of 1917 there to escape the intense Milanese heat, and they returned the following summer. · "I can't tell you right now where it was": All mail to and from the front was subject to censorship, and General Staff locations were particularly classified information. · Ugo Ojetti (1871–1946) was a journalist with *Corriere della Sera* from 1898 on and its editor in chief in 1926–27, when the Fascists installed him to replace Luigi Albertini. AT considered him vain and superficial (see letter of 5–6 February 1937).

My dearest Carla

I am extremely ill at ease over the impossibility of getting at least vague information, however imprecise, about troop movements. No one here knows anything. Tomorrow I'll go to Rovigo, where all of the Second Army's disbanded infantry is concentrated, with the artillery at Este and Monselice and the Corps of Engineers at Sanguinetto. I would be deeply sorry not to see the Magnis' son. I'll leave no stone unturned. I was at Baone; I saw Walter, whom I found in excellent condition, and spent Wednesday with him. I left the same evening, because his colonel had been warned to be ready to leave Baone in order to go toward or beyond the Po if he received a further message from headquarters. I thought that the warning was the result of the Germans having crossed the Piave, but when I got to Padua I learned of our resistance—a resistance that will continue, I hope, for many more days and avoid having Treviso, Padua, and Venice fall into the hands of those brigands. I gave Walter three hundred lire, and he was as happy as could be. He would have been happy with less, he said. But since he hadn't yet been paid—the money hadn't been withdrawn at that point—the warning to be ready to leave made the probability of being paid ever more remote; I persuaded him to keep the three big hundred-lira notes. At Baone I saw a player from my Cormons orchestra. Sad, desperate, penniless, and sorrowful over the loss of his double bass—a good instrument by a craftsman. I gave him fifty lire; he thanked me, in tears. I would be so happy if I could see the Magnis' son. But I'm afraid I won't manage it. I'll go see Mario in Sanguinetto to make Virginia happy. I asked after Riccardo, or rather after his battery, at the Artillery Headquarters in Baone, but it hadn't yet arrived. Nor have I heard anything of Benvenuti. The confusion is fearful, and no one knows anything. And I've accumulated such sadness in my soul that I could cry every five minutes. On the streets of Padua signs have been posted with the names of soldiers who were shot in the last few days for disobedience, rebellion, or lawbreaking. I read the names fearfully, afraid of seeing those of people I know. I've seen Ojetti, Civinini, Fraccaroli, Amendola, and Benedetti. I haven't seen De Maria; he left yesterday. I went to his hotel, but he habitually went out early in the morning and came back late in the evening—nor was anyone able to tell me where his wife was hospitalized. Today I met Baldo Rossi; his hospital seems about to be moved. I went to the High Command to talk to His Excellency Badoglio, but I gave up because of all the people there who had the same intention. I don't know whether to try again when I come back from Rovigo.

I see in the Corriere della Sera that Caruso hasn't yet replied to my telegram. That pig!!! You would have made the announcement at once, right? If you phone Mrs. Voghera, tell her that her sons are showing me every kindness, and that as soon as I return to Milan I'll go thank her for the consideration that she, too, has shown me. She had written to tell Tullio of my arrival in Padua, so that he would make her room ready for me. I'll return home on Monday.

Ciao, my dear Bocchio—I can't wait to get back. What I see around me is sad and makes me feel terrible. They've already emptied Venice and Padua of their marvelous artworks. Tomorrow morning they'll take down Donatello's statue of Gattamelata and send it to Rome to keep Marcus Aurelius company. Doesn't all this make you want to cry? I embrace you, my dearest, and I kiss dear Wally and Wanduccia.

Your Arturo

Greetings from the Vogheras

After the Austrian victory at the Battle of Caporetto (24 October 1717), the shattered Italian army pulled back southward and westward in order to regroup and establish a resistance to the enemy's onslaught. Even today, the word "Caporetto" rings worse in Italian ears than "Waterloo" in French ears. AT had been conducting a military band at Cormons during the Austrians' attack and had been forced to escape with his musicians at the last moment; his despair over the situation is almost tangible in this letter. · The Magnis, Mario, Virginia, Benvenuti, and Dr. Baldo Rossi were all family friends; Riccardo was probably Riccardo Polo, son of Enrico and Ida and therefore AT and CT's nephew. · Arnaldo Fraccaroli and Giovanni Amendola (1882–1926) were journalists; the latter became well known as an anti-Fascist during the early years of Mussolini's regime and was subsequently murdered by the Fascists. · General (later Field Marshal) Pietro Badoglio (1871–1956) emerged from World War I as one of Italy's leading military men, but his place in Italian history would later be compromised by his support of Mussolini; of this and later aspects of Badoglio's career, more will be said in due course. · Tullio Voghera, a young Italian musician, had been one of AT's staff conductors at the Met during the 1909–10 season. · Donatello's statue *Gattamelata,* normally located next to Padua's Basilica of St. Anthony, was to be temporarily shipped to Rome so that it could not be damaged or captured by the Austrians in the event that they took the city—which they did not.

TYPED COPY OF JOINT LETTER, (MI?), N.D. BUT PROBABLY DECEMBER 1917 OR JANUARY 1918; TO HIS EXCELLENCY MINISTER AGOSTINO BERENINI, ROME; LIBRARY OF THE GIUSEPPE VERDI CONSERVATORY OF MUSIC, MI

Your Excellency,
The undersigned are taking the liberty of sending Your Excellency the attached circular, from which you will learn of the effort they have undertaken to aid needy musicians.

We hope that Your Excellency, the natural protector of Art and artists, will grant them your respected moral support and the material support of the ministry that you direct, in accordance with enlightened wisdom and fervent patriotism.

With devoted homage
signed: [Giuseppe] Gallignani
[Arturo] Toscanini

This letter was probably written to enlist the support of the Ministry of Public Education for a series of concerts that AT had undertaken to conduct at the Milan Conservatory early in 1918, for the benefit of musicians whom the war had left unemployed. · Giuseppe Gallignani (1851–1923) had directed the conservatory since 1897.

POSTCARD WITH PHOTO OF AT AND PRINTED INSCRIPTION (IN ITALIAN): "TO TOSCANINI/SOUVENIR/TRAVIATA — FALSTAFF/BUSSETO 1913", (MONTEBELLUNA? [NEAR TREVISO, IN THE VENETO]), N.D. BUT PROBABLY MAY 1918; TO PAOLA MONTANI TOSCANINI; NYPLTL

Dear <u>Mamma</u>
I'm here near my Big Walter, whom I found in great shape. He thinks of you affectionately and sends his greetings. He hopes to go home on leave any day now. It was my wish to go back with him, but he'll have to stay on a few days longer. I'll be in Milan tomorrow evening. I hope and trust that you and all the others at home are well. I embrace and kiss you.

Your <u>Arturo.</u>

This is the only piece of correspondence known to me between AT and either of his parents.

POSTCARD WITH PORTRAIT OF A CHILD, (MI?), N.D. BUT PROBABLY MID–1918; TO WRT; NYPLTL

Dear Big Walter,
Have you received Emerson's Autobiography? Reading it has given me much peace and enjoyment. I'm also sending you this book by Papini on Carducci. I find it truthful and interesting. Don't worry: I'll dash over to see you before I get down to work. It's something I very much want to do. Bye. I embrace you affectionately.

Papà

AT was a voracious reader of novels, poetry, essays, literary biography, and much else besides; Emerson and Carducci were among his favorite authors. Giovanni Papini (1881–1956), a Florentine writer, was well known in his day.

NOTE BY AT ON BACK OF VISITING CARD OF MAJOR GUY LOWELL, DEPUTY COMMISSIONER, AMERICAN RED CROSS IN ITALY, ROME; E.P. CANTONIERA DELLA PRESOLANA, 11 SEPTEMBER 1918; TO EK, 30 VIA PRINCIPE UMBERTO, MI; WOT

<u>Sweetest</u> Elsa
My thoughts are saturated with you. I love you and I'm afraid of loving you. Why? And you, are you thinking of me? Do you love me? I give you a long kiss on the mouth. I hope to see you tomorrow.

Elsa Kurzbauer, a young Viennese woman, was married to the Czech-Italian composer and pianist Riccardo Pick-Mangiagalli (1882–1949); they lived in Milan, and she and AT were having an affair at this time.

(MI?), N.D. BUT BEFORE 1920; UNSIGNED; TO EK, (MI?);
ORIG. ENG. (ALL ERRORS HAVE BEEN PRESERVED); WOT

My <u>dearest Elsa</u> How can I ever, with my poor handful of senses contrive to express perfectly the joy which filled my heart to day at seeing you, at hearing you? Do you realize the overjoy of my soul? I kiss you a hundred times to the minute. Oh dearest how I love you and how I am fond of all of you! I can't coordinate any thought on the paper[.] I write without knowing what I am writing . . . At random. I only know that to morrow at five in the afternoon we shall meet again and, who knows? I hope to kiss your sweet velvet lips <u>under the very nose of S. Antony</u> [St. Anthony; the reference is unclear]. Oh! God! what a holy bliss I am going to enjoy! Fly, fly tedious and lazy hours and let that ineffable moment come speedly! My soul is intoxicated remembering that magical spell of your unforgetable eyes. You are a witch [i.e., enchantress] and you have bewiched me. But I am pleased and happy of it. I <u>love you</u> and <u>desire you</u> to <u>nympholepsy!</u> Do you understand? and I <u>want you to love me and desire me with the same frenzy.</u> If everything in the world were dark round us, do you think could kisses tell us quite well all that we wish to know of each other? I think they should. Meanwhile you know I love you also in sunlight and I have no room in my heart for anything more. You have swallowed up all my qualities, I have none left. Give me back crumbs of myself.

DOCUMENT IN ANOTHER HAND BUT SIGNED BY AT; WOT

The undersigned, son of Claudio, born in Parma 25 March 1867, domiciled in Milan, resident in Milan, Via Durini 20, well-to-do, having all the prerequisites for eligibility indicated by the current electoral law, declares that he accepts the candidacy for the Milan area in the national elections that will take place on 16 November 1919 within the "Fascist group" that is recognizable by an emblem depicting a sheaf of twigs with an ax in the middle.

Arturo Toscanini

Milan, 25 October 1919

[followed by notary's certification and signature: Alberto Drasmid]

Despite his personal difficulties with his father (who had died in 1906), AT inherited Claudio Toscanini's radical-libertarian political ideals and stood by them throughout his life. In 1919, in the midst of the harsh and often violent economic and social upheavals that followed the war's end, Benito Mussolini (1883–1945), a renegade socialist journalist, formed a new party that advocated the abolition of the Italian monarchy, the upper house of Parliament, all titles of nobility, and compulsory military service; the formation of an international constituent assembly; universal disarmament; women's suffrage; election of judges; dissolution of limited-liability companies; abolition of the banks and closing of the stock exchange; limitation of private capital and confiscation of unproductive capital; land for the peasants; direct union participation in the management of industry, transport, and public services; an 80 percent tax on war profits; heavy death duties; and confiscation of unused houses and ecclesiastical property. AT endorsed this platform, which was far to the left of the Italian Socialist Party's program; he gave his support to the new Fascist Party and agreed to run on its first ballot, not in order to achieve elected office (his name was sixth on the ballot, and the new party hoped at best to elect its number one candidate, Mussolini) but to demonstrate his support for the platform. In any event, not even Mussolini was elected; he quickly moved his platform from the far left to the far right, and AT abandoned official political life forever (see letter of 18 March 1938).

MI; TO GAETANO CESARI, MI; PC; EC

From home   1-1-1920

My dear <u>Cesari</u>

Happy New Year!

The violinist Prihoda will play this evening at Pick's home. Both Maestro and Mrs. Pick request that I ask you to spend the evening at their place, if this wouldn't take you away from previous engagements. I shall be there, too. The subscription is going very well. It has already reached 4,000, of which 2,500 will be paid to you. Greetings and heartily affectionate good wishes from your

Arturo Toscanini

[. . .]

Gaetano Cesari (1870–1934), a leading Italian musicologist, was chief librarian of the Milan Conservatory. · Maestro and Mrs. Pick were Riccardo Pick-Mangiagalli and his wife, Elsa Kurzbauer, who, unbeknown to her husband, was AT's lover at that time. · Váša Přihoda (1900–60) was a virtuoso Bohemian violinist who had been reduced by circumstances beyond his control to playing in a Milan café orchestra; AT helped to organize this private concert and was very impressed with Přihoda's playing. His warm recommendation led within a matter of months to a major Italian and international career for Přihoda. · The subscription was to underwrite a projected edition of early Italian music that Ricordi was willing to publish but could not hope to finance through sales; AT had initiated and made a monetary contribution to this project, which was to be carried out under the auspices of the Milan Conservatory's library, and therefore of Cesari.

[. . .]

Midnight

Mainardi has played well. His tone is beautiful[.] He has qualities of musical charm. He played Beethoven's Sonata with glibness, clarity and technical finish. He lacks, perhaps, in individuality. His playing comes by studying not through the heart. I did not enjoy anything. <u>You were not there!</u> I had like to have left the concert so much I was disappointed[.] Good night dearest—come in my first dream!!!

Enrico Mainardi (1897–1976), the best-known Italian cellist of his generation, would later play a major role in AT's life, albeit indirectly.

Saturday <u>morning</u> [10.4.20]

You did not come in my first dream. I had a sleepless night. However I dreamt at open eyes so intensively of you that I reached the same aim. I love you and I am hoping to see you to day. Who knows? Oh! come, come to my aching and loving heart! Who keeps you so long afar from me?

Afternoon

It seems the brightest sun is shining at Como for the happiness of my beloved Elsa who is merrily forgetful of a soul with is panting after her coming homeward!! Instead the wheather here is rainy, and the sky gloomy . . . I am, as ever, a lone in the worst temper one can imagine[.] God knows when you will come to bring me some glimpse of joy! I wish I could have at least some line of yours for the feast of my eyes—or a little picture to kiss it at any moment. But I have any [i.e., none] of it all. I have burned your long letter of last year, do you remember? and only its meaning I keep in the innermost recesses of my soul. Do write me sometimes . . . You will make me the happiest man on the world. I am reading Shakespeare'[s] loves sonnets. So fancy took me to write you in English. Could I understand Germany [sic] and you would convey the most beautiful thoughts in your language, so I should enjoy the flavour of their very meaning and to know how they were conceited [conceived] in the inmost of your heart—but to my shame I never endeavoured to succeed in learning your mother-tongue, sure of my failure[.] Somebody is coming. Later I shall write you again. Meantime I borrow from Shakespeare's sonnets two verses which I shall, I will repeat to you <u>ever and ever.</u>

"So are you to my thoughts as food to life,"
"Or as a sweet-season's showers are to the ground"

<u>Midnight</u>

I am tired and sleepy—I have read and studied too much. I go to bed not before sending you all my best thoughts. Catch them for caressing your heart and trust that in every word I have written there is a beat of mine. Turn all them into kisses for the joy of your dear lips and sleep well—. Good dreams! . . .

<u>Sunday afternoon</u> [11.4.20]

Oh! yes! Some sweet magnet keeps you still from me. However gloomy, rainy may be the wheater you are glued to your friend and in no-way anybody has a hint of your coming back. My beloved I am sad at heart and I don't know what to think at. From this moment I have but a faint gleam of hope to see you again before my starting for Firenze. It seems you are going to stay there at least three months, as you did last summer at <u>villa Crespi.</u> <u>There is no place like home:</u> is not your device [i.e., motto], nor your husband's, but only mine, as I am seeing—This time I flattered myself you would have come home after a week as you told me by phone, and I was wrong to believe it. Perhaps I had better to give up any remembrance [*sic*] of you and keep myself afar from the circumstances to meet you and your husband. I struggled to do it last month but I failed as soon as your witching eyes stared at mine. Oh! I want you to love me and me alone! Do love me in every way—<u>ideally, materially</u>—as you like[.] Come, come in all speed. My soul is getting such a silly answers to all sorts of doubtful inquiries about your staying away, and feels in need to <u>have, to hold trust in your love.</u> In the inner of <u>my very self</u> long ago had taken root that your simpathy for me was but a whimsical one—to-day I am at a loss what to think at. You would assure me about it on our next meeting. Only, come and come! I am hungry, thirsty of you—of your kisses[.] I hanker after your mouth, lips and your little dearest self. I love you. I long for all you[.] I <u>dote</u> on you. My eyes, my mind, <u>are gloating upon your little, girlisch body</u>. I will kiss it. I will kiss, caress its most hidden corners. <u>I shall find out some precious nook still unrevealed</u> . . . Certainly I do. God, I am <u>exausted</u>!!! Dearest of dearests my heart waits on yours.

<u>Monday night</u> [12.4.20]

No news—Ever and ever waiting!!! It seems you are sticking at your friend's house, I am endeavouring to weaken the rimembrance of your wondrous eyes of your unforgettable kisses.

Dearest Heart in the wide world

I get home in this very moment! I came back from the Arena—What a beautiful night[.] The moon was shining in full glory of splendour. Why, you were not there!? She doesn't sleep yet—However I wish to write you a few sweet words and send many big kisses before going to bed. My lovely and loving Elsa! Ours dayly meeting soar my soul to the sky . . . My soul feels itself blessed by the entrancing love's letter of yours—But they put on fire my blood which is stormful into my veins. We cannot go on in this way. We want something most fitted to quench our overgrown and overpowering desires!

Your kisses, your lips (oh! sweetness) your mouth inflame ever and evermore at the utmost my frenzy to have you under my libidinous caresses—kisses—suckings—lickings—bitings, all over your girlisch body—I am dying and lusting for every part nook—crevice—hole—holy hole of your lovely person. I long to finger every sensible and hidden doted spot of you. I will pass over all you like a river of fire! God! I am going crazy! I feel something swelling and cooking[.] Where is your hungry mouth, tongue—lips—hands? Where is that little doted spot of all raptures and deliriums?

Come in my bed Elsa mia! Come! We will find a new Paradise! I kiss everywhere of your adorable self.

Thine

The *she* of this letter's first paragraph is obviously CT.

10-April 920

My dear Marchesi

Do me the great favor of going, or sending someone, to the Music Publisher Schirmer and buying me the parts (not the score, which I already have) of the Trois poèmes juifs by Ernest Bloch. The parts cost 10 dollars, but since doublings are needed—that is, 7 more 1st Violins, 7 Seconds, 5 Violas, 5 Cellos, and 5 Basses—the price will be nearly double. Tell Schirmer to send on consignment to one publisher or another (Ricordi, Sonzogno, or Carisch) the parts and scores of Bloch's compositions. I would make them known in Italy. In the meantime, bring me those of the Trois Poèmes juifs, which I'm counting on performing in Bologna and Padua at the end of May and in June.

I've heard that you were ill, and I was very sorry. I, too, haven't been free of seasonal disturbances. A trip to Turin brought me influenza, a dreadful cough with fever, and a thousand other nasty things. I had to give up concerts and opera performances in Prague, and only now am I beginning to get my strength back and to feel like working. Did your son bring you a photograph of me to give to <u>my dear and faithful Smith</u>? If you see him again, give him my affectionate greetings. Remember me to your wife, and accept, along with my thanks, an embrace from your

Affectionate A Toscanini

P.S. Give my greetings and remember me with the greatest affection to Farrar, <u>unforgotten</u> and <u>unforgettable.</u> Ciao.

(MI, MAY 1920); TO ANTONIO SMAREGLIA (MI); G. GORI AND M. PETRONIO (EDS.), *ANTONIO SMAREGLIA — LETTERE* (ROME: EDIZIONI DELL'ATENEO, 1985), P. 88

Dear Smareglia,

I've had to go out suddenly and don't know when I'll be able to return home. I'm sorry not to have had time to let you know.

I'm leaving you a roll of paper in which you'll find the pages of that very beautiful lament: Simonia. Take it with you and have your son play it for you. Tomorrow after two we'll be able to see each other without fail. In the meanwhile, I'll fix the little piano score so that it matches the big orchestra [score].

Greetings your A. Toscanini

Arrigo Boito (1842–1918), Verdi's last and best librettist and the composer of the opera *Mefistofele*—a popular work in AT's day—had been an admirer of AT's artistry since the 1890s; as a member of La Scala's board of governors, Boito had pushed through AT's nomination as principal conductor in 1898, and the two men had remained friends. For many years, Boito had worked on a second opera, *Nerone,* but despite the encouragement of AT and others from the turn of the century on, he had not managed to finish it. Senator Luigi Albertini (1871–1941), Liberal, editor of Italy's most influential daily newspaper, *Corriere della Sera* (Milan), was Boito's testamentary executor; he had invited AT to take responsibility for the completion of *Nerone,* and AT had turned to the composer Antonio Smareglia (1854–1929) for assistance. According to the editors of the book from which this letter is taken, the letter demonstrates that AT had decided to have Smareglia collaborate on the *Nerone* project "although their relations had already been strained by misunderstandings." Smareglia was blind and thus needed others to play through music so that he could familiarize himself with it. This awkward arrangement did not work out, and AT completed the task with the assistance of Vincenzo Tommasini (1878–1950). *Nerone* received its premiere under AT's direction at La Scala in 1924.

My dearest <u>Carla</u>

I'm writing to you in the deepest, most anguished sadness. Grubicy is very ill. I can't make predictions because it makes my heart ache too much. The diabetes has taken hold of him with all its malignant vehemence. Then there are his asthma, his irregularly functioning heart—he can't rest, and he is so exhausted that one suffers with him but without knowing what to do to alleviate the discouragement that's annihilating him. Yesterday, in a moment of despair, he wrote to Vicenzi, the director of the museum in the Sforza Castle, to come quickly (which he in fact did), and he donated to him his eight big paintings and paintings by many other artists. For the castle, of course. He wrote to Benvenuti, Tosi, and a pupil of Lione's [*sic,* for Lionne]; the latter rushed over in response to the desperate call. We're awaiting Tosi and Benvenuti.

The signing up of the orchestra is proceeding regularly enough, excepting the rank and file of the first violins, still rather spotty in comparison with what I'd had in mind, because everyone wants to be concertmaster. But I'll fix that. The music from Paris has arrived. Nothing from Germany. I've written to ask Signora Elsa to help me to find what I need. Serafin (1st Oboe) will come to Italy if we pay his return fare from B[uenos] Aires. I'll have to yield to him, because I can't figure out who else to turn to. On Friday I was finally able to talk to Signora <u>Toeplitz.</u> She welcomed me very kindly; she promised to intervene in the business, and in fact that very evening her husband phoned to ask me not to talk to other banks until he and I have had a chat, which will most likely take place one day during the coming week. I wonder whether he will want to offer the whole sum on behalf of the Commerciale. His wife <u>flattered</u> me greatly when she said that the Commerciale had undertaken to give La Scala a million on condition that I become the artistic director. In short, I'm very hopeful.—Bistolfi left Saturday evening. He had many annoyances on this jury, and he had reached the point of resigning as its president—but then everything went in accordance with his wishes and with his intelligent artistic probity, to the general delight of the members of the jury itself. I met the sculptor Baroni, creator of the magnificent, moving model "The Infantryman," and I introduced him to De Finetti, an enthusiastic admirer of his. The model and the tale that accompanies it create, together, a real masterpiece. I hear that you like it there—or rather, that all of you like it there—and this makes me happy. I would like to be able to get to you soon, because it would mean that Grubicy is out of the danger that now hangs over him. Love me, and kiss all the kids. A special hug to the two Cifùs!

A kiss from your

<u>Arturo</u>

The medieval but often redone Sforza Castle (Castello Sforzesco) is one of the principal monuments in central Milan. · Benvenuto Benvenuti (1881–1959) was a well-known painter who had been a pupil of Grubicy's and had embraced pointillism. Arturo Tosi (1871–1956) was a Milanese painter and a lifelong friend of AT. · Enrico Lionne (1865–1921) was another pointillist friend of Grubicy. · Two or three weeks before this letter was written, the administrative council of La Scala, which had not had a regular season since 1917, had met and nominated AT "plenipotentiary director." Plans were completed for forming a new house orchestra and taking it on a tour of Italy and North America, and other plans for the creation of a new repertoire system were formulated. Through the summer of 1920 AT was involved in selecting the new orchestra. · "Signora Elsa" may have been EK but was more likely Elsa Muschenheim, wife of the owner of the Hotel Astor in New York and a good friend of the Toscaninis'; AT was trying to obtain printed music from abroad. · Leandro Serafin, brother of the conductor Tullio, was one of the finest Italian woodwind players of his generation. · Giuseppe Toeplitz (1866–1938), a Warsaw-born Jew, was the managing director of the Milan-based Banca Commerciale Italiana, which in the 1920s as now was one of Italy's leading financial institutions. La Scala, in its reconstituted form, was to be financed through ticket sales, donations from businesses and individuals, and subsidization at national, regional, provincial, and municipal levels. AT was successful in enlisting the Banca Commerciale's support for the new plan. · Leonardo Bistolfi (1859–1933) was one of the leading Italian monumental sculptors of his day—among the creators of the Liberty (Art Nouveau) style in his country—and he was a close friend of the Toscanini family. The family's tomb at Milan's Cimitero Monumentale was designed and partly built by Bistolfi after the death of Giorgio T. · Giuseppe De Finetti (1892–1951), a pupil of the Viennese architect Adolf Loos, was an important Italian architect, urban planner, theoretician, and, later, militant anti-Fascist. · Grubicy died shortly after this letter was written.

E.P. MI, 13 AUGUST 1920; TO CT, SEIS (BOLZANO); EC

My dearest Carla

I'm writing to you with my soul sadder than it's ever been before.

The continuous, endless worry that has been afflicting me for months when I observe Walter's ashen look (he was in the full flower of youth when he returned from the front)—his half-extinguished, almost glassy gaze, the somnolence that very often seems to take hold of him—made me think it was a matter of amatory overwork that nature would have overcome and remedied later on, once the acute phase was past. Unfortunately, by a very strange coincidence, which I'll tell you about in due course, as of today I know with absolute certainty the real cause of Walter's state! This dear, good, but weak son of ours has been taking cocaine! It's a terrible habit, hard to get rid of when one wants to escape from its temptations, the more so in someone of weak character like our son; in itself it isn't as grave a danger as morphine, or so I think, and yet I'm frightened and saddened by it, and I felt I had to talk about it with Dr. Guzzi, who will write to Walter about it. Keep your eyes open. I was assured that he sniffs cocaine very frequently. I've never noticed it, and I've never caught him in the act of raising his hand to his nose. Look in his pockets when he's asleep. He will surely keep a few little containers of it on him. I haven't found any trace of it here in the house. Alert Wally, too—she should also be on the watch. In short, you understand what and how much needs to be done in such a case. Be persuasive and gentle with him, and let's hope that we're in time to keep his condition from worsening. It seems that he has a companion in this misadventure; I wasn't told his name, but looking coldly at the matter I would guess that it's Leo Polo. He looked terrible, as pallid as Walter, at Grubicy's funeral. [. . .] I'm sorry to embitter the few days of rest that you've allowed yourself, but the fact worries and saddens me unbelievably. Write to me immediately, immediately. Kiss Wally and Wanduccia. I embrace you affectionately

Your Arturo

13-8-920

I have not been able to ascertain whether or not this worry of AT's about his son was justified. Walter died in 1971, and Walfredo Toscanini, his son, was not aware of this episode until 2000, when he read this letter. Leopoldo Polo, the youngest of Enrico and Ida's children, was known to have drug addiction problems, and he died young.

(MI); TO CT, PROBABLY AS IN THE PREVIOUS LETTER; EC

17-8-920

Dearest <u>Carla</u>

It wasn't the Didurs who warned me, nor do I think it was only a single occasion, as you've said, that could have brought Walter to his present state. I had been observing him for many months, and it gave me unspeakable anguish—and yet I figured that his way of life explained it, and I cherished the hope that nature herself would have done her job in the end! No, as I've said, it wasn't the Didurs but rather a person toward whom he had felt affection who told me—adding that neither pleas nor advice had served to dissuade him from this ruinous habit.

Keep your eyes open—and Wally must do the same.

I'm impatiently awaiting the letter that you announced [via telephone or telegram, presumably]. I don't know whether or not Dr. Guzzi wrote to him. He left yesterday with his mother and aunt, and I didn't see him before he left, to ask whether he had done it.

My mother seems to have a cystic fibroma in her lower abdomen, or rather it's certain, inasmuch as Dr. Guzzi examined her. Guzzi says that it's been there for at least twenty years. She only began to notice it a little recently, as a result of the bandage that she's wearing, and there's nothing to be done about it. Yesterday morning, however, since he was about to leave, Guzzi brought Dr. Zanuso along with him in case of emergency. Mamma was a bit alarmed, but then she understood the reason and calmed down. Another problem that we could have done without. [. . .]

"The Didurs" were presumably the bass Adam (Adamo) Didur (see the note accompanying the letter of 26 January 1914) and his wife. · AT's mother lived another four years, to the age of eighty-four.

(MI), N.D. BUT CLEARLY WRITTEN SHORTLY AFTER THE PREVIOUS LETTER; TO CT, ADDRESS PROBABLY AS IN THE LETTER OF 13 AUGUST 1920; EC

Dearest Carla

Your optimism about Walter is strange! Don't you see how pallid his face is, how sallow the pallor? When all of you were back here when Vittore died, I couldn't see the slightest sign that would have indicated his having been breathing good air for more than a week! His color was as ashen as before! And those eyes staring at nothing! Be watchful, and Wally, too.—Regarding Professor Principe, try to get information from him about a pupil of his, one Bastia. Yesterday I auditioned another pupil of Principe's here at the house, with Nastrucci. Absolutely shocking!

I sent a short, brusque note to Ranzato that ought to make him rethink his decision. We shall see! While I'm writing, a horn player is here doing a sort of audition. But he seems to be a bit of a dog!

I've received from Scandiani, who is in Venice, the contracts for London with the altered fee. Instead of 500 pounds sterling for four concerts they would now agree to giving me 700 (Quinlan[?]). What do you think? At today's rate of exchange, it seems to me a good deal. I think that at La Scala they will soon have cut off that part of the proscenium indicated in the report, and we'll proceed to listen to the orchestra to determine whether or not to make the modification final.

[. . .] Mamma came here to lunch yesterday and seemed to me free of that pain in her lower abdomen. I'm so-so—I have no appetite. I've been notified that other packages of music have arrived from America. I don't remember whether or not I told you in my previous letter that Ugo Ara wired me to send him a cablegram with the specifics of our tour. But I don't think it's been completely organized yet. I should be seeing Engineer Albertini soon, and I'll find out from him. [. . .]

Remy Principe (1889–1977) and Virgilio Ranzato (1883–1937) were leading Italian violinists; the latter was the Scala orchestra's concertmaster during its 1920–21 tour. · Angelo Scandiani (1872–1930), a former baritone, had been appointed general manager of the newly reorganized Scala ensemble; throughout the 1920s he functioned as AT's right-hand man. · I do not know what concerts AT had been offered in London in 1920; there may have been a plan to take the new Scala orchestra there. In any case, the concerts did not take place. · Ugo Ara (1876–1936) had been violist of the celebrated Flonzaley String Quartet and was living in the United States. · Cesare Albertini was La Scala's chief engineer.

26 August 1920

My dear friend,

This Sunday the 29th, at 9:30 a.m., I'll have the first orchestra rehearsal to try out La Scala's acoustics after the removal of the proscenium. I expect you there without fail.

Hearty, affectionate greetings.

your A. Toscanini

Ferruccio Calusio (1889–1983) was one of La Scala's coaches and staff conductors.

TG, (MI?), ON OR SHORTLY AFTER 23 NOVEMBER 1920;
TO GABRIELE D'ANNUNZIO, (FIUME [RIJEKA]); FIORDA, P. 45

Nothing I know of can equal the harmony of your bewitching words, the energy of your victorious work. With the devoted and grateful heart of an Italian and an artist, I hope that your vows will be fulfilled. For beautiful Italy, for great Italy, for her noblest son, for his valorous comrades, eja, eja, eja, alalà!

Toscanini

AT had known the poet and First World War hero Gabriele D'Annunzio (1863–1938) for many years. In 1919 D'Annunzio and a group of war veterans, dissatisfied with the section in the Treaty of Versailles that had assigned the ethnic Italian port of Fiume (Rijeka), in what is now Croatia, to the newly created Yugoslavia, occupied the town. AT, who favored the incorporation of Fiume into Italy, took the newly formed Scala orchestra to perform there in November 1920, near the beginning of its marathon national and international tour. This telegram is a reply to a telegram of thanks that D'Annunzio sent AT after he and the orchestra had left Fiume.

P.S., "COSULICH"/SOCIETÀ TRIESTINA DI NAVIGAZIONE/TRIESTE/ON
BOARD/S.S. *PRESIDENTE WILSON;* TO CT, (MI?); NYPLTL

Algiers 2-December 920

Dearest Carla.

The voyage is going excellently so far. Everyone is happy. It can be said that no one is suffering—not even [Leandro] Serafin, who has a lifelong subscription ticket to seasickness. I'm glad that you've found D'Annunzio's letter. Have it photographed and send the copy to the Metropolitan. [. . .]

AT and his orchestra had embarked at Naples on 29 November 1920 and arrived in New York on 13 December 1920. · The letter in question was probably the tribute to AT that D'Annunzio had given him when the orchestra had performed in Fiume; it bore the title "From Montesanto to Fiume/XX November MCMXX."

TG, NY, 29 DECEMBER 1920; TO WALTER DAMROSCH, NY; ORIG. ENG.;
LOC, DAMROSCH-BLAINE COLLECTION

TO YOU[,] MR. FLAGLER AND THE WHOLE SYMPHONY ORCHESTRA THE MOST
GRATEFUL THANKS FROM MYSELF AND LA SCALA ORCHESTRA FOR YOUR
NEVER TO BE FORGOTTEN BROTHERLY RECEPTION
TOSCANINI

The conductor Walter Damrosch (1862–1950) was an influential figure in American
musical life; among other accomplishments, he had persuaded Andrew Carnegie to
finance the building of Carnegie Hall, and he was for many years conductor of the New
York Symphony Orchestra, which later (in 1928) merged with the New York Philharmonic. Harry Harkness Flagler was the NYSO's great benefactor. Damrosch and Flagler had evidently organized a reception in honor of AT and the Scala orchestra.

P.S., HOTEL ASTOR/NEW YORK; N.D. BUT WRITTEN 26 JANUARY 1921;
TO CT, (MI?); EC

Dearest Carla, Yesterday evening I gave the last of the three subscription concerts at the Metropolitan. In addition to these three I gave one at Carnegie
Hall on January 3 and a second at the Hippodrome on the 16th, and we will
surely do others when we return from the big tour that begins this very day,
the 26th, in Albany, and will end in Chicago on February 27. Scandiani won't
come along with me; he's leaving on Saturday. Lucky man! This is a great loss
for me, because in addition to being pleasant company he has spared me many
troubles. From now on, unfortunately, I'll have to enjoy them all, and with
interest. But enough! Let's hope for the best. It's just that I now realize that
I've taken on a responsibility, also toward myself, that's too big and too long
lasting. When will the end of June come? And what will my nerves be like?
I'm more and more convinced that it would be madness to tie myself to La
Scala for a long time. I mentioned this to Scandiani, too. I must confess that
although I've had many annoyances over here, I've also enjoyed much satisfaction. Scandiani will be better able than I to tell you about how wonderfully the
audiences of the various cities that we've visited have greeted us. In Boston
they again asked me, through the Consul General, to become Conductor of the
Symphony. Yesterday, during a private encounter with Madame Kahn, I was
invited to return to the Metropolitan for at least six or seven weeks. Naturally,
I replied that conditions at the Metropolitan have worsened rather than
improved since I was here and that I thought my coming back would be useless and perhaps downright harmful, because it would disrupt everyone's peace
and quiet. At that point, Mrs. Kahn made me promise at least that if the Philharmonic orchestra is reorganized at the end of this season, I won't deny her
the pleasure and honor of announcing to the public that I would accept to
come for a few weeks, when I please, as guest conductor [last two words in

English in the original]. I accepted but put off a final acceptance until I've arranged my situation at La Scala.

You ought to have received from Maestro Tanara my letter with the two checks. A bit later you ought to have received another check for 83 thousand lire, sent by Marchesi. I'm now holding on to five thousand dollars, which I would not like to change for another few days because the exchange rate has gone down a few points—but I don't know whether this is a good idea or a bad one. I received letters from Wally and Vercelli yesterday. I know that you're all well, and this is a great relief for me. I was intensely sad for D'Annunzio, and I can't think without horror and disgust about the cowardice of our Government and—let's admit it—of the Italians. We have always worn our Fiume medals, and we continue to wear them proudly. Ciao, my dearest. I regret not having you here, but on the other hand I console myself with the thought that I've spared you many upsets. I kiss and embrace everyone with nostalgic affection. Your

Arturo

During World War I the Boston Symphony Orchestra had communicated with AT in Italy about taking over the conductorship; he had not accepted because of his commitment to the war effort. He did not accept this new invitation because of his commitment to La Scala. Nor did the invitation to be a guest conductor with the New York Philharmonic pan out until the 1925–26 season. · The Italian government had had D'Annunzio and his troops removed from Fiume early in 1921.

PHOTOGRAPHIC REPRODUCTION OF AUTOGRAPH DRAFT OF TG; (MI), N.D. BUT PROBABLY 14 DECEMBER 1923; TO THE MINISTRY OF PUBLIC EDUCATION, ROME; IN *L'ILLUSTRAZIONE ITALIANA*, MILAN, 13 JUNE 1948.

Maestro Gallignani, who did what no Minister or Director General was capable of doing for our Conservatory, has committed suicide. Gentlemen of the Ministry of Public Education, Ministers and Directors General: I tell you that this suicide will weigh upon your consciences forever.

For a note on Gallignani, see page 96. Gallignani, who had shown no sympathy toward Mussolini's fourteen-month-old Fascist government, had been abruptly dismissed from the directorship of the Milan Conservatory and had promptly gone home and jumped off the roof. The minister of public education at the time was the ardently pro-Fascist philosopher Giovanni Gentile (1875–1944). This draft is the earliest known documentation of what was to be a two-decade-long battle between AT and the new regime, although there had been conflicts between them even earlier.

H[is] E[xcellency] Mussolini
Rome
Maestro Gallignani victim of a ferocious act of injustice on the part of the
Minister of Education committed suicide this morning[.] with broken heart
and all my tears I protest against this Minister who did not have even the
slightest respect for a man who gave all his marvelous activity for the Conservatory's welfare[.]

Arturo Toscanini

There are other, less complete drafts of the same telegram.

His Excellency Mussolini (Urgent, Personal)
via Rasella
Rome
I feel I must draw your attention to the sudden and wholly unmotivated firing
of Professor Cesari from the position of librarian of the Milan Conservatory.

Clearly His Excellency M[inister] Gentile must be unaware of Cesari's
worth; I consider him the very best among Italy's finest musicologists. I know
that Senator Mangiagalli, Professor Scherillo, and Count Casati have lodged
protests with the minister on this matter. With great fervor I ask Your Excellency to see to it that the provision is withdrawn, and it will be an act of justice toward an artist.

With unchangeable devotion and affection.

Arturo Toscanini

For Cesari, see the note following the letter of 1 January 1920. When Cesari had seen
a wreath from Gentile being placed on the hearse at Gallignani's funeral, he had
insisted that it not be attached: like AT, Cesari considered the Ministry of Education
responsible for Gallignani's suicide. Word of this incident reached the ministry in
Rome, and Cesari was fired. Mangiagalli, Scherillo, and Casati were non-Fascists who
held administrative positions during the regime's early years and were looked upon
favorably by Mussolini. Cesari was reinstated.

TG, MI, 14 JANUARY 1924; TO ILDEBRANDO PIZZETTI, (FLORENCE);
B. PIZZETTI, *ILDEBRANDO PIZZETTI: CRONOLOGIA E BIBLIOGRAFIA*
(PARMA: LA PILOTTA, 1980), P. 208

I HAVE BEEN THINKING A LOT ABOUT YOU IN RECENT DAYS ALSO LOOKING OVER THE NEW DIRECTION YOUR LIFE IS TAKING[.] WELL THEN DEAR MAESTRO INSIST ON THE TERMS REQUESTED OF THE MINISTRY AND ACCEPT WITHOUT FURTHER HESITATION[.] THE GENTLE HOLY SPIRIT THAT WATCHES OVER YOU DESIRES IT AS I DO

From the early 1920s to the mid-1930s, Ildebrando Pizzetti (1880–1968) was one of the contemporary Italian composers most heartily supported by AT, who conducted the world premieres of two Pizzetti operas at La Scala and performed five of his orchestral pieces as well. In this telegram, written exactly one month after Gallignani's death, AT gives his blessing to Pizzetti's assumption of the directorship of the Milan Conservatory, a position he held until 1936. Pizzetti's beloved first wife had died sometime earlier; when this telegram was written, he was about to remarry—thus the "new direction" mentioned by AT. Later there was a falling-out between the two men. AT felt that Pizzetti's work had declined in quality, and he could not stomach the composer's blatantly opportunistic attitude toward the Fascists. There were rumors, too, that Pizzetti's second wife had been AT's mistress before she married Pizzetti and that Pizzetti found this out only many years later. But Walfredo Toscanini writes: "I think Rirì"—the second wife—had "just flirted" with AT, and Carla introduced her to Pizzetti "to distance her" from AT.

TG, MI, 4 MARCH 1926; TO ARTHUR JUDSON, NEW YORK PHILHARMONIC
SOCIETY, NY; ORIG. ENG.; NYPA

AM SORRY BUT I CANT REHEARSING NINTH AT CARNEGIE AND PERFORMING FOR FIRST TIME AT METROPERA BECAUSE OF DIFFERENT ACOUSTIC
TOSCANINI

AT had made his first appearances with the New York Philharmonic as a guest conductor in January–February 1926, and his success was so extraordinary that he was immediately invited to return the following season, for as long a period as possible. In this telegram to Arthur Judson, the orchestra's manager, he protests against the decision to hold his projected performance of Beethoven's Ninth Symphony at the Metropolitan Opera House after having rehearsed it in Carnegie Hall. As usual, he had his way: the rehearsals and two performances took place at Carnegie.

(BUSSETO?), N.D. BUT PROBABLY SEPTEMBER 1926; TO WRT, (MI?); NYPLTL

My dear Walter

In case they should continue to send the Corriere della Sera, please refuse it. I doubt that they'll continue to send it after the note I sent to the editors, which I copy for you here.

Administration of the C. della S:

The undersigned requests that the Adm[inistration] suspend the delivery of the Corriere from now on, for the simple reason that he is even more disgusted by the newspaper as it's run by the millionaire Crespi Bros. than he was when it was run by the no less wealthy Senatore Borletti.

Thank you.

Arturo Toscanini
Musician, always tuned to the same pitch

I embrace you affectionately

your aff. Papa

Are you coming to Busseto on Saturday?
Kisses to Wally and Wanda.

When the Fascist regime began to muzzle the Italian press, Milan's influential *Corriere della Sera* underwent a political purge. Anti-Fascist journalists were fired, and the obstinately liberal editor in chief, Senator Luigi Albertini, a friend of AT, was forcibly replaced by the compliant Ugo Ojetti. AT canceled his subscription, and this act did not pass unnoticed in Rome. · The transfer of the newspaper's ownership from the Borletti family to the Crespi family seems not to have been politically induced, inasmuch as neither was anti-Fascist. Senatore Borletti (1880–1939) was a Milanese industrialist who had been accused of profiteering during World War I. A few years later, he became a rabidly nationalistic Fascist, helped—through the pages of his ultraconservative newspaper, *Il Secolo*—to hound Albertini out of the editorship of *Corriere della Sera,* and was eventually ennobled. But he was also a music lover and a useful liaison, in fascism's early, unstable years in power, between the fledgling dictatorship and AT's unbendably "apolitical" La Scala. My guess is that AT put up with Borletti and perhaps had a glimmer of admiration for him, because he was one of AT's few adversaries who wasn't afraid of expressing disagreement with him in no uncertain terms. AT was much happier insulting the regime before a highly placed Fascist like Borletti than when he was in the company of people who shared his political point of view. · In September 1926, AT conducted members of the Scala ensemble in special performances of *Falstaff* in Busseto, Verdi's hometown, to commemorate the twenty-fifth anniversary of the composer's death.

AUTOGRAPH NOTE, (MI?), N.D. BUT ALMOST CERTAINLY LATE SEPTEMBER 1926, WRITTEN ON THE BACK OF A LETTER DATED 22 SEPTEMBER 1926 TO AT FROM THE JOURNALIST RAFFAELE CALZINI; NYPLTL

[. . .] It was Figner who advised me to come to Milan (at that time—1886—I was living in Genoa). It was he who introduced me, with enthusiastic declarations, to the publisher Giovannina Lucca—and she introduced me to Maestro Catalani, who believed me capable of conducting his Edmea at the Carignano in Turin, Autumn 1886.

Calzini, a journalist for *Corriere della Sera* and friend of the Toscanini family, had written to ask AT how the Russian tenor Nicolai Figner, who had sung with AT during his debut conducting season in Rio de Janeiro in 1886, had helped to launch AT's career after their return to Italy. The above note was AT's typically terse reply to career-related questions. Giovannina Lucca (1814–94) was one of Ricordi's rivals in the music publishing business until the latter bought her out. The Turin premiere of *Edmea*, which AT conducted, was his Italian debut.

TG, BAVENO (NOVARA), 23 AUGUST 1928; TO ARTHUR JUDSON, NEW YORK PHILHARMONIC, NY; ORIG. ENG. (ALL ERRORS HAVE BEEN PRESERVED); NYPA

AFTER NEXT SEASON Y [*SIC*, FOR "I"] TAKE LEAVE DEFINITELY FROM THE THEATRE YOU MAY REPLY [*SIC*, FOR "RELY"] UPON MY COOPERATION FOR CARRING OUT TOUR SPRING OF NINETEEN THIRTY
ARTURO TOSCANINI

Tired of the tremendous burden of his work at La Scala, fed up with the growing strength of the various theater unions (he supported their financial demands but not their demands to take part in decision making), and disgusted with the "fascistization" of the country as a whole and the arts in particular, AT made up his mind to resign the artistic directorship of La Scala in the spring of 1929 and to concentrate on the directorship of the New York Philharmonic. He was particularly interested in the prospect of showing off his orchestra in the European tour planned for the following year.

DRAFT OF TG, (NY), N.D. BUT ANNOTATION IN ANOTHER HAND: "FEBRUARY 1929"; TO ANGELO SCANDIANI, TEATRO ALLA SCALA, MILAN; EC

I spoke to Simons. Stop—As I foresaw[,] Gigli can't come with us to Berlin[.] He's a real clown. Repertoire all right[,] only I can't see with which tenors[.] Choose those you think best among the prime donne for Ballo and Trovatore. I would like a third [soprano] whom I don't know. I'm rather worried about this tour. Let's hope that everything will proceed well. Greetings.
Toscanini

The Scala ensemble gave extraordinarily successful performances in Vienna and Berlin in the spring of 1929, AT's last performances as the company's artistic director. · Simons was presumably an artists' agent. · Beniamino Gigli (1890–1957) was one of the most beloved tenors of his time, but AT rarely performed with him. In the end, Giacomo Lauri-Volpi (whom AT did not much like) and Aureliano Pertile (whom he very much liked) were the principal tenors chosen for the tour. Giannina Arangi Lombardi (1891–1951) was the prima donna in *Il trovatore; Un ballo in maschera* was not taken on the tour.

TG (MI, LATE MAY OR EARLY JUNE 1929); TO BENITO MUSSOLINI, ROME;
ARNALDO FRACCAROLI, "LA SCALA A VIENNA E A BERLINO (MAGGIO 1929)"
(PAMPHLET), MILAN, 1929, P. 93

The demonstration of your satisfaction and kindness reaches my colleagues
and me while the echo of the joyful welcomes in Vienna and Berlin still
resounds, and it is the occasion of lively and profound joy for all of us.

I very gratefully thank Your Excellency, also in the name of my faithful colleagues. Today, as yesterday and as always, I serve and will continue to serve
my art with humility, but with intense love, certain that in so doing I am serv-
ing and honoring my country. Sincerely yours
Arturo Toscanini

When AT and the Scala ensemble returned from their trip to Vienna and Berlin, Mussolini sent a typically pompous telegram to the Maestro; he said, among other things,
that "La Scala's performances made known not only the great historic virtues of an
artistic organization, but also the new spirit of Contemporary Italy, which unites to its
will to power the necessary harmonious discipline required in every field of human
activity." AT understood the implication that in contributing to La Scala's glory he
was also contributing to the glory of the new Fascist society. As he wrote the last sentence of his reply, he must have been thinking that at that moment in history he preferred to serve his country from abroad rather than at home, because his resignation
from La Scala had just been announced. The next time AT performed with an Italian
ensemble, Mussolini and his Fascist society were dead.

TG, MI, 24 JULY 1929(?); TO ZOLTÁN KODÁLY, SCHILLERHOF, BADGASTEIN,
AUSTRIA (FORWARDED FROM BUDAPEST); PC; EC(?)

putting together programs i would like to know for sure whether i can hope
for a composition of yours to present in premiere my forthcoming concerts
america greetings toscanini

This is presumably the request that resulted in AT's giving the world premiere of the
revised version of Kodály's *Nyári este* (*Summer Evening,* originally written in 1906) with
the New York Philharmonic in April 1930; see the next item. It was one of four works
by Kodály in AT's repertoire.

TG, NY, 4 APRIL 1930; TO ZOLTÁN KODÁLY, ZÉNEI FOISKOLA, BUDAPEST;
ORIG. GER.; PC; EC(?)

THIS EVENING HAVE SUCCESSFULLY CONDUCTED YOUR SUMMER EVENING
WHICH I TRULY LOVE AND THE AUDIENCE LISTENED AND APPLAUDED WITH
LOVE HEARTY GREETINGS ARTURO TOSCANINI

AT conducted Kodály's *Summer Evening* during the New York Philharmonic concerts
of 3 and 4 April 1930; he repeated the piece when the orchestra played in Budapest on

21 May 1930, during its triumphal European tour. · Someone evidently translated this message into German for AT.

TG, (NY, 16 OR 17 APRIL 1930); TO OTTORINO
RESPIGHI, (ROME?); DELLA CORTE, P. 229

PASSACAGLIA HAS HAD GREATEST SUCCESS: IT IS MASTERFULLY ORCHES-TRATED. BRAVO RESPIGHI! GREETINGS — TOSCANINI

AT commissioned Respighi—another contemporary composer whose work interested the conductor—to orchestrate Bach's Passacaglia and Fugue in C Minor for him to perform with the New York Philharmonic. The arrangement was first performed in New York on 16 and 17 April 1930 and was repeated by AT and the Philharmonic five times during their European tour.

AUTOGRAPH DRAFT, 4 JUNE 1930; P.S., SAVOY HOTEL/LONDON; TO THE
MEMBERS OF THE NEW YORK PHILHARMONIC; EC

My dearest friends, members of the Philharmonic Orchestra . . .
My heart is sad!
The thought that this evening we will give the last concert of a successful tour and that tomorrow we will have to separate after seven weeks spent in affectionate, familylike cordiality moves me profoundly. But that's life. It's almost always made up of bitter separations. When one isn't separating from loved ones or dear friends, one is separating from some illusion or other.
This time, however, the illusion that our tour has been a magnificent artistic statement won't leave us. I am very sure that all of us will always keep this sweet memory. But what I most want to tell you and express to you is the great joy that I have experienced in becoming more aware every day of the enthusiasm and the faith that you've brought to making every concert turn out better than the previous one, and you have never given the slightest sign of tiredness! You have really been marvelous, and I thank you and tell you that today not only am I proud of you but I love you as faithful friends.
And now I wish you an excellent crossing, and see you in November.
Arturo Toscanini

London 4-6-930

Just as the Scala ensemble's performances of Italian opera under AT had created a furor in Vienna and Berlin the previous year, so the New York Philharmonic's performances in May–June 1930 had made a tremendous impact throughout much of Europe. AT's rare sense of satisfaction is evident in this message to his players.

Dearest Walter

[. . .] I'm well enough—better than the first few days, when I couldn't sleep. I'm working a lot and waiting for the day when I'll have to leave for Bayreuth. The thought of such a long train trip frightens me! I'd like to go as far as Nuremberg by airplane! Enough! I'll see. [. . .]

AT was not able to rest after the Philharmonic's tour: in July he was to become the first non-German-school conductor to perform at the Wagner Festival in Bayreuth, and he spent the intervening weeks at St. Moritz, trying to avoid physical exertion but studying and restudying *Tannhäuser* and *Tristan.*

Milan <u>23 June 1930</u>

I, the undersigned Arturo Toscanini, in full command of my faculties, order that in the event of my death the sole Heir of everything I possess be my wife Carla De Martini, with due respect being given to the legitimate claims of my three children, Walter, Wally, and Wanda, with the wish that the house in Via Durini 20 be preserved for the use of my above-mentioned spouse. Within the limits of her economic possibilities, she should treat generously the Istituzione Toscanini (connected to the Scala Theater), which is close to my heart.
<u>Arturo Toscanini.</u>

It is unclear whether AT returned briefly to Milan before proceeding to Bayreuth or simply wrote "Milan" on this testament. · The Istituzione Toscanini was a fund to help finance fresh-air camps and educational projects for the children of La Scala's employees; it had been created in 1928 to honor AT on the occasion of the thirtieth anniversary of his debut as La Scala's principal conductor, and he himself contributed considerable sums to it. À propos AT's generosity toward the people who worked with him, the conductor Gianandrea Gavazzeni (1909–96) told me that members of La Scala's orchestra would often turn to CT whenever they found themselves in financial embarrassment, and that she had standing orders from her husband to help them out, with no questions asked.

My dearest <u>friend</u> Daniela

I don't agree with you regarding the lighting at the change from the <u>Venusberg</u> to the <u>valley,</u> and I am transcribing for you the very words of R. Wagner about this scene change: "The great transformation scene takes place all at once as follows: after the stage darkens, suddenly the massive cloud decoration is raised; the scrims are removed quickly after that, at which time the personage who bursts onto the scene with great energy takes in the new scene, the valley bathed in midday sunlight at its brightest. The effect of this valley decor, which is to materialize in precise accordance with the instructions in the score, must now be so overpoweringly fresh, scintillating, and familiar that the poet-musician may be allowed to leave the spectators to their impressions for a good long while."

My dear friend, the book you sent me with the extremely nice dedication is delightful. I'm devouring it. Many thanks. Continue to be as fond of me as I am of you!

Arturo <u>Toscanini</u>

AT faced many trials and tribulations at Bayreuth in 1930; nevertheless, Wagner's children and stepchildren—who had heard all of the principal Wagner interpreters from the composer himself onward—were overwhelmed by AT's performances. In particular, Daniela Thode, Cosima Wagner's daughter by her first husband (the conductor Hans von Bülow), and Eva Chamberlain, Wagner and Cosima's daughter, became fanatical admirers of AT. · Daniela and her half brother, Siegfried Wagner, had created a new *Tannhäuser* production that had included a gradual light change from the Venusberg to the Wartburg, whereas AT insisted that the change be sudden, as Richard Wagner had requested. (AT cited the Wagner quotation in the original German in his note to Daniela; it was translated for me by Philip Wults.)

DRAFT OF A NOTE, (BAYREUTH, END OF JULY OR EARLY AUGUST 1930);
TO COUNTESS BLANDINE GRAVINA, (BAYREUTH); EC

Dearest Countess Gravina

With my nerves in their present state, stretched to the breaking point, it is impossible for me to take on so demanding and, above all, so unpleasant a job as that of making records! My aversion to this type of work is so great that since last winter I have broken off all relations with the Gramophone [RCA Victor] of New York. So try, dear, good lady, to persuade the gentleman not to persist further with his request as I really don't like it.

Countess Gravina was another of Cosima Wagner's daughters by von Bülow; she was an intimate member of the Wagner circle but had lived for many years in Florence and thus spoke Italian more fluently than the other Wagner daughters and stepdaughters. The gentleman who tried to persuade AT to make some recordings at Bayreuth was almost certainly the legendary Fred Gaisberg, pioneer of the phonograph. AT's description of his own dislike of the recording process in those years can certainly be taken at face value, but in fact he was so dissatisfied with the Bayreuth orchestra in 1930 that he would not have wanted its work to be preserved. Yet the fact that Gaisberg's hopes were not fulfilled means that we lack any trace of AT's work at Bayreuth. The draft of this note was written on a blank page at the end of an obsequiously praiseful letter to AT from Leopold Reichwein, conductor of the Vienna Konzertverein.

TG, (MI?), CIRCA I OCTOBER 1930; TO SERGE KOUSSEVITZKY, SYMPHONY
HALL, BOSTON; ORIG. ENG.; LOC, KOUSSEVITZKY COLLECTION

Can I safely produce Prokofieff Sinfonietta December eleven in New York or
do you intend playing it previously there[?] please cable Maestro Toscanini
Milano Best wishes

The "Sinfonietta" was in fact Prokofiev's Symphony No. 1 ("Classical"). Koussevitzky
cabled back on 4 October that AT could go ahead and program the work, but in the
end AT did not do so. (He had first conducted it with the Philharmonic in 1929, and
he did not conduct it again until 1939.)

(ABOARD THE STEAMSHIP *VULCANIA*, I NOVEMBER 1930);
TO CT, ROME/MI; EC

My <u>dear Carla</u>
As I telegraphed you, I'm happy about Wally's news. Despite the fact that the
sadness that settled in my heart some weeks ago is so profound that it doesn't
give me a moment's peace, your certainty that Wally, in the new life that she's
about to enter upon, won't have to experience any of the annoyances that are
sometimes part and parcel of the special conditions of marriages like hers
allows me a brief glimpse of light at the end of the tunnel.
    [. . .] I'm working and working to pass the time. I'm terrified of the great
task before me, yet I can't wait to throw myself headlong into this work,
which is my joy and my torment! The trip has been magnificent so far. Luigi is
doing well. Max and I dine in the <u>grill-room.</u> So far, we're alone, excepting a
blind Swiss gentleman. This evening, former Minister Volpi will embark.
They say that he's alone. One Ravenna, who is said to be His Excellency's secretary, is already aboard. And how long are you [plural] going to stay in
Rome? I'm sending this letter to Milan in the certainty that it will find you
back there. And Carla, remember to take care of yourself and above all not to
get upset. Be calm with our children. Even from far away, I want to know that
you are tranquil and serene, and you must believe that you're in my soul, as
you've always been at every moment in our life. I love you and I've always
loved you. You're still my Carla of long ago, and you will always be <u>above</u>
<u>everything</u> for me. Kiss our children, tell Wally that she is ever deeper in my
heart; and for you, all my affection—Arturo.

CT, who was deeply depressed and, in addition, still experiencing pain in her leg,
which she had broken at Bayreuth the previous summer, remained in Italy in the fall
of 1930, when AT went to New York for his Philharmonic concerts. · Wally and
Count Emanuele di Castelbarco had been a de facto couple for more than a decade, but
Castelbarco was married and had children—and Italian law did not recognize divorce.
In 1930 he finally managed to obtain a divorce in Hungary, and in January 1931 he

and Wally married there, in the home of Zoltán Kodály, because they could not marry in Italy. AT was a nonpracticing Catholic but nevertheless did not believe in divorce; he ostracized several friends who divorced and remarried, or who remarried too soon, in his opinion, after the death of a spouse, but for his beloved Wally he made an exception—of course. · Luigi was a valet who had been engaged to look after AT in Carla's absence. · Max Smith was the Toscaninis' American journalist friend from the Met days. · Count Volpi di Misurata was a leading Fascist financier and sometime government minister.

P.S., M/N *VULCANIA;* TO CT, (MI?); EC

Saturday 8-11-930

My <u>dear Carla</u>

We won't be able to disembark until tomorrow morning. We'll arrive in New York this evening at 10. I'm a little sorry, but there's nothing to be done. The last three days the sea was rough and agitated and the wind was blustering, so we made little progress. There were many <u>victims,</u> among them His Excellency Count Volpi, who is very good at turning his sails to the prevailing wind on dry land but demonstrated less ability at sea. I chatted with him a few times, and he was always very pleasant with me. He reminded me that Walter and Wanda had been to his home in Venice a few times. It is said that his trip to the United States may be a pretext, presumably for [a request for] a loan to Italy. He, however, is as silent as a tomb on this subject; he says only that he must be in London early in December for some very important business. Luigi was another of the bad weather's victims. I didn't see him for three whole days, and he appeared this morning because the most beautiful sun is shining over the most marvelous sea. Max is very well. We see each other at mealtimes, and for a few days we met at the cinema, but then I began to take Murri's powders and I had to give up my favorite travel amusement. I studied the new scores, but so far I don't feel a great desire to encounter my orchestra and begin to work!! I would gladly stay on this same ship and go back home. I hope that this state of mind will change tomorrow, on contact with that marvelous instrument, and that I'll be relieved, at least in part, of this state of anxiety which tortures me. [. . .]

Augusto Murri (1841–1932) was one of the leading Italian physicians and medical scholars of his generation, and at some time, probably in the 1920s, he had examined AT.

11-11-930

My dearest <u>Carla</u>

All our faithful friends were on hand for my arrival. Despite the early hour, even the biggest sleepyheads didn't fail to show up [. . .]. And then many orchestra members with Maestro Kleiber, Van Praag, Zirato, Davies from Philadelphia, etc. [. . .]

At Mackay's invitation I attended Kleiber's last concert. Not bad at all. He was quite warmly received. I talked with Judson today about having him re-engaged. I also spoke about Zirato with Mackay, who engaged him on the spot for the Philharmonic. You can imagine that good fellow's happiness and gratitude!

I had my first two rehearsals yesterday. I found the orchestra enthusiastic about getting back to work with me. I immediately rehearsed the Brahms symphony, and in the afternoon also the Bach chorales [one or more pages missing here].

[. . .] My dear Wally—how deep in my soul she is! I have two photographs before me—one of all of us taken in Bayreuth on the terrace of our house, the other, which Margherita gave me, of Wally and Wanda as little girls taken on the terrace of the house in Via San <u>Vincenzino,</u> and I get tears in my eyes over the many sad and happy memories that they stir up.

My dearest, I can't tell you how many people have asked about you! And all with affectionate interest.

Bori has just come in. A moment earlier I had received a basket of fruit from her, while I was writing this letter, and she came up behind me while I was writing about Wally, suddenly, precisely at a moment in which I could not hold back my feelings!! [. . .]

Erich Kleiber (1890–1956) had been the Philharmonic's guest conductor since early October; these concerts constituted his American debut. The concert that AT heard on 9 November comprised works of Ernst Křenek, Richard Strauss, Schubert, Mozart, and Josef Strauss. "Not bad at all" was high praise indeed from AT, and Kleiber did in fact return the following season. · Clarence H. Mackay was chairman of the Philharmonic's board and its leading benefactor. · Bruno Zirato, who had been Caruso's secretary, was much liked by AT and CT and became a sort of "Minister in Charge of Toscanini" with the Philharmonic. He continued to work for the orchestra long after AT left it. · AT's first program of the season included three Bach chorale preludes orchestrated by Respighi and the first symphonies of Beethoven and Brahms. · "Margherita" was Margherita De Vecchi, an American-born woman of independent means whose father had emigrated from Italy. She had become a close friend of AT and CT since he had begun working with the Philharmonic, and for much of the rest of his American career she acted as a sort of amanuensis to him and his family. There are frequent references to her in AT's correspondence. · For Lucrezia Bori, see the note accompanying the letter of the end of December 1911.

Dearest <u>Carla,</u>

The good-luck telegrams from all of you brought me luck. I had them with me, indeed on me, through the whole concert. The orchestra played marvelously. The Brahms symphony (no. 1), which I was conducting here for the first time, made a great impression. Everyone is praising the performance as one of the best. [. . .]

I'm so agitated that I can't write—my hand is shaking. It's the tiredness of these first days of rehearsal. The day before yesterday I called a doctor, one Eckmann, to massage my right arm, and it did me good, but just now my writing is indecent. Please make do with my good intentions.

Kiss my dear Wally and Wanda, remember me to Walter, and accept all my affection.

<u>Your Arturo</u>

Friday <u>evening 14-11-930</u>

This performance of the Brahms First was AT's first anywhere. Although the Second and Fourth Symphonies had been part of his repertoire for over thirty years, he did not conduct the Third until 1929 or the First until 1930. · Throughout the following year, AT's arm and shoulder pains would increase until they became unbearable.

My dear <u>Mrs. Stokowski</u>

I feel greatly distressed at not being able to accept your friendly and sympathetic invitation to be Godfather for your baby—the more so as I am particularly fond of children and my heart goes out to them always.

I trust, however, that you will understand my position when I tell you that for years I have made it a rule not to officiate as Godfather, even in instances of colleagues very close to me such as Ildebrando Pizzetti [word illegible]. Under the circumstances it would be an injustice towards others if I were to break a precedent of long standing. Thus, I am convinced, you will appreciate and accept my assurances that I feel thoroughly and gratefully the spirit that animated you in asking me to take into my arms the new little life you have brought into the world.

For little Sadja and her lovely mother I wish the greatest good fortune.

Very sincerely

For an explanation of this letter, see the next letter and its note.

My dearest Carla,

It was a real joy for my soul to have heard your voices. I couldn't wait. Too bad that you were so nervous that you couldn't talk a little more. I'm happy to know that you are well again and sleeping better than before. I'm well enough, but as for sleep, that's another story! As usual, the nights are eternal. I get up six or seven times a night. I wander from room to room, I read, I look at a few new scores, I look for all of you but I find you only in my thoughts and at the bottom of my heart. All of our friends continue to be extremely kind to me—I might almost say too kind and solicitous. My God, I'm very sorry to say it—in fact, I'll say it only to you, and softly—if they would let me breathe a bit and live in complete solitude, I think I would live much better! Even in Philadelphia things are quite different. I feel that I can breathe easier. For pity's sake, don't let any of what I'm telling you be known to Margherita (from whom I've just this moment received a basket of fruit from New York), if you write to her or to anyone else; I would be very sorry, after all, to offend good friends who offer the very best they can and think that they're helping me to feel less lonely because they don't know the [Latin] proverb: <u>Beata solitudo— sola beatitudo</u> [O blessed solitude, sole bliss].

[. . .] This morning I had my second rehearsal with the Philadelphia orchestra. Everyone is enthusiastic over this poor old maestro. Hmmph! And to think that I would love nothing better than to drop everything and withdraw in peace! I'm torn by a thousand different thoughts. They're already inviting me to come back to Philadelphia next year, and not only that, but also to do a California tour after the regular season. These people think I'm eternal! You want to hear a good one? Four or five days ago I received a letter from Stokowski's wife asking me (can you imagine?) to be godfather to her recently born baby. Of course I replied in the negative. In the meantime, he—the husband—published an article full of praise for my art, with indescribable enthusiasm. So I've been told, because I haven't read it. Great charlatans, both of them. And all this happened one or two days before I came to lead his orchestra and he mine. [. . .]

Leopold Stokowski (1882–1977), who had been conductor of the Philadelphia Orchestra since 1912, traded orchestras with AT for the last week in November and the first week in December 1930. AT enjoyed a tremendous success in Philadelphia, but Stokowski had a difficult time with the Philharmonic's musicians, who did not like him. Before the exchange took place, however, Stokowski wrote an article in which he praised AT's "divine fire," "subtle and flexible and vibrant" rhythm, "clear and eloquent" beat, finely sculpted melodic line, and "originality of conception," which was the result of "expressing the essence and soul of the score, instead of merely the literal notes." He also had his second wife, the heiress Evangeline Brewster Johnson (part of the Johnson & Johnson family) invite AT to be godfather of their second daughter (see previous letter). Rightly or wrongly, AT was convinced that this was all a publicity ploy on Stokowski's part, and Stokowski certainly had the reputation of being interested in publicity.

E.P. NY, 4 DECEMBER 1930; TO CT, D2OMI; EC

[Philadelphia,] 3-12-930

Dearest <u>Carla mine,</u>

The nights are terrible! Here I am pacing the rooms, whereas I had really hoped to rest, given the tiredness caused by this evening's concert. That damned Heldenleben of Strauss kills me. I've already conducted it six times between here and New York, and I can't stand it anymore!

[. . .] Tomorrow morning, after the rehearsal, I'll go to New York, and I'll come back at ten in the evening. I want to see my little apartment again, where all of you have lived. [. . .]

In today's Times I read news of strikes in Turin and of people being arrested in Rome, among them the poet De Bosis's wife, an American woman. Do you know anything about all of this? Do the newspapers talk about it, or do they pretend to know nothing?

[New York, 4 December 1930] [. . .] Monday evening (8 December) I have my last concert for the Philadelphia [Orchestra's] Pension Fund, and as soon as the concert is over I'll leave for New York, as I have a rehearsal at Carnegie [Hall] on Tuesday morning. Margherita tells me that she received a letter from Wally, who assured her that her marriage is set for 20 December. How is it that you tell me that it will take place in January? My dear Wally—it seems impossible not to see her anymore in my house, in <u>her house!</u> I never realized how profoundly I love her! But what have I ever known about myself, my heart—my being!!!

Embrace her with the most affectionate tenderness and tell her how dear she is to me and how much I adore her! There: at this very moment I'm overwhelmed with deep sadness, desperate sadness, and I would like to have you near, to be able to reveal my mind to you and clear it of all the bitterness that's pouring into it! [. . .]

AT evidently did not know that the poet and translator Adolfo De Bosis (1863–1924) was dead; it was true, however, that his widow, the American-born Lillian Vernon, had been arrested for anti-Fascist activities. She was released not long afterward, but her son, Lauro De Bosis, died the following year, at the age of thirty, in a suicide mission during which he flew over Rome distributing anti-Fascist leaflets. Lauro was romantically involved with the celebrated American monologuist Ruth Draper (1884–1956), whom AT admired. (He persuaded RCA to record some of her monologues.) The fascinating and moving account of De Bosis, Draper, and their circle is told in detail in Iris Origo, A Need to Testify (New York: Harcourt Brace Jovanovitch, 1984).

Dearest <u>Carla</u>

Here I am back at the Astor. I've finally finished the two Philadelphia weeks, too. What boredom, what sighs, what sadness!!! Warm welcomes, triumphs, applause are worthless when one's soul is sad. Stokowski's two weeks in New York didn't bring him good fortune. Public, press, and Philharmonic Orchestra—none of them were nice to him. In fact, the orchestra doesn't want him to conduct the concert that he's supposed to conduct in March for the <u>pension fund,</u> so great is the antipathy he aroused in all the musicians! Quite the contrary happened yesterday evening at my last concert (they took in nearly 10,000 dollars): the Philadelphia orchestra [members] were sad to see me go and said that they had spent two heavenly weeks playing good music in a way that they had never known. Not to mention the audience and the press: the latter verified that never had the orchestra given so much of itself. Stokowski was there and came to congratulate me. I excused myself again for not having been able to grant his wife's wish. [. . .]

No, my dearest, it's not for <u>life's negligible little things</u> that I need you, but for <u>life's</u> most <u>important</u> things—those that can truly make life worth living! My dear Carla, thirty-three years of life together must surely have some value for good, honest souls like us! And if clouds have sometimes darkened our happiness, the depth and sincerity of our feelings have never been undermined.

In my solitude in Philadelphia, I thought many times of the evening when you came [there] in secret to a performance that I was giving with the Metropolitan company, and when I got back to New York I didn't find you at home!!! How wrong you were to have doubted me then! The person you suspected at the time is now dead, but I'm alive and I'm telling you the truth.

But enough of such melancholy stuff.

I rehearsed this morning; I was tired as a result of a bad night, yet I had a very good rehearsal, and the orchestra welcomed me with shouts of joy. I was really moved. [. . .] [Zirato] is a thoroughly good fellow, helpful above all, intelligent, and prudent. I had dinner at his home one evening. His wife and sister-in-law are also adorable. You can imagine how many invitations I've had. At this very moment [I've learned that] Mrs. Vanderbilt wants me for New Year's Eve, and so do the Schellings. The day after tomorrow, after the concert, I'm going to the home of old Lewisohn, that gentleman who supports the Stadium concerts. He wanted to make it a big event, with five or six hundred guests, but I told him, through the wife of Gilman, the music critic, that I wouldn't accept, and so he is inviting only about fifty people, most of them friends of mine.

But that's enough of this chattering; I have to study for tomorrow's rehearsal. [. . .]

It is amusing to observe AT letting himself go, gloating over Stokowski's misfortunes in New York, and even quoting the critics, whom he usually claimed not to read. It is true, however, that the Philharmonic's invitation to Stokowski for the following March was canceled. · I have not discovered the identity of the woman of whom CT had been jealous twenty years earlier; her jealousy in that particular case may have been misdirected, but AT's blanket disclaimer was hypocritical, to say the least. · I do not know which of the prominent New York Vanderbilts invited AT to dinner. · The American composer, conductor, and pianist Ernest Schelling (1876–1939) worked often with the Philharmonic in those years, and AT performed his *Impressions from an Artist's Life* in 1929 and 1932, with the composer as piano soloist. · Adolph Lewisohn, a New York music lover, had provided much of the funding for the Lewisohn Stadium concerts every summer since 1918; as many as 22,000 people attended each of these performances. · Lawrence Gilman (1878–1939) was a great admirer of AT; he published a book called *Toscanini and Great Music* (New York: Farrar, 1938).

E.P. NY, 15 DECEMBER 1930; P.S., HOTEL ASTOR/NEW YORK;
TO CT, D2OMI; EC

Monday <u>15-12-930</u>

[. . .] This morning I've already had a rehearsal for the Wagner concert for the pension fund on Thursday evening—and meanwhile I'm on the verge of leaving for Philadelphia, Washington, and Baltimore. Margherita is here having lunch with me. I'm leaving with Zirato; I'm leaving Luigi at home. He's very nice but a bit of a goose. In fact, I'd say he's quite a goose.

[. . .] Tell Walter that I'm getting information about the radio that he wants, and so is Margherita; in fact, I have to go to dinner one of these days at the home of one of the big radiophony bosses; I've long avoided this invitation, but I'll accept for Walter's sake. [. . .] [one or more pages missing] [. . .] [about a dinner:] We ate badly (or so Margherita says, because I was so distracted I didn't notice, to the point that instead of putting croutons in the broth I put in <u>walnuts and almonds</u>). [. . .]

AT's brief trip to Philadelphia, Washington, and Baltimore was for concerts with the New York Philharmonic. · "Radiophony": The radio was still in its infancy in 1930, and AT uses the word *radiofonia* to indicate what modern Italians would simply call *la radio*. My guess is that the "boss" in question was David Sarnoff of RCA, because he and AT had many friends in common; within the next few years he would be playing a large part in AT's life, and there will be more information on him below.

(NY), P.S. AS IN PREVIOUS LETTER; TO CT, D2OMI; EC

<u>5-1-931</u>

My dearest Carla, At this moment I've received a letter from Wally that has moved me deeply. Never have I felt her soul so strongly through my own. God bless her for all the good she has done me. I would like to express to her all that I feel, but I'm impotent to do so. I firmly believe that the best part of me, that which could best shed light on my soul, is and will forever remain unexpressed. It is given only to truly superior beings like Dante, Shakespeare, Leopardi, Beethoven, Verdi, Wagner to express themselves completely, for the joy of all humanity. But she knows and you know that I am good and that I love you both so much and that you are as essential to my life as air and light. I didn't understand why the wedding was being postponed every two weeks while you were both writing to me that everything was ready, and I was about to wire you when Wally's letter arrived. Now I'm calmer. You were right to spend the New Year's period in Switzerland. I had four concerts in a row from Christmas day onward, and again beginning on New Year's Day until yesterday, the 4th. On the evening of Christmas Day I went to the Muschenheims' after the concert; on New Year's Eve I was supposed to go to Lucilla's, but I was very tired—I'd had two rehearsals that day and a stubborn cough was shattering my head and chest. So I stayed home. [. . .] A very comical thing happened to me. I had called Dr. Howe to have him order some cough remedy or other for me, and in fact he gave me an elixir to be taken every hour, one spoonful. That's what I did the last night of the year. I didn't get a lot of rest, but enough that I didn't feel tired, as I had the previous evening. In the morning, after having had my coffee with milk, I swallowed a spoonful of that elixir and jumped into bed again. I slept three whole hours in a row. Zirato came by to wake me at noon, reminding me that I was supposed to have lunch at Signora Elsa's at one. I flung my legs off the bed but wasn't able to stand up—impossible! My head, legs, arms, everything was asleep; I couldn't keep my eyes open. But what most worried me was that I couldn't stay on my feet, and I was thinking about that evening's concert. I dragged myself to Elsa's, however, in part in order to put up some resistance to that unusual somnolence. I again called Dr. Howe, who gave me an injection—of what, I don't know—behind my shoulder, and that brought me back to life a bit, but that evening I was in a bad way at the beginning of the concert. I managed to reach my podium slowly, and I climbed onto it circumspectly and nonchalantly, but my legs barely held me up. After the Sammartini sym. I got a grip on myself, and by the end of the Haydn sym. I felt much better. During the intermission, Dr. Howe gave me an intravenous injection, and I was able to finish the program magnificently. It seems that that elixir contained opiates to keep the cough down; indeed, the cough had subsided, but my body and soul had been put to sleep. I'm continuing with the injections every day. I'm a tiny bit tired. On the whole, however, I'm well, and everyone finds me rejuvenated. Yesterday evening, too, at supper at Zirato's, I met Maestro Sturani, whom I hadn't seen in years, and he said it was miraculous that I had no lines in my face. His hair has turned completely white—but he married, recently, a woman much younger than himself.—Today I had Lange start the rehearsals for the [next] concert. Here at the hotel I rehearsed the two women [singers] in the Requiem. The soprano has a nice voice but is a potato dumpling; the mezzo-soprano is old, painted up, and a dog. That's the way it goes!!! The other day I listened to the tenor, Chamlee. Not bad. Pinza will be the bass. We'll do two performances. Thursday and Friday, January 15–16. The last concert will be on the 18th, after which I don't know what I'll do. I was hoping to have all of you here at that time and to go to Miami or somewhere else in Florida. But that's not to be! Enough—we shall see! [. . .]

Hubert Howe was AT's physician in New York for a quarter century and, in the 1940s, he also made Toscanini's batons, as a hobby. · AT's New York Philharmonic concert program of 1 January 1931 began with Sammartini's Symphony no. 3 and Haydn's Symphony no. 31 in D Major ("Horncall") and also included works by Tommasini, Sibelius, and Martucci. · Giuseppe Sturani was a staff conductor at the Met. · Hans Lange was AT's assistant conductor at the Philharmonic; as the orchestra's schedule was grueling (usually five rehearsals and four concerts per week), AT would sometimes have Lange conduct the first rehearsal or two in a series, to work out the rough patches before he took over the remaining sessions. · The "potato dumpling" soprano in his performances of Verdi's Requiem on 15–16 January 1931 was the celebrated German-born Elisabeth Rethberg (1894–1976), and the "painted dog" of a mezzo-soprano was the almost equally highly regarded Hungarian-born Margarete Matzenauer (1881–1963), who had often sung with AT during his Metropolitan Opera years. The American tenor Mario Chamlee (originally Archer Cholmondeley; 1892–1966) was widely admired at the Met during the 1920s and 1930s, and the Italian bass Ezio Pinza (1892–1957), who had sung several roles under AT at La Scala during the 1920s, was one of the best-loved artists of his day.

TG, S.S. BREMEN, 25 JANUARY 1931;
TO ANITA COLOMBO, LA SCALA, MI; PC; EC

DE SABATA REFUSES RESUME HIS POST—I'LL TRY AGAIN TO PERSUADE HIM. AFFECTIONATE GREETINGS

TOSCANINI

Anita Colombo had been an important administrative aide to AT at La Scala in the 1920s, and after Scandiani's death in 1930 she served briefly as the ensemble's general manager. · Victor De Sabata (1892–1967), who is generally considered the finest Italian conductor of the first half of the twentieth century, after AT, had succeeded AT at La Scala. AT had conducted two of De Sabata's symphonic poems when the younger man's principal interest had been composition, but he did not approve of De Sabata's conducting style, which he considered visually overactive, or of many of his interpretations. On the other hand, he was more concerned about La Scala's well-being than about his personal tastes, and he knew that De Sabata was the best person available for the job of principal conductor (and virtual artistic director). As a result of a dispute with the orchestra, De Sabata had left La Scala only a few months after having taken over; AT tried to persuade him to return, and indeed De Sabata did return the following season.

Affection that binds me to you makes me insist asking you revoke your decision because damaging to you [and] to theater. Listen to my advice. Toscanini

Dear Mr. Judson:

I find that with the great number of concerts which the Philharmonic-Symphony is compelled to play during the season that it is physically impossible for me to conduct all of the rehearsals and concerts. In such cases, it is the practice in Europe, and I believe also in America, with such orchestras as the Philadelphia, to have an assistant conductor who devotes his time only to conducting rehearsals and in emergencies.

I wish very much that the Philharmonic-Symphony Society would authorize the engagement of an Assistant Conductor to relieve me at rehearsals and also be prepared for emergencies and that they would engage Mr. Hans Lange for this purpose, relieving him from any playing in the orchestra. I have observed Mr. Lange's work for several years when he has had occasion to rehearse for me and I shall be delighted if he can be given such a position.

Yours sincerely,

Arturo Toscanini

General Musical Director

Lange was the orchestra's assistant concertmaster, but in the 1930 European tour program he was already listed as assistant conductor as well; see also the letter of 5 January 1931. The request was simply to formalize a fait accompli. AT was asking to be relieved of only a few rehearsals, not of most or all of them.

Following the base assault I suffered in Bologna, foreseeing either systematic silence on the part of the press or erroneous and tendentious information about the incident, the next day (May 15) I sent the Head of Government the following telegram, which reflects in brief, but faithfully, the truth of what happened the evening of the 14th.

To His Excellency Benito Mussolini

Yesterday evening, while going with my family to Bologna's Teatro Comunale to carry out a kind act of friendship and love in memory of Giuseppe Martucci (having been invited there by the mayor of the city for a solemn and artistic commemoration, not for a gala evening), I was attacked, injured, and repeatedly struck in the face by a contemptible gang. The undersecretary of the interior was present in Bologna. Not fully satisfied with this, the gang, its ranks swollen, stood threateningly under the windows of the Hotel Brun, where I was staying, uttering every sort of insult and threat against me. Not only that: one of its leaders enjoined me, through Maestro Respighi, to leave the city by six a.m., not being able to guarantee my safety otherwise. I am communicating this to Your Excellency so that despite the silence of the press or false information Your Excellency will be able to have precise news of the deed, and so that the deed be remembered.

Salutations
Arturo Toscanini

The Head of Government did not reply. On May 16 my passport for going abroad was taken away from me and my house was put under surveillance.

Today, to repudiate the press's false declarations and to put an end to foreign newspapers' repeated requests for interviews, I am breaking the silence that I had imposed upon myself and, reaffirming what I wired to the Head of Government, I am adding some other attendant facts as a corollary and for further clarification.

The Deputy Mayor of Bologna, Professor Giuseppe Lipparini, with whom I had undertaken last August to conduct two concerts commemorating Giuseppe Martucci, announced to me only on the afternoon of the 14th, shortly before the concert, that Their Excellencies the ministers [Costanzo] Ciano and [Leandro] Arpinati would be present at the aforementioned concert, and that it would therefore be necessary to play the national anthems. This happened a few minutes after the last rehearsal, at which I had warmly exhorted the members of the orchestra to take their places only two minutes before the performance, with a maximum of concentration, in awareness of the reverent and loving demonstration that they had been called upon to participate in—in order that no sounds other than Martucci's music should make contact with the public. I concluded, "Gentlemen, be democrats in life but aristocrats in art." I could not, therefore, accommodate Professor Lipparini's request—as unexpected as it was out of place—and allow the concert suddenly to take on a gala or political character, since no preliminary sign or newspaper advertisement had announced this. Instead, I very readily accepted the conciliatory proposal later formulated by the prefect of Bologna together with the deputy mayor, which they communicated to me at five in the afternoon. The proposal was set forth in these terms: when the ministers entered the theater, a band would play the national anthems in the lobby of the Comunale. But at eight o'clock the situation changed. The conciliatory formula did not satisfy the ministers, and there was a return to the earlier order; and I remained more steadfast than ever in my conviction about maintaining the commemorative character of the evening. At nine-thirty [the concert's scheduled starting time], Mr. Brianzi of the municipal administration telephoned me [to say] that I could go to the theater, advising me that Their Excellencies would refrain from attending the concert.

And I fell right into the ambush.

But the lesson that they wanted to teach me, according to certain hack reporters, was to no avail, nor will it be to any avail in the future, for I would repeat tomorrow what I did yesterday if the same conditions prevailed in Italy or in any other part of the world.

I know perfectly well how great the moral, political, and patriotic value of a national anthem played at the right time is—and I have never refused to play that of the nation to which I belong, in any situation, so long as its moral and patriotic meaning was unmistakable.

Did I not cross Italy and North America shortly after the war, at the head of the Scala orchestra, in a long series of concerts of national propaganda, playing my country's anthem everywhere? And have I not conducted it innumerable times, in my forty-five-year career, for patriotic events (at the Milan Arena in August 1915, for instance), gala evenings, and exposition openings, in the presence of the monarchs? And did I not conduct it on Monte Santo under enemy fire? I have been accused of having performed the English anthem in London on my European tour with the American orchestra. But, by God, that concert was given under the august patronage of the English sovereigns! And if the Queen of Italy, in Rome, very graciously considered the concert a purely artistic event, didn't the same thing happen a few days later in Brussels before the King and Queen of Belgium? And so?

To conclude: Am I, then, to take newspapers like the Resto del Carlino [Bologna] or the Corriere della Sera [Milan] seriously when, overnight, they replace the Hosannahs to Toscanini with the Crucifixus? When they, like the Popolo d'Italia [official Fascist newspaper], even find me unsuitable for commemorating Giuseppe Martucci? And all the others who have actually called me unpatriotic? How tiny these people are, and of what little value is all this business, barely worthy of my compassion!

"The spine bends when the soul is bent." It is true. But the conduct of my life has been, is, and will always be the echo and reflection of my conscience, which does not know dissimulation or deviations of any sort—reinforced, I admit, by a proud and scornful character, but clear as crystal and just as cutting—always and everywhere ready to shout the truth loudly—that truth which, as Emerson so rightly says, always comes into the world in a manger, but is rewarded by having to live until it is completely enslaved by mankind.

The story of the "Bologna slaps" has been told in my own and others' books on AT and was even the subject of an entire book published in Italy on the sixtieth anniversary of the episode, which was one of the greatest international prewar embarrassments to Mussolini's regime. In part, it is recounted in the above letter, which AT gave his daughter Wally in St. Moritz (where he was trying to relax after his passport had been given back and before his second Bayreuth season) to distribute to a foreign newspaper in Milan; as soon as she had reached Milan, however, her father phoned to say that he had changed his mind about having it published. Six years later, she showed it to Crown Prince Umberto and his consort (see the letter of 22–23 October 1937), and forty years after the event she allowed Guglielmo Barblan to publish a holographic reproduction of the document in his book *Toscanini e la Scala*. This was fortunate, because in the mid-1980s, the letter, which Wally kept in a plastic wrapper in a special box, caught fire, and nothing remains of it but tiny crumbs of scorched paper.

(BAYREUTH), 5 JULY 1931; TO CT,
(PALAIS HALBMAYRHAUS, MARIENBAD?); EC

My dearest <u>Carla</u>

I haven't had any more orchestra rehearsals since you left. They've begun the ensemble rehearsals for the Ring in the theater, and I have rehearsed the individual singers for each opera. The disaster here is that one can never have a whole ensemble for the rehearsals. The singers come when they please, and even the Ring was rehearsed by the orchestra practically without the principal singers. I was supposed to have had my first ensemble rehearsal for Parsifal today, but I vehemently declined, since I haven't heard the singers <u>even individually.</u> Amfortas and Klingsor haven't yet arrived. I'll probably agree to rehearse the third act tomorrow, Monday, afternoon, because the lady doesn't sing in it (Ohms doesn't arrive until Tuesday), and I'll make do with <u>that French woman,</u> who seems very intelligent and a quick learner. I rehearsed Tannhäuser, too, without Müller and Pilinsky, who was ill, and while awaiting Melchior. In short, much patience is needed, and that's not precisely my forte. The other evening I was at dinner when they came to announce the first Parsifal ensemble rehearsal; that was the end of the dinner, of course, and I relieved my hunger by taking an automobile ride to calm my nerves. [. . .]

<u>5-7-931</u>

CT was taking a cure at Marienbad during AT's rehearsal period at Bayreuth; he was conducting *Tannhäuser* and *Parsifal* that summer. This letter gives a glimpse of the conditions at Bayreuth that caused AT to declare, at the end of that summer's festival, that he would not return. Of the roles or singers he mentions here, Amfortas was Herbert Janssen, Klingsor was Gotthold Ditter, Elisabeth Ohms sang Kundry (it is not clear who AT meant by "that French woman"—presumably an understudy for Ohms), Maria Müller sang Venus, and Sigismund Pilinsky and Lauritz Melchior alternated as Tannhäuser.

28-7-931

<u>My dearest,</u> How is your cure going? Mine leaves me neither hot nor cold, as far as <u>results</u> are concerned—because it does make me hot: I sweat as much as when I conduct Tannhäuser! Every day I go to the hospital; the doctor asks me whether I feel any improvement (it's clear that he thinks there should be some after even a few days), and he is surprised that this isn't the case. Yesterday I saw [Countess] Gravina's son (Guido), the poor devil! He's declined terribly since last year! But he seems quite resigned to his fate!! I haven't yet received a letter or card from Wally and Wanda to tell me when they're arriving! Here in my study I held a few more Parsifal rehearsals with the singers, and this morning I have a Tannhäuser rehearsal. Friday morning at eleven I'll rehearse Wagner's <u>Faust Overture</u> with the orchestra and I'll leave immediately for Marienbad. [. . .]

The pains in AT's right shoulder worsened dramatically at Bayreuth, and he was forced to conduct some performances using only his left arm. · Blandine von Bülow Gravina's son Guido died of tuberculosis the following December at the age of thirty-five. · Regarding the *Faust* Overture: AT was to have conducted this piece as part of a concert to mark the first anniversary of Siegfried Wagner's death, but a series of misunderstandings led to his abandoning the dress rehearsal and not participating in the concert.

5 August 1931

Dear Baron Hans Paul von Wolzogen,
No word of praise could have been more dear to and desired by me than yours; if my interpretation of <u>Parsifal</u> was able to awaken in you an echo of that memorable one of 1882, it is the most I could hope for in achieving my ideal dream, that is, to come as close as possible to expressing the author's thoughts. You, friend and faithful, wise disseminator of that <u>Supreme One</u>'s ideas, could not have given me a greater reward; <u>your praise</u> has moved me deeply and I thank you with all my heart.

Please accept my reverent greetings and believe in the admiration and affection that I have felt toward you for very many years, although I do not know you personally.

Arturo Toscanini

Wolzogen (1848–1938) had been a friend and disciple of Wagner and, after the latter's death, one of his most important propagandists. He had attended every Bayreuth festival since the first (1876), including—as is clear from this letter—that of 1882, during which Hermann Levi had conducted the world premiere of *Parsifal* under Wagner's supervision. AT rarely replied to letters from admirers; here, his thanks seem heartfelt.

TG, NY, 17 NOVEMBER 1931; TO CT, 14 [RUE] ALFRED ROLL, PARIS; EC

DISEMBARKED VERY LATE YESTERDAY EVENING UNPLEASANT TRIP FOUND YOUR TELEGRAM THANKS ARM STILL PAINFUL AFFECTION
ARTURO

TG, NY, (LATE NOVEMBER OR EARLY DECEMBER 1931); TO CT, 14 [RUE] ALFRED ROLL, PARIS; ORIG. ENG. (ALL ERRORS HAVE BEEN PRESERVED); EC

= AM OVERJOYED YOU COULD HEAR CONCERT WHILE MY CHOUGHT WAS SO NEAR YOU BUT SEEMS TO ME IMPOSSIBLE GOING ON WITH MY ARM IN SUCH BAD CONDITIONS LOVE AND KISSES ARTURO =

DRAFT OF TG, (NY), 16 DECEMBER 1931; TO SENATOR FRANCESCO RUFFINI, TU; EC

Deeply moved I embrace you and your illustrious university colleagues for your proud and noble behavior (stop) the backbone bends when the soul is bent. Greetings.

Arturo Toscanini

[at bottom, in Margherita De Vecchi's handwriting, in English: "not sent"]

In the fall of 1931 Mussolini had insisted that all university professors sign an oath of fidelity to fascism, and in all of Italy only twelve professors refused to do so. Francesco Ruffini, a senator and jurist who taught law at the University of Turin, was among that select dozen. "For reasons of conscience and the most basic consistency with my academic and political past, I cannot swear the oath demanded of me. . . . It is absolutely clear that for me such an oath would be an obstacle to the free exercise of my political functions as a senator of the kingdom. . . ." AT evidently wanted to show his solidarity with Ruffini, but he was probably advised that doing so could have endangered the senator's already precarious position.

[. . .] Get hold of Manfred parts and score. My arm still the same am in despair.

AT had decided to program Tchaikovsky's "Manfred" Symphony with the Philharmonic the following season; their performances of the work in March 1933 were not
only his first performances of "Manfred" but also his first performances of any music by
Tchaikovsky since 1900. From then on, he gradually brought several of the Russian
composer's works into, or back into, his repertoire.

BEST WISHES TO YOU AND MARIA EGIZIACA MAY EVERYTHING GO AS YOU
WISH I EMBRACE YOU TOGETHER WITH ELSA =
TOSCANINI.

On 17 March 1932 Respighi conducted a program of his works—including the world
premiere of his "mystery" *Maria Egiziaca*—with the Philharmonic; Elsa was his wife.

[. . .] Gelsa will have brought you the final payment on my account. I send you
my affectionate greetings and a hearty embrace. Arturo Toscanini anti-Fascist

Dr. Rinaldi had successfully treated AT's right arm and shoulder in the winter and
early spring of 1932, and the two men had found themselves in complete agreement
on political matters. AT continued to return to the village of Piazze for treatment
until 1935, when the doctor was assassinated in what is believed to have been a political crime committed by Fascists.

Dear Mr. Judson:
Upon my arrival here I realized even more deeply than before the conditions
existing in the country and the serious problems the Philharmonic-Symphony
Society will have to face for the coming season. Zirato also told me of the
splendid spirit in which the orchestra, management and office staff have
agreed to make a donation in order to meet this crisis.

Under such circumstances I, too, should like to do something to help and I wish you would tell our Board of Directors that I should be glad to contribute $10,000. to the Philharmonic-Symphony Society to be taken off from my salary of $110,000. for my next year's periods of my conducting here.

With best wishes and regards, I am,
Sincerely yours,
Arturo Toscanini

AT had had to cancel the second half of his 1931–32 season because of his shoulder pains, but after having successfully undergone Dr. Rinaldi's treatment he traveled by steamship to New York at his own expense, conducted a single Philharmonic concert on 28 April 1932 for the benefit of unemployed musicians, and returned home. (See the following telegram.) During his brief stay in New York, he learned that the Depression had caused such severe problems among cultural organizations that the Philharmonic's players and staff members had all voluntarily taken a 10 percent pay cut rather than put the entire operation in jeopardy. He asked to participate in the plan. (AT's income tax and travel expenses were paid over and above his $100,000 or $110,000 Philharmonic salary, which he received for fifteen weeks of work a year. This would be roughly equivalent to earning $2,000,000 net for fifteen weeks' work today.)

TG, NY, 28 APRIL 1932; TO CT, (D20MI); EC

CONCERT OBTAINED TRIUMPHAL ARTISTIC AND MATERIAL RESULTS AM VERY PLEASED ARM VERY WELL HOPE MEET YOU PARIS AFFECTION = ARTURO —

TG, BAVENO (NOVARA), 19 MAY 1932;
TO DANIELA THODE, GARDONE-RIVIERA; RWGSB

WINIFRED COME AND GONE THE MOST BEAUTIFUL CALM SKY IS STILL SHINING[.] I SHALL CONDUCT FIVE PARISFALS EIGHT MEISTERSINGERS[.] I HOPE THAT WAGNER'S DIVINE SPIRIT WILL PROTECT ME I EMBRACE MY DEAR FRIENDS EVA DANIELA WITH GREAT EMOTION HAVE A GOOD TRIP
TOSCANINI

At the end of the 1931 festival, AT had declared that he would not return to Bayreuth in 1933 (no festival was scheduled for 1932). Although there was no love lost between Winifred Wagner, Siegfried's widow, who had taken over the festival, on the one hand, and her sister-in-law Eva Chamberlain and half sister-in-law Daniela Thode on the other, they joined together to persuade AT to return in 1933; this telegram announces his decision.

(MI?), SPRING OR SUMMER 1932; AT WAS REPLYING TO A QUESTIONNAIRE
FROM THE NEWSPAPER *BERLINER BÖRSEN-ZEITUNG*;
DELLA CORTE, PP. 245-6

I love and admire all the works that I conduct, symphonic or operatic,
because—I conduct only those that I love. My preferences in the symphonic
field are for the greats, Haydn, Mozart, and Beethoven. In recent years I have
thoroughly studied Bruckner's monumental symphonies. I gladly leave modern works to other conductors. Among operas, I value those of Wagner and
Verdi above all. It is difficult to state a preference for one of Wagner's operas. I
have noticed that if I am conducting one or another of Wagner's operas, or
playing it at the piano, whichever one it happens to be takes possession of my
heart. And yet, every time I glance at the score of Parsifal, I say to myself: This
is the sublime one. In Verdi's operas, I appreciate not only the richness of the
melodies but also the effective and sure power of the musical drama. When I
conduct Falstaff at Busseto I think about the possibility of a Verdian Bayreuth,
along the lines of Wagner's Festspielhaus. These two masters are the real representatives of German and Italian national music.

E.P. STRESA NOVARA, 3 AUGUST 1932; POSTCARD WITH PHOTO OF THE
ISOLINO SAN GIOVANNI; TO LAVINIA SALVADORI, ASP; SR

Dear Lavinietta, How is life in Piazze without us? Have the two gravedigger
sisters left? Cured or gone downhill? And has the very pleasant Lawyer De
Paolis managed to improve? Is my dear friend Lucilla still there among you?

From this earthly paradise we frequently sigh as we think of Piazze's heart,
which is that of our delightful friends Gelsa and Lavinia. Remember me to
Daria, to Nella, to your mamma—the silent observer—and to everyone.

Affec. Arturo Toscanini

The Salvadori family ran the only *pensione* in the village of Piazze, where AT went as
often as possible to be treated by Dr. Rinaldi. He flirted—but nothing more—with
the very young Salvadori sisters. In this note and in his first notes to Lavinia's sister
Gelsa he used the formal *Lei* form of the second person singular; in later correspondence with them he used the informal *tu,* whereas in their letters to him they continued to address him formally, and always as Maestro, never by name. · Lucilla De
Vescovi Whitman, a close family friend, was an Italian who had married an American
and who developed and designed the "Countess Mara" line of men's ties. · Beginning
in that summer of 1932 the Toscaninis rented from the Borromeo family a tiny island
(Isolino San Giovanni) with its own monastery—long since converted into a private
residence—in Lago Maggiore. Until 1938 and then again from 1947 to 1952, the
Isolino San Giovanni was one of AT's favorite spots in the world.

VERY HAPPY[.] CONTRACT SIGNED[.] FIRST CONCERT [WENT] EXCEL-
LENTLY[.] ARM RESPONDING PERFECTLY[.] HUGS KISSES TO ALL = ARTURO

[. . .] As I told you and cabled you, I'm tired, very tired. This work is no longer
tolerable for me. Having a rehearsal and often two rehearsals every day, four
concerts a week—rarely three—isn't the sort of life for someone my age, the
more so when one gives a hundred percent at every rehearsal as at every concert. I can never go out for a breath of air. Only once did I go with Zirato,
Nina, and Margherita for an automobile ride outside New York, but since
then I've always been holed up in these rooms at the Astor, working. I still
have eleven concerts, and then, God willing, on the thirtieth I'll board the
Bremen. [. . .] Ansbacher has written to me about an honor from Germany! I
see that he is much happier about it than I am. Wonderful!

   If I could avoid going to Berlin I would be extremely happy. I'll write about
this to Tietjen. Did you know that poor Mrs. Thode was hit by a bicycle, with
serious consequences, it seems? [. . .]

Nina was Zirato's wife and a Metropolitan Opera soprano from 1920 to 1935 (under
the name of Nina Morgana). · Luigi Ansbacher was a Milanese lawyer and music lover,
for many years president of Casa Verdi (the rest home for aged musicians founded by
the composer), and a fanatical admirer of AT. It is not known which of the many honors AT received—most of them unsought and unacknowledged—this refers to. · The
projected trip to Berlin was probably to discuss the 1933 Bayreuth season with Heinz
Tietjen, the musician and theater administrator whom Winifred Wagner had engaged
to help her run the festival (and who, according to family history, was her lover).

31-3-933

My dear Mr. Neuer
Not only you can use my name but if there is no objection and if it is possible
I would like to have my name put at the head of the subscribers of this
message.

Greetings and compliments from
Arturo Toscanini

At the end of January 1933, Adolf Hitler had become chancellor of Germany. The quickly initiated distancing of Jewish musicians from their positions deeply offended AT, and when, late in March, he was asked to sign a message of protest from musicians active in America that would be cabled to Hitler, he answered with this note. (AT meant "signatories" rather than "subscribers.") Most of the other signatories were Jews; thus his gesture was particularly strong and much appreciated. Their recordings and broadcasts were immediately banned by the German radio.

TO ADOLF HITLER, (BERLIN); ORIG. ENG.; RWGSB

Newyork 29-4-33

Your <u>Excellency:</u>—For your very friendly writing I want to thank you heartily, only I greatly regret that I could not answer it sooner.

You know how closely I feel attached to Bayreuth and what deep pleasure it gives me to consecrate my "Something" to a genius like Wagner whom I love so boundlessly.

Therefore it would be a bitter disappointment to me if any circumstances should interfere with my purpose to take part in the coming Festival Plays, and I hope that my strength, which the last weeks here taxed severely, will hold out.

Expressing once more my thanks for your kind expressions of thought, I subscribe myself as Your Excellency's sincere

A.T.

Winifred Wagner was a close friend of Hitler; she persuaded him to overlook AT's protest cable and to try to persuade the maestro to return to Bayreuth that summer, as planned. AT's initial response, above, was made in the hope—held by many—that conditions in Germany would quickly return to normal.

DRAFT OF LETTER, (MI? ISG?); TO BAYREUTH FESTIVAL; RWGSB

28-5-933

The sorrowful events that have wounded my human and artistic feelings have not yet undergone any change, contrary to all my hopes. Thus it is my duty today to break the silence I had imposed on myself for two months and to let you know that for my peace of mind, for yours, and for everyone's, it is better not to think anymore about my coming to Bayreuth.

With unchangeable friendship (and affection) for the house of Wagner (your)

<u>Arturo Toscanini.</u>

This communication marked AT's final break with Bayreuth and Germany. (In his entire life, his only performances in Germany took place in 1929 [La Scala ensemble in

Berlin], 1930 [New York Philharmonic concerts in Munich, Leipzig, Dresden, and Berlin, and Bayreuth Festival], and 1931 [Bayreuth].) · The words in parentheses in the draft were removed from the final version. · Richard Strauss stepped in to conduct AT's *Parsifal* production, and Karl Elmendorff took over what was to have been AT's *Meistersinger* performances.

Part Three

JUNE 1933–
MAY 1936

1933   Makes first guest appearances with Vienna Philharmonic (returns every
        year through 1937).
1935   Makes first appearances with a British ensemble—the BBC Symphony
        Orchestra, London (returns 1937–39); conducts *Fidelio* and *Falstaff* at
        Salzburg Festival.
1936   Resigns directorship of the New York Philharmonic.

This and the following two sections of the book are dominated by AT's letters to Ada
Mainardi, *née* Colleoni (1897–1979), a Milanese-born musician and descendant of a
prominent family from Bergamo. She studied piano at the Milan Conservatory, where
she was generally considered gifted but not brilliant, and singularly beautiful. At the
conservatory, she met Enrico Mainardi (1897–1976), a handsome young man who was
to become the most highly regarded Italian cellist of his generation. They fell in love,
married young, and led what appeared to be a fairly privileged existence: frequent
concert tours all over Europe, abundant encounters with the highest echelons of artistic and aristocratic society, and all the other trappings of celebrity. They often performed as a duo, but by the mid-1930s Ada's public appearances had become rare.
Their marriage seems to have been troubled almost from the start, and they both had
numerous extramarital affairs. Although only AT's side of his correspondence with
Ada exists—except for a few items—some of his statements demonstrate that she had
told him that the physical part of her relationship with Enrico had ended long since
and that she had had several lovers; he specifically mentions Count Aldrovandi, who
had been Italy's ambassador to Germany during the last years of the Weimar Republic, but he also refers to others, without naming them.

Yet, as one person who knew the Mainardis has said, although Enrico and Ada had
a hard time living with each other, they couldn't live without each other. (I shall continue to refer to them by their first names, to avoid the confusion of using "Mainardi,"
which is the surname that Ada used to the end of her life.) They never officially
divorced, and when Ada was dying, she left the material that she had received from
AT—letters, telegrams, photographs, concert programs, and newspaper clippings—
to Sela Sommer-Mainardi, the woman who had been Enrico's companion in his last
years.

AT had met Ada and Enrico at least as early as 1917, and he later declared that
from the first he had considered her the most attractive young woman of her generation, so much so that he had been jealous, not so much of Enrico himself as of Enrico's
presumed happiness. Milan was where the Toscaninis and the Mainardis spent more
time than anywhere else during the 1920s and early 1930s, and inasmuch as they frequented similar circles they must inevitably have encountered each other on many
occasions. Ada was friendly with both of AT's daughters: she was less than three years

older than Wally and a little more than ten years older than Wanda. AT himself, on the other hand, was a towering figure in the musical world by the time the young Mainardis had begun to insert themselves into that world, and Ada seems to have revered him with something approaching awe. But their relationship changed dramatically in 1933, when she was thirty-six and he was sixty-six.

Putting the pieces of their love story together is difficult because AT destroyed Ada's letters to him (although he held on to some of them for weeks, months, or perhaps even years after having received them), just as he destroyed virtually all of the letters that he received from other lovers. About the beginning of the affair, the letters reveal only that during a visit to Rome, probably very shortly before the correspondence began, AT encountered Ada at the home of friends, and during that encounter the two of them spoke together of private matters, including oblique references to the marital dissatisfactions that each of them faced; at some point that day, AT hinted that he was in love with her (see his letter of 28 July 1933). It is not unlikely, however, that AT dropped such hints to many women ("He cast his nets wide," as his grandson says), and their relationship might have gone no further had Ada not made a bold move: on 9 June 1933 she sent AT a telegram in which she evidently managed to communicate feelings for him that went beyond both friendship and admiration. Before long, their love story became highly serious on both sides, and during the following seven years AT sent Ada nearly a thousand letters and telegrams that trace his professional, private, and involuntary political life during a particularly turbulent period. Although I have incorporated, in chronological order, AT's letters to others from the same years, his letters to Ada dominate this period.

E.P. PS, 10 JUNE 1933; TO AM, HQR; FSD-FOF

9-6-933

It was a sweet and pleasant surprise. Your telegram's few words were good, very good, for my soul.

It was like pouring gasoline onto a fire. Thank you, dearest Ada—you are beautiful, good, and kind. I hope we will see each other soon. Be fond of me. In friendship

Your A Toscanini

TG, PS, 19 JUNE 1933; TO WYT,
CLINICA DE MARIA, LUGANO, EC

PROFOUNDLY MOVED BUT HAPPY I EMBRACE YOU WITH TENDERNESS AND AFFECTION = PAPARINO

AT's elder daughter had given birth that day to a daughter, Emanuela di Castelbarco, his second grandchild (Walfredo Toscanini, the son of Walter Toscanini and his future wife, Cia Fornaroli [1888–1954], prima ballerina at La Scala, had been born on 16 August 1929). "Paparino" is facetious—roughly equivalent to "Daddykins."

Your affectionate morning greeting arrived twenty-four hours after it was sent, because the telegraph office read <u>Piazza</u> di Siena instead of <u>Piazze</u>—but I had already felt it through the numberless, infinite "whispers of the aethers." So if my vanity was punished, my sensitivity won the day. Thank you, dearest Ada. Can you feel that you are ever dearer to me? You, too, are a musician, highly sensitive to the whispers of the aethers, thus also to the subtlest vibrations of the human soul. [Musical quote: *"Sul fil d'un raggio etesio"* (On the edge of a sea-wafted ray)—Verdi, *Falstaff,* III, 2]

On the edge of a sea-wafted ray I send you endless affectionate messages. Remember me from time to time and be a little fond of me.

With friendship, your

A <u>Toscanini</u>

<u>19-6-933</u>

Herewith, dearest Ada, I'm returning Zweig's book on Mary Stuart. I liked it. It seems to me one of the best of its genre. Thank you and arrivederci. A Toscanini

The Austrian author Stefan Zweig (1881–1942), one of the most popular writers of his day, became a devoted friend of AT a year or two later.

<u>Tuesday night</u>

Do you realize, my dearest Ada, the joy and the emotion that even the simplest of your affectionate words gives me? How will I ever be able to do without them from now on? <u>Ever affectionately,</u> you telegraphed me. I was pleasantly troubled! "Be a little fond of me, too," you wrote to me. I gaze confusedly in front of me. I'm afraid that I don't understand. In fact, I'm sure of it! But I am very fond of you! Beyond the most affectionate friendship!!! Ada, my sweet friend, will I see you again? Will I be able to talk to you again, to gaze for an instant into your beautiful eyes, which give me a sense of heavenly purity? Will you stay awhile in Milan? How long? Who knows!

If these lines find you in Milan, send me a few words. I'm leaving Piazze on <u>Saturday morning</u>.

[Musical quote: *"Du bist der Lenz"* (You are the springtime); Wagner, *Die Walküre,* I,3]

See you in a few days.

Your AT

E.P. MI, 11 JULY 1933; TO AM, 46VMPMI; FSD-FOF

10-7-933

My beloved Ada, I give <u>weight</u> and <u>value</u> to every word that you send me through the mouth of the <u>Divine One</u>! I no longer know what world I'm living in! I'm daydreaming!

I had thought that my age had gently laid its hand upon my heart, like a harpist placing a hand on the strings to extinguish the vibrations, but you are working a miracle! There is still much unexpressed music in my heart, and you are making it sing melodies that have never yet been heard.

Do you remember Keats's marvelous verse: "Heard melodies are sweet, but those unheard are sweeter"? [English in the original]

And again I ask you, why have you appeared upon my path—this path that the sun illuminates with the reflected light of dusk? Are you happy to have done this?

The Isolino was enchanting yesterday; you were in my thoughts. And who would be able to count how many times you'll return to them during these long summer evenings, when infinite splendor reigns over the lake and the surrounding mountains, and I, deep in concentration, will live in intimate communion with the <u>mystery</u> known to you and me alone?

It is a month today since you sent me the <u>first</u> telegram that awakened the <u>first</u> agitation in my soul.

Who pushed you to do it?

Write to me, Ada, write to me and tell me something, open your soul to me a little. Tomorrow I'll leave Milan; when will we see each other? It's terrible!!!

May I write to you from time to time, freely? You may [write to me]. Change and vary how you address [the envelopes]. Use the typewriter sometimes, write by hand at other times. Sign the name Maria. For me, your pseudonym will be <u>Maria Anadid</u>.

I kiss you on the eyes and on your enchanting smile.

A

AT and AM had seen each other in Milan in the period between the previous letter and this one; their relationship, however, had so far remained "chaste." · It is unclear whether the "Divine One" refers to God or to Dante; AM may have quoted Dante in the letter that AT was answering. · The Keats quotation is from "Ode on a Grecian Urn" (II, lines 1 and 2). · When AT says, "It is a month today since you sent me the *first* telegram," he is forgetting that the telegram arrived on June 9, not 10, and he continued to make the same mistake throughout the correspondence. · "Maria Anadid" is, of course, a not very clever anagram for "Ada Mainardi."

"Despair lies in reality: anxiety, trouble, sadness, and horror of lying."

This last word echoed lugubriously all night in my soul. Yes, my adored, my beloved Ada, one ought to have the strength and the courage to go right down to the bottom of one's own being. Then we would all become better, we would be happier because we would be more indulgent. But, accustomed as we are to false principles and laws, we stop, uncertain, on the shores of our internal high sea, incapable of reaching the bottom once and for all and of destroying the original sin of the lie that is in us. Oh, if only our souls could reveal themselves in all their nakedness! To be what one really is: [then] what our spirit most needs—freedom—would no longer be alien to us. Truth is synonymous with freedom, falsehood with slavery! Were Dante, Michelangelo, Goethe, Verdi, Wagner unfamiliar, perhaps, with falsehood? I doubt it! My love for you was born spontaneously, like a flower opening up or a star lighting up; could I destroy, by my own hand, this unanticipated happiness that [musical quote: the Fate motif from Wagner's *Ring of the Nibelungen*] reserved for me, at a moment of supreme uneasiness? My Ada, I will never be able to thank fate enough for having sent you to me. Ah, **if you** could love me! Or if I could at least look into your inner self, for consolation and rest. But our most intimate thoughts are like an immense, endless sea in which the deep drama takes place in all its inscrutable depth.

And so? One must have faith. And I have it, in you—great faith. I kiss you with great passion. Write to me at length, open your heart and strengthen mine. The Isolino is enchanting; only you are lacking to make it **divine.**

The quotation at the beginning of this letter is from a letter that AT had received from AM, and it obviously refers to the horror of the lies and subterfuge that a serious extramarital relationship would necessitate for both of them. AT's thoughts on the subject are straightforward enough, despite his not entirely felicitous metaphors.

16-7-33

[. . .] Some days ago I began to study Bach's Mass in B minor again. The deep emotion aroused by the Kyrie has equaled and surpassed what I felt the first time I heard it. At that time, I wept the hottest tears of my life. The phenomenon has [now] repeated itself, years later.

The Kyrie, the Qui tollis, the Incarnatus, and the Crucifixus are among the most divine things ever conceived and realized by the human mind. Beethoven, in the same numbers of the Mass in D, is a long way behind. He is to Bach as Mont Blanc to the Resegone! Never has a more profound and desperate human cry been raised up to God than in Bach's Kyrie! Every day, the human beings who cover the earth's five continents ought to offer up this invocation to the Eternal Father, in a formidable voice, to redeem their sins!

What a marvel! At that moment, Bach must have been in direct communication with his internal Daemon or God! Most modern composers, even if they are good musicians, have no internal voice to listen to; no revelation comes to them from a world of the spirit, as it came to Bach, Beethoven, and Wagner! Poor wretches, why do they continue to daub at paper? By the time I was twenty years old, I had grasped perfectly well the futility of my efforts!

Ada, my dearest, how I would love to have you near when I study these masterpieces! I think you would help me to understand them better!

Vain hope! Yesterday (Friday), I finally moved my carcass off the Isolino and mailed two letters. I had hidden them among the pages of the Masses of Bach and Beethoven. They underwent their purification! [. . .]

AT was studying the Bach and Beethoven masses because in the course of his 1933–34 season with the New York Philharmonic he conducted the *Kyrie* from the Bach work and the entire Beethoven work—both for the first time in his long career. He went on to conduct the Beethoven many times, but he never again conducted any part of the Bach. The fact that he so adored the Bach masterpiece but never performed it seems to confirm the opinion, expressed elsewhere by this writer and others, that AT performed Baroque music infrequently because he felt uncertain as to how it ought to be interpreted. · The Mont Blanc–Beethoven and Resegone-Bach metaphor is backward, inasmuch as Mont Blanc is the highest peak in the Alps, unless AT meant to say that the Resegone is more dramatically beautiful than Mont Blanc.

E.P. PN, 21 JULY 1933; TO AM, 46VMPMI; FSD-FOF

Friday <u>21-7-933</u>

[. . .] Today, the 21st, first performance at Bayreuth, with Meistersinger. My thoughts rush there nostalgically and sorrowfully. You can well understand. Oh, this cursed, nasty muscle of ours called the heart. How unforgiving it is toward those who violate it, and how it makes them suffer! Since yesterday I've put Beethoven and Bach to rest and I'm up to my neck in Chopin's studies, nocturnes, mazurkas, waltzes—and I'm <u>obsessed</u> with one mazurka, this one, in A min[or]: [musical quote from op. 17, no. 4]. Its sadness is consonant with mine. In the middle, there is a bit of joy darkened by a bit of regret, and then the infinite sadness comes back! Study it, my Ada, play it always; you'll play it for me some day. [. . .]

E.P. PN, 26 JULY 1933; TO AM, 46VMPMI; FSD-FOF

Saturday <u>evening 22-7-933</u>

I've had people here the whole blessed day today. This morning it was Maestro Voghera, who stayed for lunch with the Pizzetti couple and Ugo Ara. In the afternoon, Huberman came to show me his letter in reply to an invitation from

Furtwängler for concerts in Germany. A very nice, dignified, humane letter—of refusal, naturally. Then my Polo in-laws arrived with Riccardo and his wife. That Huberman—how ugly and greasy he is! It seems impossible that there have been women who have gone crazy over him! [. . .]

Sunday 23-7-33

[. . .] "Beautiful and terrible" (you say of our mystery), "because sin" (of which we are innocent, so far) "is mixed in with the lightheadedness, anguish with the sweetness, ill with the good." It's true—as in everything human!!! I think that deep in our being there must certainly exist a cause or a reason, stronger than ourselves, for secret life, which is one of the supreme necessities of Creation and of that limitless sea of love into which we have been swept. It is very probable that special powers must be released from it, to work on us mysteriously, like invisible fluids, and at a given moment in life they flow together impetuously and drag us onward, like bits of straw blowing aimlessly. [. . .]

For Tullio Voghera, see note, page 95. By 1933 he was working in Sweden, and he was visiting AT to try to persuade him to guest conduct the Stockholm Concert Society Orchestra; his efforts were fruitful. · Ugo Ara (see note, page 106) lived on the Isola dei Pescatori, not far from AT's Isolino, in Lake Maggiore; AT was very fond of him. · Bronisław Huberman (1882–1947), one of the most celebrated violinists of his day, often spent his summer holidays near Luino, on the eastern shore of Lake Maggiore. During the summer of 1933, he was trying to persuade AT to accept an invitation to conduct the Vienna Philharmonic for the first time, to strengthen the protest against Austria's neighbor, Germany; Huberman's attempt was ultimately successful. · During the same summer, the outstanding German conductor Wilhelm Furtwängler (1886–1954) was trying to demonstrate that art could remain above the political fray, even in Nazi Germany, and he had invited Huberman, a Polish Jew, to help prove his point by continuing to perform in Germany.

E.P. STRESA NOVARA, 29 JULY 1933; TO AM, 46VMPMI; FSD-FOF

Friday 28-7-933

[. . .] Yes, I feel that I am ever closer to you, [and] you, too, must feel that you're inside my soul, and still more, in my living flesh, in my blood. All my thoughts live on nothing but you; you are my sole, incessant, lacerating thought. As I write to you, I feel my heart in my throat, and it's beating so violently that I feel as if I were suffocating. You are the good news of the autumn of my life, and I will never be able to bless enough the fate that has sent you to me. Ah, to submit to this mysterious power that wants us to be united forever—yes, forever—is a superhuman thing! I would never have believed that life held so high and unhoped-for a prize in store for me. And you, are you happy now? In Rome one morning, we were in a car together (do you remember?). We were silent more than we spoke. We touched upon a deeply intimate subject; a few words from you made me see the sadness of your soul. I would have liked to know more, but I preferred not to ask. The whole revelation was sorrowful. **I had always thought you were happy!** I wanted to tell you at that moment how much I loved you, but I didn't dare! I then murmured it to you a few hours later, in the pine grove of Respighi's villa. Do you remember? [. . .]

E.P. STRESA BORROMEO NOVARA, 2 AUGUST 1933; TO AM, 46VMPMI; FSD-FOF

[. . .] Since Sunday I have been <u>oppressed</u> by visits. Today, too, Mrs. Szigeti arrived with her daughter. I don't know how long she'll stay. I can't write to you and tell you all that I'd like and that I have to tell you, but you know that I love you so much—<u>you feel, you can be sure</u> that you are at the <u>center</u> of my sweetest thoughts, or rather, the **circle** that contains them all! [. . .]

<u>Tuesday afternoon</u> [1.8.33]

Wanda Szigeti was married to the celebrated Hungarian-born violinist Joseph Szigeti (1892–1973). Their daughter later married the Russian-born pianist Nikita Magaloff (1912–92).

E.P. PN, 4 AUGUST 1933; TO AM, AOLCV; FSD-FOF

Thursday <u>3-8-933</u>

"I cannot believe it," Ada. "Why would you love me? But why do you love me? Is what you say true? You're not fooling me? You're not lying to me a little, to make me smile?" (Maeterlinck) [French in the original]

Ah, this internal gnawing, this nightmare that never leaves me—how cruel it is. I know that I'm gravely offending your loyalty, and I can't rid myself of [the thought]! All my life long, I have never known how to grab the truth off the face of things in such a way as to fix it tenaciously and forever in my soul. Neither the delightful enchantment of your letters nor the supreme joy of your sweet assurances of affection can dispel my sadness and free my heart of the nightmare that oppresses it. I'm a real wretch. I inherited from my mother the unhappiness that oppressed her all her life. A week ago you were here. I ought to have been happy; I wasn't, and neither were you. You were suffering and I could have died! Our souls were swollen with love and passion, and we had to use barbarous violence against them, externalizing them, in keeping with others' vulgarity. We were clumsy. I don't remember having looked into your eyes as I would have wished. I don't know how we had the nerve to go into my study alone. And we didn't kiss, even though our mouths were parched for kisses! What a <u>disaster</u>!! Won't we ever be able to meet among other people without trembling about giving ourselves away? [. . .]

Friday <u>morning</u> [4.8.33]

Wanda Szigeti has left. She and her daughter stayed three days on the Isolino. I don't know whether you've met her. She's a beautiful Russian woman, still young—35 years old—has a 13-year-old daughter and a husband who is <u>not at all simpatico.</u> He's a handsome man and he is an artist—a bit inexpressive—but above all he must be frigid and a pedant. I think that a respectful and even affectionate friendship exists between them, but nothing more. She, too, can't be happy. She arrived unexpectedly! I have something too **absolute** in my heart today, and I have to make a great effort to put up with all that is relative that comes my way every day. If I were alone on the Isolino or, better still, with you, my Ada. . . . . Vain dream! Who knows when we'll see each other again? Certainly not among other people. [. . .]

This is the first of several occasions on which AT tells AM that he inherited his unhappy nature from his mother. (AT's daughter Wally told me that her grandmother, who lived until Wally was twenty-four, was a "grumbler.") And he later expressed the opinion that he had passed this characteristic on to Wanda, his younger daughter.

E.P. PN, 5 AUGUST 1933; TO AM, AOLCV; FSD-FOF

Friday night <u>4-8-933</u>

Elucidate, my Ada, this disquieting passage from your last letter: "Woe grows out of sorrow." What woe will I cause or suffer? "But I don't want the woe that defrauds good faith through subterfuge and lies." I think I understand, but I'm still uncertain. I feel that I love you more and more for <u>your</u> **straight** <u>character,</u> which doesn't tolerate faking. No, you aren't doing nor will you do ill to anyone, and I don't know who could do it to you. "But I don't want the woe that defrauds": do you mean, are you alluding to, the <u>painful condition</u> of finding ourselves facing people to whom we are tied by bonds of affection? Clarify your thoughts for me.

I don't think I'll hang around much longer, here on the Isolino. I'm not alone, as I would have wished. And my heart is full to bursting. I live in a continuous, tormenting anguish. The days seem endless to me; I have no more desire for music or books or the company of friends or relatives. Everything and everyone disgust me. I intend to go to Salzburg toward the middle of the month, to a performance of Goethe's Faust staged by <u>Max Reinhardt.</u> But how will I receive word from you? [. . .]

AT was interested in the work of Reinhardt (1873–1943), the great German director, and in the following few years they met on several occasions.

[. . .] Thursday 9 [*sic*; 10]-<u>8-33</u>

I was greatly saddened by the death of a friend from my first years at the conservatory, whose friendship was obscured and interrupted after the regrettable Bologna incident.

Monday morning, a telephone call from his family in Milan communicated the sick man's wish to see me before he died. I went, he recognized my voice, he groped for my hand and I stroked his arm, which was already cold, and from which I could feel the life rushing out of him minute by minute. I can't begin to describe everyone's anguish. He died four hours later. It was terrible, terrible, to see his family's despair. It was Carla's birthday, I had to return to the Isolino, where we had guests, too. On Tuesday I went back to Milan for the funeral. [. . .]

11[.8.33] <u>Friday night</u>

[. . .] I won't go to Salzburg after all. The thought of not <u>being alone</u> and of having to be without your sweet news kills my intention of leaving the Isolino. I have an indomitable desire to work. In November I'll go to Stockholm for two concerts (the 8th and the 10th), I'll very probably arrange a few concerts in Paris, also in the fall, and I have persistent requests from California. I need to work, otherwise I would die! Life on the Isolino is very different from last year. I enjoyed seeing people then; now they disturb me, irritate me, make me irascible! I live for one sole thought, and I don't want anyone to take me away from my contemplation. I ought to be happy, and instead I am very unhappy! To work means to go farther and farther from you. Not to work barely increases the probability of our seeing each other. One must suffer, in any case! [. . .]

E.P. ISOLA BELLA, 18 MARCH (1933); TO AM, AOLCV; FSD-FOF

Morning <u>17-8-933</u>

[. . .] No, I won't go to Salzburg or anywhere else. I'll stay on the Isolino, which, instead of being an <u>oasis of peace,</u> has turned into a <u>torture chamber.</u> Everyone lands here. Miecio, invited by C[arla], has been here for four days. How little and how badly I'm understood, and for so many years! I need solitude, to look at the sky, the lake, and down to the bottom of my thoughts. [. . .]

"Miecio" was the nickname of Mieczysław Horszowski (1892–1993), a Polish-born pianist who spent many years in Italy and was friendly with AT and his family.

Monday <u>21-8-933</u>

My joy, whether sad or happy things are in my mind, they are always associated with and then transformed by the thought of you. You are the diary of my every day and every moment. Everything turns toward and goes toward you. This morning, as usual, I went down to the garden very early, at six. During the last few days the morning air has been very hot. The sky and the lake are covered with a light layer of fog. But at that hour, the Isolino enjoys its real guest: <u>Silence!</u> [. . .]

1-<u>September</u>

[. . .] Wanda went alone to St. Moritz, but she stopped for a day at Sils-Maria, where she visited the Piatigorskys, Horowitz, and Menuhin with his whole family. I've stayed on the Isolino with C[arla], not <u>alone enough</u> and <u>all for myself,</u> as I would have liked. Have you ever experienced the voluptuous joy of being alone and all for yourself? I have, and it's only then that I can let my little boatful of thoughts be pushed hither and yon by the wind, in the sea of marvels that leave you speechless. Only then can I let my soul land on the mysterious shores that it alone knows how to reach!

I still haven't sent back the signed contract for the Stockholm concerts, and I'll have to do it. The thought of facing a new orchestra paralyzes me. The same for Vienna. At my age and after so many years in my profession, it's incredible that I'm still a slave to such exaggerated timidity! Blessed are the shameless! They don't suffer—on the contrary! Paris, too, is asking me to come for the second half of October. [. . .]

"The Piatigorskys" refers to the renowned Russian-born cellist Gregor Piatigorsky (1903–76) and his second wife, Jacqueline, *née* Rothschild. The Russian-born pianist Vladimir Horowitz (1903–89), a lifelong friend of Piatigorsky, had first played with AT earlier that year, in the New York Philharmonic's subscription series. Yehudi Menuhin (1916–99), the celebrated violin prodigy, was seventeen years old at the time.

Tuesday evening [5.9.33]

Thus another sorrowful, profound vacuum has been created in the circle of people dear to me, with the death [three days earlier] of Leonardo Bistolfi, my very dear friend for fully forty-six years! A laconic telegram Sunday morning announced the fact. I hadn't seen him in three years, I think, since the last concert I gave in Turin three years ago, with my American orchestra.

Since then his mind had clouded over. Little by little, his fine intelligence was extinguished. And little by little his speech, too, became shakier and shakier. He barely recognized people any longer, even his friends [he recognized] only with difficulty. I knew about this and I didn't have the nerve to see him. Still, he kept on working, according to his family. I know, however, that a year ago the City of Turin took away from him the job of [creating] a monument to the soldiers who died in the war. They had created a vacuum around him and his name—as with me. The modernists did it to him, the politicians to me. He was very much distressed by this, because he was a very weak man and had a feminine nature, although he was a most elect artist—but he was a slave to and victim of publicity and superficial appearances. I laugh at them and will continue to laugh, because I've always been happy to swim against the current and to do battle for my spiritual and moral independence. The backbone curves when the soul is curved.

Yet for all his weaknesses, my friend Bistolfi was a great, great artist, a poet in marble, and he spoke with his own voice. Despite fifty years of strenuous work, he died poor! All this is sad, sad!! On returning from Turin I wanted to send you a telegram, as I had intended for two days, but it wasn't possible. You understand: I wasn't alone for even a minute. I'm writing the telegrams in English because I have to use others' services, and at the tel. Office [in Pallanza] no one understands the language. [. . .]

For Bistolfi, see note on page 104.

E.P. PN, 20 SEPTEMBER 1933; TO AM, 25VBMMI; FSD-FOF

[. . .] 18-9-33

[. . .] Have you ever read the life of Goethe written by Ludwig? This morning, I happened to pick up the edition that Ludwig himself gave me and I saw, underlined: "the most cultivated man has no better occasion than married life for proving the sweetness of his soul." [French in the original]

And a few pages earlier:

"Fate sometimes has questionable plans. Reason and virtue, duty and everything sacred seek in vain to bar its way: something has to happen that seems wrong to us but right to it, and that ends up by seizing whatever barrier we set up and escaping." [French in the original] The words are Charlotte's, in the "Elective Affinities." And she was a rather cold woman!

I've had some news that has very much disturbed me, these last few days.

Horowitz has asked to marry Wanda. What an idea—a foreigner, and of a different religion!! What should I do? Continue to suffer! My children certainly don't fill my life with joy!! [. . .]

Emil Ludwig (1881–1948) was a popular German-born biographer. · As to Wanda and Horowitz: AT was not pleased with the marital choices of any of his children, although he soon changed his mind about Horowitz—for a while, at any rate.

My joy, what can I tell you that I haven't already told you to satiety, to the point of boring you? The days are gray, it's raining, the lake is sulky and swollen, its level is up by almost two meters. All this is true, but my soul is radiant, full of sunshine. [. . .] On Saturday we'll return [to Milan]. This morning all the Pizzettis, including the <u>misunderstood genius,</u> will come to lunch. Will you call me back? Will we repeat the delicious hours that we spent together last Monday? Just as Anteus's strength was renewed for his formidable struggle with Hercules once he had touched the earth (his mother) with his shoulders, so all my doubts and my sadness disappear through contact with you, and I draw new strength to put up with the suffering that cruel distance holds in store for me. [. . .]

"Misunderstood genius" refers to Ildebrando Pizzetti's older son, Bruno (1910–2000), whom AT did not like.

8-10-933

<u>My joy.</u> You were my first thought as I began to rehearse Daphnis et Chloé!!! The murmuring of the flutes, harp, and clarinets was like a gentle caress to my soul, which was longing for you, far away. The orchestra behaved well. I rehearsed the Ravel piece in a detailed enough way and gave a good shake to Berlioz's Queen Mab. My nightmare is over, God willing. I'm getting back into my skin. But what suffering, my dear! It's ridiculous, but I don't know how to get the better of myself, nor have I ever known how. At times, I'm so unhappy that I'd like to quit once and for all. As soon as I have the program of the two concerts, I'll send it to you; it ought to be a minor <u>masterpiece.</u> I saw the galleys at <u>Astruc</u>'s yesterday, and they filled me with enthusiasm.

Everything is already sold out, and they're insisting that I do a third concert for a vast audience at the Trocadéro. We shall see! [. . .]

The printed program for these concerts was elegantly designed and included a woodcut portrait of AT on the cover. · Gabriel Astruc (1864–1938), one of the most artistically astute French impresarios of the twentieth century, had been a fervent admirer of AT at least since 1910, when AT had made his Paris debut with the Metropolitan Opera Company. · AT did give three concerts in Paris in October 1933, but they all took place at the Théâtre des Champs-Elysées.

13-10-933

My **real** and **only** treasure, the first concert is finally over! What nervousness! What a black day, and how many times I cursed the moment when I accepted to conduct! This is no longer the life for me! The contrast within me is too great; I'm old in years, young in spirit, and it's a battle that leaves me exhausted, that annihilates me! This morning I had a rehearsal for the Wagner concert. As usual in Paris, I found myself with six first violins and other parts missing, because they're engaged at other theaters, etc. I stormed out of the rehearsal—naturally.

Yesterday evening's concert went well enough. On the whole, the orchestra is good and was very attentive. I'll send you the program. And you, what are you doing amid those Teutonic delinquents? Are you thinking of me? Do you think it's a good idea to love me a bit? Do you know how much I love you? My dear creature, beautiful and good, I don't know whether you've realized yet how much I love you, how much I like you, how much I would like to live with you at my side, to get to know better and better your goodness, your sweetness, and to feel that you really love me and will love me still more.

I'm writing to you at a metronome speed of 208. Excuse me, but for loving you the highest metronome speed isn't enough. Write to me and tell me pleasant things. I kiss you passionately.

Arturo.

write to me—don't be lazy.

Two hundred eight beats per minute is the highest speed possible on the traditional mechanical metronome.

22-10-933
Sunday

My Ada, I've begun the rehearsals with Beethoven's 7th and the Brahms variations. The orchestra is good—not excellent, like mine in New York, and above all not as disciplined. You can tell that it's not accustomed to being in good hands. However, it's flexible, because at the first rehearsal it immediately modified itself so as to maintain the rhythm strictly, and it has responded perfectly to all of my demands. But I'm bored, I'm not enjoying myself. Even the applause, the articles full of enthusiastic praise, don't make me want to continue, and I would happily give up Stockholm—the more so since Horowitz tells me that the orchestra there is second- or even third-rate. To be without vanity, as I am, is almost painful, because one experiences only the annoyances of one's position.

Yesterday, while I was walking all by myself in Vienna, wandering into the shops—an unusual thing for me—I heard Wally calling me; she was with her husband, Wanda, Tonio Puccini, and his wife, and she sort of pointed to Castelbarco. We greeted each other. I shook his hand, because it would have been terrible not to do so, but . . . I can't change the feeling of repulsion that I have for him. This saddens me for Wally, whom I love to distraction, but I can't get the better of myself!!!

I have a nasty character, which makes me suffer a lot and makes others suffer.

[. . .] Yesterday evening I went to the Opera to hear Strauss's Arabella (noblesse oblige). What desolation! What wretched stuff! What a shame for an artist like Strauss to sink so low!!! I didn't have the nerve to go see him. [. . .]

This was AT's first professional encounter with the Vienna Philharmonic, which quickly came to love him as it had and has loved few if any other conductors in its history. Recordings from those years, with other conductors, demonstrate the correctness of AT's assessment: the ensemble had a beautiful sound but often lacked the sort of rhythmic sharpness that AT always demanded of orchestras and that was a major factor in giving his performances their distinctive vitality. · That AT was capable of vanity in some of his human relationships is undeniable—he refers to it himself in other letters—but he was not being dishonest in saying that he had no vanity with respect to music making. He considered himself a better conductor than virtually all of his colleagues and considered his musical motives to be beyond reproach, but he nevertheless felt that he was inadequate to the great task of interpreting great music. · Since 1924, when AT had found out about his daughter Wally's affair with Count Emanuele di Castelbarco, a married man, he had refused to meet him, and his refusal continued even after Castelbarco's divorce from his first wife and marriage to Wally in 1931. The event described in this letter was the first occasion on which he behaved civilly toward his son-in-law, and he continued to treat him decently thereafter, however unwillingly. · Antonio (Tonio) Puccini (1886–1946) was Giacomo Puccini's son. · Although five of Richard Strauss's tone poems figured frequently in AT's repertoire, the only Strauss opera that he ever conducted was Salome, and he conducted only one production of it. The performance of Arabella to which he refers was the work's Viennese premiere, on 21 October 1933 (the world premiere had taken place in Dresden the previous summer); Clemens Krauss conducted, and the all-star cast included Lotte Lehmann in the title role, Luise Helletsgruber as Zdenka, Alfred Jerger as Mandryka, Richard Mayr as Count Waldner, and Helge Roswaenge as Matteo; Lothar Wallerstein was the director, the sets and costumes were by Alfred Roller, and Strauss himself was present.

<u>Monday evening</u>

<u>23-10-933</u>

<u>My love,</u> I am very tired. There is a price to pay for three hours of intense rehearsal, and with nerves taut from striving toward relative perfection. A bit of life goes with it. Everyone marveled over my strength! The other conductors, they tell me, conduct differently and demand nothing at rehearsal; then they clown around at the performance, in front of the audience. Unfortunately, at my age I can't change my method. I know that I give more than my strength ought to allow. I'm always going into debt with myself; I'll pay the debts off eventually. It is a dear thing to me to note, from the demonstrations shown me by the whole orchestra, Rosé first and foremost, that I haven't yet started to go soft. Let's keep hoping! [. . .]

Arnold Rosé (1863–1946), longtime concertmaster of the Vienna Philharmonic and first violin of the Rosé String Quartet, was married to Gustav Mahler's sister and had played under most of the famous conductors of his day, from Wagner's disciples to those born in the 1890s.

<u>23-10-933</u>

<u>11 in the evening</u>

<u>My Ada,</u> Before I shut my eyes I want to send you my thoughts. I'm alone. Everyone went to the theater to see Moissi. I couldn't. I was too tired. I had supper with Schnabl-Rossi and an American friend, and now I'm already in bed.

Dress rehearsal at 10 tomorrow morning, concert in the evening. Oh, if only you were here! Maybe I'd be too nervous! Maybe I'd be awkward!! I don't know how I would be able to conquer the feelings that would come over me from knowing that you were in the hall!

And yet it would be dear to me. [. . .]

Alexander Moissi (1880–1935) was one of the great German-language actors of his day. · Count Riccardo Schnabl-Rossi, an old friend and confidant of Puccini's, had known AT for many years and lived in Vienna.

<u>Thursday 26-10-933</u>

[. . .] I'm working, and the work is tiring me! I've even written to postpone the Stockholm concerts, but I don't know what the upshot will be. Introducing myself to new orchestras and to new audiences is the cause of immense and painful sorrow—so why not avoid it? I rehearsed La Mer, so far, and the Brahms Third. Tomorrow I'll do the Pines and Anacréon. I had plenty to do to make Debussy clear and comprehensible; I think I succeeded. The whole orchestra broke into a great ovation. I was happy. Yesterday evening I dined tête-à-tête with an old friend, Countess Thun, who was a great friend of Cosima Wagner and Eleonora Duse. She has all of Boito's letters to Duse. I read some of them, and I have transcribed a short one and a longer one, which I'm sending you so that you can get an idea of Boito's nobility and goodness and of the fatuity of Duse, whom I could never stand because of her insincerity. She had fallen in love with a Russian painter, then with D'Annunzio. Excuse the rush. I kiss you and I love you. Don't make me suffer as Duse made Boito suffer. Write to me without fear. My joy, hold me in your arms.

"Pines" refers to Respighi's *Pines of Rome;* "Anacréon" is the Overture to Cherubini's *Anacréon.* · AT's partisan attitude toward Boito is understandable, but not everyone who has read the Boito-Duse correspondence—which was published many years after AT read it—would agree with AT's assessment of Boito's relationship with the great actress Eleonora Duse (1858–1924).

<u>27-10-933</u>

[. . .] After many years, I've seen Elsa Pick again; she hasn't remarried, as people were saying. At this moment she's out shopping with Carla and Wanda. [. . .]

<u>30-10-933</u>

As soon as the concert ended, your divine letter was delivered to me—the <u>grand prize for my labors.</u> But the audience was calling me out for another bow, and I took my bow, radiant with a joy that no one knew about, except my heart, which was beating as fast as it could. [. . .]

For the moment I've freed myself from Stockholm, but those people don't want to turn back the box-office receipts they've already taken in. So the concerts are postponed to 29 November and 3 December. At least I can breathe, however! I can't stand any more of the ghastly life I've been leading for three weeks! Photographers on the streets, at my arrival at the station, autographs, people who follow you down the street, who barge into your bedroom—it's enough to drive you crazy. I must have signed hundreds of albums and photographs! I'm rabid, and if I don't go home quickly I'll go mad. This isn't the sort of life I love. I've always hated it. On my arrival yesterday evening, I was surrounded by more than twenty cameras. Kodály and his wife were waiting for me. I ran off, swearing like a longshoreman. I jumped into a taxi, leaving behind everyone, including Carla, who caught up with me later, and I came directly to this hotel, although I'd reserved an apartment in another—in order to shake those cursed pests!

I absolutely could not have gone on; without permission to postpone Stockholm I would have become ill. I can't begin to tell you what an enthusiastic and affectionate welcome I was given by the Viennese audience! Yesterday—I'm telling you this in confidence and a little shamefacedly—I wept a bit. But I managed not to show it. I was really moved. And the orchestra players demonstrated that they adore me, and they're happy that I've promised to conduct two concerts with them in Salzburg next August.

And you? How long will you stay in Berlin? My God, how sad it makes me that those damned Germans have you in their midst! Isn't it possible for E[nrico] to find work in another country? Will I see you in Milan? [. . .]

On 30 October 1933 AT and the Vienna Philharmonic repeated in Budapest the concert they had given in Vienna six days earlier. Zoltán Kodály and his first wife, Emma (*née* Sándor, originally Schlesinger), were devoted to AT and his family.

E.P. MI, 14 NOVEMBER 1933; TO EK, 6 FRANKGASSE, VIENNA; WOT

13-11-933

My <u>dear Elsa</u>. . . . The two volumes of Goethe's Elective Affinities, in a most beautiful edition, reached me from Paris yesterday, and the two magazines from Vienna [arrived] this morning. You've been more active and intelligent than my booksellers (Baldini e Castoldi), who, as late as yesterday, told me that the Goethe book was not to be found. What can I tell you? Thank you is too little; that you are a treasure, you know; that I still love you, you can't imagine—but it's the pure and simple truth.

My dear, my sweet and beloved Elsa, you'll never know, nor will I ever be able to tell you, of my deep, immense joy at seeing you again after more than ten years! I found you as beautiful and dear as back then. The years have left no trace on your beautiful face. Your unique eyes have kept their deep mysteriousness, your graceful body is still fascinating. You are still adorable, and the hours spent together remain the nicest memory of my stay in Vienna. For ten years, silence surrounded you, nor did I dare to break it. People had told me that you had remarried, that you were married to a rich gentleman, but nothing else. I received your telegram for Nerone, but then nothing else. This silence seemed to confirm the rumor that you were happily married. My two appearances in Vienna—first with La Scala, then with the American orchestra—brought me no news about you, thus I really thought that you had forever forgotten the past and the <u>dear friends who were part of it.</u> Nor did I ever have any information that would have allowed me to give you a sign of life. How gladly I would have done so!

I would have liked to be freer in Vienna, to talk to you and to explain facts and circumstances that were sorrowful for the two of us. But we'll see each other again in Vienna, and we'll have a few free hours, tête-à-tête. We'll clear up many things. <u>One thing is certain.</u> We were trifled with, betrayed, ignobly ambushed. Not knowing what had happened, we probably even betrayed ourselves. But let's not trouble ourselves over this now! Did you love me a little? Do you still, although I've grown old? I'm still fond of you, as before—more than before. I've always kept you in my memory with infinite tenderness, sorry for what I'd done and allowing myself no excuses over having been the cause of disaster and unpleasantness for you. Oh, my Elsa! How many dear memories were awakened in my soul during those days in Vienna! And how lucky for us that my whole family re-encountered you with such pleasure! I'll write you again before I leave Milan. Send me your news. Be careful to <u>type your address.</u> Let's not be <u>foolish.</u> Love me even if I'm not <u>as I was then.</u> My <u>heart is the same.</u> As for **desire**—who knows!

I lovingly kiss your beautiful mouth.

<u>Your Arturo</u>

AT's affair with Elsa Kurzbauer had ended abruptly in circa 1920–21, when her husband was informed of it. I have been told that the informer was Carla, and that Pick-Mangiagalli divorced his wife in what was then the "free city" of Fiume (Rijeka), inasmuch as divorce, as mentioned earlier, was not allowed under Italian law. Elsa had then returned to her native Vienna. · This letter, of course, calls into question the sincerity of AT's love for AM at this early stage in their relationship; my opinion is that that relationship became the all-consuming one in his life toward the end of 1934 and remained so for about four years.

E.P. MI, 19 NOVEMBER 1933; TO AM, PH22MB; FSD-FOF

[. . .] Wednesday <u>15-11-933</u>

I read in the life of Burns (a Scottish poet and man of letters) that in 1788 "the number of his letters was exceptionally increased by his entanglement with Mrs. M'Lehose. To her alone in less than three months and a half of this year he wrote at least thirty-six letters." [In English in the original.] I know <u>another person</u> who has written an equal number (I believe) of letters in an equal period of time! Do you know him? I adore you and I desire you, oh! very much! Infinite big kisses on your beautiful mouth.

Wanda and Wally have arrived from England. Wanda is radiant—she seems to be in a state of grace. I've never seen her so happy. May God protect her and preserve for her the happiness that has always been denied to me. How very much I see myself reproduced in this dear young daughter of mine!

Like me, she seems not to be very expansive, and yet you must realize that we're both far from being as we seem!! I hope that her wedding will take place around 21 December. On the 28th, they'll leave from Cherbourg for America—we'll leave from Genoa on the same day. Unfortunately, five painful months will separate me from you!! I'd like to become ill to stay here, in the sweet, self-flattering hope that you would come visit me. What madness this love is, and at my age. [. . .]

E.P. STOCKHOLM, (?.?.) 1933; P.S., GRAND HÔTEL, STOCKHOLM; TO AM, 46VMPMI; FSD-FOF

1-12-933

My love, some time ago I received the telegram and letter. I don't know what you've been going through, but I well know how much I've suffered from not being able to write to you every day, as I had been doing for almost six months. She [Carla] has glued herself to my side, and I can barely draw a free breath. The foreign, hostile language has practically paralyzed her. She moves only in tandem with me. Add to this the fact that here it's already nighttime at four in the afternoon—and so one stays home and doesn't move. This is the first day she's ventured away from home on her own. I'm taking advantage of it to tell you something new. I love you, I love you more and more, I suffer, I despair over not seeing you at my side, the sole creature who still makes me believe that a little joy exists in life. Without you, everything would be dark, shadow, nothing!! Those hours in Berlin!! What a tragedy, what suffering, what humiliation!! I listened to the music he [Enrico] was playing, I didn't dare to touch you, I felt the warmth of your adored body, but I didn't dare think of you, I wanted to be near his mind and not to betray him. What suffering, what misery!!! Nevertheless, I love you and can't do without you—I can't live.

Love me, love me, Ada. I'm worthy of you and of your love—believe me!!!

I'll arrive on Thursday (7th) at eight in the evening.

I cling to you tightly and I give you a long kiss, with infinite desire. Oh, your beautiful mouth!—Arturo

Thanks to an invitation made through the good offices of Tullio Voghera and his wife, Iwa, the daughter of Tore Aulin, a well-known Swedish musician, AT had gone to Stockholm as guest conductor of the Konsertföreningens Orkester (Concert Society

Orchestra), later renamed the Stockholm Philharmonic; one of the programs was repeated on tour in Copenhagen, and AT returned to Stockholm in 1934 and 1937 to conduct the orchestra. · En route from Italy to Sweden, AT and his wife had evidently made a stopover in Berlin, and during that stopover they attended a performance by Enrico Mainardi (probably a private event at the Italian Embassy).

E.P. STOCKHOLM, 3 DECEMBER 1933; P.S. AS IN PREVIOUS LETTER; TO AM, 46VMPMI; FSD-FOF

2-12-1933

My dearest, Horowitz had frightened me about the skill of the Stockholm orchestra, but, perhaps because of the immense pride of these players, who understood that they would have to play under a musician whose reputation is almost that of a pestiferous ball-breaker, they have certainly given the best of themselves, in order not to make me think with regret of the orchestras of Paris and Vienna. And the public has been extremely kind and enthusiastic. From the king to the man on the street—as you would have seen—they were all on their feet to applaud me after the first part of the program and at the end. All in all, I couldn't have wished for a more enthusiastic welcome.

I've come back at this moment from a lunch given in my honor by the orchestra. I was moved by everyone. And I'm surprised that at my age I can still interest and win the love of people who knew me only by name until a few days ago. It means that simplicity and truth still have value and power over the masses. One doesn't always need rifles or violent means to make one's worth felt. [. . .]

WRITTEN DURING A WESTWARD TRANSATLANTIC CROSSING; P.S., REX; TO AM, (25VBMMI?); FSD-FOF

29-12-933

The further my poor body is dragged away from you, the more desperately my soul clutches at yours.

Oh, don't leave me, don't abandon me, write to me, write to me, keep alive in me the hope, the certainty that I'll see you again, my lover, my friend, my daughter, my all!! Too many months will separate me from you, and who knows what will become of you? You'll forget me. I've found all my friends [aboard]. The Molinaris, the Milsteins, the Menuhins, and then Wanda and Horowitz, Piatigorsky. They all bother me—my only thought is You, my only adored creature, light and blessing of my soul.

I adore you.

Nathan Milstein (1903–92) was among the finest violinists of his age.

6-1-934

[. . .] I heard my orchestra again yesterday. Marvelous. Tommasini was with me. I can't wait to begin rehearsals. Monday I'll start with the Brahms 4th, then Beethoven. Oh, if only you were here! What a joy it would be to know that you were attending my rehearsals. Imagine how many things you would tell me! What you liked best and also what you didn't like, right? [. . .]

9-1-934

My love, The second rehearsal, too, was a pleasure. [. . .] After having re-rehearsed the last movement of the Brahms 4th (the marvelous Passacaglia) and having given a once-over to Tchaikovsky's Romeo and Juliet overture-fantasy, I rehearsed the Lento assai from Beethoven's last quartet, which I intend to play with string orchestra at the first concert, together with the Vivace from the same quartet. I can't begin to describe the emotion! In its day, it was played after Beethoven's death. (He heard it only as sung by the Angels within his beautiful soul.) I hope to achieve something decent. But it's very difficult for us mortals to achieve divinity, and in this case we are really beyond seventh heaven. We shall see. [. . .] Everyone is awaiting my interpretation of Tchaikovsky, because I've never had the desire to conduct this Leoncavallo of the classics. [. . .]

AT had in fact conducted a few orchestral pieces by Tchaikovsky in the last years of the nineteenth century, not to mention the Italian premiere of *Eugene Onegin* at La Scala in 1900. Since then, however, Tchaikovsky had disappeared from his repertoire until 1933, when he had made the first of quite a few forays into the Russian master's symphonic music. In private, AT often used the music of Ruggero Leoncavallo, the composer of *Pagliacci*—which AT had conducted at its world premiere in 1892—as a paradigm for heart-on-sleeve, unsophisticated art.

12-1-934

[. . .] I've just now come from Carnegie [Hall], where I repeated yesterday evening's concert. Today, too, everything went well. The orchestra is marvelous. I wasn't happy with myself in the Lento from the Quartet. Too little time for concretely expressing what there is spiritually in this sublime music, and which I feel that I possess only in my spirit, so far. I'll repeat it later, and maybe I'll be able to realize it as I feel it.

All the same, it made a big impression. I'm sending you this newspaper clipping (sent to me anonymously), not out of vanity—may God preserve me from it—but so that you can get an idea of the vast difference that separates these critics from our know-it-alls. I've underlined the last sentence, because I think it describes me correctly. [. . .]

Article by Lawrence Gilman *(New York Herald),* entitled "Toscanini Returns and Is Acclaimed at the Philharmonic Concert." The sentence underlined by Toscanini is "And again Mr. Toscanini reminded us that what is true of the religious believer is true of the supreme artist: that faith, as a great poet has remarked, is only knowledge transcended."

E.P. NY, 19 JANUARY 1934; TO AM, 25VBMMI; FSD-FOF
[PICTURE POSTCARD SHOWING AT SEATED AT THE PIANO;
ON THE OTHER SIDE:]

Sweetest creature of my beautiful dream, You were constantly in my thoughts during the concert. I think the orchestra brought off the Eroica better than at other times. If you had been there, what a reward it would have been for the orchestra and me!! I'm tired. The Friday matinée repetition of the program is always wearying for me. Menuhin played well, too.

The seventeen-year-old Menuhin had played the Beethoven Violin Concerto with AT and the New York Philharmonic on 18 and 19 January.

E.P. NY, 27 JANUARY 1934; TO AM, 25VBMMI; FSD-FOF

26-1-934

[. . .] Today I conducted Beethoven with greater inspiration. I had the Devil in my body, or the Holy Spirit in my soul, I don't know which. [. . .]

Did you enjoy yourself in Barcelona? Was this your first time there? Write to me, tell me something about your life, how you spend your days, etc., etc. I heard that the Pizzetti boy is still ill, and this makes me feel very badly for poor Rirì and the maestro. I think Tommasini wants to leave New York around February 3 and go to California. I'll send you a clipping that will interest you. At this point, I'm an honorary Jew. Will you continue to love me? My dear, my dear, I embrace and kiss you with enormous passion, and I continue to love you. It's the best thing I'm capable of doing.

Your Arturo

AT was much fonder of Ippolito Pizzetti, son of the composer and his second wife, than of the composer's first son, Bruno. Ippolito became one of Italy's leading experts on gardening. · In several of his later letters to AM, AT berates her for her anti-Semitism, but in others he indulges her with remarks meant to amuse her on the subject. · The clipping was from the *New York Times* [?] of 24 January 1934: "JEWS PAY TRIBUTE TO TOSCANINI HERE—Conductor Gets Certificate of Inscription in Golden Book of Jewish National Fund.—HIS BAIREUTH [*sic*] BAN HAILED—Honor sent from Jerusalem Is Presented by Committee at Musician's Hotel." The article reports that Toscanini's name has been inscribed in the book "in recognition of his magnificent act in refusing to direct the 1933 Wagner Festival at Baireuth [*sic*]. [. . .] In response, Mr. Toscanini said he was deeply touched by the honor, and was glad to know that the Jews in America had thought of him at the time when he acted according to the dictates of his own conscience. Until the persecution in Germany of innocent people ceased, he said, he would continue to refuse to participate in any musical activities in that country."

E.P. NY, 31 JANUARY 1934; TO AM, 25VBMMI; FSD-FOF

Tuesday <u>30-1-934</u>

<u>My dear</u> joy, I have every right to say that I live only for you and my work—but the latter is killing me, whereas you give me life. You are truly my soul's most precious medicine. I'm impatiently waiting for tomorrow to come. The Rex [ocean liner] is arriving. Will it bring me your dear news? Oh, certainly! You can't disappoint me, you love me and don't want me to suffer even more horrible pains than the worse-than-horrible pain of distance. The Horowitzes arrived yesterday. Wanda was a little pale and tired, they had traveled from Saint Louis to New York with a four-hour delay due to wind and snow. He has a recital this evening, and tomorrow he's off again. After the concert we'll all go to the Heifetzes' home.

Have you ever met Heifetz's wife, the former <u>Florence Widor,</u> a cinema actress? She is a very dear woman, besides being beautiful and <u>charmante;</u> she is not Jewish. But she's not like my dear Ada, you <u>are unique,</u> your eyes, your grace, your beautiful mouth, everything gracious that emanates from your little self forms a special, unique, <u>unmistakable,</u> and <u>incomparable</u> whole.

This fourth week is a little bit too much for me, and I'm more and more convinced that I ought to take a year off. As you see, I'm talking as if I still had a long enough life ahead of me to be able to subtract years from my work. Still, next year I don't want to come back. I'm not saying anything for now, especially since a campaign to raise a fund of <u>500,000 dollars</u> is under way, in order to cover the deficit of the last two years and future [deficits] as well, and if such a piece of news were to be bandied about it would be a disaster and everything would fall apart. But once the thing has succeeded, I'll see to it that my point of view is understood. My hide, too, ought to be worth something! [. . .]

Regarding Wanda's pallor: She may not have known it yet, but she was pregnant (the Horowitzes' only child was born the following October). · Jascha Heifetz (1901–87) was arguably the greatest violinist of the twentieth century.

TG, NY, 6 FEBRUARY 1934; TO MRS. JOHN ALDEN CARPENTER, ARTS CLUB, 410 N. MICHIGAN AVE., CHICAGO, ILL.; ORIG. ENG.; WOT

I AM SORRY I AM UNABLE TO BE PRESENT PERSONALLY TO GREET AND HONOR ARNOLD SCHOENBERG AND MRS. SCHOENBERG STOP WILL YOU KINDLY EXTEND TO THEM MY BEST WISHES
ARTURO TOSCANINI

This was a reply to a telegram dated 4 February 1934 from the Arts Club of Chicago inviting AT to attend a dinner in honor of Schoenberg—whose music AT detested and never conducted—and his wife.

TG, NY, 26 MARCH 1934; TO PRESIDENT FRANKLIN D. ROOSEVELT, THE WHITE HOUSE, WASHINGTON, D.C.; ORIG. ENG.; FDRL

DEEPLY APPRECIATE YOUR MESSAGE ON MY BIRTHDAY STOP MY SINCERE THANKS AND HEARTFELT WISHES THAT THIS COUNTRY TO WHICH I AM SO DEVOTED AND INDEBTED MAY HAVE THE BENEFIT OF YOUR STRENGTH AND WISDOM FOR MANY YEARS TO COME
ARTURO TOSCANINI

E.P. NY, 30 MARCH 1934; P.S. WITH PHOTO OF AT; TO GS, ASP; SR

29 <u>April</u> [*sic,* for March] <u>934</u>

My <u>dearest Gelsa</u>

I would like my words to bring you peace and a good mood, and I would like the shadows to be dispersed forever from before your beautiful eyes. I would like the sun always to illuminate your beautiful soul—not the sun that gives us light and heat, but rather the one that gives light and heat to <u>the soul</u> that's in love. And you're lacking that sun—or so I'm guessing. At your age, every-thing ought to smile; there should be no shadows, either before your eyes or wrapped around your soul. So write me a letter that's not so sad, that's gayer, as befits your youth!! Leave sadness and darkness of the soul to me, the old maestro. I've worked like a dog, and I <u>still have a month to go.</u> I'll finish on April 29 and will board the <u>Ile-de-France</u> liner on May 5. Shortly after May 15 I'll go to Piazze. I want to see whether my presence will bring you a little joy. You know that I'm fond of you, very much so; you know that I'm capable of understanding you—and you know many other things—<u>isn't that so?</u> Write to me. Say hello to all my dear friends and continue to be fond of me. Your A Toscanini

31-3-934

[. . .] I won't be going to California. I'll finish my concerts on April 29. I've worked like a dog and I'm tired. Next week [there is a] break, then I have the last twelve concerts. I won't be able to leave till May 5 with the Ile de France. I can't stand it any longer. [. . .]

Something—an upsetting remark or perhaps no word at all—had made AT break off his correspondence with AM after 1 February, but a telegram from her on his birthday (25 March) had rekindled their love affair. He later revealed that he had had a brief fling with another woman during the two-month interval; he did not identify the woman in question, but she was probably the soprano Lotte Lehmann (1888–1976), whose letters to him reveal that they had an affair at about this time.

Wednesday May 30 [1934]

[. . .] I work and work. It's the only way to make life possible and to forget its miseries. And I'll work continuously. Always, until I draw my last breath. I still have a great deal of vitality. And the work doesn't weigh me down. This morning I rehearsed for three full hours, Wagner and the Bach Passacaglia. I was very tired, but after a few hours I was as fresh as at the start, ready to begin all over again. What a shame that you're not here. [. . .]

AT's Paris concerts at the Théâtre des Champs-Elysées on 3 and 6 June included some Wagner excerpts and Respighi's arrangement of the Bach Passacaglia and Fugue in C minor.

Dearest Gelsina

Thank you for your long letter! I'm not at ease for you. I feel that you are agitated and heavy-hearted. This shouldn't be so, at your age. I can understand that you live in a village that's not suited to your sensitivity. But you have a head that works very well, that can reason and is therefore capable of self-control and of overcoming life's harshness. Just think, dear Gelsina, that more or less all those who want life to be tolerable must make a little effort to pick themselves up and distance themselves from the banality and mediocrity of human society. We'll talk about all this again in Piazze in a few days, and I hope that I'll convince you and bring a bit of peace to your spirit. Be fond of me, as I am of you. Say hello to Lavinietta, Daria, and everyone—mamma, Nella, Italia. A big kiss from your

Aff. A.T.

P.S. I received the purple violet in time. Thank you.

E.P. PS, 23 JUNE 1934; TO AM, HQR; FSD-FOF

<u>My dearest,</u> yesterday was a dreadful day. They had put the idea in my head that the swelling in my cheek was caused by a bad tooth, and I was all ready to leave Piazze and go to Milan. Rinaldi wanted me to be examined by a doctor, a friend of his, who in fact came, but I was against it. I've never gone to dentists, and certainly not in this case, in which I knew the real cause—also, I could clench my teeth without feeling any discomfort. For two days I continued to use very hot compresses of water with salt, then mush with flour and linseed. Then yesterday evening I rinsed with salol and naphthol mixed with alcohol and I got rid of the swelling of the gums, and today I'm feeling much better. My cheek is less swollen and my state of mind less black. I had before my eyes the vision of an operation of the sort that Castelbarco had to put up with. Molinari has arrived. Since he had to phone Mary, I suggested that he tell the Finzis to come to Piazze for lunch tomorrow, and to bring you along.

We shall see! In the meantime, I've suspended the other treatment and even Rinaldi didn't want me to start it again today. And I'd hoped to come to Rome this evening! I'm sad, sad! [. . .]

Mary was Molinari's wife. · The Finzi family—Roman Jews—were friends of the Toscaninis and the Mainardis.

E.P. MI, 4 JULY 1934; TO AM, 46VMPMI; FDS-FOF

My <u>sweetest one,</u> if I were still of an age when certain kinds of impulsive actions can be understood and empathized with, oh, how tempted I would be to commit some. But at my age one mustn't let down one's defenses against the ridiculous, therefore one must suffocate, suffocate, not breathe, or at best breathe with great difficulty!

I'm sorry to say it, but coming back to my family is always depressing, oppressive. It gives me the impression of entering a penitentiary! I feel that my every glance, my every gesture, my every movement are looked at, spied upon, discussed, weighed. It makes me want to leave again. [. . .]

Sunday 15-7-934

I thought I'd find a bit of peace up here, but the inferno, with all its unspeak-able torments, is burning in me! I didn't know, I was unaware that still, at my age, after so many vicissitudes, so many disillusionments, after having put behind me adventures of every sort, I am still a dreamer, a romantic, still capa-ble of deluding myself, of creating castles in the air for myself, like a school-boy! My sole creature, who dominates my whole, poor soul—no, you don't know how much I'm suffering at this very moment. And if I told you that you are the cause of my suffering, you wouldn't believe me—but you can well believe that the suffering, too, is dear to me, as is everything else that comes from you. Even the weather is nasty and cold. I'm up here at the Albertinis' with Walter, Tessa, Rusca, and his wife. Tomorrow morning (Monday) I'll take Tessa to Milan. I'll try to phone you. Will you or won't you be in Milan? What will I say to you? Who knows! [. . .]

Delio Tessa (1886–1939) was a highly regarded Milanese dialect poet of openly anti-Fascist opinions. Luigi Rusca was an executive with the Milan-based Mondadori pub-lishing house, where Walter Toscanini was employed.

18-7-934

My dearest Gelsa
I'm writing while facing the beautiful lake at this beautiful twilight hour.

It is a luminous twilight, and it's suitable for my poor eyes, which are rather unwell. It seems a century since I left all of you, and it's only been sixteen days!! Now that I'm far away I realize that I'm fond of all of you!—Especially you, my Gelsina—you who have the **toupet** [in French in the original] (which, translated into Tuscan, would be faccia tosta [effrontery]) to ask me whether I still remember you or whether you're one of the many commonplace episodes amidst the whirl of people who surround me! No, my dear, you aren't a com-monplace episode, but rather a dear girl who wins everyone's liking, affection, and tenderness. I love you like one of my daughters—too bad I was born too early; you understand me, right? I don't want to say more so as not to compro-mise my seriousness. Seriousness is the cross I bear.

The flight from Rome to Milan was excellent. Carla and Wally were wait-ing for me at Taliedo[?]. I stayed in Milan for several days. I worked like a dog. Shut up in my nice study all day long, I didn't suffer from the heat. Then I came to the Isolino, where I found little Emanuela bursting with health and cheerfulness. Carla left immediately for Venice. It was the second time in less than ten days. I think she'll come back tomorrow. It's very probable that I'll spend about three weeks in Trent for ocular <u>irrigations.</u> I'll suffer from the heat, but I hope to profit from the stay. Give me your news from time to time. You know that it will give me joy. Hug and kiss Lavinietta and Daria for me. Remember me to everyone, including Wandina. I embrace you tightly with indescribable affection. Big kisses from your old

<u>Maestro</u>

TG, SILS MARIA, 22 JULY 1934; TO DANIELA THODE (AND EVA CHAMBERLAIN), BAYREUTH; RWGSB

THANK YOU FOR EVERYTHING STOP I AM NEAR YOU DEAR FRIENDS IN THE SUFFERING YOU ARE NOW GOING THROUGH STOP IF ONLY JESUS CHRIST WOULD CHASE THE PHARISEES FROM THE TEMPLE TOGETHER WITH THE PER-JURER RICHARD STRAUSS I EMBRACE YOU BOTH AFFECTIONATELY — ARTURO TOSCANINI

The "Pharisees" were the Nazis. Strauss's sin, in AT's eyes, was that he had kowtowed to the Nazis by conducting what was to have been AT's *Parsifal* production at the Nazified Bayreuth festivals of 1933 and 1934. AT probably knew that Frau Thode and Frau Chamberlain were pro-Nazi, but this did not stop him either from making anti-Nazi statements to them or from continuing to treat them as respected friends.

E.P. TRENT, 2 AUGUST 1934; TO AM, HLBVB; FSD-FOF

[. . .] I don't even have the strength to despair—my strength, my desires, my thoughts are completely exhausted. Never in my long life have I found myself in such a predicament. To desire a dear creature whom one adores, to the extreme heights of desire, and to force oneself at the same time not to see her is the apex of heroism and <u>of absurdity.</u> And I live amid absurdity. I love you even though I feel that you <u>aren't close to me,</u> as I would like, as I would wish you to be, in simple, affectionate, confidential abandon, from one creature to another, both hungering for intimate understanding. And [I wish] that you could see me as <u>I really am,</u> not overlaid with that patina that the world, people, and the many years of my artistic life have thrust upon me and that I wish could be destroyed with some corrosive acid or other, so that I could appear before your eyes with that kind-hearted simplicity that I consider the best side of <u>my real</u> self. All this I would like, but how is one to go about it? You certainly wouldn't deny that in art I have a certain exquisite sensibility! Well then, the same sensibility stands guard and functions even more in the sweet, intimate relations between two people who love each other, and I must admit to you something that I would have preferred not to say, but that I must tell you at this moment of inertia of the will, of exhaustion of all desires whatsoever: I must confess to you that many times, just when the passion, the desire to embrace you, to tell you with a kiss how much fondness, how much affection, how much love was filling my soul, something emanating from you has paralyzed me and made me think, no, Ada doesn't love me as I would like; <u>she puts up with me,</u> she doesn't <u>have the nerve to tell me what a mistake I've made. She's good, she's gentle, gracious, refined, as her nature demands, but she doesn't love me.</u> And <u>a few times</u> I've had the sensation that you were avoiding my kisses.

AT was staying near Trent to undergo eye treatment at a special clinic.

E.P. TRENT, 10 AUGUST 1934; TO AM, HLBVB; FSD-FOF

6 p.m.

Yes, dear, sweet, <u>unique creature,</u> for whom I feel the joy of living. Every time my thoughts envelop you in my mind (and that's often!), the recollection of one of Bellini's most beautiful and purest melodies comes to me instinctively. I wanted to tell you this in Rome, that day when I sat at the piano at the Finzis' home and played a few of the best bits of I Puritani and became enthusiastic about demonstrating their beauties. Do you remember? You, too, were listening to me, standing behind my back. You then praised, to my immense joy, the sweet expression that I imprinted on that music. And I played, specifically, this melody: [Musical quote with the words *"Qui la voce tua soave mi chiamava e poi sparì,"* from Part II; AT has written *"tua"* (yours) instead of *"sua"* (his), so that the words read, "Your gentle voice was calling me here, and then it disappeared."]

As you can see, this beautiful, sweet, pure, <u>not sensual</u> melody comes to mind every time you enter my thoughts. [. . .]

E.P. PN, 8 SEPTEMBER 1934; TO GS, ASP; SR

<u>8-9-934 from the Isolino</u>

[. . .] Why do you write, "I would be happy to be with you forever, but since this isn't possible, may my sweetest thoughts reach you, <u>to be taken the right way."</u> How am I to understand this? And what is the right, true way? Please tell me. <u>Be good—make an effort</u> and send me a few lines as soon as you receive this letter. [. . .]

13-9-934

[. . .] I'm angry with you because you haven't written to me. Give a lot of kisses for me to Lavinia, Daria, Don Guglielmo, the carabinieri on duty, Rinaldi's serva padrona, the mayor of Rocca Cannuccia [fictitious provincial village]—in short, to everyone. For you, none.

Maestro

15-9-934

[. . .] So peace has been made. You say: you Tuscans [*Toscani*] have tenacious hearts; you don't forget. And I add: Not more tenacious, however, than those of the Toscaninis!

Not even if I were crazy would I guess the real, true meaning of those words [see the letter of 8 September 1934] and then write it to you who know how and why they issued from your heart. Don't ask the impossible of me, who has always barely been able to do things that are possible—and not always well. [. . .]

19-9-934

[. . .] I wish you could have come to San Cristoforo, to get to know this pretty locale that cheers me in my solitude, with its romantic lake and the silence that surrounds it! I was disturbed by my unexpected encounter with Luisa Baccara at Levico. All at once, I saw my illusions about your possible little trip over here disappear. But you say that, on the contrary, her presence could serve as a pretext for the little trip—and in that case, praised be the encounter and let's thank this good friend, whom I really found quite aged—and not only that, but I wouldn't have recognized her if she hadn't been the first to rush over enthusiastically to greet me. I hadn't seen her in eight or nine years, since I took Forzano to the Vittoriale to look after the arrangements with D'Annunzio regarding the performance of Saint Sebastian at La Scala! [. . .]

The pianist Luisa Baccara (1892–1985), a graduate of the Milan Conservatory and later a pupil of Leopold Godowsky, lived with D'Annunzio from 1920 until the end of his life. · Giovacchino Forzano (1884–1970), librettist and playwright, had acted as a sort of resident stage director at La Scala from 1923 until shortly after the end of AT's tenure there. · The Vittoriale was the palatial but kitschy home on Lake Garda where the Fascist government had ensconced D'Annunzio; he had been provided with a gen-

erous state pension on the understanding that he would behave himself politically. ·
Debussy and D'Annunzio had collaborated on *Le Martyre de Saint-Sébastien* and had
jointly invited AT to conduct its premiere in 1911; but he did not conduct it until
1926, at La Scala.

23-9-934

[. . .] Baccara told me that you will come here on Wednesday. I looked pleasantly surprised.

I take my meals at the same table with her. Now I'm beginning to redis-
cover the person I knew. She's still rather pretty, although a little aged. This
morning I received from Vienna a request to conduct Verdi's Requiem Mass on
28 October, in memory of Dollfuss! Of course I've accepted. [. . .]

Two months earlier, in a period of grave political instability, Engelbert Dollfuss
(1892–1934), the Christian Socialist chancellor of Austria, had been assassinated by a
pro-Nazi group that was attempting to seize power. AT accepted an invitation from
the Austrian government to conduct the Verdi *Requiem* at Salzburg in memory of the
slain leader; he saw the event as an anti-Nazi protest. But Dollfuss, who had become
chancellor in 1932, had fought the rising Nazis with their own weapons—in other
words, by using undemocratic methods: he had abolished Parliament, abrogated the
constitution, governed by emergency decree, allied Austria with Fascist Italy (he and
Mussolini were trying to use each other as buffers against Hitler), savagely put down a
rebellion by Social Democrats and workers, and declared the Social Democratic Party
illegal. In short, he had behaved like a dictator. AT had seen Dollfuss as the lesser of
two evils, but today his decision to participate in a solemn commemoration of the
chancellor seems ill advised.

[. . .] I phoned home the other day. Were you told? I wanted to know how
Wanda is doing. Since the princess was born, I thought she might have been
followed by little Sergio. [. . .]

From Vienna I've received the chancellor's thanks. These Viennese seem to
me like sandaled friars. They're always looking for handouts. I think Wanda
miscalculated by a month. Is it possible? Might the child want to be born on
the 28th? I'm nervous. I feel as if I, too, were having labor pains. [. . .]

Maria José, consort of Italy's Crown Prince Umberto, had recently given birth to a
daughter, and AT was joking that Wanda and Vladimir Horowitz's expected baby
ought to follow in short order. Whether or not Wanda had miscalculated is not
known, but "Sergio" (who turned out to be a girl and was given the name of Sonia) was
born only five days later, on 2 October 1934.

(TRENT), 27 SEPTEMBER 1934; TO GABRIELE D'ANNUNZIO, (GARDONE);
CARLO SANTOLI (ED.), *GABRIELE D'ANNUNZIO E ARTURO TOSCANINI: SCRITTI*
(ROME: BULZONI, 1999), PP. 43–4

My dear and much-loved D'Annunzio,

for a long time I had been exhorting myself—at times in a somewhat friendly way, at others rather brusquely—"You must go pay a visit to D'Annunzio," when your letter, together with your "most recent amulets," reached me. Thank you for the latter and even more for the former.

Now I can come to see you without fear of disturbing and offending your high-minded solitude, and I shall come on Saturday. You will see me on Saturday, and you will see on my face the joy that I cannot express to you at this moment.

It has been too long since we last saw each other! Too many years! And I believe that at our age, the years pass by too quickly.

We must see each other more often. Afterward, I shall be more courageous in coming to disturb your solitude, in interrupting your frequent fasts.

I'm sorry to learn that you are a bit ill in the flesh—as you say—and very ill in spirit. The spirit of Gabriele D'Annunzio, agitator of the masses and of souls, must never diminish, much less become ill. You have written to me, "It is beautiful and infinitely rare that you stand erect in your glory, with such firmness and purity." Not in glory, my dearest d'Annunzio, but in my disdain and contempt for mankind!

So then, we'll see each other the day after tomorrow.

Luisa seems to have benefited from the cure here, but the real, definitive one, the one that will make her as good as new again, is the one by the dramaturge of Piazze.

I embrace you in faithful, affectionate friendship
Your Arturo Toscanini

What trinkets or other items accompanied D'Annunzio's letter is not known to me. · AT had evidently advised Luisa Baccara to see Dr. Rinaldi in Piazze for whatever muscular problems she was having.

E.P. TRENT, 28 SEPTEMBER 1934; TO AM, 46VMPMI; FSD-FOF

28-9-934

I really can't stand it any longer. This Via Crucis three times a day is too much—more than 120 kilometers a day!

Tomorrow morning I've got the last appointment at 9:30, for my field of vision and other oculistic observations. Then I'll go directly to the Vittoriale. I think that Luisa Baccara and her sister will come with me. Lunch and chat with the Commander, then I'll rush to Milan. Regarding the Commander, in his long letter there were some interesting points, to which I think I replied simply but perhaps struck at the heart. Among other things, he wrote, "And it is beautiful and infinitely rare that you, with such firmness and such purity, stand erect in your glory." My comeback: "Not in glory, my dearest D'Annunzio, but in my disdain and contempt for mankind." I hope it registers. Other interesting points had their just replies, but as always I never remember what I've written or said, and it's not worth the slightest effort to bring back to mind a single word, if I haven't preserved it. [. . .]

"Via Crucis" refers to the constant traveling AT had to do between his hotel and the eye clinic where he was being treated. · AT uses ironically the title "the Commander," which D'Annunzio had given himself fifteen years earlier, when he and his irregular troops had occupied Fiume. AT admired but did not love D'Annunzio's poetry, and he could not stomach the poet's compromises with Mussolini; but he also knew that D'Annunzio's self-aggrandizement was in part self-mockery.

E.P. STRESA BORROMEO NOVARA, I OCTOBER 1934; TO AM, 46VMPMI; FSD-FOF

Milan is decidedly hostile to me. It would have been horrible if I hadn't taken advantage of those few minutes yesterday. Today I haven't been able to phone you, nor will I be able to later. I'm leaving, I'm going to the Isolino; I have to work. Invitations from all over have flooded me here, people everywhere are bothering me—even Senator Casati, who wants me to come to lunch [at his home] outside Milan, to get to know Benedetto Croce. I'm going to escape! escape! escape!

Senator Alessandro Casati (1881–1955), a Milanese count and Crocean liberal, had been minister of public education in 1924–25, during the early phase of Mussolini's prime ministry, but had since become an outspoken opponent of the regime. Benedetto Croce (1866–1952) was the most respected Italian philosopher of the first half of the twentieth century, and within Italy his antifascism was probably even better known than that of AT.

E.P. VIENNA, 18 OCTOBER 1934; TO AM, 46VMPMI; FSD-FOF

Are you still alive? Am I still alive? I've read your last letter for the second time—I'm desperate!!! Since C[arla]'s arrival I haven't been alone for a moment. Everyone loves me, everyone adores me, no one leaves me for a moment. I'm exhausted from work and from the burden of humanity.

No, it would have been useless for you to be here. I would never have seen you, except during the very first days, while I was alone.

Schnabel [*sic,* for Schnabl-Rossi], Zingarelli, Elsa Pick [Kurzbauer] [are here] at all hours, at all meals, at all the rehearsals!!! My God! If this hasn't killed me it's because God has given me ferocious powers of survival.

Write to me, but address [letters] to

Wiener Philharmoniker
Canovagasse 4

Tell me you love me, even if it's not true. I can't live without you. You've bewitched me. You're making me mad. I desire you to death, as I've never desired any woman. I'm a wretch. Take care of me. Only your love can relieve my immense suffering. I don't see and don't understand what I'm writing. I'm in a hurry, I'm in a hurry. I adore you.

Your Arturo

"Zingarelli": Probably the Neapolitan journalist Italo Zingarelli, who was active in Milan and Vienna during the 1930s.

E.P. VIENNA, 19 OCTOBER 1934; TO AM, 46VMPMI; FSD-FOF

Elsa Pick has gone shopping with Carla. She brought me this article by a writer who, she says, is very well known, also for having written novels. It's not a musical article—so she says—but it's very interesting. You'll tell me about it. She says that he talks about my smile. I hope he's not one of those unmentionable types. Elsa Pick assures me that the contrary is true.

[. . .] I'm tired. The ninth symphony kills me, but I adore it. [. . .]

The article was from an unidentified German-language newspaper: Felix Salten, "Feuilleton. Portraits from the Concert Hall. Toscanini." Salten (the nom de plume of Siegfried Salzmann, 1869–1945) was a journalist and fiction writer whose best-known book is *Bambi*.

In several instances, AT's girlfriends became friendly with his wife when their affairs with him ended, and this was the case with Elsa.

E.P. VIENNA, 27 OCTOBER 1934; TO AM, 46VMPMI; FSD-FOF

[. . .] I can't stand it any longer. I hate everyone around me, I hate myself, I have no love, sweetness, or immense passion except for one being who perhaps doesn't love me and who makes me suffer. The mass has been postponed as a result of a sort of plot here against the commemoration, instigated perhaps by Maestro Krauss. Meanwhile, I can't leave here until Thursday. I can't write to you as I'd like to, I've always got to hurry, anxiously and fearfully. I can't call you on the phone, I can only adore you, hate you, too, and be your slave for all eternity!

Arturo

The conductor Clemens Krauss (1893–1954), a musical disciple of Richard Strauss, was strongly pro-Nazi and is believed to have attempted to sabotage Toscanini's work in Vienna and Salzburg on more than one occasion. Late in 1934, when Furtwängler feuded with the Nazis and abandoned the direction of the Berlin State Opera, Krauss promptly took over the position.

TG, VIENNA, 28 OCTOBER 1934;
TO ZOLTÁN KODÁLY, ANDRASSY 89, BUDAPEST; PC; (EC?)

MASS POSTPONED PLEASE WIRE ME [WHETHER] SOPRANO BATHY ANNA'S VOICE RIGHT TO SING REQUIEM GREETINGS TOSCANINI

Anna Báthy (1901–62) was at that time the Budapest Opera's leading dramatic soprano, and she did indeed sing the Verdi Requiem with AT and the Vienna Philharmonic on 1 November 1934.

E.P. VIENNA, 31 OCTOBER 1934; TO AM, 46VMPMI; FSD-FOF

31-10-934

My Ada, what's going on around me is horrible. I haven't received your letter of the 20th, it was certainly stolen from me. It's cowardly. From now on I'll travel alone, alone, completely alone, I no longer want to be surrounded by spies, thieves, people who aren't ashamed of stealing others' things. I'm mortified, desolate, wounded to the bottom of my soul.

Tomorrow morning, the Requiem; in the evening I leave. I'll be in Milan Friday [2 November], in the afternoon. I'll call you. I want to see you. You alone can bring calm and sweetness to my heart. I can't stand any more of this. I hate everyone. I love only you. Don't abandon me.

Your Arturo

AT sometimes persuaded himself that people were stealing letters or telegrams that Ada had sent him, when in fact she had not written to him. Sometimes, however, communications intended for AT's eyes only were accidentally or intentionally intercepted by Carla; according to their daughter Wally, Carla would rarely confront her husband head-on when she found out about his affairs, serious or otherwise, but would become irritable and agitated.

E.P. PARIS, 19 NOVEMBER 1934; P.S., HÔTEL PRINCE DE GALLES, PARIS;
TO AM, 46VMPMI (CANCELED; IN ANOTHER HAND: HQR); FSD-FOF

18-11-934

Not to be able to write to you, not to be able to receive a single word from you, is like dying. I can no longer live without having some sort of contact with you. Sorceress!!

I was in bed for two days, the stubborn cough that was beginning to torture me during the <u>dear days</u> when you were here continued to worsen uninterruptedly till it finally kept me nailed to my bed.

I leave for Brussels in two hours. I'll come back on Wednesday. Let me find a couple of lines. Have the address written by another hand—<u>Théâtre Champs-Elysées.</u> The <u>reality was more beautiful than the dream!!</u> You're divine!! Unique!! Love me, and <u>forever.</u> I can't write any more. But I love you more and more!!

<u>Arturo</u>

Ada had just visited AT in Paris, and their love affair had been consummated during that visit. (AT had experienced sexual failure at an encounter with Ada in Milan a year earlier.)

E.P. BRUSSELS, (20 NOVEMBER?) 1934; P.S., HÔTEL ASTORIA, BRUXELLES; TO AM, 46VMPMI (CANCELED; IN ANOTHER HAND: HQR); FSD-FOF

<u>20-11-934</u>

[. . .] Tell me that you'll always remember <u>November 11,</u> tell me that I didn't <u>disappoint</u> you. At the same time, I'm shouting to the whole world that you gave me the greatest, the most un-hoped-for of joys; I would have liked to die immediately, because I felt I had reached the limits of happiness. <u>My Ada,</u> you are divine, and now I can say—<u>mine</u>—truly **mine.** I'll wire you. I want to let you know at what time I can phone you. I want to hear your voice. I'm dying of desire for that.

Those Paris days were the dearest, most beautiful, most divine of my life. Love me, and forever. Be my last, supreme love. I can't write more.

<u>Very much your Arturo</u>

"I'm shouting to the whole world" meant, of course, "I would like to shout to the whole world." AT was not only afraid of public scandal, he was also (usually) chivalrously unboastful, even among friends, with respect to his amorous adventures.

E.P. PS, 10 DECEMBER 1934; TO AM, 46VMPMI; FSD-FOF

<u>9-12-934</u>

[. . .] So tomorrow, Monday, the doctor is giving me a day off. Zirato will certainly pay me a visit. Then on Tuesday and Wednesday I'll resume the cure. Not until Thursday will I be able to leave for Florence with the 8:30 (morning) train. In that case, you should leave [Rome] with the 8:18. I'll get there a few hours before you. I'll come to meet you. I think it's best to stay at the Hôtel <u>Anglo-Americano</u> rather than at the usual Moderne. It would be ideal if we could arrange for rooms on the same floor; if not, we'll work things out. It's certainly a haul for you, but on the other hand any other arrangement would be difficult. If we don't see each other during the coming days, we won't see each other till who knows when. I don't know. After New York, I'll have only a few free days before going to London. You'll be in Rome, thus it will be impossible to see each other. I wish that my arm would protect <u>our love</u> by <u>not getting better</u>!! My God! How thankful I would be to Him!!! I love you so much, and I don't dare allow my thoughts to settle for a single instant on our cruel, inexorable separation.

Ada, help me to live without you. Help me, help me! Artù

AT was in Piazze for further treatments on his arm by Dr. Rinaldi. He and Ada did manage to meet in Florence, where they both attended performances at the Teatro Comunale, across the street from their chosen Hotel Anglo-Americano, and where they managed to repeat their Parisian success. · Artù—which is how Ada had begun to address AT—is the Neapolitan form of Arturo, but to Italian ears it has a regal-mystical ring: "Re Artù," is the Italian form of King Arthur.

E.P. MI, 7 JANUARY 1935, TO AM, HAZB; FSD-FOF

<u>6-1-935</u>

[. . .] As I told you on the phone, the other evening I had some very dear friends over for dinner: Lawyer Giussani with his wife, the Rusca couple, Giulio Foligno, Accountant Marzorati, and Lawyer Tessa (a magnificent dialect poet and unique reciter). Later, the Polos, Miecio, and Engineer Albertini's family with Count Cicogna came. Tessa recited, magnificently, several poems by Porta and some of his [own] best ones—surprising for their poetic beauty, the beauty of their new, unanticipated, and above all musical movements and rhythms. The last, Caporetto, is a real masterpiece, a portrait of an appalling reality. [. . .]

Camillo Giussani was at one time president of the Banca Commerciale Italiana, one of Italy's most important financial institutions; he was also a man of letters, author of modern Italian translations of Lucretius and Tacitus. · The Folignos, a Jewish family, were among the Toscaninis' best friends. · Accountant Eugenio Marzorati was Carla's adviser on the family's finances. · Count Giovanni Ascanio Cicogna, a Milanese nobleman, was active in the city's musical life; after World War II, he was on the board of directors of Euro International Films. · Carlo Porta (1775–1821) is the best-known of all Milanese dialect poets.

E.P. MI, 8 JANUARY 1935; TO AM, HAZB; FSD-FOF

<u>Noon 8-1-935</u>

I've just this moment gotten home. I think that the people I meet on the street after I've spoken with you must notice that my eyes sparkle with joy, that I fly rather than walk—my feet barely touch the earth, like Jesus' on the water. And these people don't even see the soul, the heart, that would allow them to know how much sunshine and how much light shine forth! Oh, my adored Ada, unique, holy creature who dominates my life—what do you want to do with me? What will you do in the future? What do you think you'll do with my <u>brief future</u>?

At the telephone office they no longer allow me even to utter a syllable: as soon as he sees me, the clerk immediately says <u>Bismarck 2000 Berlin,</u> greeting me with his most gracious smile! And I patiently await my turn under the surreptitious <u>but curious</u> glances of the bystanders. It bothers me a little, but the happiness that awaits me is far greater than this little annoyance. Unfortunately, tomorrow will certainly be the last time that I'll hear the dear voice, the gentle voice that gives me the <u>shivers</u> every time I hear it—but I don't despair of being able to hear it from beyond the ocean. [. . .]

AT phoned Ada from the telephone office at Piazza San Babila, a two- or three-minute walk from his home in Via Durini, so as not to run the risk of being overheard by family members or domestics.

E.P. NY, 18 JANUARY 1935; P.S., *CONTE DI SAVOIA* (STEAMSHIP); TO AM, HMP; FSD-FOF

Wednesday <u>16-1-935</u>

So we'll arrive tomorrow afternoon—a delay of nearly twelve hours. During the first four days the crossing was ideal, the Mediterranean was enchanting. Sun, sun, sun! (And where were you, my love?) And the ocean, until the Azores, was better than on any other crossing. Then the sky became gray, the sea tempest-tossed. Today we're still dancing involuntarily. Many became seasick, Stefan Zweig among them. This writer is a lovely person, interesting as a human being to the greatest degree. He gave me his life of Erasmus of Rotterdam in Mazzucchetti's translation, which is still in galleys. I've read it with the greatest interest. Magnificent! It's about the eternal struggle of the spirit against brute force. Erasmus and Luther. The latter wins, of course. I don't know whether they'll let him publish it without creating difficulties.

If there were a <u>saint,</u> as in Albertini's novel, I would supplicate him to send my most searing prayer to God so that He would grant me just <u>one year of life with you—with you—my Ada,</u> creature of my long-dreamt dream—and then he could send Death to take me. I would greet him serenely, cheerfully, resignedly. I'm not talking like a madman, but with the conviction born of a healthy brain and ready to give the most convincing proof of health.

Ada, don't forget me for an instant. Write me and tell me about your life, how you spend your days. Study, practice the piano. Play Brahms's music. Our spirits will meet. Practice the two Concerti. I'm studying them, too, to accompany them with Horowitz (the D minor) and with Gabrilowitsch the one in B flat. [. . .]

The "saint" is a character in *Due anni (Two Years)*, a novel published in 1934 by Alberto Albertini, brother of AT's friend Luigi Albertini. · AT conducted concerti relatively rarely on his concert programs, because he disliked both imposing his interpretive ideas on solo artists and having their ideas imposed on him. Thus the six all-Brahms programs that he presented with the New York Philharmonic in February, March, and April 1935 included the only performances he ever gave of the composer's Piano Concerto no. 1 in D Minor, op. 15, and were to have included his first performances of the Second Piano Concerto in B-flat Major, op. 86, with Ossip Gabrilowitsch (1878–1936) as soloist. AT esteemed Gabrilowitsch, who was married to Clara Clemens, Mark Twain's daughter, and who had taken a strong stand against fascism; but when, shortly after this letter was written, AT heard Gabrilowitsch play the same concerto with the National Orchestral Association, he decided that their views of the work were impossibly divergent and canceled the engagement. He did not conduct the concerto until the following season, with Robert Casadesus (1899–1972) as soloist.

E.P. NY, 19 JANUARY 1935; TO AM, 25VBMMI; FSD-FOF

Noon 19-1-935

[. . .] I found my friends here, as usual, full of affection. I saw Bruno Walter, in good health and with an unusually animated expression for him, who always seems to me a <u>weeping willow.</u> He doesn't have his wife with him, and this explains everything. He's with a daughter, the divorced one. Unfortunately, I fear that this is his last season with the Philharmonic. They want to have Furtwängler split the season with me next year. There have been too many conductors this year, and not very interesting at that.

I begin rehearsals on Monday (21st). <u>Bruckner</u> 7th Symphony, <u>Strauss</u> Dance of the Seven Veils (Salome), Bach-Respighi Prelude and Fugue in D Major, the one Horowitz played at the Quartetto. I kiss you as I did that time; do you remember? Florence? [. . .]

AT enjoyed a friendly relationship with Bruno Walter (1876–1962); he was often highly critical of Walter's interpretations, but for the most part he respected him. And Walter adored AT as both musician and human being. Contrary to commonly held belief, AT frequently recognized and respected other conductors' talents even when he objected to their interpretations or to their comportment on the podium. Some months later, when he made up his mind to retire from the New York Philharmonic, he recommended Furtwängler as his successor, despite their very different approaches to music and life; his dramatic and permanent break with his German colleague came only later, when Furtwängler chose a quixotic form of internal anti-Nazi protest-cum-coexistence within Germany instead of making a clean break, as AT himself had done. · AT had conducted the Adagio from Bruckner's Seventh Symphony in Turin in 1896, in memory of the recently deceased composer, but his only performances of complete Bruckner symphonies took place with the New York Philharmonic: the Fourth Symphony in 1932 and 1934 and the Seventh in 1931 and 1935. · The January 1935 performances of Respighi's orchestration of Bach's Prelude and Fugue in D Major were the only ones that AT gave.

E.P. NY, 29 JANUARY 1935; TO AM, 25VBMMI; FSD-FOF

28-I-935

My beloved Ada, I've finished my first week's work (4 concerts). Too many for me! It's a task for the young. I'm very worried about next year. It's not true that a year is 365 days long, at my age; it's much longer, it's eternal, and I feel the fatigue even if I don't show it. I always spend more than I take in; it's been this way all my life, but when one is thirty years old one can go into debt, certain of paying it off; but at nearly 68 one may become a defaulting payer! I've already let a few words fall on the manager's ears concerning my uncertainty about taking part next year. His eyes opened so wide that I thought they were going to pop out of his head. He told me that, on the contrary, he would like to make do with only two conductors, Furtwängler and me, plus one other to replace us in case of illness. I let him talk, but in my heart I know perfectly well that I'll make whatever decision is best for me. This morning I began rehearsing the second program. Piatigorsky has arrived. Tomorrow I'll read through Castelnuovo's new concerto. I've already rehearsed it at the piano with Piati, who seems to me to perform it well. I'll fill out the program with a Händel Concerto Grosso, to open, and Schubert's Symphony in C as the second part. Everyone—orchestra, audience, friends—says that life has begun with my arrival. I'll tell you the truth, my Ada, sometimes I need these spontaneous demonstrations of esteem, because I'm always afraid of not being up to the level of the task that has been put in my hands, and of not noticing it. It would be horrible! Unfortunately, there's never been a lack of examples, nor are they lacking now. I would be mortified to learn that people were saying, poor Toscanini (as they used to say poor Faccio, poor Mancinelli), he's no longer his old self!! I would like to end my career next year, once I've finished my fiftieth year of conducting, and I would like to end it full of enthusiasm and still more refined. Who knows—let's hope! [. . .]

AT amused himself by calling Piatigorsky "Piati" because of the similarity to the name of Alfredo Piatti (1822–1901), Italy's most celebrated solo cellist. Piatigorsky and AT gave the world premiere of the Cello Concerto by Mario Castelnuovo-Tedesco (1895–1968) at the Philharmonic's concerts of 31 January and 1 February 1935. (Piatigorsky's anecdotal account of his encounters with AT on this and other occasions can be found in his memoir, *Cellist* [Garden City, NY: Doubleday, 1965].) In 1938, when the Italian government passed anti-Semitic racial laws, AT helped Castelnuovo, who was Jewish, to immigrate to the United States with his family. · Franco Faccio (1840–91) and Luigi Mancinelli (1848–1921) were among the leading conductors of the generation before that of AT; Faccio's decline, however, was a result not of age but of insanity.

Thursday 31-1-935

Neither the <u>Champlain</u> nor the <u>Aquitania</u> has brought me a single letter from you. I'm disconsolate! For me, the sun shines <u>only one</u> day of the week: the day that brings me your news. I'm extremely disconsolate. No, you don't love me as I would like, you don't suffer, you're incapable of making a little sacrifice. I must say, like Mme. de Staël, <u>"I have never been loved as I love."</u> I won't write to you again, nor will I wire so insistently, so as not to bore you.

   <u>I'm waiting.</u>

I still adore you—Artù

PLEASE DON'T FOR ANY REASON GIVE UP COMING TO NEWYORK[.] IF YOU HAVE TO DELAY ALL RIGHT BUT COME[.] REMEMBER THAT YOU [PLURAL] ARE MY GUESTS NOR HAVE TO WORRY ABOUT ANYTHING I EMBRACE YOU [PLURAL] = PAPA =

[. . .] <u>Friday evening</u> 8-2-935

[. . .] I'm besieged by importunate people. I have to work a great, great deal. I'm not as well prepared as in other years. My eyes, with their treatment, betrayed me.

   Monday I'll begin the rehearsals for the Brahms cycle. I'm conducting much of the music for the first time. The <u>Requiem,</u> the <u>Liebeslieder Waltzes,</u> <u>the two piano concerti, the two Serenades,</u> the <u>Gesang der Parzen,</u> etc. I'm behind, but I hope to make it through. [. . .]

Friday <u>22-March 935</u>

[. . .] I still have four weeks of work. Six have gone by—21 concerts; 15 to go. The Brahms cycle is going full steam. Never have there been such sold-out houses, not even, I think, with Beethoven and Wagner. It's stupefying when you think that only ten or fifteen years ago Brahms was [considered] hard to digest. The Requiem was given a magnificent performance. I think I understood it and made it understood. I didn't much like it formerly, but having had to study it in depth I realized that I had been an ass to judge it so lightly, just from the notes, superficially. It's been a good lesson for me. And you weren't here!! This tortures me. You know that I always think of you when I work, that I'm proud that you feel that I'm not <u>the last</u> in line among the intelligent people you know, esteem, and love. You see how vain I've become? I've reached the point of sending you newspapers that talk about me!! When did I ever do such things? My father and mother were desperate because they never received news of my artistic doings, neither in writing from me nor as reported in the newspapers. And now? Don't you think that I've turned into a child? And it's for you, for you alone. How can I not remember that in three days I'll be 68 years old and I have the <u>nerve</u> to <u>love a creature</u> who <u>could easily be my daughter</u>—and how can I not be <u>ashamed of myself</u>!!! I'm sad, my Ada, sad to the point of tears. [. . .]

(NY); TO AM (MI?); FSD-FOF

Friday <u>29-3-935</u>

[. . .] I'm tired, I can't stand it anymore. More is demanded of me than I can give. When I think that <u>4 concerts</u> in London await me, all sold out already, and 8 opera performances plus two concerts at Salzburg, I'm terrified. I hope that God makes me take ill. This could still be a lifesaver for me!! If only you showed more interest, more fondness, more love for me, I could stand anything. Instead, I'm afraid of boring you with my complaints, with my unhappiness, with my demands. I'm an unhappy wretch. My mother left me this sad legacy. I can't, I simply can't write anymore. I love you, Ada—oh, how much I love you, my holy, unique creature—forgive me if I make you sad. [. . .]

E.P. NY, 12 APRIL 1935; TO AM, 25VBMMI; FSD-FOF

<u>12-4-935</u>

<u>My love,</u> I've also received your letter from the Conte di Savoia this morning. Oh, how vibrant your soul is in every word of these last two letters of yours!!! One can feel the tragedy coming!! And it has exploded in the last few days. What determined it? You didn't tell me during our brief telephone communications!! And yet some motive, some misunderstanding must have determined your resolution. Am I the cause?

I want to know. I'll phone you in a few days and you'll tell me everything, right? I just now sent you a night letter. I told you that the millstone weighing on my heart is the <u>chain</u> that I've been dragging behind me for years like a condemned man, without having the strength to free myself from it. I'm not religious, but I believe!! I have my strange superstitions. I had one father, one mother, they were there when I first saw the light of day. I've always thought that the companion I chose in life, like my father and mother, should never be replaced by any other woman. I realized immediately, after a few years, that I had made a mistake in my choice; the fault was entirely mine, I've never had the nerve to blame anyone except myself. I've never wanted to make totally unhappy a person who was in no way to blame, and I have dragged along—and continue to drag along—an unhappy life, and I continue to put up with this continual tragedy of the soul that will never, never end. You could give me the happiness that I've dreamt of for years, and what could I give you in exchange at my age? What will I be to you in a few years? Ah, my Ada, what suffering, what lacerations I have in my heart!!

I love you. I can't write anything else.

The clear implication is that something had happened between Ada and her husband that was making her seriously consider leaving him.

E.P. NY, 19 APRIL 1935; TO AM, 25VBMMI; FSD-FOF

19-4-935

[. . .] I'm not well. Over the last few days my shoulder has been hurting. As I told you in another letter, I've begun the injections that the doctor in Piazze ordered for me. In fact, on Wednesday (day of the concert), I imprudently had an injection given me after supper, and just as I was about to begin to conduct the concert I felt as if I were going to faint. I didn't say a word to anyone. But while I was conducting "Nuages" I felt dizzy. So much so that when I had finished the Nocturnes, I gave the cue to begin La Mer, and to my great surprise the Flutist, whom I hadn't looked at, began L'Après-midi d'un faune. Imagine how I felt! I really felt awful. After sweating a bit, at last, through La Mer, however, it all passed, and all that remained was a great weakness in my legs. Sonzogno had a great success with the audience, [but] the press is sour. [. . .]

On Wednesday, 17 April, and Thursday, 18 April 1935, AT conducted the Philharmonic in a program that consisted of Debussy's *Nuages* and *Fêtes* from the *Trois nocturnes,* the *Prélude à l'après-midi d'un faune,* and *La Mer,* followed by Giulio Cesare Sonzogno's *Il negro* and *Tango* and the overture to Verdi's *I vespri siciliani.*

Saturday <u>morning 4 o'clock</u>

[. . .] As soon as I'd finished the Missa Solemnis I had to go home and to bed with a 38-degree fever [100.4 degrees F.]. The fever continues; it's nothing, and I hope to conduct my last concert on Sunday.

My arm is in a completely disastrous condition. I'll have to go immediately to Piazze. [. . .]

Tuesday <u>7 May</u> [1935]

<u>My dear</u> Ada, this is the first day I've left my stateroom. I slept profoundly for the first two, and I made up for the sleepless nights in New York. I stayed in bed to rest my painful and tired shoulder and arm, too. Then Carla came down with a slight bronchitis. Very high fever and pains all over her body. So I never for a moment stopped helping her and keeping her company. Now her fever is down; she's weak and resting. I'm taking advantage of this to breathe a bit of air, the more so since the sun is shining magnificently and the sea is delightful. [. . .] Tomorrow morning at eight we'll land at Cherbourg. I'll be in Paris in the afternoon. I have no desire at all to spend many hours on the train. I'll very probably take the plane Friday morning at 10:15, and if the Zurich–Milan [route] is working I'll be in Milan by the afternoon. I'll have to stay two or three days to work out once and for all the Falstaff cast for Salzburg. Pinza has said no, and I'll have to settle for Stabile, who, according to the news that's reached me, seems to be in rather good <u>form.</u> Then I'll go immediately to Piazze to <u>be made good as new</u> again. I won't be able to stay there more than a couple of weeks, if that long, as I have to be in London by the 29th of this month. Will we see each other in Florence? Is it really true? Won't I die before then? My God, if I were at least in your dear arms, [I would die] <u>of love, of voluptuousness, of infinite joy</u>!!! [. . .]

Ezio Pinza's vocal register was low for the role of Falstaff, but AT evidently considered the artist's acting and enunciation so good as to override possible objections on purely vocal grounds; Pinza, however, who turned the proposal down, was presumably unwilling to take the risk. The baritone Mariano Stabile (1888–1968), who had been AT's favorite Falstaff at La Scala throughout the 1920s, did indeed return to sing the role with AT in Salzburg, not only in 1935 but also during the following two summers.

Tuesday <u>21-5-935</u>

<u>My Ada,</u> my trip to Florence seems to be in jeopardy. The doctor insists on extending the cure by a few days. I don't have much strength for arguing with him, and for that matter I can't linger [in Florence] for a stay of a few days. I absolutely have to leave early Saturday morning. [. . .]

My adored Ada, I have to bless New York a thousand times, despite the 4,000 miles that separated me from you; at least I could write to you, send you telegrams, phone you when I wished. Here it's impossible. We're living too close together—not only with C[arla] but with Wanda and her husband, in two apartments joined together. There is no telegraph office at the hotel, as there is at the Astor; to phone is impossible, my <u>double,</u> Margherita, isn't here, and even if she were I couldn't make use of her. So I'm suffering more in Europe than in America. I knew this would happen. And so it will be in the coming months. [. . .]

Although Margherita De Vecchi was on excellent terms with Carla, she also helped AT to arrange his telephonic and telegraphic trysts with Ada and probably also with other lady friends.

<u>My dearest,</u> My ailing arm leaves me a complete wreck. The extremely short cure at Piazze didn't work. I'm writing to you with difficulty, but I'm taking advantage of Carla's absence to give you my news. Have you received a letter of mine of a few days ago? I've already done two concerts; with great effort I was able to rehearse the second program this morning. Tomorrow morning I'll have the second rehearsal, and Sunday and Monday I'll rest. Meanwhile, I'm looking after myself as best I can. My shoulder and right arm are smeared with an Antiphlogistine Dressing [last two words in English in the original] and bound up. I have to keep them like this for twelve hours. Tomorrow morning we'll see the results. Right now, the sharp pain that I had last night and today after the rehearsal has stopped. [. . .] I've found an excellent, intelligent orchestra that immediately showed me liking and affection.

The concerts have aroused much enthusiasm. They have been broadcast. Did you hear any of them? Tommasini is here. He even attends the rehearsals. [. . .]

The "excellent, intelligent orchestra" was the BBC Symphony Orchestra, which in those days was generally considered the finest British symphonic ensemble and which had been trained by Adrian (later Sir Adrian) Boult (1889–1983). At the age of sixty-eight, AT was working with a British musical organization for the first time in his life, and despite his physical problems he thoroughly enjoyed the experience.

TYPED COPY OF TG, (LONDON), 11 JUNE 1935; PROBABLY TO BRUNO ZIRATO
(WHO MAY HAVE TRANSLATED THIS MESSAGE FROM ITALIAN),
NEW YORK PHILHARMONIC, NY; ORIG. ENG.; NYPA

I CANNOT UNDERSTAND WHY PHILHARMONIC BOARD HAS NOT THE COURAGE TO FIGHT TO THE LIMIT IN ORDER TO HAVE ITS SACRED RIGHTS RECOGNIZED INSTEAD OF YIELDING AND THEREFORE SACRIFICING SO MANY MUSICIANS WHO WILL INCREASE UNEMPLOYMENT STOP IF YOU INSIST IN REDUCING ORCHESTRA I WILL HAVE TO RESIGN!
                    ARTURO TOSCANINI

The musicians union in New York was making demands of the Philharmonic's management that were causing the board to consider reducing the orchestra from 110 to 95 players. Hans Lange had been dispatched to London to put the matter before AT, and Lange communicated the details of AT's negative reaction in a letter that I quoted in my biography of AT.

E.P. LONDON, 13 JUNE 1935; P.S. AS IN LETTER POSTMARKED
5 JUNE 1935; TO AM, 46VMPMI; FSD-FOF

Thursday 13-[6-]1935

I've seen on the last page of the Corriere that many furnished apartments are available. Have you thought about it, have you looked after it for us? [. . .]

For a period that I have not been able to determine, AT paid for the rental of an apartment in Via Monte Bianco—in what, in those days, were the westernmost outskirts of Milan—where he and Ada met whenever both were in town at the same time.

E.P. PN, 5 JULY 1935; P.S., ISOLINO S. GIOVANNI,
PALLANZA (WITH PHOTO OF THE ISOLINO); TO GS, ASP; SR

4-7-935

[. . .] I have already begun the preparatory work for Salzburg. I come and go between Milan and the Isolino every day. I'm already working with the singers for Falstaff [. . .].

    [. . .] Don't you think that after all the good Lord looks after organizing our doings so as to keep them from collapsing, and that the difficulties He's trip-

ping you up with are for the best? Think about it! We're so weak, we human
beings!!! [. . .]

E.P. SALZBURG, 26 JULY 1935; TO AM, HWMC; FSD-FOF

25-7-935

My Ada—all mine—your dearest letter arrived today while I was going to the
second ensemble rehearsal (singers and orchestra) of Falstaff, as a reward for
my efforts!! Thank you, my treasure, divine, holy creature, who brightens my
life!!! I didn't read you immediately—no, I couldn't. There were too many
curious, profane eyes around! I held you near all through the rehearsal. I held
out incredibly—as I often do, for that matter, when I'm near you. Isn't that
right, my treasure? I worked with love and with holy humility, as always when
I approach this miraculous Falstaff. How I felt your presence! I believe, in fact
I'm sure, that if you were present during the rehearsals for this jewel, you
would love me much more. At this point, I'm a being who has to be loved
more spiritually than materially. I don't know, but it seems to me that no one
will ever be able to say about me that I have been, because in art I still feel that
I must become. But I would like you to judge me, to tell me whether this is
an illusion of mine or reality. [. . .]

E.P. SALZBURG, 27 JULY 1935; TO AM, HWMC; FSD-FOF

27[-7-35] morning

[. . .] My arm is no good; fortunately, the rehearsals are spread out, so that with
a few applications of antiphlogistine the inflammation is reduced a bit. [. . .] I
was satisfied, indeed very satisfied, with the Falstaff rehearsals and with all the
singers, when—wouldn't you know it—Dusolina Giannini (Alice) became ill,
and it's another piece of luck that she can be replaced with Caniglia for the first
performances. [. . .]

The references are to the well-known sopranos Dusolina Giannini (1902–86) and
Maria Caniglia (1905–79). In the end, both of them sang the role of Alice in *Falstaff*
with AT at Salzburg.

E.P. SALZBURG, 29 JULY 1935; TO AM, HWMC; FSD-FOF

Monday 29-7-935

[. . .] This evening Falstaff opens. Yesterday evening we had the dress rehearsal.
There was an audience. [. . .] Caniglia isn't better than Dusolina Giannini (the

latter is more musical and intelligent), but she has a good voice and looks good. There was enthusiasm, starting with the orchestra players, who, at the end, stood up and gave a warm, affectionate display, and the chorus on stage joined with the audience in the auditorium, increasing the enthusiasm. [. . .]

E.P. SALZBURG, 31 JULY 1935; TO AM, HWMC; FSD-FOF

31-7-935

[. . .] Falstaff was accorded a truly sincere and enthusiastic success. All the singers were calm and assured; they seemed to be singing a last performance, rather than a first one. The performance was precise, well coordinated, magnificent.

[. . .] This year I have the great good fortune of having a house. It's located three kilometers from Salzburg. It's really comfortable, delightful, in the midst of greenery with a magnificent mountain range all around. The village, Liefering, is far enough that I don't feel the burden [of being in town] but not so far as to make one feel totally isolated. Thus I've avoided the disturbances and annoyances of the hotel—admirers, male and female, always bothersome, and male and female autograph hunters, not to mention amateur photographers. [. . .]

E.P. SALZBURG, 4 AUGUST 1935; TO AM, HWMC; FSD-FOF

4-8-935

[. . .] Yesterday, too, Falstaff went well. There were lots and lots of people, everything was sold out. Elsa Pick [Kurzbauer] arrives today. Miecio is already here. My house is full: all of the Polos, with daughter and daughter-in-law; Walter with his son and Cia; Wally and Wanda with their respective spouses will be here for a few days in the middle of the month. I'm in the midst of the last Fidelio rehearsals. At the rehearsal for orchestra only, when I reached the end of the first act, Rosé, the concertmaster, stood up and said, in front of the whole orchestra, "Maestro, this is the first time that I've heard this finale at the right tempo. I've played Fidelio with Richter, Mahler, Strauss, Schalk, Strauss [sic], etc., but I've never heard it like this." The praise of this old musician gave me great pleasure. And I take pleasure in communicating it to you because you'll love me even more. [. . .]

Franz Schalk (1863–1931) was for many years principal conductor of the Vienna State Opera.

Tuesday 13-8-935

[. . .] I was very worried about my arm. I did a short-wave treatment that people told me was excellent. It was Rodzinski who suggested it to me. He got great results from it. Mine were so-so. [. . .] I left by plane for Salzburg on July 17 [. . .]. I worked rather hard; my arm behaved like a gentleman. Everything went well, with both Falstaff and Fidelio. I think they'll broadcast the two productions over the radio. On Thursday I'll have my first concert. [. . .]

[. . .] In September I'll stay on the lake to rest—I need this a lot. No one thinks about my 68 years. I evidently give the illusion of not being so old. But I am. [. . .]

E.P. SALZBURG, 28 AUGUST 1935; TO AM, VSCA; FSD-FOF

26 [*sic,* for 27-8-35] Tuesday night

[. . .] The last Fidelio performance is Saturday the 31st. I thought I'd leave Sunday, but the airplane doesn't leave until Monday. Another twenty-four hours of suffering. If only you were in Milan that day! Then I'll go to the Isolino. [. . .]

The Falstaff performances had a triumphal outcome with the audience. Never had so many people been present! And so many Italians! So many acquaintances! You alone were missing. What a tragedy for my soul!! [. . .]

E.P. SALZBURG, 29 AUGUST 1935; TO AM, VSCA; FSD-FOF

[. . .] I've met in person a cellist, one Cassadó, who, I'm told, is the lover of old Giulietta Mendelssohn. Her daughter, Eleonora—very simpatica, an admirer of mine for years, who attends a great many of my concerts in New York but whom I'd never seen—presented me with a magnificent little painting by Guardi, delightful, more beautiful than the one I already have. I'm told that she is divorced from the pianist Edwin Fischer and abandoned by a second husband. Strange! She seems to be an intelligent woman, too! It's clear that intelligence counts for little in intimate relations!!! I can't begin to tell you how many Italians came to the Festival! It was a real carnival. There were many of our common friends. Never had so many foreigners attended! Forty percent more than in previous years. They call me The Arturo! But you call me simply dear Artù, and you move me much more. My divine one, how I love you. I wanted to send you a book about me by Paul Stefan—it came out not long ago with a preface by Stefan Zweig—but how to go about it? For me to buy one myself would be impossible—it would be like buying the [illegible word]—and I don't have a Margherita here who is friendly to me; so I've given up!

They've had the preface translated into Italian by Mazzucchetti, and they tell me it's very nice because very true (according to friends and my family members), and 100 copies have been printed (not for sale), plus two copies, A. and B., for Zweig and me. I'll give you a copy in Milan. Vuillermoz, the music critic for Excelsior and Candide, was here, and as usual he practically wrote a poem about the Falstaff and Fidelio performances. All well and good, but the dearest, most adored person, the one who would have represented the greatest reward for my efforts, didn't come; she was missing. [. . .]

Gaspar Cassadó (1897–1966) was the best-known Spanish cellist of the generation after that of Pablo Casals. Giulietta Gordigiani Mendelssohn, an old acquaintance of AT, was married to a banker who was a great-nephew of Felix Mendelssohn; she had been a close friend of Eleonora Duse and had named her daughter after the great actress. According to Friedelind Wagner (the composer's granddaughter, who knew AT well from 1930 on), Eleonora Mendelssohn, who was herself an actress, had been the lover of Max Reinhardt but had then fallen in love with AT, with whom she had an affair in America during the 1940s. Her former husband was the Swiss pianist Edwin Fischer (1886–1960). · The Austrian music critic Paul Stefan (1879–1943) wrote a brief biography of AT (*Arturo Toscanini. Mit einem Geleitwort von Stefan Zweig* [Vienna: H. Reichner, 1936]); this edition was followed shortly thereafter by American and Italian editions, the latter translated by Livia Mazzucchetti (1889–1965), the leading Italian expert on German literature of her generation and an admirer of AT's art. AT was embarrassed about buying a copy of a book about himself to send to Ada. · Émile Vuillermoz (1879–1960) was a well-known French music critic.

E.P. MUNICH, 2 SEPTEMBER 1935; TO AM, VSCA; FSD-FOF

Munich 2-9-935

My sole, adored creature

The inconvenient part of this flight is the stop of a few hours here among the Germans, but today I bless it. It's a beautiful day! For some days the sun has been shining superbly. Salzburg was marvelous these last days—not a cloud in the sky. I enjoyed the light, air, and peace from the terrace of the adorable little house I was living in, because I was alone, completely alone, for many hours. This terrace is situated as if at the center of a circle, so I enjoyed the dawn's sweetness, the splendor of noon, and the sunset's luminous magnificence. You should see me—I'm as tan as if I'd been at the beach or high up in the mountains. How I thought of you, my Ada! I was thinking how divinely beautiful it would have been to make love in each of those sublime moments. To Enjoy, to Adore, to be Silent! To love! [. . .] I knew that you would be listening to Fidelio; I don't know whether you felt the fire running through my blood the whole evening. I wanted to please you. The performance was unique for warmth and enthusiasm, on everyone's part. So it seemed to me, and to others as well. Everyone was moved. Next year I'll conduct the same operas, plus Meistersinger. [. . .]

E.P MI, (9?) SEPTEMBER 1935; P.S., ISOLINO S. GIOVANNI, PALLANZA;
TO AM, VSCA; FSD-FOF

My <u>most beloved,</u>

I always forget that my Ada resembles a magnificent <u>Andante calmo</u> [calm, walking pace], and I an <u>Allegro concitato</u> [agitated, fast pace]. When I wire you at the beginning of the week to write me <u>immediately, immediately</u> at the Isolino, I ought to get it into my head that I'll receive word the following Saturday or Sunday. Instead, I always fall into the trap, never losing hope that you'll change once and for all!!! I was convinced that I'd receive your news on Wednesday. Since Carla received the mail that morning, purely by chance, and although I saw with my own eyes that there were no tricks, I took it into my head that she had removed your letter. I spent Thursday and Friday like a madman. I wanted to wire you, but then worry over learning the truth that I feared persuaded me not to do it; I wanted to go through her papers, through her purse, but this filled me with horror. I made a thousand conjectures, everything except the thought that you hadn't written to me. Saturday morning everything vanished as soon as I read the first lines of your adored letter. Naughty creature! Why do you make me suffer and push me to write you rash letters? Have you received Zweig's preface? How is it? I haven't yet read it. [. . .]

E.P. PN, 16 SEPTEMBER 1935; P.S. AS IN PREVIOUS LETTER;
TO AM, 46VMPMI; FSD-FOF

<u>14-9-935</u>

When I work, I don't have time to think about my country's sad, tragic current condition. It's a truly terrible situation. I've always thought that preaching peace and building up arms at the same time was absurd and monstrous! An arms race means war. It stands to reason that loaded firearms will go off in nations' hands one day or another. I don't know how it will end! What's certain is that we're in the hands and at the mercy of a man who's mad, delinquent, paranoid, syphilitic—and I'll put a period here, but the list could go on. [. . .]

The man described in the last sentence quoted above was, of course, Mussolini.

Wednesday 18-9-935

<u>My Ada,</u> The Isolino has become a place of enforced confinement since you've been in Milan. I can't phone you, because when I go to Pallanza everyone follows me. Everyone needs to buy something. At home it's impossible. So I eat my heart out, not to mention my soul, my guts. Saturday, I leave for Basel by airplane. I'm going to the Busches' to attend a performance of the Brandenburg C[oncerti]. I'll stay through Sunday and Monday. I don't think **she** will come. I think she asked Roberto to reserve a seat for me, not two seats. I haven't asked, but you could find out from Roberto himself. If she stays home, <u>couldn't you make the flight?</u> My God! My God! [. . .]

The violinist Adolf Busch (1891–1952) was one of the musicians most respected by AT, who also held in high esteem Adolf's brothers Hermann (1897–1975), a cellist, and Fritz (1890–1951), a very well known conductor, as well as Adolf's son-in-law, the pianist Rudolf Serkin (1903–91). The fact that the Busches were non-Jewish Germans who had exiled themselves from Nazi Germany raised them even higher in AT's estimation, and throughout the 1930s and 1940s the Busch and Toscanini families were often in touch with each other.

<u>My love</u>
I'm besieged by the Busches, but I've managed to avoid going to stay at their place. I'm distressed not to be here when you arrive. I'll be back as early as possible. My room is No. 27, second floor. Where will you be? I'm dying of desire to see you. I feel it will be as if I'd never seen you. You're always marvelously new. God bless you. Wait for me. I can't wait to hear your voice, to hear you repeat that you love me. Big kisses in advance, infinite love, ever growing madness.

<u>Artù</u>

FROM THE NEWSPAPERS YOU WILL HAVE LEARNED OF THE BARBAROUS KILLING MY BELOVED DOCTOR RINALDI AM APPALLED WILL STAY FOR FUNERAL MONDAY WILL PHONE TOMORROW MORNING AFFECTIONATELY = ARTU

Rinaldi had been brutally murdered by thugs outside his clinic in Piazze. His death was probably connected with his outspoken antifascism, but the details presented at his assassins' trial were inconclusive.

Tuesday <u>8 October</u>

[. . .] I'm looking at a symphony by an American composer that I'll have to perform later on in America, and it takes up time, and maybe it's also a <u>waste</u> of time. Nevertheless, I promised to perform it, and I'll keep my promise. My heart is grieving over the news coming in from Africa. Poor humanity! And this poor beautiful country of ours! This is the proof of how dictatorships govern countries. As soon as they can't hide their terrible and no longer disguisable internal difficulties, they distract attention with foreign war adventures. We're at the mercy of a mad criminal! Poor us! [. . .]

Which American composer AT was referring to is unclear, because he performed no American works during the 1935–36 season. · The "news coming in from Africa" refers to Italy's invasion of Ethiopia, which had begun five days earlier and ended with the capture of Addis Ababa the following May. In Italy there was widespread support for this colonialist military campaign, even among members of some of the underground parties of the left that were in other respects violently opposed to Mussolini; once again, AT's independent political opinion was "unsophisticated" but consistent.

[. . .] Yesterday I finished my work [with the Vienna Philharmonic], and I can't tell you how much effort and pain it cost me! Never in my life have I gone through a sadder period! I swear to you that I thought I would go mad. To see to what point the Italians' conscience or <u>lack of conscience</u> has reached inspires terror. If I didn't love my country, my home, and the Italians themselves madly, I swear to you that I would go off to China, to Japan, where I would be silent, and I wouldn't want to have any contact with the human race! [. . .]

The reference is again to Italy's war against nearly defenseless Ethiopia.

Friday <u>20-12-935</u>

[. . .] I worked like an automaton [in Vienna]. I hated my work, and at the same time it was my salvation. I didn't want to return to Italy anymore. But the hope of finding you was too strong. And then I had to get my equilibrium back. Will we see each other? When? Will you be alone? I'm leaving for Monte Carlo on the 27th. I don't know whether I told you that I'll conduct there on January 1, the 3rd in Marseilles, the 6th in Nice. If only you were to come to Monte Carlo, to your brother's! I love you, Ada, so very, very much! More than before! You're even dearer to my soul. [. . .]

AT performed works of Beethoven, Debussy, Wagner, and Verdi with the Monte Carlo orchestra.

E.P. NY, 20 FEBRUARY 1936; P.S., HOTEL ASTOR, NEW YORK; TO AM, 46VMPMI; FSD-FOF

20-2-936

[. . .] I'll leave off here; in a few hours I have a concert, with Serkin playing. Beethoven's 4th Concerto and Mozart's last Concerto, in B Flat. [. . .]

The concert in question, with the New York Philharmonic, was the thirty-three-year-old Rudolf Serkin's debut in the United States.

E.P. NY., 26 FEBRUARY 1936; P.S. AS IN PREVIOUS LETTER; TO AM, 46VMPMI; FSD-FOF

2 hours after midnight
26-2-1936

[. . .] This evening I conducted a concert in <u>Hartford</u> and I was thinking only about the music I was conducting and about you, who embellished every note that was unleashed by the marvelous orchestra. But you perhaps, or rather certainly, weren't thinking about me, the man who loves you madly—and not only that, but who can't blame you, however much he would like to, because nature is your friend, a cruel stepmother only to me. <u>How angry it makes me!!!</u>

Ada, have you been so cold, so indifferent toward all the men who have loved you? Why? There is a lack of sensuality in you that contrasts with the sensuality that you create in others to an incredible degree. How much suffering you cause, without any suffering on your part!!! Might this be the reason, the cause that distanced E[nrico] from you? I, on the contrary, feel more and more attracted to you, in an uncontrollable fever and delirium, and forever—I feel it, I'm sure of it. Big kisses all over your wonderful body. Artù

The concert in question—with the New York Philharmonic in Hartford, Connecticut, on the evening of 25 February—consisted of works by Weber, Beethoven, Saint-Saëns, Goldmark, and Wagner.

TG, (NY), 9 MARCH 1936; TO SERGE KOUSSEVITZKY, BOSTON SYMPHONY
ORCHESTRA, BOSTON; ORIG. ENG.; LOC, KOUSSEVITZKY COLLECTION

MY FAMILY AND MYSELF WILL BE SIMPLY DELIGHTED TO ACCEPT MME KOUS-
SEVITZKY AND YOUR VERY KIND INVITATION FOR SUPPER ON MONDAY AFTER
THE CONCERT CORDIAL GREETINGS
ARTURO TOSCANINI

This was a reply to an invitation wired to AT earlier the same day by Koussevitzky. AT
conducted the New York Philharmonic in Boston on Monday, 16 March, and Koussevitzky hosted a dinner party afterward at the Copley Plaza Hotel.

E.P. NY, 11 APRIL 1936; P.S. AS IN LETTER OF 20 FEBRUARY 1936; TO AM,
HIR; FSD-FOF

10-4-936

[. . .] Two weeks' work remain, then—all is done. I'll leave my orchestra forever, with a sorrow that words cannot tell but that you can understand. Is this
perhaps the beginning of the end? Who knows!! What's certain is that every-
one here is sad, and they can't get used to the fact that I'm leaving them
forever. As a result of a lot of idle chat and diatribes in the newspapers,
Furtwängler, who had been engaged, has had to turn down his contract. The
Jews had attacked him furiously. Four or five conductors have been engaged—
Barbirolli from London and Rodzinski, who is currently conductor of the
Cleveland Orchestra, Enesco and Stravinsky as composer-conductors, and one
Chávez, a Mexican. The season has been shortened by six weeks, reduced to 24.
I have also given up my London concerts. I wouldn't have had time to rest
before Salzburg. On the other hand, I'll go to Palestine in October. As an honorary Jew I have agreed to conduct some concerts there. And then what will I
do with myself? I don't know. I know that I still feel very active and not gone
soft at all—as they say about men my age—but I'm tired of feeling responsible toward the orchestra, toward the audience, toward myself. During the last
few days I let myself be persuaded to make a few records, after six years of
refusing. I made the Beethoven 7th, the Siegfried Idyll, Siegfried's Rhine
Journey, the two Lohengrin preludes, the Brahms variations, the Semiramide
overture and that of the Italiana in Algeri. Next week I'm doing an all-
Debussy program: an excerpt from St. Sebastian, the Après-midi d'un Faune,
the two Nocturnes Nuages and Fêtes, Ibéria, in the first part of the program;
La Demoiselle élue and La Mer in the 2nd. During the last week I'll repeat my
first program from 1925 [sic]: Euryanthe Overture and Haydn's Clock symphony, the Swan of Tuonela, Siegfried's death and funeral march, and the Pines
of Rome. [. . .]

AT's sixty-ninth birthday had taken place barely more than two weeks earlier, and the fiftieth anniversary of his professional conducting debut was coming up less than three months later. His dark thoughts about his immediate future may make us smile, because we know that his career lasted eighteen more years, but the fact is that as he aged, he never stopped examining himself for signs of weakness. As to his successors in the Philharmonic leadership: AT had recommended Furtwängler because he respected him as a musician (although he disagreed with him as an interpreter and considered him arrogant and too hungry for public approval) but also, in all likelihood, because he knew that Furtwängler had had some serious confrontations with the Nazi regime in his native country and felt that the Philharmonic post would give him an alternative worthy of his high standing. On the almost certainly correct assumption that Furtwängler would not have wanted to conduct an entire season of twenty-four to thirty weeks, AT had recommended Artur Rodzinski (1892–1958) to share the season. The Philharmonic's board of directors had followed AT's recommendations, and Furtwängler and Rodzinski had accepted the proposal. Furtwängler, however, did not want to give up working in Germany, and this ambivalent attitude became a matter of ferocious controversy in New York, where a large percentage of the musical public was Jewish. In the end, Furtwängler turned down the position, saying that art and politics must not mix. Furtwängler's admirers never tire of declaring that their man's intellectual sophistication was much greater than AT's, but AT—who agreed that art and politics should not be mixed—quickly grasped the fact that Nazis and Fascists were not garden-variety politicians and that the issue was moral, rather than either artistic or political. He never forgave Furtwängler for not having taken a definite stand by abandoning Germany. The Philharmonic then engaged John Barbirolli (1899–1970), an Englishman of Franco-Italian descent, and Rodzinski as coconductors for the first post-AT season—a season that, without the benefit of AT's enormous popularity, entailed severe economic cutbacks for the institution and the players. · AT had been scheduled to conduct the BBC Symphony again in the spring of 1936, but contractual problems and fatigue made him cancel the engagement. · Once again we have a comment by AT about being an "honorary Jew" (see the letter of 26 January 1934), a comment that is less amusing today than he intended it to be at the time. AT here gives a fair summation of his reasons for leaving the Philharmonic: although he felt that he was still in good form, he no longer wanted the exhausting responsibility of conducting five rehearsals and four performances a week, even if only for fifteen weeks a year. · AT's Wagner recordings with the Philharmonic were made on 8 February, 1936, not "a few days" before this letter was written. The other pieces mentioned, however, were recorded on the day before and the day of the letter. · In the end, AT added two further concerts to his last Philharmonic season: a Mozart, Beethoven, and Schubert program on 26 April and a Beethoven-Wagner program on the 29th.

E.P. NY, 14 APRIL 1936; P.S. AS IN PREVIOUS LETTER; TO AM, HIR; FSD-FOF

6 p.m.

I've just this moment returned from the rehearsal. I rehearsed Iberia. The music's sensuality made my blood rush every which way. Oh, give me, give me!! No sooner did I reach the hotel than I got your letter! Do you understand now why I'm writing in blood??? [. . .]

"Dammi, dammi" ("Give me, give me") is apparently what Ada called out at moments of intense passion; AT often quotes this in his letters to her. · He did occasionally use his blood as ink for a paragraph or two in these letters.

(NY); P.S. AS IN PREVIOUS LETTER; TO BIDÙ SAYÃO, (NY);
PC; NYPLTL

Dearest Signora Bidù

I am sending you the <u>high notes</u> that I think ought to be suitable. They aren't <u>difficult</u> because they more or less follow the orchestra's melodic line. You are a good enough musician to adapt immediately to these few changes. With my most cordial greetings,

Arturo Toscanini

14-April 1936

The Brazilian soprano Bidù Sayão (1902–99) sang in Debussy's *La Damoiselle élue* with AT and the New York Philharmonic on 16, 17, and 19 April 1936. AT evidently made some adjustments in the vocal line of this early work, presumably because he felt that the voice would not be heard otherwise.

TG, NY, 30 APRIL 1936; TO AM, HIR; FSD-FOF

IT WAS A UNIQUE UNFORGETTABLE PROFOUNDLY MOVING EVENING AND I FEEL DEEPLY THE SADNESS OF AN EPOCH ENDED NEVER TO RETURN STOP I WANT TO HEAR YOUR VOICE AGAIN I'LL CALL YOU SAME TIME I CAN'T STAND ANY LONGER NOT TO SEE YOU LOVE YOU WORSHIP YOU GIVE ME GIVE ME MORE AND MORE

AT was commenting on his farewell concert, the previous evening, as principal conductor of the New York Philharmonic, a concert that so many people had wanted to attend that mounted police had had to keep the crowds from storming Carnegie Hall.

E.P. NY, 1 MAY 1936; P.S., HOTEL ASTOR/TIMES SQUARE/NEW YORK;
TO PRESIDENT FRANKLIN D. ROOSEVELT, THE WHITE HOUSE,
WASHINGTON, D.C.; ORIG. ENG. (ALL ERRORS HAVE BEEN PRESERVED); FDRL

May 1-1936

Dear <u>Mr. President</u>

I am deeply touched to receive your letter. It will remain among the most precious of the souvenirs which I shall take from your country where I have spent so many happy years.

I shall never forget with that kindness and true understanding I have been received by the American people. I leave with sadness in my heart but with memories to enrich the year to come.

Faithfully yours,
Arturo Toscanini

Part Four

JULY 1936–
SEPTEMBER 1937

1936   Adds *Die Meistersinger* to his Salzburg repertoire; goes to Palestine at his own expense to conduct inaugural concerts of new orchestra (today's Israel Philharmonic) made up of Jewish refugees from Central Europe (returns in 1938).

1937   Adds *The Magic Flute* to his Salzburg repertoire.

DRAFT OF TG, (MI?), N.D. BUT EARLY JULY 1936;
TO BRUNO ZIRATO, (NY); PC; NYPLTL

I HAVE HEARD WAGNER RECORDS THEY ARE SHAMEFUL FOR VICTOR[,] FOR
MUSICAL EXPERTS WHO APPROVED THEM [AND] FOR ME WHO SHOULD HAVE
TRUSTED ONLY MY OWN EARS (STOP) I AM SURPRISED THEY ARE ALREADY
BEING SOLD I WOULD LIKE TO WARN THE PUBLIC NOT TO BUY THEM (STOP)
PLEASE ADVISE VICTOR THAT ROSSINI BRAHMS (BEETHOVEN) WILL HAVE
TO HAVE EXCLUSIVELY MY (APPROVAL) I REPEAT ONCE AGAIN WAGNER
RECORDS ARE SHAMEFUL ON ANY APPARATUS ELECTRICAL OR OTHERWISE—
GREETINGS

TOSCANINI

AT had made a series of recordings with the New York Philharmonic during the early
months of 1936. He later changed his mind about the quality of the performances
and/or the sound; presumably he had listened to the discs on inferior equipment. AT's
Philharmonic recordings are generally considered to be among his greatest, and some
of them are widely held to be among the greatest orchestral recordings ever made.

E.P. PN, 4 JULY 1936; P.S., ISOLINO S. GIOVANNI; TO AM, 46VMPMI; FSD-FOF

3-7-1936

"Pleasures tasted sparingly and with difficulty have always a higher relish,
whilst everything that is easy and common grows stale and insipid."

Héloïse [in English in the original]

[. . .] I need [to relax] before setting about the fearful Salzburg task. Twelve
opera performances, two concerts, and respective rehearsals in a little over
a month seem to me quite a tour de force for a young guy of nearly seventy! [. . .] In my youth I read the love letters of Abélard and Héloïse, but in
French; the other day, at Isola Pescatori, my friend Ugo Ara, who didn't know
them, was reading them in English. The excerpt I've transcribed attracted my
attention. Héloïse has come to help me. [. . .]

E.P. PN, 11 JULY 1936; TO AM, 46VMPMI; FSD-FOF

[. . .] Wednesday evening, while you were leaving the beautiful lake, I was
working full steam; amidst the Meistersinger's sublime notes, my thoughts
ran to the sweet mental image of you, from time to time. In the brief moments
of truce, I re-evoked the few, holy, dear, sublime hours that we've spent
together—too few and far between, alas! Then, around 1 a.m., I went to bed.
The photograph you know was close to me all night long. How beautiful you
are, Ada! How much I like you. More and more, you are ever more in my
blood. Yes, I love you, Ada, I can't do without it—loving you is my life, my

health. You bring me joy, you make me young, I forget my age and the sadness that comes over me now and then. Today, as you see, I'm no longer as I was the day we saw each other. I feel bitterness in my heart, just as there is bitterness in my mouth right now because of bad digestion. I need to get back to work, to kill myself with work or to have you near. These are the only ways to get my dark thoughts to give me a truce. Yesterday I worked with the singers for Falstaff—all day long. [. . .]

TO BRUNO WALTER, (PROBABLY IN SALZBURG);
NYPL, BRUNO WALTER PAPERS, JPB 92-4, SERIES I, FOLDER 589

Salzburg 17-7-1936

My dear Maestro and friend Bruno Walter

Before getting together with you and turning red with shame, I'm sending this letter ahead as a request to be forgiven for the unpardonable fault of never having adequately expressed to you all my gratitude for the kindness and solicitude you have shown me and for having taken the trouble to listen to so many singers and to give me a detailed account of them! Thank you! My dear friend Walter, one of my greatest faults is that I don't write, and throughout my life it has created much unpleasantness for me. Yet I haven't improved so far—I always depend on the compassion of good people. You are certainly one of them—take pity on me and accept my gratitude, although it is late in reaching you. Without your friendly intervention, I would never, ever have returned to Salzburg! I must be grateful to you for this, too. I look forward to seeing you, then, in a few days. Cordial respects to your wife. An affectionate embrace from your friend

Arturo Toscanini

Some matter or matters regarding Salzburg had upset AT in the spring, and he had threatened not to return to the festival that summer. Walter had been dispatched to visit him, and the problems had been resolved.

E.P. SALZBURG, 18 JULY 1936; TO AM, 25VBMMI (CROSSED OUT; IN ANOTHER
HAND: HÔTEL SAVOIA PALACE, CHIANCIANO BAGNI, SIENA); FSD-FOF

Salzburg 18-7-1936

[. . .] Every time I go back to work, my lack of confidence in myself comes over me, and it seems to become greater and greater. I put too much faith in myself and my strength. I accept too many engagements that are a great responsibility. I forget my age, and I'm wrong to do so. [. . .] I have many cast rehearsals of Meistersinger. On Monday the 20th I'll begin to rehearse the orchestra alone. Two rehearsals, however: at 10 [a.m.] and 4 p.m. In the evenings, [I rehearse] the Falstaff cast at the piano. [. . .]

<u>19-7-1936</u>

[. . .] I think (and maybe this is vanity and conceit on my part) that I alone am worthy of you; I think that I'm not banal, like most people! Correct me if <u>I'm too presumptuous</u> about myself. But I'm sure, I'm convinced, that if you had been my wife neither you nor I would have looked elsewhere to correct the direction of our happiness. Write to me, my treasure; respond to these thoughts that cross my mind! Tomorrow I'll begin the real task: I think that two orchestra rehearsals of Meistersinger will kill me. I hope that the good Lord will protect me. If you were here, how much easier everything would be. How many things you would tell me, and how joyfully I would listen to you! I remember that in Rome, you understood, as I did, E[nrico]'s defects. I hope that the cure in Chianciano will make you stronger and **more beautiful.** My God: how will poor Artù be able to preserve what little sense is left in him?! [. . .]

I do not know when AT and Ada had both heard Enrico play in Rome, but it was probably before their affair began. · Chianciano, a spa in southern Tuscany, is near Piazze, where the late Dr. Rinaldi had had his clinic.

<u>Thursday 30-7-936</u>

My <u>adored Ada,</u>

This morning was the Falstaff dress rehearsal, which went very well. As a whole, it has improved since last year. Alice (Somigli), Nannetta (Oltrabella), Doctor Cajus (Tedesco) have added a new dimension to the ensemble, which was already good last year. At the same time I am rehearsing Meistersinger, which is quite a task. Singers and orchestra alike—everyone sings and plays in a routine way[? The original is unclear.]. And then I'm worried about the singer who's taking the role of <u>Sachs,</u> the <u>Bar[itone] Schorr;</u> he seems a bit old, and he's hoarse and breathless on the high notes. He always sings softly, and when I called on him to sing full voice like the others, he said that he had a cold. Of course, the management has already begun to search among the few available [replacements]. Let's hope for the best. I'm telling you, however, my dearest, that this is the last time that I'll take on the theater. It's too great an effort for me. My demands are too great, I have an increasingly hard time satisfying myself!

Franca Somigli was the stage name of the American soprano Marion Bruce Clark (1901–74). · Augusta Oltrabella (1897–1981) was an Italian soprano. · Alfredo Tedeschi (not Tedesco; 1882–1967) was an Italian tenor. The Hungarian-born American Friedrich Schorr (1888–1953), arguably the finest Wagnerian bass-baritone of his generation, was not yet forty-eight years old during the summer of 1936, and he had sung with AT as late as the previous year, in Brahms's *German Requiem,* in New York. There is no reason to doubt AT's negative judgment: Schorr may merely have been going through a bad patch, because he did not stop singing Wagner roles until 1943. In the end, he was replaced by Hans Hermann Nissen (1893–1980), a German bass-baritone of excellent repute.

(SALZBURG, 31 JULY 1936); TO AM, (CHIANCIANO); FSD-FOF

[. . .] You're lucky to have Ugo Ara's company! He is a dear person, unique for his goodness. I've already read—in French and English—the book he wants to give me. Miecio gave it to me before my last departure for America. It's an excellent book and it interested me very much, so much so that I reread it in a second language. I think that Carrel himself, whom I met in New York, wrote it in both French and English. [. . .]

L'Homme, cet inconnu (Man, the Unknown), by the French biologist and surgeon Alexis Carrel (1873–1944) (New York: Harper, 1935), championed the intellectual elite as rulers in a scientific utopia. It was published in French and English initially and aroused considerable interest, thanks, in part, to Carrel's friendship with Charles Lindbergh. Carrel was appointed director of the Foundation for the Study of Human Relations that had been created by the Vichy regime in France, and he later denied charges of collaboration with the Germans. He died shortly after the liberation of France.

E.P. SALZBURG, 5 AUGUST 1936; TO AM, 25VBMMI; FSD-FOF

Wednesday 5-8-936

[. . .] I've lived through some infernal days. The heavy workload that weighs upon me, with its various annoyances (I had to fire a singer, Schorr, and I even wrote him a consolatory letter, but it all caused me great pain), and the feverish wait for a letter from you were driving me crazy, making me unreasonable, and all the most incredible imaginings ran through my head: that you didn't love me anymore; that you had certainly found someone more interesting than me; that you had fallen hopelessly in love. Then I thought that you had fallen ill. I couldn't sleep—I was like a madman. Add to this the terribly rainy, nasty, cold weather, and you'll have an idea of the state of my poor old heart!!! [. . .]

E.P. SALZBURG, 8 AUGUST 1936; TO AM, 25VBMMI; FSD-FOF

Friday 7-8-936
Midnight

My great, sole love, in two sessions today I did the Meistersinger dress rehearsal. From 10 in the morning until 1 p.m., the first and second acts; from

3:30 to 5:15, the long third act. Everything came off well. Orchestra, singers, chorus, staging, lights, stage action, thanks to my anything-but-easy efforts and tenacity, responded in a way that I wouldn't have dared to hope for. The enthusiasm in all of us spread to the numerous audience members who attended the rehearsal.

But what a waste of human life all this costs this poor little man! How much irritation, anxiety, trepidation! If you could see me right now—oh so tired, with my thin, dried-out face and sunken eyes—you would pity me. Do you remember at the [Hôtel] <u>Prince de Galles</u> in Paris, after the rehearsals for the concerts? You told me then that you liked to see me in that state, that you liked my elongated, tired face—and you crouched between my knees, and I caressed your hair and kissed your adored head! Do you remember? [. . .] I'm sleeping very little; I spent whole days in a state of irritation as a result of some of the singers' deficiencies. Lehmann was ill the other evening and had to be replaced in Fidelio, and I was afraid of having to replace her in Meistersinger. I'm sad, so sad. Your letters are a great comfort during my sleepless nights. [. . .]

Lotte Lehmann had first sung with AT in a New York Philharmonic concert in February 1934; at Salzburg she sang the title role in *Fidelio* and the role of Eva in *Die Meistersinger,* both under his direction.

E.P. SALZBURG, 9 AUGUST 1936; TO AM, 25VBMMI; FSD-FOF

<u>Midnight</u>

<u>My adored</u> Ada, It was a moving performance. I don't think I've ever obtained a better performance of Meistersinger. Can you imagine that the singers were crying at the end of the opera? Bruno Walter came back after the 2nd act; he told me that we had brought off a miracle! I'm so happy to tell you this. Now that I've managed to bring this immense, fearsome work to a successful conclusion, I can give myself a little pat on the back. But I was quite frightened. Now I can still hope to have the **strength to love you** for some time, my Ada. I'm not <u>entirely old</u> altogether. [. . .]

Besides Nissen and Lehmann, AT's *Meistersinger* cast in 1936 included Charles Kullman as Stolzing, Anton Dermota as Zorn, and Kerstin Thorborg as Magdalena.

E.P. SALZBURG, 12 AUGUST 1936; TO AM, PVBCA; FSD-FOF

<u>12-August 936</u>

[. . .] This morning I performed Brahms's Tragic [Overture] and German Requiem. They were broadcast on the radio. I was thinking the whole time that you and the Pizzettis were listening. How close you [singular] were to me! Humility and vanity were combined in me. I think I did well. The chorus certainly sang magnificently. The two soloists and the orchestra also did well. With this Friday's Meistersinger performance I'll be halfway through my task. I have no further rehearsals except for the concert on the 28th. I'm beginning to breathe. [. . .] After the first Meistersinger performance I was in a daze for two days! I was dead tired. Now I've recovered. I can truly compare myself to a good American car—my Cadillac, for instance—I have a good, ready pickup. When I see the good Bruno Walter, I really feel that I'm ten years younger than he! After Salzburg, however, I want to spend a few days at Badgastein. I'll certainly need it. If you could join me then, what a joy it would be for both of us. But I fear that Horowitz, too, wants to go there to recover at the same time that I'm there, and in that case I would feel like giving up the idea. [. . .]

The Toscaninis were renting the same house in Liefering, near Salzburg, that they had rented the previous summer. · The soloists who "did well" in the performance of Brahms's German Requiem were the Hungarian soprano Anna Báthy (see my note following the telegram of 28 October 1934) and the Hungarian baritone Sándor Svéd, also known as Alexander Sved (1904–79). · As AT knew, Bruno Walter was his junior by nine and a half years.

(SALZBURG); TO AM, (PVBCA); FSD-FOF

15 August 1936

[. . .] Yesterday evening, after Die Meistersinger, Bebe from Lugano said to me: What joy you must feel, Maestro, to know that you've communicated joy to others in such great measure! I would have liked to slap her. She must have understood my wish from the way I looked at her. I was exhausted from the effort, with a long, changed face, full of suffering, as if I had done battle against forces greater than my own. Stupid thing! No: when I'm working I don't have time to feel joy; on the contrary, I suffer without interruption, and I feel that I'm going through all the pain and suffering of a woman giving birth. [. . .]

Bebe Baslini was the daughter of friends of the Toscanini family.

E.P. SALZBURG, 18 AUGUST 1936; PICTURE POSTCARD WITH PORTRAIT PHOTO OF TOSCANINI; TO AM, PVBCA; FSD-FOF

16-8-936

This photograph was taken at the Fortezza station when I was coming back from Berlin in June 1929, with the Scala ensemble. I was hailed by the Fascists at every station after having been denounced by C[ount] Aldrovandi for having turned down an invitation to the Fascist Headquarters in Berlin and spoken irreverently about the <u>Duce</u> and <u>Fascism.</u> I'm still alive. Where has that worthy functionary disappeared to? He's not even named in the litanies of the Fascist saints!!!

AT was confusing two events. The photo in question was indeed taken at the railroad station in Fortezza, at the Italian border, at the time of the Scala ensemble's re-entry after its colossally triumphal visits to Vienna and Berlin in the spring of 1929, but the unpleasant Berlin episode took place in 1930, when AT was conducting the New York Philharmonic's first European tour. At that time, Arturo Bocchini, the chief of Mussolini's political police, received a memorandum containing the following information: "Having been asked repeatedly to attend a reception that was being organized in his honor at the [Berlin] headquarters of the local [Italian] Fascist Party organization, the Maestro continually replied that he could not participate because he was tired. When pressed, and when asked whether he would authorize the sending of a telegram in his name to the Duce, in which he would state that he did not agree to [attend] the function only <u>because he was tired, he replied sharply that he was not attending because he was an anti-Fascist, because he held Mussolini to be a tyrant and oppressor of Italy, and that rather than break with these convictions he was prepared never to return again to Italy.</u> . . . This document was shown to Mussolini, who underlined the lines as reproduced here and scrawled across the page: "Contact <u>His Excellency Grandi.</u>" (Dino Grandi was Italy's foreign minister.) (Document 446 in the Fascicoli personali [confidential files], Divisione Polizia Politica [Political Police Division], Direzione Generale di Pubblica Sicurezza [General Administration of Public Safety], Ministero dell'Interno [Interior Ministry], Archivio Centrale dello Stato [Central State Archive], Rome.) Count Aldrovandi, who was Italy's ambassador to Germany at that time, was evidently responsible for having passed this information on to Rome, and it is clear that, six years after the event, AT had not yet forgiven him—the more so inasmuch as he knew that Aldrovandi had been one of Ada's lovers.

<hr>

E.P. SALZBURG, 19 AUGUST 1936; TO AM, PVBCA; FSD-FOF

<hr>

<u>18-8-936</u>

[. . .] Oh, my Ada, I don't want to utter the usual sentence that all lovers have uttered and will continue to utter for centuries: <u>"Never have I loved like this."</u> But just as I'm convinced that despite my age and my fifty-year-long career, the artist in me—according to those who can judge me—has improved and become more refined, rather than diminished, so I think that the man in me has never been capable of loving with greater sincerity, with more passion. And I owe it to you, Ada. I've never been vain; I've never had a weakness for myself as man or artist. But I must confess that today, for you, I'm guilty of this weakness! I want to please you as an artist and as a man! Don't think badly of me; be good and understand me. The letter I received this morning showed you to be full of passion. Be like that always!! Don't just let yourself be adored, but do some adoring yourself. Today I have the third Meistersinger performance. Every note—and there are many of them—will bring you a loving thought. I'll write to you again tonight. I kiss you ardently, the way you like, and at length. Artù [. . .]

<u>22-8-936</u>

<u>My holy love,</u> during the last few days I've been distressingly irritated; I feel every possible woe right to my very bones. [. . .] What with friends, relatives, admirers, I'm under attack every day, even here in Liefering, and I don't know how to protect myself. I feel more tired and worn out than when I conduct Die Meistersinger. Yesterday, I hated myself. At the last performance of Falstaff that I conducted, I even hated the music. When the orchestra comes back to me after having been with other conductors, it's in bits and pieces. I can tell you that the other evening, the hatred was flashing from my eyes against myself, against everyone. Fortunately, no one in the audience realized it; on the contrary, the enthusiasm was greater than at the other performances. I can't begin to tell you how many Italians, and especially Milanese, have come! The Princess of Piedmont has been here for a long time. She's heard <u>every-thing,</u> including the Brahms Requiem, Falstaff twice, I think, and Die Meistersinger. She wanted to see me, but I took umbrage. Wally, Ida Visconti, and Maria de Senna [da Zara] managed things cleverly in order to save me. I don't want to see people who wouldn't have the courage to say hello to me in Italy. In addition to Borletti, General Caviglia also came to my dressing room. He received a rather cold welcome from the undersigned. How sad life is, my Ada! Each day brings a new disappointment! May the day never come when I have to mistrust even myself! I must confess that during the last few days I felt something awakening in the depths and darkness of my unconscious that frightened me. The least noble instincts that are hidden there came over me, rose to the surface. I can understand how weak men can be swept away by such states of mind. [. . .] This evening is the last performance of Meistersinger. I'll keep you near me; every note will be a thought directed toward you. Let me <u>adhere to you,</u> keep me **in you**; as you wrote to me, I'll <u>die of voluptuousness.</u> Wholly your Artù

Princess Maria José (1906–2001), daughter of King Albert and Queen Elisabeth of Belgium, married Italy's Crown Prince Umberto in 1930. She loved music, and she was believed to nurture anti-Fascist sentiments. Nevertheless, she was a representative of the Italian royal family, which had officially sanctioned and indeed continued to profit politically from the Fascist regime, and AT refused to receive her. · General Enrico Caviglia (1862–1945), another music lover, was a World War I hero and a for-mer minister of war who had been on friendly terms with AT, but his fence-straddling attitude toward fascism had put him on AT's blacklist. · AT does not reveal exactly what was irritating him so terribly, or whether the temptation to do something ignoble was personal, professional, or political. We do know, however, that at some point during his stay in Salzburg that summer, he was asked by Mario Labroca (1896–1973), one of the more liberal and honorable of Fascist Italy's music bureau-crats, whether he would like to work again in Italy. "I expected one of his violent reac-tions," Labroca recalled many years later. "Instead, he answered with naturalness, 'Of course I would!' 'So why don't you come back?' I persisted, moved. He remained silent, and he, too, was moved. He said, 'Thanks, Labroca,' and didn't add another word. I persisted; I assured him of the welcome he would have, of the certainty that no untoward incident would take place. He listened as if the invitation interested him but didn't speak again." (Mario Labroca and Virgilio Boccardi, *Arte di Toscanini* [Turin: ERI, 1966], pp. 142–3.) Perhaps the "least noble instincts" to which AT refers in this letter were his longings to contribute once again to the musical life of his beloved Italy. At times, these longings became almost unbearably intense, but AT never gave in to them.

E.P. SALZBURG, 25 AUGUST 1936;
(LETTER BEGUN IN THE EARLY HOURS OF 23 AUGUST 1936); TO AM, PVBCA;
FSD-FOF

one a.m.

Two hours ago I finished the last performance of Meistersinger. I'm tired and sad. Who knows when I'll conduct it again! You were near me, you know. Very near! Emilio had given me your last letter, with the beautiful photographs (bravo Bruno) just a moment before I headed for the theater. I read it by fits and starts in my dressing room, whenever I was able to be alone (not an easy thing). Then I put it in my left pants pocket, and I can't begin to tell you how carefully I caressed it, for fear of damaging it and the photographs! [. . .] I don't know why, but Mrs. Cerruti and her husband came to see me this time; she threw her arms around my neck, kissed me effusively, and spoke most exaggeratedly. Why didn't she show her face in Paris? All the world's a farce.

Monday 24 August 1936

[. . .] The photographs are really beautiful, you know. I think they're the most successful things Bruno has done among his many and variegated activities (music, poetry, short stories, painting, cinema—before long he'll turn up as a singing teacher!). Poor Pizzetti! There wasn't much phosphorous in his loins when he fecundated that dear, good creature who was his wife!—But I not only read your last sweet letter and became enchanted by your beautiful, tousled head. I even locked myself in my room for fear of unexpected visits; I spread out on the bed all ten of the letters I've received in Salzburg, read all of them, and reread one of them (the one that bears the No. 3). I put the photograph you sent from Rome (the bigger enlargement) on my pillow, and I went to sleep with the light on, so that I'd have the joy of waking up and seeing immediately your dear, adored face!

Childish stuff, you'll say; senile doings, others would say. Well, say whatever you like: I'm happy, cheerful, proud to feel life in me, as I still do, and I hope that you and the good Lord will keep me thus for many more years to come.—Yesterday, I allowed myself a bit of relaxation. We went to the Wallersee, not much more than twenty kilometers from Salzburg, to have lunch with the Busches. They're all here, including little Ursula, two months old. They attended three Meistersingers, two Falstaffs, and one Fidelio. Adolf was moved, which gave me much pleasure. His praise convinces me that I can still continue to work. If you could see what his daughter has become—it seems impossible! She isn't yet twenty years old, but she's colossal! We won't even mention her chest (that's natural—she's nursing), but the posterior section, which has no particular function in nursing, is actually a threat! I don't know what would have become of me, of my life, if a joke like that had been played on me when Carla had Walter! I would have been in despair! [. . .]

I adore Bruno's photographs. You're marvelous. I want to see you disheveled like that the next time we have a sweet hour of love together. I never tire of looking at you. I wish that no one else had these photographs. When I think of your youth, an infinite sadness comes over me and a lump forms in my throat. If only we had been able to spend our lives together. What a life of art and love it would have been! We would each have been made better by it. How often this thought crosses my mind! Haven't you ever considered this dream, which I've nurtured for years? I'm thinking far back over the years, and I see myself as a young man (30 years old), during the first year of my marriage, already troubled—you understand me—uncertain whether the fault was on my side or the other, but certain that matrimonial life didn't appear the way I'd wanted it, the way I'd believed it would be. I've been a good, honest, but unfaithful husband. C[arla] has never understood me, nor has she ever tried to improve, but she has always been good, honest, and faithful. In a life lived together, that's not everything—you know something about this! I don't know why I've taken this plunge into painful memories. Be indulgent toward me! Maybe it's because I've always thought, since far-off 1917, that you would have been my ideal, the woman of my dreams. You would have understood me, we would have adored each other, you would have made me better, as I've already said, and I would have done the same for you. But you were born too late, I too soon. Today, we're suffering the bitter results! But we adore each other, isn't that so, Ada? We like each other in every way, and will continue to love each other and to suffer   Artù

Mrs. Cerruti was the Hungarian-born actress Elisabeth de Paulay and the wife of the career diplomat Vittorio Cerruti, who was at that time Italy's ambassador to France. AT implies that in Paris, where her husband occupied an important official position, she had been unwilling to be seen with Italy's most renowned anti-Fascist, whereas in Salzburg, as an audience member like any other, she was only too happy to be seen with Italy's most renowned musician. · AT's irony is aimed not only at Bruno Pizzetti, whom he did not like (see the letter of 28 September 1933), but also at Bruno's father, Ildebrando, whose work AT had admired in the 1920s and early 1930s but who was too much the ascetic (real or self-proclaimed) for AT's tastes. In the opera world— especially in AT's day, when the demand for capable singers was so great—the profession of singing teacher was sometimes exercised by amateurs or even out-and-out frauds, thus AT's sarcastic reference to Bruno Pizzetti as a potential *maestro di canto*. · For the Busch family, see my note accompanying the letter of 18 September 1935. Ursula was the first child of Irene Busch and her husband, Rudolf Serkin.

Monday <u>31-8-936</u>

[. . .] Your very dear last letter reached me Thursday evening while I was at the theater, getting ready to listen to Tristan. You can imagine my despair at having to keep that treasure in my pocket and not be able to sample it, enjoy it!! I was <u>furious</u>! And I couldn't leave the performance, because I was near B. Walter's daughters and wife. The torment of Tantalus!! [. . .]

This evening is the last performance of Fidelio and of the season. Tomorrow I'll be at Badgastein, <u>Hotel Kaiserhof.</u> Will we see each other there? In Vienna? In Italy? Where can you go? [. . .]

Margarete Wallmann, the choreographer and stage director, recalled in her memoir, *Les Balcons du ciel* (Paris: Laffont, 1976), sitting with AT at one of Walter's *Tristan* rehearsals that summer. Toward the end of the long love scene in the second act, AT turned to her and said, "If they were Italians, they would already have seven children; but they're Germans, so they're still talking."

<u>My Ada,</u> **I'm desperately full of love.** This evening you were even more deeply in my flesh than at any of the other performances. It was the last Fidelio and the last performance of the season. I thought you might be listening to the radio, that maybe you would have heard my voice following the unfolding of the sublime music, and that if I had dared to say—Ada, I love you—you would have heard me! But at least I dared to do something. I removed the little photograph holder from my pocket, I looked at your beautiful face, and I brought it surreptitiously to my lips during the spoken dialogue! Oh, my adored lover, divine Ada, I'm crazier and crazier about you, and it's odd that every evening, when I come back tired, weary, exhausted, after having given all the best of my life, <u>the desire for you comes violently over me, the desire to hold you close, clinging to me, to possess you in every way, until I gasp my last breath!!!</u> We must, we must spend a night of love, of endless voluptuousness, together, without anxiety, without fear! But when, when? In Vienna? [. . .] Why is it that my brain, my nerves, my blood don't give me the strength to bring off a gesture that would make us happy! My will struggles eternally with my conscience. I hate myself and I'm disgusted with myself. [. . .]

Friday <u>4-10[sic]-936</u>

[. . .] I began the cure on Wednesday. The doctor who saw me found me completely all right, physically. As Prof. Murri used to say: my dear Toscanini, you were <u>born well.</u> In fact, my heart and lungs are very healthy, my blood pressure is 140. I hope to continue to work well for a long time to come. This morning I took three baths of fifteen minutes each and had one shortwave session. Badgastein is beautiful; in this magnificent weather it's the ideal mountain locale. There are magnificent walks in the woods; too bad that my Ada isn't here! Only one thing is wrong: the cure ends in the morning; the afternoon is long, the evening eternal. I don't have a piano, I don't have books, I don't have a car. You know that I can't sleep during the day, so it takes some doing to get through all those hours! I've run into many, many acquaintances. Fortunately, none of them is at my hotel, which is far from the center, where everyone gets together. I've seen the Kreislers, Wanda Szigeti with her husband and daughter, Sauer, Rosenthal, Huberman, and several Italians, including Count Cicogna—who gets uglier and uglier—Toeplitz, accompanied by a Roman countess who is said to be his lover, and several others whose names escape me. Horowitz is here with Wanda—he's better, but he still walks badly. The doctor, however, is sure that this cure will help him greatly and guarantees that he'll soon be able to begin practicing again, to start his tour early in November. I'm spending a lot of time with them—in fact, we take our meals together in the room. The two little girls, Sonia and Emanuela, are here, too. They're real loves! There I was, afraid of all the work that awaited me at Salzburg, but now that it's all finished I feel as if I hadn't worked at all! And to think that on every performance day I was sighing and swearing to give up all my activities! That's what excessive pride does to one: continual doubts, no confidence at all in oneself!! [. . .]

For Dr. Augusto Murri, see my note accompanying the letter of 8 November 1930. · The Austrian violinist Fritz Kreisler (1875–1962), the German pianist Emil von Sauer (1862–1942), and the Austro-Ukrainian pianist Moritz Rosenthal (1862–1946) were among the leading concert artists of their time. For Toeplitz, see note on page 104.

Monday afternoon [7.9.36]

[. . .] Adored Ada! The doctor has found that I've improved in a few days. The <u>heart</u> is the same as ever, <u>according to him.</u> But I know that it is much more in love, <u>incurably</u> in love.

Blood pressure: 135 instead of 140—the pressure of a young man, the doctor says. I accept the compliment, but I <u>sigh</u> deeply. Weight, the same as always: <u>173 kilograms.</u> Prospects: I'll be able to hang on for a few more years without worrying! [. . .]

AT meant 73 kilograms (160.6 pounds) rather than 173.

E.P. BADGASTEIN, 8 SEPTEMBER 1936; P.S. AS IN PREVIOUS LETTER; TO AM, PVBCA; FSD-FOF

Tuesday <u>8-9-936</u>

[. . .] I'm awaiting the arrival of Wanda and the little girls at any moment; my eyes follow what I'm writing, my ears are listening for the footsteps and little voices that are getting nearer. You never tell me anything about Rirì, about Pizzetti. Is the maestro working? And isn't Rirì surprised by the frequency of the letters that come to you from Salzburg and Badgastein? In one of your letters you tell me that Rirì is very good and discreet. I should hope so! She was once fond of me; now I don't know. I've just this moment received a telegram from Vienna; I'd thought it was to set the date for the 1st Fidelio, but instead they're asking me if I would agree to conduct Beethoven's <u>Missa Solemnis</u> at the beginning of October. Indeed! The more those Viennese eat, the hungrier they get!

I really must leave you—I hear little Sonia calling her <u>grandpa.</u> [. . .]

Concerning Rirì Pizzetti, see my note accompanying the telegram of 14 January 1924. · AT conducted two special performances of his Salzburg *Fidelio* at the Vienna Staatsoper in September 1936 as a tribute to Bruno Walter, who had recently become the ensemble's chief conductor. In the end, he agreed to conduct the *Missa Solemnis* as well, but at the end of November.

E.P. BADGASTEIN, 10 SEPTEMBER 1936; TO AM, PVBCA; FSD-FOF

[. . .] Ada, why were you born so late? If only you could at least have been born ten years earlier. Wagner married Cosima, who was twenty-four years younger than he! But not even by that standard do our accounts tally! [. . .] You know, I'm not jealous of anyone—only of E[nrico]. Do you remember Goethe's <u>Elective Affinities</u>? Have I ever spoken with you about it? Have you ever read it? [. . .] I'll finish my cure this coming Monday, and Tuesday the 15th I'll leave for Vienna. [. . .]

4 <u>in the morning</u>

[. . .] [Your letters] are my <u>gospel,</u> they contain <u>my whole faith</u>! I reread them, and then I feel that I am the happiest man on earth, the most enviable, the one who possesses the most marvelous treasure; but as soon as my gospel disappears from my line of vision, I go back to being the <u>unhappiest</u> of men, incredulous that a creature like you can feel attracted by my love, by my boundless passion! Just as in artistic matters! My suffering repeats itself before each and every rehearsal. As soon as the rehearsal has ended, I feel that I'm worth something—then the phenomenon repeats itself, with ever-increasing suffering. Men like Furtwängler suffer from too much vanity; I suffer from too little! That's my life. [. . .]

E.P. BADGASTEIN, 10 SEPTEMBER 1936;
POSTCARD WITH PORTRAIT PHOTO OF TOSCANINI; TO AM, PVBCA; FSD-FOF

My Ada, the realization of that dream of spiritual and sensual harmony that we all look for, from the threshold of adolescence to the eve of marriage, often dissolves the day after, or not much later, and forever. I think that this is <u>our case.</u> Marriage has to be considered a sort of adventure, fortunate or tempestuous (glücklich oder stürmisch); at some point, we must find a <u>modus vivendi</u> if we want to make it to the end of the end of the adventure. And you're still with E[nrico], I with C[arla]. Artù

E.P. BADGASTEIN, 12 SEPTEMBER 1936; P.S., DER KAISERHOF, BADGASTEIN;
AM, PVBCA; FSD-FOF

<u>12 September 1936</u>

[. . .] Yes, I remember very well the evening at the Alpino when I heard for the first time the ensemble from the 2nd scene of the 3rd Act of Fra Gherardo. So beautiful!! And I thought at the time that Respighi would never have been able to write anything of the sort. He lacked Pizzetti's wisdom and <u>heart</u>! Fra Gherardo reminds me of another evening, but I think it was the following year—an evening at the Pizzettis'. Besides the Tos. and Polo families <u>you</u> were there, and so were D'Annunzio and Clausetti. How jealous I was! Why? With what justification? How beautiful you were! And you promised the Poet that you would go visit him at the Vittoriale! That visit has always weighed upon my heart! And [you say that] at that time you considered me <u>unapproachable</u>! But tell me, Ada—<u>answer this</u>—had you ever thought about even a tiny probability that you could love me? The name, the fame (my God, what an ugly word) of Maestro Toscanini—weren't these titles more repellent than attractive? And you had the holy inspiration! And to think that I destroyed that telegram! Why? Maybe things weren't yet clear in my brain. What things? I don't know. I feel the palpitations of my heart again, as I felt them then; I see myself glued to the table, holding your telegram, my eyes staring off into space. Something marvelous, a distant, ever-so-distant dream, was about to materialize. I must leave you—I'm going to the doctor for the "short-wave" cure. I'll write again this evening. [. . .]

The Alpino, a hotel in the mountains above the western shore of Lake Maggiore, was frequented by the Pizzettis and Toscaninis during summer holidays in the 1920s. Pizzetti's opera *Fra Gherardo* was given its world premiere by AT at La Scala on May 16, 1928; thus the episodes in question probably took place during the summers of 1927 and 1928.

E.P. VIENNA, 18 SEPTEMBER 1936; P.S., HOTEL BRISTOL, WIEN; TO AM, HBM; FSD-FOF

17-Sept. 1936

[. . .] Enrico has sent me a very nice letter to introduce me to a conductor from Frankfurt; it was a real pleasure, as you can imagine. I was truly surprised! There is something of your handwriting in his. Yours is much more expressive and shows open intelligence. I repeat that I almost had a heart attack. [. . .]

The conductor from Frankfurt may have been Hans Wilhelm Steinberg (1899–1978), who had been general music director of the Frankfurt Opera but who, by the mid-1930s, had been reduced by the Nazis to music director of the Jewish Culture League in Frankfurt and Berlin. Not long after AT wrote this letter, Steinberg went to Palestine to train the new orchestra that was Huberman's brainchild and that would be inaugurated by AT.

E.P. VIENNA, 18 SEPTEMBER 1936; P.S. AS IN PREVIOUS LETTER; TO AM, HBM; FSD-FOF

18-September 936

[. . .] Fidelio went well yesterday evening! It was quite another thing from Salzburg. The acoustics here are noble. So everything was better blended, nobler, more musical. Enormous audience—enthusiastic. After the performance I went, or rather we went, to dinner at the home of the Polish ambassador or minister or whatever he is—his wife is the daughter of Frassati, the ex-proprietor of "La Stampa" of Turin. Unfortunately, when I got back to the hotel I couldn't converse with you, read your letters, look at your portraits, as I did in Salzburg. I'm staying in a magnificent suite, the one the king of England stayed in a few weeks ago—you can imagine how honored and reverent I feel! But unfortunately, I didn't have a separate room, so I had to be satisfied with thinking and thinking of you, my joy, my life, my everything—but it's quite another thing to be able to unburden oneself by writing down one's thoughts. I'm overexcited, and I'm writing like an epileptic. Excuse me, my spirit isn't at peace, I don't know what I've got inside me, but I am very agitated, as if some other nasty thing were about to happen to me!

My God, what a life! And to think that many people envy me! They see nothing but the exterior, which glitters in appearance, but a person's interior, soul, heart—what unknown, unexplored things they are!!! [. . .]

Luciana Frassati Gawronska (b. 1902) was the daughter of Alfredo Frassati (1868–1961), the founder of the Turin daily *La Stampa;* she married a Polish diplomat named Gawronski who, at the time this letter was written, was Poland's ambassador to Austria. Her brother, Pier Giorgio Frassati (1901–25), was an ardent anti-Fascist and liberal Catholic who was later canonized. She published *Il Maestro* (Turin: Bottega d'Erasmo, 1967), a factually confused, badly written, but beautifully illustrated book on AT.

E.P. VIENNA, 20 SEPTEMBER 1936; P.S. AS IN PREVIOUS LETTERS; TO AM, HBM; FSD-FOF

20 Sept. 1936

My Ada. **Mine???** I couldn't explain your silence! After [having sent] several special delivery letters, I've just this moment received your tel[egram] in English. The concerts that have been announced are for next November, the 15th, 22nd, and 29th, and in this last one I'll conduct the <u>Missa Solemnis.</u> This evening is the second and last Fidelio performance, God willing. I'll stay on tomorrow because the singers (I think) and I, and Bruno Walter, have been invited to lunch by Minister <u>Pertner.</u> On Tuesday morning we'll return by car to Milan, the Isolino, etc.

I don't know how to describe what sort of state I'm in, and I wouldn't tell you even if I knew how. I'm annihilated, Ada, annihilated, by a piece of news that I would have liked to have heard from you. I'm not a <u>child</u>—I could be your father—and one can confide in a father! Is it true that you want to divorce in order to marry Zingarelli—that you both have a furious <u>crush</u>? Why didn't you tell me so yourself? Can you imagine my soul's state? Oh, Vienna, Vienna! If you wish, send word to me at the Isolino.

I love you so very, very much! You know it—you must feel it in every fiber! But I suffer, I suffer so much. I kiss you ecstatically.

<u>Artù</u>

For Italo Zingarelli, see my note accompanying the letter of 18 October 1934. · Hans Pertner, the Austrian minister of education from 1934 to 1938, was directly responsible for the vicissitudes of the Salzburg Festival. He was thrown out of office when the Nazis came to power, spent three years in a concentration camp, and, during 1944–45, was actively hunted because of his participation in the Resistance.

20 Sept. 1936

My Ada, I start Fidelio in an hour! I leave you to imagine what state my heart is in! I'm in a blind despair that gnaws at me and from which I don't know how to extricate myself. I can't wait to leave. I want to see my Italian sky, my lake, my Isolino again; I can't stand foreigners anymore.

I'm not at all jealous—I don't feel even the smallest symptom of that terrible disease. If I thought that such a decision could give you happiness, well, I would almost wish it for you. But I'm suffering, suffering. Why don't you tell me? Why keep it silent? Oh, my Ada! I love you so much. Do you feel it? I'll call you from Milan or from the Isolino; I want to hear your voice, I'm dying of desire to see you, to know the truth. I kiss you, I kiss you, I kiss you desperately. Write to me at the Isolino. I beg, I plead, I supplicate.

Yours alone Artù

28-9-1936

[. . .] I thought I'd have the Horowitzes here early in October, but instead they're staying on in Venice, and I don't even know whether they still think they'll go to Capri. What I know for certain is that he doubts that he'll be able to begin his tour early in November—and not only that, but he's uncertain about taking part in my Paris concert, which is set for December 10!!! I can't figure anything out! [. . .]

Ada had reassured AT that the rumors about herself and Zingarelli were completely untrue, and he had accepted her explanations. · Vladimir Horowitz was in the midst of the first of what were to be several major breakdowns that forced him to withdraw from the keyboard for years at a time. He did not play with AT in Paris, then or later.

3-10-936

My love, [. . .] I'm truly saddened that you are leaving Milan for good. Has the Pizzettis' departure perhaps influenced this decision? This will be a reason for me to live even more like a gypsy. I'll wander around the world without respite. I'll never get used to the idea that Milan no longer houses my Ada! Yes, my Ada—mine alone—I'm sure of it—I can't doubt it! If only you knew how much good you did me yesterday! We talked so much, about so many things, and I still have so much to tell you—but when, when will I be able to do so? Love me and write to me, Ada, keep me alive—you alone can do it. Without you there is death, <u>physical</u> and <u>intellectual.</u> I kiss you, I kiss you, I kiss you with passion! You know which way! Artù

The death of Respighi earlier that year had cleared the way for Pizzetti to become director of the Accademia di Santa Cecilia in Rome, a position he quickly assumed. Enrico Mainardi, who had occasionally taught master classes at Santa Cecilia since 1932, was offered the position of principal cello professor; he accepted it, and this meant that the Mainardis' professional and domestic axis became Rome–Berlin instead of Milan–Berlin.

E.P. MI, 10 OCTOBER 1936; TO AM, HIR; FSD-FOF

Friday <u>9-10-1936</u>

[. . .] Lalla is getting married tomorrow. Walter [Toscanini] and Riccardo Polo are the best men; I'm functioning as father—I'll accompany her to the altar. It will be the cause of intense emotion for me. A few tears will flow. May God grant her every joy that my heart wishes for her and keep it for her <u>forever</u>! But marriage is always a blind jump into space! We will never marry each other, therefore we'll live eternally in the <u>full light</u> of our luminous love. [. . .]

Lalla was the daughter of AT's friend Giuseppe Gallignani, the director of the Milan Conservatory who had committed suicide thirteen years earlier; she married the art critic Gillo Dorfles.

E.P. MI, 20 OCTOBER 1936; TO AM, PFB; FSD-FOF

20-10-1936—<u>5 p.m.</u>

[. . .] I'm working, I'm drowning myself in work, and the holy flame of art has been relit. I'm already thinking about what I'll do and how I'll do it. Doubts and trepidation begin, my blood is stirred up, and I'm returning to the life I live when you are far away! I'll stay [in Milan] until the 27th, then on the Isolino until the <u>Fascist hubbub</u> ends. In the meantime, you can think of me at home, working, all day—only toward seven in the evening you can follow me to Castoldi the bookseller's, in the Galleria. [. . .]

A major Fascist Party festival was scheduled for Milan at the end of the month, and AT, who lived in the city's center, couldn't bear the thought of being in town while it was in progress. · The nineteenth-century Galleria, Milan's famous glass-roofed arcade, stretches from Piazza del Duomo (Cathedral Square) to Piazza della Scala. The booksellers and publishers Baldini e Castoldi had a shop there, and AT used to frequent it, both to satisfy his bibliomania and to chat with the fellow anti-Fascists who congregated there.

Tuesday <u>27-10-936</u>

[. . .] After two days of unanticipated revelry last week (I was at the Albertinis' at Parella and the Riboldis' at Brunate), I caught such a cold—head, chest, with a cough that killed my throat and chest—that I had to stay in the house for four days in a row, desperate because I had absolutely no way of communicating with you. Not even by telegram. I couldn't have Emilio at hand for even an instant. So I was hurling curses at every corner of heaven and all the saints. [. . .]

Saturday <u>31-10-1936</u>

[. . .] I'm still tormented by the ferocious cold that kept me shut in the house for four days, partly in bed and partly up and about. My throat hurts, I have shooting pains in my ears, and the cough doesn't leave me in peace for a moment. Add to all this an exasperating state of agitation—why? You can well imagine! It's certainly true that I fled Milan so as not to be present at the carnival of <u>that cowardly flock of ill-born slaves</u>—but my thoughts were poisoned by it, all the same. I can't stop thinking about it. I ought to have been immersed in some work, in obligatory occupations. And then the Isolino is overflowing! Just as one reads in the Decameron that an honest group of seven women and three men decided to head for a place atop a hill near Fiesole, to flee the sadness and danger of death in those pestilential times, narrating stories and singing songs, so a group of friends of both sexes has left pestilential Milan for four or five days and has taken refuge on the Isolino. Here, however, we don't create stories or sing songs, but rather imprecate against that **Judas** who once, in a short preface to a brief life of <u>John Hus</u> that he had written, concluded with these words:

"In delivering this booklet to the printers, I formulate the wish that it may arouse in readers' hearts <u>a hatred for any form of spiritual or secular tyranny whatsoever, be it theocratic or Jacobin.</u>

"Milan 1913 = B.M."

But why am I poisoning you, too, my love, with my own poisoned state of mind? [. . .]

And the little red handkerchief? Since I can't quench my thirst directly at the <u>delightful fount,</u> I'm hoping for the <u>surrogate.</u> Don't forget. Artù.

The libertarian quotation is from Mussolini's *Giovanni Huss, il veridico* (John Hus, the soothsayer, probably published in Milan in 1913). When, as dictator, Mussolini decided to consolidate and broaden his power by making Roman Catholicism Italy's state religion and submitting to other compromises with the Vatican, he suppressed this anti-Church and antiauthoritarian booklet; AT, who was both anticlerical and antiauthoritarian, here expresses his scorn for the middle-aged Mussolini's betrayal of the young Mussolini's freethinking principles. The publication was reprinted by Edinac in Rome in 1948, three years after the Duce's ignominious death. · "The little red handkerchief": At this time, AT began to send Ada one of his handkerchiefs each month, with increasingly insistent requests that she stain it with her menstrual blood and send it back to him. She often complied.

E.P. PN, 2 NOVEMBER 1936; TO AM, PFB; FSD-FOF

[. . .] The Isolino is overpopulated. There were twenty-four of us yesterday. The Horowitzes and Castelbarcos left today, but the little girls have stayed on. Walter, Cia, and the little boy will leave later. Carla, too, is going to Milan. I'll stay until Milan has been **cleansed** of its <u>pestilential Mussolinian atmosphere.</u> Then I'll go back, after having touched the <u>specifically male features of my anatomy,</u> a great and highly efficacious remedy against the evil eye, and I'll stay there until the 8th, inclusive. The days are magnificent—a real triumph of sunshine and of the most fascinating light! And while human beings are tearing themselves to pieces and the whole world is upside down, cold and inscrutable Nature is silent about our troubles, and laughs. [. . .]

E.P. MI, 7 NOVEMBER 1936; TO AM, PFB; FSD-FOF

[. . .] Senator Albertini visited me today, accompanied by Maestro Carlo Gatti, who wanted my advice regarding the publication of some Verdi letters—that is, the correspondence between Verdi and Boito during their collaboration, from the redoing of Simon Boccanegra to Falstaff. I think I perceived in Gatti a bit of rancor toward Verdi over the much-debated controversy as to whether Verdi was or wasn't Stolz's lover, and whether or not this was the cause of the Verdi-Mariani quarrel! These poor great men aren't left alone even when they're in their graves! I have always adored Verdi as artist and man, since my adolescence. Today, I have an almost fetishistic love for Him! Why should I get bogged down in <u>such useless</u> details of his life, which bring him down to the level of other men? And if he liked women, what harm was there in that? He wrote Falstaff when he was eighty years old, Otello when he was seventy-four; do you think that a man of such a fiber would be satisfied with doing nothing but reciting the Ave Maria? In Busseto many, many years ago—I was very young, not yet 19 years old, and had just left the conservatory—I met an old man who had been a close friend of Verdi's, ten or more years younger than the Maestro; but he was **filthy-mouthed,** swore like a real trooper, and said whatever was on his mind without circumlocutions of any sort. In any case, from him I learned—or rather, we learned, because there were several of us friends present—that Verdi loved women to an exaggerated degree, and not only that, but this rich, filthy-mouthed farmer said <u>that he learned from Verdi</u> to like <u>a certain kind of kiss</u> that until then he had never given any woman. And just because of that, should I have stopped adoring that Great Man? So why stick one's nose into others' boudoirs? I gave Gatti my frank opinion. Judge the man and the artist—his life, as honest and upright as his art—but for pity's sake, stop short of the bedroom threshold. [. . .]

Carlo Gatti (1876–1965) was a musicologist, composer, and musical administrator. · During the 1860s and 1870s, the Bohemian soprano Teresa Stolz (1834–1902) sang leading roles in the Italian premieres of Verdi's *Don Carlo* and *Aida* and in the premiere of the revised version of *La forza del destino;* she was also a soloist at the world premiere of Verdi's *Requiem.* She had been engaged to marry Angelo Mariani (1821–73), one of the finest Italian conductors of his day, but the engagement was broken off, probably as a result of an affair she was having with Verdi. Verdi's long friendship with Mariani ended at that time, and the composer's vindictive behavior toward the conductor constitutes one of the least edifying episodes in Verdi's life. · For the sake of pedantic exactitude: Verdi was still seventy-nine when he finished *Falstaff* and seventy-three when he finished *Otello.* · Busseto, Verdi's hometown, is in the *provincia* (the equivalent of an English or American county) of Parma, whose seat was AT's hometown. · Concerning AT's attitude toward what was and was not permissible to biographers, see my introduction.

E.P. MI, 7 NOVEMBER 1936; TO AM, PFB; FSD-FOF

7-11-936

[. . .] My highly excitable nature, which pushes me toward excess, is the cause of my suffering, my jealousy. I descend directly from Heaven to Hell, with no intermediate stops, and by the same token I take the same road in reverse [. . .].

E.P. VIENNA, 11 NOVEMBER 1936; TO AM, PFB; FSD-FOF

Wednesday 11-11. S. Martino

[. . .] I've had the <u>first</u> orchestra rehearsal: Cherubini and Ravel—but my thoughts were distracted from the music. An entirely different sort of music was singing in me; I was living entirely in you, and in every other way I was a machine. I was conducting more out of habit than consciously. Your image rose up in me and extinguished every other idea, just as the rising sun obliterates all the stars. [. . .] Oh, if only I could transform myself into an <u>infinitesimally small ovule</u> and live forever inside you, never seeing the light of day! Ada, destroy—destroy this letter full of <u>nonsense</u>. [. . .]

AT's Vienna Philharmonic program of 14–15 November 1936 included Cherubini's Symphony in D Major and the Second Suite from Ravel's *Daphnis et Chloé.*

[. . .] I received our <u>Holy Shroud</u> just as I was going up the stairs in the Musikverein. I conducted the concert with it jealously hidden in my pocket, and it was a real inspiration. I'm crazy with joy. Only one negative point, one <u>thorn,</u> stuck in my heart: that you might judge me as other than what I am. For the love of God, Ada, it's you who bring me to such excess. Only you could exalt me to the point of dreaming up such fantasies. If only you had seen me at the moment when my eyes gazed upon that diaphanous veil, sprinkled with your blood! [. . .]

"Holy Shroud" and "diaphanous veil" were among the euphemisms that AT created to name the handkerchief stained with Ada's menstrual blood.

Friday—20[.11.36] morning
Here is the letter that arrived a little while ago! I can't tear it up, so I'm sending it back to you. Thus your [two illegible words] had told me everything. My letter must have shocked you greatly: tear it up, destroy everything. Words . . . and after more than three years in which we have exchanged and combined[?] those that we thought were the only ones and the true ones, here we are unable to understand each other any longer.

How stupid you must think I am if you tell me that I'm making fun of you. What horror—enough—good-bye—<u>Ada</u>

[IN AT'S HAND, N.D.:]

So be it, as you wish.
I'll never bother you again.

<u>Artù</u>

What a sad comedy life is!!!

Whatever it was that caused this near break, the problem was soon smoothed over thanks to a few telegrams and probably one or more telephone calls; the correspondence resumed.

<u>Saturday evening</u> [5.12.36]
<u>My Ada,</u> I'm writing to you as best I can and when I can! [Carla] has attached herself to me, she's glued to me like an oyster to its shell. Here, unlike in

Vienna, there is no Elsa Kurzbauer to take her off my hands. [. . .] Oh Ada, I feel that you love me less than before, since I forced you to send me that diaphanous veil. You have judged me to be what I am not and have never been: a degenerate. No, Ada! Love me and keep me always in your highest esteem—I deserve it. You are good, much more so than I—I know. But you must understand me, interpret these excesses of mine, which may seem inconceivable in a man who would seem to be well balanced. I can't explain it either, until I think that never in the world have I loved or appreciated a creature like you. Ada, I swear to you by the holy memory of my adored Giorgio, no woman has so completely conquered me. I've told you on other occasions: I don't know whether you are really and truly as you appear in my imagination, and I don't care to know—but I know that not being able to live at your side makes me suffer, and that I am now jealous, too, of everyone and everything that approaches you. And I live an unhappy life, hating whomever impedes me from achieving my supreme happiness. To have you, to live near you, to have no other human being near, to love you, to adore you, to be your slave. Ada, I suffer, I suffer, and I love you. Oh, how I love you. Give me your mouth and all of you—

Artù

AT was in Paris to conduct concerts at the Théâtre des Champs-Elysées on 8, 10, and 13 December; these were his last engagements in France. · "My adored Giorgio" was, of course, Arturo and Carla's third child, who had died of diphtheria in 1906 in Buenos Aires at the age of four, and from whose death neither of them ever completely recovered—nor did their marriage.

E.P. PARIS, 11 DECEMBER 1936; TO AM, PFB; FSD-FOF

Monday night 7-12-936

[. . .] Have you been faithful to me through these three years, as I have to you? Can you swear it to me? I can, on the things and people I most adore and hold most holy! I was unfaithful to you only in February '34. But I still didn't know my beautiful Ada—all beautiful and adored—completely and intimately. [. . .]

E.P. JERUSALEM, 30 DECEMBER 1936; TO AM, PFB; FSD-FOF

28-12-1936

[. . .] I arrived here on the 20th instead of the 19th. We left Brindisi six hours late, and instead of stopping in Alexandria we stopped in Athens. As luck would have it, we arrived at sundown, and I enjoyed a truly fantastic spectacle. The Acropolis was illuminated by the dying sun, and in the last rays the divine Parthenon was the color of old marble. Divine!!!

And you weren't there! You horrible thing. Why don't you have the strength to bind me to you like a slave, to bind me to your whims; why don't you threaten to withdraw your love if I leave you behind once again!! You're too sweet, divinely sweet! Or else you don't believe, don't feel, that it would be worth the effort!

On arriving in Tel Aviv I immediately received the most enthusiastic of welcomes. It was as if their Messiah had finally arrived!

I got to work the very same day. I found that the orchestra had been well prepared by Maestro Steinberg. With little effort, I got it to do what I wanted. I can't begin to tell you the enthusiasm that the two concerts, given on the 26th and 27th, aroused. I'm writing too hurriedly and with my heart too agitated to tell you what I would like to be able to tell you more calmly. I want to say, however, that on the 26th (St. Stephen's Day), my thoughts were with you in a special way. Do you remember St. Stephen's in 1933, my lovely, dear Ada? How divinely human you were!!! I can't continue. Be patient, my dear, and love me; don't tire of me. I'm living in a house far from Tel Aviv, where, besides not being free to write, I can't even mail things easily. I love you even more madly. All these difficulties sharpen my love. You are the divine music of the highest spheres of my paradise. I kiss you—I kiss you as I did then.—Artù

In New York the previous February, Bronisław Huberman had told AT of his plan to create a symphony orchestra in Palestine, an ensemble that would consist mainly of some of the excellent Jewish musicians who were fleeing Germany. He was appealing to American Jews to raise money for the project, and he asked AT whether he would be willing to conduct such an ensemble. AT assented enthusiastically and even insisted that he would travel to Palestine at his own expense and conduct the orchestra's inaugural concerts without drawing a fee. Word of AT's gesture not only persuaded potential orchestra members to throw in their lot with the new group but also persuaded many American and Western European Jews to contribute to what had the makings of a serious project. Thus, to a considerable extent, the Israel Philharmonic (as the former Palestine Orchestra has been called since 1948) owes its existence not only to Huberman's idealism but to AT's concrete assistance.

E.P. JERUSALEM, 4 JANUARY 1937; P.S., KING DAVID HOTEL, JERUSALEM; TO AM, PFB (CANCELED; IN ANOTHER HAND: HOTEL ALERON, PRAGUE); FSD-FOF

4-1-1937

My love, my adored Ada, sole and unique creature toward whom my troubled soul strains, why aren't you here with me? From the moment I set foot in Palestine I've been living in a continuous exaltation of the soul. Why aren't you near—you, who would understand, who would enjoy, who would be exalted by everything that's filling your Artù with joy and stupor?!! I have neither the time nor the tranquillity to tell you, to describe to you, everything that I've seen and continue to see. I'll do it the first time we meet, and I'll have the peace of mind necessary for expressing the almost religious feeling that comes over my soul at this very moment. I'll say only that even today, Palestine continues to be the land of miracles, and that the Jews will eventually have to <u>thank Hitler</u> for having made them leave Germany. I've met marvelous people among these Jews chased out of Germany—cultivated people, doctors, lawyers, engineers, transformed into farmers, working the land, and where there were dunes, sand, a short time ago, today these areas have been transformed into olive groves and orange groves. You see new settlements everywhere, and the earth flowers again. A beautiful German girl told me yesterday, in one of these settlements; "My dear Maestro, my mother and I wept, we were in despair at having to leave Germany; now we're a hundred percent happy, and we noticed that there are seven pianos in our settlement. Music remains, still, our spiritual bread." I can't begin to tell you what blessings have been and continue to be invoked on my behalf. They've presented me with a piece of land, where an orange grove will be planted and a common-house built in my name. I'm including the translation of the document, from the Hebrew. [. . .]

[IN AT'S HAND, IN ITALIAN:]

The Palestine Orchestra Trust, together with the inhabitants of <u>Ramot Hashavim,</u> presents to Maestro A. Toscanini, the brilliant conductor and friend of humanity, a piece of land at Ramot Hashavim as a demonstration of recognition and veneration on the part of the Jewish Yishuv of Palestine and as an eternal gift. Half of this land will continue to be an orchard, producing oranges, and the other half will be dedicated to the building of a <u>common-house</u> bearing the name "Toscanini House." From now on, the celebrated maestro will be an eternal citizen of the Holy Land, frequently visiting its inhabitants and eating the fruit from his land.

20 Teveth 5697
3 January 1937

TG, CAIRO, 13 JANUARY 1937; TO SC, 29W85NY; ORIG. ENG.; SCBU

WIRE CATARACT HOTEL ASSUAN TILL SEVENTEEN REGARDS
TOSCANINI

This telegram, sent in answer to a request for contact, initiated one of the most significant musical developments in America during the second quarter of the twentieth century—as will be seen. · Samuel Chotzinoff (1889–1964) was born in Russia but brought to the United States as a small child. He was accompanist to such celebrities as the soprano Alma Gluck and the violinists Efrem Zimbalist and Jascha Heifetz, and he was later music critic for the *New York World* and *New York Evening Post*. He married Pauline Heifetz, Jascha's sister, in 1925, and became personally acquainted with AT and his family during the maestro's Philharmonic years. Early in 1937, Chotzinoff was asked by David Sarnoff, president of the Radio Corporation of America, to try to persuade AT to return to America to conduct a new orchestra that would be created for him; all concerts would be broadcast nationwide by RCA's subsidiary, the National Broadcasting Company (NBC), and the orchestra would make a series of recordings for RCA. Like Chotzinoff, Sarnoff (1891–1971) was a Russian-born, New York–raised Jew. He had left school at the age of fifteen, but by the age of thirty-nine he was at the helm of RCA and its subsidiaries. The development of the electronic media in America probably owes more to him than to any other individual.

TG, ASWAN (EGYPT), 16 JANUARY 1937; TO SC, 29W85NY; ORIG. ENG.; SCBU

SHALL BE MILAN ON THIRTY THINK TO MY AGE TELL ME IF IT IS WORTH
WHILE TO ACCEPT NEW ENGAGEMENTS CABLE LUXOR INTER HOTEL =
TOSCANINI

Chotzinoff had cabled AT that he wanted to talk to him about a new project; this was AT's response.

E.P. CAIRO, 25 JANUARY 1937; P.S., SEMIRAMIS HOTEL, CAIRO;
TO AM, 25VBMMI (CANCELED; IN ANOTHER HAND: HOTEL IMPERIALE,
ROMA); FSD-FOF

24-I-1937

[. . .] When I had finished my work, on 12 January (12 concerts in 18 days, preceded by 6 days of long rehearsals), I was advised to go take a rest in Upper Egypt. In fact, I went by train to Aswan (590 miles from Cairo) with the intention of staying in the magnificent <u>Cataract Hotel</u> on the Nile, but then the mania for familiarizing myself with and visiting temples, tombs, and all the antiquities of Upper Egypt took hold of me, and so, after a two-and-a-half-day stay in Aswan, I left—but not before having visited the main sites—and I went to Luxor aboard the steamship Arabia: two delightful days of sailing on the Nile (one can't travel by night).

My arrival in Luxor coincided with the arrival of the very young king of Egypt (17 years old—an extremely good-looking boy), who was seeing the country and its monuments for the first time. I stayed 6 days in Luxor. I can't begin to tell you all the things I saw and visited! I'm dead tired—tired in my head and in my legs! What marvels—what colossal marvels! It seems impossible that in such remote times (2,000, 2,500, 3,000 years before Christ) man had the intelligence, the genius, not only to conceive such admirably prodigious things, but also to realize them!!!

Tomorrow will be my last day in Cairo. I had thought I'd attend Busch's concert, [but] Busch is in Alexandria, ill for some days (a very bad cold with very high fever). I phoned him. We're both very sorry not to see each other.

Once he's feeling well, he'll have to cancel a recital here in Cairo for lack of time, as he has to leave on the 30th. I'm taking advantage to make a quick trip (three-quarters of an hour by car) to Lakkara to see the Step Pyramid, the oldest in Egypt and the world, 2,490 years before Christ. It's enough to make you mad. The ancient city of Memphis was near here. Naturally, the site is covered with tombs, temples, and statues strewn all over the place. They tell me that there is a gigantic statue made for Ramses II, whom they call The Great because Egypt owes him not only many victories but also its most popular and numerous monuments. He lived to be 85, reigned for 67 years, and as a pastime he fathered 162 children—111 males and 51 females. And among his many wives were three of his sisters and two of his daughters. Not bad! Were morals better back then or today? Who knows!!!

I'll leave the morning of the 26th with an Ala Littoria airplane. The evening of the 26th I'll sleep in Benghazi, the 27th I'll be in Rome, where I'll stay for a day or two, as I have to be in Milan on the 30th to meet a friend who's coming from New York, sent by someone or other, to present a plan for me to go back there. [. . .] I must tell you that my mind has been enriched by so many things that I had known only in embryonic form, but my heart has been enriched by so very much affection! If only you knew how much good my presence did in Palestine! Modesty doesn't allow me to elaborate, but I can assure you that I won and was enriched by much love. [. . .]

The "very young king" of Egypt was Farouk (1920–65; deposed 1952), who did not in fact officially become king until the following July. · Adolf Busch had gone to Egypt for some recitals but had had to cancel them because of illness. · The friend from New York was Samuel Chotzinoff, of course, and the "someone or other" who sent Chotzinoff to Europe to talk to Toscanini about a new musical proposal was David Sarnoff.

E.P. MI, 30 JANUARY 1937; TO AM, HIR; FSD-FOF

Saturday 30-1-1937

[. . .] During my short stay in Rome, I received a sadly inexplicable letter from Rirì, which will perhaps help to establish a quite different line of demarcation in our old friendship! Beware of women when they're stupid! They're worse than men. [. . .]

E.P. MI, 4 FEBRUARY 1937; TO AM, HIR; FSD-FOF

Tuesday 2-2-1937

[. . .] I've already said this other times and I don't tire of repeating it: you still don't know, you've never realized, the immense sincerity of my love. You've always believed me only halfway. From time to time, you confuse me with those who have seen only the superficial side of your being. You're wrong. [. . .]

Wednesday aft.

I've just come back from Maly's house. I hardly ate, and what little I did eat wasn't good. A little yellow rice—bad—and some Cremona mustard. On the other hand, I chattered a lot. I was in the right vein. [. . .]

As I phoned you this morning, I thought I would go crazy. After <u>forty</u> minutes of anguishing waiting, I finally got into the booth and found myself talking to someone with the number 62-425. I could have exploded with bile and indignation. With immense sorrow, I have to give up calling you! I can't stand that feverish wait under the curious, questioning glances of idiotic people. I almost reached the point of canceling the call. I was in a cold sweat. And to top off the grotesque irony, a guy approached me to propose some concerts in South America. [. . .]

Maly Falck, the daughter of a major Italian industrialist, was a family friend.

E.P. MI, 8 FEBRUARY 1937; TO AM, 46VMPMI; FSD-FOF

<u>Friday night</u> [5–6.2.37]

This evening I received from Dr. Rusca of Mondadori the galleys of a little <u>book</u> of <u>aphorisms</u> by Ugo Ojetti, entitled "Sixty <u>Aphorisms</u>"!!! He certainly has a good deal of the fickle clown in him!! It's as if he considered himself a Marcus Aurelius or Pascal—upright people, all of a piece! I wouldn't think of reading these aphorisms. I used to know by heart a caudate sonnet that someone wrote in '16, in the war zone, after the taking of Gorizia, at the time when he was awarded a bronze medal; now I can only remember the last tercet, but it fits him to a T:

> On the Carso, where there are threats all around,
> And the foot soldier crosses th' Isonzo with verve,
> To deny you a medal would be most unsound,
> For Ugo, you sure have a hell of a nerve.
>
> [Original: Dove sul Carso incombe la minaccia/E il Fante passa il contrastato Isonzo/La medaglia risplende alla tua <u>faccia</u>,/Ugo, di bronzo.]

[. . .]

For Ugo Ojetti, see my note accompanying the letter of 1 September 1917. His writing was fluent and at times stylistically brilliant, but his thinking was too superficial to allow him to realize his desire of entering the company of Montaigne and other great aphorists. AT sized him up reasonably accurately, although his dislike of Ojetti for his faithful support of Mussolini's regime certainly colored his thinking.

(MI?); TO DAVID SARNOFF, (NY); ORIG. ENG.
(ALL ERRORS HAVE BEEN PRESERVED); PC; NYPLTL

February 8—1937

My dear <u>Mr. Sarnoff</u>

It is useless to repeat once more my great happiness to have accepted your invitation . . . But now I begin to realize how hard and difficult [it] must be to put together a very fine orchestra worthy to rival with those of Newyork—Philadelphia and Boston. Your undertaking is not a commercial but an artistic one and only under **this** point of view it must succeed anyway . . . So every attempt have to be done in order to select the best musicians amongst the many good ones which are living in United-States.

My good friend Chotzinoff will be happy to join you in this difficult task and I beg you to do your utmost for realizing all that which is now hoped for. This will be and happy event on your part to put with the many which happened in your life.

Very cordially believe me
Yours **Arturo Toscanini**

The string quintet must be at least

12 first violins
12 second
10 viol[as]
8 celli
7 basses
2 Flutes
1 Petite Flutes [i.e., piccolo] (playing 3d Flute)
2 Oboi
1 English Horn
2 Clarinettes
1 Bass Clarinet
2 Bassons
1 Contrabasson
4 Horns
3 Trompettes
3 Trombones
1 Basso-Tuba
1 or 2 Harps
1 Timpani
1 Cymbals
1 Drum-Triangol

Zirato—Newyork

I am surprised at your surprise my acceptance radio proposal (Stop) I feel no
obligation to be courteous toward the Board of the Philharmonic and that
boorish individual [Arthur Judson] who advises it (Stop) I won't say a word
either for or against the Philharmonic to Mr Sarnoff who will act in accordance
with his interests as the Philharmonic has always done and continues to do.

Greetings Arturo Toscanini

The New York Philharmonic's directors had reacted with alarm to the news that AT
was returning to New York at the head of a different orchestra, and they had ordered
Zirato to ask AT to protect their orchestra's interests. At the time, AT was angry with
the Philharmonic's management because John Barbirolli had been chosen as the new
conductor over AT's first choice, Artur Rodzinski, and without the news having been
communicated to him officially. Zirato replied to this telegram by telling AT that he
did not consider the radio the right "altar for the god of the musical world." This further angered AT, who replied with the following telegram.

N[ight] L[etter]

Zirato—New York—

Whether officiant's altar is Saint Peter's in Rome or the most modest little
church in the tiniest Italian village doesn't count for the priest who knows
what the true faith is—Stop—Evidence, rather than others' bad faith or false
information, prohibits being courteous to gentlemen of the Philharmonic

Greetings—Toscanini

BY THIS TIME YOU WILL BE AWARE I AM ALREADY ENGAGED WITH RADIO NEW
YORK NEXT SEASON STOP HAPPY YOUR KIND INVITATION SORRY OBLIGED
RENOUNCE IT HAVE THANKS CONVEYED TRUSTEES TOO

TOSCANINI

This was in reply to a telegram (12 February 1937) from Koussevitzky in Boston to
AT in Milan: "THE TRUSTEES JOIN ME IN INVITING YOU TO BE OUR GUEST CONDUC-
TOR NEXT SEASON. LAST YEAR YOU GAVE OUR AUDIENCES MEMORABLE PLEASURE

BUT IT IS THEIR AND OUR DESIRE TO HAVE YOU CONDUCT BOSTON ORCHESTRA. STOP I PREFERRED TO SEND YOU THIS INVITATION MORE INTIMATELY BY LETTER BUT AM ADVISED TO CABLE BECAUSE OF RECENT ANNOUNCEMENT IN PRESS THAT YOU WILL RETURN TO AMERICA. MAY I REPEAT THAT MY SUGGESTION ALSO TRUSTEES' ACTION PRECEDED KNOWLEDGE OF YOUR RETURN. I HOPE YOU WILL JOIN US IN SINCERE FEELING THAT BOSTON SYMPHONY MUST SHARE IN YOUR ARTISTIC CAREER. MOST CONVENIENT TIME WOULD BE FORTNIGHT BEGINNING JANUARY TEN. WITH LOVE SERGE KOUSSEVITZKY." Despite the many invitations (including another personal one from Koussevitzky for the 1948–49 season) that he received from Boston and his known admiration for the Boston Symphony, in the end AT never conducted the ensemble.

(MI); TO AM, (MI); FSD-FOF

Saturday 20-2-1937

I just left you and the blood is rushing through me even more tempestuously than a few minutes ago, when I felt your divine, voluptuous mouth on mine. The mysterious voice that has been saying to me, over and over, the last few days:

> "Ada, my sweet love, believe me,
> This is the last time I will see you"

has been ringing inside me just now, like a prophecy of death! Why suffer so? Am I committing such a great, criminal sin by loving you? But I can't retreat by even a hair, nor do I want to. I lack the courage! I need you and your love too much, Ada. It makes my blood surge, makes my heart beat energetically, gives consciousness to my life, which (you know—I've told you) was gradually slowing down, extinguishing itself. You, my divine, cold woman, have performed these miracles! [. . .] I love you, Ada! The sweetness of profound sensations, which I had never yet experienced as in these last few days at our dear friend's home. Why? Artù

AT and Ada's trysting place was evidently in Milan, but I do not know who the friend in question was.

E.P. MI, 25 FEBRUARY 1937; TO AM, HIR; FSD-FOF

My love and despair

I was telling you this morning about the unforgettable impression I had at the time of Verdi's death, as if the world had shrunk—an impression that was repeated at the time of Carducci's death. Well, the same, sorrowful impression has repeated itself with your deserting Milan. I can understand how a man could turn to drink or gambling out of an inability to stand pain! Saturday night, while you were traveling, I was getting drunk on music. Dear Busch, after dinner, was good enough to delight me with three quartets: <u>Haydn, Mozart, Beethoven</u>. Of the last, the Quartet Op. 59, no. 2, in E Minor, in the molto adagio, my thoughts were so much in you that I felt as if the divine notes were whispering the most sublime words of love in my ear. Oh, Ada, why can't we be clasped together in one of these superhuman instants? To listen to the music of heaven while looking into each others' eyes! Busch made me spend the first three days of your absence in a continuous state of musical drunkenness. May God bless him! But now! What and how can I tell you about my state? I feel like a sleepwalker! I go out with no destination and come back home just as aimlessly. I don't touch the piano or look at any music or read anything. I've often sat down to write to you, [but] then my thoughts pile up like furious waves and there I am, inert, with pen in hand and my mind upside down, staring far, far away and feeling thankful to anyone who comes around and draws me out of this state of suffering [. . .]. I feel lost in Milan without you. You are my light; you project a luminous, ample circle around me, but outside of it lie disquieting shadows. Now you've left; we're not breathing together the air of our adored Milan, nor will we ever again breathe it together. Don't let the light pale, if you want me to live, my Ada! Write to me, keep my mind, my heart, my flesh alive. [. . .]

E.P. (MI?), 26 FEBRUARY 1937; TO AM, HIR; FSD-FOF

[. . .]

<u>6 o'clock p.m.</u>

I heard the broadcast—all of it. The first part left me very cold. And at the beginning [Enrico] seemed not to be in the right vein, to me. I warmed up toward the end of the Bach—but I don't like him in Bach—he's not free enough and lacks inspiration. I liked him a lot in the Bréval. The Sarabande and Gigue? He didn't even play them well. Why doesn't he play the last piece in A Major? It would be more brilliant, and better still if the tempo were quicker. But I would have given a few swift kicks to that accompanist. [. . .] Hold me close to you, on your breast—<u>one sole being</u>—<u>and for a long time</u>—doing, if we could, as concert artists do—<u>lots of encores!!!</u> [. . .]

AT had listened to a recital of Enrico Mainardi's that had been broadcast on the radio. One notes with interest that AT, who adored Bach's music but felt too unsure of his interpretive perspectives on Baroque repertoire to perform much of it, believed that it had to be done freely, not stiffly. I do not know which pieces by Jean-Baptiste Bréval (1753–1823) were on the program, or for what reason AT felt that Mainardi ought to have played one of them in a different key.

[. . .] I've just arrived. It was a long trip, boring as always, when I travel by train. I found Dobrowen at the station; he kindly came to meet me. Tomorrow I'll start the rehearsals. [. . .]

AT had accepted an invitation to conduct the Residentie-Orkest in The Hague, and the Russian-born conductor Issay Dobrowen (1894–1953) was on hand to be of linguistic assistance as an interpreter.

My love,

I'm writing to you in devilish haste and with my nerves in such a state that I would like to destroy myself if I could. This morning, at the height of exasperation, I walked out of the rehearsal, just like that, with my mind made up to leave The Hague this very evening. The orchestra is crude, lacking in discipline, and accustomed to playing as heavily as a millstone. I spent a ghastly day, besieged by everyone trying to persuade me to resume the rehearsals and not to give a moral slap to the orchestra and to the city that supports it. And then there is a terrible rivalry with Amsterdam, so that this would be a sort of victory for Mengelberg, whose invitations to conduct his orchestra I've always refused. I couldn't stand up to the pleas of these gentlemen. They've postponed the concert to Monday the 8th, and tomorrow I'll resume the rehearsals, somehow or other. But what pain, what suffering, what martyrdom for me! It's a well-deserved lesson, and I'll profit from it! Yesterday, Tuesday, I received your divine letter. I was beside myself. I would have liked to write to you at length, but . . . the life I'm leading with her [Carla] drives me mad, to despair. I could cry out of sorrow and anger. [. . .]

Willem Mengelberg (1871–1953) had been conductor of the Concertgebouw Orkest in Amsterdam since his twenties; during the 1920s, he had also been principal conductor of the New York Philharmonic—until AT's astonishing success with the orchestra put Mengelberg's considerable accomplishments in the shade. The Hague's Residentie Orkest was not considered nearly as good an ensemble as the Concertgebouw, and AT had been distressed to discover that it was far below his expectations; yet he did not want either to destroy the orchestra or to give Mengelberg (whom he disliked—and the feeling was mutual) the satisfaction of a triumph by default.

<u>4-3-1937</u>

[. . .] This morning I resumed the rehearsals. The orchestra was transformed. Fear of losing me made them decidedly better. [. . .]

7-3 1937

[. . .]

<u>afternoon</u>

I was so pleased that you participated in Enrico's concert! Continue, Ada—do it out of love for me! Yesterday evening I had a concert in Rotterdam. I can't begin to tell you how warmly I was received! On getting back to the hotel, I found the main room of the suite full of flowers and wreaths, among which there was one from Mengelberg. À propos this clown: from Rome, he sent me a telegram welcoming me to his country, but the press here published it before I had received it! I haven't replied yet, and I'm still not sure whether or not to do so. What a charlatan!!

I am very happy to have made this orchestra happy, after they sent me a moving telegram to ask me to come back. But I went through some very nasty, painful hours. I'll send you a photograph taken unbeknown to me at a moment when things weren't going so well, it seems. And you—why don't you send me a few little snapshots?? And haven't <u>your days of grace</u> come yet? Or else you've forgotten the <u>solemn promise</u>. And the tiny flowers from Ada's little garden? **I'm awaiting it all in the greatest excitement.** Your letters have been arriving slowly, too slowly. Here, everything is sent via air mail! I'll be waiting for letters in Stockholm. Give all of yourself to me—<u>feel me</u> in you and feel my voracious mouth on your marvelous, divine mouth. Artù

The "days of grace" referred to Ada's menstruation and the "souvenir" she had promised; the "tiny flowers" were pubic hairs.

I'm leaving Holland on the 10th

8-3-937
3 o'clock in the morning

My Ada, I've been in bed for three hours. As always, I have with me your little photographs and your latest letters, burning with passion, which set the inferno loose in my bloodstream. I haven't been able to close my eyes for even a minute. She [Carla] is sleeping deeply. I hear her breathing regularly, in a monotonous rhythm that makes me certain that I can write a few words to you, to give vent to and lower the fever in my blood. Don't be shocked, but try to understand my acute state of sensuality, which has been under control for so long. I want, I desire you—all of you. I feel that my veins are going to burst! Your letters drive me to frenzy. You desire me, you want me, and I can no longer contain my voluptuous craving. I want to kiss you from head to foot, suck every corner of you, every meander, however hidden, of your adored body. Your words "My man, my God, my everything, I cling to you to kiss you, to kiss you to the point of despair, until you beg me for mercy"—they take away my ability to reason, I can't see straight, I'm like a madman, I could commit a crime!! Ada, I love your mouth and your kisses—those unearthly ones that drink my life. But to possess you, while I'm deep inside you, when we are one sole being, as I look into your eyes, seeing, looking into those magnificent eyes of yours, that slowly develop little black circles around them, as if they were defeated, exhausted by the voluptuousness that you've enjoyed—oh, you don't know how divine it is, how superhuman, for your Artù! You don't know what you are to me! I wish that I could be Ada and you Artù—only then could you understand how immensely, transcendentally voluptuous it is to possess, to enjoy so gracious and beautiful a creature as you! You say that I dig deep within your soul, but you dig deep within my soul, my body, my whole life. But when, oh when, will we be able to possess each other completely, clinging together, deep inside each other, our mouths gasping, united while awaiting the supreme voluptuousness at the same moment? When—when? Tell me, Ada. Will this miracle ever happen—to have full pleasure at the same moment? After that, let God give me whatever he wishes, even death!

"I have such a need to give you and give again everything I have in me, and that is yours, because you are the one who gives me life and enriches me with love by revealing it to me. When, when, Artù? Every hour without you is a lost, desperate hour. Why aren't you here with me?" This is what you've written me; how could I not go out of my mind? [. . .]

<u>Friday</u>
12-3-1937

[. . .] Tomorrow the rehearsals begin. Tuesday the 16th is the first concert. Saturday the 20th is the second. Sunday I'll fly to Milan. Why not to Rome? Cursed Rome. <u>Mussolini, the Emperor-King,</u> and the Pope. **Pigs, all of them.** [. . .]

Italy's King Victor Emmanuel III (1869–1947) had recently become emperor of conquered Ethiopia, and this gave AT, who was already ill disposed toward monarchies in general and the House of Savoy in particular, a fresh reason for expressing his loathing. Like many nonpracticing Italian Catholics before and after him, AT looked upon the Vatican's enormous influence on national matters as a terribly negative force in his country's development, and Pius XI (1857–1939) was the then-current representative of that force.

<u>Wednesday</u>
17-3-1937

My dear and <u>good friend.</u>

I'm sorry to have to give you a sad burden, but I can't avoid it, time being short and my work for the second concert being urgent. I <u>feel tired</u>—truly tired—and I don't have either the courage or the strength to resume rehearsing tomorrow morning. The rehearsals would have to be rushed, given the very few days that precede the concert. I would need a few days' rest. I put too much faith in my physical strength, and I've been punished. If I had enough time available, I would say, let's postpone the concert to next week; but as you well know, I must be in Milan next Monday, thus I am obliged to be in debt for this missed concert—a debt I shall pay back in the near future, when more time will be available—that is, as in the past, when we did one concert a week.

So I beg you, my dear friend, to communicate my great regret to the Directors of the Konsertföreningen for this unfortunate mishap. Please excuse me, dear Signora Iva—continue to be fond of me as I am of you, and accept a world of friendly affectionate greetings.

Your <u>Arturo Toscanini</u>

A further explanation of AT's decision to cut short his stay in Stockholm is contained in the following letter.

<u>Wednesday</u>

17-3-1937

My love, contrary to all my predictions, my second concert won't take place on the evening of Saturday the 20th; instead, at 4 p.m. that day I'll already be in Milan.

After the first concert I was so disgusted that I begged the directors of the Konsertföreningen to release me from my engagement. Every day I become more impossible toward others and even more so toward myself. Art for me is a <u>lot of sorrow</u> and <u>little joy</u>. I didn't feel up to the task of getting this orchestra to play Mozart and Debussy well in a few hurried rehearsals. I'm sad and upset. [. . .]

<u>Saturday 27-3-1937</u>

Yes, my love, I wrote to you every day, and yesterday I gave you a substantial account of my birthday, and I also told you that it affects me strangely to hear myself called a <u>seventy-year-old.</u> I told you about how moved I was by Busch's <u>boundless</u> goodness toward me. I told you many things, but then the fear of boring you, the fear of continuing an <u>eternal monologue</u> with myself, makes me destroy this outlet <u>almost</u> angrily (once I have given vent to the need to pass some time with you, to talk with you) after having held on to it for a few hours. I told you, in addition, that while I was enjoying the demonstrations of affection that reached me from all over, a secret, blind agitation invaded my soul; the agitated [opening] phrase of Mozart's Symphony in G Minor was like a <u>nightmare</u> that kept coming back at every moment, making the blood in my veins pulsate desperately! [. . .]

But today I couldn't stand it and I rushed to the telephone, unsure whether I would find you at home. God was merciful. I heard your divine voice, and it seemed to me full of love. May God bless you! Come, yes, come to Milan. Tomorrow I'll spend Easter on the Isolino, then I'll go to Milan, because an envoy from Paris is waiting for me so that we can reach an agreement on a future Pelléas there! Come, Ada, and <u>make me forget my seventy years. You alone can do it. Divine woman! Angel, demon, sorceress!!</u> But you are so beautiful, and I love you so much. Artù

The Busch Quartet had come to Milan to play for AT on his seventieth birthday. · The envoy was from the Paris Opéra.

29-3-1937

[. . .] Yesterday I was thinking a lot about you. The day was rainy, nasty. I sat at the piano for a couple of hours, going over Pelléas. The very idea of having to present it in Paris in October makes me go out of my mind. I want to be capable, once again, of interpreting it in an exceptional way, to please you, before everything and everyone else! My Ada! You alone can keep me alive as an artist and a man. Your love will work this miracle. [. . .]

You know, I was moved, talking on the phone with your sister Vittorina. She was very kind. So she knows that we love each other. Tell me, isn't she shocked that such an old goat is so crazy? Doesn't she feel sorry for you? [. . .]

Dearest, most adored Ada

I'm sending you this letter from Alceo Toni (???)—such Fascist courage! And I'm also sending you my answer. Everyone at my house was against my answering. I was of a different mind. He's a marionette—and he doesn't even bother to hide his strings. [. . .]

Alceo Toni (1884–1969), a composer, critic, and functionary, held important positions in the Fascist musical bureaucracy. The following is AT's handwritten copy of AT's note to Toni; Toni's letter to AT is missing.

26-3-1937

Dear Maestro Alceo Toni

Excuse me for replying with a slight delay to yours of the 22nd. Come by all means, whenever it's most convenient for you, morning or afternoon, any day of the week, as long as you let me know by telephone. Even if our conversation doesn't lead to an agreement on the subject that's close to your heart and that makes me heartsick, it will be nice to see you again after so many years. Thank you for your good wishes.

Believe me sincerely yours etc.

Friday 2-4-1937
5 p.m.

[. . .] I'm having quite a job answering, at least in part, the many people who have thoughtfully sent me messages. Many telegrams have already been sent off, and letters, too. I received telegrams and letters from all over the world; the Austrian, Romanian, and Czechoslovakian radio networks referred to my 70th birthday (aren't you afraid, Ada?), [but] the Italian radio and official Italy were silent—which makes me feel highly honored! Thomas Mann, Stefan Zweig, and Benedetto Croce were thoughtful enough to send me messages. Zweig wrote me a magnificent letter, accompanied by a Schubert autograph. [. . .]

Tomorrow Landormy, a musician, writer, and philosopher, and Lehmann, a highly intelligent man of the theater, are coming from Paris, on a mission from the French government to reach an agreement with me on performing Pelléas in Paris. We shall see what comes of it. I've read an article by Reynaldo Hahn, full of praise for Fanny Heldy, who was my Mélisande and Louise at La Scala. Do you remember her? I admired her very much. Yet she has never sung Mélisande in Paris! For what reason, I don't know. Now, I don't think that the voice [illegible word] can still be what it was, but I think that it ought to be good enough for Mélisande.

[. . .] I am agitated, restless; the atmosphere in our country is infected, men are disgusting worms, the few whom I love and esteem are dispersed hither and thither. Some days I am capable of putting up with this stench, this plague-bearing rot. Other days—today, for instance—I would like to spit poison in the face of all mankind. I can't stand it any longer. I think of those poor young men who are going off, fooled or forced, to get themselves killed in Spain—and for whom? Not for their country, but for delinquents named Mussolini, Hitler, Stalin. My Ada, I'm desperately sad, and if it weren't for the hope of seeing you I would leave Italy tomorrow morning. Artù

AT probably met Thomas Mann (1875–1955) for the first time at the 1935 Salzburg Festival. · Paul Landormy (1869–1943) was head of the music division of the 1937 Paris Exposition; AT's *Pelléas* production was to have been presented under the Exposition's aegis. · Maurice Lehmann was involved primarily with the Théâtre des Champs-Elysées. · Reynaldo Hahn (1875–1947) was a Venezuelan-born French composer and conductor. · The Belgian-born soprano Fanny Heldy (1888–1973) was considered one of the most capable and beautiful actresses among the singers of her day; she had sung in AT's historic productions of *Pelléas et Mélisande* and Charpentier's *Louise* at La Scala in the 1920s. AT's words "good enough for Mélisande" mean merely that the part does not require either an extraordinarily beautiful voice or vocal pyrotechnics, but rather good singing joined to tremendous musical and communicative abilities. · The political reference is to the Spanish Civil War.

(MI); TO AM, (VB8R); FSD-FOF

Sunday 4[-4-37]

Read these pages, which Croce has sent me. There are still some men (few, but they exist) who stand erect, because their souls aren't curved!!

You, too, are one of us, Ada, isn't that so? You couldn't love me, otherwise.

I'm going to hear [Haydn's] <u>The Seven Last Words of Christ.</u> You must listen to the only three words I can say to you: <u>I love you.</u> They are just as holy.

Artù

The essay (four typed, mimeographed pages), in Italian, is entitled: "Replies to the questions of the 'Republic' magazine of New York," and is accompanied by some handwritten corrections, presumably made by Croce, who signed the pages in ink. AT inserted some comments and underlinings. At the end of one paragraph ("But moral, intellectual, aesthetic, and political problems do not exist outside us, like rain or sunshine: they exist within us, thus it makes no sense to ask, with respect to them, what is more or less likely to happen; instead, one must simply make up one's mind, and work—each according to his own conscience and his own ability."), AT wrote, "(what about those who have no conscience? And there are many such!)." At the end of another paragraph ("It reminds me of the anecdote about a man who went to a friend and asked: 'Someone has given me a slap; what do you advise me to do?' The friend answered: 'Keep it.' It is clear that anyone who can raise a question about his human dignity has already given up defending it, inside himself."), AT wrote, "(how true!)." And in the following phrases, AT has underlined words as indicated: "Liberalism . . . is the adversary of democracy when the latter tends to replace <u>quality with quantity</u> or numbers, because it knows that, in so doing, democracy prepares the way for demagogy and, unwillingly, for dictatorship and tyranny, thereby destroying itself. . . . Those who <u>work for an ideal</u> have <u>in it their hope and their joy.</u> [AT's comment, in the margin: "(it's true)."] Under the world's present conditions, the cumulative intellectual and moral capacities are still great, and [. . .] <u>liberal rules are maintained in great and powerful countries that will be able to face the dangers to which they are exposed, and to serve as signposts for the reconquest and the general recovery.</u> In this way, and not at all through obedience; by knowing how to stand up to *death in order to strive toward a greater life,* human works are truly animated by a military, heroic spirit." AT's comment, in the margin: "(holy truths)."

E.P. MI, 8 APRIL 1937; TO AM, VB8R; FSD-FOF

Monday [5.4.37] <u>five o'clock p.m.</u>

<u>My love,</u> I've just returned from the telephone office. You can imagine the state of my heart, the state of my nerves! I knew in advance that I wouldn't find you, but I tried. I had prepared a telegram to let you know, but the telegraph office in S. Babila was closed; I didn't feel like running to the central post office. I felt like stamping on the people I saw on the street. I have a phobia toward others—banal, stinking people who set their eyes on you, look you up and down with impertinent curiosity.

No, my Ada, I must give up talking to you; I can't stand the suffering that people's unhealthy curiosity brings me. Nor will I go again to mail letters at the central post office, because this is really becoming a sickness. My liver is swollen and I feel tired, my face is long and drawn, as after a three-hour rehearsal or a performance of <u>Meistersinger.</u>

Yesterday, despite having received that wonderful special-delivery letter, I was extremely nasty. I need solitude, I need to see no one from now on. Even the people nearest and dearest to me bother me, disturb me. I heard twice Haydn's Seven [Last] Words of Christ played (excellently) by the Busch Quartet. The first time was at 4 p.m. (St. Paul's church, amid the crowd—there are no places apart, as at the Conservatory—therefore with a concentrated rage against everything and everyone). I had given up the idea of going [again] in the evening. While I was about to write to you, Madame Busch arrived at the house, begging me to attend the performance and telling me that Adolf was nearly desperate. I listened while sitting on a stepladder behind a door, unseen by anyone. Ada! Ada! Ada! Do you feel my despair? [. . .]

E.P. MI, 8 APRIL 1937; TO AM, VB8R; FSD-FOF

[. . .]

Tuesday morning [6.4.37]

I foresaw a bad night! I didn't sleep, but no matter! At 4 I was in my study. She [Carla] was sleeping a deep and musically futuristic sleep. I reread all your letters from Rome. I found the one in which you told me about Enrico's not being well, but I had remembered only the illness that you suffered. Among your many very dear letters, a short one, written when you were saying good-- bye to the city in which you were born, struck me more than the others because of a sentence that ought to replace, from now on, the motto "Never ceasing—still beginning [last four words in English in the original]." It is: "I want to tell you of my voluptuous fidelity, and that every moment of my life will always be taken by you, full of you."

My divine one, if you were near me my state would frighten you. My head no longer works right. I feel tired and have no more willpower. I would like to go to the Isolino, to distract myself and to work, but my piano rejects me instead of attracting me—the humidity has made it impossible, at least for my hands. Something must make me get the stabbing thought of you out of my head, or I'll go crazy! Maybe I could phone you from there. Here it's impossible; I can't stand any more of the suffering I've had to go through. I've shut myself up in the house; I no longer go to Baldini e Castoldi, so as not to know about everything that's going on in the world! [. . .]

AT was being facetious in describing CT's sleep as "musically futuristic": the reference is to the Futurists' inclusion of everyday noises and rumblings among musical sounds, thus AT means that his wife was snoring. · For Baldini and Castoldi, see my note accompanying the letter of 20 October 1936.

Wednesday 7-4-1937

[. . .] I continue to stay in the house. I look over a lot of old but good music, symphonies and quartets of Haydn. I've realized that all the Italian and foreign quartets <u>always</u> play <u>the same five or six quartets</u> by this author—famous ones, if you will, but they're not the only marvelous ones. And the symphonies? In fact, as a protest against the distinguished Maestro Toscanini, I'm going to replace Mozart's symphony in G Minor with one [no. 98] in B-Flat by Haydn (concert of June 14 [in London]). To think that we students at the Parma Conservatory used to play this Haydn symphony, and it was a joy for us. I can truly say that I acquired my classical culture during my conservatory years. I haven't progressed beyond it: Beethoven, Mozart, Haydn, Mendelssohn, and a good deal of Schumann and Schubert were my usual repertoire. Bach was little known. I think that even in the music library there wasn't much in those days.

On <u>18 April</u> I'll be in Vienna to audition singers. I'll attend a performance of <u>Zauberflöte.</u> I'll leave on the 17th. Will we have seen each other? Who knows! Renzo Bianchi came to lunch today. He played me a part of an opera of his that they'll perform at La Scala next year. He says it was chosen by a commission in which Pizzetti participated. Do you know anything about this? The other day, in a bad-humored moment, I sent Bianchi the attached telegram. I know that the moment one mentions the head of government [Mussolini], the telegrams go directly to Rome—and I couldn't wish for anything better. Artù

[DRAFT OR COPY OF THE TELEGRAM, IN AT'S HAND:]

<u>Renzo Bianchi</u>
Chignolo Po—(Pavia)

I'm very happy inclusion your opera La Scala program (stop) Word reaches me don't know whether believable Head of government very wisely intends replace present manager Scala for proven artistic incompetence it is said. (stop) I would be personally happy for the dignity of art and for the love that I have felt and still feel for that theater. I hope to see you soon—Greetings—Toscanini
　　[. . .]

Renzo Bianchi (1887–1972) was a composer, conductor, and member of La Scala's board of directors; the opera in question was *Proserpina*. La Scala's general manager from 1932 to 1942 was Jenner Mataloni, a Fascist official. As an artistic enterprise, La Scala sank into one of the worst periods in its long existence from approximately 1935 until the end of World War II.

Saturday morning 10-4-1937

[. . .] I spent a delightful evening at Count Casati's in a peaceful and cordial atmosphere. Benedetto Croce and many male and female friends, all right-thinking, were there. I found Croce rather low in spirits, and this made me feel bad. I know that times are discouraging, almost without a hope for seeing change, for those of us of advanced age! But that word almost leaves a fissure of light, a breath of faith that mustn't be suffocated, and that, on the contrary, must be nourished, so that the fissure becomes a breach and the breath a storm that overwhelms and destroys everything. I'm incapable, completely incapable, of becoming discouraged; I hate and I curse. Croce doesn't know whether his answers to the questions put to him by that American magazine were published. At this very moment, to my great surprise, I've received a letter from Paola Ojetti. And the surprise is all the greater because included with it is a short letter from Oxford University, as follows:

[ORIG. IN ENG.; COPIED OUT BY AT:]

Dear Sir: I have the pleasure to inform you that the Hebdomadal Council yesterday resolved to propose to Convocation that the Degree of Doctor of Music, honoris causa, should be conferred upon you. If you are willing that this proposal should go forward the Degree would be conferred on a date to suit your convenience between April 26 and June 19. Yours faithfully

Douglas Veale

This little letter was given to Dr. Gabriel Paresce (press officer at the Italian Embassy in London), to send on to me. Instead, he charged Paola with sending it to me, with his compliments. Could this Dr. Paresce, too, be one of the many who fear compromising themselves by approaching me?

I had had word of this honor here at home, purely by chance, because I accidentally opened a telegram written by my wife, who, in agreement with our children and acting as interpreter of my thoughts regarding honors, had already asked an influential person in London to ask Oxford University, very politely, to desist from conferring this title on me.

Note, however, that the strange thing about this matter is that the note from Douglas [Veale] bears the date March 16. In a P.S. to her letter, Paola says, "The Oxford letter is old, but it has just now reached me." What do you, as an intelligent woman, certainly sharper than I, think of this? It seems to me a malicious game. My friends here, including Croce and Count Casati, want me to accept, especially inasmuch as at this very moment the great Delinquent has received the same honor from the University of—Lausanne! But I'm deaf to such requests! I would begin to feel awful, living an agitated and unhappy life! Better to say no! [. . .] Do you know how many times I've imagined, in my thoughts, what my life would have been had I been able to spend it with you? And then, in my imagination, I see it as an infinite, uninterrupted succession of days, weeks, months, and years full of sun and serene beatitude! Just as when I look back at the years of my adolescence! I don't remember a day without sunshine, because the sunshine was in my soul.

Did I tell you that I had Piatigorsky and his new wife here for dinner? Yes indeed, I found her very simpatica. She doesn't talk much, she's rather timid. I told her so, and she agreed. I've been told that one morning she went to see Wally and Wanda's little girls, and that she stayed there with Wanda for three-quarters of an hour without the two of them exchanging a word. You know Wanda! You can imagine the scene! [. . .]

Paola Ojetti, a Florentine writer, was the daughter of the journalist Ugo Ojetti. Inasmuch as an honorary doctorate from Oxford University was considered far more significant than one from the University of Lausanne, Croce and Casati were thinking of the potential embarrassment to the Fascists if AT were to receive the former at about the same time that Mussolini was receiving the latter. But AT hated all such honors, no matter what their value to himself or others. · Piatigorsky's new wife was Jacqueline Rothschild. · Wanda Toscanini Horowitz was capable of being either taciturn or overbearing (and at times even charming), depending on her mood.

(MI); ON A PIECE OF PAPER WITH A GLUED-ON LITTLE PHOTO OF AT IN HIS EARLY THIRTIES WITH WALTER AS A SMALL CHILD; TO AM, VB8R; FSD-FOF

Sunday eleventh [11.4.37]

[. . .] Walter and I in 1899 in Val di Lanzo, Piemonte (Groscavallo). You were two years old. It was the month of August. I was extremely busy studying Siegfried, which was supposed to be the first opera of the 1899–1900 Scala season, and it was also the first time it was being performed in Italy. So as not to lose time with my morning toilette, I had let my beard grow. No one knows this photograph; I myself didn't remember it. A few years later, on the other hand, I had to give myself a completely clean shave: Walter, who was already a good-sized child, cut off half my mustache as a joke, and so the other half had to go, too. But the beard, like the absence of a mustache, lasted only a few months. [. . .]

E.P. MI, 14 APRIL 1937; TO AM, VB8R; FSD-FOF

13-4-1937 Tuesday evening

[. . .] Yesterday evening I went to Rachmaninoff's concert. It interested me greatly and I enjoyed it. Bach, Beethoven, and Chopin were interpreted by an elect artist. The second part of the program was much less interesting, musically: 4 études composed by him, music of Liszt for a Petrarch sonnet, [a piano arrangement of the] Magic Fire Music from Die Walküre, and an étude in E Major by Paganini-Liszt; but the pianist's virtuosity was a success.

On Saturday I'll leave by airplane for Vienna. [. . .]

Do you know Bebe, who lives in Lugano? She came to visit me yesterday. She was the only simpatica person among the many who annoyed me. Toni, too, returned, but he left empty-handed. What a fool! How many useless words, merely to leave me unpersuaded! [. . .]

AT admired the great Russian pianist and composer Sergei Rachmaninoff (1873–1943) but never performed with him. · For Bebe Baslini, see my note accompanying the letter of 15 August 1936. · For Alceo Toni, see my note accompanying the letter of 26 March 1937.

E.P. MI, 14 APRIL 1937; TO AM, VB8R; FSD-FOF

14-4-937 Wednesday morning

[. . .] Yesterday evening two Gabriellas—Foligno and Robilant—were here for supper, and so was Ania, that friend of Volodya's (she's a Russian pianist). She's here all the time, morning and evening. I would go to the Isolino despite the piano, which repels me, but I'm sure that everyone would come pouring down on me there. I certainly am a magnet [calamita, in Italian], and the others are a calamity [calamità]. On top of this, a fever to read through music has come over me, and, as in everything else, I go overboard; I suffer if even an hour is taken away from me. Yesterday, they stole my whole day. After supper, yesterday evening, the five Polos, Miecio, and Palazzi, the painter, came over; the last, in fact, was here for lunch, too. I could have retired to my study, but you know how it is: I can't study when I know that others are listening to me. I have a modicum of shame!!! [. . .]

Gabriella Foligno and Gabriella Robilant were family friends. · The Odessa-born pianist Ania Dorfmann (1899–1984) played Beethoven's Choral Fantasy and First Piano Concerto with AT and the NBC Symphony in 1939 and 1944, respectively. · The Sardinian-born Bernardino Palazzi, who lived in Milan, was one of AT's many painter friends and acquaintances.

TG, MI, 16 APRIL 1937; TO SC, 29W85NY; ORIG. ENG.; SCBU

WOULD BE HAPPY CONDUCT BOSTON ORCHESTRA STOP DONT THINK ABOUT PALESTINE HORN STOP TELL ME IF BOLOGNIN[I] HAS BEEN ENGAGED LOVE TOSCANINI.

Koussevitzky had evidently gone directly to Sarnoff and/or Chotzinoff with his invitation to AT to conduct the Boston Symphony, but despite AT's willingness the engagement never took place, for reasons I have not been able to discover. · The reference to the Palestine horn player is unclear. · AT admired the playing of violinist Remo Bolognini, who had been his assistant concertmaster with the New York Philharmonic but had since become a staff musician at NBC; AT was eager to have him engaged by the new orchestra, and Bolognini remained for the entire seventeen years of the NBC Symphony's existence.

E.P. VIENNA, 18–19 APRIL 1937; P.S., HOTEL BRISTOL, WIEN;
TO AM, VB8R; FSD-FOF

Saturday afternoon 17-4-1937

[. . .] The life I'm living is intolerable. The people around me—all of them, <u>do you understand?</u>—disturb me. I feel that I no longer love anyone. My life is concentrated on a single idea: to live with you, to be near you. I can't stand it anymore. I live uncomfortably in my own home—too many people. I'm like a deluxe object, a rare, precious item that <u>arouses others' vanity.</u> And yet we don't have the courage to make a vigorous, decisive break with all the stupid social conventions, and to live once and for all for <u>ourselves alone.</u> Everyone thinks I have a strong character, whereas it's nothing if not weak. [. . .]

In Friday's letter I told you that after an opinion I had voiced about [Fosca] Leonardi was reported to her by someone or other, my wife commented that everything I say or write is repeated by a thousand mouths and scattered to the four winds, and as proof she quoted a sentence that she said I wrote to someone some time ago—a sentence that I remember having repeated to you several times, in my letters, regarding "<u>the misunderstanding</u> of <u>thirty-six years of marriage.</u>" It will be forty, this year, so it must have been a letter written in 1933. Believe me, Ada, I don't blame you if you confided in Rirì [Pizzetti] or Maria Teresa [Ada's sister]. I wish I had a friend with whom I could let off steam about the fullness of my affection and my sorrows! I'm saying it so that you can see the complete lack of refinement and the meanness of spirit of the people who surround me. And à propos the people who surround me: today I saw Mrs. Gawronska; or rather, more than seeing her, I <u>practically lived</u> with her. She came to pick me up in her car at the airfield [in Vienna], she kept me company at lunch, and not only that, also at supper, at the Imperial's restaurant, where I found the Piatigorsky couple, who were celebrating his 34th birthday. I saw Elsa Kurzbauer, who looked rather aged, and badly so. She's becoming deafer and deafer. It made a very painful impression on me. Tomorrow morning I'll go to Bruno Walter's concert; in the evening, to the Staatsoper, to hear the Magic Flute. <u>Novotná</u> is singing Pamina, and she is supposed to be my [Pamina] in Salzburg. I think I'll stay here through Tuesday. Wednesday I'll return home, by airplane. Why does the good Lord mock us so? I'm alone and I don't have you. A huge bed awaits my nonsleep. And you're not here. And I desire and want you so much—you, Ada, not just any woman! There are many women who have a hard time behaving themselves. I don't know what to do with them; on the contrary, they don't interest me! It's you for whom I'm <u>slowly dying</u> of **voluptuous passion.** You don't know yourself! The near lack of <u>real sensuality</u> in you brings a man to paroxysms of desire. That's what you do to me—and I'm not even a sensualist. [. . .]

Fosca Gemignani Leonardi (1880–1968) was the daughter of Puccini's wife, Elvira, by her first husband, Narciso Gemignani. She married Totò Leonardi, a singer and impresario, and had three children, the youngest of whom was the well-known Milanese stylist known as Biki (or Bicchi). AT and his family were close to the Puccini family. · "Mrs. Gawronska" was Luciana Frassati Gawronska; see my note accompanying the letter of 18 September 1936. · The performance of *The Magic Flute* that took place at the Staatsoper on 18 April 1937 was conducted by Josef Krips; its cast included Jarmila Novotná as Pamina, Helge Roswaenge as Tamino, and Alexander Kipnis as Sarastro (the same singers who would sing the same roles under AT's direction at Salzburg the following summer), in addition to Margaritha Perras as the Queen of the Night and Hans Duhan as Papageno. According to Gawronska, AT did not like Krips's account of *The Magic Flute:* "He solemnly announced to me that he was going to sleep that evening at the opera. [. . .] But as soon as we had entered the box, with the first notes of the prelude [*sic,* for overture], something that sounded more like Fafner's reawakening than the sound of a magic flute issued from his mouth. 'What a fool!' he roared. So much for the promised sleep!" (Luciana Frassati, *Il Maestro* [Turin: Bottega d'Erasmo, 1967], pp. 242–3.)

E.P. VIENNA, 21–22 APRIL 1937; P.S. AS IN PREVIOUS LETTER;
TO AM, VB8R; FSD-FOF

<u>Wednesday afternoon 21-4-1937</u>

[. . .] I worked this morning. With the orchestra, I rehearsed the Pastoral and the Haydn symphony in B Flat. I don't know the reason, but I feel better, and a much better person, than yesterday. I look at our future with less despair. [. . .]

I'll return to Milan immediately on Monday the 26th. In the afternoon, I'll be able to call you <u>at the Hotel Manin.</u> I don't know whether I've told you that I've been asked whether I want to do a concert or two in Paris, with the program repeated. I wouldn't want to do it at the Salle Pleyel, which I hate and detest, but at the Opéra or the [Théâtre des] <u>Champs-Elysées.</u> I'm told that there's demand on the part of a great many people, and that it would suffice to publish my name without a program to have a complete sellout. Wanda is there and will see whether or not it makes sense. [. . .]

While in Vienna to listen to singers, AT was prevailed upon to give a concert with the Philharmonic, and on this occasion he was able to perform the Haydn symphony that he had mentioned to AM in his letter of 7 April 1937. He then dropped it, however, from his London concert of 14 June and did not reschedule it until the following January, in New York.

(VIENNA), N.D. BUT POSSIBLY LATE APRIL 1937;
P.S. AS IN PREVIOUS LETTERS; TO BRUNO WALTER, (VIENNA);
NYPL, BRUNO WALTER PAPERS, JPB 92-4, SERIES I, FOLDER 589

My <u>very dear Walter</u>

I am truly sorry! For some days already, I've had an engagement for lunch on Sunday after the concert. I've tried to get out of it, but I've found it impossible. Believe me, dear friend, that I'm <u>angry</u> about this. In any case, I thank you very much. Lotte Lehmann has replied to my tough telegram—she <u>guarantees</u> that she'll be in Salzburg on July 21 for the morning rehearsal.

Cordial greetings to your wife—remember me to your beautiful daughters—for you, an affectionate handshake.

<u>Arturo Toscanini.</u>

E.P. VIENNA, 23 APRIL 1937; P.S. AS IN PREVIOUS LETTERS;
TO AM, VB8R; FSD-FOF

<u>Friday 22-4-1937</u>

[. . .] My rehearsals have gone well. Tomorrow at 3 p.m. I'll do the dress rehearsal, with audience. The concert is Sunday at 11:30. Monday without fail I'll leave by airplane at 1 p.m. [. . .] One can't have twenty-four hours of peace. The other day I was so tranquil, whereas today I'm as dark as Vienna's sky. [. . .]

DRAFT OF LETTER THAT AT WROTE FOR HIS WIFE TO COPY AND SIGN;
(MI?), N.D. BUT PROBABLY SPRING 1937; TO ERWIN KERBER, (VIENNA?); EC

Dear <u>Dr. Kerber</u>

I am replying in my husband's name to your letter, to express to you his wholehearted <u>satisfaction</u> over the new plans regarding the building of the Salzburg Festspielhaus. In fact, I am including some observations that my husband has made with respect to Dr. Rehrl's plans. My husband asks that you do him the favor of getting information on a young coloratura singer (Julie Osváth) in Budapest. They say that she would be a very good "Queen of the Night" for the Magic Flute. They also say that she is young and pretty, which <u>can't do any harm!</u>

Erwin Kerber was administrative head of the Vienna Staatsoper and the Salzburg Festival. · AT had agreed to help raise money for the new Festspielhaus that was being planned in Salzburg. · Dr. Rehrl was the governor of the province of Salzburg. · Young Julia Osváth did indeed sing in AT's Salzburg *Magic Flute* in 1937.

27-4-1937

<u>My love,</u> It's like a dream to hear your voice again in Milan—<u>your city</u>—not Rome, that of the <u>great Delinquent.</u> [. . .]

Tomorrow I'll phone you at 70562. Will you then go to the Hôtel Manin? I can't wait—it's like a dream, to see you again after two endless months! Do you still love me? You didn't lose your love when you flew at over 5,000 meters? I'm crazier and crazier about you.

Biggest possible kisses—Artù

2-5-1937

[. . .] Pelléas! My God, what can I tell you? The singers were nothings—zero. The orchestra? It was like all Italian orchestras—<u>bourgeois,</u> undistinguished. The interpretation? Most of the tempi seemed right, and the tone colors, too, but taken as a whole—boredom!!! The music was lacking. It's the same as in poetry, when all the words are what they ought to be, the verses feel right, the rhyme scheme works, but the essential—<u>the poetry</u>—is missing. It leaves me "avvilito e calpestato" [mortified and trampled underfoot], as Don Basilio says [in Rossini's *Il barbiere di Siviglia*], and I feel that I, too, am among the last of the losers, with no enthusiasm, and I no longer see any light that could dissipate the shadows that envelop my brain. I'm mortified. The curiosity that pushed me to attend this performance has been repaid. The frequent lowering of the curtain, too, is intolerable. I don't know why I couldn't have managed to devise a less humdrum method in my performances at La Scala! And now this thought tortures me.

I saw lots of people! I was at Placci's house, where I saw Mrs. Cerruti, Giulietta and Eleonora Mendelssohn, the new academician Papini (whom I didn't know personally). In fact, we chatted a lot, and at the theater yesterday evening Placci told me that I had made a great impression on him [Papini]. I had supper at the Leccio with the Passiglis. Whereas I had lunch all alone at <u>our very own table,</u> here at the hotel! My dear, sweet friend, how you dominate my thoughts, and how much tenderness you wring from my heart! I saw Paola Ojetti; I strongly deplored the discourteous way in which her friend <u>Paresce</u> sent me the letter from Oxford. Your <u>friend</u> [empty space, in the original] also came to say hello. We met at the [Hôtel de] la Ville [in Milan] the other evening, when I was going to see you, but he pretended not to see me. Is he perhaps one of your many adorers? Tell me, Ada—don't keep anything from me. <u>I tell you everything.</u>

Instead of stopping at Portofino, I'll fly to Milan—to you. [. . .]

The performance of *Pelléas et Mélisande* that AT attended at Florence's Maggio Musi-cale on 1 May 1937 was conducted by Albert Wolff (1884–1970), a Frenchman. Its cast included the baritone André Gaudin (1902–86) and the very young soprano Janine Micheau (1914–76) in the title roles, with the baritone Claude Got (1906–40) as Golaud; the production, directed by Jean Mercier, had been borrowed from Paris's Opéra-Comique. · Carlo Placci was a journalist friend of AT's. · For Mrs. Cerruti, see my note accompanying the letter postmarked 25 August 1936. · For the Mendels-sohn ladies, see my note accompanying the letter of 29 August 1935. · Giovanni Pap-ini was an important Florentine writer (see AT's postcard to WrT, p. 96). · The Passigli family has been active in Florentine musical life for generations; members of its various branches cofounded and still direct the Amici della Musica, which every year provides the city with its most substantial series of solo recitals and chamber music concerts by outstanding foreign and domestic artists.

E.P. PARIS, 9 MAY 1937; TO AM, VB8R; FSD-FOF

9-5-1937

[. . .] My coming here was necessary. Yesterday evening I betook myself to two theaters, the Opéra and the Opéra-Comique. I heard two acts of Boris at the Opéra, to get an idea of the protagonist, whom I was supposed to choose as Golaud. [I heard] the last act of Bohème at the Opéra-Comique, where Bour-din, who should be Pelléas in my performances, was singing. The latter is good. The former, although a good singer, isn't right because his voice lacks a certain roughness that the part of Golaud requires.

Today I'll hear two women, one for Geneviève, the other for the boy, Yniold. This evening I'm having supper with Fanny Heldy. This is the thorny point. They tell me that she's singing quite out of tune now. She isn't much liked in theater circles! They say that she's capricious, lacking in steadiness, etc., etc. I can't say the same. I always found her ready and willing, well pre-pared at all the rehearsals, enthusiastic about her work. It certainly is a bit embarrassing for me, as I have to try, very tactfully, to get an idea of her pres-ent vocal state! Enough—we shall see!

Write to me directly at the Hotel Claridge in London—don't fail, don't make me suffer. The distance in itself is enough to embitter me. Don't worsen my spirit's already depressed state. [. . .]

Tuesday morning I'll leave Paris by airplane; I'll arrive in London alone. Carla will follow by train. [. . .]

The performance of *Boris Godunov* at the Paris Opéra on 8 May 1937 was conducted by Philippe Gaubert (1879–1941) and had the bass André Pernet (1894–1966) in the title role. *La bohème* at the Opéra-Comique that evening was conducted by G. Cloez and had the baritone Roger Bourdin (1900–74) in the role of Marcello.

E.P. LONDON, 14 MAY 1937; P.S., CLARIDGE'S/BROOK STREET, W.1;
TO SC, 29W85NY; ORIG. ENG. (ALL ERRORS HAVE BEEN PRESERVED); SCBU

May <u>14—1937</u>

My dear <u>Chotzie</u>

How are you? and my dearest Pauline? and everybody at home? Well? I hope so!! It seems you are <u>very stingy</u> in sending news! I answered all your cables but so far I don't know anything about the new orchestra! Did you find the first horn? Is the <u>horns quartet</u> quite first <u>rate</u>? Who is the concertmaster? the first cellist? By this time is everything settled? Do you think the orchestra will be a wonderful one? It must be so—otherwise we shall make a <u>colossal fiasco</u> and everybody <u>will laugh at our expenses</u>! Please, be kind, and send me word on this matter. And what else about Boston? I am here to conduct several concerts—26-28 May: 2-4-14-16 June . . . After I go to the Isolino resting and waiting for Salzburg. In October I have to conduct Pelléas and Falstaff in Paris! . . . théatre Champs-Elisée. November to Palestine—Dicember (?) Newyork. As you see the <u>old maestro</u> is still alive and thinks to be so for many years to come! <u>Don't laugh!!!</u> Remember me to all at home, a **mamasha** (specialmente)[.] Give to Pauline a very big kiss—if happens to see Margherita embrace her for me . . . Where are Jascha and Florence and Elsa? Love and greetings to all and especially to my dear Chotzie. A. Toscanini

"Mamasha" was Mrs. Heifetz, mother of Jascha and Pauline; the latter was Chotzinoff's wife. Florence was Jascha's wife. Elsa was Jascha and Pauline's sister.

E.P. LONDON, 24 MAY 1937; P.S. AS IN PREVIOUS LETTER;
TO AM, VB8R; FSD-FOF

<u>24-5-1937</u>

[. . .] I began the rehearsals last Wednesday. The [BBC Symphony] orchestra is excellent—better than two years ago. You'll probably hear the broadcast—I'm very happy about that. I hope it will at least be good. [. . .]

E.P. LONDON, 31 MAY 1937; P.S. AS IN PREVIOUS LETTERS;
TO AM, VB8R; FSD-FOF

<u>31-5-1937</u>

[. . .] The two concerts went very well. Tommasini arrived in time to hear his Carnevale di Venezia, in the morning at the dress rehearsal, in the evening at the concert. The audience very warmly demonstrated its enthusiasm. I pointed to Tommasini, who was sitting near Carla in the hall, and, having been forced to stand up, he received an extremely warm ovation. I got a tremendous kick out of it. Were you able to hear the broadcast of this 2nd concert? It's odd that from my house in Milan they heard the first one, too! Maestro Mortari sent me a telegram from Venice as well, after the first one.

If only you knew how happy I am with this orchestra! It's a real joy to be working! From New York I've received the list of the new [NBC Symphony] orchestra's members. It seems to me to be made up of the best individuals to be found there. Money is no object. They're paying astonishing salaries! I have also received, during the last few days, an article by Lotte Lehmann that is supposed to be published in English in "Vanity Fair." [. . .] Send me the plan and a photograph of your home. I want them—I want to have an idea of where you live. I know from Tommasini that you had supper with him before he left Rome. I've met a delightful lady friend of his here—a truly dear person. She enthusiastically attends all the rehearsals. Miecio gave his concert last Thursday. My whole gang attended. It seems he played well. I read a very good review in the Observer newspaper. [. . .] Have you had any word from little [Maria] Salata? They tell me that that clown, Ojetti, is greatly exercised over the lack of commas in modern literature!!! There's another individual who never knows when to keep quiet! Like his head of government.

I'm using a pen that's making me suffer the torments of the damned. It slides so on the paper that it's torture to restrain it. [. . .]

Works by the composer Virgilio Mortari (1902–93) were frequently performed in Italy during the 1930s and 1940s. · Maria Salata was the daughter of Italy's ambassador to Austria; she was a friend of AM and was said to be Ugo Ojetti's mistress. The "head of government" was, of course, Mussolini.

(LONDON); P.S. AS IN PREVIOUS LETTERS; TO AM, VB8R; FSD-FOF

Tuesday 1 June 1937

[. . .] I've been through a nearly sleepless night. [. . .] I began to doze off this morning at 7, but I had a rehearsal at 10. I had no desire for it, but the Pastoral and then the Eroica swept me away, and everything disappeared in the divine enchantment of those works. Tommasini and Miecio were present, and they expressed their wonderment at how the orchestra understands me and responds to my every sign. [. . .]

E. WITH ILLEGIBLE POSTMARK (LONDON); P.S. AS IN PREVIOUS LETTERS; TO AM, VB8R; FSD-FOF

10-6-1937

[. . .] I was outside London for a few days [. . .]. The Oxford concert was in the daytime, at 3 p.m. To avoid being honored with investitures and Latin orations, I preferred donating a concert to the university, all to benefit one of its funds. The earnings were more than £1,000. After the concert (just think, I wasn't at all tired!) we went to Windsor by car and crossed the famous park (what a marvel!) in all its length and breadth, together with Roberto, my whole family, and the Guttinger couple. Mrs. Sandra G. wears the same perfume as yours—"Arpège." I almost went mad! You were in my thoughts! I felt that you were near. I closed my eyes to feel the illusion—but I didn't do any touching. This morning I resumed rehearsing. <u>Ibéria</u> was the first piece! [. . .]

The concert that AT "donated" to Oxford University on 8 June was a gigantic one that consisted of a Rossini overture and three symphonies: Haydn's No. 92 ("Oxford"), Beethoven's Sixth, and Brahms's First. · Roberto Foligno, Sandra Guttinger, and her husband were family friends.

E.P. LONDON, 14 JUNE 1937; P.S. AS IN PREVIOUS LETTERS; TO AM, VB8R; FSD-FOF

14-6-1937

My <u>divine creature,</u> I haven't been able to write to you as I had promised. I'm ready to burst in anger and vexation. I've become a victim <u>of the Jews.</u> I don't know how to defend myself. Every afternoon has been like torture for me. Never, never alone, not even for a moment! Stefan Zweig kept me at his home all last Saturday with Tommasini, to show me new autographs of truly exceptional importance: Mozart, Beethoven, Wagner, Bach, Goethe, etc., etc. Yesterday I was with the Holt sisters, who had been asking me to lunch for a long time, and what with the Holt ladies, <u>Marchioness</u> Cholmondeley (another Jewess), the Toeplitzes, and Yvonne Rothschild (can't you smell the goose salami?) I couldn't steal a moment for sending you even a telegram. Excuse me, my great treasure, love me all the same and believe me that when I can't talk to you by writing to you, it's a matter of <u>real mourning</u> for my soul—an irremediable <u>misfortune.</u> You see: I'm tired now; I've had the dress rehearsal for this evening's concert. Carla has gone to have her hair done. I'm stealing these few moments from my rest time to be with you, the <u>life, love,</u> living <u>miracle</u> of my existence. When I've finished writing this letter I'll send you a telegram, so that you won't worry or think I'm a liar.

The Holt sisters were presumably connected with the Harold Holt concert agency. · The marchioness of Cholmondeley (Sybil, <i>née</i> Sassoon; 1894–1989) and Yvonne Rothschild, both young Jewish or part-Jewish heiresses, were in love with AT; about both of them, more later.

18-6-1937

[. . .] I couldn't wait to leave London and the English. I couldn't stand it any longer. The concerts were a triumph with respect to audience and even performance. The orchestra is truly admirable for its discipline and ability. What a shame that you didn't hear the Eroica! You really would have loved me more than usual. I think that I've never conducted it better. The orchestra was possessed, like me, and like the audience afterward. It seems that after the last concert—all Wagner—the newspapers said, "the program was made up entirely of old music that's been <u>heard and heard again,</u> but it seemed new." I can't begin to describe the audience's frenzy. Despite everything, I couldn't wait to go back to my beautiful country. Oh, how I adore Italy, my Ada, and how I suffer because I adore it so! This is my fate. For me, loving means suffering! [. . .]

E.P. MI, 19 JUNE 1937; P.S., ISOLINO S. GIOVANNI, PALLANZA;
TO AM, VB8R; FSD-FOF

19-6-1937

[. . .] The Paris Pelléas has faded over the last few days. I think this was a maneuver by Rouché, Director of the Opéra, to force me to give Pelléas and Falstaff in his theater. They realized only recently that the electrical system of the <u>Champs-Elysées'</u> stage is inadequate and unfixable! Everyone, including the government, is begging me to go to the Opéra. I have definitely refused. Instead, I'll go to London again in October for two concerts: Brahms's Tragic Ov. and Requiem in the first, Beethoven's 1st and 9th syms. in the second. [. . .]

In 1924, Jacques Rouché had proposed a visit of AT's La Scala ensemble to the Paris Opéra, but financial considerations and the problem of adapting sets to the Opéra's stage, which is smaller than that of La Scala, had caused the plan to fall through. It is unclear why AT so greatly preferred the Théâtre des Champs-Elysées, where he had never conducted an opera, to the Opéra or even the Théâtre du Châtelet, at both of which he had conducted the Metropolitan Opera ensemble in 1910, before the Champs-Elysées theater was built.

E.P. MI, 20 JUNE 1937; TO AM, VB8R; FSD-FOF

19-6-1937

The day after tomorrow, 21 June, **40 years** of marriage!
  How many lost illusions.
  How much emptiness!

How much solitude!

If it weren't for you, Ada, what would I be?

Mea culpa? Maybe!

I'm very sad and I love you very much! I've given vent to my soul, briefly but deeply. Keep it to yourself, Ada.

Your Artù, who adores you above everything and every living creature!!!

E.P. PN, 23 JUNE 1937; TO AM, VB8R; FSD-FOF

Wednesday 23-6-1937

[. . .] Monday we had many friends on the Isolino! It was a day of divine sky and blazing sun. Strange coincidence! June 21, 1897, was also a Monday. Just think, Ada, that your entrance into the world was 44 days in the future. [. . .] Among the friends who gathered here was Sandra Guttinger, she of the **disturbing** perfume. I closed my eyes and **breathed you in**. But that perfume is better on you than on her. [. . .]

E.P. PN, 24 JUNE 1937; TO AM, VB8R; FSD-FOF

Thursday 24-6-1937

My unique love, I'm alone, and on the Isolino! Do you know what it means to be alone, to me who can never be so? Aren't you moved by my divine solitude? I feel that I can breathe more freely, I feel lighter, I feel that I've shed a few decades. Do you know how many dear, sweet ghosts are wandering silently around me? A whole legion—people who have passed away, whom I knew and loved, and superior spirits whom I have known and adored through their sublime works. I work, I play the piano, and I read. I don't stay still for a moment. Yesterday evening I went to bed more tired than if I had conducted a concert. Do I perhaps need to tell you that the thought of you follows me in my every action throughout the day? And you are the one who lends beauty to everything I do. I'm coming to the conclusion that the interpretation of the Magic Flute that I'll give at Salzburg will arouse outcries of either scandal or enthusiasm. There will be no middle of the road. Did I ever tell you that I attended this opera twice (partially), in Vienna and recently also at [Glyndebourne] near London to hear it again, conducted by Fritz Busch?? Here, too, the impression was of boredom, as in Vienna! The tempi were slow where they should be moderati or andante, very slow in the Larghetti, and enough to asphyxiate you in the Adagios. And then the interpretation of the embellishments was all wrong. I'm enclosing two examples, only to persuade you that the interpretation is right when it embellishes the melody that is decorated by it. The Magic Flute is full to the brim with such cases! Ada, my dear, I realize and I'm more and more convinced that good musicians are rare, and sometimes even the good ones forget the art of knowing how to go back to the beginning, of looking at music they already know with innocent, pure eyes, like a child who is seeing things for the first time. [. . .]

afternoon

Betti and his wife (a French cellist) paid me a visit. I found them both well. He's a little fatter in the face; she, on the other hand, is thinner everywhere. They were both satisfied with my impression. He was a very good friend of Ugo Ara, and, like me, he doesn't have the nerve to go to the Isola dei Pescatori. As you can imagine, I don't even have the nerve to call the friends we had in common at the Albergo Verbano! That dear, beloved ghost, too, is often near me. I still can't make my peace with his so silent passing away!

[. . .] Did you hear the broadcast of Aida from Berlin? Don't you think it was scandalous? I blushed for everyone. What ensemble! The chorus was barking instead of singing. And the singers? Everyone went off in a different direction. Poor art! But why talk about art? It's politics that count today. Everything is the slave of damned, dirty politics! I would be curious to know what the German newspapers and critics think about these performances by La Scala. La Scala in Berlin makes me think of Tietjen, the Staatsoper's director, and thinking of him makes me think of Winifred Wagner, his lover, and of Winifred's older daughter, Mausi, who is in England, studying English, and has written to me a few times, with so much friendly feeling that it makes me marvel. Well, she came to see me in London—she stayed through my last week, attended several rehearsals of the Wagner program and the concert. I can't begin to describe how affectionate she was. The last time I'd seen her, in '31, she was a little girl; now she's a young lady of 19, still a bit enormous, as she was then, but tall and with a pretty, smiling face! [. . .]

AT was correct in his predictions regarding his *Magic Flute* performances in Salzburg: they were so unorthodox, in their day, that they shocked some listeners and sent others into ecstasy. · The Italian violinist Adolfo Betti (1875–1950) had been first violin of the legendary Flonzaley String Quartet. His wife, Emma d'Archambeau, was presumably related to the quartet's cellist, Iwan d'Archambeau, and she often wrote to AT. · Ugo Ara, another former Flonzaley member, had died the previous year. · The Scala ensemble under De Sabata performed in Berlin in 1937, and Hitler attended one of the *Aida* performances to which AT refers; the leading tenor was Beniamino Gigli. · The Algerian-born Anglo-German Heinz Tietjen (1881–1967), stage director and conductor, directed the Prussian state theaters from 1927 on; according to more authoritative sources than AT, Tietjen was indeed Winifred Wagner's lover after the death of her husband, Siegfried, and he was the first artistic director of Bayreuth who was not a member of the Wagner family. He was a consummate political opportunist and power player, for which reasons AT did not like him, and on this matter AT was in complete agreement with Furtwängler. · Friedelind ("Mausi") Wagner (1918–91), Richard Wagner's granddaughter and the second of Siegfried and Winifred's four children, was strongly influenced by AT's anti-Fascist and antiracist attitudes and soon became an anti-Nazi renegade in her family.

<u>25 June 1937</u>
Tel. 81-78

[. . .] It's a magnificent day. After yesterday's rain, the good Lord has regaled us
with the sun in all its glory. The beautiful azure lake and the green mountains
that surround it melt into a splendor of light and divine harmony. If we lived
a little more in contact with nature, how much better we would be!! I think
you asked me how long I would stay on the Isolino and how it happened that
C. has left me alone. I owe these days of peace and spiritual tranquillity to
Wally, following an exchange of opinions that we had in London regarding
Carla's health and the abnormal state of her nerves. Both Wally and Wanda
understand and admire my ability to adapt. But they don't know—and it's a
good thing—about the tragedy that preceded my ability to adapt! Can you
imagine, my Ada, that for almost thirty years (since before Wanda's birth) I
haven't been able to have physical contact with her? Marriage, too, ought to
have its <u>book of etiquette.</u> A mere nothing can demolish the enchantment, the
poetry of the most powerful love. But to return to the subject: Carla, like all
women of a certain age, ought to think about reestablishing, through some
cure or other, or through rest, the physical equilibrium that wears away with
the passing of the years and that is also reflected in damaging wear on the
psyche. Wally certainly spoke to her and recommended that she leave me here
alone, with no hangers-on from the family. And I feel so calm and tranquil this
way! My brain is rested, although I keep it active all the time. Everything I see
and hear is so much in harmony with my spirit that I hardly notice being in
almost perpetual motion all the blessed day. And you're not here! And you
aren't familiar with the beauty of my Isolino! It's romantic, you know, besides
being beautiful! Poor Ugo, in his little book on the Borromean Islands, says,
in speaking of the Isolino, that the young couples who came to visit it would
murmur, "The Isolino is your heart." What an unrealizable dream: the Isolino
and my Ada! [. . .]

AT does not say whether the thirty-year absence of physical contact between himself
and his wife, since sometime in 1907, was caused by a physical problem or a psychological one on CT's part, or was perhaps the result of a decision taken by her as a conse-
quence of her husband's philandering, or even, possibly, of his inability to make love to
her. In any case, this revelation goes a long way toward explaining AT's subsequent,
cast-your-nets-wide approach to extramarital sex. · Ugo Ara's book referred to is *The
Romance of the Borromean Islands: An Italian Suite* (New York: Frederick A. Stokes, 1930).

29-6-37 Sts. <u>Peter and Paul</u>
[. . .] I've asked you whether you're religious, whether you believe! I do—I
believe—I'm not an atheist like Verdi, but I don't have time to go into the

subject. I'll do it some other time. If I've shaped you with my own hands, you've done even more for me—you've worked directly on my life, you've re-created it, since it was nearly extinguished. And you know it. You must never forget the miracle that you've worked, and you must be proud of it. You've given me back the strength to grasp my art again. A woman like you can do much for the life of a sensitive artist like me!! And you have done so. Oh, that June 10, 1933! There is now a sort of obstinacy, of vanity: I want to continue to be someone, in the first place for you and then for others. I want to be your joy; I want to be the best of artists, again for your joy, and the one most loved by all the audiences in the world, in order to please you more and more. My Ada, my soul, my joy and despair.

I'll write to you at greater length as soon as I can. A bigwig from the BBC is coming today. The last day [in London], I recorded twice the first movement of the Pastoral to see whether they make records well. This gentleman is com-ing to show me that they make them better than in New York. [. . .]

So far as one can discern, AT's religious beliefs were intellectually pantheistic but, at a gut level, closely related to the superstitious and image-oriented Roman Catholi-cism typical of the time, place, and class in which he grew up. He was not, however, a practicing Catholic and is not known to have attended a mass after the age of seven-teen or eighteen, except for the weddings or funerals of people close to him, and, in his last years, the commemorative masses on the anniversaries of his wife's death, as she had requested. · The gentleman from London may have been Fred Gaisberg, the mov-ing force behind His Master's Voice in England. The "Pastoral" Symphony was com-pleted and issued, and several other excellent BBC Symphony recordings were made by AT.

TRANSCRIPT IN UNKNOWN HAND OF AT LETTER, ISG, JUNE 1937;
TO FRIEDELIND WAGNER, (LONDON?); ORIG. ENG.
(ALL ERRORS HAVE BEEN PRESERVED); RWGSB

My dearest young friend Mausi
Daniela very often told me that you were a nice good-hearted girl—having the deepest affection for her and Eva . . . I was touched and happy for it . . . The two good and old lady deserve wholly your love and affection. Now that I met you—spoke to you looking at your beautiful face I can say that I was able to read in your eyes the goodness that your heart conceal[s]. This I wanted to say and nothing else. Your letter pleased me for it's contents and also because [it] was written by your hand. Don't believe Mausi, I can understand everything[.] I am sometimes short-minded as I am short-sighted!

Where are you going to spend the summer? Have you not any idea to go for a little while to Bayreuth?

Bayreuth! the deepest sorrow of my life . . . Are you aware of the reason which compelled me not to go there in 1933? And I thought, Bayreuth must have been the joy of all my life! . . . Helas!

When you have <u>nothing else better</u> to do send me news of yourself . . . It would ever be a joy for your old friend.

I remain here till July 15 then—**Festspielhaus Salzburg.**

A big kiss from your

A. Toscanini.

PHOTOSTATIC REPRODUCTION, (LONDON?), N.D. BUT ENCLOSED IN FOLDER DATED JULY 1937; ORIG. ENG.; NYPLTL

This is an appeal to all lovers of music, to help in an hour of need—Madame Gerda Busoni—the widow of one of the greatest musicians of our time— Ferruccio Busoni. I shall be personally grateful for your contribution

Arturo Toscanini

Copies of this open letter were distributed privately but internationally.

E.P. PN, 3 JULY 1937; TO AM, VB8R; FSD-FOF

2. July 1937

<u>My soul,</u> I wrote to you—I wrote to you and I tore it all up. I've got the Devil in me. From Vienna, they're driving me crazy. I've sent a telegram as follows:

"Dr. Kerber—Staatsoper. I'm surprised that the Austrian government keeps you at the head of the State opera. Find a conductor to replace me in Salzburg."

I want to see how he gets out of that! And if I have to give in, so as not to ruin the season, Mr. Kerber <u>will have to resign from the Salzburg theater.</u> Ada, I am completely beside myself. [. . .]

And Maria S. is in Rome! To meet the academician? Lucky them! At least one of them is free. She can move around how and when she pleases. But us! Have you noticed that Maria is forty years younger than he and you are thirty years younger than I? But love is blind, therefore it doesn't even see age. I'm worried about Enrico. Poor devil—why must such a young man suffer so much? Will he need an operation? I hope not. And will you and I see each other? I feel so bitter today. Everything looks black to me. Even the weather, which has resumed being <u>beautiful,</u> makes me angry because it's out of tune with me even more than Schönberg's music is out of tune with my ears. [. . .]

Regarding AT's confrontations with the Salzburg Festival's administration in the summer of 1937, see the following letters. · "Maria S." and "the academician" were AM's friend Maria Salata and the journalist Ugo Ojetti, a frequent butt of AT's barbs—the more so since he had become a member of Mussolini's Accademia d'Italia, which AT considered a farcical imitation of the Académie Française.

Saturday 3 July 1937

[. . .] I've never been a sensualist. Wagner was, to the highest degree. He couldn't go for two weeks without females. His letters are strewn with pleas to females—not to women. After [Mathilde von] Wesendonck, Maria the <u>maid</u> was perfectly fine for him: he wrote to her [the following quote is in English in AT's original letter]: ["]Now my best sweetheart, have everything in the house very nice and in the lovely study. Everything must be quite tidy, and well warmed. Perfume it nicely; buy the best bottles of scent, so as to give a nice odour. Ach Gott! How delighted I am to be able to rest again with you there. (I <u>hope</u> **the rose-coloured pants are ready**?) Aye, aye! You must be very pretty and charming. I deserve to have a thoroughly <u>good time</u> once more. Many kisses to my sweetheart. Au revoir.["]

As a young man, I stayed in the house for months and months, working, without getting near a woman and without suffering from it. When I saw you as a girl, many years ago, your face, your eyes attracted me; later, your voice, your gracious little self. I liked you better than any other girl at that time; I envied your adorers, but you didn't arouse any sensual thoughts in me. I adored and liked you as one adores and loves a beautiful work of art. I looked at your beautiful face more than your figure, at your eyes more than your shape. Innumerable other "nuances" were pleasing to me—your way of walking, of looking (ah!), of smiling. You were my favorite among the girls of your time, and I was hurt when people spoke badly of you or pointed out physical defects, etc. My admiration was unconditional—it left neither time nor space for analysis or reflection.

After four years of sick, incurable, mad love, thwarted by cruel fate, I cling to you more than ever, held tightly in an erotic knot that nothing can loosen by so much as a thread, let alone sever. [. . .]

TO BRUNO WALTER, (SALZBURG?);
NYPL, BRUNO WALTER PAPERS, JPB 92-4, SERIES I, FOLDER 589

Isolino S. Giovanni
<u>Lake Maggiore</u>

3. July 1937

My <u>very dear friend Bruno Walter</u>
By now you will be aware of my nasty telegram to Dr. Kerber. I was quite right to do it. He is a boorish peasant who doesn't know what it means to live uprightly among people who always act by the light of day!

I believed the inclusion of Furtwängler in the Salzburg program, which was done unbeknown to me, to be a clever move in order to obtain more easily those German singers who are needed for the festival. Only in such a case could that inclusion have been excused and accepted. But this was not at all what happened. We are navigating in very difficult waters, today, to complete the casts for the operas Meistersinger and Zauberflöte. But if the government and administrators of the German theaters deny their singers permission to come to Salzburg, why are the <u>Austrian government</u> and the <u>director</u> of the <u>Vienna Staatsoper</u> inviting this <u>most humble servant</u> of Messrs. Hitler, Goebbels, and company? It's a mystery! <u>Artistically,</u> there was no need! There were <u>three</u> of us capable of giving the cosmopolitan Salzburg audience a performance of the 9th Sym. And so? These Austrian gentlemen ought to be <u>sincere,</u> for once—they must not continue to do conjuring tricks. Either in or out. Either for or against Nazism! Either the devil or the holy water. As for me, I am withdrawing forever from the theater. Its atmosphere makes me suffocate!

Excuse me, dear friend, but I felt it my duty to tell you the above. Be fond of me, as I am fond of you. Remember me to your wife and to your lovely daughters. An embrace from your

Arturo Toscanini

For AT's attitude toward Furtwängler's political stand, see my note accompanying the letter of 19 January 1935. One cannot stress too strongly, however, that until the previous year, when their views on how to react to international fascism had collided, AT had always supported Furtwängler's career, despite their utterly dissimilar personalities and aesthetic points of view.

TWO VERSIONS OF DRAFT OF TG — ONE IN ITALIAN, IN WRT'S HAND, PROBABLY DICTATED BY AT; THE OTHER, COPY OF A GERMAN TRANSLATION, ALMOST CERTAINLY THE VERSION SENT; (ISG? MI?), N.D. BUT CLEARLY EARLY JULY 1937; TO DR. REHRL, GOVERNOR OF SALZBURG PROVINCE; NYPLTL

Governor Dr. Rehrl, Salzburg

Thank you for your courteous telegram[.] I believe futile your coming [Isolino] San Giovanni because I can confirm my departure for Salzburg as soon as I am assured giving up conductor 9th Symphony [Furtwängler][.] inviting him unbeknown to me has deeply offended me.

Arturo Toscanini

E.P. PN, 5 JULY 1937; TO AM, VB8R; FSD-FOF

<u>Sunday morning</u> [4-7-37]

[. . .] I ought to confide something that's been in my heart since London, but I don't know whether or not to do it. Would you tell me if someone wrote that he loves you, that you are his life and his despair? Have you told me every-thing during these four years? You haven't hidden anything from your Artù? I am sinless. And if a sin was committed, it was at a time when I thought you were lost. Oh, the impression made by that telegram that arrived on 25 March 1934. It was so unexpected! Like our whole love story, it is dominated and ordered by an occult power. You'll see, my love, nothing in the world will be able to separate our souls, and who knows—I hope, I believe—maybe one day the harshness, the hardships that dog our footsteps today will cease. I think that you are not much of a believer, or not at all. I am—to the point that I don't believe at all that everything ends with death. God will protect us! You'll see! [. . .]

Carla is coming with the Guttingers today. Every once in a while, Carla becomes hysterical about people. Never before have these Guttingers been underfoot so much as in recent times! [. . .]

What had been in AT's heart since his time in London was the story of Sybil Chol-mondeley's and Yvonne Rothschild's love for him.

E.P. PN, 6 JULY 1937; TO AM, VB8R; FSD-FOF

Monday 5-7-1937

My love, I received your dear special-delivery letter just this morning, while I was about to take the motorboat to Stresa to meet little Sonia. At the same time, I received a registered letter from Minister Pertner in Vienna, to whom, on Saturday, I had wired in the following terms:

"German government [and] director Tietjen in Berlin refuse German artists for Salzburg out of hatred myself. Thus I judge inclusion German conductor Furtwängler Salzburg program a weakness, an error, a lack of respect toward me against which I rebel. Mr. Kerber had obligation to let me know. Most respectful salutations. AT"

It seems, from the letter, that they're sending Bruno Walter here.

I'm so agitated and restless that I can barely hold the pen to write! I'm also including the note to Carla from that fool the mayor of Milan. Rage has made my heart stick in my throat! Why can't one be understood for once? Why don't they let me live with my beliefs, be they good or bad? Do I ever try to persuade others to change their values in politics, in art, or in life? My Ada, I even feel sick to my stomach, I'm trembling inside, and I'm writing in spasms, like an epileptic. But I want to tell you everything, I want to vent my bile, and maybe your nearness will calm me! [. . .] I'm bombarding you with letters, with futile questions. You, in your great goodness, put up with the constant siege from this love-maddened man. Much of the fault is yours. When have I ever done this sort of thing? To whom in my life—all of it—have I sent articles and photographs as I do to you? To my parents? Never, never. To my family? Never! Never! To my friends? Decidedly not! You tell me that I've made and modeled your soul, but you have completely remade me—and please note that it was much more difficult for you, who had an old wreck to work on. [. . .]

[LETTER—COPIED BY AT ON A SEPARATE PIECE OF PAPER— FROM MAYOR OF MILAN:]

<u>1-7-37</u>

Dear <u>Donna Carla</u>
   I know that our friends <u>Rocca</u> and <u>Toni</u> will have the pleasure and privilege, within the next few days, of a private exchange of thoughts with the dear Maestro, so as to ensure, at last, the return of the fullest light and the most restorative and reparative sunshine.
   You, who know what my first wish was, the moment I arrived at Palazzo Marino [Milan's City Hall], can easily sense what prayers and thoughts I send along, in spirit, with our friends. May the voice of our Country and of Milan once again illuminate the heart and mind of our great Maestro! We shall look after the rest!
   With infinite friendship and devotion, Your

<u>Guido Rasenti</u>

"Rocca" was probably Gino Rocca, a musician who was on the Scala board; for a note on Alceo Toni, see AT's letter to AM of 30 March 1937.

DRAFT OF TG; (ISG), N.D. BUT SHORTLY AFTER 3 JULY 1937; TO HANS PERTNER, AUSTRIAN MINISTER OF EDUCATION; NYPLTL

N L T [NIGHT LETTER]
MINISTER PERTNER—VIENNA
BEG PARDON FOR NOT REPLYING TO YOUR GOOD KIND LETTER STOP WITH REFERENCE TO TELEGRAM SENT TO YOU 3 JULY I CONFIRM THAT FURTWAENGLERS INCLUSION SALZBURG FESTIVAL WAS MISTAKE WEAKNESS AND LACK OF RESPECT TOWARD ME AGAINST WHICH I PROTEST STOP I HAVE NOTHING PERSONALLY AGAINST COLLEAGUE FURTWAENGLER ONLY WANT TO STATE THAT THERE WAS NO ARTISTIC REASON FOR HIS PARTICIPATION (STOP) IN ANY CASE MISTER KERBER SHOULD HAVE LET ME KNOW IMMEDIATELY (STOP) UNDER THESE CONDITIONS TO MY GREAT SORROW I MUST GIVE UP SALZBURG. MOST DISTINGUISHED SALUTATIONS

TOSCANINI

E.P. PN, 8 JULY 1937; TO AM, VB8R; FSD-FOF

Morning <u>8-July</u> [1937]
[. . .] As I told you on the phone, no further news has reached me from Vienna either from Minister Pertner or from Bruno Walter. I wish it were all over. But

that won't be the case—unfortunately! Clowns, all those Austrians! Hitler will do well to swallow them up—then he'll croak from indigestion! [. . .]

E.P. PN, 10 JULY 1937; TO AM, VB8R; FSD-FOF

Saturday 10-7-1937

[. . .] Nothing from Vienna yet. I ought to have found out on the 6th whether or not the German government would release the singers. But the Furtwängler question, unanticipated by the good Austrians, intervened. In fact, about this fellow I'm sending you a letter from Bruno Walter that arrived yesterday in reply to a rather violent but, as always, sincere and straightforward one of mine. [. . .]

The Bruno Walter letter is not to be found among AT's letters to AM.

E.P. PN, 12 JULY 1937; TO AM, VB8R; FSD-FOF

Saturday 10 o'clock in the morning

[. . .] For forty years and more I've been hearing words of admiration, exclamations of wonder, and I've always been and will always be the same wretch, always unsure of myself, worried and anxious over the choice of a tempo or a coloring! That's your Artù!! Poor devil!

Your letter moved me right from the beginning; it made my heart beat faster and nearly brought tears to my eyes. My dear Ada, I understand—oh, how I understand—your whole internal tragedy! And to think that at the time of your marriage, I envied you and Enrico! I couldn't have imagined a more handsome, happier, and more fulfilled couple! If, today, my love gives you the "courage to put up with disgust at too many things," I couldn't wish for a higher reward, believe me. [. . .] How I like your calling me "pure-impure." I tell you everything that crosses my mind.

Sunday afternoon

[. . .] From Vienna and Salzburg they send me telegrams as long as letters, but if they don't liquidate Furtwängler I won't move from here! I want to teach a lesson to those ill-bred Nazis. I thought that the inclusion of F. was a political decision, in the sense that through him they would get the singers needed at Salzburg, but on the contrary, it's to please him. Let him stay out in the cold! [. . .]

<u>Tuesday morning 13-7-1937</u>

[. . .] Little <u>Sonia</u> is a dream of a child—adorable! She has a very fine ear; I realized this last year in Salzburg, when she wasn't yet two years old. The nanny would sing her Brahms's lullaby, and what do you think: she looked at her while she was listening, and then took it up in <u>exactly the same key,</u> without missing a detail.

My love, not having children was a real tragedy in your life! Today, you would have a goal, and the aridity of marriage would have its compensation. (I'm jumping from one subject to another because I have the first page of your very long and most divine letter before my eyes, and I feel my heart swell with sadness.) [. . .]

<u>Tuesday afternoon—13-[7.37]</u>

[. . .] I've just this moment received a telegram from Minister Pertner! They've obtained the German singers. One must always threaten in order to get what one wants! [. . .]

On this occasion, however, AT did not get exactly what he had wanted. The German singers needed for his opera performances were allowed to go to Salzburg, but Furtwängler's participation in the festival was part of the package and Kerber retained his position.

<u>22-7-1937</u>

<u>My love!</u> I'm angry with you, very angry! I wouldn't have written to you if I hadn't received at least a word from you first! How is it possible that after my last telephone call, made with a swollen, exacerbated heart—I was almost on the verge of crying with rage and disdain—you left me all these days without a single kind word, without even taking an interest in my uncertain, sorrowful position [with respect to the Salzburg Festival]—because, in the meantime, I would have liked to let everything go to the Devil. I felt what a disaster my absence would have created here in Salzburg. You've been nasty, nasty. There it is—these are the moments when you show yourself to be <u>cold, glacial.</u> You've made me suffer, these last few days, almost as much as that jackass peasant of a Dr. Kerber!

Work on the new theater has been under way for several months, here, and I can't begin to tell you with what <u>fervor</u> and <u>enthusiasm</u>! Dr. Rehrl, the governor of the Salzburg province, is in charge of everything, and he wants everything done in keeping with my criteria. From the very first day, he has been taking me to see what's been done, and, to tell you the truth, I'm open-mouthed over the speed of the work. The rehearsals are going well, one after another. The Zauberflöte cast is excellent, of the highest order; that of Fidelio is much better than in past years: Marzelline, Rocco, Florestan—all are better than in the other years. This evening I'll begin rehearsing the Magic Flute with the orchestra (one rehearsal only). Tomorrow, Friday, there's the Fidelio dress rehearsal. Meanwhile, I'm also rehearsing Falstaff. I love you and I want to have your letters—long, very long ones—immediately. [. . .]

The "excellent" *Magic Flute* cast included Helge Roswaenge as Tamino, Jarmila Novotná as Pamina, Willi Domgraf-Fassbaender as Papageno, Julia Osváth as the Queen of the Night, and Alexander Kipnis as Sarastro. Kipnis was also the "better" Rocco in Fidelio (Anton Baumann had been Rocco in 1935 and 1936), whereas the new Florestan and Marzelline were Helge Roswaenge and Harriet Henders, respectively, replacing Koloman von Pataky and Luise Helletsgruber. · AT certainly had more than a single orchestral rehearsal of *The Magic Flute*. His words "one rehearsal only" may mean that he had only one rehearsal that day or (less likely) that he was running only a single rehearsal of each act with the orchestra alone before beginning the ensemble rehearsals.

E.P. SALZBURG, 24 JULY 1937; TO AM, 25VBMMI (CROSSED OUT; IN ANOTHER HAND: HÔTEL DEUTSCHER KAISER, MUNICH); FSD-FOF

Friday <u>night</u> [23.7.37]

<u>My treasure,</u> You know, I'm still in a state of agitation, as if I had a presentiment of some disaster. I still can't free myself of the uneasiness that that d—— Kerber arouses in me! This afternoon there was the dress rehearsal of Fidelio. Everything went normally and well: as I already wrote to you, this year's version is much better with respect to the Florestan, Rocco, and Marzelline! Tomorrow morning I have a Falstaff ensemble rehearsal with the same people as last season, and tomorrow evening the festival opens. I've already seen many Italian cars around town! I've also had many visits from Americans! Will I be able to see my Ada this year? If only God were willing! <u>Strobl</u> is a little village on the St. Gilgen Lake. I remember passing through there last year. [Lotte] Lehmann has a villa at St. Gilgen. How long will you stay in Milan? Will you then go on to Germany? Damn that country! You two are poisoned by those big, rude, massive Germans! I hate them. I've always hated them, since long before Hitler. But Enrico has a sort of weakness for them. I remember how he spoke about them, one evening in Berlin in the fall of '33! [. . .]

Saturday night [24.7.37]

[. . .] Everything went marvelously [at the first <u>Fidelio</u> performance]. I received your dear telegram after the first act. My old friend [Daniela] Thode is also here. I can't begin to tell you how moved she was. The poor thing was crying with joy. She hasn't set foot in the Bayreuth Festival for two years! She has a nasty character, like mine. But you love me even though I am the way I am, and so nothing else matters! [. . .]

Tuesday night [27.7.37]

[. . .] Falstaff had an excellent performance, better, perhaps, than in previous years. Many Italians were present, and among them were the Duke and Duchess Visconti di Modrone, the Borlettis, etc. It was broadcast in America. Our dear Margherita telegraphed me, as soon as the performance was over, that she had heard the 1st act perfectly! This morning there were other telegrams from friends of mine in <u>Hollywood</u> who told me of their joy over the performance and the excellent quality of the broadcast. And you heard nothing! I would like to work only for you, but only rarely do I have that joy. This morning I had the ensemble rehearsal for the 2nd act of the Magic Flute. Tomorrow morning the one for the first act will take place, and Thursday the dress rehearsal. I hope to achieve something good artistically. The cast is excellent. I'm having the three youths sung by three children. Those children's voices contrast delightfully with those of the ladies-in-waiting. I'm curious to see how my interpretation will be received and judged! I feel that I'm in the right! I hope I'm not fooling myself. We shall see!

I mentioned, in a letter, something that had happened to me in London. You asked me to tell you <u>everything.</u> You have the right. But I've dithered until now as a result of a feeling that you can well understand. The woman is a friend of <u>Wally, Wanda, and Horowitz</u> who has followed me everywhere for two years: Paris, Vienna, Salzburg. In fact, she has been here for some days and will stay until Saturday. I always thought that she admired me as an artist, but instead it seems that she admires the man, too. I've tried to give her paternal advice, but it's all been futile. I find myself in an embarrassing and slightly ridiculous situation. It's always difficult and painful for a man to get himself out of certain situations. I'm sending you, separately, two letters that will give you an idea of my comical status with respect to this kind, dear lady, with whom I have always had a most cordial friendship. Love me, Ada—write to me and tell me everything—you, too. We mustn't have secrets from each other. I kiss you lovingly. Your Artù

The roles of the Three Youths in *The Magic Flute* were often sung by three women for the sake of musical security, but using three well-trained children—which AT decided to do—is common practice today. · Included with this letter was a very beautiful love letter on engraved stationery—Hôtel de Crillon, Place de la Concorde, Paris—from Sybil, marchioness of Cholmondeley, *née* Sassoon, granddaughter of Baron Gustave de Rothschild; it is dated 30 June 1937. Her touching declaration is, among other things, an extraordinary testimonial to the impact of AT's personality even on people accustomed to associating with the highest echelons of international society: political, economic, and cultural.

E.P. SALZBURG, 29 JULY 1937; TO AM, 25VBMMI (CROSSED OUT; IN ANOTHER HAND: HÔTEL RIESSERSEE, GARMISCH, GERMANIA); FSD-FOF

29-7-1937

My dear

This is a very short little letter, and also a bit funny. Do me the kindness of playing these four numbers in the lottery—80-3-57-44—on the Rome and Milan wheel. I'll put 25 lire on each wheel—**quaterna secca.** They must be played for <u>two</u> weeks. [. . .]

This is not the only proof among AT's letters that he occasionally played small sums of money on the lottery. *Quaterna secca* is maximum risk for highest gain: you win only if the four numbers you have chosen come up in the order in which you have chosen them.

E.P. SALZBURG, 30 JULY 1937; TO AM, HRG; FSD-FOF

Friday <u>30-July</u>

[. . .] The <u>Zauberflöte</u> dress rehearsal was magnificent, with a very large audience that <u>filled</u> the hall <u>beyond bursting</u>—residents of Salzburg, all. The first performance is this evening. I think it's being broadcast. I would be very happy if it is! It was a very good idea of mine to have the part of the <u>youths</u> sung by three children. If only you could hear how adorable those <u>childish, pure voices</u> are!!! When they join together with Pamina's, they're moving! [. . .]

E.P. SALZBURG, 31 JULY 1937; TO AM, HRG; FSD-FOF

<u>Friday night</u> [30.7.37]

[. . .] Yes, you were in my blood with every note of the Magic Flute! I think I did a good job. Bruno Walter came to my dressing room after the performance. He was moved and most interested in all the ways in which my interpretation differed from the usual ones. In certain things, especially with respect to the embellishments, it seemed to me still very unready! Strange to say! Were you able to listen? [. . .]

E.P. SALZBURG, 5 AUGUST 1937; TO AM, HRG; FSD-FOF

Wednesday evening 4-8-1937

[. . .] I had to get Die Meistersinger back in shape in two ensemble rehearsals. At first I found it a bit of a wreck, especially the orchestra, which, since the four Salzburg performances last year, has performed this opera eight or nine times under other conductors and has fallen back into the same old errors and carelessness. I rehearsed two acts yesterday, and today from two to five I rehearsed the third, which is the longest. I hope that I've straightened them out. But what a strain! Isn't there a radio in the hotel over there in Garmisch? Is it possible that you can't manage to hear anything while everyone else from as far away as America, not to mention Switzerland and here in Austria, hears magnificently and enjoys it? Maria Salata has been in Strobl for several days and has written to my assistant, Leinsdorf, to get her a ticket for tomorrow evening. I don't know whether she'll be so lucky. [. . .] This year Carla has stuck Elsa Kurzbauer permanently before me. I have nothing against her (because, on the contrary, I feel that I am to blame for her present state), but it bothers me to have her underfoot every day and at every meal and at every rehearsal! [. . .]

The Austrian-born conductor Erich Leinsdorf (originally Landauer; 1912–93) was AT's chief musical assistant during his three Salzburg summers; he later held important positions in the United States and elsewhere. Another of AT's Salzburg assistants in 1937 was Hungarian-born Georg Solti (1912–97), who went on to an even more glorious conducting career than Leinsdorf's; Solti also played the glockenspiel in the 1937 *Magic Flute* performances.

E.P. SALZBURG, 6 AUGUST 1937; TO AM, HRG; FSD-FOF

[night of 5–6.8.37]

[. . .] I am still all vibrant from my efforts. The performance [of *Die Meistersinger*] took place in an infinitely poetic atmosphere. I can't begin to tell you of the joy of the audience and performers, all of them! After the first act, Eva Chamberlain (Wagner's second daughter) came with tears in her eyes and said to me, "My dear friend, I feel as if I were hearing Die Meistersinger for the first time. Never, not even in Bayreuth's early days, has it made so great an impression as this evening." And she kissed my hands, bathing them with her tears, which seemed unending. Poor friend—I found her very much aged!

[. . .] I certainly feel exhausted, but tranquil enough for having once again done my duty as an honest artist. And the audience feels it! And you ought to have seen with what smiling faces the performers, from the orchestra to the last minor extra, looked at me! General Caviglia came but didn't have the nerve to show his face. Now that he, too, has <u>degenerated</u> he feels his conscience gnawing at him! But the reason is that as long ago as last year I didn't receive him with my former cordial enthusiasm. Unfortunately, I'm incapable of pretending! Ada, my dear, I foresee and predict a sleepless night. My nerves are still tense; as I write, I have to stop every once in a while, because my hand jerks, as if from epilepsy. [. . .]

For General Enrico Caviglia, see my note accompanying the letter of 22 August 1936.

E.P. SALZBURG, 11 AUGUST 1937; TO AM, HDKM; FSD-FOF

[. . .] I hate people more than ever! It would have been a disaster if I weren't living in this little house, which is a delight and in a delightful position! I would already have fled Salzburg! I can't stand being looked at any longer. Yesterday I wanted to attend the dress rehearsal of the Marriage of Figaro, out of respect for Bruno Walter. I couldn't hold out—I rushed home out of despair, before the rehearsal began. [. . .]

E.P. SALZBURG, 13 AUGUST 1937; TO AM, HDKM; FSD-FOF

<u>12-8-937</u> Two in the <u>afternoon</u>
<u>Dear Ada,</u> Everyone has gone for a nap; I can't, I'm so agitated and nervous that I can't tell you why. I'm fed up with Salzburg. I can't wait till I'm done here. Apart from the Requiem and the last concert—music of Brahms—I have no further interest in the repeat performances. [. . .] Meistersinger in a few hours! Inspire me, be near me, don't ever leave me. May your sweet image waft around me.

I kiss you, I kiss you!!!—Artù

<u>Thursday night</u> [12.8.37]

You've done a very unpleasant thing to me. You might have spared me this. Why have you gone to Bayreuth? You weren't obliged to go. Who invited you? Furtwängler?

You and your husband have stomachs of iron!

I can say no more to you tonight.

<u>Artù</u>

<u>16-8-1937</u>

My <u>love</u>, You made me suffer, I repeat, but your dear, most dear letter has brought peace back into my heart. And then, just now any trifle can disturb me, I see everything askew, I'm fed up with myself, not to mention all the people who surround me! The last Meistersinger performance [so far] was a tragedy—I don't know how I managed to conduct it. My thoughts were fixed on you and Bayreuth, and I was saturated in rage. Your special-delivery letter from Munich was delivered to me just as I was about to start the [Verdi] <u>Te Deum</u>. I didn't have time to open it. I had it on me through the whole concert. I was able to read it only many hours later.

My Ada, I can't wait to finish. Every day I become more nervous and savage. I hate people, but they crowd desperately around me! I can't begin to tell you how many people have invaded my little house during the last few days! Yesterday evening I had to attend a sort of concert of early music played on old instruments, given in the town hall, and as I <u>read</u> the <u>program</u> I realized that it was given in honor of Bruno <u>Walter, Knappertsbusch,</u> and myself. You can imagine my state. I refused to sit in the chair of honor that had been reserved for me, to avoid being exposed to curious glances; then at supper I didn't eat or drink anything, nor even open my mouth! The whole government was there, from Schuschnigg on down. Even that vain Salata fellow. Everyone was so <u>bandaged</u> with decorations that it was actually funny to see them! I wanted to write to you when I got home, but I didn't have the strength nor was I in the right mood. [. . .]

AT conducted Verdi's *Te Deum* and *Requiem* at Salzburg on 14 August 1937 with a remarkable quartet of soloists: Zinka Kunc (who soon changed her last name to Milanov), soprano; Kirsten Thorborg, mezzo-soprano; Helge Roswaenge, tenor; and Alexander Kipnis, bass. · Hans Knappertsbusch (1888–1965) conducted *Elektra, Der Rosenkavalier,* and two concerts at Salzburg in 1937. One wonders whether Bruno Walter knew that Knappertsbusch had been only too pleased when, in 1933, the Nazis had chased Walter out of Munich, and that he had been among those responsible for forcing Walter's friend Thomas Mann into exile. · Kurt von Schuschnigg was Austria's chancellor from 1934 to 1938.

<u>Monday night</u> [16.8.37]

My **marvelous** <u>love</u>!!! I love you to death!! I hope I've found an orchestra seat for you for the last Meistersinger performance. I'll know tomorrow. I'll send it to you immediately. Or rather, I'll look for a second one, for Maria. I think that after the performance there won't be a train to take you to Strobl. Maria could be of use, for the car—isn't that so? I'll also look for a place for you for the last Falstaff performance. I want you to hear these two masterpieces! It's too bad that you didn't hear Zauberflöte. <u>My</u> dear <u>little joy,</u> how will I be able to conduct, knowing that you're there? I'm afraid that I'll be thinking <u>so intensely</u> of you as to lose the light of reason. But if I conduct badly, you'll love me all the same, no? [. . .]

E.P. SALZBURG, 18 AUGUST 1937; P.S., ISOLINO S. GIOVANNI, PALLANZA; TO AM, GHS (CROSSED OUT; WRITTEN IN, BY AT: SCHLOSS NEUDECK, NONNTHALHAUPTSTRASSE 51, SALZBURG); FSD-FOF

Tuesday night [17.8.37]

God bless you, my holy, beautiful creature. Do you know how much you were in my heart yesterday evening during the performance of Zauberflöte? I don't know whether you could see that several times I held the little portrait carrier in my hand and brought it to my lips. Well, at those moments I said to myself: if only my Ada were in the theater! And I tortured myself over not having been able to find a ticket to give you. But I was happy all evening. I conducted with joy. And you were there, and you saw me! And you were <u>pleased</u> with me! <u>I'm jumping out of my skin.</u> When I received your telegram, I couldn't believe my eyes. I had just left the Euryanthe dress rehearsal and was going back to <u>Liefering</u> in the automobile when Emilio handed me your telegram. I felt immediately that it had to be yours because of the way my heart was beating, but I was a thousand miles from imagining that you had attended the performance! How and where did you manage to get the ticket? Were you alone or with Maria? I already have a seat for you for Meistersinger, and tomorrow morning I'll know whether I'll have one for Maria. In any case I'll send them to you by <u>special delivery.</u> I'm crazy with joy. My dear, dear, adored Ada—<u>tell me, tell me</u> that you were pleased with me, that I'm worthy of being loved by you, my soul, my life, my all. Your love will keep me forever young and in love with my art. No one will ever say, <u>in watching me work, "old Maestro Toscanini."</u> The miracle worker will be you and your marvelous love! [. . .]

Weber's *Euryanthe* was conducted by Bruno Walter at Salzburg that season.

E. NEITHER STAMPED NOR CANCELED; (SALZBURG, 19 AUGUST 1937); TO AM, SNNS; FSD-FOF

<u>My dear,</u> **marvelous** <u>soul</u>

Yesterday I received your telegram before the special-delivery letter, and I hurried to cross out the address on mine, to Strobl; I didn't want it to get to you a day late. I wasn't able to read your <u>tempestuous</u> letter until tonight. I could have destroyed the day, extinguished the sun. I spent the day at Kammer, at Eleonora Mendelssohn's, with the Busches and other hateful people. I stole a few moments from them, but I could read only a few lines, and in a disorganized way, from whichever page fell under my glance. In the evening I had to be present at Euryanthe (noblesse oblige). I can't begin to describe the tragedy in my soul. After the opera, all the Busches came to dinner at my house. At one a.m., all alone, I was able to face the tempest of your beautiful soul. I <u>slept no more.</u> **White night** [i.e., sleepless night], with neither moon nor stars. But dark, tempestuous. How you stirred up my blood, Ada! How I suffered, happy to suffer <u>your</u> suffering multiplied a **hundredfold** by my own. I went through all the names in the telephone directory to find where you're staying. <u>Meran, Johanna,</u> Tel. St. 6v.[?] 20-90. But I couldn't write. My thoughts overtook one another like waves in a tempest-tossed sea. I'll come see you later—if I don't <u>die first</u>. Artù

E.P. SALZBURG, 24 AUGUST 1937; TO AM, SNNS; FSD-FOF

Monday night [23.8.37]

<u>Dear Ada, my sole, sweet,</u> **desperate** <u>love,</u> why am I here all alone, sad, my heart so swollen that it could burst from despair, as if over some unanticipated misfortune or some criminal act? And yet this evening, when the last chord of Falstaff had stopped resounding, I saw the orchestra musicians, afire with sacred enthusiasm, showing me their joy through their applause. I, who had <u>pressed</u> them <u>implacably</u> morning, noon, and night, received their joy and gratitude in exchange. Ada mine—Falstaff is an incredible, incomparable masterpiece—you understand it—but it doesn't allow for mediocre performers. This evening, all the performers—singers, chorus, orchestra, and the old maestro who kept them in line—seemed to me to have brought off wonders. We all had the Devil in us, as Verdi often said when he was happy with a performance. You were there, Ada my dear, and I wanted to do the impossible to extract the best, better than the best, of their abilities. <u>You'll tell me</u> whether I succeeded! Did you feel me in your blood? I did—I had you in my heart. Not a bar vanished without having first been cajoled and caressed by you! After the opera, many Italians came to my dressing room. I listened to a <u>lot</u> of banalities—the usual ones that everyone utters. Busch alone said nothing, but his eyes were swollen with tears. Maria S. was there with her father. Only you were <u>apparently</u> missing. But I felt you <u>inside.</u> Oh, how I felt you! And now? Don't I deserve to have you near? Even without talking to each other, [only to] look at each other, breathe each other in, meditate on the mystery of our marvelous love! I'm sad, my Ada, so sad!!! Artù. [. . .]

Wednesday <u>25 morning</u>

[. . .] Toward the end of the first movement [of Beethoven's "Pastoral" Symphony], at the big fortissimo that just precedes the clarinet and bassoon's bars, I felt a sort of confusion. I closed my eyes to get a grip on myself. Didn't it seem to you, Ada, that the Andante followed as if in a dream? Oh, my holy creature, love me, adore me, be mine forever, let's be each others' until my very last day, and you'll see your Artù getting better and better. <u>I'll accomplish wonders.</u> I want to astonish everyone. I want to astonish <u>myself.</u> You can't imagine how moved I was to know that you were in the hall, amid the multitude, with your beautiful heart beating in unison with mine. I feel you, you know—oh, how I feel you! Yesterday, I felt that you were guiding my arm! After the concert I was really tired, more than after Falstaff the previous evening. I was overcome with sleepiness at half past 10. The others were playing scopa [a card game]; I went to bed and fell deeply asleep, but I was already awake at two. What to do? Write to you? I had such a confusion of things in my brain that I couldn't have chosen among them. I preferred to read all of your dear, adored, delightful letters. To hear so many dear, sweet assurances of love repeated to me by the creature I like and love best in the world seems almost impossible to me! When you say, <u>"What are you? Man or god?"</u> I feel that you're addressing someone else. Do you perhaps not know that I feel very much inferior to what I would like to be? Because I feel that I can never reach the point that I ought to reach, that ought to be reached??? That's the cause of my suffering! You see? Bruno Walter, Furtwängler, enjoy their work; you see them smiling, almost fainting, while they conduct. I, on the contrary—you can see me suffer. Bistolfi's medal, with that frowning look and hollow cheek, perfectly illustrates that suffering. In short, I'm like a <u>woman giving birth!</u> I know joy when I'm near you. Then it's divine ecstasy—I walk like Orpheus in the <u>Elysian Fields.</u> Ada, do you feel my desire? My mouth is thirsty for yours, hungry and thirsty for <u>all</u> of <u>your beautiful body</u>—all of it—every corner—every secret and <u>concealed entry.</u> When?

Big kisses, pure and impure—Artù

Monday <u>night 30-8-1937</u>

[. . .] Everyone is saying, unanimously, that the last concert (Brahms) was the best of all those I've conducted here during these years! Bruno Walter, Polo, Bruno Walter's family, many Italian and foreign friends, were moved to tears. None of them knew the cause, the real reason. **I did,** and so do you, right? The **Adartù** unison can work miracles! [. . .]

From this time on, AT and AM often conjoined the names Ada and Artù as Adartù.

After the last Zauberflöte performance [31.8.37]

My love, I've come home just this minute, tired, sad, and discouraged. I went to supper with Italian friends. I nearly fell asleep! I would have liked to make a beeline for home after the performance, but there was no way out. Sadness over things coming to an end is a tragedy for me! I don't know how to rid myself of it; I can't do it. I'm a defenseless victim of it. Last year, too, I had requested that they end [the festival] with Bruno Walter, but box-office requirements ran counter to my wishes! [. . .]

The performance was excellent. The audience gave everyone an extremely warm reception. When I think that you were able to stay in Salzburg for so many days and to hear four opera performances and two concerts conducted by me, it still seems to me like a dream, and if I weren't still feeling all the sweetness I wouldn't believe in the reality. You see, Ada dear, sometimes God protects. We ought to be grateful to him. The thing that flits fleetingly across my mind every once in a while (and that seems a vain, mad dream) will one day come true. God is and will continue to be with us!

I'm leaving Salzburg tomorrow morning at ten, alone, alone, alone. Carla is going to Cortina with the three Polos and Wally's little girl; they'll deposit the child at the Pizzettis' and proceed from there—Carla for Abano and the Polos for Milan. Wanda is in Venice, Horowitz in Lucerne. At this point, we're all dispersed. I need solitude more than I need air. I can no longer stand having people around! [. . .]

Wednesday 1-9-37

My Ada, I've arrived this very moment. Here's a line before I go to the doctor. I love you more than I did yesterday; tomorrow I'll love you more than today, and so it will be forever. [. . .] Come, come here. Don't let me down. Is Enrico in Germany? When do you have to be there? Until when will you stay among those louts? Aren't you afraid of losing all your beauty, of becoming like Freia in Das Rheingold? Write at once, if you haven't already done so. [. . .]

Friday evening 3 September

[. . .] Badgastein is beautiful. The marvelous weather makes it even nicer. There are fewer people here. I began my baths two days ago. The doctor found me well enough. Heart, lungs, liver, spleen, etc., are in perfect shape. Only my blood pressure was a little low (110). This is a result of the sustained efforts of the last month. 12 opera perfs. and three concerts, with respective rehearsals, are in any case something for a man of my age. But in a few days everything will return to its normal state. My right arm and shoulder are better than last year. So you really want to come see me? I think I'll go mad if I dwell even a little on that thought! It already seems like a thousand years since I saw you— so much so that I was in despair over not receiving letters from you, and you left Salzburg only on Monday! Ada, I need to look at you, but in peace, without hurry or the fear of being seen or heard. Oh, the indescribable suffering of those few, fleeting moments on the morning of the 18th in your room in Salzburg! While, with a heart swollen with passion and trembling with desire, I was lost in your dear arms, nearly dying of voluptuousness, I was assailed by the thought of being <u>heard</u> or <u>spied on,</u> and this made a moment of divine poetry into something nearly banal! No, never again that way. You've made me so desperate, these last few days, that I've given myself entirely to Leopardi, the poet I love best after Dante! And in the <u>"Pensiero dominante"</u> I've found lines that I would have liked to create for you, my <u>dominant thought:</u> here they are.

> Angelic beauty!
> Every lovely face, where'er I gaze,
> Seems almost a false image
> That mimics your face. To me
> You seem the only source
> Of all other charms; <u>sole true beauty.</u>
>   etc. etc.

Yes, my Ada, all the beautiful forms that grace other women are united in you. For me, you alone are real beauty. And I kiss you, and I kiss you <u>all over, because in you everything is beautiful.</u> Artù

AT quotes lines 130–135 of "Pensiero dominante" ("Dominant Thought"), no. XXVI of the *Canti* of the great Italian poet Giacomo Leopardi (1797–1837); my translation. (I do not pretend to be an expert translator of poetry, but I find the other English translations that I have seen of this poem even worse than my own.)

E.P. BADGASTEIN, 4 SEPTEMBER 1937; SMALL PHOTO OF AT, GLUED TO UPPER RIGHT-HAND CORNER OF FIRST PAGE; TO AM, 25VBMMI; FSD-FOF

Morning 4-9-937

Oh, my soul, my sweet love! I must transcribe for you the ending of the <u>"Pensiero dominante"</u>! It's as if it were welling up from my soul:

> Since first I looked upon you,
> Were you not the ultimate goal of all
> My serious concerns? How much of any day goes by

Without my thinking of you? How many times
Has your sovereign image
Been missing from my dreams? Lovely as a dream,
Angelic apparition
In an earthly dwelling,
On the soaring paths of th' entire universe,
What could I ever ask, what hope for,
What desire, other than to see your eyes?
What sweeter to possess than the thought of you?

My adored Ada, there is nothing beautiful, no sublime music, no winged poetry that doesn't recall your sweet image to my mind, to my thoughts! You are my life's supreme goal. All I ask of God is that he preserve your love for me. Yesterday I was the unhappiest of men, almost on the verge of despair, because I was without news from you and thought I had already been forgotten! Today my soul is full of sunshine. [. . .]

The poetic quotation is the concluding verse (lines 136–147) of Leopardi's "Pensiero dominante"; my translation.

E.P. BADGASTEIN, 5 SEPTEMBER 1937; TO AM, 25VBMMI; FSD-FOF

Saturday <u>five o'clock p.m.</u> [4.9.37]
[. . .] I'll certainly stay here until the 17th or 18th, because I have to do the cure for at least 15 days, and with the rest periods that are required every now and again I'll be here till around the 20th. You have to be in Berlin (hateful place) around September 15. Fine—the dates coincide beautifully! Here at the Kaiserhof there are far fewer people than before. Among those I know, there is only Carlo Placci, who is leaving in four days or even earlier, and Engineer Guttinger and his wife (whose perfume is the same as yours) and son, who will leave in a week. There will be no one to disturb us. [. . .]

How do I spend the day? Doing little or nothing. The cure occupies very little time. A fifteen-minute bath at half past six in the morning. I go back to bed, as the doctor has ordered, and stay there till nine. I have a coffee with milk. I perform my ablutions and stay in my room until half past eleven, reading Leopardi. Besides the Canti I have here with me the first volume of the "Zibaldone," a big volume of <u>1549</u> pages, fancy that! There's a whole world of things. He talks about literature, art, science, poetry, etc. <u>Thoughts</u> that Leopardi noted down each day, throughout his life. Then I take a walk for an hour and a half. I come back at <u>one</u> for lunch, which I take <u>all alone</u> in my room. I spend the afternoon partly on a terrace, in the sun, and partly in my room, reading again and writing to my <u>sweet friend,</u> to my <u>dear daughter,</u> to my **sublime lover.** I'll <u>never</u> tell you <u>who she is.</u> [. . .]

Sunday [5.9.37]

My <u>dearest Ada,</u>

Marvelous, divine Leopardi has taken me by the throat, by my brain, and by all my nerves. The poet I adored most in my youth, after Dante! I remember that I read his marvelous Correspondence aloud to my mother, and that both of us wept buckets of tears over some of the desperate letters written to Pietro Giordani. The receipt of the <u>Canti</u>—with Flora's annotations and commentary, and with a dedication that disturbs my modesty more than a little—and of the Zibaldone has thrust me far back to the days of my youth. I leave off reading only with difficulty. The first four lines (over) are the <u>first</u> poetic motif of the <u>Holiday Evening,</u> the last nine are the <u>second:</u> the one about the nocturnal song that dies away as the distance increases.

> (1st) Mild and clear is the night, and without wind,
> And quietly o'er the roofs and amid the orchards
> Sits the moon, and reveals from afar
> All the peaceful mountains.
>
> . . . .
>
> (2nd) All is peace and silence, and all the world
> Rests, and we dispute no more about them [the ancient Romans].
> In my early youth, when a festive day
> Was eagerly awaited, just as soon
> As it had ended I lay sadly awake,
> Pressed into my feather bed; and a song
> Heard late at night along the pathways,
> Receding further, dying out little by little,
> Even then clutched in like way at my heart.

[. . .] Such divinity! Don't you think that they're among the highest poetic inspirations of all times and that Leopardi had been touched by superhuman grace at that moment, as Flora says? My Ada, have you read much of Leopardi? Do you know the Correspondence, besides the Canti? And to think that D'Annunzio can't bear him and that he criticizes him because he drafted a prose version of a poem before setting it in verse! But Leopardi couldn't write at the drop of a hat, as Gabriele can, or <u>versify</u> at any hour of the day. "If inspiration does not come of its own, water could more easily flow from a dead trunk than a single line of verse from my brain. Others can always versify as they like, but I do not in any way have this faculty, and however you might beg me, it would be futile, not because I would not want to satisfy you, but because I could not. What is certain is that to ask for verses from a difficult, infertile nature like mine (<u>sic</u> [by AT]) is the same as asking me to grant an Episcopal see: the latter is not mine to give, and the former I cannot compose except by chance." And <u>Carducci was the same.</u> My love, adored Ada, I've even missed my afternoon walk! I feel as if I were <u>25 years old</u> again, when I shut myself in the house for months and months, studying and reading a little of everything. At that time, <u>no one</u> wanted me as a conductor, and I spent many a month inactive, <u>by others' lights.</u> They didn't deny that I had a certain amount of talent, but they were frightened by my <u>nasty character</u> and my exacting demands. Today everyone wants me, unfortunately, and they steal from me what ought to be my life—<u>to work for myself, study, learn</u> the many things that I don't know and that interest me so very much, since I don't have <u>much more time</u> before me to provide for this [desire to learn]. I'm very upset about having to go to Vienna before long! It seems to me that these Austrians are taking advantage of me at every moment and in every way! When I think that from October until well into March I'll be on the go without rest, I ask myself whether I'm really an intelligent man or rather an imbecile! My excellent health fools me and gives me illusions that I absolutely ought to consider <u>deceptive</u>! I forget that I completed my seventh decade several months ago! And that from one moment to the next my age could really demand its natural rights! But I want to convince the Vienna Philharmonic's president, <u>Burghauser,</u> in a kind and persuasive way, to forget about these two concerts— which are really four, because the dress rehearsals are open to a paying audience! [. . .]

I've read this thought in the Zibaldone, I like it, and I'm transcribing it for you:

"In love's transports, in conversation with the beloved woman, in the favors that one receives from her, even the ultimate ones" (and poor L. must always have paid for those he received), "you are always looking for [love's] happiness rather than experiencing it, your agitated heart always feels a great lack, a bit less than what it was hoping for, a desire for something more, or rather for much more. Love's best moments are those of soft, sweet melancholy, when you cry and <u>don't know why, and you almost resign yourself peacefully to a misadventure</u> without knowing which one. In <u>that repose,</u> your <u>less agitated spirit is nearly full and almost experiences happiness.</u>"

I'm not with him in the first part of this thought. In the second (the "best moments," etc.), I'm wholly with him. [. . .]

Francesco Flora (1891–1962), an Italian literary historian, was an anti-Fascist who, after the war, published an anthology of poetry written by partisans. The verses quoted by AT are lines 1–4 and 38–46 of "La sera del dì di festa," no. XIII of Leopardi's *Canti.* · Pietro Giordani (1774–1848) was a writer, scholar, and patriot who had befriended the isolated Leopardi. The quotation from the *Zibaldone* (which means "hodgepodge") is from no. 142. My translations.

(BADGASTEIN, SEPTEMBER 1937); TO LUIGI RUSCA, (MI?);
SACCHI 1951, P. 99

My dear friend Rusca. I also received the three books, almost at the same time as your letter. You could not have given me a gift I would appreciate more than in sending me the first volume of the Zibaldone. Excellent, and thank you for the other books, too. I'll read them later. In the meanwhile, the Zibaldone has completely taken hold of me, as have the <u>Canti</u> in Francesco Flora's edition, which he sent me a few months ago with exquisite kindness. I am enthusiastic about and full of admiration for his knowledgeable and profound commentary on these divine <u>Canti.</u> Read his commentary on <u>L'infinito.</u> It's a masterpiece! Reading Leopardi in recent days—after a long hiatus—has taken me back to my now-distant youth, when I used to read the Letters to my mother, poor thing—and we would be moved to tears by some of the desperate letters to Giordani. [. . .]

E.P. BADGASTEIN, 7 SEPTEMBER 1937; TO AM, 25VBMMI; FSD-FOF

6-9—Monday night

[. . .] Carlo Placci is leaving tomorrow morning. He's been good company. He made me talk as I hadn't done for some time. This evening we took a long walk. We were a bit out of step. He walks slowly, I, on the contrary, full steam ahead. I suffered more than a little! This has been a rather out-of-kilter day. Sad thoughts were going through my head. I thought badly of myself because I was thinking <u>bad things</u> of you. Why are you hanging around Milan? Who is keeping you there? What business can you have? Not even your mother is there. So why didn't you stay in Como? I'm very agitated. I'm extremely jealous, of everyone, of the air that you breathe!!! Because, you see, it seems to me, it's as if the friends who want you with them are <u>stealing</u> from me something that is rightfully mine, <u>all mine, like the light of your eyes, your divine smile</u>! Oh, Ada, if I think of the coming months it's enough to make one cry! [. . .]

E.P. BADGASTEIN, 8 SEPTEMBER 1937; TO AM, 25VBMMI; FSD-FOF

Tuesday <u>7-9-1937</u>

[. . .] I saw the doctor at eleven this morning. Rest today, after the fifth bath. He was very pleased. My pressure is already up to 120, my heart perfect. "With a heart like that," he said, "you can live to be 120 years old!" You'll be 90. Without a doubt, we would still be head over heels in love, like now, and who knows whether we'd be able to make love and be **Adarturo** together every once in a while. All miracles are possible with you. Haven't you re-created me? [. . .]

<u>Wednesday afternoon</u> [8.9.37]

[. . .] I'm sending these few lines to Rome. I want them to be there when you arrive in the <u>enemy city</u> that has **stolen** you from me. Cursed be the Rome–Berlin axis. I wish that there were rather an <u>axe</u> between Rome and Berlin and that it would chop off the heads of <u>both</u> those **Delinquents** (note the capital letter). And you—<u>you beautiful, you dear,</u> you <u>marvelous creature</u>—live in those two capitals! [. . .]

<u>9-9-1937</u> <u>Thursday night</u> at one

Dear love, I can't sleep. For me, the night is always too long. I read, but my eyes are tired. I would gladly go wandering, but it's drizzling. This morning I had lunch at <u>Hof-Gastein</u> with my young colleague Rodzinski and his wife. I spent a good part of the day with them. [. . .] From Salzburg I have received the enclosed <u>clipping.</u> A letter from your friend Furtwängler, a big clown and big self-advertiser! Taken as a whole, the letter could be considered absolutely right and right-thinking if Furtwängler himself hadn't been the one to impose a political character on his artistic activity by accepting (at a pay of 10 or 12 thousand marks a year) an inevitably political <u>state position.</u> Thus the letter is meant only to throw dust in the eyes of simpletons, of which the world is full. I, however, shall be as silent as the tomb. I don't want to fuel gossip. I told him what I needed to tell him. Enough! Now I understand the various telephone calls, over the last few days, from journalists in Vienna and London. All of them remained unanswered, naturally. It seems to me that this letter could get him into a bit of trouble with his government! What do you think of it?

[. . .] Countess Carla Visconti arrived two or three days ago. I haven't seen her, nor will I see her. It's very easy to <u>avoid</u> people in this hotel. They tell me that she's in very bad health. The doctor doesn't allow her to take the baths; maybe later. She's alone with her maid, her beauty is spoiled, she has aged, she's unrecognizable. Once she was among the most beautiful women in Milan. I met her when she was a girl, in 1896 in Turin, when I was rehearsing the Bohème premiere. You weren't <u>born yet.</u> She was very friendly with Fosca Leonardi, and they were always together. I couldn't <u>stand them</u>! The former because she was as <u>yellow</u> as if she had jaundice, the latter because she had a voice like that of an old alcoholic.

And your voice—what does it resemble? Tell me if you know! Why didn't you take advantage of such a beautiful gift? Think of Vera Vergani, with that ordinary voice of hers! And yet she's had quite a career! You've been a real sluggard! Indolent! Lacking in enthusiasm—which is a mortal sin! Aren't you a bit sorry now? Am I right in saying that you've betrayed yourself?? You had only one pressing aim: <u>to Get Married!</u> Did no one who heard you speak ever advise you to study recitation? Didn't you yourself ever think that you might have succeeded in being something more than a piano teacher? Too bad that I had no occasion to approach you at that time—1916–1917. And I already found you so pleasing! [. . .]

For more on Rodzinski, see my note accompanying the letter of 10 April 1936 and subsequent references. His wife, Halina Lilpop Rodzinski, wrote about her and her husband's relations with AT in her memoir *Our Two Lives* (New York: Scribner's, 1976). · The contents of Furtwängler's letter are not known to me, but clearly Furtwängler was trying to dissociate himself, in AT's eyes, from the policies of the Nazi German government. AT did not doubt Furtwängler's sincerity, but he understood that by accepting an important position with an organization the German government subsidized, Furtwängler was automatically compromised. · Countess Carla Visconti was a member of one of Milan's leading aristocratic families. · For Fosca Leonardi, see my note accompanying the letter of 17 April 1937. · Vera Vergani was a well-known Milanese actress only two years older than AM.

E.P. BADGASTEIN, 13 SEPTEMBER 1937; TO AM, VB8R; FSD-FOF

Sunday <u>10 p.m.</u> [12.9.37]

[. . .] After ten days in a row of sun, ideal atmosphere, tepid and fragrant air, the leap into total winter is truly disconcerting. And please note that I love everything that nature sends me. Sun, rain, snow, storms—each has its fascination for me. For that matter, my sadness is not the result of the bad weather, but of several causes: I'm not happy with myself, I don't know how to get hold of myself. When I'm working, I'm restless; when I'm not working, I'm more so. I'd like to turn my back on everything and retire for good, so as not to have that endless <u>nightmare</u> that kills me every time I have to face an audience or an orchestra. This happens every time, and I never manage to get used to it. The more time passes, the worse I get. And then I can't tell you how homesick I am for my country! It <u>kills</u> me! During these last days here, alone, I can't tell you what sorts and quantities of things have gone through my brain! I am the <u>only Italian artist, truly</u> and <u>wholly Italian</u> musician, who must, who is obliged to remain <u>outside</u> his country!!! You know, Ada, the effort I make to keep this atrocious thought hidden down, down in the depths of my soul, is nearly <u>inhuman.</u> I get to the point of dulling my own senses by working here, there, and everywhere, interspersing my work with no pauses, you could say, but I don't manage to <u>forget.</u> And when I hear certain opera performances or concerts on the radio, conducted by those <u>irresponsible artisans</u> who like to think of themselves as <u>my colleagues,</u> it's a <u>humiliation;</u> and I'm almost ashamed of myself to be part of this gang of <u>commonplace</u> and <u>humdrum</u> musicians, <u>still,</u> at my age! And I'm unhappy about many other things, too. It would be awful if I weren't sure of seeing you in a few days! I would escape from here immediately, and I would barricade myself on the Isolino with cannons and machine guns! [. . .]

AT WROTE ON E. ONLY: "TO ADA MAINARDI";
IN ANOTHER HAND: 14 SEPTEMBER 1937;
HE EVIDENTLY GAVE THIS LETTER TO AM WHEN SHE ARRIVED IN
BADGASTEIN; FSD-FOF

14-9[-37] <u>Tuesday night</u>

[. . .] I despair and revolt, I become <u>perfidious,</u> in my troubled and <u>vain</u> waiting, but the antidote to my perfidy is to fling onto paper all that's <u>ugly,</u> the <u>worst</u> of my <u>ego.</u> I empty out a bag full of horrors, of enormities, of abuses aimed <u>against you,</u> then I tear them up, I destroy them, and I go back to being a reasonable man. I have a <u>nasty character,</u> my Ada, but a <u>good</u> and <u>honest</u> one. As to what I think about your <u>ability</u> to be something superior, you haven't persuaded me <u>at all</u> of the contrary, despite your <u>most convincing proofs.</u> We'll talk about it again if the good Lord allows us to see each other! In the meantime, tell me: Have you sacrificed (note well, <u>sacrificed</u>) <u>hours, days, months, years</u> to continuous, unremitting, wearying study at your piano, and of music in general? I mentioned Vera Vergani not as a <u>brilliant goal</u>—on the contrary!—but as an example of a woman with neither special talent nor culture, and with a commonplace voice working against her, who at least tried to get away from the <u>humdrum,</u> monotonous life without a goal that nearly all women accept whether they want to or not. You, on the other hand, had and have talent, culture, and an adorable voice, and you write charmingly. Who says that you couldn't have been a magnificent actress or a writer? I am absolutely certain that you have betrayed yourself, if not out of laziness then out of apathy! Maybe you had no one to urge you to work, maybe <u>no one</u> understood how much you were indubitably capable of <u>doing</u> and <u>giving.</u> I alone <u>know</u> you and understand you. <u>Believe me!!</u> Do you think that I knew, when I was fifteen or sixteen years old, what sort of intellectual development I would undergo, or how, via what route, and toward which goal my future would be directed? I practiced the cello, which I didn't love, and I studied it to make my teacher happy; he saw <u>much more</u> in me than what I was, but I had an <u>inexhaustible thirst to familiarize myself with music,</u> to <u>get to know it</u>—**all music!** And even then, as now, I was always dissatisfied with myself. My schoolmates jokingly called me <u>"genius."</u> I enjoyed everyone's esteem, but it was of no importance to me. Then as now, I tried to achieve the maximum, and I couldn't do it, and I still can't do it today—which is why neither your dear words of praise and enthusiasm nor the audience's applause, not to mention exaggerated newspaper articles, can ever free me from the discontent and the torment that I have in me eternally! I hear and listen to everyone, and I am grateful to all of them, but I pay attention only to my conscience, which is <u>implacable!</u> Now, however, I have no desire to start working again! Especially in Austria! I'm agitated and worried about the work—too much of it—that I have to bring off. This very day, a telegram from The Hague reminded me that they wrung a promise out of me to go back there. I tell you, Ada, I'm more agitated than when I got here. I don't know what's gotten into me, but I feel troubled, upset! I continue to fear something, but I don't know what. I don't eat, or not much. I went to the doctor this morning. He found me well. My blood pressure has gone up again, from 120 to 126 over 80. I've already done twelve baths. He's ordered six more for me, but I'll do only five. I would like to leave Badgastein on the 20th. I <u>badly</u> want to go back to Italy. I can't stand it any longer! [. . .]

Part Five

SEPTEMBER 1937–
SEPTEMBER 1939

1937   At age seventy becomes principal conductor of the National Broadcasting
        Company Symphony Orchestra, New York, with which he remains for
        seventeen years (except 1941–42 season).

1938   Withdraws from the Salzburg Festival after first hints of Austrian
        government's compromise with Nazi Germany; conducts first concerts of
        Lucerne Festival, founded as a result of his willingness to participate in it
        (returns in 1939 and 1946).

Afternoon 19-9-1937

My Ada—all mine

I'll never again in my life watch you leave! I'd rather die!

Yesterday I ran away like a man in despair; I didn't have the nerve to turn around. It was as if the train that was taking you away wanted to pull me along with it, while a desperate, mysterious power kept pushing me forward, forward! I can't recall a moment of greater despair! Not even when we separated that last evening in Milan in Via Bianca Maria, before your departure for Rome, was it so terrible! You were leaving, but there was still **Milan,** where you were born and grew up, and whose adoptive son I have been for fifty years. It's entirely different! Believe me! I came back to the hotel in despair. I couldn't tell you which streets I took, but I went up and down many, many of them, sweating like an ox. I didn't take any of our usual ones, so I got lost on all of them and had to go back and forth on them several times. I got home eventually. I haven't left the room since. [. . .]

From the Isolino 22 Sept. night

Dear joy,

[. . .] You know that we'll have to pay with the cruelest distance for the joy, the happiness, the divine ecstasy of those unforgettable days, which we had sighed for and desired for years. When will we see each other again? There is a clutch at my heart, and a knot of tears fills my throat. Ada my dear, can't you feel my desperate love? I don't know how to bear the anguish that weighs upon my soul. Yet I ought to be happy! How much love, how much passion you have poured into my soul, my dear Ada, my unique, holy creature! How many times did I see your beautiful face illuminated, transfigured (day and night) under my ardent, voluptuous caresses! How much loving exaltation drove us into each others' arms! Do you remember? The last night, we <u>couldn't</u> detach ourselves from each other, nor did we <u>want</u> to. We were overcome with voluptuous furor! And afterward? How sweet it was to become soothingly drowsy, holding each other tight, and how bitter it was, on the other hand, to tear ourselves away from that embrace, because we would have liked to **blend together** yet another time! Yes, my love, I have all of you with me, as you have all of me. During those dear days we belonged to each other as never before. Never were our bodies so united, never had we known each other so intimately. And our souls? They will **never** separate from each other, neither with the passage of time nor with changing events. Do you feel that every fiber in me is reaching out to you, as is every palpitation and every slightest thought of mine? Although I am at home, the internal agitation that you know so well hasn't ceased. My mood is of the darkest sort. I don't want to see anyone around me! I even avoided a visit from Zweig to the Isolino, although he is very dear to me! I myself don't know what's taken hold of me this time, and I'm upset at not being able to conquer it! Telegrams from Vienna were waiting for me, asking for my programs, but I can't make up my mind—and I won't go! [. . .]

E.P. MI, 27 SEPTEMBER 1937; TO AM, PFB; FSD-FOF

One should choose as a wife only the woman one would choose as one's friend, if she were a man.—Joubert [original in French]

24 Sept. afternoon

[. . .] My brain is like a forge. Everything in it is inflamed and inflammable. I can't get away from whatever thought is torturing my poor soul. I see no one; I haven't read the newspapers in four months, and I don't turn the radio on. I want to not know, to be unaware of things. But there's something poisoned in the air that manages to get inside me. I read in the Rivista musicale that in Germany they interrupted a performance of a Requiem by Hugo Kaun because it contains a chorale on the words "Jesus, in whom I have placed my faith." This is an outrage to the dignity of Nazism. One must place all one's faith only in Germany. And in the meantime millions are being spent in Berlin and Munich to receive in a worthy manner the **great Delinquent** [Mussolini]—this was told to me by the head of the Grand Hotel in Gardone (who seemed to be German and who had news directly from Berlin). And you, angel, most delicate flower, vision of heaven, my soul's soul, you are breathing that **putrid** air. You are in contact with that people that has never had or known a **sense of the ridiculous.** No, I can't hold out, not even here; I want to escape. I'll get back to work. I'll toil, I'll kill myself, but there's nothing except work that can give me back a little peace. I'll do the two concerts in Vienna. I haven't yet replied, I haven't yet decided on the programs, but the program for me, for my life in the coming months, is this: work, work, kill myself, if necessary. [. . .] Carla has resumed her marvelous activities after having taken the cure at Abano. She's thinking about making the Crema estate livable. How do you like that? Walter is working. Wally is being a countess and lives amid those highly placed and overrated scoundrels. Wanda has come to meet Horowitz in Milan and is going back to Venice. They've told me that D'Annunzio has accepted the Presidency of the Accademia d'Italia, replacing Marconi, after having shown contempt for it when it was created and not having wanted to participate in it! **Stinking old wreck!!!** He already has one foot in the grave, but he can't stop being an obscene, repulsive clown. How shameful! How humiliating for human beings to have such representatives! Horror. Disgust! Ada, love me, I deserve it, yes, I deserve it! [. . .]

The choral works of Hugo Kaun (1863–1932) were popular in Germany. · CT had invested some of AT's earnings in the purchase of an estate at Ripalta Guerina, near Crema, some 40 kilometers (25 miles) southeast of Milan. He speaks scornfully here of CT's domestic doings, but he soon grew to love the estate (see the letter of 31 March–2 April 1938).

E.P. BUT POSTMARK ILLEGIBLE; TO AM, PFB; FSD-FOF

24 September [1937] <u>afternoon</u>

<u>My love,</u> I've just this moment received your short letter of Wednesday. I have a long one that I wanted to send you now, but as you can see, yours has been <u>censored,</u> so I'll wait before I send you mine. My name is suspect to <u>thieves</u> and <u>delinquents</u> but not to upright, honest people. I wish to know first whether my letters reach you uncensored. [. . .] Now, if this business of opening the letters continues, I'll <u>completely</u> lose <u>control.</u> I don't want to create difficulties for you—I won't talk about delinquents anymore—but I'm extremely annoyed that <u>scoundrels</u> can know about my intimate matters. So tell me, even by telegram, whether my letters reach you <u>uncensored.</u> All my love, for you; for me, despair.

<u>Adartù</u>

E.P. PN, 28 SEPTEMBER 1937; TO AM, PFB; FSD-FOF

Monday night
<u>27 Sept.</u>

[. . .] Carla has stayed in Milan, and on Thursday she'll go to Venice with Polo and probably Roberto, for Horowitz's birthday (October 1).

It seems that he feels like playing that evening. Wally will have guests. I know that they're looking for a <u>Steinway.</u> Polo, who heard him at my house the other evening, wrote me enthusiastically, saying, "He's a colossus." He has become even better! God grant that he'll decide to put himself back in circulation! I, on the other hand, will stay here all alone on the Isolino. I'll send an affectionate telegram, but I don't feel like facing my daughter the <u>countess's entourage</u>! The <u>Volpis,</u> the <u>Cinis,</u> and the <u>old Morosini woman</u> bring me to the point of <u>vomiting.</u> (It would be more refined of me to use the word <u>nausea,</u> but for the likes of them the other term is more appropriate.) [. . .] I'm a completely different man since I decided to get back to work. I will decidedly never reach the point of becoming <u>neurasthenic.</u> I feared it during the last few weeks! I was thinking back to 1915, when I left the <u>Metropolitan.</u> Then, too, I wanted to be done with the theater, with music. I felt <u>old, finished,</u> and I was only 48 years old. Our entry into the war was like a whiplash. I got back to work with real vigor, and with the enthusiasm of someone much younger than 48. I don't know whether you remember the famous patriotic <u>mammoth con-</u>

cert at the Arena, with an all-Verdi program! You were too young and probably not yet interested in concerts. But that one was truly memorable and moving. At the end of the concert I turned toward the audience, and I don't know how I managed to exert influence on it, but I do know that it began, under my direction, to sing the patriotic anthems as if with one voice, with infinite feeling and enthusiasm, and poor Boito came to embrace me, crying like a child. In those days I didn't turn up my nose at conducting the anthems. And in those days the anthems meant something; they had a holy, high, patriotic goal—not like today, when our national anthem is served up the moment any moron shows his face! In short, Ada my dear, the poisoned air that one breathes around here (and also where you are, you know) worked on me like a whiplash across my face; it was a good antidote to the poison that had infiltrated my veins. I'm counting on being in Vienna on October 7. I'll fly there, naturally. [. . .]

Roberto Foligno was a family friend. · On 26 July 1915, two months after Italy's entry into the war against Germany and Austria, AT had conducted massive choral and orchestral forces in an all-Verdi concert at Milan's outdoor arena; the event was attended by 40,000 people and raised 70,000 lire for the war effort.

E.P. PN, 29 SEPTEMBER 1937; TO AM, PFB; FSD-FOF

Tuesday night 28—September
[. . .] It did my soul a lot of good to know that you [plural] were far away from Berlin in recent days! I don't know why, but I was afraid that that jerk of a [diplomatic] minister A[ldrovandi] had required that you attend—for love of fascism—the monstrously grotesque celebrations that the Madman, the Teutonic criminal, has prepared for the Great Delinquent from the Romagna, compatriot of the celebrated Passatore, whom the old people of Forlimpopoli may still remember. Self-exaltation to the point of blindness, of absurdity, of monstrosity, belongs to the hegemonic mentality of people like those two, whom I dare not name. And we look on, impotent, at the loosening and lowering of nearly the whole world's moral forces! It's frightening! The coalitions that were created in the past against imperialism and dictatorships seem unrealizable today! How will we be judged fifty years from now? Goodness knows! But let's not think about it now. Today, when my spirit is feeling so light and my humor is so serene, I don't want to return to the theme that poisons me more than anything else! My joy, in an instant I truly defeated a state of mind that was as painful for me as for those who have to be near me. It's a true miracle of my healthy nature ("You were born well"), which is still able to react! My internal upheaval, my dissatisfaction with myself, with everyone and everything, has been implacable lately, and there was no defense against it. I was filled with a general sense of oppression over everything; even my will felt oppressed. For months a degree of strain had been under way, a suppressed

rage, and always for <u>moral reasons.</u> I pretended not to notice, but as often happens when you're following the thread of one thought, another one insinuates itself into your subconscious, develops, takes hold, and all of a sudden becomes the <u>protagonist that obsesses you,</u> so I was the victim of such a thing, lately, and I had decided to drop <u>everything.</u> Every once in a while, I repeated mentally the words I had said to a tearful Wally in New York in 1927, at an analogous moment: **"for everyone, the end must come."** Back then, too, I was perplexed, uncertain of and about everything. Strange to say, these crises repeat themselves roughly every ten years: 1915—1927—1937! Who knows what 1947 holds in store for me! Poor <u>Giovanni Cena</u> said to me, in 1915; "My dear Toscanini, <u>one must dive deep into one's sorrow until one touches the bottom,</u> if one is to <u>give a push with one's feet and return</u> to the <u>surface.</u>" Golden words!! As long as there isn't muck and mire at the bottom! [. . .]

I'm deeply into the <u>ninth symphony.</u> I'll have to <u>surpass myself</u> again, hop up a bit higher in order to stay at the same level. <u>The Adagio!</u> Elysian Fields, Paradise—I feel what is inexpressible. It lifts me off the earth, removes me from the field of gravity, makes me weightless; one becomes <u>all soul.</u> One ought to conduct it on one's <u>knees.</u> [. . .] Do you know that at the modulation to E-flat I always conduct with my eyes closed? I see extremely bright lights far, far away; I see shadows moving around, penetrated by rays that make them even more disembodied; I see flowers of the most charming shapes and colors. And the very music I'm conducting seems to descend from up there—I don't know where! It's all a mysterious spell that wraps around me during those sixteen bars, and it changes at the next modulation into the main key, when the second <u>divine</u> variation begins. The picture, the landscape is transformed, but it's still another small part of the Elysian Fields. From this you can imagine the life I'm leading on the Isolino. Excepting a short visit of a few hours last Sunday from the Polos together with Mrs. Motta, no one has come to see me. Carla saved me from the Guttingers and from many other friends who wanted to see me. And now I'm completely alone. Little Walfredo and the silent Cia left me on Monday because school is about to begin. So I have no one to talk to. My heart is full of you. And the <u>fullness is such</u> that there is no room for anything else. You're jealous? I'm glad. When one loves, one is jealous even of the air that touches one's beloved's face. [. . .]

"Minister Aldrovandi": see my note accompanying the letter of 16 August 1936. · Mussolini and "Il Passatore," a celebrated brigand, both hailed from Italy's Romagna region, and AT enjoyed joking about the coincidence. The town of Forlimpopoli is only 15 kilometers (9 miles) from Predappio, Mussolini's native village. · Giovanni Cena (1870–1917) was a journalist, poet, and novelist who was also active in the campaign to increase literacy among the peasants. · Mrs. Motta was a family friend.

<u>Wednesday night</u>
<u>29 September</u>

[. . .] When I think that by next Monday, or Tuesday at the latest, I'll be in Vienna, and that from then on an unbroken chain of travels and stops won't bring me back home until April, I feel chills go up my spine and my blood congeals! Seven months! Seven months without seeing each other, without hearing each others' voices, without . . . It seems impossible and monstrous. And I'm the one who causes these troubles! To save myself from evil, to defend myself from moral disaster, from illness of the spirit, I have to <u>work,</u> and so even what seems a God-given miracle—"<u>cancel the years</u> or <u>renew them,</u>" as you say in your letter of 6 July—turns into a punitive sentence for me. One <u>year only</u>—to <u>live with you</u> for only a year—and after that, what would death matter to me? Won't we ever have the courage? I have been too altruistic all my life; today, this <u>continuous, stabbing</u> thought that has been eating away at my heart for several years (and it's wrong of me to tell you this) gnaws more and more at my pour soul, and it is one of the crosses on my sad Calvary. I'm not sorry, dear Ada, to be good, but sometimes the price of the sacrifice is dear, oh so dear! [. . .] I hope and wish that Enrico is well and will be able to work again. I would give him <u>my liver</u> if I could; I have so many healthy parts that I could get used to having that one be ill. [. . .] I'm extremely agitated—as you can imagine! My thoughts and desires are clashing furiously. Now that I have to leave in a few days, I'm cursing the moment when I made this decision. I'm a wretch, an unhappy, dissatisfied man who ought to put an end to it once and for all, retire to private life, forget and be forgotten. [. . .]

<u>30 September Afternoon</u>

[. . .] It's a gloomy day—it's raining, there's no light. I've written a couple of lines to Horowitz for tomorrow, his birthday—his 34th! Who can remember being 34? You can, my dear, but not I! [. . .] What are you doing besides looking after Enrico? Do you practice the piano, read, see people, go to the theater? When will Enrico begin to work? I've never known what Enrico's Berlin activities are, never had a clear idea about them. Does he still have something to do with the orchestras, as he once did? Does he give private lessons? Does he have a manager or an agent who organizes a certain number of concerts for him in various German towns or outside Germany? With whom is he under contract in London? Hasn't he ever played with the BBC? Answer these questions, don't forget. You know, today it crossed my mind to transcribe for you, by heart, that beautiful lyric piano piece of Catalani's, "Sogno" ["Dream"], so that you would learn it and play it while I'm far away from you. I'll do it one of these days. I want you to have before your eyes something that I love a lot and that I practically saw being born. We must have something that unites us spiritually, even in music. I won't say that no day passes, but probably no week passes without my playing that piece. It's a way of reapproaching that dear spirit who adored me and to whom I owe the beginning of my conducting career in Italy—in Turin, with <u>Edmea, November 1886.</u> And you'll like it, I'm sure—it can't fail to please you. They are really dream notes. Who knows: maybe one day we'll take turns playing it. We'll challenge each other. You're more of a pianist—I've never been able to play a scale twice with the same <u>fingering.</u> I was the despair of my teacher. I loved the piano only because it gave me the means of getting to know music. I can't tell you how many times Catalani had me play it [the piece]. He always ended by saying, "It's as if the music were yours. I, who wrote it, don't get out of it what you do." [. . .]

Horowitz's official birth year was 1904, but AT and other intimates of the pianist knew that the correct year was 1903. · Catalani's *melodia* "In sogno!" ("In a Dream!") was published in 1889 as the second of a series of ten piano pieces called *Impressioni*.

E.P. PN, 1 OCTOBER 1937; TO AM, PFB; FSD-FOF

1 October morning

[. . .] Last night, too, I turned the light off at three. Do you know what I did? I transcribed Catalani's "Sogno" by heart! I think I talked to you about it in a previous letter. I didn't have music paper, but there were some sheets of paper already written on in pencil. I worked with the eraser and I believe that I've reproduced the <u>beautiful lyric piece</u> without mistakes, so that you can play it and fix it in your memory as it is in mine—and may it be a sweet, ideal recollection in our thoughts during our cruel separation! [. . .]

I can't begin to tell you what it's like to live alone on the Isolino! You know, not a word crosses my lips all day long! Yet every corner of this paradise is populated with dear spirits. My study, with the precious autograph manuscripts of Leopardi, Beethoven, Verdi, and Wagner, which I often read; every lane, every corner has its mysterious fascination—and I can hardly count the number of people with whom I am in ideal contact. But you are always beside me; you are my sweet guide, my dear inspirer. You <u>never</u> leave me, nor would you want to. I've never been so undisturbed as this, and it's very painful that I'll have to tear myself away in a few days. A visit from Flora and Oberdorfer, accompanied by Rusca of Mondadori, has been announced for Sunday. Flora wants to see three or four autograph letters of Leopardi, and Oberdorfer wants to talk to me about the letters of Wagner and the king of Bavaria, which were recently published, and which I lent him. [. . .]

The letter I received from you this morning had not been opened.

You see? Now that the <u>Delinquent</u> has left Berlin, they're not taking the trouble to spy! [. . .] Emilio showed me the <u>reproduction</u> in the Corriere della Sera of a photograph of Mussolini's meeting with D'Annunzio at the station in

Verona. Is it possible for a man to be reduced to such a state of decay?! Can't you just smell his <u>breath</u>! Fortunately, they haven't yet invented a way of reproducing it in a <u>photograph.</u> It's true that I go for months without looking at myself, but I don't think that the good Lord is holding such a <u>horrendous surprise</u> in store for me! [. . .]

For more on Francesco Flora, see my note accompanying the letter of 5 September 1937. · Aldo Oberdorfer (1885–1941), a translator (from German to Italian) with a strong interest in music, was a socialist, anti-Fascist, and Jew who died in internal exile during the war. He had published a book on Wagner in 1933, thus his interest in the subject.

E.P. PN, 3 OCTOBER 1937; TO AM, PFB; FSD-FOF

Saturday <u>afternoon</u> [2.10.37]

[. . .] Yesterday evening I turned the radio on. They were performing the <u>ninth symphony</u> in London, with the BBC's choral and orchestral forces. The same ones I'll have next month. The conductor was <u>Henry Wood.</u> I was courageous enough to drink the bitter chalice to the dregs! Shouldn't the Penal or Civil Code deal with crimes that are committed to the detriment of musical master-pieces? You can't imagine what that gentleman managed to do! And besides calling himself a maestro, he is also a <u>Sir.</u> Incredible! The first movement was a <u>funeral march.</u> The scherzo—consider that the metronome marking indi-cates 116 to the dotted half note—<u>just right.</u> Well, now, I actually measured it with metronome in hand—it was played at 138 to the dotted half. Now, I tell you—it's all very well <u>not to stick</u> strictly to the letter. Play it at 120, at 112, at 126—which is already too fast—<u>but at 138</u> you go completely off the rails! The adagio was adagissimo, therefore very **borsaiuolo** [boring?], as they say in Parma and Bologna, and the Finale was so choppy that it made me angry. At the end, I found that I had fallen asleep. I didn't hear the <u>solo</u> quar-tet at the end!

What will Mr. <u>Wood</u> say when he hears it done by me? That I'm wrong. [. . .]

Sir Henry Wood (1869–1944) was one of the most important forces in the develop-ment of British orchestral life during the first half of the twentieth century. In Febru-ary 1936, AT had conducted Wood's orchestration of Bach's Toccata and Fugue in D minor with the New York Philharmonic.

E.P. PN, 4 OCTOBER 1937; TO AM, PFB; FSD-FOF

Monday <u>morning</u> 4. <u>October</u>

[. . .] Yesterday morning [. . .] I got your long letter and the two beautiful postcards with the reproductions of Dürer's paintings. How many years do I have to go back to remember those paintings? Very many. You weren't born yet. 1895! The year of my first disappointment in those <u>German know-it-alls.</u> That was when people in Italy were proclaiming that Wagner performances in the theaters of Munich and Bayreuth were perfect! [. . .]

This letter indicates that AT first went to Germany, to hear how Wagner was performed there, in 1895, shortly before he conducted (in Turin) the first Italian production of *Götterdämmerung,* his own first major Wagner production. But there was no Bayreuth Festival in 1895; he did not attend one until 1899.

E.P. VIENNA, 11 OCTOBER 1937; TO AM, PFB; FSD-FOF

<u>From bed Thursday night</u> [7.10.37]

<u>My</u> only and blessed <u>friend</u>

Despite the work, which pleasantly distracts me, I continue to be overcome by dejection, which I defeat and get over because of the element in me that is a little <u>diabolical</u> and <u>satanic,</u> and that doesn't give in and won't give in. But the disturbance, the agitation in my blood are there—it's not a case of imagination—and they wear me out and give me no peace. I can't sleep. I turn over and over; I turn the light on and off, but it's all the same. I ought to turn off something that's burning inside me, but it's not within my power, and God often and gladly forgets about me.

[. . .] Today the horrible disaster that's happened to Huberman has upset and terrified me! If such a misfortune were to happen to me, I wouldn't want to survive, I would prefer death to continuing to have some sort of awful nervous condition all my life! His poor mother—what a terrible shock, if she suddenly learned about it from the newspapers! My Ada, my heart is breaking—I no longer recognize myself. At the same time I wonder at my ability to muddle on rather well and to work, despite continual lack of sleep. You know, I don't manage to sleep even four hours a night, and <u>discontinuously.</u> And it's futile to talk about resting during the day! [. . .] I'm a wretch, incapable of rebelling against old moral theories invented by abject, stupid, false men, not by nature, which binds two beings not by laws but by love! [. . .]

From Boris Schwarz, *Great Masters of the Violin* (London: Robert Hale, 1983), p. 314: "Huberman suffered a near-fatal accident on October 6, 1937, in a plane crash on Sumatra (Dutch East Indies). His hands and arms were injured; for a time the doctors thought that he would never play again. The recovery was slow, but he was able to retrain his hands, using the violin as an 'orthopedic rather than a musical instrument' (as he wrote to George Szell)."

E.P. VIENNA, 11 OCTOBER 1937; TO AM, PFB; FSD-FOF

[. . .] The concert went well. But I'm not interested in the audience, the music, or myself. Only you are in my thoughts, only you count in my life, only you can arbitrate over my joy and sadness alike. [. . .]

In mid-October 1937 AT conducted two concerts in Vienna and one in Budapest with the Vienna Philharmonic; these proved to be his last appearances with that orchestra and in that part of Europe.

E.P. VIENNA, 16 OCTOBER 1937; TO AM, PFB; FSD-FOF

Saturday morning [16.10.37]

[. . .] Yesterday evening I saw Maria S[alata]. We were invited by the consul Rochira[?]. The Gawronska woman was also there, without her husband. I gave her a piece of my mind! She's stupid. She's a real cow, good for making children and milk. She confided that she's pregnant for the seventh time! I couldn't have cared less!

[. . .] Don't worry about my trips by air. My hour has not yet come. We have to live that year together, after which let whatever happens happen! [. . .]

For Luciana Frassati Gawronska, see my note accompanying the letter of 18 September 1936. · The words "My hour has not yet come" bear out Walfredo Toscanini's description of his grandfather as a fatalist who firmly believed that one's allotted lifetime is virtually predetermined, and that until that time is up one can live as one wishes without having to suffer fatal consequences. See also subsequent letters.

E.P. LONDON, 20 OCTOBER 1937; TO AM, PFB; FSD-FOF

Sunday 17-10-937   after the concert

I've finished here [Vienna], but the day after tomorrow I'll begin there [London]. And I still have no desire for it. But when I'm in front of the orchestra, I come alive and the quicksilver circulates again in my blood. Wally came by yesterday, all worried about my trip to Palestine. I don't live in the world of the living, I know nothing, I'm unaware of everything. But she and the Horowitzes are worried about my trip, and it seems that they have sent a telegram to Weizmann in Tel Aviv, asking for advice. I put myself completely in the hands of my fate. I have complete faith in it. Haven't I found you along my path, after all? And who, if not fate, decided to send me this blessing!

Wednesday morning [20.10.37]

You see? I haven't been able to finish a letter begun on Sunday and to tell you so many things that I'd like to say. Let's be patient! You, too. It's the virtue of donkeys, and one must sometimes envy them. I've begun rehearsals. I'm happy with the chorus—very good. [. . .]

Chaim Weizmann (1874–1952) was a leader of the World Zionist Organization from World War I until the creation of the State of Israel, of which he became the first president (1948). In 1937 there were serious skirmishes between Jewish settlers and the native Arab population in Palestine, thus the worry on the part of AT's family. · AT's work in London began with three days of recording sessions. His two concerts, on 30 October and 3 November, consisted entirely of music by Brahms and Beethoven, respectively.

E.P. LONDON, 20 OCTOBER 1937; P.S., LANGHAM HOTEL, PORTLAND PLACE, LONDON, W.I.; TO AM, PFB; FSD-FOF

Wednesday <u>20-10-937</u>

[. . .] The trip by air was delightful. I arrived in London with the sun shining magnificently. I immediately asked about the Palestine business, and I'll have definite word within a few days. In the meantime, I'm waiting for an answer to the telegram that Wally and the Horowitzes sent to Tel Aviv—and if I have to postpone my departure, thus shortening my stay there, we should think seriously about <u>meeting again,</u> don't you think? [. . .] I've found the chorus well prepared and together. I'm hoping for a good performance of the <u>German Requiem.</u> Maybe you'll be able to hear it on the radio. It will be the evening of Oct. 30 at 8:15.

When does Enrico have to come to London? Where is he playing? For whom is he playing? Piatigorsky is playing here on the 28th with Beecham— Boccherini['s Cello Concerto in B-flat Major] and [Bloch's] <u>Schelomo.</u> [. . .]

The BBC Choral Society's conductor was Leslie Woodgate.

E. WITHOUT STAMPS OR POSTMARK; TO AM, PFB; FSD-FOF

[. . .] The two concerts here are <u>more than sold out.</u> It seems that there were fourteen thousand requests, and they ended up holding a sort of lottery to distribute the tickets fairly. So the <u>old maestro</u> is still of interest. And I'm not at all happy about it. I would like everyone to forget me, except you. I would like to live only in your thoughts, in your memory. If you had attended my last concert in Vienna, you would have liked me. Despite my having been sad and somewhat listless, the music managed to pull me up. Music has the same effect on me that you have. It rejuvenates me, it gives me what nature <u>takes away,</u> at my age. My blessings on both of you, forever.

Have you seen Furtwängler? Do you know that it always bothers me to write your Berlin address because I have to repeat, twice, that **Fur.** The <u>insipid vacuity</u> of that man with the <u>pear</u>-shaped head disquiets me. And he has certainly pursued you. This exasperates me. [. . .]

AM's Berlin address was Pension Fürstenhaus, 69 Kurfürstendamm; thus the double *fur.* During the previous eighteen months Furtwängler, whom AT had previously respected, had become one of AT's principal *bêtes noires* over political issues and he would remain so for the rest of their lives.

<u>21-10-937</u>   Thursday <u>night</u>

[. . .] I really like this hotel [the Langham] better than Claridge's, and now that you've told me that you stayed here I'd like to discover your footprints, so that I could bow down and kiss them, my dear love. I'm staying in rooms 201, 203, and 204. [. . .]

My dear, I haven't yet seen <u>that lady</u> who wrote the letters—I think she's in <u>Cannes</u>—but I'll certainly see her, because she won't want to miss my concerts. I haven't heard from her since the two illustrated postcards she sent me in Salzburg. Maybe because I've played dead with her. But I'm glad that you talk to me about it. [. . .]

"That lady" was almost certainly Sybil Cholmondeley.

<u>Friday night</u> [22.10.37]

[. . .] The enclosed telegram has arrived from Palestine. Weizmann isn't there. He's here in London. Yesterday his wife sent flowers to Carla. Tomorrow Carla will go visit her and talk about whether or not it's opportune for me to go. I know, however, that Weizmann is about to go there with his wife. I understand very well that he symbolizes the general of an army that's at the front. It's his duty to go to the front lines. Enough—we shall see. But as I wrote to you, I'm a fatalist, and I won't hesitate to leave when the moment comes. Wanda is beside herself over that telegram. I expected it. My not going there would be <u>disastrous.</u> [. . .]

Saturday <u>morning</u> [23.10.37]
<u>very early</u>

[. . .] I've forgotten for many days to tell you something that you certainly don't know, and that no one knows, I think. Did you know that Wally had a conversation with the Crown Prince? Oh, yes—he called her to find out whether I would condescend to talk with him and to let myself be persuaded to conduct in Italy! You know that Wally is never lacking for words or for subjects to talk about, so she persuaded him that the attempt would be in vain. In fact, since May 1931 Wally had been holding on to a long explanation of the facts [of the Bologna incident] that I wrote and that was to have appeared in a foreign newspaper (but, as always happens, I then gave up the idea); she decided to send it to the Princess, and the two of them [i.e., the prince and princess], after having taken note of the truths set forth in it, were more than ever convinced that I acted and act in the most serious, correct, and consistent way imaginable! The princess had wanted to talk to me as early as last year, at Salzburg, but she didn't dare. And she was right! Did you know this? None of it had leaked out to me! Wally let me in on it recently, in Venice.

Have you ever come upon an Italian writer named Ignazio Silone? To my shame, it was Stefan Zweig who introduced me to him during the last few days—not personally, but by giving me two of his novels. One, the short "Fontamara," has been translated into every language—<u>French</u>, <u>Spanish</u>, <u>Portuguese</u>, <u>Flemish</u>, <u>Dutch</u>, <u>Norwegian</u>, <u>German</u>, <u>Polish</u>, <u>Czech</u>, <u>Hungarian</u>, <u>Romanian</u>, <u>Croatian</u>, <u>Russian</u>, and <u>Hebrew</u>. Sorry if that's not enough! Look for it in Berlin and read it! The other one is "Pane e vino" ["Bread and Wine"], which has also been translated into German, English, Danish, Dutch, Czech, and Hungarian, so far.

You know, Weizmann's family is also begging him not to leave. Isn't this funny? I'll leave by airplane on November 8—Rome, Brindisi, Athens, Rhodes, Haifa, Lydda. Leaving on the morning of the 8th, I'll be in Tel Aviv on the afternoon of the 9th. This time I won't stop in Egypt. <u>Your benediction</u> will go with me, your love, all the best thoughts will be my faithful and trusty escorts.

[COPY IN AT'S HAND (ON P.S. OF THE LANGHAM HOTEL) OF THE ABOVE-MENTIONED TELEGRAM; N.D.:]

European reports concerning Palestine situation doubtless greatly exaggerated. Would not esitate [*sic*] to renounce if we felt any personal risk maestro—Otherwise consider cancellation unwarranted view enormous public support already secured coming season inspired by maestros [*sic*] announced participation. Of course if maestro or signora desire cancellation shall accept decision—Shall ourselves take initiative to inform maestro if anything should occur to justify [*sic*] our present view. Wire sent after consulting Palestine orchestra trustees, <u>Colonel Kisch</u>—<u>maître Seinberg</u>—<u>Horowitz</u>—<u>Simon</u>.

In using the term "condescend," AT was enjoying a little joke at the expense of Crown Prince Umberto and his consort, Princess Maria José, but he was also enjoying his own astonishment at the fact that the future king and queen of Italy were trying to get him to come back into the fold—an attempt that merely strengthened his resolve not to exercise his art in his native country as long as the Fascists were in power. AT seems to have had no particular dislike for Umberto or Maria José (the latter was the daughter of King Albert I and Queen Elisabeth of Belgium, and Elisabeth was among the few monarchs of whom AT thought highly), but he detested Umberto's father, King Victor Emmanuel III, whom considered responsible for fascism's continued stranglehold on Italy. · The document in which AT described and explained the 1931 Bologna incident is the one reprinted in this book (see late May 1931, p. 128). · *Fontamara* (1930) and *Pane e vino* (1937) remain the best-known novels of Ignazio Silone (*nom de plume* of Secondo Tranquilli, 1900–78); one may safely assume that AT liked them not only as works of literature but also for their strongly anti-Fascist sentiments. They were not published in Fascist Italy, and AT's suggestion that AM look for them in Nazi Germany was probably naive.

Sunday night [24.10.37]

My <u>holy love,</u> This afternoon Weizmann came to see me. He was furious about
that telegram from Tel Aviv. And he told me that for the moment I mustn't
make a move, that I absolutely must postpone going to Palestine until things
there have been resolved or at least improved, and that he was sending a
telegram to Tel Aviv this evening advising them not to insist any further. So
I'll go there in March, after America. I've already wired Milan to cancel my
tickets. Are you happy? Weizmann is leaving in November. He has postponed
his already announced departure by a few weeks, to distract attention. It seems
that that <u>criminal</u> delinquent of a <u>Mussolini,</u> who has played a part in stirring
up the riots that are taking place in Palestine and Egypt, spread the rumor
that Weizmann wants to become <u>king</u> or <u>emperor</u> of Palestine. This was
meant to whip up the Arabs' <u>already furious</u> hatred of [Weizmann], so much
so that for some years there has been an award of $2,000 offered to anyone who
kills him.

[. . .] Won't you tell me anything about your life in Berlin? How do you
usually spend your days? Do you play, practice the piano? And our "Sogno"—
have you learned it by heart? Have I told you that I've had some sessions with
the orchestra to make new records? I did Beethoven's Pastoral and first symphonies. I'll also do Brahms's Tragische Overture and something else that I
haven't yet decided on. Tomorrow morning I'll begin rehearsing the ninth.
I'm already all full of dread at the thought of confronting that <u>colossal, marvelous first movement</u>. I always feel that I'm doing it for the first time, and
that I've never understood it well enough! In the score, [at the opening of] the
last 35 bars, where there begins a sort of march that concludes that tragic
movement, I've written in pencil:

Per me si va nella città dolente.
Per me si va nell'eterno dolore
Per me si va tra la perduta gente.

Every time that I play or conduct those bars, the well-known Dantean terzina
rings in my brain. Dante and Beethoven! It's enough to make you quake!

Monday night. [25.10.37]

My Ada, I've had a very work-filled day; I couldn't either finish or mail this
letter. Two long orchestra rehearsals of nearly three hours each knocked me
out. In the first, I worked on the Brahms Tragische and the first movement of
the ninth Symphony; in the second, only two and a half hours later, I made
records of Beethoven's first symphony and the Brahms overture. These recording sessions are killers for me! I even end up with a headache—an illness virtually unknown to me. At six p.m., on returning from the rehearsal, I found
<u>your big letter.</u> It's not <u>just what</u> I was waiting for, but it's adorable, like

everything that comes to me from you. My dear, adored one, now you'll be at peace! As you see, my trip to Palestine has been postponed to a date yet to be determined. As I was telling you, Weizmann was most indignant over that telegraphic reply, and he said, "Those asses don't understand that if by chance anything were to happen to you, even if it were only something unpleasant, we Jews would attract the whole world's hatred!" I'm telling you, he was furious—like you, my love! [. . .]

AT uses modern Italian spelling in his Dante quotation (the first stanza of the third Canto of *The Divine Comedy*), but the quotation is otherwise exact. (Words over the Gate to Hell: "Through me one goes into the sorrowing city, / Through me one goes into eternal sorrow, / Through me one goes among the lost people.") He knew much of the work by heart. · Regarding Fascist Italy's attitude toward Palestine, Denis Mack Smith says (in *Mussolini's Roman Empire* [London: Penguin, 1977], p. 33): "Mussolini backed his colonial claims by a forward policy in the Middle East. He tried to persuade King Fuad to copy fascism and suspend the Egyptian constitution; he made use of Italian Jewish settlements in the eastern Mediterranean for the penetration of the Levant by Italian propaganda; and young Catholic missionaries were exempted from military service as part of an attempt to replace French and Spanish influence by Italian in the Holy Land. An Italian right of patronage over the holy places of Jerusalem was claimed by mediaeval tradition, though this was rejected by the British, who held an international mandate for Palestine."

E.P. LONDON, 27 OCTOBER 1937; P.S. AS IN PREVIOUS LETTERS;
TO AM, PFB; FSD-FOF

Wednesday 27-10

[. . .] I'm sending you only a few, hurried lines. At three p.m. I have an orchestra rehearsal. A little ninth sym. and then a once-over on the [German] Requiem, with orchestra only.

Rehearsals here are spread out over many days.

Tomorrow at three I have an ensemble rehearsal for the Requiem.

It's very easy to rehearse with this orchestra. For me, it's superior to all others, at least for its magnificent discipline. Friday at three, dress rehearsal. Saturday evening at eight, concert. I hope you'll be listening to it over the radio. [. . .]

E.P. LONDON, (30?) OCTOBER 1937; P.S. AS IN PREVIOUS LETTERS;
TO AM, PFB; FSD-FOF

two o'clock Thursday night [night of 28–29.10.37]

My Ada, I've just come back from a magnificent performance of Shakespeare's Richard the Second. Excellent artists. Staging and sets in exquisite taste and thoroughly worked out. The protagonist is the actor John Gielgud, who is also the director—marvelous. It put my nerves back in order. Today's rehearsal was a disaster. I stopped after three-quarters of an hour. That first movement of the ninth always makes me despair. This orchestra played it a month ago with Henry Wood, very badly and in an incorrect way. I heard it on the radio.

Despite my agitation, it seems that something a little out of the ordinary emerged, because Cortot, who attended the rehearsal with his young mistress and Stefan Zweig, came to me with tears in his eyes and couldn't speak for the emotion! It was the first time that he was attending one of my rehearsals. Too bad that the state of my nerves didn't allow me to resume the rehearsal. I immediately went back to the hotel, where I was greeted by a telegram that shocked me! It came from Marshall Field, the New York Philharmonic's president. I'm transcribing it for you:

> Just had first meeting of season of Philharmonic symphony[.] board and myself send you greetings and welcome. Would be much honoured if madame Toscanini and you would dine with entire board and all members of the orchestra at first available date after your arrival here in December. Please cable me what date would be convenient for you. Kindest personal regards.
>
> [Quotation in English in the original.]

These gentlemen, after having nearly called me a traitor for having accepted to do the concerts for the <u>National Broadcasting Company,</u> and having gossiped unfairly in the newspapers, suddenly make this about-face. Why? What has happened that's new on my part? I've already prepared an answer. I'm awaiting word from <u>our Margherita</u> before I send it. Here it is: "Mrs. Toscanini and myself send hearty thanks to you and to the board of the Philharmonic Symphony for your greetings which we reciprocate. Regret not being able to accept any engagements till after our arrival in Newyork [*sic*]. Best regards." [Quotation in English in the original.] What do you think, Ada my dear? Are they or aren't they clowns, even over there? [. . .]

That Furtwängler [and] that Mrs. Furt bother me. After your magnificent, concise, definitive critique, I didn't even want to set my eyes for a minute on the musical themes of that foolish <u>friend of yours,</u> or at least <u>admirer of yours.</u> His former secretary has let Dr. Kerber know that next year he won't conduct in Bayreuth. And I add: Hitler permitting. [. . .]

The production of *Richard II* that AT attended in London was considered one of the most important events in the long career of John (later Sir John) Gielgud (1904–2000). · The Swiss pianist Alfred Cortot (1877–1962) was one of the best-known keyboard artists of his generation; his approach to musical interpretation was very different from AT's, and the two never worked together. · The reference to Furtwängler and his first wife, Zita, *née* Lund, is unclear. Furtwängler's "former secretary" was Berta Geissmar; she had left Germany because she was Jewish.

3-11-1937 <u>Wednesday morning</u>

[. . .] I'm sending you these two notes from the women who are in love with me. One is older than I am, think of that! You'll know her name—Lady Asquith (Margot), who wanted a photograph of me with the dedication: To Margot—<u>with love.</u> Now I ask you, Ada, is it possible that a woman should still have <u>subversive</u> notions at the age of 74? But you know, she pursues me more than if she were young. <u>Yvonne Rothschild,</u> on the other hand, is very dear and very correct, as a well-brought-up woman should be! She is a friend of Wally's—they're the same age, and I met her last season here in London. She came to Salzburg two or three times this summer. She often sends me flowers, but, as I told you, she is very <u>reserved</u> and <u>restrained.</u> And I'm happy about that!

[. . .] You've only realized now how vacuous Ojetti is? That guy is a dirty sack of vanity. He is nothing but <u>superficial</u>! And little Maria [Salata]? My God, she isn't much, either! We really have something superior and profound, Ada my dear. We are inspired. Nothing is external, <u>everything is internal.</u> [. . .]

Margot Tennant Asquith was the second wife (widow, since 1928) of Herbert Henry Asquith, the British prime minister from 1908 to 1916.

<u>Wednesday afternoon</u> [10.11.37]

[. . .] Yesterday evening at nine-thirty I broke off [listening to] the broadcast of Falstaff from Bologna to try to get Belgrade. In fact, little by little I managed to hear a cello play the Adagio in F from the Schumann Concerto, through the first fifty bars of the final Allegro—then a more powerful station prevented me from hearing the rest of the piece. But I was happy to be able to be a little closer to you, this way. [. . .] The life I lead in Milan is always the same. You know all about it. I spend most of the day at home. I'm studying Sibelius's 2nd Symphony, which I've never performed, and the Tchaikovsky 4th, which I've never wanted to conduct because I like it very little, but which I've promised to perform in America. I go out, but <u>not every</u> evening, to see my friends at the Baldini-Castoldi bookshop. The Clausetti couple came to me for supper yesterday evening, this evening I'm going to their place. The Riboldi couple and Ravasio were here for supper. Wanda comes every once in a while with a Venetian friend (Luciana Magrini), I occasionally see Roberto [Foligno], also at supper or lunch. Giulio [Foligno] seems to me a bit aged. His face is like parchment. Always <u>allegro molto moderato.</u> The Polo family is always here, like part of the furniture. As for musicians, [I see] a few of my old orchestra players from La Scala and two of my assistant conductors, Calusio and Votto. That's all! [. . .]

Yes, you're right, we're bound together by something that neither you nor I can explain. For me, too, it's <u>all</u> a miracle and a dream! You ask, "Why me?" I answer: Because you are the <u>only</u> woman in the world who contains within herself everything that my mind could <u>imagine</u> and my soul <u>adore,</u> and I could paraphrase the Dantean terzina from the last Canto of the Paradiso:

> "In te <u>la somma grazia—in te beltate,</u>
> In te <u>la gentilezza, in te s'aduna</u>
> <u>Quantunque in creatura è di bontate.</u>"

And so I love you. Everything that is a natural gift in you I've found scattered through <u>hundreds</u> of women. How would it be possible not to be faithful to you and not to feel sorry for all the women who try to approach me? How could I not be crazy about you, not ask even the <u>absurd</u> of you—that which no man must ever have asked? Do you understand me, Ada? Yes, I am very different from other men, but am I not thus in <u>many other</u> ways? We've been bound together intimately for four and a half years, and by now you know me thoroughly. You know my few <u>good</u> qualities and my many unpardonable weaknesses. You have to take an average. Put everything on the scale and see which side is heavier. I feel that you are very much in love in these dear letters of yours; I feel as if I were clasping you, throbbing, to my chest, and the emotion and illusion are so strong that I have to stop writing to let my blood resume its regular course.

[. . .] If only I could throw America to the four winds! Some problems between the MBC [*sic*] and the unions have sprung up over there. I don't have time to explain them to you, but this copy of a telegram that I've already sent will allow you to understand approximately what has happened.

Oh, if only I could free myself! I can't continue to live that sort of life. That continual <u>nightmare</u> of standing before orchestras and audiences kills me, makes my life a hell!

Feeling that one is <u>no good</u> has a high price! [. . .]

[COPY IN AT'S HAND OF MESSAGE SENT TO SC; ORIG. ENG. (ALL ERRORS HAVE BEEN PRESERVED):]

Chotzinoff
29 West-85 St. Newyork

I received yours and John cable together with the American Radio Telegraphists Association one—Stop—As I hate to be the cause of any trouble and my engagement seems to have been the reason of discharging numerous employes I feel my coming to Newyork under such conditions will put me in the most troubling state of mind so I beg you to suggest Sarnoff to cancel my engagement. Deeply sorry. Love—AT.

The broadcast from Belgrade that interested AT was of a live performance by Enrico Mainardi. · AT conducted Sibelius's Second Symphony for the first time in January 1938, with the NBC Symphony Orchestra; he conducted it again, later that year, with the BBC Symphony Orchestra, and in 1939 and 1940 with the NBC, then set it aside forever. He never did conduct the Tchaikovsky Fourth, or any other Tchaikovsky symphony except the Sixth. · Carlo Clausetti was codirector of the Ricordi Company. · For the Riboldi couple, see my note accompanying the letter of 13 March 1905. · For more on Calusio, see the letter of 26 August 1920. · The common musical term *allegro molto moderato* (fast, but very moderately) means "not terribly cheerful" in modern Italian. · Antonino Votto (1896–1985) had a considerable conducting career of his own after having worked as AT's assistant, and he later taught Claudio Abbado and Riccardo Muti. · AT was paraphrasing lines 19 to 22 of *Paradiso,* Canto XXXIII. His version reads: "In thee *supreme grace—in thee beauty,*/In thee *kindness, in thee are united*/*Every goodness that a being can have.* · "John" was John N. Royal, vice president of NBC. AT had received a message from Kendal E. Davis of the American Radio Telegraphers Association, who declared that the assumption of personnel to create the NBC Symphony Orchestra for him was causing other NBC and RCA personnel to lose their jobs and was a "vicious open-shop" and "antilabor" move. As a liberal, AT had felt duty bound to withdraw his participation in the project.

TO BRUNO WALTER, (VIENNA?); NYPL, BRUNO WALTER PAPERS, JPB 92-4, SERIES I, FOLDER 589

Milan 12-November [1937]

My dear and good friend

In the last conversation that I had with Dr. Kerber, it was decided that I would conduct two concerts during the next Salzburg season; in one of these, Beethoven's Missa Solemnis, in the other a program of modern music. I've now been thinking that next year it will be exactly twenty years since the death of my friend Claude Debussy and that it should be my duty to do a commemorative concert made up entirely of his music—and I think that it would arouse great interest in the Salzburg audience, which becomes more numerous every year. What do you think, my dear friend? Speak about it with Dr. Kerber. I think it is an excellent idea and at the same time a duty for us to remember this exquisitely brilliant musician and truly great artist!

As you see, I have had to give up Palestine—on the advice of Dr. Weizmann when I was in London. I'll go there in March if things calm down.

I embark for New York on December sixth.

I hope that you are in good health and working hard. Remember me to your wife and daughter.

A hearty embrace to you from your

Arturo Toscanini

I am aware that the statement cabled from the A.R.T.A. and not signed by anybody of its members is entirely false. Shame on you.

Arturo Toscanini

AT did not want to give up the NBC project and allowed himself to be mollified on the labor question by heated protests from the company's representatives. As we have seen, however, the ARTA's message had indeed been signed (although a second, unsigned telegram may also have been sent to AT), and a few jobs (but among musicians, not radiotelegraphers) were probably lost as a result of the creation of the new ensemble. On the other hand, quite a few jobs were created.

15-11 Monday <u>morning</u>

[. . .] The unpleasant American incident has been fixed up. I can't tell you how many <u>kilometers</u> of telegrams I got, all of them desperate. So I'll have to leave on December sixth!

The other evening I had the two Folignos here for supper with a Russian ballerina, a friend of the Rothschild lady—one <u>Nikitina,</u> who now wants to debut as a singer. Do you know her? She told me that Yvonne will probably come to New York with her. Maybe Sybil will come, too. The two rivals who now, for love of me, have made peace with each other!!! Poor Artù—can you imagine the diplomacy I'll have to use? [. . .]

The Russian-born Alice Nikitina (1909–78) danced with Diaghilev's Ballets Russes, studied singing in Italy, sang as a coloratura soprano at Italian opera houses beginning in 1938, and eventually opened a ballet school in Paris.

Wednesday <u>17-11-937</u>

[. . .] Yesterday afternoon I went to try out the records I made in London of <u>Brahms's Tragische Ov.</u> They came out well. Baccara happened to come in, and she listened to them; she also listened to the Pastoral. She said that she and the Commandant [D'Annunzio] heard the broadcast [from London] of the ninth symphony with great pleasure. By the way, Ada, when you talk about my interpretations, don't express yourself as the Furtwänglers, Mengelbergs, etc. do when they say <u>my fifth, my Ninth,</u> etc. Say your interpretation of the Pastoral, of the Ninth, etc. etc. I hate to see the names of miserable mortals put on a part with those of the Gods!

Wanda and little Sonia have left. They're going to Zurich for a few days, then they'll go on to Paris together with Volodia. It seems that he's decided to play this winter. He wants to begin in some provincial place. Maybe in Switzerland. I think he wants to play here at the Friends of the <u>friends</u> of music! [. . .]

For Luisa Baccara, see my note accompanying the letter of 19 September 1934. · AT was clearly making a joke about the Amici della Musica (Friends of Music) association by calling it the "Friends of the *friends* of music," but the reference is unclear.

TG, MI, 17 NOVEMBER 1937; TO SC, 29W85NY; ORIG. ENG.; SCBU

SORRY HAVE BEEN THE INNOCENT CAUSE MUCH TROUBLE TO YOU BUT WAS TERRIBLY UPSET STOP AM ANXIOUS TO HEAR NEWS ABOUT ORCHESTRAS DEBUT LOVE

TOSCANINI

The NBC Symphony Orchestra had made its formal debut on 13 November 1937 under the baton of Pierre Monteux (1875–1964).

E.P. MI, 18 NOVEMBER 1937; TO AM, C/O BOOTH, 28CSL; FSD-FOF

---

morning, Thursday <u>18-11-1937</u>

<u>My love,</u> You're traveling to London at this moment. Your teacher, L. Maz- zuchetti, has <u>just now</u> sent me an article from the "Basler National Zeitung" that she translated. Naturally, although the incident is true, it's told in a com- pletely distorted way. [. . .] Ten days ago I received a letter from <u>Vuillermoz,</u> who reminded me that next year will be the twentieth anniversary of the death of <u>Debussy</u> and asked whether it would be possible to commemorate him with a concert in <u>Salzburg.</u> I answered him, consenting enthusiastically. So in the two concerts, I'll do Beethoven's <u>"Missa Solemnis"</u> on the first and all Debussy on the second! [. . .]

Yesterday evening [. . .] I agreed to go to the [Teatro] Manzoni: they were doing the premiere of Adami's <u>Ninetta del Verze.</u> The protagonist, naturally, was old, rancid <u>Dina Galli.</u> What stupidity! what wretched stuff! what banal- ity! What need was there for that popular Milanese historical figure, defini- tively immortalized by Porta, to be put on the stage by an Adami, who demonstrates that he hasn't understood a thing about Porta's greatness? But it was a <u>fiasco</u>!!! I hadn't seen Adami in years! He shamelessly came out for a bow after the tepid applause for the 2nd act. What a <u>pig's</u> face he has put on! Fat, fat, red to the point of bursting. I could almost smell the <u>nasty odor</u> of his body!

Do you know Porta well? I'm crazy about him! He is a rare sort of poet, of enormous imagination and the greatest humanity. My friend Tessa (who is also a dialect poet of great worth) comes to see me from time to time. Then we gather several friends together and he recites <u>superbly</u> what he considers to be the best of Porta. [. . .]

Italian translation of the *Basler National Zeitung* article (signed "Walter") mentioned above by AT. At the end of a story that says that in London AT had punched a photographer, AT wrote, "(Pure fabrication)." Following the sentence "Yesterday, when, after the Brahms Requiem, the audience began to applaud, he angrily threw down his baton, left the podium, and didn't appear again," AT wrote, "(A historical fact that never happened)." After the sentence "Toscanini is marvelously untopical," AT wrote, "(Maybe!)." Following a sentence in which the journalist complains about the fact that modest people such as AT are ever rarer "while impudence spreads," AT wrote, "(And what is to be done about it?—the world has always been this way)." And after the sentence "Since the world, beneath the surface, is richer and more powerful in its aspirations than its noisy heralds would lead one to suspect," AT wrote, "(Do you believe this, Ada? I don't)." · For Vuillermoz, see the letter and note of 29 August 1935; about the planned Debussy concert at Salzburg (which never took place because AT did not return to Salzburg), see the letter of 12 November 1937. · Giuseppe Adami (1878–1946) is remembered today as the librettist of Puccini's *La rondine, Il tabarro,* and (together with Renato Simoni) *Turandot,* but in his day he was well known in Italy as a playwright. · Dina Galli (1877–1951) was one of the most famous Italian actresses of her generation. · *La Ninetta del Verzee* was the story of a Milanese prostitute. · For more on Porta, see my note accompanying the letter of 6 January 1935. · For more on Tessa, see my note accompanying the letter of 15 July 1934.

E.P. MI, 24 NOVEMBER 1937; TO AM, C/O BOOTH, 28CSL; FSD-FOF

[. . .] The thought that Berlin is about to swallow you up again, to absorb all of you, makes me raving mad! I hate that city—I've always hated it—but now my hatred is white, livid, poisonous, made of prussic acid. Woe to a German, to a Prussian, if I were to spit in his face! He would drop stone dead on the spot! And we—I mean the Italians of . . . (be careful not to say his name without having taken the <u>usual measures;</u> now I can do it)—the Italians of the <u>Great Delinquent</u> are allied and enjoying a honeymoon with those descendants of Attila, Barbarossa, and so on. And you have to live among them! [. . .]

E.P. MI, 27 NOVEMBER 1937; TO AM, PFB; FSD-FOF

<u>Saturday evening</u> [27.11.37]
[. . .] I've never feared death; on the contrary, one could say that I think of it every day with a certain indifference. My family, my children, no longer need me—but <u>there's you, Ada,</u> **there's you** who makes me want to live, and to live <u>as long as possible.</u> And I shall live—you'll see—I'll live for you, and with <u>continually</u> renewed, **faithful** affection that will never languish. I'm leaving

off unwillingly. Some friends are coming to supper this evening. They're all from Parma, and some of them were students together with me or at the same conservatory. [. . .]

E.P. MI, 29 NOVEMBER 1937; TO AM, PFB; FSD-FOF

Sunday morning [28.11.37]

[. . .] Yesterday evening, among my old friends, I put a very substantial mask on my face. I didn't want to throw a pall over their joy at seeing me, but I could have wept. That <u>brother-in-law</u> of mine, how **empty** he is. My God, how empty he is. A big **fascist**! That will suffice to make you understand. The other friends—<u>not one of them</u> [is a fascist]! They stayed till 1 a.m. I went to bed at four. I couldn't tell you what the devil I managed to accomplish in those three hours. I reread your letters, I wrote to you—or rather, I chatted with you and destroyed [the letters], as usual—but I knew that I'd write to you this morning. I sat by the radio, in communication with New York, and I was able to hear Mozart's sym. in G minor played by the MBC [*sic*] orchestra (mine). At seven, my old Nena brought me my black coffee. [. . .]

The brother-in-law was, of course, Enrico Polo. Among the former schoolmates of AT who came to dinner that evening was Guido Zavadini (1868–1958), an oboist who became well known for his research on Donizetti. · If AT heard Mozart's Symphony in G Minor on the radio, he was tuned in to the wrong station: the NBC Symphony Orchestra concert (conducted by Pierre Monteux) of 27 November 1937 did not include any works by Mozart.

E.P. MI, 5 DECEMBER 1937; TO AM, PFB; FSD-FOF

Sunday morn. [5.12.37]

[. . .] Yes, I want to tell you everything on that subject—on that person [Count Aldrovandi], who irked me from the moment I met him, with that enormous <u>vanity</u> that characterizes all of those empty, empty, <u>superficial</u> people who care only about their **nobility**, which, in reality, exists only on their visiting cards. Only yesterday evening, at dinner (I don't know how the conversation stumbled onto him), Rusca, of Mondadori, in talking to Walter, related that he [Aldrovandi] showed up one day while his latest book was being printed, and in a tone of voice that showed that he was half annoyed and half offended, he pointed out that whoever had sent him the galleys had shown a lack of respect and consideration. In what way? asked Rusca. And this fool pulls out a certificate that <u>authenticated</u> that on such and such a day, his father (or grandfather) had had the title of <u>Count</u> conferred on him, therefore he couldn't bear the fact that letters or packages were addressed to him—given <u>the position he had occupied</u> (ambassador to Berlin)—without his various names and titles! And you loved such an imbecile! A nothing, a worthy representative of that elect bunch of vain people, of civil and moral vacuities, who have always infested the world, today more than ever! You were going through a bad period in your life, my friend. A moment of truly great mental weakness! You, who are so _intense_ in your _internal_ life, next to that fearful piece of aristocratic emptiness! It's clear why he was able to accept your sincerity with gratitude, as you say, without despair, and to continue to write to you (perhaps to demonstrate once again his cultivation and his unlimited vanity), but what I have never been able to understand is that _you_ can still bear to have him underfoot, although you know it causes me great, profound displeasure! But let's not speak of it anymore. I'm writing you in a rush—I'm not even looking at what I write. My house is full of people, and I can't make head or tail of what I'm saying.

I'm going to Genoa this evening. I'll board ship at 9:30 tomorrow, and we weigh anchor at eleven. How do I feel about leaving? Can you imagine? Sadder, more desolate than in all the previous years. It's a real tragedy! You write to me blinded by tears; I, on the other hand, am not crying through my eyes, but my heart feels like bursting! [. . .]

E.P. NY, 22 DECEMBER 1937; TO AM, 25VBMMI; FSD-FOF

Wednesday 22-12-937

[. . .] I can't describe how I was received on my arrival here. Friends, acquaintances—even enemies, I think—all seemed to have gone mad. I, however, had only one sole thought: whether or not a letter of yours had arrived. I got one two days later! I thought I was becoming ill. I felt a fever in my bones. Everyone thought I'd caught a chill the morning of my arrival. But it was internal turmoil, anger, disappointment that had made me feverish. [. . .]

E.P. NY, 23 DECEMBER 1937; TO AM, 25VBMMI; FSD-FOF

Wednesday night [22.12.37]

[. . .] This evening all the Busches came to supper. What good, honest, simple, peaceful people! When I compare myself to them, I see all my _infernal nastiness._ And recently I've been perfidious even toward you. I was already aware of it back in Milan. I didn't want to hear your voice! Therefore, I was perfidious toward myself, too. But I had the Devil in my blood. Unreasonable jealousy, and the atrocious notion that you read my letters only carelessly, threw me into despair. And then I keep thinking that you hide things from me that I really ought to know, that you're not as sincere with me as I am with you! Now, tell me the truth. When you left Berlin and stopped in Munich, wasn't it to attend a concert that Furtwängler was giving? Tell me the truth, Ada—

tell me the whole truth! I know that that individual has been and still is court-
ing you. He takes advantage of every opportunity (I remember Paris) to visit
you, and I know from Mausi (Winifred's daughter) that he spares no woman,
be she young or old, pretty or ugly! You must tell me everything, as if I were
your confessor. Don't I do the same with you? Look: I've heard from Wally
that that English lady (Sybil) is supposed to come to New York; I don't know
how, but the rumor has spread that she's coming because she is in love with
me. I wouldn't be at peace with myself if I didn't tell you—I would feel that I
had done a bad deed if I hid this from you! My love, how I would like you to
get to know this marvelous, fantastic New York! It seems even more marvelous than before to me. I can't describe the welcome I've received. The entire
personnel of the NBC, from President Sarnoff (a truly exceptional man) and
the board of directors down to the doorman, are enchanted with me and treat
me like their God. If I weren't the wretched creature that you know me to be,
I would swell up with vanity, like a Lucifer. Instead, it all leaves me nearly
indifferent, and I feel unhappier and more wretched than before. Oh, my Ada,
if I had you near maybe I would enjoy this, too, thanks to the joy that you
would bring me. Can you imagine that the enthusiasm toward me is such that
people are already sending checks to Carnegie Hall to reserve seats at a concert
that hasn't yet been announced, but that they know I'll be giving for the benefit of the theater that's being built at Salzburg!

The orchestra is of the highest order. Their manner of playing together is
already magnificent. The strings are first class, beyond any description! Working is a delight. [. . .]

Although here and in subsequent letters AT's descriptions of the reception that
greeted him in New York demonstrate his desire to impress AM, he was by no means
overstating the matter. One does gather, from the tone of the original Italian, that he
was even more astonished than pleased, and his delight over the new orchestra's abilities is as genuine as that of a child who has just been given the most remarkable toy in
the world.

E.P. NY, 25 DECEMBER 1937; TO AM, 25VBMMI; FSD-FOF

25 Dec. Christmas 1937

[. . .] Everyone welcomes me here, everyone is in a state of delirium for me! It's
as if they were seeing and hearing me for the first time!! It's impossible for me
to tell you about all the presents that I've received and that Carla has received.
It is really moving—yet I'm not moved and, wicked man that I am, I must
confess to you that my soul is sad and anxious. I have my first concert this evening. I hardly need to tell you, but you can imagine how nervous I am. I'm the
eternal beginner, perhaps the only person who doesn't hold me in esteem. And
the work costs me an effort—not material but spiritual—and I always suffer
like a woman giving birth, I think. [. . .]

The [printed] programs here aren't like those of the Philharmonic. They don't have explanatory notes. There is an announcer who explains and talks, thus everything is put on a little piece of soft cardboard with the names of the pieces and so on. The program for next Saturday (New Year's) is Schubert's symphony in C Major, the Adagio and Scherzo from Beethoven's last quartet (string orchestra), and Strauss's Death and Transfiguration. I'll tell you the programs as they come up.

Who do I see here? The usual friends. Our Margherita, every day. I haven't yet seen the Heifetzes. They live outside New York. As always, I stay in. I work with the new orchestra—which is truly exceptional—with great pleasure and satisfaction. I can't describe the enthusiasm of the musicians and of all the members of the NBC board. It seems impossible that an old conductor like me can still stir up enough enthusiasm to form a new orchestra in a country that already has many of them, and good ones! I'm leaving you because I hear people in the other room. I'll write at [i.e., to coincide with the departure of] every passenger ship. [. . .]

E.P. NY, 26 DECEMBER 1937; TO AM, 25VBMMI; FSD-FOF

<u>Sunday 26</u>   <u>6 o'clock in the morning</u>

<u>My sweet</u> love, I'm just this moment getting home. After the concert, which ended at eleven-thirty, I went to the home of the President of NBC, <u>David Sarnoff,</u> who had invited a great many people in my honor, and I stayed until five in the morning. [. . .] I received many kisses (beautiful young women are glad to kiss the <u>famous old maestro,</u> you know, but only out of vanity), but if I could have told them all the wish that was tormenting me, they would have taken it very badly! The concert went off very beautifully. There was much enthusiasm. Back at home I found a great many congratulatory telegrams. Many of them were sent by radio listeners (my son in Milan among them), and many by people who attended the concert, including all of the Busches with Serkin, who sent an extremely moving telegram. The orchestra played marvelously well. You ought to hear what a noble sonority this orchestra produces! It is truly made up of members of the highest order. In Italy, we could never put together an orchestra of this sort. Too bad—and it's really too bad that you weren't here, my Ada. But I was thinking of you while I was conducting. With every beat, you were present in my thoughts. I had brought along everything of yours. Besides the little portrait case that you'll recall, I had the photograph that was taken at the Pincio, with the little hat, and the last diaphanous, magic veil! As you can see, I was well protected against bad luck. I'm happy to send along the graceful, elegant program, specially made on silk to avoid all noise. And I'm dissatisfied to find myself alone in this little room, so far and separated from you. [. . .]

The "magic veil" was a handkerchief stained with AM's menstrual blood. · The NBC's first program was indeed printed on silk, and along with program listings and other basic information, it reads, "Since the modern microphone is extremely sensitive, your co-operation in maintaining strict silence during the music is urgently requested." The concert comprised Vivaldi's Concerto Grosso in D Minor, Op. 3, no. 11; Mozart's Symphony no. 40 in G Minor; and Brahms's Symphony no. 1 in C Minor.

E.P. NY, 29 DECEMBER 1937; TO AM, 25VBMMI; FSD-FOF

29 <u>Decem. 1937</u>

[. . .] My Ada, I'm happy that you're finally leaving Germany and going back to our country! It's real torture to know that you're among those crude Germans <u>of the horrid chant</u> (as Tacitus called them). How is it possible that Enrico has never found a way of carrying out his artistic activity outside Germany? I couldn't live there! I never loved it before Hitler's advent, but now I detest it. Those brutal people, made from the same mold, all alike—and as Heine justly said, when you've met one German, don't trouble yourself to meet others, because they're all alike. The Italians, no: each one has his own personality. When you've met one, you still have to meet all the others. If Heine were alive today, he would change his mind about us. But who could have imagined the birth of that <u>Great Criminal,</u> whose name I can't mention without touching the **two amulets**?

[. . .] Ada, if you heard this orchestra, you would think your Artù is better than he seems [*sic*]. The strings are magnificent. They have a delightful sonority. It's a joy to work with such players. On the other hand, my ex-Philharmonic is sad to hear. It no longer seems the same orchestra. [. . .]

The New York Philharmonic under John Barbirolli was not doing as well at the box office as it had done under AT, but its playing had not declined seriously. Like many other performers, AT was often disinclined to distinguish bad (to his way of thinking) interpretations from bad playing.

E.P. NY, 12 JANUARY 1938; TO AM, VB8R; FSD-FOF

11 <u>January</u>

[. . .] This evening on the Ile-de-France, Wanda, too, arrived—alone. I invited her together with her husband for Wally's birthday on January 16 (38 years old). But Horowitz had to stay in Paris, having begun a cure that he can't interrupt for the time being. Wally is still in California (she went with Castelbarco, who is showing his paintings), but Saturday morning she'll be here among us. There's a woman who can (and does) say that she's enjoyed life so far! Wanda is very different! Like me, she has a more internal life—she is <u>never</u> truly happy. She says that Horowitz's father can no longer communicate with his son. It seems that [Vladimir's] brother wrote a letter urging him to take no further interest in them, not to send any more money (because they don't need it), and urging him to return home. Naturally, the letter has the flavor of having been written <u>under duress.</u> It's fearful, what a world we live in! The only thing to do is to work, to work without letting up, if one wants to live and forget a tiny bit! I'm frightened by the obligations I've taken on! In Palestine, they're still <u>upside down.</u> Will I go? Won't I go? Who knows! There are moments when my sadness is practically <u>tragic</u>! Everyone here adores me and they fight with each other to make themselves useful and dear, yet I hate everyone fiercely. I would like to be alone, always. I have a phobia about people. And I'm obliged and constrained to live among them! It's really tragic. And I'm always and forever hearing people say, "How happy Maestro Toscanini must be, to be adored by the whole world!"

I'll send you some newspaper clippings, under separate cover, so that you can see that your Artù isn't yet ready to be thrown on the rag heap. The article in the Times by Olin Downes, who stayed home and listened to the last concert on the radio, is interesting. Dorothy Thompson spoke about me on the radio. She is a highly intelligent woman who writes articles on politics for the New York Herald. A woman who writes about politics doesn't make me feel too sure of her femininity. [. . .]

Olin Downes (1886–1955) was a music critic for the *New York Times* (and for many years chief music critic) from 1924 until his death; he greatly admired AT. · Dorothy Thompson (1894–1961) was one of the best-known liberal American political columnists of her day; she loved music, but her praise of AT was directly connected to his antifascism. As to his final comment: he may have been ahead of his time in believing that women of talent had an obligation to themselves to set themselves goals beyond that of getting married (see the letters of 9 and 14 September 1937), but many of his ideas were much more old-fashioned.

E.P. NY, 15 JANUARY 1938; TO AM, VB8R; FSD-FOF

Friday night   14-1-938

<u>My adored</u> Ada,

I'm just getting back from an extremely boring musical evening. I swallowed three piano and violin sonatas (Bach, Debussy, and Beethoven) to please Maria Carrera[s], who plays badly, and the violinist, who played worse. I had finished a very laborious three-hour rehearsal (from four to seven); I had no need for such a mess. Sibelius's Symph. in D Major is a tough nut to crack. It's a beautiful thing. The orchestras here—or, not to mince words, the conductors— have the bad habit of dragging tempi, and this symphony, which is often performed, suffers more than others because it's full of warmth and spontaneity and needs to be performed with simplicity and inspiration. There's a <u>record</u> of this symphony by Ku {i.e., Koussevitzky} that is simply scandalous. That record destroys him as musician and interpreter. On this program I'm doing

Tommasini's Carnevale di Venezia and Busoni's Rondò Arlecchinesco. I'm starting with Brahms's Tragische. I can't describe how much interest these concerts have aroused. I get hundreds of letters of admiration and thanks.

Didn't I tell you that I'm giving two benefit concerts at Carnegie Hall? The first is on February 6 with the 1st Parsifal Prelude, joined by the theme [musical quotation] to the Good Friday Spell. Then the ninth symphony. This concert is for the benefit of the <u>Italian Welfare League.</u> The second will take place early in March with the Verdi Requiem and will benefit the <u>Salzburg</u> theater. The poor old maestro, your poor old Artù, is still good for something! As soon as the concert was announced, even before the program was made known, Carnegie [Hall] was besieged. Twenty-plus days ahead, it's all sold out. My love, please tell me that you're happy with me even though I do <u>nothing</u> for you. [. . .]

You can believe me, Ada—I don't lie easily—and to you (may God strike me blind) I can only tell the truth. You're my first <u>great</u> passion, <u>immense</u> passion. In saying it, I feel moved to tears. I wish you could see me at this very moment—it would make you feel sad and happy—and you ought to feel a bit flattered at having subjugated a man who has certainly known and enjoyed life! But what you have given him comes from another sphere. It's like music. You may have been familiar with everything that was written in the two centuries before Wagner, but when Wagner set down this simple A major chord [musical quote: first chord of the Prelude to Act I of *Lohengrin*] for the Violins and Woodwinds, I've always imagined that at a moment of great, sublime inspiration he disappeared from the earth, went up to heaven for a time, and came back down bringing that magical chord, of whose existence no one before him had dreamt. To me, you are that divine chord. You came into my life and brought me what no woman had been able to give me. You are my ideal creature, the one I dreamt of in my far-off adolescence. [. . .]

The pianist Maria Carreras and the violinist Ronald Murat had given a recital that evening at the home of Carolyn (Mrs. Lionel) Perera, a good friend of the Toscaninis.

E.P. NY, 19 JANUARY 1938; TO AM, VB8R; FSD-FOF

Sunday <u>morning</u> [16.1.38]

<u>My love,</u> The fourth concert, too, is finished. I don't know how I managed to conduct. I only know that I had death in my heart, and I still haven't been able to free myself of the nightmare that's been racking me since yesterday morning. A telegram to Carla mistakenly got into my hands. It was from Walter, who declared that for several months Horowitz's father has been either in prison or deported. The news was communicated to Walter by Countess <u>Cicogna,</u> whose sister is in Moscow, married to someone at the Embassy.

Wanda was near me while I was reading the telegram. Imagine the sorrow and turmoil I felt throughout my being. Naturally, I didn't pass the sad news on to anyone.

I've kept and am still keeping everything inside me. Today is Wally's birthday; she arrived from California yesterday, full of enthusiasm and moved by Wanda's surprise arrival. How could I poison this day with such a piece of news?

I'm half dead with fatigue and emotion. I leave it to you to imagine how I managed, with so much sorrow in my heart, to conduct an extremely tiring rehearsal from 4 p.m. to six-thirty and then the concert from 10 until eleven-thirty!

It's fearful to think about what sort of world we live in, my love—and I no longer hope to live to see it change. [. . .]

From Harold C. Schonberg, *Horowitz: His Life and Music* (New York: Simon & Schuster, 1992), p. 145: ". . . Samuel Horowitz {Vladimir's father} was arrested during one of Stalin's purges. Nobody knew the reason for his arrest. . . . Natasha Saitzoff {Horowitz's cousin} said that when Horowitz's sister, Regina, got permission to visit her father in the gulag, he was in so deplorable a condition that he did not recognize her. He died in the prison camp."

E.P. NY, (?) JANUARY 1938; TO AM, VB8R; FSD-FOF

Saturday <u>22-1-1938</u>

[. . .] My total lack of vanity is practically my ruin, while for others it's a stimulus and perhaps the achievement of an ideal. To believe in themselves and in those who praise them! Look at <u>Furtwängler,</u> De Sabata, Molinari. And à propos the last: Do you know to what extent his successes in Germany have gone to his head? Polo went to say hello to him after a concert in Milan. Mary of course found the Milanese audience thirty years behind the time because it didn't applaud Petrassi's music, and Bernardino, all proud and full of himself, having been received more warmly than formerly, expressed himself to my brother-in-law in the following terms: "They (the Milanese) are finally realizing that I have a pair of b[alls] this big." And a gesture duly indicating the <u>proportions</u> accompanied the description of <u>that pair,</u> etc. My dear, it's enough to shock you. When on earth has such a sentence ever passed across my lips? When have I ever spoken with such shameless presumption about myself in front of [other] artists? Such ignorance and such self-satisfaction! And from him, poor Bernardino, who, apart from music, is fearfully ignorant. Go to his house—you won't find a book, an objet d'art. Apart from those few notes, he doesn't know a thing—I don't know anyone who can equal him for lack of cultivation. I've recommended him for the NBC here. I think they've signed him up, and I also believe that he asked for too much money. And the Furtwängler case! Can you imagine that after our conversation on August 27, when I very clearly defined our situation in Salzburg, he's shamelessly resumed begging for a concert for the coming season? And the Viennese and Minister Pertner are again daring to take the subject up and trying to persuade me to allow him that concert? But what are made men of these days? Certainly not of the courage of lions. Oh, what a bad race we are! It's always been so, but it seems to be worse today. Tell me where I come from, Ada. I feel that I'm so different from others! Or am I wrong, am I deluding myself? [. . .]

For more on Molinari, see my note accompanying the telegram of 18 December 1915. · Goffredo Petrassi (b. 1904), who studied with Molinari, is a well-known Italian composer. AT was familiar with some of his works but found them uninteresting and did not perform any of them.

E.P. NY, 9 FEBRUARY 1938; TO AM, VB8R; FSD-FOF

Sunday night   6-2-938

I've just come back from a dinner at the home of friends. I feel like talking to you before I lie down. I'm very tired but radiant with joy. You were in my thoughts, in my blood all through the concert. I was a devil. I conducted, I believe, as never before in my very long career. I had quicksilver in my blood, in my veins, as Verdi used to say. The orchestra did wonders. The chorus, the solo singers, everyone was at one with me. My Ada, you often ask me whether I'm a man or a devil or a God; but I, in turn, must send the same question back to you: What are you for me, dear soul, a human being or a divinity? You work magically on me from far away, and you make something marvelous of me. This evening, everyone found me miraculously improved—everyone was saying that the ninth symphony has never had a better performance, even bearing in mind my most recent ones. Busch was moved and he moved me. Even I, who am never satisfied with what I do, felt that something approaching perfection was taking place before my eyes this evening. [. . .]

Carnegie Hall was packed, maybe more so than at my last Philharmonic concert. The box-office take was enormous, $27,000, of which $22,000 was netted for the Italian Welfare League. I'm really happy.

It was a rather tough week. I worked hard. I had to have a few intravenous injections. My blood pressure went down from 130 to 118 and 116, but I'm hoping to recoup the lost points, if not all of them, next week. The program isn't difficult:

Euryanthe overture
Brahms's 2nd symphony
Siegfried Idyll and the Sorcerer's Apprentice won't give me much to worry about.

I'll leave you now because I feel I must go to bed. I won't sleep. My nerves are still trembling. But I'll rest my bones. [. . .]

THE CURRENT POLITICAL EVENTS IN AUSTRIA OBLIGE ME TO RENOUNCE MY
SALZBURG FESTIVAL PARTICIPATION. GREETINGS.
                    TOSCANINI

On 12 February 1938 Austrian Chancellor Schuschnigg met Hitler and bowed to
some of his demands: he accepted Artur Seyss-Inquart, a leading Austrian Nazi, as
minister of the interior, and he aligned Austria's foreign and economic policies with
Germany's, in the hope that these concessions would allow his country to remain independent. The politically unsophisticated AT understood immediately where these
compromises would lead and, to the surprise and regret of many of his Jewish and
otherwise anti-Nazi friends in Austria and elsewhere, broke with the Salzburg Festival. (I have written about this matter at length in the chapter "Toscanini, Hitler, and
Salzburg" in my book *Reflections on Toscanini*.)

TG, NY, 20 FEBRUARY 1938; TO AM, VB8R; FSD-FOF

HAVE GIVEN UP SALZBURG FOR GOOD EXTREMELY SADDENED BUT IT WAS
INEVITABLE YOU CAN UNDERSTAND WHY [. . .] = ARTU + +

DRAFT OF TG, (NY, 21 FEBRUARY 1938);
TO BRUNO WALTER, STAATSOPER, VIENNA; NYPLSC

Futile that I await your letter[.] my decision however painful is final stop. I
have only one way of thinking and acting. I hate compromise. I walk and shall
always walk on the straight path that I have traced for myself in life. Cordial
greetings

Bruno Walter had cabled AT, asking that he wait to read a detailed letter that he was
sending him before making up his mind for good.

DRAFT OF TG (NY, ON OR SHORTLY AFTER 2 MARCH 1938);
TO SALZBURG FESTIVAL ADMINISTRATION, SALZBURG; ORIG. GER.; NYPLSC

I AM SURPRISED BY YOUR INSULTING TELEGRAM AND I AM SURPRISED THAT
THE FINALITY OF MY DECISION WAS NOT ALREADY UNDERSTOOD FROM MY
FIRST CABLE.
                    A. TOSCANINI

On 2 March 1938 AT had received a telegram from the Festival administrators
requesting that he meet with the Austrian consul general in New York and that he
then confirm his decision one way or another by 10 March. This telegram was AT's
reply.

DEAR MAX REINHART [*sic*] THANK YOU FOR THE HIGH ESTEEM WITH WHICH YOU HONOR ME I HAVE REFLECTED ON YOUR PROPOSAL BUT MY AGE DOESN'T ALLOW ME TO TAKE ON A NEW ACTIVITY IN THE THEATER STOP THE CONTRACT SET DOWN IN THE LAST FEW DAYS WITH THE N.B.C. ELIMINATES ANY POSSIBILITY OF MY ACCEPTING OTHER ENGAGEMENTS. VERY SORRY I GREET YOU HEARTILY.

A.T.

For more on Reinhardt, see my note accompanying the letter of 4 August 1933. This telegram was a reply to a very long telegram (4 March 1938) in which the famous German director, who had fled to the United States, proposed creating a "new Salzburg" in California; had AT agreed to participate, financing could have been arranged immediately.

AT THE CLOSE OF ALMOST THREE MONTHS OF CONCERTS I FEEL A GREAT SADNESS IN LEAVING THESE COLLEAGUES WHO WITH GREAT DEVOTION AND A SPIRIT OF SERVICE TO OUR ART HAVE WORKED WITH ME TO THE REALIZATION OF THIS FIRST SERIES OF CONCERTS. I HOPE THAT WE HAVE SATISFIED THE PUBLIC AND THAT WE HAVE BROUGHT ALSO TO VARIED DISTANT REGIONS AND IN HUMBLE HOMES, SERENITY AND THE MAGIC JOY OF AN HOUR OF MUSIC.

I AM CONSOLED IN THE SADNESS OF REALIZING THAT THIS SERIES OF CONCERTS HAS ENDED BY THINKING OF NEXT OCTOBER WHEN I RETURN TO WORK WITH SUCH PERFECT MATERIAL[.]

DEAR SARNOFF, THANK YOU, AND PLEASE THANK FOR ME, MR. LOHR AND MR. ROYAL BECAUSE I CAN SO WELL UNDERSTAND AND APPRECIATE HOW MUCH YOU HAVE ALL DONE TO SPARE ME ANY ANNOYANCES AND TO GIVE ME THE GREAT HAPPINESS OF WORKING WITH YOU ALL. AND ABOVE ALL, THANK YOU FROM THE BOTTOM OF MY HEART FOR THE GREAT GENEROSITY OF THE NATIONAL BROADCASTING COMPANY ORGANIZATION WHO, WITH MAGNIFICENT GESTURE PUT AT MY DISPOSAL THIS SUPERB ORCHESTRA FOR THE PURPOSE OF GIVING TWO BENEFIT CONCERTS.

DEAR FRIENDS, THIS IS NOT GOODBYE, BUT A VERY TENDER AND AFFECTIONATE "ARRIVEDERCI AND GRAZIE."

DEVOTEDLY
ARTURO TOSCANINI

This is not an absolutely precise translation of the original letter, which AT wrote in Italian, but it is close—and it is the version that Sarnoff and his colleagues read.

<u>17 March</u>

[. . .] For some time I haven't been living. That is, I feel the <u>uselessness</u> of living. If I didn't have you, I wouldn't mind at all passing on to the next world at this very moment. What has happened during these last weeks has made me lose every hope for the slightest improvement in humanity. I am ashamed of belonging to the human race. The <u>delinquents</u> who govern the peoples are beneath all imagining, however low. And I lump them **all** together, from all countries, of all opinions and of all parties, of all races. The Italian head of Government? He is even lower than I had judged him to be! Open all the prisons—you won't find a delinquent or a criminal who is <u>more of a delinquent, more of a criminal</u> than that **ignoble animal**! Poor Italy! And the Italians? They disgust me! If it weren't for you, I would never again set foot in my country. [. . .] Ada, I don't know whether I'll go to Palestine. A telegram from Huberman (who recently had a conversation with Weizmann) tells me to postpone to a more propitious time. But I would like to fulfill this promise as soon as possible. I need to have no ties with anyone, or promises, or word given. I'd like to live in a desert, or on a faraway island, like <u>Robinson Crusoe.</u> I hate the human race! [. . .]

AT was in The Hague for his second (and last) series of appearances with the Residentie-Orkest. · The cause of his particularly strong outburst was the *Anschluss,* Nazi Germany's annexation of Austria on 11–12 March 1938. His particular disgust had to do with the fact that Mussolini, who had previously set himself up as a protector of Austrian independence, had backed down (like the leaders of other nations) in the face of Hitler's *fait accompli.*

18 <u>March 1938</u>

[. . .] I don't know why, but this morning I looked at myself in the mirror, after I don't know how many months, and I looked old, ugly, and unwell to myself. I'm not ill, I'm not well, but I have something worse than having a real illness. I'm working out of necessity, not out of love. All the people around me get on my nerves, and unfortunately there are <u>many</u> of them. The nicer they are to me, the more I'd like to kick them. The events of these last weeks drive me crazy. Read the enclosed article. <u>Prostitutes,</u> the ones who do it for five lire a night or even less, care more about their honor and are more likely to keep their word. What are the Italians saying after the great Delinquent's shameful speech? My love, I'll never be able to remain silent about the truth and not defend it.

I've never been and will never be involved in politics; that is, I became involved only once, in '19, and for Mussolini, and I repented even before he came to power in '22. Of course I think and act as my conscience tells me. I can't alienate myself from life. I've never taken part in Societies, either political or artistic. I've always been a loner. I've always believed that only <u>an individual</u> can be a gentleman; <u>two</u> individuals—two friends; <u>three</u>—there's a traitor among them. I can't exempt myself from expressing what I think. If others take advantage of it for other ends, that's not my business. Everyone ought to express his own opinion honestly and courageously—then dictators, criminals, wouldn't last so long. [. . .]

I do not know which article AT sent along with this letter, but the "great Delinquent's shameful speech" was Mussolini's backtracking on the question of Austrian independence. This letter contains one of AT's few extant references to his support for Mussolini in 1919, when the renegade socialist journalist turned politician advocated an extreme-left platform. Many of Mussolini's original supporters remained faithful to the man when he moved to the extreme right; AT remained faithful to the original antimonarchic, anti-Church ideals.

E.P. MI, 30 MARCH 1938; TO AM, VB8R; FSD-FOF

30 <u>March 1938</u>

[. . .] I'm <u>desperate</u> and I no longer even have the strength to despair, as the circumstances would require. I feel annihilated!!! Everything that happens to me throws my being into a sort of moral stupefaction, so that at times it seems to me that I don't understand the value of evil, of good, of good and bad. Where could that letter of yours have gone? Into what horrible, sinful, criminal hands can it have fallen? I had a feeling that you wouldn't have wished to send it, in these times, when my name was being profaned by Farinacci, that two-bit <u>Cato</u>! [. . .] Ada, I can't begin to tell you of my unhappiness, my <u>profound</u> unhappiness. A whole battle of feelings is taking place in me, and it's torturing me. I love and hate my country and the men who are <u>dishonoring</u> it. I don't know what to do, how to live anymore. And everyone tortures me, they praise me, they admire me, and they continue to be **cowards**—oh, what cowards they are! But I mean <u>everywhere,</u> you know. <u>All over</u> the <u>world.</u> People are the same in <u>every nation.</u> [. . .]

Roberto Farinacci (1892–1945), one of Mussolini's leading henchmen, wrote and published several anti-AT articles in his newspaper, *Il regime fascista.* The comparison is presumably with Cato the Elder, either because of his warmongering or because of his epithet, Cato the Censor; AT would not have compared Farinacci with Cato the Younger, who was a model of political rectitude and republican virtues.

[. . .] A ray of hope had crossed my heart when I received a telegram from Huberman and Weizmann that freed me of my obligation in Palestine. I was dreaming of a happy, sweet stay in Capri! In Capri with you!!! You <u>alone with me</u> on that island of dreams! Instead, those <u>tentacles</u> have taken hold again and have sucked a final yes out of me!

Well, if that was to be my fate, let it happen once and for all and let it be done forever. I know that I'll be giving much joy to those poor, unfortunate musicians, all of them young, down there, and that makes less cruel the sorrow of having to give up the beautiful dream that had crossed my mind for a moment. Ada, my Ada, you have to love me, I think I deserve your esteem, your love, as no other man in the world can deserve them. It's true that my unhappy nature sometimes makes me doubt you, but believe me, it's not nastiness and it's not because I think you're bad or disloyal. No, my Ada, it's nothing but my <u>lack of faith</u> in myself and my absolute lack of vanity, and above all because I haven't been able to give you <u>any joy</u> in these nearly five years, and it seems nearly inhuman to me that a woman could sacrifice herself for a man who, above all, is also an old man. [. . .]

Thursday <u>31-[3-]1938</u>

[. . .] The shouts of the newspaper vendors announcing the speech by the D—— (interpret it as you please) to the Senate reached me in my study yesterday evening. I was exasperated! Can you imagine those senile old men dressed in brown, on their feet, squawking and singing "Giovinezza"? Could people be more cowardly and vile? Old Silvestri, Salmoiraghi, Falk, etc., etc. Poor Senate! It used to be represented by intelligent men chosen by the King and nominated by Parliament. Now it's become a barracks for drunken noncommissioned officers from the fascist militia. How disgusting! How disgusting! What degradation for the human race! That's the way it is—that's the way humanity is. Maybe it's always been that way, and the few good ones must suffer for the bestiality of the many.

Saturday <u>2-[4-]1938</u>

[. . .] I was interrupted by a visit by Count Casati, who brought Benedetto Croce along. I spent half an hour that did me good, like pure morning air in the Alps. Up, up high, toward the clouds and the sky. I needed it. I found Croce much better in health and, I must say, in spirit than the last time I'd seen him, and this gave me much pleasure, because at that time he left me feeling very upset. That time it was I who was encouraging him; this time it was the opposite. But he lives such a different life from mine—his world is so much the opposite of mine—that he can and indeed must manage more easily than I to find peace for his soul.

A philosopher is a little like an astronomer. The latter searches the skies amid the numberless stars; the former searches inside the human spirit, studies the first causes and how they unfold. Both are perfectly able to withdraw from normal life and, if they so wish, to avoid any contact with the cowardly human race. But I, with my artist's life, haven't been able to avoid carrying out my activity among people. It's very difficult, my dear Croce, I told him the other day, to find the serenity necessary to put up with everything horrible, grotesque, and tragic that the world has to offer today, when you're obliged to live in the midst of it, and every day!

I replied last night, to some extent, to the sweet reproofs in your second letter, but I have before my eyes two declarations by two very great men that reflect my thoughts, and I'll transcribe them for you as a finale and epilogue to this troublesome subject.

I would truly be guilty of a crime if, for fear of death or of anything else, I were to desert the post that God has assigned me. (Plato)

I would cheerfully destroy everything I've composed if, in so doing, I could hope to advance the cause of Liberty and Justice. R. Wagner

My adored Ada, I don't have even the palest shadow of their genius, but my heart—yes, it is like theirs. And that's why you love me. Isn't that so? And you will always love me because I'll never change, or rather—I'll improve—**continually!**

Yesterday I went to see our property in Crema. Wally is looking after furnishing it. What peace, what divine peace that magnificent green countryside exudes. A religious silence. It's situated far from the main road, thus also from all noises, and the eye delights in the infinite sky space. Too bad that I won't have the time to enjoy this peace, what with my wandering life! The Isolino is more romantic, more poetic, but not more restful—you still feel life too much around you, and the presence of people! **Disgust!**

And speaking of people and of their purity of spirit, do you know how many proposals reached me after I quit Salzburg—to create, to found a new Salzburg? From Hollywood, Max Reinhardt sent me a closely written two-page telegram to tell me that millions were already available for founding a theater. I thanked him, excusing myself on the grounds that at my age one ends things, one doesn't begin them. Holland made the same proposals (two of them). Switzerland. Everyone forgot that I was at Salzburg because Mozart was born there, just as I was at Bayreuth before that because Wagner's theater was there! Everyone saw the business side, the personal publicity; poetry and the Ideal are a dead letter.

Did you receive the clippings that I included with several of my letters? The one from Le Figaro? The one by Vuillermoz? When I arrived from America, two secretaries of the minister of fine arts received me in Paris to communicate an invitation to do concerts in the coming months and to repeat the request to give Pelléas. I refused, and there was no falsehood in my refusal, because I am really very busy, first in London, then in America, where I'll have to go much earlier than last year. Did you know that the City of Lucerne has sent me a magnificent letter in which I'm requested to conduct a concert in August at Tribschen, near Lucerne, where Wagner lived for six years? It's where he created Die Meistersinger, the Siegfried Idyll, etc., etc., in addition to two children, Eva and Siegfried. The program, for small orchestra, should include, in addition to the Siegfried-Idyll, a Mozart Symphony—one of those that he wrote when he was 16 or 17—and something by Beethoven. Maybe the Septet, with four violins, four violas, three cellos, two basses, Clarinet, bassoon, and horn. So far, so good: there's a certain sort of poetry in the idea of this concert in that setting—but that's not enough—the good Swiss want to exploit something, that rare animal, Maestro Toscanini, and they immediately propose a concert with a big orchestra, and I waver, or rather rebel. We shall see. [. . .]

"D" was *Duce* or, in AT's vocabulary, *Delinquente.* · For more on Count Alessandro Casati and Benedetto Croce, see the letter of 1 October 1934, and the accompanying note. · The invitation to AT from the city of Lucerne launched what has proved to be one of the most durable and serious of Europe's many summer music festivals.

E.P. HAIFA, 14 APRIL 1938;
P.S., MOUNT CARMEL, HAIFA; TO AM, VB8R; FSD-FOF

13-4-1938

[. . .] Will you stay in Rome during the filthy celebrations that the Great Delinquent is preparing for his worthy comrade? I hope not. I wish that all Romans except officialdom would stay shut up and buried in their homes and not take part in those Nero-like or Borgia-like festivities, fit for a people of slaves that's reached the lowest level of ignominy. Leave Rome, Ada, leave it, don't breathe the infected air during those days. Come to Milan, or if you like we'll go to Switzerland, maybe to Lugano, so as not to breathe Italy's air during those horrible, dishonoring days!

I'm happy to have come to Palestine. If you had attended the dress rehearsal yesterday evening for the first program, you would have loved me even more. You would have understood how much joy and how much gratitude issued from the breasts of 2,500 workers, men, women, children, their hands reaching out to me; they shouted like mad people in the most affectionate excitement, their eyes full of tears! The rehearsal was scheduled for 8. At seven-thirty the hall was already packed. I began at seven-forty-five. This morning I came here to Haifa by automobile. This evening is the first concert. I traveled with Carla in Weizmann's (armored) car. It wasn't necessary. But they are taking every precaution. In front of my auto and Huberman's there was another one, full of police. I felt like laughing, and I think that I could go around all by myself and no one would touch a hair on my head. [. . .]

[. . .] I've reached the halfway point in my concerts. In ten days it will all be over. As I already wrote, I'll leave from Haifa on the morning of Wednesday the 27th, but I'll stay on Rhodes all day Thursday. Friday morning I'll take the airplane—not the hydroplane—and at one-thirty of the <u>same day</u> I'll be in Rome. [. . .] Today I rehearsed the second program. The orchestra has made progress since last year. Tomorrow, Tuesday, I'm going to lunch at Weizmann's after the rehearsal, and then I'll go to Jerusalem in his <u>armored</u> car, and not only that, but with a rifle between me and the chauffeur.

I see from the newspapers that every once in a while people are killing each other, but I'm not worried. <u>My time</u> has not yet come. Did you know that Rirì [Pizzetti] wrote me a letter? She might have saved herself the trouble. She's still a fool, especially when she thinks of herself as the <u>great artist</u>'s wife. To hear the word <u>pride</u> spoken by someone [i.e., her husband] who has accepted the Mussolini Prize makes me laugh and feel pity at one and the same time. [. . .]

Thursday <u>21-4-1938</u>

[. . .] I read in the newspapers (unfortunately I can't exempt myself from doing so) about what's happening in Vienna. My heart is torn in bits and pieces. When you think about this tragic destruction of the Jewish population of Austria, it makes your blood turn cold. Think of what a prominent part they've played in Vienna's life for two centuries! And remember that when Maria Theresa tried to expel them, Great Britain and other nations protested through diplomatic interventions. Today, with all the great progress of our civilization, none of the so-called liberal nations is making a move. England, France, and the United States are silent! [. . .]

From Lois C. Dubin, *The Port Jews of Habsburg Trieste* (Stanford, Calif.: Stanford University Press, 1999), p. 42: Maria Theresa "tried expulsion—of the long-standing Prague Jewish community in 1745—but local and international pressure led her to rescind the order."

Saturday <u>21-5-938</u>

[. . .] This morning I began to rehearse the second program. First the Fifth Symphony, which I hadn't conducted in a few years, then some bits of Don Quixote, which I also hadn't conducted in six or seven years. The orchestra applauded at the end. Are you happy that they applaud your Artù? Tomorrow morning I'll rehearse the 2nd Brandenburg Concerto. Besides the four soloists (violin, flute, oboe, and trumpet) I'm using a small string orchestra—4 first violins, 4 seconds, 4 violas, 3 cellos, 2 basses, and harpsichord. I think it will sound good! Too bad you're not here to judge. [. . .]

AT had last conducted Beethoven's Fifth Symphony in 1934 and Strauss's *Don Quixote* in 1931; his soloists in the latter in the 1938 BBC Symphony Orchestra performance were the great cellist Emanuel Feuermann (1902–42) and the orchestra's outstanding principal violist, Bernard Shore (1896–1985). AT programmed Bach's Second "Brandenburg" Concerto on only three occasions: with the New York Philharmonic in January and February 1936, with the BBC Symphony Orchestra in May 1938, and with the NBC Symphony Orchestra in October 1938.

E.P. LONDON, 24 MAY 1938; TO AM, VB8R; FSD-FOF

[. . .]

Tuesday <u>morning</u> [24.5.38]

It was a very good concert. I wonder whether you were able to have a clearer broadcast! And to think that I conduct for you, for the joy of pleasing and satisfying you.

Feuermann played very well. I've discovered after several years the way to interpret a trill at the end of the andante of Bach's ["Brandenburg"] concerto [No. 2] in F! I trill in the violin part, right in the last bar, which everyone including Busch omits. I'll send you the bar in question under separate cover! And I made the discovery very early yesterday morning, while I was sitting at the piano (but not playing), and you can't imagine my joy at having discovered that I learn something every day. [. . .]

E.P. LONDON, 26 MAY 1938; TO AM, VB8R; FSD-FOF

Wednesday <u>night</u>   <u>25-5-1938</u>

<u>My Ada,</u> I'm tired and I can't sleep. I had two rehearsals of nearly <u>three hours</u> <u>each</u> for the Te Deum and Requiem. Even my shoulder is tired and painful. [. . .]

I'm so happy that Wally and Wanda are fond of you. They certainly understand why I love you and how necessary you are to my life and my art! You make me young and better. They see and hear it. But what did you talk about in almost two hours on the phone with Wanda? Can you tell me? [. . .] After the first concert I went to dinner at Sybil [Cholmondeley]'s. That evening I met Eden and his wife. He is very simpatico and very natural. She seemed to me pretty but very timid. [. . .]

AT conducted Verdi's "Requiem" and "Te Deum" with the BBC Symphony Orchestra on 27 and 30 May 1938; the soloists were Zinka Milanov, Kerstin Thorborg, Helge Roswaenge, and Nicola Moscona. · AT's daughters had evidently become privy to their father's affair with AM, but the nature and extent of their complicity are not known. · Anthony Eden (1897–1977), a future British prime minister, had been foreign secretary in the Baldwin and Chamberlain governments, but he had resigned three months before this letter was written in disagreement over Chamberlain's policy of appeasement toward Germany and Italy; this fact alone would have made him "simpatico" to AT, even though Eden was a Tory.

E.P. LONDON, 26 MAY 1938; P.S. AS IN LETTER OF 21 MAY;
TO AM, VB8R; FSD-FOF

Thursday 26-5-938

[. . .] I'm tired, the night brought me no rest. My shoulder was horrendously painful. The <u>Requiem</u> kills me, but I adore it more and more. I think I perform it as Verdi conceived it. The **Dies Irae** is <u>fearful.</u> That marvelous man knew how to touch <u>every</u> string. And the Agnus Dei? What sweetness! What gentleness! And it's all, all <u>marvelous.</u> And to think that **He**, too, loved to give a <u>certain type</u> of kiss! But he can't ever have reached the extreme limit of <u>all mad desires,</u> like your Artù. But I can say with absolute certainty that he can <u>never</u> have <u>loved</u> and **been loved** by so beautiful a creature as you, my Ada. <u>Stolz</u> was a peasant. <u>Strepponi</u> was a cultivated woman but very masculine. I <u>kiss</u> you, <u>Ada.</u> Artù

E.P. LONDON, (30?) MAY 1938; P.S. AS IN PREVIOUS LETTER;
AM, VB8R; FSD-FOF

Saturday 28-5-938

[. . .] Despite a <u>horrible</u> final rehearsal of the Requiem that took away my sleep and peace of mind, yesterday evening everything <u>went along</u> as it should have. Did you have a clear broadcast? Tommasini has arrived. He told me about the clear broadcast of the second concert. He didn't come to the concert yesterday evening, but he heard it on the radio, marvelously, it seems! And you, my dear, I wonder whether you were happy with me! I'm very tired. As usual, I had a terrible night. After the concert I went to supper (with the whole Italian gang) at <u>Yvonne Rothschild's.</u> Everyone was enchanted with the magnificent house, luxurious but in superior good taste. [. . .]

Thursday <u>night 2-6-1938</u>

[. . .] Tomorrow I have the final rehearsal for the fifth concert and the perfor-mance in the evening. I've put Rossini's "La scala di seta" overture before Mozart's Jupiter because it goes better there than before Sibelius's second sym-phony. For the last program, on the other hand, I've put Tommasini's "<u>Le donne di buon umore,</u>" with music by D. Scarlatti, before Sibelius. Tommasini knows nothing about this. It's a surprise that I'm doing for him. But I can't stand anymore. It's not so much the physical tiredness as that of being sur-rounded by people who adore you but who break your etc. etc. etc. [. . .]

This evening I learned from a letter of Walter's that the second performance of Verdi's Requiem wasn't broadcast outside England. My poor Ada—and you had probably invited Mrs. Cerruti and Maria Salata to listen to the Concert! I'm so sorry! If I had known I would have wired you!

Today I had two recording sessions. These sessions tire me more than rehearsals for concerts. I did the Magic Flute overture, Weber's Invitation à la Valse, Rossini's overture to "La scala di seta," and the last movement of Beethoven's First symphony, which hadn't turned out well last season. My shoulder is painful, but much less so. That compress that I showed you at Badgastein (oh, sweet memory!) has helped me a great deal! As I write, I feel its beneficial warmth. [. . .]

Thursday <u>evening 9-6-938</u>

[. . .] I am my own <u>assassin.</u> Eternal doubt, incessant hypercriticism reduce me to nothing. This morning they had me listen to the new records. The <u>Magic Flute</u> overture, the <u>Scala di seta</u> overture, the last movement of <u>Beethoven</u>'s 1st <u>symph.,</u> and Weber's Waltz. Everyone is enthusiastic. I was too much on edge to be able to judge. A session to record Brahms's second symph. was scheduled for today, but after less than twenty bars I left the rehearsal and came back home. My nerves couldn't take it, and tomorrow morning I have the final rehearsal and in the evening the concert. It's too much!! I don't want to make records anymore! [. . .]

Saturday <u>evening 18-6-[38]</u>

[. . .] Yesterday evening I heard the concert (but not all of it) that the two music conservatories of Rome and Berlin exchanged! Why is it that they didn't give the name of the cellist who played Boccherini's Largo (I suppose he was a student) or of his teacher? Wasn't he a pupil of Enrico's? But the pianist who was accompanying should have had his brains bashed in! What a pounder! Judging from the broadcast, at any rate. I asked you on the phone the other day whether you had heard the concert of Molinari's that was broadcast from New York. I had the most disconcerting experience of how one can destroy, annihilate a composition through a totally and fundamentally wrong pace! More so with a _slow_ movement beyond belief than with a _fast_ movement, also beyond belief. While I was listening, I kept repeating to myself, "It's odd that I don't remember this [symphony] in A Major.! I know all of Mozart's symphs., from the first in E-flat. written at the age of 8 to the last, 'Jupiter.' " I think there are 34 in all. Well, my friend, I couldn't make head or tail of it, and I concluded that either I didn't know that symphony or I no longer remembered it. Then the Andante, first, followed by the Minuet and finale revealed to me not only that I knew it but that I had conducted it several times. Our poor Bernardino, who boasts of having two big, hard b———, and who indicated to Polo their vast size, through gestures, I think that Bernardino is really the victim of the disproportionate weight and size of his accessories, because the blood, exiting from his brain and infiltrating down below, leaves his intelligence very anemic—and isn't his always going too far in one direction or the other the proof? The excessive weight **unbalances** him, so to speak. He makes the first movement—which is an All. moderato that must be interpreted alla breve, even if it is mistakenly written in tempo ordinario in four beats to the bar—into an All. moderato at quarter note = 126. But it's a bore! I interpret it at 84 to the half note. Mozart is really the downfall of all conductors, including Bruno Walter, although he is considered a specialist. Why should one specialize, as doctors or lawyers or engineers do? Did I tell you that in London I heard my records of the G minor symph.? The first movement, minuet, and Finale seem good, but not the Andante—it lacks lightness, refinement. I'll redo it. I care about this symph. If only it were of use to someone! But I don't believe it. I'll send you examples, under separate cover, taken from the symph. in A Major that Molinari conducted. Say something about it, whether you think I'm right or wrong. [. . .]

AT's sense of tempo for the first movement of Mozart's Symphony No. 29 in A Major, K. 201, was correct: in the composer's autograph score, the meter is given as _alla breve_ (two beats to the bar), rather than 4/4, as it appeared in the published versions available in AT's day.

E.P. PN, 1 JULY 1938; TO AM, VB8R; FSD-FOF

Thursday morning
30-6-938

[. . .] You moved me by speaking to me about Enrico. I would never have imagined that he had (as you say) a great desire and need to see me, and to live near me a little. You suffer from it, you say, and I feel remorse and pain even as I write—I feel almost guilty, as if I had betrayed a friend. I fear that I'll blush when I encounter him. Yet I haven't stolen you from his love, just as you haven't stolen me from Carla's. I could repeat the same words that you've written, that is: "Because our love shouldn't <u>wound</u> anyone, because from a love so intense and made up only of **renunciations,** everyone ought to extract only the good part." Golden words.

For the moment I won't go to Lucerne, as I told you I would. Lawyer Ansbacher has taken it upon himself to send Busch (who was bombarding me with telephone calls) my parts of the program, because he wants to start making the players (strings) whom he has gathered together in addition to the quartet practice. I don't know, for that matter, what he wants to make them practice! It's easy music that they know, which will quickly be ready with very few rehearsals. But the Busches are maniacal! And now they have the occasion to play under my direction! They're jumping out of their skin. The program is made up thus: Rossini—La scala di seta [overture]; Mozart—Symphony in G Minor (which Wagner loved so much); Prelude to the 3rd act of Die Meistersinger; Siegfried Idyll; and Beethoven's 2nd Symphony. The concert will take place on August 25 (Cosima and Wagner's wedding day) in the park of the villa at Tribschen. Since the place is big enough for barely more than 500 people, I've given in to the entreaties of those Swiss fellows to repeat the concert the next day in a bigger venue. [. . .]

E.P. PN, 4 JULY 1938; TO AM, VB8R; FSD-FOF

Friday 1 July

[. . .] Walter, that ass, brought a friend of his here to me on St. Peter's [i.e., June 29, the feast of Saints Peter and Paul]—<u>Alfredo Segre,</u> a writer of novels that are said to be rather good—and I had to put up with him at lunch, at supper, during an outing to the Isola dei Pescatori, and always touching on the same subjects: politics, fascism, persecution of the Jews, and on and on with these subjects that poison me and embitter my existence! My soul is upside down, all the bad blood that I'd felt during the past months and had pushed down into the depths of my being—where all the corruption in my nature separates and hides from the little bit of good stuff, which floats—has come back to the surface.

Since I left London I've paid no attention to what's going on in the world; I don't read the newspapers of any country, I don't turn on the radio except when I'm interested in hearing some music—and I'm almost always sorry to have done that—I try to live with my ghosts, with those dear spirits named Dante, Shakespeare, Shelley, Keats, and I'm also reading, these days, Croce's latest book: "La storia come pensiero e come azione."

Alfredo Segre was Jewish and soon found himself in America, like the Toscaninis. His substantial article "Toscanini: The First Forty Years," which appeared in *Musical Quarterly* (1947/2), was one of the first attempts to write seriously about AT's early career; Walter Toscanini provided Segre with the information. · Croce's *La storia come pensiero e come azione* (History as Thought and as Action) (Bari: Laterza, 1938), was published in English in 1941 as *History as the Story of Liberty*.

In the <u>late afternoon</u> [Saturday, 2 July 1938] [. . .] I've had a piece of good news from Wanda. Horowitz, on the advice of his doctors, seems to have decided to resume his activities in October. In fact, he wants me to put together a program for October 1 (his birthday) here on the Isolino (as for Pizzetti in 1933), and we should already begin to think about <u>sending out the invitations.</u> It's a ray of light that's entered my soul. I want it to shine in yours, too. Kisses, <u>Artù</u>

Monday <u>4-7-938</u>

[. . .] The weather has gone back to being <u>beautiful</u> since yesterday. Unfortunately, it has been the cause of a great many visits—some of them unexpected, such as Count <u>Cicogna,</u> who brought along some damned Milanese nobleman whose name escapes me; my neighbor, the beautiful Mrs. Ceretti, with her brother and his wife; also Nino Rota, who brought along two young musicians. [. . .] Fortunately I'm alone today, but I'll be even more so this evening, because Carla and her sister are going to Milan. [. . .] You can't imagine how much work I do in a day when I'm alone. I go to bed at night, always very late, at two or even three, dog tired. I play the piano, a bit of everything, I read, going from one author to another with a devilish fever. The day is always too short. And I congratulate myself, because I very often find in each book observations [that I wrote out in the past] that I rarely if ever want to change. And it makes me marvel, because I who am so insecure, so unsure of myself, realize that even in those far-off times I had the same impressions and made the same comments! Consequently, I can say that even back then <u>I wasn't a fool!</u> Which makes me feel good. On a separate sheet I'm copying out for you some stanzas of Dante, Virgil, Carducci, and Byron. You, my love, who have an exquisite musical sensibility, see and hear all the marvelous music in that Dantean terzina and compare it to the music of Virgil's Latin verses. Both describe a moment of <u>exquisite poetry.</u> In Virgil, it's still night; in Dante, the dawn begins to break. But the music of that <u>"tremolar della marina"</u> and that of the <u>"splendet tremulo sub lumine pontus"</u> is one and the same. Dante was influenced by Virgil {here}. Don't you think?

And observe, further, the divine Ave Maria of Carducci's <u>Chiesa di Polenta.</u> Compare it with that of the 3rd Canto of Byron's Don Juan. If I didn't know and esteem Carducci's uprightness and honesty, I could judge his [Ave Maria] to be a piece of plagiarism. But Carducci wasn't D'Annunzio. [. . .]

In the end, Horowitz chose to resume performing by sharing a program with the Busch Quartet in a benefit concert in Zurich on 26 September 1938; the performance on the Isolino never took place. · Nino Rota (1911–79), known today above all for his film scores for Fellini and other master directors, had been a child prodigy, and on AT's advice he had been sent to Philadelphia in 1930 to study composition with Rosario Scalero at the Curtis Institute. The "young musicians" whom he brought to the Isolino to meet AT were Samuel Barber (1910–81) and Gian Carlo Menotti (b. 1911); AT later influenced Barber's career by conducting two of his works, with much success, and Menotti's by declaring his admiration for some of his work. · The quotations copied by AT on a separate sheet of paper are from (1) Carducci's "La chiesa di Polenta," beginning with the line ". . . il campanil risorto" and ending with "Mormoran gli alti vertici ondeggianti / Ave Maria"; (2) Byron's Don Juan, Canto 3, beginning with "Every sound of revelry expired / Ave Maria!" and ending with "Are gathered round us by thy look of rest"; (3) an Italian translation of the Byron quotation; (4) Dante's Purgatorio, Canto 1, the terzina that begins with "L' alba vinceva l' ora matutina"; (5) Virgil's Aeneid, Book 7, the lines "Adspirant auræ in noctem nec candida cursus / Luna negat, splendet tremulo sub lumine pontus"; (6) an Italian translation of the Virgil quotation.

E.P. PN, 9 JULY 1938; TO AM, VB8R; FSD-FOF

[. . .] Saturday morning   9-7-938

[. . .] I had Vera Vergani and Linda Muschenheim (daughter of the proprietor of the Astor Hotel) here for two days. They've left by car for Venice; they were going to Wally's. I found Vera less aged than I'd thought! She seems to be closer to fifty than to forty—isn't that so? But how easy it is to see and hear that she was a real <u>leader</u> in her art! Not a thought about the past, as if it had never existed! She talks only about her husband (a handsome man, but . . . a <u>boor,</u> so there!) and her children. But she remains a good-looking woman! At least that! [. . .]

For more on Vergani, see the letter of 9 September 1937 and the accompanying note; she was forty-three in 1938. AT's description of her as a "leader" was sarcastic, of course. · AT probably did not know that his son was having an affair with Linda Muschenheim.

E.P. PN, 10 JULY 1938; TO AM, VB8R; FSD-FOF

Sunday morning [10.7.38]

[. . .] Why don't you <u>bare</u> your soul (which is mine), as I have always bared mine (which is yours) before you? Even if sometimes the <u>ugliness</u> that is certainly hidden in every soul should come to the <u>surface,</u> what difference does it make? It's a way of <u>feeling lighter!</u> To confess to a friend, to a sister spirit, is better than confessing before God! We all have a layer of criminality at the bottom of our being. It would be terrible if our souls always <u>showed their naked selves</u>! No one would have anything to do with his fellowman, and perhaps not even with himself! [. . .]

TRANSCRIPT OF LETTER; (MI?); TO ADOLF BUSCH, (BASEL?);
IRENE BUSCH SERKIN, *ADOLF BUSCH: LETTERS — PICTURES — MEMORIES*
(WALPOLE, N.H.: ARTS & LETTERS PRESS, 1991), P. 377.

August 1, 1938

My dearest Adolf:

How are <u>Irene</u> and <u>Rudi</u>? I hope that by now they're out of the hospital and on the mend. The <u>bars</u> from the <u>concerto</u> seem to me <u>excellent.</u> I'm sending you the same bars with a harmonic interpretation of mine that maybe <u>is even simpler.</u> You'll decide whether I'm right or wrong!

I'm happy to have spent a few hours in your and dear Frieda's company. Many affectionate greetings to you and <u>everyone</u> in the family. A caress to <u>little Ursula</u> from your affectionate

A. Toscanini

Busch's daughter Irene and her husband, the pianist Rudolf Serkin, had both had their tonsils removed; Ursula, their daughter, was two years old. The concerto in question was Reger's Violin Concerto, which Busch was reorchestrating; a sheet of music paper with AT's version of a passage accompanied the letter.

E.P. PN, 3 AUGUST 1938; TO AM, HBG; FSD-FOF

3 <u>August 1938</u>   Wednesday morning

Ada <u>my dear,</u> I haven't written to you in many days, nor have I written to you as I habitually do, for my sole use. I would have had to say too much, and I preferred to say nothing. I haven't even read your last two letters—the one that contains the hidden veil and the other, which is postmarked Gstaad on the 28th–29th. I don't deserve anything.

Tomorrow is your birthday. Thinking of it always fills me with tenderness, and I always think of your mother with indescribable emotion. My dear! I don't know what I've done during these long, eternal, suffocating days. My soul was absent. Whereas this miserable body of mine was offered up to the many, too many pests who are crowding the Isolino. I feel empty, as if my bodily shell were dissolving, evaporating. I try to clutch at the two days (although not whole ones) spent with you in Lucerne. I try to hook my present life onto them, but in vain; I can't manage to find again the meaning of those hours as they were!! Why? Without knowing it, and (maybe) without intending to, you killed the illusion I had of myself. The illusion that our intimacies had to grow ever more intense and profound was extinguished, it died forever. Something in me repels you, distances you from me, eludes you! For two nights we slept like two strangers. We, who have lived for years suffering from desire and distance. Nor did I see you, as at other times, crouching at my knees in a sweet act of love.!!! Why? Tell me. What is it in me that repels you, Ada? What is it? This tormenting thought, which doesn't give me a moment's peace, has stuck in my heart and flesh like a poisonous, gluttonous snake. I heard your voice again, asking me whether I still love you, as if love were a handkerchief or a trinket that could be lost along the street. Today, perhaps, I wouldn't know how to answer you. There is an indefinable lacuna in my spirit. It's as if my soul were dilated. My thoughts form, wander, and lose themselves in an uncertain atmosphere. I'm experiencing a sort of flimsy, empty stupor. I feel as if I were emerging from a serious illness and beginning a convalescence that will never come to an end. I was very glad to see Enrico again, and I didn't feel the sense of embarrassment that I had feared. I liked your friend. What is her name? I'll see her again in America. And you were so pretty that I could have eaten you up with kisses. But afterward, on the train! **Alone!** Thinking over those previous days, those three days of martyrdom! I can't describe my suffering! I didn't want to read your letter, I didn't want to see our adored magic veil, and even today it remains closed in the letter of the 28th–29th, in the secret briefcase! Ada, until when will you stay in Gstaad? We're waiting for Wally and Wanda, who will be here on the 7th (Carla's birthday), then I'll dash to Milan for a few days, to look for music for the new programs in America. On the 15th I'll go (alas) to Lucerne. Wagner, Wagner, what a price I have to pay for you!!! And then? Will I come back here??? I don't know. I really don't know what I'll do with myself. I embrace you, I kiss you, I love you, with tears in my eyes and in my heart. Artù

AT had gone to Lucerne to meet the Busches (see the previous letter) and work out the details of the first Lucerne Festival, and there he had spent some time with AM. Despite subsequent temporary improvements, that encounter marked the beginning of a general decline in their relationship, although exactly what transpired cannot be determined.

E.P. PN, 5 AUGUST 1938; TO AM, HBG; FSD-FOF

Thursday night [4.8.38]

[. . .] The Lucerne concert is threatening to give birth to another! The Busches give me no quarter. When they're not writing to me, they're phoning me. [. . .]

[. . .]

Saturday morning [6.8.38]

[. . .] I envy my brother-in-law [Polo], who sleeps from <u>ten</u> in the evening until <u>nine</u> in the morning, and <u>after</u> lunch until <u>four</u> in the aft. He admires Mussolini's genius and maybe Hitler's, too, and he doesn't give a damn about the rest of life and anything in life that gives signs of movement! That's a healthy man; I'm not—maybe he was born luckier than I, who suffer and have suffered all my life! Ada, my head is no longer functioning, believe me, I can't get a <u>reasonable</u> thought into it, I see everything distorted, cross-eyed, on a slant! Yesterday I got two letters from the Busches, one from Adolf, the other from Frieda. There's another family that I envy! They live for <u>themselves</u> and <u>music.</u> The inferno that's in me isn't present in them! May God always preserve their enviable peace! But the difference in feeling, in the way of feeling, between a German and an Italian is enormous, even when there are <u>points</u> of <u>contact</u> between them, as between Adolf and me! I'll tell you in another letter something about his and my musical tastes. [. . .] I heard an act of *Tannhäuser* on the radio, broadcast from Salzburg. A horror! An obscenity! This evening *Falstaff* opens! [. . .]

At the Nazified 1938 Salzburg Festival, the new *Tannhäuser* production that was to have been conducted by AT was conducted instead by Knappertsbusch, as was the *Fidelio* production that AT had conducted since 1935; his *Falstaff* production was conducted by Vittorio Gui and his *Meistersinger* by Furtwängler; his *Magic Flute* production was not revived. The two symphony concerts (Beethoven's *Missa Solemnis* and a Debussy program) that AT had planned, as well as those planned by Bruno Walter and others, were scrapped in favor of different programs, conducted by the three above-named maestros plus Edwin Fischer and Karl Böhm.

My <u>dearest friend</u>—

The marvelous drawing by Lenbach has become my daily joy. No other gift could have been dearer to me. I was lacking a souvenir of your great Father, the incomparable Artist. The fact that it came from His worthy daughter, my very dear friend Daniela, makes it even more precious to me. Thank you! Thank you, and I hope to see you very soon.

Affectionate greetings   A <u>Toscanini</u>

Franz von Lenbach (1836–1904) was the leading German portrait artist of his time. Daniela Thode's father was the celebrated conductor Hans von Bülow (1830–94).

Saturday 10-10[*sic,* for 9]-938

[. . .] The week in Milan revealed to me still more sweetness, still unknown aspects of our love. Ada, don't you think we're marvelous? But it's wrong of me to say "we're marvelous." <u>You're marvelous!</u> You continue to <u>re-create</u> me, you bring me back to that life that would otherwise be extinguished forever. [. . .]

<u>Noon</u>   12-10[*sic,* for 9]-938

You know why I'm leaving my country in a great hurry, you know the state I'm in, you're aware of it—and despite everything you haven't managed to give me a sign of the affection of which I'm so much in need at this moment. I've tried to phone you. Your telephone was silent. You've <u>tired</u> my soul, I can't stand it any longer! This continual drawing everything out of you <u>with the forceps,</u> this continual <u>towing</u> has <u>almost annihilated</u> me. I no longer desire anything except to leave. If you want word of me, others can provide it—not I! Kindness and grace are external things in you, inside you're <u>dried out.</u> Too bad! I forgive you all the harm you're doing me.

Artù

Mussolini had been enraged by the fact that many, many Italians, including the crown prince's consort, Maria José, had traveled to Lucerne to hear AT's concerts; on top of that, during one of AT's telephone conversations with AM—a conversation tapped by the secret police—he had described the Italian government's new anti-Semitic edicts as "medieval stuff," and when this was reported to Mussolini, the latter had ordered that AT's passport be confiscated. This is when AT realized that he had to leave his country for the duration of the regime's existence, and he knew that the regime might well last beyond his lifetime. This explains his extreme nervousness.

27[.9.38] <u>morning</u>

[. . .] No news regarding my freedom of movement. From Margherita in America I've received notice that says that attempts are being made to do something concrete, but so far everything is as it was to begin with. At this <u>tragically difficult moment,</u> with these threats of war, of a European conflagration, even the <u>Great Criminals</u> have other things on their mind. And never have I felt so <u>impeded</u> by family ties as I do now. You know and understand what I'm alluding to. One false step on my part could involve everyone. God, God, what have we come to! [. . .]

[. . .] I feel that we're heading toward terrible, tragic days. It's a horrible thing to say, but to free ourselves from those **Monsters** who have subverted, degraded, and most shamefully enslaved millions and millions of beings, we've almost come to the point of wanting war—a horrible, fearful thought that makes the most hidden fibers of our being tremble!

I am followed and spied on as never before. Why? I've never been a part of secret societies, either political or artistic. I've always believed that an individual can be a man of honor, two can be very good, faithful friends, but three—one of them is bound to be a traitor. This is why I've always hated societies and have always refused to belong to any. I am always responsible for what I think and say. I learned this morning at Baldini and Castoldi's that a Commissar of public safety recently inspected the bookshop and mentioned the names of people who from now on must never again meet as before in that shop. My name is among them. In fact, if I happen to be there at the same time as one Baroni (the head of a pasta company), Baldini and Castoldi have to denounce me. I'll say no more, my dear Ada! I only wish that my family, all of it, adults and children, would take refuge in Switzerland, because I very much fear that with the outbreak of war they won't leave me in Milan. And if I'm not alone, you understand, I can't do absolutely any of what I have in mind! And what will you do if Germany goes to war? Won't you leave Berlin? Do you think that our alliance—the Rome–Berlin axis—will break up? I still have faith in the Italians' hearts! Vittorina has just now phoned to say that she needs to see me! I'll meet her at 5 p.m. Will she have some message from you? At the same time, Wanda phoned from Zurich to have little Sonia leave immediately. Maybe she fears the way events are heating up and the inevitable consequences! My Ada! My Ada, what tragic circumstances for this unhappy human race. I went to the cemetery this morning. I hadn't gone there in a long time. I wanted to say good-bye to my dead relatives, also to a few friends— among them the painter Grubicy, who[se ashes are] in the crematorium. Opposite his urn, there is one that holds the remains of a little girl who died at the age of six. On the plaque I read the following epigraph:

> The little bones of Linda Zaccheo
> And Her mother's joy
> Are contained in this urn.
> Of life, Linda knew only games;
> The sorrows that might have come to her
> Were inherited—all of them—by her mother.
> Happy Linda! Unhappy mother!

It made me weep more than I can say. The epigraph was signed by Carlo Dossi. And not later [*sic*] than yesterday I was reading his Desinenza in A. He is

Milanese, and a marvelous prose writer. Perhaps you know nothing that he has written, and perhaps <u>not even</u> his <u>name.</u> It would be a bit shameful for <u>a</u> <u>Milanese woman</u>!

[. . .] Yesterday I sent the following telegram to America: <u>At this point it is</u> <u>futile to hope I think it is more prudent to replace me.</u>

<u>No</u> reply has come yet. Through this telegram I want to pull the wool over the eyes of you know who—you understand? My Ada, I don't sleep, I don't work, I rack up kilometers in my study, my brain hurts because of the thousands of mad, sad, senseless thoughts—<u>all of them</u>—that besiege it. [. . .]

The Munich Conference was taking place when this letter and the next one were written, and on 30 September an agreement was signed whereby Britain and France "sold" Czech independence to Nazi Germany in order to avert war—for less than a year, as things turned out. · AT hesitated to create an international stir over his state of virtual house arrest because he justifiably feared repercussions for his family, but he let NBC know that he was unable to leave for New York as scheduled. · Vittorina was one of AM's sisters. · Carlo Dossi (1849–1910) was a novelist and short story writer; *La desinenza in A* (1878) was a series of satirical "human portraits."

E. WITH NO STAMP OR POSTMARK, (MI); TO AM, PFB; FSD-FOF

<u>Thursday 29[.9.38]</u>

Ada <u>my dear,</u> Yesterday evening I heard your dear voice, but I felt I was hearing it reproduced on a <u>record.</u> It was cold, and you will have heard that mine was awkward and without a doubt colder than yours. How can one make love in the presence of others? In the car yesterday, Vittorina was rummaging around in back on the suspicion that there might be some apparatus that was recording our words! I thought about the <u>empty room</u> near the living room that you had at the Hôtel de la Ville! But what does all this <u>spying</u> count for <u>us</u>? Am I not responsible for everything that crosses my lips?

They've forced Giulio Foligno to resign, and <u>he himself</u> signed his resignation. I would have done the opposite. I would have forced them to fire me. The offense would have been entirely the government's responsibility. Giulio didn't understand that in forcing him to resign because he is Jewish, his company ridded itself of the obligation to close its accounts with him and to pay him a rather <u>huge sum.</u> If only he had at least declared his contempt!

[. . .] Did you know that they want to deprive the Jews of their <u>citizenship</u> and to allow them only to be <u>subjects</u>? The <u>Inquisition</u> was less of a torture. And everything will be taken away—taxes, taxes, and more taxes will be imposed on them.

Thieves!!!

This demonstrates conclusively what many people have long suspected: AT was aware that his telephone was tapped and that he was spied on in other ways as well, but he nevertheless continued to say openly what he thought. · The Folignos were among the Toscaninis' closest friends.

<u>Thursday 29[.9.38]</u>

[. . .]

<u>6:30 p.m.</u>

My Wally has just this moment arrived from Venice. She says that <u>Suvich</u> spoke to the **beast,** informing him of the scandal that would explode in New York and all over the world when it will be known that etc. etc. The <u>monstrous beast</u> replied that after the scandal he will give back the <u>passport.</u> Or else they must come up with some new factor to make the <u>said beast</u> change its mind. New factor? What could it be? The <u>princess</u> of Piedmont, for instance, could make a personal request. That's all we need! I don't want either princes or princesses helping out. Tomorrow Carla will go to the prefect to find out how [i.e., whether or not] I'm supposed to answer the American telegram. That's all. If the answer is no, so much the better. Oh, if only I were alone right now! [. . .]

<u>Artù who adores you</u>

Fulvio De Suvich was Italy's ambassador to the United States. · The "beast" was, of course, Mussolini. · The "American telegram" was a message from NBC asking AT when he would be leaving for New York.

[Le Havre or aboard ship] 6 <u>Oct. 1938</u>

My **vast** and **unlucky** love. Yes, my Ada, you weren't lucky in finding along your path a man like me who couldn't offer you <u>any</u> of what you deserved or <u>any</u> of what he would have liked [to offer]. Oh, my angel, my sole, real, great love, I am to be pitied, so pity me from your beautiful, generous heart! Tuesday morning [4 October 1938] I was at Venegono Superiore for the funeral of a friend of mine (Maestro Giulio Setti, who was for many years my [word illegible; presumably "assistant" or "chorus master"] at the Metropolitan), who died after a second, extremely painful operation that had revealed the presence of a carcinoma!

When I got back home, around one, to my surprise joy was gleaming in everyone's eyes and I found that my passport had been returned.

In less time than it takes to tell the story, two suitcases with basic necessities were packed, a phone call was made to Paris for the cabin [on a passenger liner], seats were reserved on the 5 p.m. train, and at 5 p.m. Carla and I left for Paris. I didn't have time to wire you or even to see Vittorina, to see her and thank her in person. I did it by telephone. To flee, to flee—that was the consuming thought! To flee in order to breathe freedom, life!

At Domodossola a police commissar came on board, asked whether I was Maestro Toscanini, took my passport, and requested that I follow him, with my suitcases. Please note that I couldn't miss that train, because the next morning at nine-thirty I had to leave Paris for Le Havre. No use. I got off with Carla, and we went to a sort of barracks where some creatures with mugs more like those of life-sentence servers than of cops had congregated. I asked whether my passport was going to be taken away again or whether some formality hadn't been looked after, and I was told that the office hadn't been advised to let me leave and that only a telegram from the Milan Police Headquarters could cancel their orders. I asked them to phone at my expense. They phoned. The reply was favorable, but it wasn't enough; a confirmation in **code** was required. I couldn't resist saying: That's why Napoleon lost at Waterloo: Grouchy's excessive zeal **screwed him**. But so be it! After all, I wasn't about to lose a battle—nothing but a train and, at worst, a steamship. My wife was on tenterhooks; her fear that I would compromise myself was making her blood pressure suffocate her. They searched the suitcases. **In great detail!!!** Even the little secret one. The three packets of your letters, each fastened with a rubber band, were looked at; they separated letter from letter, maybe trying to see whether there was money. I was on the verge of exploding with indignation. Then I said to myself: I'm cleverer than you talentless spies. There is money, I have it, but not amidst those adored letters, **but rather at my feet**. And in fact, I could feel something between my socks and my skin that seemed to be laughing at those scoundrels.

My Ada, my heart is sick, my blood is green with bile, I feel ten years older. At last the telegram arrived. Luckily, we were able to catch the deluxe train. I informed Wanda, in Paris, to spare me the trouble of changing the embarkation ticket so that I could proceed from one station to the other. And that's what happened.

And here I am alone—alone and with death in my heart. Carla left [for Milan] yesterday evening to prepare everything for the real departure for America. She'll leave aboard the Savoia on the 12th, with Walter, his wife, and their little son. The house, or rather the houses, will be **empty!** For how long? Ada, there's a lump in my throat, and I wish you were near. Your voice, your words of consolation would bring off the miracle of reconciling me with life, which I've come to hate and which I wouldn't mind losing at this very moment. The thought of never again returning to Italy is fearfully horrible! I had never faced it before. I felt profound pity for all those Italians who, like Count Sforza, Borgese, Salvemini, and many others had lost the joy of seeing their country again. How will I be able to get used to it? I don't know. I fear for myself. To drown myself in work? Today I'm afraid of not having the strength. The effort is great. Conducting and giving what I'm accustomed to give have always killed me, at every period of my life. Today the weight is greater! The responsibility is greater! The NBC [Symphony Orchestra] is based on my name and my efforts. No one ever thinks about my age. I alone think about it, and I'm afraid of it.

[. . .] At five-thirty p.m. we disembark. I've been in continual telephone communication with the NBC. They've arranged to have me avoid encounters with journalists. By agreement with the chief steward, I'll leave the liner via the staff's exit, with <u>sailors, cabin boys, scullery boys,</u> etc. Will I find a few words from you? [. . .]

Domodossola is the last town in Italy before the Swiss border on the Milan–Geneva–Paris route. · For more on Sforza, Borgese, and Salvemini, see the wartime letters that follow. · This letter marks the beginning of AT's nearly eight-year-long exile from Italy.

E.P. NY, 13 OCTOBER 1938; TO AM, C/O BOOTH, 28CSL; FSD-FOF

Thursday <u>13-10-938</u>

[. . .] I would like to be alone, alone with my savage heart, which is set against the human race, against the beast called man, that is, the most refined, most perfect <u>predatory beast</u>! Isn't the word "progress" absurd, then?

This morning I received a letter from Sybil [Cholmondeley] in London, together with your letter. I'm sending it in a separate envelope. You'll see from it how she, in unison with me, feels shame for her country's representative, a senile old man, unworthy of belonging to so liberal a country as England! Ada, tell me that you, too, think and feel as I do, tell me that you, too, are human, that you would give everything, give up your personal well-being for freedom, justice, the rights of the world's peoples! A sentence in one of your letters (the one of the 1st, I think) <u>hurt</u> me <u>very badly,</u> very badly. "Over a question that was of only indirect interest and prestige for most of the nations, Europe was on the verge of catching fire," etc., etc. Oh, if only it had caught fire, and if only the fire had burned away forever those two wild beasts, thirsty for human blood! But this didn't happen. **It will.**

You see, Ada? Do you understand this torment? I don't have a moment's peace. I don't sleep, I don't eat—and they find me even better than before. How nice! I've begun to work. I cabled you that news. The orchestra is better still than last year. Improved in the horn and trombone sections. The balance is magnificent. I can't tell you how overjoyed everyone was to see me again. I ought to be happy to feel so loved and adored! Instead, I am and I feel that I am an unhappy being, the most unhappy of men. And you are so far away! I can't wait till the 17th comes and you go far away from that lurid country, no longer to be contaminated by proximity with that <u>crude, coarse</u> people, the descendants of Attila, the <u>scourge of God.</u> [. . .]

The "senile old man" who represented England was Prime Minister Neville Chamberlain (1869–1940), who was two years younger than AT. Sybil Cholmondeley had written that the weeks of the Munich Conference with Hitler had been "a nightmare of horror & *shame*," and that she knew that AT would not be "lulled into a sense of false security by the turtle-dove cooings of the Gangsters. [. . .] Now we shall have a few months of respite I suppose but at what price?" · AT was given a hero's welcome by his orchestra on his return to New York in the fall of 1938, because everyone knew that he had been virtually a prisoner of the Fascists after his passport had been confiscated. When he walked onstage for the first rehearsal, the musicians rose to give him a great ovation; he indicated his thanks, but when he gestured to stop the applause and cheering, the players, for once, paid no attention to him. Several minutes passed before the rehearsal could proceed. · AM was leaving Germany (temporarily) for England, which is why AT's first letters to her from New York are addressed to London.

E.P. NY, 18 OCTOBER 1938; TO AM, C/O BOOTH, 28CSL; FSD-FOF

Monday 17-10-938

[. . .] My work, you say! Yes, Ada, I'm working, and they say that I'm still the same Toscanini. But what does that do for me? Nothing. In order to forget, I'd have to work 24 hours a day. I tried to find a different sort of distraction. But disgust rises from the tips of my toes to the hair on my head. Women, all of them, disgust me! Carla, Cia, Walter, and Dedè are arriving the day after tomorrow. And you, Ada? When will you arrive? [. . .]

The name of the woman with whom AT sought distraction is perhaps contained in the letter of 4 November 1938. · Dedè was the nickname of AT's grandson, Walfredo, Walter and Cia's son, who was nine in 1938.

E. HAS STAMPS BUT NO POSTMARK, (NY); TO AM, C/O BOOTH, 28CSL; FSD-FOF

Tuesday 18-10-938

[. . .] A woman's love is always superior to a man's love. Its essence is nobler, it aims toward divinity. We are nearly always banal, earthbound; we take the best a woman can give and don't care about anything else. Oh, what a vile race we are! So what can I do? What do you want me to do? Suggest what you would be most pleased to have me do and I'll do it. [. . .] When I think of the wretched life, with no satisfactions, that I impose on you without wishing to do so, shame rises to my face and I'd like to disappear from your life. [. . .]

E. WITHOUT STAMPS OR POSTMARK, (NY);
TO AM, C/O BOOTH, 28CSL; FSD-FOF

Friday 21-10-938

[. . .] Carla, Walter, Cia, and Dedè have arrived and are already settled in. I'm pleased on the one hand, but displeased on the other! I've lost my peace and my solitude! With Carla, <u>Disorder</u> has arrived. For **41 years** I've suffered from this disorder of hers!!! Such goodness and such patience! The world wouldn't believe it. A good, patient Maestro Toscanini! Yet it's so!! I'm working with my orchestra, which is better than last year—much better. Some musicians have been changed. Trombones and Horns are very much better. I live on my work and my solitude (a bit disrupted now). [. . .]

E.P. NY, 28 OCTOBER 1938; TO AM, PFB; FSD-FOF

Wednesday <u>26-10-938</u>

[. . .] I'm jealous of <u>Enrico.</u> I think it's absurd that he can live beside you and not <u>possess you every ten minutes.</u> If I had his youth, I would do it. I would reduce you to a pulp. You're too beautiful, dear, and lovely, and I'm <u>too old</u> to prostrate myself and honor your beauty <u>the right way.</u> Ada, pity me, I'm in an abnormal state. I work but I don't eat or sleep. I could, I should be content with the affection, esteem, and veneration that surround me, and instead I have only bitterness and sadness in my heart. I live like a bear, shut into the two rooms that are mine—<u>study</u> and <u>bedroom.</u> Excepting the few hours of rehearsals, I stay here like a prisoner, with no other wish than to be left to my thoughts, undisturbed.

[. . .] Ada, Ada, I'm a madman, a delinquent, for not having the courage to tell Enrico that I love you with a love that he doesn't know and whose existence on earth he couldn't ever have imagined. [. . .]

E.P. NY, 2 NOVEMBER 1938; TO AM, PFB; FSD-FOF

Saturday night after <u>the concert</u> [29.10.38]

<u>My love,</u> I'm in pieces. This evening, for the first time in forty years I conducted Tchaikovsky's Pathétique [Symphony]. I was afraid of not being able to do it, of not being capable of getting anything out of that music! Must I confess? I was nervous, uncertain, as fearful as someone making his debut! As always, after the first few bars my nervousness, uncertainty, and fear disappeared. I threw myself into it as one throws oneself courageously into water for the first time, to learn to swim. I had nothing before my eyes but Tchaikovsky, his unfortunate, tragic life, and you, my angel, that day at the [Hôtel de la] Ville, when, to my declarations of antipathy for that music, you timidly answered, "But <u>don't you think that the last movement of the Pathétique is beautiful</u>?"

Yes, my Ada, you were right, it is not only beautiful but <u>profoundly</u> inspired. And while I was conducting it this evening, I wept like a <u>man in despair.</u> At the phrase in D Major [musical quote of bars 38–42, written out by AT in short score] I couldn't contain myself. Tears flooded my face and mixed with my sweat, luckily, because the stupefied musicians were looking at me. But what could I do? As the whole orchestra little by little took over that phrase in its powerful crescendo, I was at the peak of despair. I was thinking of you, of me, of our <u>desperate</u> situation, which has no way of escape. The darkness before us <u>is impenetrable.</u> What will become of us? I won't return to Italy ever again as long as the present regime lasts, and what can you do? Can you, will you be able to join me outside Italy? [. . .] Oh, my old heart was absolutely right to produce tears this evening—and at this very instant I feel that I can't stop the immense emotion that comes over me with unheard-of violence! Ada, I make you sad, I know; have pity on me. I've never in my life been so weak, so unreasonable. Nothing can bring me back to reason, and each day begins worse than the previous one. [. . .]

Monday <u>31-10-938</u>

Here I am, still open-mouthed at reading that after 42 [*sic;* actually 45] <u>years</u> since the day the Pathétique was [first] performed I have revealed it! I'm including one of the many articles that are repeating the same thing!

It's true that I was in an exceptional soul state the other evening. Since I left my country, I've been living in <u>such spiritual agitation</u> that I really don't know how I manage to go about my task with a fair degree of ease. The thought that gnaws at me and eats me up—not knowing <u>when</u> we'll see each other again, and <u>if</u> we'll see each other again—doesn't allow me to think straight anymore. [. . .] Imagine that a few days ago, Carla, knowing that we're still at a loss for a first cello, said to me, "Why don't you propose <u>Mainardi</u> for the post?" I was disconcerted, and I could only say that Mainardi doesn't intend to go back to orchestra playing, as in the past in Berlin. I can't tell you how my heart was beating at that unexpected question! [. . .]

BLANK E.; ONE OR MORE PAGES MISSING FROM LETTER, OTHERS SPOTTED, WITH SOME WORDS OR PARTS OF WORDS ILLEGIBLE; (NY); TO AM, (BERLIN? ROME?); FSD-FOF

Friday <u>4-11-938</u>

[. . .] I didn't tell you that a young woman was traveling aboard the Normandie—one Colette d'Arville, who they say is simultaneously the lover of Martinelli (tenor) and Maestro Deems Taylor. Well, she's really a pretty little lady who looks Spanish but is French. She took a fancy to me, and she bombards me with books of poetry, Rimbaud, Verlaine—but that's nothing. She had the nerve to have an Italian friend of mine accompany her to my cabin, and at one point he disappeared, leaving me alone with her. My Ada, at that moment, I felt nausea—I'll say no more—and when you feel nausea <u>every</u>

<u>other appetite goes away.</u> She continues to send me books. I don't even thank her. But I did feel tempted to free myself from my <u>obsession with you.</u> [. . .]

Giovanni Martinelli (1885–1969) sang under AT in Italy and the United States. · Deems Taylor (1885–1966) was an American composer and critic.

E.P. NY, 15 NOVEMBER 1938; TO AM, VB8R; FSD-FOF

Tuesday <u>15-11-938</u>

[. . .] I don't know how I manage to make my brain work on music; maybe I'm so accustomed to <u>conducting notes</u> that I do it unconsciously, and the audience is unconsciously so accustomed to thinking I'm good that it mistakenly goes on! [. . .]

E.P. NY, 10 FEBRUARY 1939; TO AM, VB8R
(ADDRESS TYPEWRITTEN); FSD-FOF

Thursday <u>night 9-2-939</u>

[. . .] I feel that I'm no longer the same man, something that I can't precisely define is missing from me and leaves me perplexed, uncertain, and incapable of looking ahead to my near future. The state of my health is normal, but the state of my spirit is really **abnormal.** I'm not living, I have no peace, I feel that some misfortune will happen at any moment. I take no more joy in my work. Everything is an effort. [. . .]

My last concert is on February 25. In all likelihood I'll take the orchestra to Washington on March 2 or 4, but I don't yet know what I'll do after that. The thought that I'll at least be able to live for <u>myself alone</u> is comforting in itself. Never have I <u>hated</u> my fellow human beings as I do now. I'm lost among people. Since just after the first concert I haven't allowed anyone to come see me in my dressing room, and except for a few dinner invitations I've always gone right home as soon as the concert was over. Not to receive any more letters from you, not to write any to you was as if all of a sudden <u>life had ceased</u>! [. . .] I couldn't imagine that there was no way to get word to me in order to let me know of the sad situation you were in. And maybe you were lacking a bit of wisdom, or maybe you were more or less <u>petrified</u> before a fact that bears witness to the moral poverty that the Italians have fallen into. And that <u>gentleman from the censorship department,</u> who concealed his identity and whom you described in a way that is almost kind—he ought to be ashamed of himself for exercising that profession. [. . .] And your friend Pizzetti—he, too, has been one of the greatest disappointments of my life! What horror! What horror! How alone I feel! <u>Ever more alone!</u> [. . .]

[. . .] You hurt me when you say that you don't love the Jews. Tell me, rather, that you don't love the <u>human race</u>! Jews or Catholics, Protestants or Anglicans, men are all the same! Nasty and selfish. The <u>two delinquents</u> aren't Jews, but something much worse! [. . .]

AT's Washington, D.C., concert with the NBC Symphony Orchestra took place on 14 March 1939. · AT received few communications from AM from mid-November 1938 to late January 1939, and he became increasingly unsure of and angry at her. Eventually he learned that she had had trouble with the Italian police censors; their correspondence resumed its previous rhythm, but he had to use ruses in his way of addressing letters.

E.P. NY, 25 FEBRUARY 1939; TO AM, VB8R; FSD-FOF

Friday <u>24-2-939</u>

[. . .] Since <u>February first,</u> when you set foot on Italy's beautiful soil, you haven't had the courage to [send me another letter], despite the <u>new address.</u> So be it! Just for the record, I have to tell you that I continually receive from Milan letters addressed <u>simply with the name</u> "Maestro <u>Arturo Toscanini.</u>" It's clear that the <u>Roman censorship department</u> is even more worthy <u>of the Head of the Fascist Government</u> (respectfully speaking, while <u>touching something very delicate</u>!!! You never know!).

If you wish, you could address letters to Margherita De Vecchi, 333 <u>East 57 St.</u> A last attempt, and if it fails, we'll await the <u>wheel of fortune.</u> You certainly <u>are inside my soul</u> to an extent that makes me angry. You avenge all those unfortunate women who believed in me. I love you desperately, although I would like to hate you for your lack of blood, life, enthusiasm, passion, which makes you able to stand more than I can. [. . .]

Tomorrow evening will be my last effort. Finally! Even my art bores me now. I don't know what I'll do afterward. I would like to find a "cottage" [word in English in the original] on the banks of the Hudson, amid the greenery. To distance myself as much as possible from people, whom I hate, hate, hate!

Wanda is supposed to come with Sonia next month, Volodia at the beginning of April!

The letters I receive from <u>all over</u> with requests for help, help, and more help drive me mad with pity and rage. Never say again that you don't love the Jews! In what way do they differ from us Catholics? Not in cowardice—the proof is overwhelming. <u>Look at the Italians of today.</u> Their leader hasn't yet come to the point of requiring that they put holes in the seat of their pants, but if he requests it all the tailors will immediately adapt to <u>that style.</u> By the way: does Enrico give lessons dressed in the usual way or in a Fascist uniform? I'm curious to know, because it seems to me that he didn't want to submit to that imposition. Excuse me, Ada, but I'm in a pitiable state. Do you know how many times I wish that I would come down with an illness that would finish me off for good? If only I were cowardly enough to commit suicide. [. . .]

E.P. LONDON, 6 MAY 1939; TO AM, VB8R; FSD-FOF

Saturday 6 May

[. . .] Ada my dear, if you had told me frankly, "Artù, I don't love you anymore, Artù, we must put an end to all our intimacies, I no longer feel anything for you," all this would have caused me <u>much less sorrow</u> than to hear that you were afraid of <u>communicating</u> with me, afraid that the Fascist government would discover our friendship, our intimacy. For <u>two months</u> I had no doubts about you, about your sincerity, about the superiority of your character. I only <u>believed</u> and <u>suffered.</u> After the two letters from Belgrade and [empty space], and <u>despite my new address,</u> you delayed in writing to me for another month. And so the idea seeped into my brain that you were <u>no different from the others,</u> that is, from those who are afraid to be my friends for fear of <u>compromising themselves.</u> That did it. If you no longer valued me as man and artist, or if you didn't have the courage to act in accordance with your <u>conscience,</u> [it meant that] you were losing yourself in the company of people whom I **despise** as men of no faith or moral principles, like the Pizzettis, Molinaris, Panizzas, and the whole mob of bad and good artists who infest Italy and the world. Artists who don't deserve to be counted as men, but rather as slaves. How could our intimate relationship have interested the <u>censors</u>? Not at all. Doesn't the <u>Number 2 delinquent</u> have lovers? Because you took into account the advice of that gentleman from the censorship department and not of my <u>despair.</u> Because you, too, are the victim of the <u>entourage</u> in which you live, the victim of general human cowardice. And I have bled with suffering, because I had placed you so high in my thoughts, you were in a solitary niche where **no one** could reach you—only my <u>boundless love.</u> Excuse me, my dear, if I have upset you. Even two solitary words in a telegram will always be welcome. <u>Artù</u>

Héctor (Ettore) Panizza (1875–1967), an Italo-Argentine composer and conductor, had been one of La Scala's conductors during AT's tenure there in the 1920s and later worked at the Met. In 1938 he conducted at the Berlin Staatsoper, and this was presumably the cause of AT's inclusion of him among the "men of no faith or moral principles."

E.P. LONDON, 4 JUNE 1939; TO AM, VB8R; FSD-FOF

Sunday 4 June [1939]

[. . .] I'm leaving London <u>tomorrow.</u> I'm going by airplane to Basel; from there Emilio is coming to get me, to take me to <u>Kastanienbaum,</u> a little village <u>near</u>

<u>Lucerne.</u> We have rented a Villa on the lake (Villa Althaus). If only I could see you, talk to you—we both need this, isn't that so?

E.P. KASTANIENBAUM (LUCERNE), 9 JUNE 1939; TO AM, VB8R; FSD-FOF

<u>Kastanienbaum   Villa Althaus   Wednesday</u> [*sic,* for Thursday] <u>8-6-939</u>
[. . .] I've been here for three days. The place is nice, peaceful, on the lakeshore, the house is comfortable, large, well furnished, far enough from Lucerne not to have b——breakers here often but not so far as not to be able to reach the city in a few minutes by automobile. But it's not my Isolino, it's not my lake, my sky, my mountains—in short, it's not my country, and my homesickness is profound. I'm in a black, black mood, as sad as a November day. [. . .] I was hoping to be able to find not only tranquillity but also sleep, which I've lost over months and months—but not even this silence restores either calmness of spirit or peacefulness of soul, and I manage to sleep only if I take some <u>drug,</u> and I nevertheless <u>often</u> wake up after two hours, and sleepless nights are <u>frequent</u>! [. . .]

E.P. KASTANIENBAUM, 23 JUNE 1939; TO AM, VB8R; FSD-FOF

Friday <u>23-6-1939</u>
[. . .] For many months I haven't managed to balance my faculties. The sorrow of not being able to come to Italy, not being able to see my home, also contributes to this continuing unbalance. It's become impossible for me to make my internal life mesh with my external life. The lack of activity, however necessary it may be, allows tempests to gather in my restless spirit! Those two or three hours of sleep that I manage are upset by <u>nightmares</u> that destroy me. I keep dreaming that I'm conducting music that I don't know, and that I don't have enough rehearsals. [. . .]

E.P. KASTANIENBAUM, 5 JULY 1939; TO AM, VB8R; FSD-FOF

[. . .] Leonora Mendelssohn has been here for two weeks. She phoned to ask whether she could come to say hello. She came, and she planted herself in a little Hotel in Kastanienbaum, but morning and evening <u>she eats at our place.</u> Without being invited. One of these days, I'm going to explode. [. . .]

Wednesday aft.   19-7-939

[. . .] I keep conducting the <u>same music</u>! I can't get modern music to enter either my head or my heart! I'm too old, and my faculties have <u>calcified.</u> Some evenings ago I heard some music of <u>Petrassi</u> on the radio. <u>A big, bad joke!</u> Now, that's the kind of person to <u>put in jail.</u> And Molinari is enthusiastic about that senile young man! [. . .]

AT was spending some time at the Alpine resort of Vermala.

Friday morning   28-7-939

[. . .] Emilio came punctually to pick me up Wednesday morning, and I left the Hotel Forest at exactly nine. I went to <u>Gstaad,</u> I found everyone very well—Wanda, Horowitz, and little Sonia, who becomes more and more a <u>treasure,</u> a <u>real love,</u> and she adores me as you can hardly imagine! She's hoping to come see my rehearsals. She already conducts. Even back in New York I would sit at the piano, I would play something that she knew, and she would beat time with absolutely correct rhythm. She adores music, and she has an ear and rhythm that are truly remarkable. I stayed until five, got back into the automobile, and reached Kastanienbaum in a little under three hours. Who do you think I met there immediately? Leonora Mendelssohn. That woman has become a boarder at my house.

Yesterday evening, however, Carla went crazy, because not only does she [Leonora] come for supper every day, but we also have to answer telephone calls from her friends. Yesterday morning Mrs. Hofmannsthal phoned from London. It seems that she wants to come for the concerts, and naturally she, too, wants to stay at Kastanienbaum. Carla lost her self-control. <u>Nothing</u> was left unsaid: that we took this villa far from Lucerne specifically to be alone and to enjoy a bit of rest and peace far from everyone after so many months of life on the move and at everyone's mercy; that just yesterday we had warned Wally not to bring here a whole mass of her <u>Venetian</u> friends, because I, yes I, want tranquillity, especially during this period of rehearsals and concerts.

Leonora wept floods of tears. The dramatic scene took place before supper, while I was working in my study. But she sat with us <u>imperturbably</u> at supper and stayed with us until eleven, like every other evening! Carla thinks she won't show up today; I don't believe it. We shall see. [. . .]

Enough. In a few days I'll start working again. I'm as nervous as ever when I think about the first rehearsal. I'm <u>still the eternal beginner</u>! My God! I'm beginning the rehearsals on Monday afternoon with <u>La Mer.</u> I'll keep you informed. [. . .]

[3.8.39]

[. . .] I'm dead from the rehearsals. Two a day, 3 hours each.

Three hours this morning, too!

But I love you so much and want to see you—after the concert <u>this evening.</u>
I'll think intensely of you during the <u>Andante sostenuto</u> of Brahms. [. . .]

Between 3 and 29 August 1939 AT conducted six concerts (five different programs) at
the Lucerne Festival. The *andante sostenuto* of Brahms referred to here is the second
movement of the First Symphony.

Monday <u>afternoon</u> [14.8.39]

Ada <u>my dear,</u> I've managed to scrape up a ticket for the Requiem. If it's of use
to you, take advantage of it. I can't stand being in Switzerland any longer! The
thought of having to leave Europe at the end of next month without having
seen my house and country again drives me crazy. It's the first time since I
began to travel and work abroad that this is happening to me. I don't think I'll
be able to stand up to the task that awaits me. After the two performances of
the Messa da Requiem I would like to go away for a few days. The obligation
to attend others' concerts kills me. Listening tires me as much as if I myself
were conducting. I've never felt so old as during recent days. [. . .] I would like
to go alone to the sea, to Cannes, for instance, but I don't have my passport
because I sent it to be renewed. I have no idea where I could go. Could you
suggest someplace where we can meet? I see no other possibility than staying
in Switzerland because <u>you couldn't come</u> to <u>France,</u> right? [. . .] I see Tommasini from time to time, but my God, look at what he, too, has turned into!
The other day, we were talking about events in Italy, or rather in the world. He
was speaking so softly and mysteriously that at one point, tired of trying to
hear him, I said, "Excuse me, Tommasini, don't you know, don't you feel that
you're in a free country, among free people? Speak up and speak your thoughts
clearly. You see, this is exactly how the Italians have become slaves. They're
even afraid to think!" Would you believe it? He still went on talking in
the same mysterious tone, to such a point that I could no longer hear him!
Poor Tommasini! Even he makes me angry! Yesterday evening I had a long
ensemble rehearsal—chorus and orchestra—in the <u>Gesuitenkirche.</u> One must
become accustomed to the unusual acoustics of that venue. After three hours,
it seemed to me not too bad. It seems that there are no echoes! But I've had
them make a wooden riser for the orchestra, <u>50 centimeters</u> above the stone
floor, for the string instruments' resonance. At tomorrow evening's rehearsal
we'll see how much it's helped. [. . .]

AT's performances of the Verdi *Requiem* took place on 16 and 17 August 1939.

[16.8.39]

[. . .] Can you stay through Friday? I'm still planning to go to France, either Cannes or Cap Martin. Try to get a visa for France <u>here</u> in <u>Lucerne.</u> Wanda did it. And she left for <u>Deauville</u> today with Horowitz. This evening in the Offertorio, at the **Hostias,** think of me; I'll be totally with you, inside your soul and body. I kiss you, I kiss you.

<u>I love you</u>   Artù

<u>Friday 25-8-939</u>

<u>Ada my dear,</u> Isn't it ridiculous that I'm "alone" for the second time and don't have you with me? For some time now, everything, but everything has been going wrong!

I really can't stand it any longer. Having seen you for a few moments after the concerts, and those minutes before your departure from Lucerne, was a very gentle ray that penetrated the depths of my soul, but the darkness remains there. [. . .] I'm still under the extremely sorrowful impression of Grete Walter's tragic passing. I can't forget it. I see her in my study at Kastanienbaum with her beautiful smile, and it seems to me unreal that only three hours later she had ceased to exist. I dreamt of her last night, but as I had seen her at Salzburg. My sadness is deepened by the horrible news of recent days about this miserable Europe's horrible condition, which is worsening from hour to hour. I'm going back to Lucerne this evening. I'll attend Busch's concert, in which Huberman is taking part. I have no desire to hear music, much less to make it. I made a mistake in coming up here, the weather is as terrible as my mood. [. . .]

AT was again spending a few days at a resort. · Gretel Neppach, Bruno Walter's beautiful younger daughter, had been having an affair with Ezio Pinza, as a result of which her husband, a film set designer, had killed her and then committed suicide. Carla and Wally Toscanini were among the first to hear the news, and they took upon themselves the grim task of communicating it to Bruno Walter. · Mobilization had begun in much of Europe, and a week after this letter was written Germany invaded Poland, thus initiating World War II. As far as I have been able to determine, AT and AM never saw each other again after the fleeting encounters at Lucerne to which he refers here.

= I LEAVE LUCERNE TOMORROW[.] GOING ABOARD MANHATTAN IN BORDEAUX
SATURDAY[.] MAIL TO MARGHERITA DE VECCHI 333 EAST 57 STREET[.] YOU CAN
IMAGINE MY STATE OF MIND[.] I EMBRACE YOU = ARTU ARTURO TOSCANINI

VERY GREAT DIFFICULTY OBTAIN SIMPLE CABIN TWO BEDS [. . .]
TOSCANINI

With the onset of war, so many people were trying to leave Europe quickly that book-
ing passage was difficult.

= WE LEAVE IN A FEW HOURS[.] HUGS = TOSCANINI =

This was probably the last piece of correspondence that AT sent from Europe until
May 1946.

Part Six

OCTOBER 1939–
MARCH 1946

MAJOR EVENTS IN TOSCANINI'S LIFE DURING THIS PERIOD

1940   Takes NBC Symphony Orchestra on South American tour.
1946   11 May: Conducts inaugural concert at restored La Scala, which had been
       bombed during the war.

= LEFT TWELFTH ARRIVED YESTERDAY[.] IMAGINE MY STATE NOT BEING ABLE COMMUNICATE ANY MANNER WITH YOU[.] I EMBRACE YOU — ARTU =

24 October 1939

[. . .] By the greatest luck I'm no longer living at the Astor. This way I see hardly anyone now. I'm living in a magnificent large villa in Riverdale, 25 minutes from the NBC, where I work. It's situated in an enchanting position, facing the Hudson, with a magnificent park abounding in big trees and terraces where I can enjoy the sun and the silence!! Oh, my Ada, I wish you could get to know this marvelous place. It makes me think of the Isolino. But the fact is that the Isolino is unique, and it's in Italy! [. . .]

I've already done two concerts. Impossible though it seems, I can tell you that the orchestra has improved even more. I've brought the number of cellos up to 12. The first stand is excellent, made up of two new players. The first, one Miller, a young man—he isn't yet thirty—is magnificent. On the last program there was Brahms's Double Concerto, a piece that isn't too easy for the cello, as you know; well, he managed it magnificently.

Now I'm starting the Beethoven symphonies, and I'll be doing them on the next six programs. On one of the programs I'll be playing the Septet with six Violins, 5 violas, 4 Cellos, and two Double basses, because I never loved this marvelous, youthful music as played by seven instruments. I think that the Clarinet, Horn, and Bassoon are better balanced over a large base of strings! [. . .]

AT and CT had rented and moved into a spacious turn-of-the-century imitation Tudor house, the Villa Pauline, at 655 West 254th Street, in the elegant Riverdale section of the Bronx, in the northwesternmost part of New York City. · Frank Miller was twenty-six in 1939 when he became principal cello of the NBC Symphony Orchestra; he remained with the orchestra until it was disbanded in 1954, then became principal cello of the Chicago Symphony Orchestra under Fritz Reiner, Jean Martinon, and Georg Solti. · Beethoven wrote his Septet in E-flat Major, op. 20, when he was in his late twenties.

Saturday aft.   28 October [1939]

[. . .] I'm starting the Beethoven programs this evening. Oh, how hard it is to repeat the same music after a short lapse and to find a way to make new life flow into all of it! I can still bring off this miracle! At least I think so!!! [. . .] I try not to read the newspapers and know as little as possible about the infernal tragedy that is hanging over the poor human race—but I can't ignore the delinquents who have been preparing it over the last few years. My hatred for these brigands, monsters, delinquents <u>has no limit.</u> I think that the beginning of the end has come for them. Unfortunately, <u>too many young lives</u> will have to be consumed, but the <u>redde rationem</u> [roughly equivalent to "moment of reckoning"] is coming for <u>these people beyond all human laws.</u> That includes <u>the one</u> who is now playing <u>second fiddle.</u> But let's change the subject, otherwise my liver will swell up! I also think a lot about the <u>material</u> condition of you both, and it makes me feel bad. I think I heard you say that all of Enrico's savings are in Berlin and that he can't take advantage of any of them. Is that still true, or has he been able to cash them in, in a sensible way? And the concerts he had in former years—have they or haven't they been canceled? Tell me something in your next letter; who knows when it will arrive! This year the mail will drive everyone crazy. The fast steamships aren't departing—we'll have to take advantage of the airplanes.

Sunday morning [29.10.39]   <u>Three o'clock</u>

The concert was magnificent. The orchestra played marvelously! How I would have liked you to hear the broadcast! I saw Castelnuovo-Tedesco and Liuzzi. Castelnuovo-Tedesco will play his concerto for piano and orchestra next Thursday with the Philharmonic. He is happy to be here with his family. I think he'll find a way to situate himself well. Heifetz will be a great help to him. [. . .]

The composers (and brothers-in-law) Mario Castelnuovo-Tedesco and Ferdinando Liuzzi were Italian Jews who had immigrated to the United States after the promulgation of the 1938 racial laws. Jascha Heifetz, who was an American citizen, had provided an affidavit for Castelnuovo; AT and his wife, although they never became American citizens, helped Castelnuovo, Liuzzi (who was also an internationally known musicologist), and many other Jewish and anti-Fascist émigrés from Europe in a variety of moral and material ways, and provided affidavits for some of them.

E.P. NY, 3 NOVEMBER 1939; TO AM, VB8R; FSD-FOF

Thursday <u>morning</u>   <u>2 November</u> [1939]

[. . .] the <u>eighth Saturday</u> [concert] is 2 December, then I'll turn over the baton to Defauw for 4 weeks, Molinari for 5, and Bruno Walter for 5 others. I'll resume working on 2 March and finish on 5 May with a concert in which Horowitz will play. As you see, I have 14 free weeks. [. . .] I'd like to go visit California, which I've never seen, while Wanda and Horowitz are there, but as I told you, I haven't made any plans so far. In bygone times I would have gone to Italy, as I always did when I was conducting the Philharmonic, but today? [. . .]

Désiré Défauw (1885–1960) was a Belgian conductor who had immigrated to the United States in 1938. · AT's NBC Symphony Orchestra 1939–40 season ended on 6 May 1940 with an all-Brahms concert in which Horowitz played the Second Piano Concerto.

E.P. NY, 4 NOVEMBER 1939; TO AM, VB8R; FSD-FOF

Saturday morning   4 Nov. 939

[. . .] I forgot to tell you that I did a rehearsal of the <u>Aida Overture</u> and I decided that it would be worth performing on a concert. I don't know whether you knew that Verdi had written an Overture after the nice little Prelude that is usually played, and he would have replaced the latter with the former if he had judged it favorably; but that's not how things went. On the contrary, his opinion was extremely severe. Too much so, I think. In an excerpt from a letter of 1875—we don't know to whom it was addressed—one reads the following words: "There is no Aida Overture. You may have heard people say that at one of the Aida rehearsals in Milan I had a piece played that had the attributes of an Overture. The orchestra, too, was good, willing, and obedient, and the piece could have produced good results if it <u>had been solidly constructed.</u> But the orchestra's excellence wasn't enough to make the <u>pretentious silliness</u> of this self-proclaimed Overture turn out better." Always marvelously honest, in art as in life, Giuseppe Verdi. Something of his character, not of his genius, lives in me. [. . .]

Many who have heard the *Aida* Overture, however, would agree with Verdi's severe judgment. For more on this issue, see the draft telegram of 30 March 1940.

E.P. NY, 15 NOVEMBER 1939, BUT AT LEAST THE FIRST TWO LETTERS IN
THE ENVELOPE PREDATE THE POSTMARK; TO EK, 26W68NY; WOT

My <u>dear Elsa,</u>

Can you still love me a little[?] Although my heart has aged, it <u>still</u> beats as it did <u>then.</u> Do you remember, Elsa? Our furtive evening walks? Your eyes <u>still</u> have the <u>magnificent power</u> of times <u>now long past,</u> and I feel chills go up my spine <u>every time</u> they gaze at me. Sorceress!! I still love you, and I desire you even more intensely. <u>You make me feel young again.</u> When will we be able to enjoy Brahms's sublime music as we wish? Give me your mouth as you did then. I <u>kiss you until you faint.</u>

Your very own.

[In the same envelope:]

<u>Dear Elsa,</u> I don't know why, but I am devilishly fearful of sending you these words. I would have preferred to give them to you by hand. In any case, come

what may, whatever happens will happen. Listen, my dear, I wouldn't want your friendship with <u>Cia</u> to make you imprudent. If we keep our secret, we'll be able to love each other in peace, otherwise, for pity's sake—a tragedy at this time and at my age would be a disaster and **ridiculous.**

<u>Let's love each other silently</u> and <u>suffer</u> in silence, too. Love me a lot—I adore you and you <u>delight</u> me <u>more</u> than <u>before,</u> if such a thing is <u>possible!!!</u> Come quickly to finish the Aida parts, so that I can at least hold you close and kiss you furtively on the mouth and on your very beautiful eyes. <u>Give me, give me everything,</u> let me <u>kiss your whole adorable little body.</u> Think of Brahms—the appassionato first movement of the <u>third symphony</u> [the notes of the melody of the first bar and a half of the principal theme appear here]. I kiss you <u>everywhere,</u> in the <u>most hidden recesses.</u> God! God! God!—Ar—

[In the same envelope:]

Elsa <u>my dear,</u> I suffer indescribably by being near you and not being able to caress you, talk to you, and repeat every moment that I love you, I adore you, and I don't live through a <u>single</u> minute of the day or the night without <u>invoking</u> your <u>name,</u> without desiring a <u>kiss from you.</u> Elsa, I don't know whether you suffer the same form of suffering that I do, but I know that every day our situation becomes sadder. To turn back is impossible for me, I love you as I never loved you before, and you delight me more than any other woman, more than anything else. What <u>is there,</u> <u>what is there</u> in your eyes, what is there in your dear little self, in your flesh? You drive me crazy with desire and make me do absurd things that are inconceivable for an old man like me! Give me, give me your caresses, your mouth. Give me <u>everything—everything!!</u>

[In the same envelope:]

<u>Elsa dear,</u> It's real, cruel torture to have you near and not cover you with kisses, clasp you furiously to my heart, suck your voluptuous lips, as bees suck flowers. God! What torture! Call me, call me Tuesday afternoon, tell me to come to you. My blood is in revolt. I adore you, Elsa, and you delight me to <u>death.</u> [. . .] Don't <u>lose time.</u> Maybe <u>before long</u> God will take away even the <u>little bit</u> of <u>virility</u> that's left me. And then? What misery! [. . .] Till tonight. <u>Your very own.</u>

AT had clearly given up hope of seeing AM again, at least in the relatively near future. He wanted some sexual activity and looked for it where he was quite sure he could get it without being betrayed. · Regarding the *Aida* parts, see the next letter and my accompanying note.

(NY); TO AM, VB8R; FSD-FOF

Friday <u>10-11-939</u>

[. . .] Castelnuovo-Tedesco made his debut last week as pianist-composer. I heard it over the radio. Both pianist and composer irritated me! He is forever the victim of a continual musical <u>dysentery</u>. And he writes music that <u>grips</u> no one, it runs off you just like it runs out of his . . . pen. The reviews were mixed. Liuzzi is here, too, but I haven't yet seen him. He came to a concert of mine, he wrote me a nice letter, but I'll see him very soon. Elsa Kurzbauer is here. She gives a few Italian lessons and copies music. She copied the orchestra parts of the Aida Overture for me and she is now trying to come within the immigrant <u>quota</u> so that she can get a work permit. We've helped her in every way. I signed an <u>affidavit</u> for her. She'll have to go to Havana for a while in order to re-enter the United States and stay for good. She will then be able to work and, I think, to <u>earn well</u>.

[. . .] The Horowitzes arrived in Los Angeles this morning and we old people are keeping with us <u>delightful</u> little <u>Sonia,</u> who fills us with joy. [. . .]

Thursday 23
Thanksgiving day

Today is a holiday in New York, and nature, too, is having a holiday. It's one of those days full of light, sun, and such beauty that for a moment it makes you forget the horrible tragedy that weighs upon humanity. If you could see the view from this marvelous villa, you would be as moved as I am at this instant, as I write to you. I'm alone and can write to you freely. Carla has gone into the city with little Sonia, who is invited to lunch with other children at the Astor and then to watch from the hotel's terraces the <u>parade</u> that goes along Broadway. Sonia continues to be a love of a child. She has begun to take piano lessons. The other day, while she was alone in her room (everyone thought she was asleep), she cut her hair—all the curls are gone. She turned herself into a little boy. You can imagine the displeasure of everyone here at home. I didn't speak to her for two days, although it was hard for me. She would steal a glance at me, and I would pretend not to notice. Then, when she came to excuse herself, I can't tell you how many kisses I gave her. As far as I'm concerned, she looks better now than when her hair was long. She looks like a little boy, and she says that she wants to be a <u>boy</u> and not a <u>girl.</u> It's a real joy to have her with us, and it goes a long way toward filling our lives! Walfredo we see on <u>weekends,</u> on the other hand. He comes to us here on Friday evening and stays until Sunday evening. He goes to school, and it seems that he is doing very well. He, too, is very intelligent and has an excellent character. From Milan, however, I've had the bad news that Emanuela will probably have to have an <u>operation</u> for <u>appendicitis</u>! I didn't know that such risks could be faced at that age as well as by adults. Poor Wally is rather frightened. I'm hoping that an all-out preventive treatment will allow them to avoid the operation.

Thursday <u>night</u>

As usual, I can't sleep; while I write to you I'm listening to the radio (shortwave) very softly, so as not to disturb anyone, and the BBC station in London is giving bad news. Ships sunk and human lives lost. My God, this terrible, deaf, cowardly, inhuman war—when will it cease and how will it end? There will be neither losers nor winners, but rather infinite mourning, misery, and greater hatred. And I doubt that I'll be able to return, not only to Italy but also to Europe. This thought is enough to destroy my sleeping and waking hours and to make me wish to disappear from the face of the earth. A <u>man,</u> a **beast,** an **outlaw** has managed to throw Europe into such a fearful abyss, backed up by other bandits and by the ignorance and sloth of the so-called **democrats**—senile old men! [. . .]

Castelnuovo-Tedesco was extremely prolific, but few of his compositions are still played. · AT evidently meant that he had not had occasion to talk seriously with Liuzzi; he had seen him briefly after the concert of 28 October 1939. · The reference to Sonia's saying, at the age of five, that she wanted to be a boy is interesting in view of the fact that she grew up to be a lesbian. She had a difficult life, psychologically: her incredibly egocentric and unloving father was a homosexual, and her moody, selfish mother seems not to have taken much interest in her; both parents often left her with governesses for long periods while they traveled around on Horowitz's tours, tormenting each other. Sonia seems to have been happiest when she stayed with her grandparents.

E.P. NY, 24 NOVEMBER 1939; TO AM, VB8R; FSD-FOF

Friday morning   <u>24-11-1939</u>
[. . .] Margherita will send you "Life" where you will see some good photographs of me and of Sonia. I was in <u>good humor that day.</u> How could one not be with that dear, adorable creature? You'll see the faces she makes when she wants to <u>clown</u> around! She is really a <u>most amusing</u> character. This morning, or rather half an hour ago, she came to show me the <u>gold star</u> that her piano teacher put in her notebook for the magnificent lesson she'd had.

And her father and mother are enjoying themselves in California. They are really a couple of savages, they don't have their own home, that is, they've had several and have always given them up—they have a daughter, and she almost always lives with her grandparents! They're really funny, the <u>two</u> of them! [. . .]

AT seems to have had no idea (at that time) of just how "funny" his own daughter and son-in-law were.

(NY, 27 NOVEMBER 1939); TO EDWARD JOHNSON, GENERAL MANAGER, THE METROPOLITAN OPERA, NY; METROPOLITAN OPERA ARCHIVES

My dear <u>Johnson</u>
In 1915 I was the cause of our poor friend Bodanzky's arrival at the Metropolitan, on the recommendation of Busoni. He [Bodanzky] was to share the Ger-

man repertoire with me. My artistic views, which clashed with Gatti-Casazza's commercial ones, made me decide to leave the Metropolitan, thus the collaboration with our friend never took place. He, however, remained in the saddle for twenty-four years.—

Today I would like to bring to your attention Mae. <u>Hans Steinberg.</u> Steinberg is a <u>born</u> opera conductor.—. I believe him to be the best among the young generation. I'm attaching a sort of <u>curriculum vitae</u> so that you can get an idea of his previous activities in several German opera houses. These activities are not limited to conducting the orchestra and singers but also embrace the whole artistic and stage ensemble.

In short, have a look, dear Johnson. On Wednesday we can talk in greater detail. Meanwhile, I'm glad to greet you heartily and to wish you a good beginning to your season and an even better continuation. Your

Arturo Toscanini

27 November—1939

The Austrian conductor Artur Bodanzky (1877–1939) had become one of the Metropolitan Opera's chief conductors in the fall of 1915, just after AT left. · Edward Johnson (1878–1959), a Canadian tenor who, as Edoardo Di Giovanni, had sung in Beethoven's Ninth Symphony with AT in Italy in 1919, was general manager of the Met from 1935 to 1950. · This letter was written only four days after Bodanzky's death. For Steinberg, see my note accompanying the letter of 17 September 1936. He had trained the new Palestine Symphony Orchestra in 1936, before AT's arrival, and AT was so impressed with his work that he brought him to the NBC as his assistant conductor. In the United States, Hans Wilhelm Steinberg changed his name to William Steinberg and had a major career, but he did not conduct at the Met until 1965.

E.P. NY, 29 NOVEMBER 1939; TO AM, VB8R; FSD-FOF

<u>Monday 28-11-939</u> [*sic,* for Monday 27 or Tuesday 28] [. . .] The last concert, last Saturday the 25th, you were very close to me during the whole divine <u>Lento</u> of <u>Beethoven's quartet in F</u> [op. 135]. It's the first time that I <u>may</u> have done it moderately well. It's an extremely difficult piece. I've never heard it played well. Not by the [blank space; name missing] or the Busch quartet or the Flonzaley. I tried a few years ago with the Philharmonic, two years ago with my present orchestra, also in London. I was <u>never</u> satisfied. I even made a record, which I had rejected and then, on the advice of musician friends, accepted, but I've bitterly repented and would like to withdraw it from circulation. But it's too late. [. . .]

Mon. Dec. 18 [1939]

[. . .] I'm facing one of nature's most marvelous spectacles! It's impossible to describe this miracle, which only God and nature can make. I was never able to write to you from California, another dream country! [. . .]

Tuesday 19—Dec.

Ada my dear! I'm drunk with beauty. It would be impossible to find a more fantastic and unreal marvel than this Grand Canyon. Yesterday evening at dusk and this morning at sunrise there were tears in my eyes from the emotion that this miracle of nature has given me!! Even the people here, as in California, seem better. How I would like to have you here, my adored creature, and enjoy in silence, hand in hand, this sublime, grandiose, fearful miracle that God, Nature, and Time have forged over millions of years!!! [. . .]

[. . .] Friday 29-12-1939

This evening I'll conduct a little orchestra made up of players from mine, plus Heifetz, Busch, Milstein, Feuermann, and Wallenstein. I'm doing a sort of café-chantant program. A Moment musical of Schubert with Loin du bal by Gillet, for strings, Strauss's Pizzicato Polka with a polka by Shostakovich that's all dissonances, Ries's Moto perpetuo played by all the violins accompanied by [the rest of] the orchestra, and a Mozart Divertimento for strings and two horns, full of wrong-note passages. Suffice it to say that the last chords are played in a different key by each instrument. Wanda, made up as Toscanini, was supposed to conduct the moto perpetuo, but at the rehearsal yesterday evening she didn't have the nerve to do it. I, on the other hand, will come out not made up but dressed in a long overcoat, an 1830s-style collar, a huge necktie with stickpin, and old-fashioned dark glasses. I'll have a huge handkerchief of colored silk (I have one that Wagner used, a gift to me from Mrs. Thode), which I'll ostentatiously pull out of my back pocket for laughs. All the musicians will be dressed like children, in shorts, some with long stockings, others bare-legged. Can you imagine Adolf Busch? Before us, there will be some vaudeville scenes in which all of the Chotzinoffs—which means the whole Heifetz family, including the old mother—will take part. Feuermann, Horowitz, Tibbett, and Heifetz have a very funny scene in a theatrical agency, where they have to audition. Horowitz is very funny. Wanda made up as Toscanini is also very amusing—too bad that she doesn't have the nerve to come out and conduct the last number. It would certainly be a big success. [. . .]

The entertainment that AT describes was a benefit event for the Chatham Square Music School on Manhattan's Lower East Side, and so far as is known it is the only professional musical satire in which AT ever took part. · Alfred Wallenstein (1898–1983) had been AT's first cello in the New York Philharmonic; by 1939, however, he had embarked on a career as a conductor. AT had an affair with Wallenstein's wife, Virginia, but I do not know when. (There are several undated letters from her to AT.)

E.P. NY, 20 JANUARY 1940; TO AM, VB8R; FSD-FOF

Saturday 20-1-1940

[. . .] They've cabled me from Lucerne to ask whether they can count on me for the coming festival. How do they have the nerve to think about what will happen in August?

Here they're preparing a plan to take my orchestra and me to South America! Fourteen concerts, 8 in Buenos Aires, 4 in Rio de Janeiro, 2 in São Paulo. I would like it, to keep my spirit and nerves occupied until they're used up. But unfortunately I fear that difficulties will arise. [. . .]

The Lucerne Festival did not take place in 1940, but the NBC Symphony Orchestra's South American tour did materialize.

E.P. NY, 24 JANUARY 1940; TO AM, VB8R; FSD-FOF

Wednesday 24-1-1940

[. . .] The other day I gave Mary Molinari a piece of my mind. She came at exactly the right moment. I had attended a rehearsal of Pizzetti's Concerto dell'Estate and I was furious over Bernardino's way of rehearsing. He stops the orchestra every three or four bars, and he does so not only at the first reading but at the last rehearsal. Whether the orchestra is good or bad, it's all the same—just like Bruno Walter, he can't go on, he has to stop every moment. It's antiaesthetic to look at him, with his head always buried in the score. I let off steam with that cretin of a woman, who never ceases to ask me, "How did the rehearsal go? Are you happy with Bernardino?" "No," I told her, "I'm not happy, and I'm surprised that after thirty years of conducting he hasn't yet learned how to deal with a self-respecting orchestra. And I'd like him to attend one of my rehearsals of brand-new music to show him how to deal with an orchestra like the one he's conducting, and how much more he would get out of it in very little time." But in any case it would be time wasted, or at least so it seems to me. I try not to go too often to rehearsals, so as not to upset myself. Can you believe that a musician from the orchestra told me that in the first movement of Tchaikovsky's fourth symph. he [Molinari] went back between seventy and eighty times? And here in America all the orchestras can play that symphony by heart!!! Fortunately, the orchestra is magnificently disciplined and follows him patiently without showing signs of boredom. But they can't wait for me to come back. Even when I'm on edge and I maltreat them, they're happier than living peacefully but in boredom!

Poor Liuzzi is ill and in the hospital. I'll go see him soon. I wrote to him and sent a photograph, which he had asked for with much solicitude. I think that his family hasn't been told, <u>in keeping with his wishes.</u> [. . .]

Liuzzi, knowing that he was mortally ill, gave up a teaching position at Columbia University and returned to Italy, where he died the following October.

DRAFT OF TG, (NY); TO ANGELO CARRARA VERDI (SANT'AGATA?); NYPLTL

NOTARY ANGELO CARRARA   30-3-1940, 4:30 O'CLOCK P.M.
SURPRISED BY YOUR CURRENT ATTITUDE [ONE OR TWO WORDS CROSSED OUT] AS YOU HAD [CROSSED OUT: AT THE TIME] LET ME KNOW THROUGH MY SON WHEN HE GAVE YOU BACK THE MANUSCRIPT THAT I ALONE WAS TO DECIDE ABOUT THE PERFORMANCE STOP ONLY AFTER THIS AUTHORIZATION ON YOUR PART DID I DECIDE TO PRESENT IT AND SINCE IT HAS ALREADY BEEN ANNOUNCED I THOUGHT INAPPROPRIATE CANCEL THE PERFORMANCE CORDIAL GREETINGS
ARTURO TOSCANINI

Carrara Verdi, who was Verdi's surviving heir, had evidently protested against the performance of the *Aida* Overture (see the letter of 4 November 1939), which AT gave with the NBC Symphony Orchestra on the day this telegram draft was written.

E.P. NY, 3 MAY 1940; P.S., AT; TO OLIN DOWNES, 9 E. 10TH ST., NY;
ORIG. ENG. (ALL ERRORS HAVE BEEN PRESERVED); ODUGA

My dear <u>Olin Downes</u>
Many and many thanks for your telegram . . . You made me very happy. I am sorry you missed the <u>Sibelius fourth</u> . . . I have the illusion it was well performed and according [to] the intention of the composer.

When can I see you and Madame at Riverdale? Can you not spare one morning next week end to have lunch with me and my family? It would be <u>very nice</u>!!! Send me word, please . . . My telephone is: Kingsbridge 9-7674 and 9-7918.—My best regards to Madame that I shall be very happy to meet very soon and affectionate greetings for you from the old maestro
<u>Arturo Toscanini</u>

May <u>3—1940</u>

Downes (1886–1955), as I have said, was the chief music critic of the *New York Times;* he idolized AT and occasionally sent him letters charged with emotion and gratitude. AT in turn demonstrated a degree of esteem for Downes.

DRAFT OF TG OR LETTER, POSSIBLY FROM ABOARD STEAMSHIP *BRAZIL* OR
FROM SOUTH AMERICA, SHORTLY AFTER 10 JUNE 1940;
TO PRESIDENT FRANKLIN D. ROOSEVELT, (WASHINGTON, D.C.); ORIG. ENG.
(ALL ERRORS HAVE BEEN PRESERVED); NYPLTL

To President <u>Franklin Roosevelt</u>

"The hand that held the dagger has struck it in the back of its neighbor[."]
With these words, you made the perfect moral picture of the Italian dictator. I
thank you in advance for all you will do in order to destroy and forever these
two wild beast that commonly are called dictators.

<u>A Toscanini</u>

On 10 June 1940, Italy attacked France, which was on the verge of being defeated
by Germany; Mussolini, observing Germany's easy conquest of much of continental
Europe, wanted to get his share of the spoils before it was too late and therefore
decided to bring Italy into the war. AT and the NBC Symphony Orchestra were
aboard ship, en route to South America for what was to be a memorable tour. AT was
so ashamed and angry over Italy's cowardly action that he locked himself in his cabin
and refused to come out for a few days. This message, which was intended not only to
thank Roosevelt for his expression of outrage over Mussolini's deed but also to encour-
age him to bring the United States into the war effort, is not to be found in the
Franklin D. Roosevelt Library and may never have been sent.

(ABOARD STEAMSHIP *URUGUAY*), 22 JULY 1940; TO THE MEMBERS
OF THE NBC SYMPHONY ORCHESTRA, ABOARD THE SAME SHIP; ORIG. ENG.
(ALL ERRORS HAVE BEEN PRESERVED); PC; NYPLTL

My <u>dear friends</u>

To-morrow our trip will be over . . . To-morrow we will be separated after two
months we lived day by day the same life. It is very sad indeed, but that is life!
One thing remains still to me, namely, to look forward to next November
when I shall resume the conducting of my beloved orchestra. I wish I could
express my feelings and my thanks personally to you . . . but it is impossible—
My throbbing heart would raise up to the throarth chocking my poor voice . . .
Mr. Chotzinoff will be so kind as to read these few lines to you . . . While writing I feel sad at heart and it will be always so when beautiful things come to an
end, but it is a sadness caused by happiness. If I think to our concerts they
seem far far away . . . They are like dear, sweet memories of time long past . . .
Anyhow they were beautiful! You have never played so well, so inspired in
three seasons that I am with you. We have never been so linked, so all one, as
in these 16 concerts . . . We must be proud of what we have done! I can't say
which of these concerts has been the best! I only know that the next to the first
was better, and so on. I hope you will never forget them. Memories of beautiful, dear things are the poetry and the sweet perfume of our existence.

Good bye, dearest friends.

God bless you all.

Arturo <u>Toscanini</u>

<u>22 July—1940</u>

In the course of what had been a triumphal tour, AT and the orchestra had performed in Rio de Janeiro and São Paulo (neither of which he had revisited since his debut season in 1886) in addition to Buenos Aires and Montevideo.

E.P. NY, 11 AUGUST 1940; P.S., AT; TO AM, 25VBMMI; FSD-FOF

10 <u>August 1940</u>

Ada <u>my dear,</u> When Margherita read me your telegram I thought I would <u>faint</u> with joy. I fell on my knees, pressing my hands to my heart, which I thought would jump out of my throat! Those words of yours, so full of affection, revealed you to me just as you were and as I wanted to find you again. No, you don't seem to have changed. Your feelings are the same ones that I knew. I doubted you very much, and I beg your pardon. It's difficult these days to live life as one feels and wishes. Only strong people are able not to change— those who are truly good and honest are capable of suffering, of going beyond all limits of suffering! <u>I feel that I am one of them.</u> For some months my life has no goal. To be like a **useless tool** humiliates me and makes me ashamed of belonging to the human race. While millions and millions of beings are being swept away by the most fearful tragedy that the world has ever known, I sit here, a ridiculous spectator, with my hands folded, sighing, hating, but an inert and useless tool. I live far from everyone. Here in Riverdale I see hardly anyone except Margherita, because I don't get along with anyone. The other day—in fact, the very day I arrived from South America—I sent my son out of the house. I don't want to see him again! He wanted to list all of England's wrongdoings!!! I couldn't stand it. I called him a bastard and sent him out of the house. England is fighting to save Europe from the slavery, the subjection that threatens it. This is enough to make me love her!! I'm enclosing a clipping about a letter of Garibaldi. I've always thought and felt **His** way!!! I was never able to send you a message or even programs from South America. I was living in too much togetherness with everyone, and I didn't have a <u>Margherita</u> at my disposal, unfortunately! The tour went magnificently. The orchestra was beyond all praise. Never had it played better. Every concert was a revelation! I don't know what the newspapers said. I'll send you, however, a clipping taken from the New York Times of a few days ago. You'll like it because I know that you love me, however **neglected** I feel since December 12, 1939. I can't figure out whether you're obeying a natural feeling or some **order** from outside, but certainly no servant has ever been treated as <u>you have treated me.</u> You didn't even give me a week's notice! But so be it! I love you all the same. [. . .]

AT's rage against his son abated after a couple of months. · The first of the above-mentioned newspaper clippings is entitled "Garibaldi's Curse"; it is a letter to the *New York Herald Tribune,* dated 1 August 1940, and signed with the initials G.P.A. It quotes Garibaldi, who wrote, in 1854, ". . . if ever England should be so circumstanced as to require the help of an ally, cursed be the Italian who would not step forward in her defense." The second clipping, from the *New York Times* (no date on the clipping), tells of AT's return from South America, of the death of the NBC Symphony violist Jacques Tuschinsky (who was killed in a traffic accident in Rio at the end of the tour), and of the musical campaign of AT, "who has known how to rebuke the arrogance of dictators, who has set his face sternly against racial and religious intolerance," etc.

E.P. NY, 14 AUGUST 1940; P.S., AT; TO AM, 25VBMMI; FSD-FOF

Tuesday 13-August [1940]

[. . .] I'm very worried over the fate of my dear Mausi, Siegfried's daughter, who is in London. She wasn't sent to a concentration camp, no. I had an immigration permit sent to her from Buenos Aires, along with a contract at the Teatro Colón. I've sent recommendations to Argentina's ambassador [to Great Britain] and to [Joseph] Kennedy, the United States' ambassador [to Great Britain]. Everyone knows the feelings of this girl, who is not only against Hitler but also against her mother, and who refused to return to her country. I've done everything that was humanly possible for me to do for her; now <u>we must wait.</u> But that 22-year-old girl is marvelous; she has a **strong and loyal** character, and I love her like a daughter. Let's hope!

I won't resume my activities until November. The first concert is set for the 23rd at Carnegie Hall, with Verdi's Te Deum and Requiem. The NBC's concert season, however, begins around mid-October with Maestro Steinberg. In the meantime, I'm preparing a few programs. I look through new music, but then I stick to the old. [. . .]

E.P. NY, 4 SEPTEMBER 1940; P.S., AT; TO AM, 25VBMMI; FSD-FOF

Wednesday 4-Sept. 1940

My dear <u>and adored Ada</u>

<u>I'll write, I'll write</u>—these are the words you repeat in your delayed telegrams! When will you telegraph, "I've written a letter"? Maybe never again! Last year, too, by both <u>telegraph</u> and <u>telephone,</u> your mouth repeated this music. Poor me. I can no longer believe in <u>anyone.</u> The friends who surround you may be nice people, perhaps even honest, but they are cowardly and without a trace of **civil courage.** For shame!!! But you, you who admired the purity of my feelings, my courage in confronting the <u>threats of the bandits</u> who <u>lord it over Italy,</u> and what's more in feeling contempt toward them, in not giving a damn about them—you, you, Ada, are unwittingly showing solidarity with them, and you're afraid of compromising yourself by writing to me. Poor creature! I feel sorry for you and I love you all the same! What is the honest but **pusillan-**

imous Tommasini doing and thinking? What sorrow, what sad suffering it is <u>not to be able to love</u> one's own country any longer, and to feel contempt for all the Italians—the good ones because <u>they're cowards,</u> the perfidious ones because they're evil. I can't stand life any longer! It's truly a heavy burden! But how can one rid oneself of it today, when the struggle to preserve civilization is taking place? I feel so humiliated to be a useless tool at this moment that I'm ashamed of the air I breathe! I live here in Riverdale, which is enchanting, a dream. Only the Isolino surpasses it for beauty and poetry. A few friends come to see me. Relatives? No, they're all far away. Wanda is in California with that egoist of a husband of hers! I haven't seen Walter and Cia again, nor does this make me cry, only I would like to see the two little creatures Dedè and Sonia, but . . . Sonia, however, will come back before long! I'm sending you a photograph that an orchestra member took during a rehearsal. Ada, do you still love me??? Give me proof! Don't make me suffer and doubt!

Your very own Artù

(NY), 22 JANUARY 1941; P.S., RIVERDALE-ON-HUDSON/NEW YORK;
TO BRUNO ZIRATO, (NY); NYPA

My <u>dear Zirato</u>
I know that the Philharmonic's Board of Directors is meeting today to discuss the choice of guest conductors for the coming 1941–42 concert season. Just as I recommended Maestro Fritz Busch in 1936 to Mr. Marshall Field (to whom please make my excuses again for not having been able to see him last week), so I repeat my recommendation today, knowing that I am persevering in my support of an artist who is worthy of leading an Orchestra like the Philharmonic. I hardly need to repeat how <u>delighted</u> I am about <u>my return</u> on the occasion of the centenary of the oldest musical organization in the United States, only I don't want to make a formal decision today. Thus I ask you to inform the honorable Mr. Marshall Field about this; I send him my sincerest regards.

For you, an affectionate embrace.
Yours entirely
<u>Arturo Toscanini</u>

22 <u>January 1941.</u>

After the Furtwängler debacle in 1936, AT had recommended that the New York Philharmonic choose Fritz Busch as his successor. An offer was made, but at that time Busch chose to remain in Europe (like his brother Adolf, he had exiled himself from Nazi Germany, but he had chosen to live in Denmark). Busch did indeed conduct several concerts with the Philharmonic during its centennial season (1941–42), and AT also returned to his old orchestra as guest conductor.

TG, NY, 12 MARCH 1941; TO FRIEDELIND WAGNER,
C/O UGARTE, TEATRO COLÓN, BUENOS AIRES; ORIG. ENG.;
NEILL THORNBORROW ARCHIVE, DÜSSELDORF

READ WONDERFUL NEWS YOUR SAFE ARRIVAL AFTER MANY MONTHS ANXIOUS
WAITING WILL SEE YOU IN MAY LOVE AND KISSES —
TOSCANINI

Friedelind had finally been released from detention as an enemy alien in Britain and
had made her way to Buenos Aires, thanks to AT (see his letter of 14 August 1940). ·
"See you in May": AT had accepted an offer to return to Buenos Aires in the spring to
conduct a few concerts with the Colón orchestra, bolstered by a few musicians he
brought along with him.

TYPED COPY OF LETTER, (NY); TO DAVID SARNOFF;
REVISED VERSION OF AN EARLIER DRAFT; ORIG. ENG.
(ALL ERRORS HAVE BEEN PRESERVED); NYPLTL

May 1, 1941.

My dear Sarnoff;
First of all I have to make my apology for having delayed so many times and
for a long while to answer your letter of February 24.

If at that time it was hard and painful for me to take a conclusive decision
about to accept or not your proposal to conduct the N.B.C. orchestra next season, to-day things are not at all changed and I feel that I am as before, in the
same state of mind. However I have come to an end. . . . . to make you and me
free of the nightmare which weighs upon us since February.

My old age tells me it is high time to withdraw from the militant scene of
Art. I am tired and a little exhausted. The tragedy which tears apart this
unhappy humanity saddens me so and makes me crazy and restless; how can I
find heart, will and strength in order to meet with new responsabilities and
new work? For me it is impossible, so that my dear David, don't be hesitating
any longer and make up your plans at once, for next season.

Later on, if my state of mind, health and rest will be improved and you will
believe my co-operation advantageous enough for the N.B.C. . . . . call me and
I shall be glad to resume once more my work. Believe me I am sad at heart to
renounce the joy of conducting that very fine orchestra you formed for me and
which gave me such great satisfaction.

My deepest gratitude for you will never be lessened. . . . . Many thanks for
the co-operation you gave me in my task as well as the facilities you placed at
my disposal.

Affectionally yours,
Arturo Toscanini.

A series of run-ins (described at length in my biography of AT) with the orchestra's
management had contributed to his decision to retire. His retirement, however, was

partial and temporary: during the 1941–42 season he was guest conductor with the orchestras of Philadelphia and New York and also gave five war-bond benefit concerts with the NBC Symphony Orchestra, whose new music director was Leopold Stokowski.

(NY); TO AM, (ROME?); THIS ITEM IS NOT PART OF THE REST OF THE AT–AM COLLECTION BUT BELONGS TO EC.

16 May 1941

[. . .] You are too poisoned by the atmosphere that surrounds you, you are all living now too much amid shame and dishonor, without showing any sign of rebellion, to be able to value people like me, who have remained and will remain above the mud, not to give it a worse name, that is drowning the Italians!!! [. . .] Excuse me, but <u>I don't believe you.</u> I believe only that you never understood me or valued me at my <u>real</u> and <u>true worth</u>! I was too far above you, and your eyesight deceived you. You mixed me up with the Molinaris, the Pizzettis, and other <u>animals</u> like them. I'll stop working. I've left the NBC for good. I'm too old, and I feel disgust at belonging to the family of artists, who, with a few exceptions, are not men but poor creatures, full of vanity. Life no longer holds any interest for me, and I would pray God to take it from me if it weren't for my firm, <u>never-diminished hope</u> to see the <u>delinquents</u> swept off the face of the earth before I go. [. . .] Live happily and healthily, if you can. [. . .]

(NY); P.S., AT; TO PAUL CRESTON; ORIG. ENG. (ALL ERRORS HAVE BEEN PRESERVED); PC; NYPLTL

Sep. <u>21—1941</u>

My dear <u>Mae. Creston</u>
Many thanks for your kindness to send me the orchestral score of your two <u>Choric Dances</u> which I love without reserve . . . I only have to ask you if you haven't any objection that I perform the second one in account of the economy of my program.

Some day I hope to perform both them.

With my cordial greetings believe me

Yours

<u>Arturo Toscanini</u>

In 1941 the Italo-American composer Paul Creston (originally Giuseppe Guttoveggio; 1906–85) had received the New York Music Critics' Circle Award for his Symphony no. 1; the Two Choric Dances, op. 17, date from 1938. AT performed the second of them with the NBC, Cincinnati, and Philadelphia orchestras in 1942 and 1943, and he performed *Frontiers,* op. 34, with the NBC Symphony Orchestra in 1943, the year of the work's composition.

Riverdale-on-Hudson
September 29, 1941

My very <u>dear Adolf,</u>
you have been <u>so quick</u> to send me the new Electric Metronome and I <u>so late</u> to acknowledge it and to thank you that I <u>feel ashamed.</u>

I want you to excuse me and to believe how happy you made me in sending to me that very useful instrument . . . I already ordered one for Horowitz . . . he will be certainly pleased . . . I embrace you friendly . . . remember me to dearest Frieda[.]

Yours
A. Toscanini

September 30—1941

My <u>dear Walker</u> .. Will you do me a great favor? . . . Ask to the librarian of the N.B.C. <u>score</u> and <u>orchestral parts</u> of the suite "**Piemonte**" by Leone Sinigaglia of my property, and make up a <u>package</u> of it, <u>ready to be sent</u> to <u>Tel-Aviv.</u> (Palestine.) To morrow morning mrs. Selden-Goth will come to your office to take that package . . . Excuse me if I give you such a trouble but be good once more again with me as you have ever been. Many and many thanks. Remember me to Madame Walker and believe me ever yours
Arturo Toscanini

Albert Walker, a physical education instructor, had been employed by NBC as a sort of bodyguard and factotum for AT. · For more on Sinigaglia and his Piedmont Suite, see the letter on pp. 81–82· Gisella Selden-Goth was active in musical life among the Jewish settlers in Palestine and later in the state of Israel.

Riverdale-on-Hudson, New York.
Saturday, October 11, 1941.

My very dear old friend Walter Price:
Of course you sent to me some time ago "The Human Situation" by William McNeill [*sic*] Dixon. I have read it and have deeply appreciated it twice . . . I am still going to read from chapters here and there from time to time and I get always more and more stupefied and astonished at the overwhelming knowledge of human mind and heart of this great thinker.

The book is always on my desk ready to be grasped when I want to obliterate the atrocious perfidy and trying to absorb my mind just a little while in a higher and more expirable air!

In those moments my thoughts are hovering very often around you. Thursday morning came quite unexpectedly the two volumes, first edition, of Newman's Wagner's life, together with your dear letter. What can I say? You are an angel and I am a devilish creature unworthy of your friendship. As an angel, you must be very good—so you will forgive my lacking, my deficiency, of expressing myself as I would wish, in order to reciprocate and in the same way the friendship you bestowed as a rare gift upon me so warmly and enthusiastically in the past years as in the present times. Maybe my poor knowledge of the English language hinders me more than inciting me to write to you so I feel quite miserable every time I cannot freely open my heart as I could do when it was possible to write to you in my own language.

My dear friend Walter Price, I need very badly to see you as soon as possible. I want to speak about something that is important to decide upon in a few days. Will you tell me when I can come to see you. As for me, any time is good. Do not write any letter but call me on the telephone. My number is Kingsbridge 9-7674. Remember me cordially to Madame and receive a huge embrace from

Your old friend,
Arturo Toscanini

Walter Price, a wealthy businessman, was on the New York Philharmonic's board of directors. He often wrote long, philosophical letters to AT. · W. MacNeile Dixon's *The Human Situation* was a collection of the Gifford Lectures delivered at the University of Glasgow from 1935 to 1937 and published in London in 1937. · Ernest Newman (1868–1959), the leading British music critic of his generation, was an admirer and acquaintance of AT. His four-volume life of Wagner, completed only in 1947, had begun to appear in 1933. · The matter that AT wanted to discuss with Price was probably the one referred to in the following letter.

(NY); P.S. WITH PHOTO OF AT; TO MARSHALL FIELD, (NY);
ORIG. ENG. (ALL ERRORS HAVE BEEN PRESERVED); NYPA

October 15—1941

My dear Marshall Field,

You cannot doubt that I have the greatest respect regard and happy association of memory with the Philharmonic-Symphony Society and I would have answered months ago to your kind invitation, but there have been complications that have made it difficult for me to determine the course I wished to pursue. To day I write you to say that I will be very glad to finish up the Centennial season with the Philharmonic for such time as you may allot not to be over two weeks. It would be much to my preference to start the season with you in 1942 (so important as the Centennial one) for say two weeks.

However, though, I leave the matter in your hands, and with my best wishes I remain

Yours sincerely

Arturo Toscanini

Marshall Field, a leading American businessman, had been president of the New York Philharmonic since the 1934–35 season and chairman of the board since 1938–39. In the end, AT conducted a complete Beethoven symphony cycle plus the *Missa Solemnis* and other pieces in a two-week, six-concert series with the Philharmonic in April–May 1942. He returned to the orchestra in October and November to conduct works by Berlioz, Wagner, Shostakovich, and others.

(NY); P.S., THE NATIONAL BROADCASTING COMPANY SYMPHONY ORCHESTRA/
ARTURO TOSCANINI/RCA BUILDING/NEW YORK;
TO LEOPOLD STOKOWSKI, (NY?); ORIG. ENG.
(ALL ERRORS HAVE BEEN PRESERVED); WOT

October 19, 1941

My dear <u>Stokowsky</u> [*sic*]
This afternoon you have vitrolized Franck's Symphony . . . Never in my long life I have heard such a brutal, bestial, ignobil, unmusical performance like yours—not even from you.

The Divine Art of Music too, has its own ganster like Hitler and Mussolini . . . Believe me, you are ready for mad-house or for jail . . . Hurry up!!!

Toscanini

Stokowski had conducted the Franck Symphony with the New York Philharmonic that day, and AT had evidently heard the performance on the radio. This letter was never sent.

(NY); P.S., RIVERDALE ON HUDSON, NEW YORK; TO OLIN DOWNES, (NY);
ORIG. ENG. (ALL ERRORS HAVE BEEN PRESERVED); ODUGA

October <u>28—1941</u>

My dear friend <u>Olin Downes</u>
I have just received the enclosed concerts-program with the love and greetings of all my english friends—all working with joy, faith, love and hope in their own fatherland—while that <u>nazi-sympathizer</u> <u>man</u> whom I do not even dare to call him by name lives here, in America protected, adulated and honoured by critics and american public . . . Truly, it is a very <u>farcical</u> and <u>deploring thing,</u> but so is life!!!

My dear Olin Downes, at the end of April 1915 I left Newyork and reached Italy just when she joined in the war (May 24)[.] Then I spent <u>five years</u> doing what my dear english friends are now doing . . . In that time through the Italian Governement I was invited to conduct the Boston Symphony Orchestra (1917) but my fatherland's love was stronger than the vanity to accept the honor they would bestow upon me and I declined the offer. To day I <u>cannot do</u> for Italy what I did in former times and with bleeding but resolute heart I say with Garibaldi: Cursed be the italian who would not step forward in the defense of Liberty. With all my friendly greetings believe me yours

<u>Arturo Toscanini</u>

The British conductor Sir Thomas Beecham (1879–1961), who is certainly the object of AT's attack in this letter, had defended Furtwängler's political position, recorded *The Magic Flute* in Berlin in 1938, and left Britain for the United States after war broke out. (It must be remembered that the United States was a nonbelligerent power until December 1941.) To deduce from this that Beecham was a Nazi sympathizer seems rather extreme—but AT was nothing if not an extremist.

TYPED COPY, RIVERDALE-ON-HUDSON, 30 OCTOBER 1941;
TO MAURICE VAN PRAAG, NEW YORK PHILHARMONIC; ORIG. ENG.; NYPA

My dear Van—
Will you be so kind as to convey my heartfelt thanks to my old friends, the members of the Philharmonic Orchestra for their cordial and affectionate telegram and tell them how glad I am to be once more their leader <u>though for a short while</u>!!! I always remember their devotion and exertion in order to obtain the best artistic achievement, and I am sure we will find in ourselves the enthusiasm of former times for attaining the same goal.

Affectionate greetings to all and many, many thanks to you, dear Van.

Yours
Arturo Toscanini

Maurice Van Praag was personnel manager and a member of the board of directors of the New York Philharmonic.

(NY); THE YEAR IS HARD TO READ: IT COULD BE 1940,
BUT 1941 SEEMS MORE LIKELY, ALSO JUDGING FROM THE CONTENT;
TO AM, (ROME?); THIS ITEM IS NOT PART OF THE REST
OF THE AT–AM COLLECTION, BUT BELONGS TO EC

25 <u>November 1941</u>[?]

Here, gathered together, are the last three of your lies (the worst ones, because the result of cynicism). They are the last of an uninterrupted series that's lasted for years! Shame!!! If my last letters didn't speak to your heart, it means that God, in creating your body sterile, also wanted your soul to be sterile. You have been properly chastised. I believe, in fact I'm sure, that we won't meet ever again during the few years of life left to me, but if the opposite were to happen <u>I'm not</u> the one who will have to blush!

Arturo Toscanini

(NY); TO CHARLES V. BANNER, BANDLEADER,
FORT MONMOUTH, NEW JERSEY; ORIG. ENG.; NYPLTL

January 5, 1942

Dear Mr. Banner:—

From Mr. Leonard Sharrow, who for several years played in the N.B.C. Symphony Orchestra under my baton, I learned there is a possibility of including him in your band. I would be very glad if Mr. Sharrow could find a place in the Army where his talents and professional ability could be exploited rightly. He is one of the best bassoon players and I hope you will enjoy having him in your band.

Thanking you in advance for anything you may be able to do for this artist.

With my best regards, I am
Very cordially yours
Arturo Toscanini

The NBC Symphony Orchestra's principal bassoon had been drafted, and AT helped to arrange for him to spend his war service in a military band.

TYPED COPY OF TG, (NY), 25 APRIL 1942;
TO DIMITRI MITROPOULOS, CYRUS NORTHROP MEMORIAL AUDITORIUM,
MINNEAPOLIS, MINNESOTA; ORIG. ENG.; NYPLTL

If during your engagement with Philharmonic it will be necessary to have guest conductor with your splendid orchestra will you kindly recommend to your Board in my name Hans Wilhelm Steinberg? STOP. You may rest assured that he will make both of us proud to have recommended such a distinguished musician and very able colleague. STOP. I count on your cooperation. Grazie et [*sic*] cordiali saluti.

Arturo Toscanini

Mitropoulos was at that time music director of the Minneapolis Symphony; AT was recommending Steinberg to be guest conductor with that orchestra while Mitropoulos was in New York (December 1942–January 1943) as guest conductor with the Philharmonic.

8 <u>May 1942</u>

My <u>adored Wally</u>
my <u>beloved Ela</u> [Emanuela]
<u>dearest Emanuele</u>

You will be pleased to know that <u>all of us</u> are well—I myself have had <u>more than adequate</u> proof of it in recent days. At my tender age, I conducted <u>six</u> concerts in two weeks with the Philharmonic—a <u>Beethoven Festival.</u> The <u>nine</u> <u>Symphonies</u>—<u>5 Overtures</u>—<u>Triple Concerto,</u> and <u>Missa Solemnis.</u> So you see that I'm in good health. My body doesn't suffer, but my soul, oh! the soul is something else!—Let's keep loving each other and hoping to embrace each other again soon. I know, I feel that it will happen. My dear, beautiful, good Wally, I kiss you, and I kiss Ela, whom I would like to see together with Dedè and Sonia, and I embrace Emanuele. And Enrico and Ida? Embrace them for me.

Your <u>papa</u>

I do not know how this letter was smuggled to Wally, since the United States and Italy were now enemy powers.

DRAFT(?), NY, N.D. BUT CIRCA 20 JUNE 1942; P.S., THE NATIONAL BROADCASTING COMPANY SYMPHONY ORCHESTRA/ARTURO TOSCANINI/ RCA BUILDING/NEW YORK; TO LEOPOLD STOKOWSKI, (NY?); ORIG. ENG. (ALL ERRORS HAVE BEEN PRESERVED); NYPLTL

My dear <u>Stokowski</u>   I do not want nor will attempt in any way to refute the arguments you display in your letter in order to prove and claim your right to give the first radio performance of Shostakowithc [*sic*] Seventh symphony.

During my long career I never urged the honor to conduct first performances of any composer! I admire Shostakowitch [*sic*] music but I don't feel such a frenzy love for it like you—Time ago I had promise to receive the new score as soon as it arrives from Russia . . . In effect two members of the Am-Rus-music corporation brought to me the film and some days later the first copy of the score . . . As you can imagine I eagerly looked into it for a few days. At once I was deeply taken by it beauty—its antifascist meaning and I have to confess [to] you also, by the greatest desire to perform it.

Don't you think, dear Stokowski, it would be very interesting for every body and yourself too, to hear the old Italian conductor (one of the first artist, who strenuously fought against fascism) to play this work of a young Russian antinazi composer? I have not any drop of Slavonic blood into my veins—I am only a true and genuine Latin!—May be I am not an intense interpreter of this kind of music but I am sure I can conduct it simply with love and honesty. Beside that this performance will have for me to-day a special meaning.

Think over it only a few minutes—and you will convince yourself not to give much importance to the arguments you display in your letter.

   With my best and cordial greetings believe me sincerely

Your

Arturo Toscanini

AT had agreed to conduct the American radio premiere of Shostakovich's Seventh ("Leningrad") Symphony with the NBC Symphony Orchestra, but Stokowski wrote to AT to request the privilege for himself. This was AT's reply.

DRAFT(?); (NY); P.S., AT/RIVERDALE-ON-HUDSON/NEW YORK;
TO LEOPOLD STOKOWSKI, (NY?); ORIG. ENG.
(ALL ERRORS HAVE BEEN PRESERVED); NYPLTL

June <u>25—1942</u>

My dear <u>Stokowski</u>—Your letter of Wednesday troubled me very much because I saw in it the complet result of some misunderstanding . . . May be my poor English language has certainly been the cause, and I am sorry for it.

   When weeks ago I told you that I planned a Brahms Festival for the next season at the N.B.C. I never intended to exclude for ever to take into consideration modern music. I only wanted to let you know my wish in order to avoid we have to meet in our programs with the same music and composers. I don't know if you are aware that in the season 1938–39 at the N.B.C. I renounced to be the first interpreter of Shostakowitch 5th Symphony because of my scanty interest in it—and I want to repeat again that this time after a careful reading of the Seventh I felt the strongest sympathy and emotion for this special work so I urged the N.B.C. to have it performed the first time by me—Try to understand me, my dear Stokowski "only because of the special meaning of this Seventh symphony["] I asked to be its first interpreter. Happily, you are much younger than me and Shostakowitch will not stop writing new symphonies[.] You will certainly have all the opportunities you like to perform them . . . Be sure you will never find me again in your way. In the interest of our friendly collaboration I believe you should prepare, at your early convenience an outline of your programs, so I shall adapt mine in accordance.

   With my most cordial greetings believe me sincerely

Your

A Toscanini

Stokowski and AT were to be coconductors of the NBC Symphony Orchestra for the following two seasons. · AT did conduct the American premiere of Shostakovich's Seventh Symphony on 19 July 1942.

(NY); P.S., AT; TO MORTON GOULD, (NY?); ORIG. ENG.
(ALL ERRORS HAVE BEEN PRESERVED); MORTON GOULD ARCHIVES

September 1—1942

My dear <u>Mae. Gould</u>

Have you any objection if I perform your Lincoln's [*sic*] Legend in my first concert at the N.B.C. on Novembre the first?

I don't know, nor I can't say to you if the music is beautiful or good—clever or well written—I leave these things to the sterile critics, incapable of procreation but never doubting about their wisdom!

I only know, and I like to tell you, that at my first looking on your score I was much taken and fascinated with the incisive and penetrating musical strokes of your Lincoln's Legend.

Isn't enough?

I would like to see you once before starting the rehearsals . . . Will you give me, at your convenience later in October, an appointment?

Many cordial greetings from your
Arturo <u>Toscanini</u>

Excuse my poor English . . . <u>but</u>. . . . I do <u>my best.</u>

AT did indeed conduct the *Lincoln Legend* by the American composer Morton Gould (1913–96) on the date suggested here. It was his only performance of any of Gould's music.

(NY), N.D. BUT 26 APRIL 1943; P.S., WAVE HILL/
RIVERDALE-ON-HUDSON; TO WYT, (MI); EC

My <u>dear Wally</u>—I'm so sorry that you received exaggerated news about my health! It was nothing but a bit of flu, which kept me from doing a couple of concerts—but almost immediately I began my usual and not yet diminished activity again, and yesterday, April 25, I gave the last concert, with Volodia. Mamma, Wanda, and Walter, like me, are all very well, and so are Walfredo and Sonia, who are both real loves. To say that our thoughts are with all of you at every moment is to say very little; not a day passes without our making vows for a quick end to this appalling tragedy that has struck poor humanity. My dear Wally, when will I be able to embrace you again, and Emanuela with you, and everyone, everyone? I kiss you with infinite tenderness and I embrace everyone with affection.

Your Papa

[Brief greetings written by Carla, Wanda, and Walter Toscanini are attached.]

In 1942 the Toscaninis had to leave the Villa Pauline; they moved into the nearby Wave Hill house, which belonged to the Freeman family and which had formerly been a residence of Theodore Roosevelt, Mark Twain, and other celebrities. · This note, like the letter of 8 May 1942, was smuggled into Italy; although AT refers to the "appalling tragedy that has struck humanity" he carefully avoids specific political references, so as not to create trouble for Wally if the letter were intercepted. Nor does he mention that the "last concert" of the season, "with Volodia" (i.e., Vladimir Horowitz), had been a benefit event that had raised $10 million in U.S. war bonds. Similar considerations are true of the next letter.

(NY); P.S., AT; TO WYT, (RIPALTA GUERINA); EC

Monday—<u>17 May 43</u>

My <u>adored Wally,</u>
I finished my concerts a few weeks ago and I am resting in this delight-ful Riverdale that reminds me so much of our dear Isolino, although in a quieter way.

I'll conduct concerts again from time to time (June 20, July 18 and 25, September 19), but only benefit concerts, because the real musical season will begin on October 31. As you can see, my activities haven't decreased at all, despite my 76 years. It's a sign that the good Lord (or someone on his behalf) is protecting me, keeping me in good health and with the ever more fervent hope that we'll see each other again much sooner than we had believed. Dear Wally, you can well imagine from the anxiety that you yourself feel for us how many times my thoughts—or rather our thoughts (because Mamma, Walter, and Wanda don't love you any less than I do)—reach out to you, eager to know how your lives are going. But, I repeat, I hope that we'll be together again much sooner than we had believed. At this point, events will close in, and are already closing in. We must withstand a little longer still the appalling disas-ter that has struck the world. The fifth act of the horrible tragedy is unfolding. The curtain will fall at last. Hearts will be uplifted.—And our dear Emanuela? How all of us would like to see her! Sonia and Walfredo are real loves. Still beautiful, very lively, and good.

I'm so happy about the <u>"Camp"</u> that you've created. Brava! You're a marvel of goodness and wisdom. And I'm happy not only for you, but for our relatives and friends. I embrace and kiss you with infinite tenderness, as I embrace and kiss all the relatives and friends.

Mamma, too, will write to you.

<u>Wholly your papa</u>

[Single sentences of greeting added by Carla and Wanda Toscanini.]

Life in Italian cities was becoming increasingly difficult because of Allied bombing raids, food shortages, and other war-related problems. Most people who were able to get out did so, and Wally went to the estate at Ripalta Guerina, near Crema, with Emanuela, the Polos, Fosca Leonardi, and other relatives and friends.

ON 13 SEPTEMBER 1943 THE EDITORIAL PAGE OF *LIFE* MAGAZINE WAS OCCUPIED BY AN ARTICLE ENTITLED "TO THE PEOPLE OF AMERICA" AND SIGNED BY AT; IT WAS THE ONLY EXTENSIVE PUBLIC DECLARATION HE EVER WROTE — AND IT WAS ABOUT POLITICS, NOT MUSIC. BASED ON THE INFORMATION AVAILABLE TO ME IN 1978, WHEN MY BIOGRAPHY OF AT WAS FIRST PUBLISHED, I STATED THAT HE HAD WRITTEN THE ARTICLE DIRECTLY IN ENGLISH, ON HIS OWN. IN THE SPRING OF 2000, HOWEVER, I CAME ACROSS MATERIAL THAT DEMONSTRATED INCONTROVERTIBLY THAT THE ARTICLE HAD ORIGINALLY BEEN INTENDED AS A LETTER TO PRESIDENT ROOSEVELT AND THAT THE FIRST DRAFTS HAD BEEN PREPARED FOR AT BY THE ITALIAN HISTORIANS IN EXILE GAETANO SALVEMINI AND GIORGIO LA PIANA, WHO WERE BOTH TEACHING AT HARVARD UNIVERSITY AT THE TIME. THEY KNEW THAT THEIR BELIEFS AND AT'S COINCIDED PERFECTLY, AND THEY WANTED THE LETTER TO APPEAR OVER HIS SIGNATURE BECAUSE HIS FAME WAS MUCH GREATER THAN THEIRS.

WHAT PROMPTED THE LETTER? A FEW WEEKS EARLIER — ON 25 JULY — IN THE WAKE OF THE ALLIED INVASION OF SICILY, THE GRAND COUNCIL OF FASCISM IN ROME HAD VOTED TO DEPOSE MUSSOLINI AS PRIME MINSTER OF ITALY; HIS SUCCESSOR, MARSHALL PIETRO BADOGLIO, HAD ANNOUNCED THAT ITALY WOULD CONTINUE TO FIGHT ALONGSIDE NAZI GERMANY. MANY ITALIANS ASSUMED, HOWEVER — AND CORRECTLY — THAT THE NEW GOVERNMENT WAS SECRETLY NEGOTIATING EITHER AN ARMISTICE OR A SURRENDER WITH THE ANGLO-AMERICANS. AT AND OTHER LEADING ANTI-FASCIST ITALIAN EXILES WERE DISTRESSED THAT THE ALLIES HAD, IN EFFECT, RECOGNIZED THE LEGITIMACY OF THE GOVERNMENT OF BADOGLIO, WHO HAD SUPPORTED MUSSOLINI'S MILITARISM AND HAD NOW BEEN CHOSEN AS PRIME MINISTER BY KING VICTOR EMMANUEL III. IN THE OPINION OF THE EXILES, THE KING HAD CONTENTEDLY LEFT ITALY IN MUSSOLINI'S HANDS FOR NEARLY TWENTY-ONE YEARS AND WAS THEREFORE AT LEAST AS CULPABLE OF FASCIST CRIMES AS THE FASCISTS THEMSELVES. IN THEIR LETTER TO PRESIDENT ROOSEVELT, THE EXILES STATED THEIR HOPES AND FEARS FOR ITALY'S IMMEDIATE FUTURE, AND THEY TRIED — AS THE TEXT ILLUSTRATES — TO INFLUENCE ALLIED POLICY TOWARD THEIR NATIVE COUNTRY.

THE TOSCANINI LEGACY AT THE NEW YORK PUBLIC LIBRARY CONTAINS SEVERAL VERSIONS OF THIS DECLARATION AND MANY DOCUMENTS ABOUT IT; OF THESE ITEMS, THE MOST IMPORTANT ARE THE ORIGINAL TYPED DRAFT (ON SALVEMINI'S STATIONERY) THAT LA PIANA SENT, WITH AN ACCOMPANYING LETTER, FROM CAMBRIDGE, MASSACHUSETTS, ON 14 AUGUST 1943, TO WALTER TOSCANINI IN NEW YORK CITY, FOR AT TO EXAMINE AND CHANGE AS HE SAW FIT, AND TWO SUBSEQUENT DRAFTS IN AT'S HAND. THE FOLLOWING ITEM IS A TRANSCRIPTION OF THE ORIGINAL DOCUMENT AS IT WAS DRAFTED BY THE TWO HISTORIANS, BUT WITH ALTERATIONS: THE UNBRACKETED, BOLDFACE DETAILS WERE ADDED BY AT IN HIS FINAL DRAFT; THE BRACKETED, BOLDFACE DETAILS WERE DELETED BY HIM. FEW OF THE CHANGES ALTER THE DOCUMENT'S SUBSTANCE; SOME MERELY MAKE THE ENGLISH CLUMSIER, OTHERS MAKE THE STATEMENT MORE DRAMATIC. ORIG. ENG; NYPLTL

Newyork August 24—1943

My dear Mr. President:

At this moment[,] when the destiny of Italy depends so largely upon the decisions and policies of the United States Government, I am taking the liberty of writing to you, **my dear Mr. President,** because of my love for **both** Italy and the United States and my faith and devotion to the **universal** ideals of justice and freedom for all peoples of the world.

I am an old artist who has been among the first to denounce Fascism to the world. I feel **and believe** I can act as [an] interpreter of **the soul of** the Italian people—that people whose voice has been choked for more than twenty years but, thank God, {is now crying out for liberty in} just now is shouting for peace and liberty into the streets and squares of Italy, and defying everything even the martial law. A people like this deserve [*sic*] the respect of every man whose brain is still able to discern between good and bad . . . A people like this must be helped in a friendly way, with understanding, wisdom, and exact conviction . . . {It is with deep emotion and deliberate mind that I convey to you} And it is with moved heart and deliberate mind that I try to convey to you, my dear President, what all Italians, worthy to be so called, think{,} and would say to you {were they free to express their minds and hearts} if they were free to express their minds and souls.

They would say:

My dear Mr. President—{The King and the Badoglio government} the king of Italy and Badoglio, both despicable men, are bound by the alliance with Germany, which they endorsed jointly with Mussolini. {They cannot dissociate themselves from that alliance and conclude peace without dishonoring themselves and their country. They cannot dismantle the militaristic and fascist clique in which they were participants. Only a revolution of the people can put in power in Italy men who have no links with the past and who can without dishonor bring back their country into the comity of free and self-respecting nations.} They cannot be dissociated in any way from the militaristic and fascist clique: They cannot be the representatives of the italian people, so, they cannot conclude peace with the Allies in the name of Italy so betrayed by them.

Italy will certainly have a revolution as a result of the current war[. Either the Allies favor, help and guide it, or they endeavor to stifle it. The Allied attitude will determine whether this revolution will result in an orderly democratic government or in anarchy and chaos. If the Italian revolution is to result in a democratic government the Allies should not discourage the democratic elements currently arrayed against Badoglio and the King. They should also announce wise and just peace terms to the people of Italy.], either the Allies will favor and help or hinder it. The Allies attitude will determine whether this revolution will or not result in an orderly democratic governement [*sic*] . . . Should this revolution result in an orderly democratic governement [*sic*], as we hope, it will be necessary for the Allies to lend support to all democratic elements currently arrayed against the king and Badoglio, offering to the reborn free Italy—along with the unconditional surrender of the Italian armed forces—equitable peace terms as tu [*sic*] include: the respect of the integrity of the national territory of Italy as it was before 1922 (the march of [*sic*] Rome) obtained through the common efforts of Italy-France England and the United States, together with their Allies in the first World war.

{These peace terms, along with the unconditional surrender of the armed forces, should include:

1) The respect of the national integrity of Italy from the Brenner Pass to

Sicily and from Venezia Giulia to Sardinia.} What a crime it would be, my dear Mr. President, to {sever} separate Sicily and Sardinia, Trieste and {Istria} Venezia Giulia from Italy! {Such a crime} It would be like driving nails into the living flesh of Italy. We shudder to think of it.!!

{2)} In our opinion it will be wise for the Allies to give fair and Equitable treatment {of} to democratic Italy (as an equal member of the free nations) in {all} matters concerning access to raw materials, colonies, {and} emigration etc. etc. and also to give

{3)} Economic assistance to the new {democratic} governement [sic] to enable it to carry the burden of {rehabilitating the country} the rehabilitation of Italy and to cooperate in the reconstruction of European society. (This number might be omitted since an artist is not expected to be interested in economic affairs)

{These conditions should be announced as soon as possible and before armistice negotiations for unconditional surrender are opened.

The unconditional surrender of the Italian armed forces will be considered honorable by the Italians only if it is stated that Italian volunteers will be allowed to fight against the Nazis side by side with the Allies under the Italian flag and under conditions substantially similar to those of the Fighting French. By so doing many American and Italian lives could be saved. In this way, my dear Mr. President, Italy will become again an element of democratic order in the commonwealth of nations.} We think, my dear Mr. President, that these suggestions should be made known independently of the unconditional surrender as soon as it is possible in order to give to the Italians faith, courage and entusiasm [sic] to act and to fight together with the Allies and so to save many and many American lives.

The unconditional surrender of the Italian armed forces will be considered honorable by us italians if it will be permitted to our volunteers to fight against the hated nazis under Italian flag and with conditions substantially similar to those of the fighting French. . . .

In this way, my dear Mr. President, Italy will become again an element of democratic order amongst the family of European Nations{.}

{We Italians have been the first to suffer the oppression of a tyrranical [sic] gang of outlaws. But thousands of men and women have given their lives and shed blood, sweat and tears to resist tyranny under the indifferent eyes of the world. Our sufferings give us the right to ask that the whole Italian people should not pay for the guilt of the Fascist criminals and of those who all over the world aided and abetted them.} Do not forget that we Italians have been the first to endure the oppression of a tyrannical gang of criminals, supported by that "faint-hearted and degenerate King" of Italy—but we have never willingly submitted to them . . . Countless thousands of men and women in Italy shed blood, met imprisonment and death in order to strive against that horde of delinquents, enduring also the apathy and indifference of the world then in admiration of Mussolini.

Our suffering, my dear Mr. President gives us the right to ask that the whole Italian people should not pay for te [*sic*] guilt of the fascist regime. . . .

[Italians expect to regain their liberty and to rid themselves not only of the Fascist regime but also of all dictatorships, be they military or clerical. This is why they are willing to suffer the death and destruction brought about by the march forward of the Allied armies in which thousands of Americans of Italian descent are involved.

We are confident in the justice and equanimity of the American people. It is with this confidence and because with equal devotion I love both Italy and this great American republic of which you are the leader chosen by the people, that I have tried, my dear Mr. President, to express what the Italians think and would say to you.]

We Italians are willing to suffer the inevitable death and destruction which accompanies the march forward of the Allies armies, in which thousands of Americans of Italian descent are included, because we expect to regain our liberty and to rid ourselves not only of the hated fascist regime but also of all dictatorship—be they military or clerical—and we are entirely confident in the justice, equanimity and understanding of the American people. And it is with the same confidence that I tried to express what the Italians think and would say to you, my dear Mr. President, if they were free to open their minds and souls, for I love my dear Italy and with equal devotion I love this great American Republic of which you are the leader chosen by the people.

With my best regards and deep respect believe me

Yours

<u>Arturo Toscanini</u>

I have not found information that would explain when and why the decision was made to convert the letter to Roosevelt into an open letter "To the People of America," to be printed in *Life.* In any case, the final version, as it appeared in print, follows herewith. The anti-Church reference to a "clerical" dictatorship is said to have been removed by the magazine's editors, whereas the reference to the "faint-hearted and degenerate king," taken from Shakespeare's Henry VI, was—as has already been shown—added by AT to the historians' original draft. *Life* appeared on the newsstands well before its official, printed publication date, which means that almost immediately after AT's editorial went to press and at virtually the same moment that it appeared, Italy officially surrendered to the Allies and the German occupation of the northern half of the country began.

LIFE, 13 SEPTEMBER 1943; OPEN LETTER ON THE EDITORIAL PAGE; ORIG. ENG.

TO THE PEOPLE OF AMERICA
by Arturo Toscanini

At this moment when the destiny of Italy depends so largely upon the decision and policy of the United States Government, I attempt to present a plea for my fellow Italians, addressing it to the American people together with the leader chosen by them, President Franklin Delano Roosevelt, because I think you are well aware of my love for Italy and the United States and my faith and devotion to the ideals of justice and freedom for all peoples of the world.

In presenting this plea I am conscious of the need for all of us to build a just and lasting peace, and that our common aim is to prepare it, and to attain it at the moment required.

I am an old artist who has been among the first to denounce Fascism to the world. I feel and believe that I can act as interpreter of the soul of the Italian people—those people whose voice has been choked for more than 20 years, but, thanks to God, just now is shouting for peace and liberty in the streets and squares of Italy, defying everything, even martial law. A people such as this deserves the respect of every man who is still able to discern between good and bad. A people such as this must be helped in a most friendly way, with clear understanding, exact conviction, and full consciousness of how to deal with them. And it is with moved heart and deliberate mind that I try to convey to you American people what all Italians, worthy of being so called, think and would say if they were free to communicate with you and to open their minds and hearts.

They would like to say: People of America, we are not your enemies and never have been your enemies in the past. We were forced into the role of "enemy" by a vicious and wicked man, Mussolini, who betrayed us for more than 20 years. We never wanted to fight against you, and today we do not want to do it. Only the King of Italy and his bootlicker, Badoglio, both despicable men, are your enemies and want to carry on this war. They are bound by the alliance with Germany, which they endorsed jointly with Mussolini. They cannot be dissociated in any way from the militarist and fascist clique. They cannot be the representatives of the Italian people; they cannot in any way conclude peace with the Allies in the name of Italy, so betrayed by them.

Italy will certainly have a revolution as a result of the current war; the Allies will either favor and help it, or hinder it. The Allies' attitude will determine whether the revolution will, or will not, result in an orderly democratic government.

Should this revolution result in an orderly democratic government, as we hope, it will be necessary for the Allies to support all democratic elements currently arrayed against the King and Badoglio, offering to the reborn free Italy—along with the unconditional surrender of the Italian armed forces—equitable peace terms, to include:

Respect for the integrity of the national territory of Italy as it was established before 1922 (the march on Rome) through the strenuous efforts of Italy, France, England, the United States, and their Allies of the First World War.

What a crime it would be to separate Sicily and Sardinia, Trieste and Venezia Giulia from Italy! It would be like driving knives into the living flesh of Italy. We shudder just to think of it.

In our opinion it would be wise to give fair and equitable treatment to democratic Italy (as an equal member of the family of free nations) in matters concerning access to raw materials, colonies, emigration, etc., and also to give economic assistance to the new government, for the purpose of carrying the burden of the rehabilitation of Italy and cooperating in establishing "a just postwar society of men and nations."

We think, people of America, that these suggestions should be made known independently of the demand for "unconditional surrender" as soon as possible, in order to give to the Italians faith, courage and enthusiasm to act and to fight together with the Allies, and so to save many, many American lives.

We ask that the Allies permit our volunteers to fight against the hated Nazis under the Italian flag with conditions substantially similar to those of the Free French. Thus alone can we Italians visualize the unconditional surrender of our armed forces without injury to our sense of honor. Give us a chance to fight along with you in your just cause which is also our own cause.

In this way, people of America, Italy will become again an element of democratic order among the family of nations.

Do not forget that we Italians have been the first to endure the oppression of a tyrannical gang of criminals, supported by that "fainthearted and degenerate King" of Italy—but that we have never willingly submitted to them. Countless thousands of men and women in Italy shed blood, met imprisonment and death, striving fiercely against that horde of criminals, enduring also the apathy and indifference of the world then full of admiration for Mussolini.

Our own suffering, people of America, gives us the right to ask the Allies that the Italian people must not pay for the guilt of the fascist regime. We are willing and ready to suffer the inevitable death and destruction which accompanies the march forward of the Allied Armies, in which thousands of Americans of Italian descent are included; for we expect to regain our liberty and to get rid not only of the hated fascist regime but also of all dictatorships—be they of a military or any other nature—entirely confident in the justice, equity and understanding of the American people.

And it is with the same confidence that I have tried to make clear what the Italians think and would say if they were free to communicate with you and to open their minds and hearts. For I love Italy, and with equal devotion I love you sons of this great American Republic which, together with the United Nations, will soon put an end to despotic wars, and bring into the renovate world a bright and more breathable atmosphere of freedom and peace.

STATEMENT (TO THE PRESS?); (NY); ORIG. ENG; PC; NYPLTL

I am overwhelmed with joy: The news of the surrender of the armed force of Italy came so suddenly that my thoughts are like waves in a stormy sea: I can only say: Blessed Italy at last you are free to join the Allies who are struggling to keep alive the flame of liberty in the world.

Arturo Toscanini
September 8—1943

(NY); P.S. AT; TO COUNT CARLO SFORZA, (NY?); NEGATIVE PC;
ANTHONY CAPRARO COLLECTION, IMMIGRATION HISTORY RESEARCH
CENTER, UNIVERSITY OF MINNESOTA

---

1 October 1943

My dear Count Sforza

From this moment on you may consider me a traitor to my country! Not even to save Italy could I compromise with the people who have shamefully betrayed her for more than twenty years! I could not even speak to or look at those two wretches [the king and Badoglio]. I feel sorry for you. Our palates are very different. Your politics may be intelligent and shrewd, but I condemn them and despise them—and I declare myself against you and the Allied government, which has fully demonstrated its complete ignorance and ineptitude in its understanding of the honest and simple Italian soul. Their policy regarding Italy has been a shameful fiasco—and, as Dorothy Thompson says, completely bankrupt. Their "unconditional surrender" is ridiculous. And now they want to put the anti-fascist forces into the hands of those who have betrayed them for long and, alas! such sorrowful years! No, dear Count Sforza, I don't believe—and I am sure of this—that Italians, the real ones, the good ones who, like me, would give their lives to save their country from the tragic scourge against which the struggle is being waged, can be happy with your attitude. I don't believe it. The Allied government may be happy with it, but that has nothing to do with us. There can be no half measures at this moment! One must stand on one side of the fence or the other! Either for the king and Badoglio or against them—there is no other way. No amount of chatter, however intelligent, can save our wretched country; only arms. Later, when the war is won, the Italian people will choose the form of government they believe best. Then you will truly be of great use—but for pity's sake, don't let yourself be taken in by the Allies' disastrous policy. Excuse my outburst, but I could not restrain myself—I would have exploded with anger and sorrow.

Believe me always your

Arturo Toscanini

Count Carlo Sforza (1872–1952) had been foreign minister in one of Italy's last pre-Fascist governments, went into self-imposed exile during the Fascist period, and was again foreign minister after the war (1947–51).

DRAFT, (NY), N.D. BUT PROBABLY NOVEMBER OR DECEMBER 1943;
TO ARMANDO BORGHI, (NY?); NYPLTL

It was fate that made my second concert [7 November 1943] coincide with the memorable date of the 26th anniversary of the Russian Revolution. Today I learn from you that it was also the 56th anniversary of the death of Eugène Pottier—and on it, I conducted for the first time the International Anthem. Could I have been any luckier? Thank you for having sent me in advance the Adunato dei Refrattari, with your "The Sources of the 'International.' " Magnificent. Moving. Excellent, Mr. Borghi. I thank you with all my heart for your dear offering.

Armando Borghi was a well-known Italian anarchist who had found refuge in the United States (thanks largely to Salvemini and AT) and who contributed to radical Italian-American periodicals, such as the Adunato dei refrattari, in New York. · Eugène Pottier had written the words to the "Internationale," which had become the worldwide socialist anthem (music by Degeyter); AT had used the piece to open his NBC Symphony Orchestra concert of 7 November 1943—an all-Russian program, in tribute to America's ally (for a while), the Soviet Union.

November 27—1943

My <u>very dear Bruno Walter</u>

Thank you for your most affectionate words, immensely dear to my heart as a father. Yes, Wally and her little daughter have been in Switzerland, and specifically Lucerne, since <u>November 13.</u> When the bad news with Wally's photograph appeared in the "Post" newspaper, we already knew the good news, but for months my heart was telling me that something nasty was developing. Too much time had gone by without direct or indirect news! And you, my dear fellow, how are you? I hope that you will soon resume your work at the Metropolitan, and I also hope to see you again with your wife and Lotte here in Riverdale. I <u>ardently</u> desire it. Think about it, and tell me when we can spend a few hours together! Remember me to your wife and to Lotte. I embrace you cordially.

Your friend

<u>Arturo Toscanini</u>

Shortly after the Germans occupied northern Italy, Wally learned that she was to be arrested and probably deported to a concentration camp; she and Emanuela undertook a dangerous nighttime escape on foot and by horse-drawn cart across the border into Switzerland, where they spent the remainder of the war. The *New York Post* had mistakenly reported her arrest, and this of course worried many of the Toscaninis' American friends. · Lotte was Bruno Walter's older daughter.

30 <u>November 1943</u>

My <u>adored Wally</u>

The terrible nightmare that oppressed us for so many months has finally vanished, and we are again breathing somewhat normally. You are with your and our dear Emanuela, in a free and welcoming country. God be praised!!! For months we had a presentiment of what was happening. In addition, it was a real miracle that the <u>bad piece of news</u> given by the newspapers arrived after the **good one,** otherwise we would have gone mad. I'm sorry that you've had to separate from your husband, our relatives, and our friends, but they weren't and aren't as precious a prey as you for those jackals. I'm absolutely certain that they won't be bothered. One thing that makes me happy is to know that you're safe and in precisely the village where we spent happy days, amid people who adore me and where we said good-bye to each other. My thoughts can easily see you, follow you, be near you—and I have a real need for that— as you can well understand—after more than four years of enforced, sorrowful distance. My dear, my adored Wally, I'm beginning to see a <u>glimmer of</u>

light, however overshadowed by the immense obscurity that surrounds this appalling tragedy. But a ray of hope lights up my heart. A mysterious voice tells me that we'll see each other again, and soon!—You can imagine the interest in you on the part of all our friends—everyone feared the worst—when the bad news came, no one knew, as we knew, that you were already safe. We now hope to have news directly from you. To see your handwriting, to hear your words will be sweeter and more convincing than all the indirect news. Mamma will add a few lines to mine, and so will Wanda and Walter, too. Everyone is well. I'm surprised at myself. I _work_ and I _work_—and it seems that I'm still managing well. At my tender age, God is still giving me the strength and the desire to work, to get angry with my orchestra, which means that the blood is still running quickly enough through my veins. Next Sunday (5 December) I'll conduct my sixth concert. Then I have a twelve-week truce, when I'll be replaced by _Stokowski_—still a clown (more so than ever, in fact). I'll begin again on March 6, for six weeks. Thus I'll end the NBC's winter season. Royal has behaved adorably with us. He got your news directly from friends in Switzerland and sent it to the State Department in Washington, which, in turn, communicated it to us. We really owe him a lot.

As you may or may not know, Walter was called to New York from Camden, and he is very happy as an NBC employee. He lives near us in a magnificent little house facing the Hudson, with a garden that makes him and Dedè happy; Dedè is a love of a boy! Sonia, on the other hand, spends weekdays in a convent run by nuns and often comes here to Riverdale to spend the weekend. There, in a jumble, is some of our news. Imagine our joy at knowing that you and your daughter are far from that inferno where those scoundrels still reign, but not for long, we hope!!!

I kiss you, I embrace you with my heart beating fast. I hug and kiss that love of an Emanuela.

God bless you, forever!

your <u>old Papa.</u>

John Royal was NBC's vice president. · Walter had been working for RCA in Camden, New Jersey, before being transferred to New York. It was at this point that he began to look after his father in a way that the aging and increasingly infirm Carla was no longer able to do.

ON 5 JUNE 1944, THE HONORABLE VITO MARCANTONIO, A DEMOCRATIC CONGRESSMAN FROM NEW YORK CITY, SENT A LETTER TO AT TO ASK THAT HE TESTIFY BEFORE A SUBCOMMITTEE OF THE HOUSE OF REPRESENTATIVES IN FAVOR OF REESTABLISHING NORMAL DIPLOMATIC RELATIONS BETWEEN THE UNITED STATES AND ITALY. A DRAFT OF A REPLY WAS TYPEWRITTEN ON 11 JUNE 1944; IT CONTAINS MANY PENCILED ANNOTATIONS BY WRT THE FOLLOWING DOCUMENT IS A TRANSCRIPT OF A CARBON COPY OF AN UNSIGNED TYPED LETTER, WHICH, I IMAGINE, WAS DRAFTED JOINTLY BY WALTER AND AT BUT WHICH CLEARLY STATES AT'S OPINIONS ON THE SUBJECT. ORIG. ENG.; NYPLTL

The Honorable Vito Marcantonio
Congress of the United States
House of Representatives
Washington, D. C.
Dear Sir:

I thank you very much for your letter of June 5th and for your invitation to appear as a witness at the hearing to testify in favor of the Resolution in which you request that the President of the United States establish friendly diplomatic relations with my country—Italy. Since I am not an American Citizen but an Italian, I do not believe that I can appear as a witness at that hearing. Also some previous engagements make it difficult for me to leave New York at the present time. Nevertheless I should like to tell you how grateful I am to you, who are a representative of the American people, for taking the initiative in this action which I anticipated in my open letter to the people of America, printed in LIFE in September 1943, and sponsored with some other Italians in a recent Italian Manifesto published by LIFE on June 12th, of which I enclose a copy.

I want to stress to you in the strongest way possible that until now the Italian people have not been free to have a democratically chosen government representative of every political current in Italy. In Rome the anti-fascist parties yesterday made the first step towards this goal, refusing to swear allegiance to the Monarchy. But still the House of Savoy is there and the lieutenancy is a legal trick which in some ways is worse than the situation which was created before. The King of Italy refuses to abdicate, and by maintaining the title of the head of the House of Savoy, he still maintains all the power and authority, because also today in the feudal rule of the Royal family, the head of the family is the only one who has despotic powers over all the members of the family, and whose will is law.

I do not want to tell you, who are an American Citizen and have been brought up with the love of liberty, how to hate tyranny and despotism. I am an old man and I can stand as a witness that the monarchy in Italy has always tried to oppose any social reform or any progressive attempt to better and improve the life of the worker and farmer in Italy, and that all the progressive reforms that were introduced in Italy were always a conquest by the people after long struggles, fights, strikes and bloody repressions.

The reasons that we Italians are now asking for a change in our government and that we are against the Monarchy are the same that have been exposed by Thomas Paine in his "Common Sense" and the same that made the American people throw off the yoke of the English Monarchy and declare their independence. In my opinion they are the same that are exposed by Jefferson in his government by the people which I quote below: "I am certainly not an advocate for frequent and untried changes in laws and constitutions. I think moderate imperfections had better be borne with, because, when once known, we accommodate ourselves to them, and find some practical means of correcting their ill effects. But I know also that laws and institutions must go hand in hand with the progress of the human mind. As that becomes more developed, more enlightened, as new discoveries are made, new truths disclosed, and manners and opinions change with the change of circumstances, institutions must advance also, and keep pace with the times. We might as well require a man to wear still the coat which fitted him as a boy, as civilized society to remain ever under the regimen of their barbarous ancestors. It is this preposterous idea which has lately deluged Europe in blood. Their monarchs instead of wisely yielding to the gradual change of circumstances, of favoring progressive accommodation to progressive improvement have clung to old abuses, entrenched themselves behind steady habits, and obliged their subjects to seek through blood and violence rash and ruinous innovations, which had they been referred to the peaceful deliberations and collected wisdom of the nation, would have been put into acceptable and salutary forms."

If your joint resolution has the aim to help the Italian people to regain their liberty and to put them again in the society of free nations as an ally and not to reinforce the tie and the power of the House of Savoy in Italy, you have my full approval and blessing!

Cordially yours,

Not until 1946, when a referendum on the monarchy was called in Italy, did Victor Emmanuel III abdicate in favor of his son Umberto II, who was perceived as less culpable in the Fascists' seizure of and hold on power. Umberto reigned for only a month because following the referendum Italy became a republic.

DRAFT, (NY), N.D. BUT PROBABLY JULY 1944; ORIG. ENG.; NYPLTL

The recording of the Star Spangled Banner as it is scored in my film is only fitted for the close of Verdi's Hymn of the Nations because the anthem starts at the highest point of its musical, orchestral and choral crescendo—and it cannot be played in that way for any other occasion be it political or warlike. [Crossed-out sentence: I could permit to use only the sound track if you can take away from the film my person while conducting.]

This was a reply to requests from Frank Capra and others at the Office of War Information (Washington and New York, July 1944) to be allowed to use AT's performance of "The Star-Spangled Banner" in Hymn of the Nations, a propaganda film made for the OWI by AT and the NBC Symphony Orchestra in 1943–44, as part of another Allied propaganda film. In a letter to the OWI (24 July 1944), WrT reiterates his father's statement and adds: "if Col. Capra needs the 'Star-Spangled Banner' for the end of his film, father would be willing to record it with chorus in the usual original version which he has also specially orchestrated, but in the normal key." There were also requests to use the film without the parts that showed Salvemini and other anti-Fascist exiles, but AT refused to have it cut to pieces. Other letters indicate that the film was shown on television (in New York and elsewhere, via hookups) on 14 August 1944; there were many letters of thanks to AT from viewers, with requests for more NBC/AT television concerts.

26-September 1944

My adored Wally
The very thought that in a few days you will receive these few lines, which I'm tracing out on these sheets of paper with a shaky hand and suffering heart, makes me breathe a little more freely. But I can't stand it any longer. It seems a thousand years since I last saw you. The complete absence of news from you makes me unreasonable. I can understand that you can't write to us—there are reasons of force majeure—but that none of our common friends can do it for you seems to me improbable. But I don't want to sadden you with my complaints. God willing, it seems to me that the beginning of the end of this appalling tragedy has already begun. Let's hope for a rather quick resolution, and that you can return home soon. Our health is good. In a few weeks I'll begin my concerts again. I'll conduct 16 this year—four more than last year. So you see that your old father is still in harness and managing to stay well enough. Last winter I made a propaganda film, which turned out very well, according to everyone. It was sent to all the Nations of Europe. Rome and Naples have already had it. I know that it has also been sent to Switzerland. Ask about it. I would love it so much if you could see it! From Rome I've had word from Tommasini. He was ill for a long time and had two operations; now he's better. Everyone here asks about you—you can well imagine! And what's become of my dear, beautiful Emanuela? I can only imagine how big she's grown! Dedè is now a handsome young fellow, as good and intelligent as ever. Sonia is a love. Dear Wally, I'm a little calmer than before. I've been able to talk to you, thanks be to God. I embrace you with all my love.

Entirely your Papa

Rome had been liberated early in June, thus the possibility of corresponding with Tommasini and other friends in that part of the country. (Northern Italian cities such as Milan and Turin were not liberated until the end of April 1945.)

9 November 1944

My adored Wally,
your long letter was like a divine sunbeam. I really needed it after long months of sorrowful waiting. My dear daughter, it was a grave error not to leave with Emanuela when we were in Switzerland! There would have been much less suffering, and today our souls would have been less anguished!—I'm writing a few lines; I can't manage to put my thoughts in order.

For today, suffice it for you to know that I began my work three weeks ago; it's a useful distraction for me, that's true, but it doesn't remove the burden and anguish in my heart, and I think of my poor, dear Italy, mishandled and massacred by enemies and friends alike, and I don't know why I'm not over there to do something more than I can do here. I guarantee you that I feel remorse. [. . .]

E.P. NY, 23 DECEMBER 1944; TO BRUNO WALTER, 965 FIFTH AVENUE, NY; NYPL, BRUNO WALTER PAPERS, JPB 92-4, SERIES I, FOLDER 590

December 23—1944.

My <u>dear Walter</u>

I have no words of comfort, nor can I repeat to you the banal good wishes that even in these tragic days pass from one poor mortal to another. No, I could curse God and all his Saints—but I simply want to be remembered to you, dear friend, and to tell you how close my thoughts have been to you during these last months, aware as I am of your inner, bitter suffering and of the absorption that your troubled soul needs. You understand me, isn't it so?

I embrace you with unalterable affectionate friendship

<u>Arturo Toscanini</u>

Elsa Walter, the conductor's wife, was mortally ill at this time.

DRAFT OF LETTER; (NY), N.D. BUT FROM THE FINAL DAYS OF 1944 OR EARLY 1945; TO H. G. WELLS (LONDON?); ORIG. ENG. (ALL ERRORS HAVE BEEN PRESERVED); NYPLTL

My dear Wells—let me embrace and thank you in the holy names of Justice and Liberty . . . You spoke wonderful and wise words—They express entirely my thought and my feelings . . . Churchill must go! He his not anymore that man we liked and loved . . . His brain is tired and softening. His ugly and shameful business with Greece and Italy is the proof[.] His association with the House of Savoy whose chief members deserve to be executed is simply criminal and prove once more his old and limited range of political views[.] His imposition of Bonomi governement too is ridicolous and clearly shows which is his own view and why he likes that kind of Italian men[.] But Italy will later frustrate all plans of the Tory Churchill—I am quite sure[.]

Once more let me thank you my dear Wells[.] Long live true Liberty[.] Down with the old Torys which refuse to be rejuvenated.

AT had met H. G. Wells (1866–1946) through Stefan Zweig in London a few years earlier. The reference here is to Wells's article "Churchill Must Go," which appeared in the *Tribune* on 15 December 1944. In it, Wells had said, "There can be no doubt of the feelings of the common people of England and the rank and file about this ugly business in Greece and other countries under the heel of slapdash British Toryism. As people have made enormous sacrifices to produce munitions for a united national effort, what is to prevent a working man asking: Why am I overstraining myself to equip our usurper government which has long outstayed its mandate to suppress my fellow workers? What are these guns and shells going to do? In the midst of a still uncertain war, this ineffable Prime Minister of ours has precipitated us into the class war—and on the wrong side. If we do not end Winston, Winston will end us." Michael Foot, in his *H.G.: The History of Mr Wells* (London: Doubleday, 1995, pp. 295–6), comments: "The invocation may sound hopelessly out of touch, but . . . six months later, the English people did, after their own fashion, end Winston, even if the reprieve came too late to prevent the inflicting of deep wounds in Greek society, which have hardly yet healed and which injured some of the people who had been our firmest friends in resisting the Fascist conquest of their country. . . . In Greece and Italy, too, the mass of the people at that stage in the war were on HG's side, not Churchill's." · Ivanoe Bonomi (1873–1951) had been prime minister immediately before the March on Rome in 1922, and AT, like many other Italian liberals, in part blamed Bonomi's incompetence in dealing with Fascist violence for Mussolini's assumption of power; the fact that the Allies installed him as prime minister after Badoglio angered AT and like-thinking anti-Fascists.

FRAGMENT OF TYPED DRAFT, EVIDENTLY WRITTEN TOGETHER WITH WRT
(CORRECTIONS ARE IN WRT'S HAND); (NY);
TO PRES. FRANKLIN D. ROOSEVELT, WASHINGTON; ORIG. ENG.; NYPLTL

February 19, 1945

My dear Mr. President:

Tonight, working in behalf of the collection of money for the National Foundation of Infantile Paralysis, my thoughts and my soul were going out to the millions of innocent Italian children who are starving, and dying by the thousands.

I know that the problem of helping the Italian people is not an easy one. It is made more hard and difficult by the necessity of war. I also know that very little has been done to solve this problem, to relieve this misery and to help Italy heal the many wounds that war has brought to her. From many sections I have been told that it was a deliberate policy that the Italian people must be made to suffer and pay for their part in the war. I would like to ask those people who are now condemning the Italians to this misery if they are so pure that they can throw stones against the Italians. I would like to ask those severe judges who are now enforcing this pitiless policy of revenge if in their consciences they knew that they did not applaud and helped the rise of fascism in Italy. The Italians were the first to endure the oppression of fascism but we have never willingly submitted to it. Countless thousands of men and women in Italy met imprisonment when they strove for years fiercely against the suppression of their [fragment ends here]

On 19 February 1945 AT and the NBC Symphony Orchestra, with Horowitz as soloist, gave a benefit concert at Carnegie Hall for the National Foundation for Infantile Paralysis. · There is no evidence in the FDR Library that the president ever received this letter; it may never had been completed and/or sent.

Dear <u>Mr Girosi.</u>

Excuse me for my delay in sending back your letter of the [blank space] of this month.

More than a quarter of a century ago I met and acted on behalf of Adriano Lualdi—and I think I was even of use to him. At the time, I believed him to be an honest man, a humble and sincere artist. I was wrong. The advent of fascism, and its spread, ruined him. All the ugliness and rot that had lain dormant in him were stirred up, so that the humility that I had found in him was transformed into limitless vanity, and he became a shameless Fascist, superaccumulator of positions, unworthy of my esteem. He was also a Fascist member of parliament for years, and in 1931 he attempted to engineer a rapprochement between his Duce and me. The <u>wretch</u>!! And now he would like to engineer a rapprochement with me! No—for me, that man is dead, <u>forever.</u> Nor does America urgently need mediocre composers and bad conductors, because it's overflowing with them.

With my most cordial greetings, believe me, Your

<u>Arturo Toscanini.</u>

(27 May 1945.)

For those who have studied Italian musical life under the Fascist regime, AT's accusations regarding Adriano Lualdi (1885–1971) seem absolutely fair. In any case, with no help from AT, Lualdi managed to remain part of Italy's musical bureaucracy well into the postwar era.

DRAFT OF TG IN MARGHERITA DE VECCHI'S HAND, (NY), 12 JUNE 1945;
P.S., 333 EAST 57TH STREET, NEW YORK (MDV'S ADDRESS);
TO JOHN STACK, ROME; ORIG. ENG.; EC

Still awaiting license from Treasury Department necessary to authorize my daughter Wally to donate one million lira [*sic*] to campaign for rebuilding La Scala stop depending entirely her good judgment that this amount goes into proper hands—thanks—greetings—

Arturo Toscanini

La Scala's auditorium, not its stage, had been largely destroyed during an Allied bombing raid in August 1943, and as soon as the war had ended the restoration of the theater became one of the city of Milan's top priorities. John Stack was an official with the Allied forces of occupation.

The echo of your message, however incomplete, has moved me to the depths of my heart. I have always been near you with all my spirit throughout these sorrowful years of struggle, mourning, and despair. Never, not even in the darkest and saddest hours, did I doubt that Italian patriots would make a generous contribution to the struggle for the liberation of the world, when the moment came for redemption from Nazi-fascist tyranny.

But the many tens of thousands of Italian patriots who fell heroically in this war alongside Allied soldiers, the decisiveness and discipline that you Milanese demonstrated at the time of the revolt, the inexorable and rapid execution of the most important fascist criminals make me certain that the republican ideals of Cattaneo, Garibaldi, and Mazzini will be fully put into action by you and by the Italian people. Every vestige of the ignominy and betrayals of the past must disappear.

Justice also demands that he who gave every form of moral and material support to the fascist tyranny, and the arms and legal powers for silencing, subjugating, and oppressing the Italian people for twenty sorrowful years, be called upon to account for his own complicity in the crimes perpetrated by the fascists in his name, and for all those violations of the Statute that made the Italian people the first victims of Nazi-fascist terror. You Milanese, who started the revolt against Germanic tyranny in 1848, have well deserved to conclude this struggle of our Risorgimento in 1945. I am proud to come back to you as a citizen of a free Italy and certainly not as a subject of the kings and princes of the House of Savoy.

Arturo Toscanini

This was AT's response to repeated requests that he immediately resume the directorship of La Scala: however much the decision cost him, he would postpone his return to Italy until the monarchy was called to account.

My dear <u>Emanuela</u>
Here is a **perfect** little typewriter for you. It's a real gem! I hope that the first letter you write with it will be addressed to your old grandfather who loves you <u>so much</u> and who wishes you all that's best in the world.

<u>Christmas 1945</u>

Wally and Emanuela had been allowed to travel to the United States almost immediately after the war's end, thanks not only to Wally's father's name but also to the fact that she had been romantically involved, during her Swiss exile, with Allen Dulles

(1893–1969), the chief American negotiator of the surrender of German forces in northern Italy.

TG, NY, 30 MARCH 1946; TO ANTONIO GREPPI,
PALAZZO DEL MUNICIPIO, MI; (PROVENANCE?)

I HAVE LEARNED WITH GREAT SATISFACTION THAT ALL THE RELICS AUTO-GRAPHS WORKS OF ART PRESERVED IN THAT JEWEL THAT WAS THE MUSEO TEATRALE DELLA SCALA WERE MIRACULOUSLY SAVED[.] I AM DEEPLY SAD-DENED TO LEARN THAT THE IMMEDIATE SETTING UP OF THIS MUSEUM HAS NOT YET BEEN LOOKED AFTER SO THAT ALL OF THOSE TREASURES THREAT-ENED WITH DETERIORATION IF NEGLECTED OR LEFT IN CRATES CAN RETURN TO THEIR HOME[.] I MOST WARMLY BEG YOU TO SEE TO IT THAT THIS MUSEUM[,] ONE OF THE MOST IMPORTANT IN EUROPE[,] BE GIVEN BACK THE LOCATION THAT IT USED TO OCCUPY AND THAT IT BE OFFERED EVERY ASSIS-TANCE NECESSARY FOR A SETUP THAT ALSO TAKES INTO DUE ACCOUNT THE NECESSITY OF EXPANDING THE MUSEUM IN THE FUTURE[.] IN THE MUSEO TEATRALE'S COLLECTIONS THERE IS THE HISTORIC DOCUMENTATION OF THE ITALIAN THEATER'S GLORIOUS VITALITY THAT WAS ALWAYS OF SUCH IMPOR-TANCE IN THE LIFE OF THE ITALIAN PEOPLE IN OUR MILAN AND IN THE HIS-TORY OF CIVILIZATION[.] GRATEFUL FOR WHATEVER YOU CAN DO I SEND HEARTY GREETINGS —
ARTURO TOSCANINI +

Antonio Greppi, a playwright, was Milan's first postwar (Socialist) mayor and was instrumental not only in the quick restoration of La Scala in 1946 but also in the cre-ation, the following year, of the Piccolo Teatro di Milano, which has proved to be Italy's finest and most enduring repertory theater ensemble. · The Museo Teatrale alla Scala, located in a wing of the opera house structure, is a repository of important docu-ments, works of art, and memorabilia regarding the history of the theater in Italy and elsewhere from ancient times to the present.

Part Seven

JULY 1946–
NOVEMBER 1956

1948 Makes first live television appearances, with NBC Symphony Orchestra.

1950 Makes transcontinental American tour with NBC Symphony Orchestra.

1952 Makes final appearances in Italy (La Scala) and Great Britain (Philharmonia Orchestra, Royal Festival Hall, London).

1954 4 April: Final conducting appearance—a concert with the NBC Symphony Orchestra at Carnegie Hall; conducts recording sessions in early June, then returns to Italy.

1955 28 February: Leaves Italy for the last time and returns to New York for declining years; devotes much time to listening to his as-yet-unissued recordings, approving some and rejecting others.

1957 16 January: Dies at home in Riverdale (Bronx), New York.

My <u>dear Pandolfini</u>

Your letter upset me. When I read it, I could hardly believe the cruel truth. My God! When I arrived in Milan three months ago, I asked many, many people—including Maria Farneti—about you, but no one, no one at all was able to give me even the tiniest piece of news. I got some only when I actually received your letter, which sadly moved and upset me. Carla will bring this letter to you, and you should tell her, dear Pandolfini, everything that might be of use to you. On my part, I will write to those who can do something for your case, and I am absolutely certain that I will get what you request.

AT had returned to Italy late in April, conducted the opening concert of La Scala on 11 May 1946—probably the emotional high point of his career (see the letter of 23 September 1946)—voted in the referendum that abolished the monarchy, and stayed in Milan and environs until mid-August. · The soprano Angelica Pandolfini (1871–1959) had sung with AT many times in the last decade of the nineteenth century and the first decade of the twentieth (she had retired in 1909; see letter of 2 November 1896 and accompanying note); she evidently was in need, as were many other retired Italian singers and musicians during and immediately after the war, and AT tried to help her and as many of the others as possible. Maria Farneti, another retired soprano, was a friend of the Toscanini family.

Saturday <u>31 August</u> [1946]

My dear <u>Carla,</u> I've waited to write to you because I wanted to be happier about living in this house. At first I felt lost in my solitude. If I had known that you weren't coming I would certainly have preferred to stay at a hotel. Now I've gotten used to it. The Horowitzes came yesterday and will stay with me for a few weeks, I think, then they'll go to <u>Hollywood</u> to make a <u>film</u> on Schumann. [. . .] Poor Frieda [Busch] died on Thursday, 22 August. I went to see the Busches and Serkin, who seemed rather resigned. Poor Frieda had been transported from New York to Serkin's country house in Vermont during the month of July, and there she died. [. . .]

Last week I spent a few days in the country with the Chotzinoffs. I now have the Horowitzes' company and I won't budge. Sonia has grown a lot—she is really pretty. Anna comes to cook for me, the <u>Schaefer</u> woman has replaced Isolina, who is still at Walter's. The house is pretty, clean, well arranged, and comfortable. Only one doesn't see the <u>Hudson,</u> as I was accustomed to seeing it at Villa Pauline and from the Freemans' house. In the autumn, when the trees lose their leaves, it will be a different matter. And how are you? Better than when I left you? I'm the same as I was; after the first baths my legs started to act up again. On top of that I now have <u>itchy eyes</u> and <u>nose,</u> with sneezing that drives me crazy. But it will all pass. Villa Pauline is still as before. It seems that the government hasn't yet given permission to begin work. [. . .]

Before leaving for Italy the previous April, the Toscaninis had bought the Villa Pauline (which they had rented from 1939 to 1943) and had moved out of nearby Wave Hill (which belonged to the Freeman family, whose young son John, later an editor of *Opera News* magazine and a composer, became a close friend of Walfredo), which they had rented in the interim. CT had decided to stay in Italy for the first part of AT's 1946–47 season; thus AT reports to her on the progress of work on the Villa Pauline. In the meantime, he was staying in another house in Riverdale, made available to him by Mrs. Knapp, a neighbor. · The government restrictions were no doubt a result of the postwar housing shortage: the pressing need to construct new homes took precedence over repairs to already existing homes. · Frieda Busch was Adolf's wife and Rudolf Serkin's mother-in-law.

[. . .] The Horowitzes stayed with me for ten days. Now they've gone back to their house. At the end of the month they'll go to Hollywood to make a film based on Schumann's life. They're giving him 100 thousand dollars. His trip to Russia won't take place. It seems that he had requested, through the Russian embassy, to go there to give some concerts. So far, he's had no reply, and it's already been three months. It seems that his country doesn't want him. Maybe they've learned that he's become an American citizen. [. . .]

I'm desperate! I've had <u>hay</u> fever for three weeks. I'm going mad. I do all the treatments they tell me. They're all impossible and futile. Poor Dedè, too, has been terribly stricken. I wanted to dedicate my time to the tenor <u>Vinay,</u> whom I heard and who made a good impression on me, but I would have to do it seriously and I have neither the desire nor the strength to spend hours at the piano with runny eyes and nose, sneezing twenty times a minute. [. . .]

Horowitz did not return to his native country until forty years after this letter was written. · AT had agreed to open La Scala's 1946–47 season with Verdi's *Otello,* but a disagreement with the theater's administration later caused him to cancel his plans. He did, however, coach the Chilean tenor Ramón Vinay (1912–96) in the title role and used him for his NBC radio broadcast recording of the opera the following February—*Otello*'s sixtieth anniversary.

23 <u>September 1946</u>

My dear friend of bygone times, I believed that anything was possible after your behavior during 1939–40, but I still—today, as I write—can't accept the fact that on my return to Italy you didn't find a way of coming to greet me, at least as a friend! I saw Enrico, and he and I were both pleased with our very cordial encounter. Tommasini, Molinari, Corti—everyone was as moved as I to see each other after several years. I immediately asked Enrico about you, and he assured me that you would come. I believed him. So much for that! I never heard anything about you during these long years of war. I was very happy to be back in Italy, very happy to have resumed contact with my orchestra and my audience at La Scala. I can't describe the emotion I felt at my first concert! I was afraid of fainting on stage! I didn't have the nerve to walk along the streets of Milan! The view was too sorrowful to bear. [I went] from my house to La Scala or from my house to the Palazzo dello Sport to attend rehearsals— nothing else.

I came back here in the second half of August to prepare the programs for the coming fall–winter season. I'll return to Milan in December to open the Scala season with Otello, then I'll come back [to New York] in February to resume and finish my concerts. After that, I'll see what's left for me to do. April 6 will be the last concert. By then, I will have passed my **80th birthday** twelve days earlier!!! My God! I think it's time to pull in my oars and begin to rest, so as not to <u>be too tired when I get to the opposite bank</u>!!! Carla has stayed in Milan. I'm alone and in a new house put at my disposal for a few months by a lady friend, while they're making ready for me an apartment in <u>Villa Pauline,</u> which I lived in from 1939 to 1943. But this house is too big for me alone, and it doesn't have the view of the Hudson, and it's all surrounded by trees that, although beautiful, suffocate me and make the atmosphere sad on rainy days. If you want to give me your news, you will give me pleasure. In my heart there is nothing but goodness and simpatia [good feelings] for you. An embrace from your old and affectionate friend

A.T.

AM probably did not reply, and this was AT's last letter to her.

(NY); TO CT, (MI?); EC

Thursday 10 <u>October 1946</u>

[. . .] I'm well enough; as usual, I eat very little. My old body has gained no weight—I vary between 156 and 160 pounds, depending on how empty I keep my intestines. As I already told you, the house I'm living in is pretty and comfortable, with nothing lacking, but . . . There's a but . . . I don't see the Hudson. On sunny days it's all right, but when it rains and I'm surrounded by all that green I feel that I'm <u>suffocating,</u> and all sorts of dark thoughts attack me. Fortunately, Walter, Cia, and Walfredo come every day for supper, and this is a great joy. [. . .]

The Horowitzes are well; every once in a while they come to spend a <u>week-end</u> with me. He gave up the film that he was supposed to do [. . .].

Friday 11 October 1946

My <u>most beloved Wally,</u> I'm ashamed for not having written until now, despite having received two letters from you. What can you expect? My state of mind since I arrived is neither gay nor good. Every time I try to write to you, a tear runs down from my eyes onto the paper—and so I stop and postpone, postpone, hoping for a more propitious moment. [. . .]

Sonia has grown bigger and prettier, and I must say that she is also nicer and more polite. Even you would be happy. But however pretty and comfortable this house is, lacking nothing, <u>everything is foreign.</u> I don't have my paintings, my books, my piano, my radios, and all those dear little things that create the atmosphere in which one feels a need to live, in order to forget for a few moments the tedium of this wretched life. [. . .]

My first concert has been postponed to October 27, thus instead of eight concerts I'll conduct seven before I leave for Italy, postponing the other seven till after I get back. The tenor Vinay has studied and is still studying Otello with me. I think I'll manage well to reach the goal I've set for myself. Graf absolutely can't come to La Scala. The Metropolitan won't allow him to do so, unless he gives up that house altogether. Why did you mention <u>Wally</u> and <u>Novotna</u>? It's true that that opera is close to my heart, but Nerone, too, is close to my heart!!! And how can I forget my <u>nearly eighty years</u>? Dear Wally, maybe it's my present bad humor and living in this house that make me doubt myself, but what's certain is that at the moment I couldn't take on greater responsibilities than those I already have. I think continually about whether or not to go on with the NBC. Who knows—maybe when I resume work next week all this will pass. Let's hope so! I'm glad that the season at the Palazzo dello Sport went well. I'm pleased for dear Ghiringhelli. How is Serafin doing? I very much fear that Ansaldo will become a sort of tsar at La Scala. I recommended him as an excellent <u>head for the technical crew,</u> but **never** as director of stage production (a position that was occupied by Caramba). Ghiringhelli should be very wary of him. I don't look favorably upon the <u>Ansaldo-Serafin</u> duo. It may have worked in Rome, but at La Scala it makes me tremble. I fear that we'll lose <u>Benois,</u> an <u>excellent, intelligent, refined man</u> who has already covered Caramba's post for several years! Ghiringhelli must keep his eyes wide open!!! [. . .]

AT had wanted the Austrian-American director Herbert Graf (1904–73), who had staged his *Meistersinger* and *Magic Flute* productions at Salzburg, to direct his new *Otello* production at La Scala. · During the postwar years, Wally carried out an ongoing diplomatic mission between her father and Antonio Ghiringhelli, La Scala's general manager, whose relationship swung back and forth from amicability to hatred. Ghiringhelli had evidently asked Wally to put a bug in her father's ear about the possibility of conducting *La Wally* by his never-forgotten friend Catalani, but AT points out that he would also like to revive his friend Boito's *Nerone*, of which he had conducted the world premiere. · Tullio Serafin was La Scala's principal conductor at the time; AT respected him as a solid, serious craftsman but did not consider him a particularly refined artist, and it must be said that most of Serafin's recordings bear out this opinion. · Giovanni, Pericle, and Rinaldo Ansaldo had been in charge of what would today be called "special effects" at La Scala for many years; I do not know which of them AT refers to here. · Count Luigi Sapelli, better known as Caramba, had been AT's chief set designer at La Scala during the 1920s, but AT had also brought in such innovative designers as the father-son team Alexandre and Nicola Benois, who had worked for Diaghilev's Ballets-Russes; the Benois referred to here is Nicola (1901–88), who created more than three hundred productions at La Scala between 1925 and 1977.

(NY); TO CT, (MI?); EC

Thursday night 24 October [1946]

My dear <u>Carla</u>—Today I had my first rehearsal with the orchestra. The orchestra was in good form. I didn't get tired. I didn't have <u>any injections.</u> [. . .] Just as in Milan, where I withstood the effort magnificently without intravenous injections, I'll do the same here. My legs are in excellent condition. Those shoes made in Milan do their job magnificently. I continue to have no appetite, and this makes me uneasy; I hate meat; I've tried to gulp down eggs in the morning, but after two or three days I have to give up. I haven't gained back the weight I lost in Milan. But it's not important. I'm well. [. . .]

My first program is

Faust Overture of Wagner and
The **Harold** [in Italy] Symphony of Berlioz.

For the second I'm doing all Mozart.

I'll write to you again. Did you know that they wanted to change the rehearsal times? To start them at <u>eleven</u> in the morning? From eleven to one thirty. I made a vigorous protest, and now everything is all right. [. . .]

(NY); TO CT, (MI?); EC

Thursday 31-October 1946

[. . .] The first concert went magnificently—I didn't get tired and had no need for <u>injections.</u> Cia is a treasure. She has even organized magnificently the domestic help's schedules. Anna, the cook, is free on Fridays, Isolina comes to replace her. Mrs. <u>Schaeffer</u> is free on Tuesdays and replaces Isolina. Walter, Cia, and Walfredo are here with me for supper every day. I always have a few guests on Sundays—the usual people you know. [. . .] The Horowitzes have stolen away a bit, or rather <u>he</u> has; he didn't even come to the concert, nor did he phone a single word, to the wonder of everyone—except me, however. [. . .] Mausi [Friedelind Wagner] is in California, giving lectures, etc., in San Francisco and Los Angeles. It seems that she's enjoying some success and that they want her to go back there. It's a good thing that she's gotten down to doing something and is now self-sufficient. [. . .] I've begun the Hypophosphyte[?] treatment to improve my appetite, but without much success so far. Write to me and love me. I embrace you and kiss you with unaltered affection

Entirely your Tosca.

(NY), N.D. BUT FROM MID-JANUARY 1947; TO CT, (MI?); EC

My dear Carla, This morning I received your dear letter, which makes my face turn red for not having written any more to you in a long time. My heart was broken and still is. Wally couldn't have given me a greater sorrow in my life. I could have expected anything except this tragedy before I die! Countess Lina is avenged. And if it's true that Emanuela and I were everything in her life, this great affection ought to have made Wally do everything to avoid this tragedy. But so be it, my dear Carla.

[. . .] I'll resume my work on February 6 and will end on April 6; nine concerts. I've already put my programs together. The last one will be dedicated to Wagner. As it falls on Easter, I'll perform the Prelude and Good Friday Spell from Parsifal and the final duet from Act I of the Walküre, with Bampton and the tenor Svanholm. [rest of letter missing]

Wally evidently had finally told her father that she and her husband had gone their separate ways, although this had happened several years earlier. · Countess Lina had been Castelbarco's first wife. · By "the final duet" AT meant the entire final scene of *Die Walküre*'s first act. · The American soprano Rose Bampton (b. 1908) and her husband, the Canadian conductor Wilfrid Pelletier, were friends of the Toscaninis. · Set Svanholm (1904–64) was a well-known Swedish tenor.

(NY); TO SERGE KOUSSEVITZKY, (BOSTON?); ORIG. ENG.;
LOC, KOUSSEVITZKY COLLECTION

April 4—1947

My dear Maestro Koussevitzky—
I thank you for your kind remembrance of me . . . It was very gratifying to be remembered in this circumstance of my eightieth birthday . . . Eighty years of age!!!

I never could have hoped to be in such full health and such activity of mind and body in this advanced period of life!

But however I have reached the assigned limit of existence I am still hoping to come one day, **personally,** to greet your eightieth birthday . . . Think of it!!!

With cordial greetings I am, dear Koussevitzky, yours

Arturo Toscanini

Koussevitzky would have turned eighty in 1954; he died in 1951, but AT was still around.

(NY); TO PAUL CRESTON, (NY); P.S., AT; ORIG. ENG.
(ALL ERRORS HAVE BEEN PRESERVED); NYPLTL

(April 30—1947)

My dear <u>Mae. Creston.</u>

May I ask you to forgive me for not having written to thank you for your kind and sweet letter of April 15 . . . ? I know that the delay is inexcusable but was not for <u>inpoliteness</u>—no—but for that <u>laziness</u> which I could never get rid [of] during my long life—I am very sorry but forgive me, please!

I was moved at heart for your words of praise and above all for the dedication of your most recent composition which I was unaware you had written in honor of my eightieth birthday . . . What can I say to show my gratitude? The apostle of Beauty, as you very kindly wanted to call me, is embarassed to find suitably words of thanking but he his <u>proud</u> and <u>happy</u> to accept this homage from so distinguished and eminent [a] musician like you.

Unfortunately I was not able to enjoy your composition as I had hoped . . . Maybe the broadcast or my grammophone were not good enough because the Viola (a very good player) was always too loud, while the Arpa sounded weak and I guessed more than I could hear the organ's part . . .

So, if you would send to me a copy of this composition I should be very grateful and I thank you in advance.

In admiration and friendship I send you my most cordial greetings.

Yours

Arturo <u>Toscanini</u>

I have not been able to discover which of Creston's compositions is referred to here.

E.P. BRONX, 1 MAY 1947; TO ELSA KURZBAUER, NY; WOT

My <u>dear Elsina</u>

I've received this letter written in German and in a script [Gothic] that I've never been able to read. I think it's someone who was with me in Bayreuth. You'll tell me what he [she?] wants. I think I figured out that he [she?] is sending good wishes for my==brrr==80th birthday and hopes that I'll make it to 100. If only it were so!!!! [. . .] How are you? Well, I hope. I haven't called you in several days, which is <u>bad</u> for you and for me. I've worked very hard on my new records. I've spent many hours downtown adding the Timpani that couldn't be heard in Tchaikovsky's Romeo and Juliet fantasy. I've approved the Faust Overture. I'm fighting to <u>persuade myself</u> that the Haffner Symphony is good, but I'm not succeeding. [. . .]

AT and the NBC Symphony Orchestra had recorded the Tchaikovsky piece on 7 April 1946, Wagner's "Faust" Overture on 11 November 1946, and Mozart's "Haffner" Symphony on 4 and 6 November 1946. All three were released, but indeed the "Haffner" recording is not as beautiful as some of his other performances of the symphony that have been preserved.

E.P. BRONX, 15 MAY 1947; TO EK, NY; WOT

My dear Elsina

Does it ever happen to you in life to find yourself unpleasant? It does to me—often. In these last weeks I have been so unpleasantly nasty that I think I even disgusted the members of my orchestra last Monday during a recording session. To such a point that I received an anonymous letter full of insolent remarks—all of them just—only the person who wrote was a coward because he didn't sign. So try to be patient, without patience it's useless to love me. [. . .]

The recording session in question had comprised Wagner's *Tristan* Prelude and Berlioz's "Queen Mab" Scherzo from *Roméo et Juliette;* neither was issued. · This is AT's last known letter to Elsa Kurzbauer, although there is an empty envelope addressed by him to her and postmarked 25 October 1948.

(NY); P.S., AT; TO PIERO WEISS, 246TH STREET AT INDEPENDENCE AVENUE, RIVERDALE, NEW YORK; COLL. OF PIERO WEISS

28 July 1947

My dear Piero . . . Yes, I remember very well that you mentioned the Agnus Dei of the "Petite Messe" to me, but I did not think that you would be so kind as to take the trouble to make a photograph of the orchestral score and send it to me . . . I thank you with all my heart, however belatedly.

To me, this "Little Mass" (which lasts much longer than Verdi's Requiem) is, together with William Tell, one of the Rossini works that I love most. After a private performance, at which I believe Meyerbeer was present, he {Rossini} himself orchestrated it—but it wasn't performed in its entirety until 1869, after his death.—Thank you again . . . Please give my greetings to your dear mother and your excellent father.

Believe me cordially yours

Arturo Toscanini

The musicologist Piero Weiss was a nineteen-year-old piano student when AT sent him this letter. Weiss and his family were exiles from Fascist Italy, and they lived near AT in Riverdale. · AT's recollections of Rossini's *Petite Messe solennelle* are correct. The work was composed in 1863 and first performed in its original version (for twelve solo voices, two pianos, and harmonium) the following year at the Paris home of Countess

Louise Pillet-Will, to whom it was dedicated; the composer Giacomo Meyerbeer, although gravely ill (he died two months later), disobeyed his doctor and attended the private event. Rossini orchestrated the work in 1867, and in that form it was first performed at the Théâtre des Italiens in Paris in February 1869, three months after its composer's death.

(NY); P.S., AT; TO SAMUEL CHOTZINOFF, (NY);
ORIG. ENG. (ALL ERRORS HAVE BEEN PRESERVED); SCBU

September 12—1947

My <u>dear Chotzi</u>

Once more again you have been exceedingly dear and sweet to send me such adorable lines which moved me very deeply . . . Thank you, my dear friend, a thousand times.

I didn't read the piece you mention written by the critic of Newyork Times. But I must say that I too I felt the unusual <u>charm</u> (not quality) of that evening—because of the symphatetic intercourse arisen immediately between performers and udience—intercourse necessary to create that warm atmosphere where music can pour out all its magic—and because of the small theatre which helps performers and public to make and enjoy music.—In short, I was happy of my "debut" at Ridg[e]field—now, my dear Chotzi, think about **Falstaff**!

I embrace you <u>and all the family</u>

<u>Arturo Toscanini</u>

On 6 September 1947 AT and the NBC Symphony Orchestra had performed in the high school auditorium at Ridgefield, Connecticut, where the Chotzinoffs had a summer home and where Geraldine Farrar lived. · AT did not do a concert performance of *Falstaff* at NBC until 1950.

(NY); P.S., AT; TO CARLTON COOLEY, (NY); ORIG. ENG.; RICHARD S. COOLEY

September 16—1947

My <u>dear Cooley</u> . . . Your sweet but unexpected letter has moved me to the bottom of my heart . . . While I am writing these lines my eyes are filled with tears—I cannot find words in order to thank you enough for your kind and affectionate expressions addressed to me (they prove you are not yet bored with the old maestro) and above all for your noble gesture, worthy only of a man and artist <u>like you</u> . . . In my turn I say: Bravo, bravissimo Cooley. My dear friend I think it is useless to tell you how much I love and admire you! Permit me to embrace you affectionately and to thank you once more again.

<u>Arturo Toscanini.</u>

Carlton Cooley was the NBC Symphony Orchestra's principal viola for the entire seventeen years of the orchestra's existence. The concert in Ridgefield had been a benefit event for a local cultural association; AT had donated his services, but the orchestra members had been paid. Cooley had sent AT a check in the amount of $40—his earnings for the evening—declaring that he had particularly enjoyed this concert and that "I could not accept a playing fee and am enclosing my check to you to be added to the general fund of the Ridgefield Association [. . .]. May God bless and keep you with us dear Maestro for a long, long time to come."

(NY); TO CIA FORNAROLI TOSCANINI, (NY); WOT

My <u>beloved Cia</u>—
Thank you for everything you do and have done for me and for the house. You are really an angel of goodness, and the least I can do is to <u>be fond of you.</u> And I am, very much so. Very best wishes for happiness
> Your very own old father of Walter.

(Christmas 1947)

AT's relationship with his daughter-in-law had gotten off to a bad start, but over the years it had become very affectionate. Oddly, in the notes to her that I have seen he never signed himself *suocero* (father-in-law), but always as *padre di Walter.*

(NY); P.S., AT; TO SAMUEL AND PAULINE (HEIFETZ) CHOTZINOFF, (NY); ORIG. ENG.; SCBU

January <u>6—1948</u>
My dearest friends <u>Pauline and Chotzi</u>
[. . .] You, my dear Chotzi, why do you write such a kind and sweet letter like this last one? You know very well that I am an old man and it is very hard for me to prevent tears running down on my cheeks!!! Like a little babe . . . So happened the other day. That you think of me so highly I am happy . . . it is useless to deny it . . . It may be also you see things about me through an aggrandizement lens, and then? Anyhow I love you and Pauline very dearly and <u>forever</u> . . .
I embrace you both with friendship and love.
> <u>Arturo Toscanini.</u>

According to some gossips among AT's circle of friends, he had had an affair with Pauline Chotzinoff, and her husband had been aware of it. According to others, AT merely enjoyed pretending that Pauline was one of his girlfriends: he would phone her late at night and describe in graphic detail all their real or imagined sexual activities.

THANK VOTTO[.] PRANDELLI SIMIONATO ALL RIGHT BUT INSTEAD OF ROSSI
LEMENI I WOULD PREFER SIEPI[.] PLEASE ALL OF YOU THINK ABOUT SIMON
MAGO STOP REASSURE US YOUR HEALTH HUGS ARTURO +

CT, who was not in good health, was returning less and less often to the United States
with her husband. · On 10 June 1948, precisely the thirtieth anniversary of Boito's
death, AT stepped into La Scala's orchestra pit for the last time in his life to conduct the Prologue and third act of *Mefistofele* and the third act and second part of the
fourth act of *Nerone;* the casts—engaged, it seems, by Antonino Votto, AT's former
assistant—included such young luminaries as Giacinto Prandelli (tenor, b. 1914),
Giulietta Simionato (mezzo-soprano, b. 1910), and Cesare Siepi (bass, b. 1923); AT
preferred Siepi to Nicola Rossi-Lemeni (bass, 1920–91). The role of Simon Mago was
taken by the young Italo-American baritone Frank Guarrera (b. 1923), who later sang
the part of Ford in AT's *Falstaff* broadcast recording, and the lead soprano roles in
both operas went to the Italo-American soprano Herva Nelli (1909–94), who sang
various important Verdi roles with AT in the United States and was one of his last
"flings." · Never again did AT conduct a staged opera performance.

21 March 1948

My dear Walter

50 years!!! On the day you were born, I would never have believed that I
would have the joy of seeing you fifty years later. I hope that the good Lord
will let you reach my age and <u>even beyond.</u>

I hug you with the greatest affection

Your old father

Unfortunately, Walter seems to have inherited his mother's longevity genes rather
than his father's—and in addition, he was a heavy smoker. He died in 1971 at the age
of seventy-three, after having spent the last four years of his life paralyzed as the result
of a stroke.

<u>MARCIA DAVENPORT.</u>

THE <u>OLD PICALAGE.</u> [*SIC;* VICARAGE?]

<u>SHIPLAKE</u>

<u>OXFORDSHIRE</u>

DID YOU HEAR THE BOITO CONCERT SORRY YOU ARE NOT YET QUITE WELL DID
NOT RECEIVE YOUR LETTER TO NEWYORK WISHES AND LOVE FROM YOUR OLD
FRIEND.

Davenport (1903–96), a writer, was the daughter of the celebrated soprano Alma Gluck; AT is thought to have had affairs with both mother and daughter.

E.P. NY, 18 OCTOBER 1948; P.S., AT; TO CT, D2OMI; EC

17 <u>October</u> 1948

My <u>dear Carla</u>

[. . .] At our age we ought to live more united, ever more united. Unfortunately, I can't abandon my work, which is my reason for living—you know it—and at this point I can only work here. In Europe there is only Milan, and at La Scala . . . I <u>no longer wish</u> to appear before either new or old audiences. I must show respect for my age, and then changing orchestras, even if only once in a while, causes me suffering!! As I cabled you, the trip was magnificent in every way. The airplane was magnificent, the flight was magnificent, and the service was excellent. Mimì Finzi was at the station in Rome together with her son and Tommasini. [. . .] Molinari came to see me, but unfortunately, although he is better physically than he was two years ago, I found his morale low. I think that he lives in an unhealthy situation that underlines the manias that unfortunately torment him. Poor Molinari!!!

Here the Sarnoffs, the Chotzinoffs, Nelli with her husband, Margherita, Cia, etc. etc. were at the airport on my arrival. I found the house in order. [. . .]

Wednesday (20th) I begin rehearsing with the orchestra only, Thursday and Friday with Volodya. By the way, Wanda, Volodya, and Sonia were also there to meet us, together with the <u>Merowitzes.</u>

Now I hug and kiss you intensely and await good news from you.

Your <u>Tosca.</u>

AT had evidently traveled by train to Rome and then to New York by plane, together with WrT. He began his 1948–49 NBC Symphony Orchestra season on 23 October 1948 with the first of six all-Brahms programs; Horowitz played the Second Piano Concerto as part of that concert. · Alexander Merovitch was a concert agent and a longtime friend of Horowitz.

E.P. NY, 25 OCTOBER 1948; P.S., AT; TO CT, D2OMI; EC

23 <u>October 1948</u>

My <u>dear Carla,</u> The first concert was a triumph for Volodya. He played like a god. The orchestra was magnificent. Volodya is now enthusiastic about the acoustics of our hall and he told me that he will play any time I like.

Everyone was enthusiastic.

[. . .]

Few musicians liked the acoustics of Studio 8-H in the RCA Building, Rockefeller Center, where the NBC Symphony Orchestra gave most of its concerts until 1950, but AT was happy there and apparently converted Horowitz to his point of view. On the other hand, after this concert father-in-law and son-in-law never again performed together.

E.P. NY, 23 DECEMBER 1948; P.S., AT; TO WYT, D2OMI; EC

20 December 1948

My most beloved Wally

[. . .] Mamma is really quite well, and it was an excellent idea to have her come here immediately after the cure at Luino. Her appetite is always so good that she could devour nails. But she always does her rice-carrot-etc. cure, never once forgetting her duty. She now has a maid completely to herself, a Tuscan woman, who, however, speaks English, French, and maybe even Spanish. She is very happy with her and we say our prayers in the hope that things will go on as they began, and that she won't change her mind. I'm now having a period of rest. I'll begin again on 12 February, and I hope to perform Aida in two concerts (the 12th and 19th). I've finally found a mezzo-soprano who seems to me good for Amneris, and what with Nelli as Aida, the tenor Tocker [sic], and the baritone [blank space: Giuseppe Valdengo], I hope to obtain a good performance. [. . .]

Eva Gustavson sang Amneris in AT's broadcast-telecast recording of *Aida;* her voice had the dramatic contralto quality that AT required of his Verdian mezzos, but she was otherwise one of the weaker cast members. · "Tocker": The famous Richard Tucker (1913–75); this was his only collaboration with AT. · Giuseppe Valdengo (b. 1914) also sang the lead baritone roles in AT's NBC *Otello* and *Falstaff* broadcasts.

E.P. NY, 11 JANUARY 1949; P.S., AT; TO WYT, D2OMI; EC

(10 January 1949)

My adored Wally

[. . .] I saw that the opening of La Scala wasn't brilliant—too bad! But I foresaw it, with that tenor! and—that maestro in Trovatore!! I received a letter from Votto, who tells me of the good outcome of Faust. I'm really pleased. I know two really good singers—Tebaldi and the basso Siepi. [. . .] Give my greetings to Ghiringhelli, and if you see anyone from the orchestra tell them of my gratitude for the good memories they have of me. [. . .]

Kurt Baum (1900–89) and Victor De Sabata were the tenor and conductor, respectively, of the new production of *Il trovatore* at La Scala. · *Faust* was conducted by Votto. · AT had given soprano Renata Tebaldi (b. 1922) her first big break by choosing her to sing under his direction at La Scala's reopening in 1946. · The Scala orchestra had evidently sent AT a grateful message.

3 March 1949.

My dear Iris

Allow me to treat you with affectionate friendship and to tell you of the joy that I feel in thinking of my dear Guido's return to his country and of your reunion. He is returning with the affection and admiration of everyone who has approached and admired him—and they are many, without even mentioning the American public. I must tell you that for me, personally, this is the first time in my long career as an artist that I've found a young man truly gifted with those qualities that can't be described but that are the real ones, those that raise an artist high, very high. I attended all of Guido's rehearsals with ever-growing interest, and the impression I had at the first rehearsal at La Scala repeated itself and continued to increase. Now I hope that God will preserve him always as he is—so good, simple, and humble—I mean humble toward his art, of course. Treasure him, dear Iris. I know that you love each other very much; this will help both of you in life and especially him in his art. I can't tell you how sorry I am to see him leave, but we'll see each other again this coming May. And next year we'll all be together here in New York. Allow me to embrace you affectionately. Your very devoted

Arturo Toscanini

AT had first observed young Guido Cantelli (1920–56) conducting at La Scala in 1948 and had been so impressed that he had immediately had him engaged for four weeks of concerts with the NBC Symphony Orchestra during its 1948–49 season. This letter to Cantelli's wife, Iris (*née* Bilucaglia), speaks for itself. AT continued to lend his support to Cantelli, who would undoubtedly have become one of the most celebrated conductors of the second half of the twentieth century had he not died in an airplane crash at the age of thirty-six.

(19 April 1949)

My dear Carla, The rehearsals are finally finished!!! After tomorrow I'll be completely free. I'm not at all worn out. It was only the thought of the rehearsals that worried me. Now I'm thinking only about the departure—what joy! The whole Chotzinoff family plus the doctor friend from Washington will leave with us. We'll make up quite a table aboard the Saturnia. [. . .]

My dearest Emanuela

I've delayed too long in thanking you for your dear good wishes and your beautiful photograph, but what can you expect? "You can't teach an old dog new tricks"—and at this point your grandfather, who isn't merely old but ancient, can't be cured of the horrible habit of not writing and, what's worse, of not answering those who write to him. So you, too—please be patient and have pity on me. Your photograph is beautiful and you are very beautiful. I'm happy to have you before my eyes. You have pride of place on my desk. But I'll soon have the joy of seeing you in person, and for me that will be a greater joy. Next Thursday I'll leave New York together with Walter and the whole Chotzinoff family. I can't wait to enjoy a little air and sun and to see again my old house and all of you who are dear to my heart. I hug and kiss you with the greatest tenderness.

Your <u>old grandfather.</u>

(Saturday 23 April 1949)

(MI? ISG?); P.S., AT; TO GUIDO CANTELLI, (NOVARA);
PHOTOGRAPHIC REPRODUCTION BETWEEN PP. 112 AND 113 OF
IRIS CANTELLI'S UN MUCCHIO DI MANI (ROME: SAMONÀ E SAVELLI, 1965)

(25-June 1949)

My <u>dear Cantelli</u>

I'm sorry not to be near you this evening—you know why—unfortunately at my <u>tender young age</u> I still suffer from shyness. In any case, I'll be near you in my heart and soul, and my applause will join with that of your fellow townspeople who perhaps honor you in that theater that I had the honor of inaugurating during the carnival season 1888–89, when I was not yet twenty-two years old. Oh, those good old days!!! I affectionately embrace you and dear Iris.

<u>Entirely yours A Toscanini</u>

Cantelli was giving a concert with the Scala orchestra at the Teatro Coccia in his hometown, Novara (not far from AT's beloved Isolino).

DRAFT IN MARGHERITA DE VECCHI'S HAND — EVIDENTLY DICTATED TO
OR COPIED BY HER, (NY), N.D. BUT 5 OR 6 DECEMBER 1949;
TO LUIGI EINAUDI, PRESIDENT OF ITALY, ROME; EC

Mr. President of the Republic of Italy—<u>Rome</u>

It is an old Italian artist, very much troubled by your unexpected telegram, who turns to you and asks you to understand that this announcement of his nomination as senator for life clashes profoundly with his sentiments and that he is forced to refuse this honor, with great sadness.

Averse to any sort of accumulation of honors, academic titles, and decorations, I wish to end my existence in the same simplicity with which I have always lived it.

Grateful and happy for the recognition that has been expressed toward me in the name of my Country, ready to serve it again in any eventuality, I ask you not to interpret this wish of mine as a rude or arrogant gesture, but rather in the spirit of simplicity and humility that inspires it. Accept my deferential greetings and respectful homage.

A.T.

This message was read to the Senate by the Hon. Ivanoe Bonomi, president of the Senate (and former prime minister), on 7 December 1949. The Italian Senate is made up mainly of elected members, but former presidents of the Republic automatically become senators for life, and current presidents are allowed to appoint lifetime members "for highest worth." This last group is the one for which AT had been nominated. Some Italians took his refusal as a moral slap in the face to his country, but this seems not to have been his intention at all: he wanted to continue to work as long as possible, and his principal place of work was far from Rome.

FRAGMENT OF LETTER, (ISG?), N.D. BUT SUMMER 1950 (AFTER 3 JULY); TO MARIA CECCHINI, (MI?); PC; EC

[first page(s) missing] At La Scala after my performance of the Verdi Requiem (which left a very bitter taste in my mouth) I heard Beethoven's Missa Solemnis and Bach's Mass in b minor with the choral and orchestral forces of Vienna. Karajan was conducting. The audience was cold at the Beethoven and warmed up at the Bach. I was bored at both. Not even Bach's divine Kyrie moved me as it did in a long-ago performance with a Berlin chorus conducted by Georg Schumann. Maybe my advanced age has hardened my heart a little! After those two performances I came to the Isolino. What a delight! What beauty! This is truly an enchanting place! It seems to have fallen out of the sky for the joy of mankind. I brought my piano, and I bang on it from time to time. I'm also leading a contemplative life! I let my thoughts go back to my past life and I look <u>seriously</u> at my future one. I say seriously, because a visit from Chotzinoff here at the Isolino upset me a little and [rest of letter missing]

Maria Cecchini (who later married the basso Paolo Montarsolo) had been engaged as a tutor for Emanuela during the latter's extended stays in America; she remained a close friend of the Toscaninis and became involved in programs for young artists at La Scala. · AT had not been at all happy with his performance of the Verdi Requiem at La Scala on 24 June 1950 (the soloists had been Tebaldi, Cloe Elmo [1910–62], Prandelli, and Siepi). · Georg Schumann (1866–1952) was for many years conductor of Berlin's famous Singakademie. · What upset AT was probably the news from Chotzinoff that NBC's Studio 8-H was being converted into a television studio that summer and that the orchestra's concerts would have to be moved elsewhere.

Deeply [sorry] unable to accept your invitation to conduct Gala opening concert Israel Philharmonic being in Europe during that period Stop My sincerest wishes for a most successful tour and heartiest congratulations for your magnanimous project Kindest regards A.T.

This message was copied out by WrT (Mi?), n.d. but from September 1950, for Margherita De Vecchi (NY). The Israel Philharmonic Orchestra made its first U.S. tour in 1951, and AT had evidently been invited to conduct its first concert.

My <u>dear Carla</u>

We were visited by Ghiringhelli and Cantelli all day yesterday, at lunch and supper; I would gladly have followed them when they left. Instead, <u>poor Toscanini</u> has to continue with his trip, however unwillingly, and whatever happens happens!!! I hope that you will continue to be well and to have the <u>healthy face</u> that you had when I left you. Don't think about <u>anything;</u> that is, think about me, because I love you a lot and already can't wait to return, although I haven't yet left.

We have a fine cabin with porch and have settled in nicely. Walter took so much stuff out of the suitcases that we could stay here for months. Yesterday he went into Naples to buy sulfur for bathing my feet, and he had to go to ten or twelve pharmacies to find it. My leg [illegible word] is going from bad to worse, and I'm worried. [. . .]

AT was using stationery from the previous spring's transcontinental NBC Symphony Orchestra tour, which had been an outstanding success. · CT's heart was giving her problems, and she once again decided not to travel to the United States with her husband. · The fact that AT often referred self-pityingly to himself as *il povero Toscanini* (poor Toscanini) had become a family joke, and he enjoyed making fun of himself by repeating the description as often as possible.

12 <u>October</u>   <u>Columbus Day</u>

My <u>dearest Carla</u>

The trip was long (twelve days) and boring. Even the sea was tedious. But we arrived in good shape. Walter did exercises every morning and went back to bed dead tired. But he did lose three or four kilos. I've stopped drinking wine because it was upsetting my stomach, and the same for coffee. Only my leg is getting worse. It's no longer as flexible as before, and I get tired when I walk as I used to do. In a few days I'll go to Dr. Stein in Philadelphia. The change of halls and concert days and times has thrown me into the same state as in 1927, when I couldn't go to rehearsals and had to give up five weeks of work. Now not being at NBC any longer makes me feel as if I were <u>not even</u> in New York and didn't have the house but rather, as back then, were staying at the hotel. I would have liked to take a plane back to Milan. I'm in a bad mood—black, black!! But so be it! The new law that makes passengers undergo questioning before disembarking, giving detailed accounts of their political past, has caused much clamor in the United States. President Truman first and foremost doesn't approve, but the Senate approved it unanimously. So Barbieri and her husband with about forty [rest of letter missing]

The reference is to the mezzo-soprano Fedora Barbieri (b. 1920).

E.P. NY, 14 OCTOBER 1950; TO CT, D2OMI; EC

13 October

My dear Carla

I'm sending you this newspaper clipping so that you can see the expression of De Sabata at Ellis Island, where he is still, and where he spent the night. As you'll read, he has the nerve to deny that he was a fascist. Shameless!!! [. . .]

I'm in a bad mood. Not to have the NBC's concert hall anymore leaves me with no desire to conduct, and, as I already told you, if my home weren't here I would return to Milan immediately. [. . .]

Why De Sabata, who had already conducted in the United States several times since the end of the war, was being detained in the fall of 1950 is hard to understand. In any case, he was released and allowed to fulfill his engagement with the Pittsburgh Symphony Orchestra. As La Scala's principal conductor after AT's departure, De Sabata had often conducted for visiting Fascist and Nazi dignitaries, toured Nazi Germany with Italian and native ensembles, and conducted at the 1939 Bayreuth Festival. De Sabata's file in Mussolini's office was slim; the most incriminating item in it was an effusive letter (1932) to the Duce in which he expressed "great emotion" for having received an autographed photo from the head of government and "profound devotion" to him.

(NY); TO CT, (MI?); EC

21 October 1950

My <u>dear Carla,</u> For pity's sake don't pay attention to the news that appears in the papers. As long ago as my letter of the 12th [*sic,* for 13th] I had told you of my refusal to conduct the concerts and the press ought to have given the news truthfully, that is, that after thirteen years of work at NBC I didn't intend to be sent away [from Studio 8-H] for any reason whatsoever, or at least I ought to have been treated as a man of my age and my artistic position deserves. Mr. Sarnoff took remedial measures too late, and when he asked to meet with me I refused to see him. [rest of letter missing]

E.P. PHILADELPHIA, 31 OCTOBER 1950;
P.S., THE WARWICK/LOCUST STREET AT 17TH/PHILADELPHIA 3, PA.;
TO CT, D2OMI; EC

Tuesday 31 October [1950]

[. . .] Here I am in Philadelphia, in the hands of Dr. Stein. Walter is here with me. I'll stay two or three weeks, as the doctor wishes. Let's hope that something good comes of it. [. . .] Don't read the newspapers, and don't believe the foolish things that they print. Here they've said every sort of nonsense—even that CBS will <u>hire</u> me. Imagine! And those idiots Chotzinoff and Sarnoff of the NBC are asking Walter if there's any truth in this news. What saddens me is that you get excited on my behalf, whereas I would like to know that you're peaceful and <u>concerned</u> with <u>your own health.</u> And if you love me, do everything to feel as you did at the end on the Isolino. Play cards and take an interest in something pleasant, but don't always distance yourself from what's going on around you. Write to me and try to be good-humored. Do it for <u>your</u> sake and also <u>for mine.</u> I think of you a lot and I would like to be near you, as on the Isolino. The only thing that worries me now is my leg. Dr. Stein gives me high hopes, but I believe him only to a certain extent. We shall see! [. . .]

Yesterday evening, from ten to eleven, we heard the second concert of my orchestra conducted by Reiner. It gave me no pleasure at all. In fact, it distressed me because of the acoustics of that venue (Manhattan [Center]), which I wholly dislike. Reiner will conduct a third concert, then come Leinsdorf and Perlea, I think. Next Monday (6 November) the Metropolitan will open with <u>Don Carlos,</u> followed by the Flying Dutchman and La Traviata, the first conducted by Stiedry, the second by Reiner, the third by Erede. I've been invited, in fact <u>you</u> and <u>I</u> have been invited, to the opening performance by Bing and his wife, in their box. Of course I thanked them but refused. Barbieri and Siepi are the only Italian artists who are singing in Don Carlos. It's not yet known whether the première will be shown on television. In that case I would go to New York. The weather is magnificent. Sun, sun, sun!!! I've much enjoyed my spacious terrace, from which I heard the beautiful music made by my sixteen canaries. You should see how beautiful they are!! [. . .]

For some time AT had been having problems with his right leg, especially the knee, and he had decided to take advantage of his self-imposed absence from the NBC Symphony Orchestra to be treated by Dr. Stein in Philadelphia. · Fritz Reiner (1888–1963) had conducted music of Beethoven, Mozart, and R. Strauss in his concert the previous evening. · AT seems to have had a degree of respect for the Romanian

conductor Jonel Perlea (1900–70). · Vienna-born Rudolf Bing (1902–97) was opening his first season as general manager of the Metropolitan Opera; he would hold the
position until 1972. Fritz Stiedry (1883–1968), another Viennese, conducted major
Wagner and Verdi productions at the Met from 1946 to 1958. Alberto Erede (b. 1909),
whom AT had at one time respected but had since turned against (perhaps because
Erede had chosen to work in Italy during the war), was making his Met debut with *La
traviata.* · Fedora Barbieri (Eboli) and Cesare Siepi (Filippo) were making their Met
debuts in *Don Carlos.*

E.P. PHILADELPHIA, 2 NOVEMBER 1950; P.S. AS IN PREVIOUS LETTER;
TO CT, D2OMI; EC

Thursday   2 November 1950.

[. . .] I go twice a day to Stein. Two injections and massages are killing me.
Walter goes with me; I limp and have to stop from time to time because I get
damnably tired. But I have to get exercise, and I'm doing my best. After the
session on Saturday I'm going to New York. I'll come back here on Tuesday,
because I want to stay home on Monday to see the Metropolitan's opening on
television. [. . .] The Carandinis are leaving tomorrow by plane. I gave Elena a
reproduction of Rietti's portrait of me. She was thrilled. [. . .]

Elena Albertini Carandini (1902–90) was the daughter of AT's old friend Luigi Albertini and the wife of Nicolò Carandini, Italy's first postwar ambassador to London; the
entire family had courageously engaged in highly dangerous anti-Fascist activities,
even in Rome during the German occupation. Parts of this brilliant woman's remarkable diaries have been published in Italy. · Arturo Rietti (1863–1943), a noted Italian
portraitist, had painted, in 1933, what has become the best-known portrait of AT.

E.P. PHILADELPHIA, 11.11.50; P.S. AS IN PREVIOUS LETTERS;
TO CT, D2OMI; EC

Saturday 11 November 1950

[. . .] I've just returned from the hospital, where they did X rays of my shoulder and back. What with X rays, injections, massages, and, for good measure,
magnesia every evening (three teaspoonsful) in hot milk with 30 drops of I
don't know what, I'm hoping that some good will come of it! It takes time,
however, and that's not lacking. But it takes patience, too. Walter is a wonderful nurse—he remembers everything and doesn't leave out a thing.

[. . .] I thought the Metropolitan's opening was better than last year. Barbieri and Siepi had a magnificent success. [. . .]

<u>Wednesday morning 2 a.m.</u> [15.11.50]

My dear Carla, I can't sleep and I'm writing you a few lines to keep you company for a moment. I've begun the third week of treatment, but so far <u>with no results.</u> Dr. Stein says to persevere, and I obey. For some time my ankles were continuing to swell despite the injections; I'm now wearing elastic socks and the result has been marvelous. Just like the tingling in your hands, the swelling of my ankles is a result of bad circulation of the blood and of <u>our youth.</u> One must be patient!

[. . .] I read a <u>very unpleasant</u> article by Confalonieri on Cantelli, in Illustrazione. Tell Maria Cecchini that I no longer like her friend. I had believed him to be more honest and more intelligent. It's a <u>real disappointment</u> to me. The ending of that article is poisonous. If Cantelli has been lucky, he owes it to his talent. [. . .]

Cantelli's quick leap to fame, thanks to an unprecedented degree of support from AT—but (as AT points out here) mainly thanks to his own ability—had of course been the object of much envy, especially in Italy. · Giulio Confalonieri (1896–1972) was a Milanese musician, music historian, and critic.

<u>Monday 20 November 1950</u>

[. . .] Today after supper I'll go back to Philadelphia for the <u>fourth</u> week. I'm not in a good mood because the results of the treatment are zero, so far. Dr. Stein is very confident, but I'm in despair. Enough—we shall see! Yesterday (Sunday) I had Barbieri and her husband, Tebaldi and her mother, and Siepi over for lunch. [. . .] Yesterday evening at Town Hall the <u>Virtuosi di Roma,</u> a group of <u>magnificent</u> Italian musicians who play early music, enjoyed a <u>great success.</u> The press gave them the highest praise. I'll go hear them Tuesday evening in Philadelphia. [. . .]

Along with I Musici, I Virtuosi di Roma (founded and directed by Renato Fasano) was one of the first small groups created specifically for the performance of seventeenth- and eighteenth-century instrumental music. These and similar ensembles enjoyed great success until the 1970s, when they began to be supplanted by the "authenticist" groups that use replicas of period instruments and try to reproduce period performance practices.

Thursday <u>Thanksgiving day (23-11)</u>

[. . .] Dr. Stein sent us back to New York today. It's Thanksgiving day, thus a day off for everyone. But he gave me a special injection and a careful examination. He wants me to stay in New York for a week, to walk for a quarter hour now and then, to conduct—at home only—and to notice whether after twenty and more minutes of work my leg becomes atrophied, as happened to me after the <u>Te Deum</u> at the Scala concert.

I heard the <u>Virtuosi di Roma</u> the other evening in Philadelphia. They played magnificently and with great success. I went to greet them after the concert. They went crazy!! They kissed me, embraced me, and wept with emotion. They left for London yesterday aboard the <u>Queen Elizabeth</u> steamship.

We left Philadelphia at four minutes past noon and got here at one thirty-eight. We found Cia doing decently, but she must stay in bed for a few weeks. [. . .]

<u>Sunday 3 December 1950</u>

My <u>dear Carla.</u> I've finally learned what it means to have a <u>toothache.</u> And I paid for it rather dearly, with the extraction of <u>two</u> teeth. [. . .] But you, Carla, you'll still love me even without the two teeth, isn't that so?

The Cantellis have arrived. He has already had two rehearsals and is very happy with the orchestra. They'll be here for dinner this evening, with Wanda and Miecio. I read today of the deaths of Betti and the pianist Lipatti, whom I met and heard at La Scala in 1946. [. . .] And Tommasini—has he recovered? My God, so much sadness! And the war! And the atomic bomb! [. . .]

AT's friend Adolfo Betti had been first violin of the Flonzaley String Quartet. · The Romanian Dinu Lipatti, one of the most gifted pianists of his generation, had died of a rare form of cancer the day before this letter was written; he was thirty-three years old. · Tommasini died three weeks later, on 23 December 1950. · The war was, of course, the Korean War.

[. . .] The Philadelphia treatment was a <u>complete failure.</u> Now there's the story of my teeth. Little by little, they've removed **three,** together with two or three roots of teeth that had gradually crumbled. I'm telling you, I'm <u>quite a mess.</u> Now they want to try a treatment with **cortisone,** which is said to be marvelous. These are injections that have extraordinary powers.

[. . .] I've already accepted to conduct the Verdi Requiem on January 27 at

<u>Carnegie Hall</u> to benefit Casa Verdi, with <u>Nelli, Barbieri, Di Stefano,</u> and <u>Siepi.</u> I hope I'll be well, but in the meantime the weeks go by and I'm forever agitated and I haven't yet tried to conduct; but <u>come what may</u> I'll find the strength to do well, at least for that evening. [. . .]

Along with the other singers named here, the tenor Giuseppe Di Stefano (b. 1921) was among the youngest singers with whom AT worked.

E.P. PHILADELPHIA, 6 JANUARY 1951;
P.S. AS IN LETTER OF 31 OCTOBER 1950; TO CT, D2OMI; EC

<u>Friday 5-January 1951</u>

[. . .] the sadness of not having been able to be with you [Carla and Wally] for Christmas and New Year's was immense, and in my heart I cursed America and my engagements. What's more, this year I feel lost. Not having the NBC [i.e., Studio 8-H] is like not having air and light!!! Those two Jews David [Sarnoff] and Chotzinoff will never know how much harm they've done me!! The failure of the treatment, the tragedy of my teeth—everything has helped to throw me into this state of affliction and agitation from which I can't manage to free myself. I see black, everything black. I have a recording session on Wednesday 10 January, and I'm terrified just to <u>think about it.</u> But I'll go, even if I have to go on crutches. I've already had three cortisone injections, directly into the guilty knee. Together with the injections I'm also getting <u>X rays</u> on the knee and kidneys. After the second, I seemed cured—I went back to the hotel on foot, marvelously. But today things went differently and I'm a bit discouraged. Tomorrow, Saturday, I'll have the fourth one, then I'll go back to New York, since no one even thinks about working on Sunday and I'll be glad to get out of this hateful city. After the recording session on Wednesday I'll come back and resume [the treatment]. Ticket sales for the Requiem on the 27th are going full steam, as was to be expected. Make my excuses to Wally for not having written to her, but I hope she'll understand. I'm very agitated, my brain is full of nasty thoughts and my heart full of bitterness. I've never felt so awful in New York. Poor Toscanini!!!—but this time <u>for real.</u> [. . .]

AT and the NBC Symphony Orchestra made a brilliant recording of Strauss's *Don Juan* on 10 January 1951.

DRAFT IN AT'S SHAKY HAND, WRITTEN ON VERSO OF ANOTHER LETTER,
(NY), N.D. BUT PROBABLY FEBRUARY 1951;
TO JOHN HOWE TREDER, HERSHEY, PENNSYLVANIA; ORIG. ENG.
(ALL ERRORS HAVE BEEN PRESERVED); NYPLTL

My dear <u>friend Dena</u> [Dener?; should be Treder]
I thank you for yuor sweet and kind letter about the Requiem and Te Deum

but I don't deserve any praise[.] I did my best in order to reach a good performance worthy of the circumstance instead I failed entirely and I was so unhappy as I cant say but the performance of both Requ and Te Deum faild to be as good as I hoped and I felt unhappy and ashamed of myself

This was a reply to a letter from the Reverend John Howe Treder, Vicar, All Saints' Episcopal Church, Hershey, Pennsylvania, who had written to tell AT that he had been in the Schola Cantorum in New York from 1936 to 1939 and had sung under AT's direction in performances with the Philharmonic; he said that the experience had been an inspiration for his whole life, including the priesthood, and he praised AT's recent performance of the Verdi *Requiem* and *Te Deum,* which had taken place on 10 January 1951, the fiftieth anniversary of Verdi's death. AT eventually allowed the performance of the *Requiem* to be released on record, although he insisted that a considerable amount of material recorded during the rehearsals replace segments that had not gone right during the performance.

E.P. NY, (24?) FEBRUARY 1951; TO CT, D2OMI; EC

24 <u>February 1951</u>

[. . .] How am I? Even I don't know. I'd like to be back home. I can assure you that never have I wished to be in my old house as much as during these months. To be in New York without working has never happened to me before. My attempt [to conduct] succeeded only halfway, and above all because I had promised you that in any case I would conduct the Requiem! I had already tested my strength with magnificent results when I worked for three hours [recording Strauss's *Don Juan* on 10 January 1951]. But after the Requiem, no one realized how much effort performing the three concerts that followed cost me, so I decided to drop the last two [after those three]. So be it.

[. . .] My leg continues to be <u>as heavy as before,</u> and even worse. One day, after a rehearsal, Dr. Howe measured my blood pressure at 165, another day at 160; they laid the blame on the cortisone. A few days later, it went down to 122, and the evening of the Requiem it was 120. Now it's normal. I've freed myself of the London engagement, however. Now my thoughts are turned toward Busseto! Can I have faith in a <u>problematic</u> improvement? Here it's a matter of preparing a whole season and having a big responsibility on my shoulders!!! I'm very agitated. Dr. Stein advises me to go to Arizona for a couple of weeks—he says I need a change of climate. I haven't yet decided; I would rather go back home, but I'm torn by the wish and the anxiety not to leave New York before I have at least some improvement. I admit that I'm very nervous and worried. I hadn't been aware of having reached the age of 83!!! Now I'm only too aware of it. Other disturbances, such as my much-weakened eyesight, bother me more than a little. [. . .]

AT had had to cancel his planned participation in the opening concerts of the Royal Festival Hall in London. He wanted to conduct Verdi's *Macbeth* (and possibly also *Falstaff*) at Busseto, with Maria Callas as Lady Macbeth, during the summer of 1951, as part of the Verdi commemorations, but this also proved to be impossible for reasons of age and health.

E.P. NEW ROCHELLE, N.Y., 25 FEBRUARY 1951; TO CT, D2OMI; EC

Sunday <u>25 February 1951</u>

My <u>dear Carla</u> I've had a very anxious day today. Bruno Walter and his daughter Lotte came to lunch. It was a magnificent day—the sun practically begged to be applauded, like a tenor. But my mood continued to darken. I went to your rooms and I could have cried—such sadness! I don't want to go to Arizona. I want, rather, to go to Milan. I have a great desire to see my house, to see you and Wally again, to hear your voices. It's terrible to be here and not work. [. . .]

E.P. NY, 14 MARCH 1951; TO WYT, D2OMI; EC

14 <u>March 1951</u>

My <u>adored Wally</u>

Day and night I read and reread your [plural] affectionate letters to feel that you are near and in my bloodstream, because I need it so much. I'm sad, ever so sad, and this sadness has dug itself into my heart since the day of my arrival here. Six months! You can imagine! I won't go to Arizona, no! Instead, I'll return home as soon as possible. Just as Antaeus needed to touch the earth to regain his strength, I must embrace you and mamma in my old house to bring peace back to my heart. I've thought of you so much, and with sorrowful homesickness—I really don't know how I've held out and stayed in New York. Only the illnesses of old age have kept me from it [i.e., returning to Italy]. I don't yet know when I'll leave. I'll certainly leave with the Cantellis during the first half of April. Maybe Wanda will come, too; she arrives this evening, after having followed her husband's concerts for a week, since his secretary died. Walter absolutely <u>must</u> stay in New York. Cia's health is too delicate and she is in extreme need of help. She stays in bed for weeks and weeks, she can't climb the stairs, can't go often in the automobile—she's really miserable and my heart aches for her, the poor thing! My knee is still the same. Despite the ten cortisone injections, it hasn't improved. And yet I would like to work. I feel that work overcomes my great age!

Is it true that La Scala gave the [Verdi] Requiem free on 27 January? Mamma raised two million [lire] from her sickbed, and La Scala <u>in action</u> presents its audience with the commemorative Requiem as a gift! Bravo, Mr. General Manager! I greatly deplored the bad outcome of La Traviata, and I'm surprised at Tebaldi and her lack of self-esteem. And that ass of a General Manager wants to give Oberto instead of Nabucco!

Please note, Wally, that I don't want to see Ghiringhelli when I arrive. One thing that made a strong impression on me was the death of my dear friend Tommasini! Who was near him? He lived by himself! I wanted to write to [Elsa] Respighi or to Ada Mainardi, who were very friendly with him, but then . . . I saw him only once this year [i.e., the previous summer]. Last year he spent a week on the Isolino. Poor, dear friend of fifty years. And that wretch of a Molinari is still alive, and in God knows what condition!

My dear, adored, Wally, let's set aside these sad things and think about seeing each other again in a few weeks. Kiss and hug Mamma, and as for you, think of how much I love you and how dear you are to me.

<u>Wholly your papa</u>

Like CT, Cia Fornaroli Toscanini was suffering from acute heart disease. · AT knew that Tommasini had been one of Ada Mainardi's many admirers; she and the composer were lovers, according to some. · Molinari died on 25 December 1952.

E.P. NY, 15 MARCH 1951; TO CT, D2OMI; EC

14 <u>March 1951</u>

[. . .] Today, in talking with Walter, I noticed that my foolishness began when I considered the possibility of doing productions in Busseto! My mind was still far back in 1913 [and] 1926. In those days productions cost a few thousand lire per performance; today they cost millions. What a fool! And no one thought of it; we had to wait until today to notice. Enough. With the Requiem at Carnegie [Hall], I managed to do something decent! You did the rest, even though you're in bed. I can't forgive La Scala for having given the Requiem on January 27 gratis. That Ghiringhelli is a real donkey, stubborn to the point of nausea. Cowardly to excess. Worthy of that secretary from whom he gets the inspiration to put together those <u>season programs à la Walter Mocchi,</u> real provincial hodgepodges, filled up with <u>a bit of everything.</u> [. . .]

There is no question but that funding would have been found for any opera production that AT had wished to conduct; Walter probably mentioned the excessive expense of bringing productions to Busseto as a way of giving AT a ready excuse for withdrawing without unduly hurting his ferocious pride. · We do not know whether AT had changed his mind about the quality of his performance of Verdi's *Requiem* (see pp. 432–433) or whether he was simply trying to reassure Carla about his physical condition. · La Scala's secretary-general was Luigi Oldani. · For more on Walter Mocchi, see AT's letter to Duke Uberto Visconti di Modrone in 1916 and my accompanying note (pp. 89–92).

21 <u>March 1951</u>

My dear <u>Carla</u>

Today is Walter's birthday. We'll all go to the Pelletiers to celebrate. He doesn't know it yet. They'll come pick us up with their automobile. Maybe the Cantellis will come; they just got back yesterday from San Francisco, where he had a memorable success. [. . .]

I can't wait to leave—and to finish this unfortunate season. Yet I must work, I can't stay idle; work is my life. Before leaving I think I'll make <u>a few records.</u> I don't want to leave Beethoven's second symphony unfinished; three movements are <u>magnificent.</u> Only the first is bad. Walter won't be able to come [to Italy] with me. Although Cia is much better, she can't <u>and mustn't climb</u> the stairs. Her heart is still a mess, and if we can't manage to install an elevator here it will be a disaster. I have high hopes of arriving [in Milan] even before the 15th of next month. I can no longer stand not seeing you and embracing you. I kiss you many, many times, and also Wally.

<u>Entirely your Tosca.</u>

In the end, AT conducted no further recording sessions or anything else before he left for Italy. · This was probably his last letter to CT.

Nigh [*sic*] letter   Via RCA

Frank M. Folsom

President Radio Corporation America

Very grateful for acknowledgment of friendship I heartily thank you for your kind letters Stop Unfortunately for my Carla there is no more hope of recovering and in these sad hours of despair the only hope is to look forward to my work with the NBC Greetings Arturo Toscanini

Folsom occasionally sent friendly greetings to AT, who was the most celebrated of all of RCA Victor's artists. CT died on 23 June 1951, two months after AT's return to Italy. · As AT's eyesight worsened, so did his ability to write; thus he increasingly depended on others to write out messages that he dictated.

My most beloved Walfredo,

It's inevitable that we have to be far apart when we would like to be more united than ever. So it goes! But you know very well that your old grandfather wishes you every possible happiness, as your goodness deserves.

I give you a big, big hug, and I kiss you affectionately.

Your <u>old grandfather</u>

16 August 1951

This was Walfredo's twenty-second birthday. He was a student at Yale University.

(NY), 3 OCTOBER 1951; P.S., AT; TO WYT, (MI); EC

My <u>most beloved Wally</u>

I can't forgive myself for having left without having first visited the cemetery! And then, the very hurried departure, without having been able to stay with you [plural] calmly for an instant poisoned the trip for me; it seemed eternal, sad, and at every moment I felt that I was suffocating—so I swore <u>never</u> to go by <u>airplane again.</u>

Nor was the arrival in Riverdale a happy one! Cia had been in bed for several days with that blessed heart of hers in a state of agitation. She doesn't yet have permission to go downstairs to Mamma's apartment. She is always good and patient.

I am as always—well, according to others, badly, according to me. I'm homesick for my old house in Via Durini! But what can I do? I want to work. In Italy I can't. The atmosphere I need for working is only here. And work I must, otherwise life is <u>intolerable</u>!! I've made two records. Nearly three and a half hours of rehearsal were enough. Howe took my blood pressure afterward—it was 122 over 80. I didn't feel tired out. Next Friday I have another rehearsal. Beethoven's Second Symph. and the Don Pasquale Overture. So you see that your old father has gotten down to work, and with enthusiasm. [. . .]

(3-10-1951)

AT always used the Italian term *prove* (rehearsals) for recording sessions. · On 28 September 1951 he had recorded Rossini's *Semiramide* Overture and the Weber-Berlioz *Invitation to the Dance.* On 5 October 1951 he completed his recording of Beethoven's Second Symphony, which he had begun two years earlier (see the letter of 21 March 1951) and also recorded Donizetti's *Don Pasquale* Overture. All of these items, as well as recordings of works by Prokofiev, Wagner, and—again—Weber, made later in October, were released.

14 [24?] October 1951

My dear Valdengo,

I believe that the puntatura that is often done in the Violetta-Germont duet in the 2nd act of La Traviata is as old as the opera itself. I have always heard it and always allowed it; in fact, allow me to say something heretical, I prefer this puntatura to the original notes written by the maestro. Only it would be necessary for the artist to sing that magnificent piece with paternal emotion and not to shout it, as is generally done.

Thank you for the short news updates that I used to receive from you every once in a while and that made my dear Departed smile and moved my heart.

Say hello to Nelli for me and thank Moscona for his dear telegram, and see you soon in New York. I embrace you heartily.

Arturo Toscanini

P.S. Excuse me, dear Signora Nannetta—my salutations to you got stuck in my pen—but I send them to you very affectionately. Your devoted
AT.

For more on Valdengo, see the letter of 20 December 1948. The present letter was sent from New York to Italy. A *puntatura* is usually a note or passage sung an octave higher than written. · The bass Nicola Moscona (1907–75) sang many times with AT during the 1940s and 1950s. · Signora Nannetta was Valdengo's first wife. · The tone of this letter gives an idea of the warm human relations that AT usually maintained with singers and orchestra musicians, despite his sternness with them in rehearsals.

3 November 1951

My adored Wally

[. . .] If I didn't have the work that keeps me here and is so necessary to my life, I would go back to my old house in Via Durini, where everything speaks to me of Her and of your [plural] childhood and adolescence! I can declare myself happy with my work. I've had five recording sessions of three hours each, without getting tired, and three rehearsals for the concert that I'll be conducting in a few hours. So you see that I'm well enough. My mood is still the same, I often take chlorate. You can guess the reason. Cia is better after five or six weeks in bed. I had Sonia here for two days, and she has really become a serious, very dear girl. She spoke on television with marvelous ease, as if it were for the hundredth time rather than the first.

What's happened to the painter Caselli and my portrait? He had promised to send me a photograph, even if [the portrait] wasn't finished, as well as other color photographs, but so far I haven't received anything. Has he finished it or not? Thank you also for sending me the photograph of my beautiful, dear granddaughter! For the record: Monday, November 5, I'll have a recording session from <u>midnight on</u>! Can you picture your old father working at that hour? [. . .]

In 1953 the Florentine painter Silvano Caselli (b. 1921) published a book—*Toscanini nella pittura di Caselli* (Bergamo: Istituto italiano d'arti grafiche, 1953)—that is illustrated by photographs and preparatory pencil, pen, and oil sketches for a portrait of AT that he did in 1951; there are also reproductions of the finished portrait, details from it, and other works by Caselli (including a portrait of Stravinsky), as well as essays by Orio Vergani, Emilio Radius, and Waldemar George. · AT made his best-known (but not necessarily best in other respects) recording of Brahms's First Symphony at that postmidnight session on what was actually November 6.

TG, NY, 14 JANUARY 1952; TO FAMILY OF AURELIANO PERTILE,
VIA SAN NICOLAO 5, MI; CASA NATALE DI TOSCANINI, PARMA, ITALY

DISMAYED TO LEARN SUDDEN PASSING MY DEAR FRIEND AND UNFORGET-
TABLE COLLEAGUE I JOIN IN YOUR GREAT MOURNING REMEMBERING HIM
WITH AFFECTION AND WEEPING FOR HIM = ARTURO TOSCANINI +

Pertile (1885–1952) did not have the most beautiful tenor voice of his era, but he was an outstanding, highly intelligent artist and one of AT's favorite singers at La Scala throughout the 1920s. Plácido Domingo has said that Pertile's recordings are "remarkable first and foremost for the modernity of their style: he would feel at home on the stage of any opera house today—which is not true of many of his contemporaries." This telegram is the only document I can think of in which AT referred to a singer as a colleague. Pertile had died on 11 January.

TYPED TRANSCRIPT OF LETTER EXCERPT, RIVERDALE, 21 APRIL 1952;
TO MARIA CECCHINI (ITALY); EC

[. . .] I'm a wretch who doesn't write, and in addition to doing harm to others I also do it to myself.

I very much need to communicate with others and <u>unload</u> from my heart all the goodness it contains, beyond its strength. But what's to be done? I've become an incorrigible old man, and you've got to be patient with me. [. . .]

E.P. NY, 3 MAY 1952; P.S., AT; TO OLIN DOWNES, THE NEW YORK TIMES,
37 RUE CAUMARTIN, PARIS; ORIG. ENG. (ALL ERRORS HAVE BEEN
PRESERVED); ODUGA

(May 1—1952)

My dear <u>Olin Downes</u>
I am not so presumptuous as to give any opinion on your "Ten Masterpieces of Operas" nor can I think that my opinion would ever ever be printed in maga-

zines or in daily newspapers. Believe me, Olin, I have never permitted anyone to print or to publish any opinion of mine, because I never gave any opinion to them and I do not want to start to day at my age.—.

Nevertheless, in explaining in words, as you said, to the public the best way to comprehend the Opera-Drama in its true significance, is to <u>help him</u> [*sic*, for "it"]: to point out in detail, as you did, the way the composers bring to the listeners their thoughts and emotions, it is, <u>the non plus ultra</u> of teaching. So I was right when I agreed with your attempts, because I was fully aware of your great musical culture and certain unfailing success.

I have read and reread the librettos of the four operas you left with me with the same interest and the most favorable impression. Especially "Die Meistersinger" fashinated me pleasingly. While reading it the music was singing in my moved mind . . . I imagine you have worked <u>hard</u> on this book, I am sure, but you have <u>succeeded</u> in your aim . . . Bravo, bravissimo, my dear Olin.

In a few days I leave for Italy. I hope to meet you somewhere there . . . God bless you my dear!

God bless you my dear!

Your affectionate friend
<u>Arturo Toscanini</u>

For more on Downes, see the letter of 3 October 1940, and the accompanying note. Downes evidently sent a copy of his book <u>10 Operatic Masterpieces</u> (New York: Scribner's, 1952) to AT. AT drafted a reply, first in Italian, then in English, and his secretary, Eugenia Gale, typed up a final version in slightly more idiomatic English. The version given above is AT's handwritten English draft, which is more pungent than the typed version.

TG, MI, 16 JUNE 1952; TO WRT, RIVERDALE; PC; NYPLTL

NINTH GOOD PHONE US IMMEDIATELY EULENBURG IN HAND =

On 31 March and 1 April 1952, two and three days after having performed Beethoven's Ninth Symphony (for the last time in his life) at Carnegie Hall, Toscanini and the NBC Symphony Orchestra recorded the work in the same venue. Back in Italy for the summer, AT evidently listened to the various takes of the work and wished to comment on them in order to put together a finished recording for release. Eulenburg published a pocket edition of the score, and AT evidently wanted to make sure that the producer with whom Walter was working on the recording would have the same edition in hand, for reference purposes.

TYPED TRANSCRIPT OF EXCERPT FROM LETTER, CASAMICCIOLA, ISCHIA,
AUGUST 1952; TO MARIA CECCHINI, (ITALY); EC

My dear Maria, what beauty, what luminosity in this village! The sun, flowers, and stars seem more luminous than back home! Dream country. Human beings could live with a fistful of grass if they had eyes for seeing and a heart for feeling. See you soon on the Isolino.

Your old friend

(NY); P.S., AT; TO WYT (MI); EC

2 <u>November 1952</u>

[. . .] I'm well—that's what the doctors say. I work, and it seems that I'm working well. Yesterday evening I gave the first concert—Brahms's 3rd Symphony and Strauss's Till Eulenspiegel—this last played as never before by the orchestra. The work doesn't weigh on me. Doctor Howe comes after every rehearsal and always finds my blood pressure good, but what I have in my heart and brain he can't see, unfortunately, but there's a sadness that can't be healed—after the sudden death of Alda I have no peace. If I didn't have my work, which forces me to stay here, I would fly home immediately.

My dear Wally, how I miss you! I think of you every moment and would like to have you always near me, like Walter and Cia, who are so good to me— poor things! Today is a sad day, and I'm thinking of all my dead, who are many, from the eldest of my sisters to my adored Carla!! [. . .]

AT's dear old friend Frances Alda, the soprano, had died in Venice on 18 September 1952 at the age of seventy-three. · Narcisa, the eldest of AT's sisters, had been dead for nearly seventy-five years.

TYPED TRANSCRIPT OF EXCERPT FROM LETTER, RIVERDALE,
16 MARCH 1953; TO MARIA CECCHINI, (ITALY); EC

[. . .] I'm working on the Missa Solemnis. If, with my enthusiasm and adoration for that <u>Saint,</u> I could accomplish something worthy, it would be the greatest reward of my long (too long) artistic life. [. . .]

(NY), N.D. BUT PROBABLY LATE APRIL OR EARLY MAY 1953; P.S., AT;
TO WYT, (MI); PC; EC

My adored Wally, I would like to come to Milan soon, but I have to stay to work more on the proofs of the records of the <u>Missa Solemnis.</u> The violinist who plays in the <u>Benedictus</u> didn't make enough sound and has to play again onto the record that we have made. Then I would like to go to Philadelphia for a few days, to Doctor Stein. I think I'll leave around the beginning of June. If Walfredo gets out of military service, everyone would come [to Italy]—Cia, Walfredo, and Walter. Anyway you know that I love you, but you don't know how much—and I'm certainly not going to tell you. Tell Maria [Cecchini] that I'll write to her and thank her for mailing to [*sic;* should be: from] Paris the marvelous reviews of the <u>Cadets of La Scala.</u> It was a very great pleasure for me. Even my friend <u>Vuillermoz</u> spoke with enthusiasm, also about Maestro <u>Enrico Piazza,</u> and this gave me great pleasure, because he deserves it. Ciao dearest, I embrace you, I kiss you till you suffocate. Your

<u>very old father</u>

The violin soloist in the *Missa Solemnis* was Daniel Guilet, concertmaster of the NBC Symphony Orchestra. · The Cadetti della Scala were young singers who participated in a training program under the direction of Enrico Piazza, one of La Scala's assistant conductors; they included such up-and-coming artists as Luigi Alva, Flaviano Labò, Ilva Ligabue, Paolo Montarsolo, and Ivo Vinco. AT had heard them rehearse Cherubini's *L'osteria portoghese* and had been very impressed with their work; thus he was pleased when Vuillermoz (see the letter postmarked 29 August 1935 and the accompanying note) praised a performance they had given in Paris.

E.P. NY, 14 MAY 1953; P.S., AT; TO WYT, MI; EC

---

12 <u>May 1953</u>

My <u>adored Wally</u>

[. . .] I've worked a lot. The Missa Solemnis kept me <u>very, very</u> occupied and preoccupied. I tried to improve since the last time I conducted it, in 1940. I hope that I succeeded—I say I hope, but I'm not sure. I was hoping to close this season and be done with it once and for all, because I can't stand being Arturo Toscanini any longer—at this point I'm bored with hearing my name—it's been heard for many years, too many, and I would like to rest for what little time remains to me and enjoy a peaceful death. Unfortunately, my ferocious resistance was beaten by the most ferocious ball-breakers, and the day that Brigadier General Sarnoff came to lunch with Chotzinoff, to start in again on their exhortations about my return, I prepared in a great hurry three programs that Walter presented to him before he could see me and talk to me. That's how the matter ended, and for me it ended badly. But I've resigned myself—this is my fate—to work until I close my eyes. And the work doesn't tire me! Twenty years ago, a doctor would come to give me an injection after a rehearsal or concert; these days, he comes to see whether my blood pressure is still good. I feel tired for an hour or two, but then I'm nimble again. But my eyes get worse and worse, my legs no longer have the already diminished elasticity of the last few years, and even my memory is no longer what it once was, but rather <u>it is what it is</u>—bad, in other words—and that's to be expected! Everyone, starting with the orchestra, says that I conduct better than before, and I really can't deny it, but I've always continued to study and have never believed that I could do without it, and right to the last day they won't see me **going soft!!!** My <u>pride is limitless</u>—and I have never been satisfied with myself, nor am I today. But can I guarantee that I'll still be able to accomplish the task that they've forced me to take on? I've already prepared my 14 programs and have already begun to study, but I'm not happy; I don't know why, but I torture myself, I don't sleep well, but on the contrary badly, and above all with continuous, fearful dreams. [rest of letter missing]

It is clear that AT accepted the "exhortations" to conduct another season because this is what he really wanted to do in his heart of hearts. Had he felt otherwise, no one would have been able to persuade him to change his mind. In the end, however, he conducted only eleven broadcasts rather than fourteen.

RIVERDALE, 16 MAY 1953; TO MARIA CECCHINI (ITALY); FIRST PART:
TRANSLATION OF QUOTATION DICTATED TO ME
BY MARIA CECCHINI MONTARSOLO IN 1977; SECOND PART:
TYPED TRANSCRIPT BELONGING TO EC OF EXCERPTS FROM LETTER

[. . .] I am not well, and no one believes me, the asses, but I'm not the same as I was. My eyes have worsened so much that I can no longer find glasses that can help me. I sleep little and badly, tormented by tragic, commonplace, or fearful dreams. All in all, a poor, unhappy man—and they have had the bad taste to force me to accept another year of concerts. And I, imbecile that I am and tired of hearing myself pestered, have given in. The American public will again have to have the patience to put up with having an old man of eighty-six before its eyes.

[. . .] [Y]ou gave me indescribable pleasure by sending such enthusiastic and well-presented reviews. I truly thank you from my heart. You can't imagine my joy in reading the well-earned praise bestowed on those dear young singers and on that dear Maestro Enrico Piazza. [. . .] You must take me [again] sometime to hear the rehearsals of those young artists. I love the young more than the old and famous. I see that Vuillermoz, too, had nice words to say about Maestro Piazza. He is a magnificent, intelligent critic, and he writes excellently. He defended Cherubini, which gave me great pleasure. In Paris there are still imbeciles, just as in Berlioz's day, unfortunately!!

I see in the newspapers that Schwarzkoff [sic] will sing Mélisande! She is a marvelous singer, but in Pelléas you don't sing, but rather speak through singing, and sing correctly in French, which I believe is impossible for a German woman. I wouldn't want to hear her for all the tea in China. I wouldn't love her anymore. I'm very sorry not to have had her for the Missa Solemnis! Excuse my horrible writing, but I'm very agitated and my hand slides around on the paper. That's the way it goes! I'm old, very old, and I can't stand it anymore! [. . .]

AT admired Cherubini and conducted several orchestral pieces by him, but none of his operas. · Elisabeth Schwarzkopf (b. 1915) was one of the leading sopranos of her generation; AT evidently considered her excellent and highly attractive. · The Canadian soprano Lois Marshall (1924–1997) sang in AT's 1953 *Missa Solemnis* performance and recording.

My <u>dearest Miecio,</u>

You worked hard with Casals and you didn't rest as you should have done! Now you're rushing away from me, to America, and you haven't even come to Italy, much less to the Isolino! I, too, went to the Isolino [only] a couple of times and have stayed put in Milan, except for four days in Rome to see Doctor Frugoni. Walter, Cia, and Walfredo are here with me, the last one traveling around Italy with Emanuela. The Chotzinoffs, too, have arrived and will stay in Pallanza for a few weeks, then they intend to travel. I am working on my programs for the coming season, which I **hope** will <u>definitely</u> be the **last** (68-year career). We'll stay here through September. In October we'll return [to America] by <u>Airplane.</u>

According to Frugoni, my health is better than during the last few years; as for me, I'm not satisfied. But so be it, as long as I can work and end honorably my too-long career!!

Best wishes to you for a good trip and an even better start for your work.

I embrace you.

Your <u>A Toscanini</u>

(3 August 1953)

Horszowski had participated in Pablo Casals's Prades Festival, in the south of France, from mid-June to early July. · AT occasionally visited Dr. Cesare Frugoni in Rome for a general checkup.

[. . .] Good to postpone dates Ballo maschera—Silveri impossible—Try Merrill putting him in hands of Marzollo. Ask Chotzi make record Schumann's Manfred marvelous performance. Please make tape Mignone's concerto—We await you with open arms—Much affection

Papa

AT had decided to conduct a concert performance of Verdi's *Un ballo in maschera* during the 1953–54 NBC season; it was eventually presented in two halves, on 17 and 24 January 1954. He had evidently considered the baritone Paolo Silveri (b. 1913) for the role of Renato but had changed his mind after having heard him; instead, he opted for Robert Merrill (b. 1917), who had sung in AT's NBC *Traviata* broadcast recording in 1946, but he wanted the trustworthy coach Dick Marzollo to prepare Merrill in the role. · AT had presumably listened to a tape of his live NBC performance (31 January 1953) of Schumann's "Manfred" Overture and wanted to have it issued; he may have forgotten that his 1946 NBC studio recording of the piece was already on the market. (The 1953 version was not in fact published by RCA.) · In 1943 AT had performed a

Fantasia Brasileira for piano and orchestra by Francisco Mignone (1897–1986) with the NBC Symphony Orchestra and may have been considering the performance for release.

TYPEWRITTEN LETTER, (NY); TO DAVID SARNOFF, (NY); ORIG. ENG.;
NBC ARCHIVES, BOX 166, FOLDER 46, REPRINTED IN DONALD C. MEYER,
"THE NBC SYMPHONY ORCHESTRA"
(DISSERTATION, UNIVERSITY OF CALIFORNIA, DAVIS, 1994), P. 370

March 25, 1954

My very dear David:

At this season of the year seventeen years ago you sent me an invitation to become the Musical Director of an orchestra to be created especially for me for the purpose of broadcasting symphonic music throughout the United States.

You will remember how reluctant I was to accept your invitation because I felt at that time that I was too old to start a new venture. However, you persuaded me and all of my doubts were dispelled as soon as I began rehearsing for the first broadcast of Christmas night in 1937 with the group of fine musicians whom you had chosen.

Year after year it has been a joy for me to know that the music played by the NBC Symphony Orchestra has been acclaimed by the vast radio audiences all over the United States and abroad.

And now the sad time has come when I must reluctantly lay aside my baton and say goodbye to my orchestra, and in leaving I want you to know that I shall carry with me rich memories of these years of music making and heartfelt gratitude to you and the National Broadcasting Company for having made them possible.

I know that I can rely on you to express to everyone at the National Broadcasting Company who has worked with me all these years my cordial and sincere thanks.

Your friend,
Arturo Toscanini

This letter was prepared for AT by Walter and (probably) others, and was signed by AT, in a shaky hand, on his eighty-seventh birthday. Copies of it were distributed to New York's music critics as they arrived at Carnegie Hall for what proved to be AT's last public performance—the NBC Symphony Orchestra concert of 4 April 1954.

DRAFT (IN VERY SHAKY HAND) OF TG, (NY), N.D.; IN ANOTHER HAND:
"JUNE 3, 1954"; NYPLTL

Maestro Bruno Walter.
Teatro Scala
Milano
I am terribly sorry not to be present at your concert and not to be able to spend a few hours with you in my beautiful country and to tell you personally how

moved I was by your dear letter Stop. I am working on some records, but I am near you in my thoughts. I embrace you in affectionate friendship, your old friend <u>Arturo Toscanini</u>

AT conducted for the last time on 3 and 5 June 1954, at a pair of NBC Symphony Orchestra recording sessions in Carnegie Hall to touch up a few segments of the *Ballo in maschera* and *Aida* live broadcast recordings.

TG, (MI?), N.D. BUT LATE JUNE OR EARLY JULY 1954;
TO COMMITTEE FOR THE FORMER NBC SYMPHONY ORCHESTRA, NY;
ORIG. ENG.; IN THE *NEW YORK TIMES*, 4 JULY 1954, P. 23;
REPRINTED IN MEYER, OP. CIT., P. 390

Please thank Don Gillis and orchestra members for their touching, kind cable. Greatly appreciate it but my age and my present feeling do not allow me to make plans for the future. Extend my best wishes to each member of the orchestra.

When AT retired, NBC dropped its symphony orchestra. Many of its musicians wished to continue to play together, and various plans were formulated; eventually, the ensemble became known as the Symphony of the Air and worked with several outstanding conductors. The players invited AT to conduct their first concert, and this telegram was his reply. · Don Gillis (1912–78), an American composer, had produced the NBC Symphony Orchestra broadcasts for ten years.

DRAFT OF TG; IN ANOTHER HAND:
"FROM MILAN TO WALTER [NY] — 24 NOV. 1954"; NYPLTL

I'm sorry about and I protest against publication Fidelio without my final revision stop. Prisoners' chorus too loud stop. Must find better rehearsal [i.e., recording made at a rehearsal] first act finale[.] Please repair this somehow. Ballo maschera—Aida—Requiem Mass had precedence over Fidelio. Greetings.

If this message is to be believed, AT's live 1944 NBC broadcast recording of Beethoven's *Fidelio* had been issued without his permission. There are worse flaws in the performance than the volume of the Prisoners' Chorus (e.g., generally harsh sound quality and bad ensemble work in the postlude to Florestan's aria), but much of the performance is so powerfully intense that posterity ought to be grateful for its existence, especially inasmuch as an off-the-air recording of AT's 1937 broadcast of *Fidelio* from Salzburg seems to have been lost forever.

I have followed you mentally through your laborious rehearsals stop = I affectionately send you my friendly blessing. I embrace you.

Toscanini.

Cantelli was conducting the Verdi *Requiem* for the first time in his life on 17 December 1954, with the Boston Symphony Orchestra.

= I WAS MOVED BY YOUR BEAUTIFUL PERFORMANCE OF MAHLER'S SYM-
PHONIES AND LIEDER PERFORMED AND SUNG BY THAT DIVINE VOICE I
EMBRACE YOU WITH GREAT GREAT FRIENDSHIP =
= ARTURO TOSCANINI.

Either AT had suddenly become interested in Mahler's music in the last months of his life or this telegram was invented for him by someone else. · The "divine voice" was that of the English contralto Kathleen Ferrier (1912–53).

Extremely moved kind remembrance please express to all members delegation my thanks and fervent hope that under their direction the renovated Coccia will continue glorious artistic tradition. Cordially

Arturo Toscanini

For Teatro Coccia, see the letter of 25 June 1949 and the accompanying note. · To my knowledge, this is the last message that AT ever wrote (or—more likely in this case—dictated). He suffered a stroke early on the morning of 1 January 1957 and died in his sleep on 16 January 1957 at his home in Riverdale.

Index

Hartford, Connecticut, 197
Haydn, Joseph, 52, 136, 237, 247, 258; *Seven Last Words of Christ*, 245, 246; Symphony no. 31 in D Major, "Hornsignal," 126, 127; Symphony no. 98 in B-Flat Major, 247, 252; Symphony no. 101 in D Major, "Clock," 41, 198
Heifetz, Florence Vidor, 256
Heifetz, Jascha, 166, 230, 256, 319, 365, 371
Heldy, Fanny, 244
Helletsgruber, Luise, 157, 271
Henders, Harriet, 271
Hitler, Adolf, xvii, xviii, 62, 138, 174, 261, 266, 269, 271, 320, 325, 342, 376; *Anschluss* and, 327; Toscanini's letter to, 138
Holland, 238–9, 330
Holt, Harold, 258
Holt sisters, 258
Homer, Louise, 80
Horowitz, Samuel, 322–3
Horowitz, Sonia, 174, 217, 270, 314, 344, 356, 368, 369, 377
Horowitz, Vladimir, 153–4, 156, 163, 166, 174, 182, 188, 211, 222, 296, 299–300, 303, 314, 320–3, 338–9, 356, 358, 365–6, 369, 371, 377, 380, 388, 402, 411, 414; NBC Symphony Brahms program with Toscanini (1948), 421–2
Horowitz, Wanda Toscanini, 61, 80, 81, 116, 143–4, 151, 154, 157, 162, 166, 174, 188, 191, 218, 222, 225, 249, 252, 295, 305, 314, 320–3, 333, 334, 338, 344, 356, 358, 365, 369, 371, 377, 411
Horszowski, Mieczysław, 152, 444; Toscanini's letter to, 444
Howe, Hubert, 126, 127
Huberman, Bronisław, 148, 149, 217, 220, 229, 302, 327, 329, 331, 358
Hungary, 88
Hymn of the Nations (propaganda film), 399

Illica, Luigi, 41–2
impresa, 9
"Internationale" (socialist anthem), 395

Isolino San Giovanni, 136
Israel, 303, 380; *see also* Palestine
Israel Philharmonic (Palestine Symphony Orchestra), xvii, 205, 220, 229–30, 306, 370, 426; Toscanini's work with, 229–30
Istituzione Toscanini, 116
Italy, xv–xviii, 3, 12, 61, 334; Badoglio government, 389–90, 393; colonialism, 196, 241, 308; fascist regime, xvii, xxi, 62, 91–8, 109–12, 114, 123, 128–33, 173–6, 182, 194, 199, 211–15, 223, 243, 249, 266, 306–8, 326–8, 353, 389–404, 427; invasion of Ethiopia, 196, 241; monarchy abolished, 399, 410, 425; police censors, 353; racial laws, 82, 183, 365; Toscanini's postwar return to, 410; World War I, 88, 92–6; World War II, 374–6, 385, 388–405; *see also specific cities, orchestras, opera companies, and theaters*

Jerger, Alfred, 157
Jerusalem, 308, 332
Jews, xvii, xxii, 82, 149, 301; anti-Semitism, xxii, 138, 166, 183, 199, 332, 337, 343, 345, 365; refugees in Palestine, xvii, 205, 229–30, 303, 380; Toscanini and, 82, 138, 165–6, 169, 180, 183, 198, 205, 220, 229–30, 258, 303–8, 325, 332, 337–8, 343, 345, 352–3, 365, 376
Joachim, Joseph, 5, 64
Johnson, Edward, 370; Toscanini's letter to, 369–70
Judson, Arthur, 235; Toscanini's letters to, 111, 113, 128, 134–5

Kahn, Otto, 83, 84, 85, 86; Toscanini's letter to, 88
Kastanienbaum, 354–7
Kaun, Hugo, 295, 296
Keats, John, 337; "Ode on a Grecian Urn," 146
Kennedy, Joseph, 376
Kerber, Edwin, 253, 270, 312; Toscanini's letters to, 253, 325
Kipnis, Alexander, 252, 271, 276
Kleiber, Erich, 120

Novara, 30, 424
Novotná, Jarmila, 251, 252, 271

Oberdorfer, Aldo, 300, 301
oboe, 103, 104
Ohms, Elisabeth, 131
Ojetti, Paola, 248–9, 254
Ojetti, Ugo, 93, 233, 249, 257, 264, 310
Oldani, Luigi, 435
Oltrabella, Augusta, 208
opera, xv–xvi, 3, 9, 12, 16, 24, 45, 136, 215; ballet following, 16; box-office, 11; copyright, 9; encoring arias in, 21; late-nineteenth century views on, 12, 16, 42, 48; literary-dramatic quality, 18–19; original language, 79; prompters, 73; publishers, 8–9, 24, 25, 27, 51, 98, 101, 112–13; stage distribution, 42; see also specific composers, conductors, musicians, operas, opera companies, and singers
Opera News, 411
Opéra, Paris, 29, 44, 242, 252, 255, 259
Opéra-Comique, Paris, 255
orchestra, xvi, 9, 16, 35, 43, 44, 53, 56–7; Toscanini's choice of players in Turin, 14–17; La Scala, 63, 65, 75, 103–8, 113, 127, 138–9, 422, 424; see also specific cities, conductors, instruments, and orchestras
Orchestre des Concerts Lamoureux, Paris, 78, 79
Orchestre Walter-Straram, Paris, xvii
Orfeo, 85
Orfeo ed Euridice, xvi, 80
Orsi, Romeo, 63; Toscanini's letter to, 63
Osváth, Julia, 253, 271
Otello, 5, 9, 226, 411, 422; La Scala production, 411–13
Oxford University, 248, 249; Toscanini's concert at, 257–8

Padua, 94, 95
Paër, Ferdinando, Sargino overture, 65
Paganini, Niccolò, 250
Pagliacci, xv, 3, 17, 55, 88, 164
Palazzi, Bernardino, 250

Palermo, 8
Palestine, xvii, 198, 205, 220, 229–30, 303–8, 312, 327, 329, 331–2, 380
Palestine Symphony Orchestra, see Israel Philharmonic
Palminteri, Maestro, 36
Pandolfini, Angelica, 28, 37, 55, 410; Toscanini's letter to, 410
Pandolfini, Francesco, 28
Panizza, Héctor (Ettore), 354
Papini, Giovanni, 96, 254, 255
Paris, xvii, 29, 61, 85, 152, 155, 163, 168, 179, 210, 222, 228, 244, 252, 255, 259, 346, 347
Paris Exposition (1937), 244
Parma, xv, 3, 4, 8, 18, 22, 226, 316
Parma Conservatory, 86, 247
Parsifal, 62, 66, 131, 132, 133, 136, 139, 171
Pasini, Camilla, 10, 11, 28, 29
Passigli family, 254, 255
Pataky, Koloman von, 271
Peirani, Giovanni, 11
Pelléas et Mélisande, xv, 17, 70, 78–9, 243, 244, 254–5, 259, 443; Italian premiere, 79
Pelletier, Wilfrid, 415
Perera, Carolyn, 322
Peri, Lina, 30
Perlea, Jonel, 428, 429
Pernet, André, 255
Perosio, 23, 24
Perras, Margaritha, 252
Pertile, Aureliano, 55, 113, 439; Toscanini's letter to family of, 439
Pertner, Hans, 221, 267, 268, 270, 324
Petrassi, Goffredo, 323, 324, 356
Petrella, 69–70
Peydro, Lola, 5
Philadelphia Orchestra, 122–5, 379
Philharmonia Orchestra, Royal Festival Hall, London, Toscanini as conductor of, 409
piano, 20, 153, 182, 217, 249–50, 296, 309
Piatigorsky, Gregor, 153, 163, 183, 249, 251, 304
Piatti, Alfredo, 183
Piazza, Enrico, 442, 443

Piazze, 134, 136, 168, 169, 195

piccolo, 15

Piccolo Teatro di Milano, 405

Pick-Mangiagalli, Riccardo, 97, 98, 161

Pilinsky, Sigismund, 131

Pillet-Will, Countess Louise, 417–18

Pini-Corsi, Antonio, 19–20

Pinza, Ezio, 125, 198, 358

Piontelli, Luigi, 6, 13, 23–6, 28, 37, 40, 45, 47, 50, 51, 55, 56; Toscanini's letters to, 5–7

Pisa, 8, 9

Pittsburgh Symphony Orchestra, 427

Pius XI, Pope, 241

Pizzetti, Bruno, 155, 165, 214, 215

Pizzetti, Ildebrando, 111, 155, 210, 215, 219, 220, 222–3, 352, 372; *Fra Gherardo,* 219, 220; Toscanini's letter to, 111

Pizzetti, Ippolito, 165

Pizzetti, Rirì, 218, 232, 251, 332

Placci, Carlo, 254, 255, 282, 285

Poland, 221; German invasion of, 358

Polese, Giovanni, 44

Politeama Garibaldi, Palermo, 8

Pollini, Cesare, 64

Polo, Enrico, xxi, 5, 10, 11, 17, 40–1, 46, 48, 53, 54, 62, 64, 69, 76, 95, 149, 191, 296, 310, 316, 342, 388; Toscanini's letters to, 4–5, 17, 38–9, 56, 69–70, 74

Polo, Ida De Martini, 10, 11, 17–20, 23–7, 34, 36, 38, 39, 43, 53, 56, 62, 86, 95, 149, 191, 310, 388; Toscanini's letters to, 14, 86–7

Polo, Leopoldo, 105

Polo, Riccardo, 95, 149

Polonini, Alessandro, 10, 11

Pomè, Alessandro, 21, 37

Ponchielli, Amilcare, *La Gioconda,* 4, 5

Porta, Carlo, 180, 314–15

Pottier, Eugène, 395

Prades Festival, 444

Prague, 102; Jews, 332

Prandelli, Giacinto, 420, 425

press, 55, 92, 125, 177; American, 87, 165, 166, 230, 321, 375–6, 396; Fascist, 112, 130, 328; German, 261; Italian, 7, 93, 102, 111–13, 130, 221, 395; Toscanini and, 48, 55,

128–31, 165, 288, 309, 314, 315, 321, 328, 338, 375–6, 389–94, 427–8, 439–40; *see also specific publications*

Prévost, Abbé, 18

Price, Walter, 380; Toscanini's letter to, 379–80

Přihoda, Váša, 98

Principe, Remy, 106

Prokofiev, Sergei, 437; Symphony no. 1 ("Classical"), 118

Prosperina, 247

Prossi, Ella, 26, 27

publishing, music, 8–9, 24, 25, 27, 51, 98, 101, 112–13

Puccini, Antonio, 157

Puccini, Elvira, 252

Puccini, Giacomo, 8, 9, 22, 32, 33, 34, 157, 158, 252; *La bohème,* xv, 3, 11, 12, 13, 19–39, 42, 50, 51, 255; *La fanciulla del West,* xvi, 61; *Madama Butterfly, xvi, 42, 61; Manon Lescaut,* 7–9, 18–19, 21, 23, 27, 30, 54, 61; *La rondine,* 315; *Il tabarro,* 315; *Tosca,* xvi, 42; Toscanini's letters to, 7–8, 9–10; *Turandot,* 62, 315; *Le villi, 24, 25, 31–5, 37, 39*

Rachmaninoff, Sergei, 249–50; *Isle of the Dead,* 89

radio, 62, 125, 231, 235; BBC Symphony broadcasts, 256–8, 301, 313, 333–5; German, 138; NBC Symphony broadcasts, 319, 386, 411, 443–6; Toscanini's broadcasts, 62, 256–8, 272, 319, 333–5, 386, 411, 443–6

Radius, Emilio, 439

Raff, Joseph Joachim, 52

Rama, Eugenia (Nena), 80

Rantzau, I, 7

Ranzato, Virgilio, 106

Ravel, Maurice Joseph, 155; *Daphnis et Chloé,* 226

RCA, 117, 123, 125, 231, 312, 436, 444

Rebuffini, 26, 27, 28, 30

Reger, Max, Violin Concerto, 340

Regime fascista, Il, 328

Rehrl, Dr., 271; Toscanini's letter to, 266

A NOTE ABOUT THE EDITOR

Harvey Sachs selected, edited, translated, and annotated the letters in this collection. He is the author of Toscanini *(1978), which remains the standard biography, and a biography of Arthur Rubinstein. He also published* Reflections on Toscanini—*a collection of essays—and two other books. He has coauthored the memoirs of Plácido Domingo and Sir Georg Solti, and he has written for* The New Yorker, *the* New York Times, The Times Literary Supplement *(London), and many other newspapers and periodicals. He lives in Switzerland.*

A NOTE ON THE TYPE

The text of this book was set in Garamond No. 3. It is not a true copy of any of the designs of Claude Garamond (ca. 1480–1561), but an adaptation of his types, which set the European standard for two centuries. It probably owes as much to the designs of Jean Jannon, a Protestant printer working in Sedan in the early seventeenth century, who had worked with Garamond's romans earlier, in Paris, but who was denied their use because of Catholic censorship. Jannon's matrices came into the possession of the Imprimerie nationale, where they were thought to be by Garamond himself, and were so described when the Imprimerie revived the type in 1900. This particular version is based on an adaptation by Morris Fuller Benton.

Composed by Creative Graphics, Allentown, Pennsylvania

Printed and bound by Berryville Graphics, Berryville, Virginia

Designed by Iris Weinstein